Stephen J. Cannell
Television Productions

ALSO BY JON ABBOTT AND FROM McFARLAND

*Irwin Allen Television Productions, 1964–1970:
A Critical History of* Voyage to the Bottom of the Sea,
Lost in Space, The Time Tunnel *and* Land of the Giants
(2006; softcover 2009)

Stephen J. Cannell Television Productions

A History of All Series and Pilots

JON ABBOTT

McFarland & Company, Inc., Publishers
Jefferson, North Carolina, and London

LIBRARY OF CONGRESS CATALOGUING-IN-PUBLICATION DATA

Abbott, Jon, 1956–
Stephen J. Cannell television productions : a history of
all series and pilots / Jon Abbott.
  p.   cm.
Includes bibliographical references and index.

ISBN 978-0-7864-4173-0
softcover : 50# alkaline paper ∞

1. Cannell, Stephen J. — Criticism and Interpretation.
2. Television series — United States.   I. Title.
PN1992.4.C24A23   2009   791.4502'32092 — dc22   2009008044

British Library cataloguing data are available

©2009 Jon Abbott. All rights reserved

*No part of this book may be reproduced or transmitted in any form
or by any means, electronic or mechanical, including photocopying
or recording, or by any information storage and retrieval system,
without permission in writing from the publisher.*

On the cover: Stephen J. Cannell in his office (Photofest)

Manufactured in the United States of America

*McFarland & Company, Inc., Publishers
Box 611, Jefferson, North Carolina 28640
www.mcfarlandpub.com*

Acknowledgments

With many of the 1970s Cannell series gone before home VCRs arrived, and many of the 1980s Cannell series given only part-runs in the U.K., this was not an easy book to research, and I was obliged to resort to a vast number of sources, friends and contacts in the television world, from the highest-placed TV executives in program buying and selling to the humblest TV enthusiasts, scribbling notes off the TV screen and begging fuzzy videotapes from the U.S. and Canada. Very few of these people are in the same jobs today, and many I haven't seen for some years, but whereas my book on Irwin Allen Productions was very much a solo effort requiring me to quietly and personally thank only a couple of individuals, the small army of much missed faces from those exciting early days of VCR, channel multiplication and satellite television who helped me finish this marathon during my years in the magazine industry of media punditry cannot go unthanked, and important acknowledgments follow.

This book would not have been possible without a number of people, who over the years have helped me out with tapes, cuttings, friendship, opinions, advice, encouragement and/or information. To list them all would be to simply reproduce my contacts book, and some wish anonymity, but they know who they are. There are some though, whom I feel comfortable openly thanking. I'm particularly indebted to Don Gale and Christine Dillon, then with MCA in London, later with ITV Program Purchases, for getting me off the starting block all those years ago, and Cannell fan extraordinaire Jackie Eason for getting me past the finishing post with an endless supply of information, tapes, fanzine cuttings, and program notes. Without Don and Chris' trust and friendship, it would never have been started; without Jackie's help and enthusiasm it would never have been finished. Also to Lynn Campion, the credits queen, for adding details and subtracting typos from the episode guides and generally helping out with research far and beyond the call of duty (get in touch, girls); also, Tony Mechele of the British Film Institute; Barbara Mack, formerly with Columbia, whose friendship and assistance with some of Cannell's more obscure contributions was invaluable; her successor, Liz Harker; S. "Fred" Hill, the toyboy, who first enthusiastically introduced me to the elusive *Greatest American Hero* and tracked down *Wiseguy* in Ireland when all the English terrestrial channels were ignoring the most impressive U.S. drama series since *Hill Street Blues;* the friendship, commiserations and insights of program buyer Jeremy Boulton, of both ITV and Sky at various times, who taught me so much about how 20th century TV actually worked (and often didn't); and Gary Davey, Richard Platt and Fiona Waters, all formerly with Sky Television, who offered both their friendship and their program records in those heady, exciting early days of satellite television. It was then, in the early 1990s, that Britain finally caught up with *The Greatest American Hero, Black Sheep Squadron, Riptide, Hunter, Wiseguy,* and others. Cannell gave the BBC *The Rockford Files* and ITV *The A-Team,* but only 1990s Sky ever recognized and acknowledged Stephen Cannell's astonishing track record of excellence in the action/adventure arena.

All episode guides in this volume have been compiled from information in the public domain from a variety of sources made available by friends and colleagues inside and outside the television industry. There is no intention to infringe copyright, and this book has been produced to advance study and appreciation, and keep the properties favorably in the public eye. We're all on the same side. In many cases, several different sources have been used, and cross-referenced. Unfortunately, spelling mistakes in credits are rife in both official and unofficial documents, and I have endeavored to keep errors to the absolute minimum. Where possible, credits have been taken directly from, or checked against, broadcast screenings; in cases where reference sources differed, and on-screen checking was not possible, the most likely or prevailing credit has been taken. No internet sites were sought or consulted.

Contents

Acknowledgments	v
Preface	1
Introduction	3

Part One: Beginnings

The Rockford Files: September 1974–January 1980	43
Baretta: January 1975–May 1978	71
City of Angels: February 1976–May 1976	82
Black Sheep Squadron: September 1976–April 1978	86
Richie Brockelman, Private Eye: March 1978–April 1978	96
The Duke: April 1979–May 1979	99
Stone: January 1980–March 1980	101
Unsold Pilots (1)	106

Part Two: The Golden Years

Tenspeed and Brownshoe: January 1980–June 1980	109
The Greatest American Hero: March 1981–February 1983	113
The Quest: October 1982–November 1982	127
The A-Team: January 1983–December 1986	131
Hardcastle and McCormick: September 1983–May 1986	156
Rousters: October 1983, June 1984–July 1984	170
Riptide: January 1984–April 1986	175
Unsold Pilots (2)	190

Part Three: From L.A. to Canada

Hunter: September 1984–April 1991	192
Stingray: March 1986–May 1987	221
The Last Precinct: April 1986–May 1986	231
21 Jump Street: April 1987–May 1991	236
Wiseguy: September 1987–December 1990	258

J.J. Starbuck: September 1987–February 1988   295
Sonny Spoon: February 1988–December 1988   305
Unsub: February 1989–April 1989   313
Unsold Pilots (3)   317

The Wrap-Up   318
Sources of Quotations   335
Bibliography   345
Index   349

Preface

The first episode of *The Rockford Files* I ever saw was "Two into 5.56 Won't Go," which turned out to be smack in the middle of the second season. I wasn't watching much television in the 1970s (or, as an incurable TV buff, perhaps I should say I was watching the least amount in my life). Most U.S. TV at that time seemed to consist of Quinn Martin cop shows, Aaron Spelling idiocies, and super-heroes who spent more time in their cheaper secret identities than their more expensive super-heroic personas. I was in my teens, and music, comics, and cinema (not to mention the other, more universal teenage pursuits) seemed far more interesting than anything going on the moribund, conservative world of the small screen. Most of the wild and wacky shows I had loved in the 1960s had disappeared, not to return until the mid–'80s as TV channels in Britain multiplied (mostly on cable and satellite), and only Universal's *Mystery Movies* and the late arrival of *Star Trek* really intrigued me. I knew immediately there was something special about *The Rockford Files,* though. Firstly, the hero was cautiously disrespectful to the authorities, and openly mocked the police and the army (unheard of for 1970s TV unless you were the bad guy, and admirably hip). Secondly, he was tough, but not too tough, very obviously not the usual looking-for-trouble TV detective seen in all the other shows. And thirdly, the scripts were laugh-out-loud witty and humorous, with unpredictable stories. Unlike the other shows of the time, you didn't know what was going to happen next, which of the regular co-stars would pop up, or for how long, or how the stories would end. In short, *The Rockford Files* was an oasis of originality in a desert of mediocrity.

With the exception of *Black Sheep Squadron,* which didn't fly into British airspace until the very late–'80s, the post–*Rockford* Universal shows all made it to the U.K., but didn't last very long either in Britain or America. Cannell's next big hit — in Europe and the U.S. — was *The A-Team* in the early '80s, which left me nonplussed. This? This from the guy who made *The Rockford Files?* A thick-ear, low-brow kiddie show? But as the other early 1980s Cannell shows trickled over to Britain in fits and starts to fill obscure time-slots, I began to see a pattern emerging that linked these two disparate shows and all the others. I was writing professionally about TV now (and even anonymously scripting the *A-Team* comic-strip for Britain's *TV Comic*), and Cannell's *modus operandi* fascinated me, the more so because most media attention at the time was on MTM productions, Steven Bochco, and the glossy night-time soaps phenomenon. Despite the excellent ratings for *The A-Team,* and non–Cannell populist series such as *Knight Rider, Airwolf,* and *The Equalizer* among others, the vigilante shows were discussed only when the tedious spectre of violence on television reared its head, not for any other cultural implications. When the extraordinary *Wiseguy* arrived in the very late '80s, ignored by British program buyers but circulating among TV buffs on videotape from Ireland (the English equivalent of Cuban cigars) I knew I had to write the book on Cannell. During the 1990s, while reluctantly giving priority to my numerous magazine deadlines, I gradually compiled the work you now hold in your hands.

It's taken a long time to get this book right, and I'd like to have seen it published earlier, but in some ways it might be more useful to look at the Cannell shows as the part of television history they now are than when they were still being produced. In the climate of reality TV, "dark and gritty" dramas (in the face of all ratings evidence, which suggests the public prefer the opposite), and humor-free, story-free, directionless character-lite series, we may be documenting and preserving a lost art. If Cannell knew anything, it was how to write great stories. They were witty, clever, and captivating, with beautifully observed characters. There was luck involved — the luck to latch onto wonderful character actors and performers such as James Garner and Robert Culp, and the luck of a good time-slot, but Cannell earned his successes because he not only knew how to write, but how to delegate, how to train new writers, and — so important — how to produce. He wasn't just a writer, he wasn't just a producer, he was a writer-producer. His work, and this analysis of his methods, is an object lesson in how to convey a message of substance and value while producing populist, non-preachy TV that the public wants to watch ... and get it right.

Introduction

For twenty years, Stephen J. Cannell was in the hero business. Or perhaps the anti-hero business. Whatever the case, his heroes were on the side of the slightly tarnished angels.

They were, and in some cases, still are, immensely popular television creations. During the late '70s and early 1980s, Cannell was the single most influential figure in populist action/adventure television. His series range from the smart, wry humor of *The Rockford Files* to the comic-book exploits of *The A-Team*. In between, he has created, co-created, and overseen such productions as *Baretta, Black Sheep Squadron, The Greatest American Hero, Riptide, Hardcastle and McCormick, Hunter,* and many more. In the late '80s he produced the critically acclaimed cult shows *21 Jump Street* and *Wiseguy*.

From his beginnings creating series at Universal Studios in the 1970s, to forming his own production company in 1980, Cannell's ideas and attitudes have guided and influenced other TV talents and — alongside such other equally prolific creator-producers as Aaron Spelling, Glen Larson, Steven Bochco, and the MTM studios — Cannell played a large part in determining the shape and the standards of U.S. TV in the late 20th century; he directed a tired and weary action/adventure detective genre away from its grim, clichéd poker-faced past toward a lighter, more humorous and knowing self-parodic approach that permeated all of American television throughout the 1980s and much cinema thereafter. However, while his contemporaries such as Glen Larson seemed to have been simply and effectively transferring successful feature film concepts to television formats (*Alias Smith and Jones, McCloud, Switch, BJ and the Bear, Battlestar Galactica, The Fall Guy, Manimal* and *Automan* all appear to have their origins in the feature film equivalents of the same period), and Aaron Spelling reveled reliably and efficiently in the dated conventions of old-time Hollywood murder and glamour he first discovered in the star-studded 1963–65 hit series *Burke's Law* (and whose later output featured numerous old-time stars in such series as *Love Boat, Fantasy Island, Vegas, Dynasty,* and *Hotel*), Cannell seems to have taken his inspiration directly from an inspired marriage of 1940s and '50s B-western plots and values to those of post–Watergate 1970s cinema. And while Larson jumped swiftly onto the passing bandwagon of the cinema triumphs of the day, sometimes producing a populist hit, sometimes not, Cannell seems to have understood the deeper significance of trends in cinema, dismissing the surface appeal that Larson so accurately emulated (special effects and swaggering stars) for their underlying message, a technique that stood him in good stead whether creating the anti-establishment *The Rockford Files* in the 1970s, or the populist vigilante series *The A-Team, Hardcastle and McCormick,* and *Hunter* in the 1980s, drawing directly from themes explored and avenues opened by Robert Altman and Clint Eastwood in the '70s, perhaps the two most influential American film-makers of the period prior to the disastrous (for serious film-makers) emergence of Lucas and Spielberg.

If MTM, *M*A*S*H,* and Norman Lear remodeled TV comedy for the 1970s, fashioning and determining a new direction for the form, it was Universal, and then Cannell at Universal, who shaped the glib, sly 1970s attitude to adventure and detective series that developed into the homage and pastiche dominant in the 1980s (and reflected in such series as *Magnum, p.i., Remington Steele, Simon and Simon, Mike Hammer* and *Moonlighting* to name just a few). As the 1970s neared their close, and MTM—with *Lou Grant* and then later *Hill Street Blues* and *St. Elsewhere*—added drama to their proven ability for humor, Cannell was turning in the opposite direction, from the straight dramatic action of *Toma, Baretta, The Duke* and *Stone* to the tongue in cheek *Rockford*-inspired humor of *Richie Brockelman, Tenspeed and Brownshoe, Greatest American Hero, Rousters, Riptide,* and *The A-Team.* Consequently, as comedy became more substantial in the '70s and '80s, adventure shows were becoming less absurdly grim and more frivolous.

In *TV Guide,* Cannell was quoted on the creation of the format for *The Rockford Files:* "I said to myself, I'm going to break every rule about a television detective—like they never work for money! What bull! My guy wants money! Lives in a trailer, doesn't have a pretty secretary but a truck-driver father who's embarrassed by what his son does! I was laughing, sitting at the typewriter, exercising all my fantasies...."

Since that day, Cannell has been laughing all the way to the bank, not only with *The Rockford Files* (which was followed by a stream of other unlikely private eyes for Universal), but with hit series like *The Greatest American Hero* (a super-hero spoof that does for comicbooks what *Rockford* did for Spillane), beach-boy detective show *Riptide,* the cartoonish kidult phenomenon *The A-Team,* the outrageous vigilante buddy show *Hardcastle and McCormick,* the obviously Eastwood-inspired anti-cop show *Hunter,* and the grim, dark, quietly horrific mob show *Wiseguy.*

"What I try and do is just make programs that appeal to me" Cannell told Louis Rukeyser in a public television interview for *Wall Street Week* in 1986. "And that way I always have a barometer for whether I feel they're being well done or not. And I pretty much try to make my television entertainment-type TV. I'm not trying to solve social problems with my shows, I'm just trying to entertain people and give them an hour away from their problems. One of the things that I try to do is put a sense of humor in my shows. And you know, most of my series, all the way back to *The Rockford Files* and those things I did at Universal, all had a sense of humor. And I think of *The A-Team* as basically a comedy. And I think that's what makes those shows timeless. If something's funny now, it'll be funny ten years from now."

But like his heroes, Cannell hasn't come out on top every time. Some of that money has been lost again, backing such brave ratings failures as *Tenspeed and Brownshoe, Rousters, The Quest,* and others. Out on his own, away from the protective environs of Universal, a long-running success such as *The Rockford Files, The A-Team,* or *Hunter* (which he ceased to have much creative input into after the first two seasons) kept his company afloat, while the modest hits that made up the bulk of his output kept the books balanced. But every time Cannell struck out, a few more millions trickled away.

"I don't really think too much about demographics," Cannell told Rukeyser later, "but then after you've made a show they help you. I really think it's a mistake for people to feel that television can be produced by getting a recipe book. If that were the case, they would never have tried *Golden Girls,* because they would have said this will be a 50-plus audience and it's not going to work. *The A-Team* is a good example of a show that should never have been a hit if you were to use the rule book. It broke every rule that I can think of ... the heroes were bizarre and unfamiliar, they were mercenaries, they were Vietnam veterans. One of them was insane and lived in a mental institution, another is a con man. One of them can't enjoy himself unless he's on the edge of disaster, and one of them is an angry black. And you know, you can imagine the strikes that you have going against you when you do something like that! But if you pull it off, you generally get a big hit. I don't think anybody really knows what a hit television show is, because if I really knew, do you think I would have made *The Last Precinct*? I mean, I've always just tried to do shows that make me laugh. And you know, *The*

Promo flyer with the cast of the aforementioned shambolic and short-lived *Last Precinct*. Clockwise, from outside to inside, starting in the lower left corner: Keenan Wynn, Wings Hauser, Ernie Hudson, Rick Ducommun, Lucy Lee Flippin, Randi Brooks, Adam West, Pete Willcox, Hank Rolike, Yana Nirvana, and Jonathan Perpich.

Rockford Files made me laugh. When I wrote that pilot I was having fun, and when I wrote *The A-Team* I was having fun."

And Cannell was clearly having fun for most of the 1970s and 1980s. As writer Tom Carson noted in a 1983 review of *The A-Team* in *The Village Voice*, "Chances are that any action show of the last few years that's struck you as slightly offbeat or weirdly contrived, or just somewhat perverse, is one he's been involved in. Some of Cannell's projects have not succeeded, i.e. the wonderful *Tenspeed and Brownshoe* ... but a surprising number were or are hits, and I can't think of anyone else in TV who's managed to get so many shows on the air that all bear some stamp of his personality." "He has to write," colleague Frank Lupo told *Variety* in 1995. "While most writers find it difficult to get to the keyboard, with Stephen you would have to shackle him to keep him away." "One of the things about Stephen is he loves to write," echoes *Rockford Files* writer and producer Charles Johnson. "He would get up at four or five in the morning and write until noon. He would come out of his office and say 'I've just written one of the best things I've ever done, let me read it to you.' He always creates colorful and interesting characters."

Discarding sacred clichés and conventions, Cannell made his TV creations tougher and more credible by making them flawed and more vulnerable. His knights in shining armor, from Jim Rockford through to the A-Team, are strong, moral, and upright in the conventional manner, but also cynical realists and often reluctant heroes. James Garner's weary look of exasperation and resignation as he was dragged helplessly into yet another convoluted comedy of deception, counter-deception and self-deception in *The Rockford Files* became a welcome trademark of the series; in *The Greatest American Hero*, schoolteacher Ralph Hinckley doesn't want to become a crusading super-hero, he has the role thrust upon him by visiting extra-terrestrials and eager beaver gung-ho FBI man Bill Maxwell. In *Hardcastle and McCormick*, racing driver and parolee Mark McCormick has also been forced into an unholy alliance, this time with the near-demented Judge Hardcastle; in *The A-Team*, tough guy B.A. Baracus (Mr. T) has to be tricked into taking the necessary air-flight to their missions, and Templeton Peck is frequently averse to leaving whatever high living or hot date he's just arranged for himself. All that Cannell's army of reluctant heroes really desire is the quiet life, but when the chips are down they deliver their heroics with flying colors. Deep down, they're all decent people, who can't resist ensuring that justice will be done.

"We asked him once about writing," William Katt of *Greatest American Hero* told *Variety* in 1995. "He said 'In the first act I put my hero up a tree. In the second act, I throw rocks at him. In the third act, I drop a house on him. In the fourth act, I get him back down the tree.'"

Like all the best television talents, Cannell was smart enough to play both sides of the fence in order to please the maximum number of viewers in a mass medium. But far from compromising his integrity and creativity, this has given his creations greater depth, complexity, and character. On the surface, Cannell's heroes are the traditional conservative icons of Hollywood mythology — cops, judges, vigilantes, military men, tough guys — but they are also renegades, rebels who prefer to buck the system (even if, as in some cases — Hunter, Hardcastle — they work within it) rather than become just another cog in a faulty machine. By making many of the characters part of the system, and supporters of traditional commonsense values that transcend politics, he shows support for, and belief in, a safe, just society ruled by benevolent, familiar bodies. By then casting his heroes as individualistic malcontents at odds with the injustices of the world, he acknowledges the imperfections that make up the system's failings. Consequently, there is something for audiences of every political persuasion to empathize with, and perhaps more importantly in the commercial environment of television, nothing threatening, off-putting, or overtly depressing. Rockford may live from day to day in a sleazy seaside trailer, the A-Team may be fugitives from the law, but they're living a good life in the meantime.

Carson goes on to discuss two first season episodes of *The A-Team*, written by Cannell's right-hand man throughout the best part of the 1980s, Frank Lupo, later a producer in his own right. "('The Rabbit Who Ate Las Vegas'), like an earlier episode about a killer SWAT team ('A Small and Deadly War'), also revealed just how much the fantasy format lets Cannell express attitudes and ideas unconventional and subversive enough that a naturalistic show would never be able to get away with them. It was just taken for granted, for instance, that Las Vegas is a city openly run by the Mafia. When one character expresses concern about the police, Hannibal Smith cheerfully implies there's nothing to worry about — getting around cops is child's play. It's easy to read too much into such implications — but even without them, *The A-Team* can still be brash and knowing enough to unsettle people's preconceptions. There's a double-edge to almost everything about the show. It isn't just that the actors are allowed to be aware of their characters' self-parodic aspects — the characters themselves are. All the characters are conceived as genial con artists — a much more basic and self-aware image in male role-playing than many people realise."

And, one might add, a prevailing and recurring character trait in all of Cannell's series. The scam is a major ingredient of the Cannell *modus operandi*. Characters such as Jim Rockford, who carries his own business card printing press around with him, Baretta and Sonny Spoon, masters of flummery and disguise (as is the A-Team's Hannibal Smith), Pappy Boyington (who, in the pilot film for *Black Sheep Squadron*, cons an entire air force into grounding themselves with just a doctor's coat and a clip-board), Tenspeed Turner from *Tenspeed and Brownshoe* and *J.J. Starbuck*, Angel Martin of *The Rockford Files*, the boys from *Riptide*, genial J.J. Starbuck himself (a Texan Columbo), *Wiseguy's* Vinnie Terranova, the *21 Jump Street* kids, and the entire A-Team are all frequently masquerading as something they are not in order to put one over on their targets. "Thing about cons is that you can never con an honest man" says Cody Johnson, repeating an old adage in "Escape from a Velvet Box" for *The Quest*—"It's the nature of the business!" But Cannell cons us all, making his larger-than-life characters so likeable, and their reaction to his preposterous plots so credible, that the audience is sucked unquestioningly into some of the most outlandish storylines in television; everywhere our heroes turn, they're falling over mobsters, hit-men, spies, swindles, and secret identities. The casts of *Riptide, The A-Team, The Greatest American Hero* and *Hardcastle and McCormick* breeze through their adventures with "this ain't for real" practically tattooed on their faces, and wily veteran actors such as George Peppard (as Hannibal Smith), Robert Culp (as reactionary FBI man Bill Maxwell), Dale Robertson (as the devious but disarming J.J. Starbuck) and Brian Keith (as demented vigilante judge Milton Hardcastle) appear to understand the nature of Cannell's shows effortlessly, giving performances so broad compared to their other work that the scams they perpetrate on their fictional targets reach out to dupe the audience as well. They keep their distance from the viewer, never turning to the camera and breaking the fourth wall like Tom Selleck on *Magnum, p.i.* or Bruce Willis on *Moonlighting*,* but never quite taking the jeopardy seriously either. They're safe as houses — they're on a Cannell show!

---

*Fred Dryer did go through a brief phase of breaking the fourth wall on Hunter.

All of Cannell's heroes endure their trials and tribulations with good humor and wry self-effacement, from Rockford and his fellow p.i. associates through to Ralph and Bill, Hardcastle and McCormick, and Hunter and McCall. It is an attribute that soon spread to other TV heroes in a similar vein, such as Phil De Guere's *Simon and Simon*, Donald Bellisario's *Magnum, p.i.*, Jay Bernstein's version of Mickey Spillane's *Mike Hammer*, and MTM's *Remington Steele*. Like their characters, Cannell's actors are role-playing broadly, but it's all done with such speed and pace that the audience never quite has the time to stop and realize they've been taken. There's just enough conviction in the performances married to a *lack* of conviction in the performances, to create exactly the right ambience. And like all good con tricks, while looking exceptionally simple, it's a very thin line indeed to tread, often marking the difference between a Stephen Cannell show and somebody else's.

This practice of drawing the audience into the game so that they almost feel like part of the sting—pawns, middle-men, or allies in bringing down the bad guys—prevails across all but the most intense of Cannell's series (late '80s entries such as *Wiseguy, Unsub, Top of the Hill* and *21 Jump Street* being notable exceptions to the rule). With *Unsub* and *Top of the Hill* in particular—interestingly, both instant flops—what you see is what you get, but with Cannell's successful shows (particularly those of the first half of the '80s, when it seemed he could do no wrong), it's not just that the characters are pretending to be something they're not, or even that the actors are pretending to be something they're not—Cannell's series *themselves* are pretending to be something they're not. The leads of *Baretta, Stone, Richie Brockelman, Riptide, Hunter, J.J. Starbuck* and *Sonny Spoon* are not typical cops or detectives, they're rebels, rule-breakers, and misfits. The same applies to the fliers in the *Black Sheep Squadron* and the military mercenaries of *The A-Team*, who are neither military nor mercenary in their manner. Cars crash with no injury to their occupants, and the bullets may as well be blanks. Cannell himself gleefully relates the story of how in one *A-Team* episode a helicopter exploded

Left, Non-Cannell productions, such as *Magnum, p.i.* starring Cannell protégé Tom Selleck (center with supporting cast, clockwise, Larry Manetti, John Hillerman and Roger E. Mosely) and right, *Mickey Spillane's Mike Hammer* (Stacy Keach, seen here with Lindsay Bloom as Velda) adopted his knowing, wink-at-the-audience approach to detective action shows.

and two goons staggered out of the fireball's wreckage dusting themselves down. The un-named "Greatest American Hero" is not a typical super-hero — like the junior detectives of *Richie Brockelman* and *Tenspeed and Brownshoe*, he's trying to live up to impossible, media-fuelled images. *Wiseguy's* Vinnie Terranova isn't even a real mobster, and the *21 Jump Street* kids aren't real schoolkids. As outsiders, Cannell's heroes are both part of the established order and resolutely removed from it. They are exiled from the system for being superior to it. "You think you're doing pretty good, don't you Maxwell!?" snaps suit-and-tie superior Carlyle in "Just Another Three Ring Circus," an episode of *The Greatest American Hero*. "Except that you're a one man band! You ignore dress codes, you crash more cars than a college fraternity.... Despite your record, you are lousy for morale here, because the other agents idolize you and your offbeat style!"

White knight cops Baretta, Hunter, and Stone are mavericks who go their own way in spite of the play-safe politics of their chiefs; Rockford and the A-Team have been wrongly incriminated by the system. Rockford, the *Riptide* detectives, Jake Axminster of *City of Angels*, and Sonny Spoon are among those persecuted constantly by dumb, stupid bad cops; very often, the authorities will coerce Rockford, the A-Team, the Riptide agency, or Sonny Spoon into taking assignments they otherwise wouldn't take (as in the *Riptide* episode "The Orange Grove," the *A-Team* episode "One More Time," or the *Sonny Spoon* episode "Semper Fi," for example). Frequently this is done by employing the methods that hero cops use on criminals in the straight cop shows from other producers (entrapment, violence, threats of violence, threats of harassment, threats to dig up past misdemeanors or initiate administrative red-tape obstructions).* Baretta, *Rockford's* Dennis Becker, Stone, Hunter, *Black Sheep Squadron's* Boyington and *Greatest American Hero's* Bill Maxwell are all harassed by mean-minded, ill-tempered, authoritarian, ladder-climbing, easy-option bosses. For these sorry specimens, the reward for toeing the line and sucking up to their own superiors is frustration, worry, irritability, and dissatisfaction. The reward for opposing officialdom is self-respect, self-assuredness, modest success, inner moral contentment and the ability to look at yourself in the mirror each morning.†

Ironically, the only other attempt to document the work of Cannell to this author's knowledge (*Adventures on Prime-Time* by Robert Thompson, published in 1990) selects Cannell as the subject because the author viewed his work as "ordinary" and "typical" in the world of U.S. television. In fact, although there is little in the book's analysis of individual series to argue with, nothing could be further from the truth. If Cannell's series are, or were, typically representative of television's output at the close of the 1980s, it was only because Cannell and

---

This cliché reasserts itself in its traditional form in Hunter, *again the exception to the rule in Cannell's '70's and early '80's output.*

†*In* Baretta *and* Greatest American Hero, *as in many non–Cannell series, these Aunt Sally superiors — there for the knocking down of — are cartoon cut-outs for the humble viewer to see his or her own personal nemesis behind. In* Black Sheep Squadron—*ahead of its time in this regard—and the late-'80s* Hunter, *a greater effort appears to be made to create a sense of genuine opposing viewpoints and priorities, an attempt to flesh out these TV stereotypes, a trend which again extends beyond the Cannell trademark. By the time we reach 1987, and the birth of* 21 Jump Street *and* Wiseguy, *the boss has become the confidant, the patient ally, the supportive buddy. This is particularly noticeable not just in* Hunter, Wiseguy, *and* 21 Jump Street, *but in the boss/hero relationships portrayed in such non–Cannell series as* China Beach, Equal Justice, St. Elsewhere, Doogie Howser, Mancuso FBI, Law and Order, *and many others; the most extraordinary transformation was that of the boss in* Cagney and Lacey, *a virulent male chauvinist pig in the early episodes, a sensitive, thoughtful pal in later years as the series' simplistic political pedantry softened. In the Cannell series, Jonathan Banks' superbly acidic superior Frank McPike ultimately takes the role of partner and confidante to Ken Wahl's* Wiseguy *Vinnie Terranova; in* 21 Jump Street, *Steven Williams' Captain Fuller is practically one of the team. Fuller plays cards with the Jump Street cops, swapping personal stories ("Chapel of Love") while McPike heads for the hills with Vinnie for some male bonding ("Call It Casaba").*

his writers had spent the previous fifteen years breaking down boundaries, deconstructing clichés, and paving the way for others to follow — providing, in fact, a fresh blueprint for others to refer to and emulate. It is telling that envelope-pushing controversial program producers MTM, Lear and Bochco were perceived as exceptional, while Cannell — aiming for populism — has been perceived as conventional (his series are only typical from Thompson's 1990 viewpoint retrospectively, by sheer force of numbers, both of Cannell series and Cannell-influenced series). Many of the critics who threw garlands at *Remington Steele, Moonlighting* and *The Sopranos,* to name but three, blithely ignored the hundreds of Cannell hours that had primed the audience and paved the way for them. From 1974 to the close of the 1980s, Cannell's series were about as unconventional and untypical as one could get. If they blend in today with the work of other studios and producers it is simply because, as derivative of previous forms of popular culture as they are, they have been extraordinarily influential leaders.

Cannell — Content and Criticism

To support the noble aims of the forces of law, truth, and justice, Cannell's heroes often find themselves placed in an adversarial position to them. As a result, Cannell's series — while on the surface appearing to be no different from the hundreds of standard TV detective action/adventure series that preceded them, or many of those that have followed them — are quietly, discreetly subversive, turning many of the accepted TV conventions of the genre almost unnoticeably on their heads. His heroes are an intriguing amalgam of 1940s Saturday serial stoicism, 1960s adversarial questioning of the authorities' methods and priorities, and 1970s post–Vietnam, post–Watergate cynicism. All of this was liberally sliced and diced into the melting pot to create something fresh but familiar for the nothing-new '80s, otherwise a decade of retreads and pastiche that offered no new film genres other than a predominance of splatter movies and a shabby attempt to rewrite the Vietnam war.

Certainly Cannell would not cite the swarm of 1980s straight-to-VCR vigilantes unleashed by the *Death Wish* series — or its real-life counterparts — as bedfellows, nor would it be accurate or fair; Cannell's heroes have not been corrupted by their surroundings, his canon of characters are too far removed from the real world for that. On the contrary, they are constantly seen to be rising above them. In the *Wiseguy* storyline beginning with the episode "Day One" and ending with "Day Nine,"* we see Ken Wahl's Vinnie Terranova drinking in the fresh air of freedom in Washington as his boss, the dour and cynical McPike looks sourly on. As all the covert, unscrupulous activity around him mocks everything the grand monuments he marvels at stand for, all seems lost until the hitherto quite plausible and very '80s storyline bursts into a ludicrous Capra-esque finale that would have done Jimmy Stewart proud. As the villains crumble before our very eyes and everyone remembers what America should really stand for, the viewer almost waits for a fireworks display and the band to strike up. Cannell's terms of reference stretch back considerably further than Bronson, Rambo, and Arnie, to a more innocent, simplistic age of heroes — to the Hollywood traditions and spirits evoked by the mythological status of the likes of Robin Hood and the Lone Ranger. In fact, what made the Cannell vigilante series considerably hipper and more watchable dur-

---

*Although it's only a four-parter, bridged by "Day Four" and "Day Seven!"

ing the 1980s was their mockery of machismo and their specific avoidance of the reactionary revisionism of the Vietnam years that permeated all the other action hero shows of the 1980s and even some of the cop shows.

Indeed, the Lone Ranger is referred to as an influence both directly and indirectly throughout Cannell's crime-busting series; Cannell and his writers fairly bludgeon the audience with references to the source material. Judge Hardcastle knowingly peruses *Lone Ranger* comic-books in the pilot film of *Hardcastle and McCormick,* and Nick Mancuso, as the anonymous hero of *Stingray,* is plainly a spiritual descendant of the legendary mystery man, maskless and yet still shadowed, thanks to modern-day methods of computerized concealment; he rides into the sunset while backs are turned in the inevitable fast car rather than on the more familiar trusty steed, his eyes hidden behind reflective shades instead of the archetypal mask! *The A-Team* (not to mention Glen Larson's *Knight Rider,* Donald Bellisario's *Airwolf,* and Michael Sloan's *The Equalizer,* among many other 1980s creations) are further obvious examples, albeit, in the case of the latter two, much more severe.*

The fabled western hero himself even puts in a personal appearance in Cannell's splendid "My Heroes Have Always Been Cowboys," an episode of *The Greatest American Hero.* Here, actor John Hart, one of the two men to play the Lone Ranger on television, appears as himself, opening a supermarket in costume and pausing to offer a disillusioned Ralph Hinck-

From the Lone Ranger and other heroes of the 1940s serials to the cynicism of later times. Left, Clayton Moore as the Lone Ranger. Right, Nick Mancuso as the anonymous *Stingray*— a modern day incarnation of the Lone Ranger, sunglasses replacing the black mask.

*Indeed, we even get to see the dark side of the Lone Ranger myth when one recurring Cannell character, John Shearin's Lt. Finn in Hunter, *is written out in Dallas and Joanna Barnes' episode "Silver Bullet," when the cop cracks up and becomes a vigilante killer who leaves a silver bullet behind at the scene of his murders.*

ley some words of wisdom on super-heroing.* An episode of *The A-Team* written by Frank Lupo is pleadingly titled "When You Comin' Back, Range Rider?," with the Murdock character paying homage to the TV hero of old throughout, and even *Hill Street Blues* got into the act with "Here's Adventure, Here's Romance," with a demented Murdock-like vigilante (Martin Ferrero, highlight of the silly *Miami Vice* as stoolie Izzy Moreno) riding around the streets convinced that he was not only the legendary TV hero the Cisco Kid, but also Duncan Renaldo, the actor who played the part!†

Cannell's contempt for red tape authoritarianism, petty rule-book waving, and intractable brainless bureaucracy is a populist and universal stance that runs through his entire output. There are many underlying themes that run consistently throughout his body of work, from the most sophisticated of his series — *The Rockford Files, Wiseguy, 21 Jump Street* — to the most heavy-handed and simplistic — *The A-Team, Riptide, Hardcastle and McCormick*. These attitudes — almost obsessions — are always secondary to the action, but ever present, an integral part of the series' success. The underlying message beneath these constants is basic — good will triumph over bad, right will win out over wrong; the virtuous and helpless, the just and the decent, will defeat the bullying, selfish, thuggish, lawsuit-threatening, politician-buying bad guys. The violence and vigilanteism of Cannell's series is tempered by his resilient oddballs, his reluctant heroes, independent loners, and system-cracking, justice-dodging villains, murderers and bullies. It's traditional frontier justice, unhampered by the legal loopholes of the courts, the wealth of the corruptors, or the ambiguities and realities of real life. Consequently, Cannell's series appeal to a gut-level right-or-wrong, black-and-white morality that is sympathetic and identifiable right across the political spectrum.

Needless to say, this stance has not only attracted satisfied viewers from all walks of life, but critics from all corners as well. Some, such as Robert Thompson (for all his strained analogies between Cannell the person and Cannell the product; television has always been a self-referential and insular environment), Robert MacKenzie in *TV Guide*, Tom Carson in *The Village Voice*, and Chris Wicking in Britain's *Time Out* magazine of the 1970s (the single U.K. publication to acknowledge Cannell) very quickly caught on to what Cannell was doing and saying. Some of the above were complimentary, others sarcastic or critical. Other commentators have inevitably either missed the point or seen only what they chose to see. Like the work of his populist cinema counterpart, Clint Eastwood, Cannell's output has attracted such colorful labels as "quasi-fascist" and "American imperialism." Some might say that it's the price to be paid for producing shamelessly populist work that becomes too big for the critics

---

Interestingly, the other actor who portrayed the Lone Ranger had been forbidden by law to appear in costume after a legal injunction taken out against him by the makers of a lousy modern film version. A perfect case of frontier justice for the A-Team, surely? But wait, what's this — in the second season episode of Phil De Guere's Simon and Simon p.i. series "The Rough Rider Rides Again," we find the detective heroes defending Stuart Whitman as an ageing 1950s TV hero who has been accused of doing away with a schlock film-maker (Broderick Crawford) who took out an injunction to stop him wearing the Rough Rider duds in public. And, like Ralph's infatuation with his childhood hero the Lone Ranger in the Greatest American Hero *episode, Rick Simon just happens to be a fanatically devoted admirer of the Rough Rider ... who, of course, rides to the rescue in full costume at the episode's end to corral the real bad guys.*

†*And it doesn't end there. Ferrero turns up again in "Leapin' Lizards," a second season episode of* L.A. Law, *as actor Julius Goldfarb, an eccentric performer who has been forbidden to appear in his costume as TV super-hero the Salamander by the copyright owners, who — sure enough — plan to make a new version with a new actor in the role. This same storyline manifests itself yet again, in "Stronger than Steele," an episode of* Remington Steele, *and "Things Get Ugly," for the short-lived* Once a Hero, *in which Conrad Janis as the former "Atomic Man" of vintage TV, and none other than Adam West, as the former TV incarnation of Captain Justice respectively, both find themselves ousted by new, legally protected versions of the characters — a situation Adam West, as TV's 1960s Batman, has experienced first-hand. Faded former heroes of times gone by also turn up in episodes of* My Secret Identity *(a* Greatest American Hero *clone) and the sit-com* Babes, *and* The Simpsons.

to comfortably ignore—driven to make a comment, they are obliged to strike an attitude, but can bear to give the work only the most fleeting, cursory glance. Some of their sniveling—about Cannell's ego (as if any writer could work without one, as if he hadn't earned his end-of-show logo) or the consequence-free violence and vigilanteism—paints them as the personification of Cannell's repertoire of humorless twits who harangue his heroes from the comfort of their safe, warm offices. At the other end of the spectrum, some fans gush mindlessly, warming to the themes of the shows (even adopting the language of the cop genre or vigilante show) without considering the content or perspective of the shows or what makes Cannell's different from his protégés or copyists, working hard to prove the complainers right. Whatever one's conclusions about Cannell's output, it is telling that in researching this book, the most complimentary and enthusiastic critics have been found to be witty, perceptive, informed, and clearly researched to the point of often displaying familiarity with characters and storylines, while the most hostile reviews have been generalized and glib, often riddled with elementary errors, simplistic, blinkered, and instantly dismissive, many of their complaints often covered in specific episodes they haven't seen because they naturally don't care to follow the shows they're criticizing. The result is a knee-jerk reaction far less resistant to serious scrutiny than any of the pop culture generalizations to be found in Cannell's productions.

A typical example concludes this offhand review of *Riptide* from 1984, which reviews two series from different producers and with different formats at once: "There isn't much space left to discuss *Riptide,* in which a couple of California beach boys play private detective when they should have stuck to volleyball, or *Blue Thunder,* in which James Farentino and his helicopter behave like beach boys, only upside down. *Riptide* has a robot that looks like a pelican, only orange. *Blue Thunder* has pretty, fascist uniforms and many hours of Pac-Man in the sky. On *Riptide,* there are many, many mermaids..." and so on, until both programs leave the reviewer "thinking about dimples." To call this cursory would be an insult to channel-surfers.

The Rockford Files has been almost universally acclaimed (most memorably and surprisingly perhaps by Britain's *Gay Times,* which praised—with just a few reservations—an episode's sane, matter-of-fact and downplayed portrayal of two homosexuals during the swish-happy '70s—hardly a fascist trait*), as indeed has the much later *Wiseguy,* the recipient of some deliriously enjoyable purple prose. In contrast, *The A-Team* was perhaps predictably universally derided, although Cannell bemusedly told his TV interviewer for *Wall Street Week:* "I'll tell you how off the money I was—I thought the critics were going to love it because it was so bizarre and different, and the public would hate it ... and it was just the other way around." As Cannell's most simplistic series, it was—of course—the most critically misinterpreted. *Tenspeed and Brownshoe* and *The Greatest American Hero* have earned grudging nods, as have *Hunter* (primarily for its durability!) and *21 Jump Street* (for its non-preachy social conscience, some might say social engineering, courtesy producer Patrick Hasburgh). *Riptide* took quite a drubbing in the U.S., while the British critics laid into *Hardcastle and McCormick* with merciless vigor and venom! Cannell's series certainly seem to get noticed ... but throughout it all, only the U.S. television trade press remained truly impartial and objective. Here's *Variety* on *Riptide:*

"*Riptide's* lead couple have laid-back appeal ... producers have added an extra dimension

---

*Cannell's "The Empty Frame," directed by Corey Allen.

in naive computer whiz Thom Bray that could be the ingredient that makes *Riptide* work ... a pair of novice private eyes (former beach boy types) get involved in a smuggling operation and eventual hijack while trying to help a pretty client.... The mystery is *not as important as the cameraderie between the three principals* (my italics)—with Bray stealing the pilot with his deft portrayal of the klutzy but smart computer expert. There are gimmicks galore ... if ami-

Revenge of the nerd ... Cannell's *Riptide* gives equal time to computer geek Murray (center, Thom Bray) alongside dashing Cody (left, Perry King) and musclebound Nick (right, Joe Penny). In the background, requisite '80s accessory, the helicopter Screaming Mimi.

ability mixed with action was the ultimate goal, *Riptide* was pretty much on target...." So was *Variety*.

Cannell's improbable, enviable fantasies are relentlessly, unashamedly masculine, and yet his production operation was one of the earliest to give women a fair deal both in front of the camera and behind the scenes. While other producers were presenting plots and dialogue for obnoxious and unreal supermen and their helpless and subservient women, and liberal supposedly progressive producers were peppering their series with aggressive and unpleasant career women who blew emasculated men off their arms as they might bugs, Cannell was quietly giving equal time to both sexes. Offstage, a number of female writers and production people were employed, with writers such as Juanita Bartlett and Babs Greyhosky graduating to producer status. Onscreen, in *The Rockford Files*, there was tough no-nonsense lawyer Beth Davenport* (Gretchen Corbett), the first female participant in an open, casual, unspoken but clearly sexual relationship on TV, without any talk of love or commitment; this character was not only a smart career woman as opposed to the standard bimbo secretary of detective mythology, but was also not cast in the negative roles of either denying or belonging to the hero. Despite their casual, adult relationship (confirmed in a brief dialogue exchange in "The Farnsworth Stratagem"), Rockford pays for her legal services, and she pays for his (referenced in early episodes "Charlie Harris at Large" and "The Deep Blue Sleep" to name but two). To call this characterization a breath of fresh air is an understatement that doesn't do the phenomenon justice; in television terms this was not only innovation, but still shamefully unique decades later. Female characters are still, thirty years on, often defined by the words yes or no. In *The Greatest American Hero* and *Hunter*, there were the equally strong (and strongly equal) Pam Davidson and DeeDee McCall (Connie Sellecca and Stepfanie Kramer), both likeable, friendly, successful women.

For this reason, and no doubt for casting attractive male leads in honest portrayals of strong—but not super—men, Cannell's masculine buddy series have picked up as many female admirers as male. Davenport, Davidson and McCall are just three of the women in the Cannell canon who are strong, independent, and intelligent, and not simply around to service the needs of the male heroes or act as "romantic interest," a phrase in Hollywood terminology that positively exudes second rate status. And just as the women in the audience can enjoy good looking guys without having their own sexuality insulted or trivialized, so are the female characters equally pleasing to the eager eyes of the male audience. Cannell has been very careful in the arena of sexual politics, and the unkindest remark that could be made of any of Cannell's female characters is that they are demographic advantages in capturing the largest appreciative audience possible. The Cannell women do frequently find themselves in the role of damsel-in-distress by the very nature of the action/adventure genre—which, after all, is all about jeopardy—but this is neatly offset by the fact that the heroes are not brainlessly macho, and also frequently captive themselves. The women in *Riptide*, for example, although often seeking the help of the male detectives for protection, do not sit on the sidelines screaming but participate in the adventure, and all the perils those exploits provide; they join in the escapades at every opportunity (actress Geena Davis, despite having made many films, cited her guest appearance in *Riptide* as her favorite role; this resulted in a deafening silence from the British chat show audience of *Parkinson*, where the series was virtually unknown). In *The Greatest American Hero*, much is made of Pam Davidson's refusal to play

---

An early predecessor of Veronica Hamel's Joyce Davenport on Steven Bochco's Hill Street Blues?

Lois Lane to Ralph's super-man, and slot in with the old-fashioned notions of a woman's role proposed by FBI agent Bill Maxwell, sentiments advocated with little conviction by a mocking Robert Culp, who clearly relishes sending them up and seems to be barely restraining himself from winking at the camera!

Following a June 2nd, 1979 article in *TV Guide* on Cannell and *The Rockford Files*, a Brooklyn viewer wrote in to the letters page realizing at last why she liked *The Rockford Files*— "It is the one truly non-sexist TV series on the air" wrote Salli B. Madden. "There are no regular female characters spouting feminist ideologies, but the weekly episodes never fail to include at least one intelligently portrayed woman in a responsible position. As far as I am concerned, the quiet, understated way in which *The Rockford Files* presents liberated females to its audience is worth more than Ann Romano (*One Day at a Time*), Edith Bunker (*All In the Family*) and *Alice* all rolled into one."

Bizarrely, despite all evidence to the contrary, the masculine nature of Cannell's series has provoked many critics to suggest that Cannell "can't write women"; Thompson cites *Black Sheep Squadron* and *The A-Team* to make his point, but in neither case was this Cannell's doing. *Black Sheep Squadron* had bimbos foisted upon it by the network to challenge the ratings power of *Charlie's Angels,* and Cannell's and his writers' response was to promptly satirize this imposition ... while it is common knowledge that in the schoolboyish fantasy *The A-Team,* attempts to include a strong woman in the team (Melinda Culea as Amy Allen) were sabotaged by series star George Peppard, who played a large part in minimizing the female characters' participation, mostly for self-serving motives, although — as with *Mission: Impossible,* the 1960s spy show that was part of the series' inspiration — there was little more for a woman to realistically do other than seduce gullible males without sacrificing credibility to political correctness, with the nature of the drama invariably leaving Culea (and then Marla Heasley as Tawnia Baker) as the delightful decoy, bimbo bait for the parade of gormless oafs who challenged the team each week. Heasley, it transpires, was summoned to Peppard's trailer for what she thought was a welcome speech and brazenly told to her face that she wasn't wanted; both women were ultimately bullied into leaving the series early, but Peppard's comeuppance came in the form of Mr. T's B.A. Baracus, who swiftly overshadowed him as the series' prime draw. One might argue that Cannell could or should have stepped in, but the less self-interested argument that a female team member was a waste of space (and production money) was undeniable, particularly as most episodes had a female guest star who, in the Cannell tradition, did not simply stand at the side of the action but took part. However, in *Hunter,* a series which more than one commentator suggested should have been called "Hunter and McCall," Cannell makes Stepfanie Kramer's tarty but tough DeeDee McCall the co-star (previously, all Cannell's series had featured predominantly all-male groups or male partnerships). Hunter's diminutive but equally dangerous and plucky partner is very much an equal in their assignments and their actions, memorably kicking off her shoes in an early episode to pursue a suspect in her stockinged feet. In those earliest episodes, before Fred Dryer shrugged off his Eastwood clone persona, McCall is amusingly portrayed as the smarter of the two, more like the partnership in Eastwood's *The Gauntlet* than the earlier Eastwood feature *The Enforcer,* which clearly served as partial inspiration for the show. Conservative male egos were partially protected in those early episodes by having McCall's logical assumptions and wisdom frequently proven wrong by Hunter's TV tradition hunches and gut feelings. By the time *Hunter* reached its third season, the Cannell studio's involvement with it was minimal in terms of creative input; *Hunter* became a much more traditional cop show, but did manage to retain most of the positive input Cannell and Kramer had injected during those heady, formative days of adventurous disarray.

First and foremost though, Cannell produced shows in the 1980s for the boys, laden with cars, vans, boats, 'planes, tanks, jeeps and bullets at a time when the media was embracing unquestioningly the more absurdly excessive assumptions of militant feminism. Consequently, it's ironic that his shows turned out to be among the least sexist on television. It's equally interesting that, having written strong women as early as 1974 when he created Beth Davenport for *The Rockford Files,* ten years later, at a time when the networks were at last filling their schedules with series either starring women, or sharing top billing with the guys (*Cagney and Lacey, Kate and Allie, Codename: Foxfire, Hunter, Scarecrow and Mrs. King, Remington Steele, Cover-Up,* etc.),* Cannell chose to introduce his two most blatantly macho boys only shows, *The A-Team* and *Riptide* (twinned in the NBC schedule on Tuesday nights). Both of these series were heavily dressed with beach bunny types with blonde hair, soft eyes and great legs, but Cannell's insistence on making his heroes regular guys rather than super-men meant that the highly-sexed characters in the shows (Templeton Peck in *The A-Team,* Nick and Cody in *Riptide*) did not always get the girl in the grand Hollywood tradition. In "Beneath the Surface" for example, an episode of *The A-Team,* Peck's arrogant over-confidence is yet again his downfall when a gorgeous woman from his youth who never had time for him before but now suddenly attempts to seduce him, is in fact only setting up the A-Team for capture by the military police. Nick and Cody are also frequently duped and conned by attractive women, but the series offers enough genuine relationships and honest women to ensure that the show never lapses into misogyny. Cannell has wisely assumed that the predominantly male audience of these shows will more readily identify with guys who "get lucky" only some of the time. The *Riptide* duo and other Cannell heroes therefore enjoy the same success rate in the dating game as the average male, and their failures, disappointments, and occasional triumphs strike a chord of recognition not present in more typical heroic adventures in which women with big doe eyes trample each other to gaze at the men.

In an interview with Alan Ginsberg for the 54th anniversary edition of *Hollywood Reporter,* Cannell explained his approach to his productions. "What I've basically been trying to do since I started in this business is action/adventure with a sense of humor. There might be some occasional heavy drama or poignant moments, but ... I put no emphasis on sex, money, or power."

Indeed, unlike say, the Aaron Spelling shows, money and power are portrayed as the trappings of the bad guys, and the root of all evil (this was no left-wing childishness though; it was the root of all evil because it's so obviously desirable). Frequently money and power will be the downfall of many a Cannell villain, while for most of Cannell's heroes any visit to the high life is strictly temporary, and received with the same urgent enthusiasm and excitement as it would be by Cannell's mass audience. Cannell's heroes don't live the high life, but once in a while they'll get a taste of it, either through a tempting offer to exchange their freedom and independence for conformity and big bucks (as in *Richie Brockelman's* "A Title On the

---

*It should be remembered that as recently as the '50s and '60s, women rarely even had their own shows named after them; with the exception of unthreatening kids like Gidget *or motherly figures such as* Hazel, *series were titled from a male perspective:* I Love Lucy, I Married Joan, Our Miss Brooks, The Farmer's Daughter, My Mother the Car, My Living Doll, That Girl, I Dream of Jeannie; *it was Darren who was* Bewitched. The Lucy Show *finally, through necessity, broke some of the wall down, until* The Mary Tyler Moore Show *and spin-offs* Rhoda *and* Phyllis *in the 1970s. Had* Cagney and Lacey *been made twenty years earlier it would probably have been called* Our Assistants, the Female Cops...!

Door and a Carpet On the Floor" and the remarkably similar "The Bargain Department" in *Riptide*), or on vacation (a frequent Cannell plot springboard in numerous episodes). In *The A-Team,* the wily Face can acquire a limo, jet, or yacht at a moment's notice, but never for keeps. As Ginsberg points out, "Cannell focusses not on the woebegone wealthy, smothered in mink, nor on heroes who have to have every dame in sight ... or even on characters looking to move up the corporate ladder.* The typical Cannell hero is a blue-collar, regular sort of guy. He may meet a girl or two, but you won't see any stacked starlets strutting their stuff on Cannell's screen."

Of course, Cannell's heroes are rarely married. The emphasis in all of Cannell's series is on freedom, and most of his heroes live enviable lives of idyllic bachelorhood in pleasurable surroundings far removed from dull suburbia and the obligations of a nine-to-five existence. Indeed, few TV heroes *are* married, for the practical and obvious reason that this restricts storylines (revealingly perhaps, married life is left to the sit-com writers), but Cannell goes one step further, with married couples in his series invariably portrayed as either mundane, quarreling, or cheating. A prime example is *The Rockford Files,* in which James Garner's Rockford lives in a trailer on the beach, living only for the TV ball game and fishing trips with his father Rocky, a genial, naive trucker. When we visit the home of harassed cop Dennis Becker and his dull wife Peggy in Juanita Bartlett's "The Paper Palace" it is to enjoy the miserable suburbanites' supreme humiliation when Rockford takes a prostitute he is protecting as his date to an icy evening meal.

Other heroes invariably find themselves with partners either divorced or deceased, but the time for sympathy is usually long past. Only Bill Katt's Ralph Hinckley in *The Greatest American Hero* is going steady (following an unsuccessful marriage) and eventually remarries — to Pam — near the end of the series. This was not the triumph of romance over cynicism; as writer/producer Frank Lupo pointed out to *Starlog* magazine in a 1982 interview, it was purely a matter of convenience — logistically, it was awkward having to pick up Pam during the course of the adventure, and far easier to have her ready for action at Ralph's house! Presumably the 1982 TV audience was not considered ready for unmarried co-habitation. Indeed, Hinckley's shallow and catty ex-wife is played by the same actress (Simone Griffeths) that Jeff Goldblum's Lionel Whitney so narrowly avoided marrying in the pilot for *Tenspeed and Brownshoe* the previous year! In that story, drab accountant Whitney, who fantasizes Richie Brockelman-fashion about living the life of a tough p.i., is whisked away to a life of adventure and intrigue by Ben Vereen's Tenspeed Turner, thus evading the altar, suburban domesticity, and the interfering in-laws in the nick of time!

While Rockford enjoys the single life in a trailer by the sea, the *Riptide* boys go one step further by actually living on a boat, and it is in this series that the bond of male friendship is continuously hammered home. In many episodes, the mere arrival of a woman into the all-male domain is seen as a threat or intrusion into the male idyll and is conveniently repelled by circumstance by the end of the episode. In "Someone is Killing the Great Geeks of America" (!— this title *never* gets into the listings mags accurately!), by Babs Greyhosky, a meeting of high I.Q. types on the Riptide is attended by a female computer wizard who Nick once had a fling with. In Tom Blomquist's "Double Your Pleasure," a young woman Cody has fallen in love with turns out to be a murderous schizophrenic with a split personality; in Frank Lupo's

---

*His one stab at it, the critically acclaimed but heartless series Profit, *a peculiar, soulless aberration that seemed ten years too late in the mid–'90s, deservedly died instantly.*

"Something Fishy," Murray falls for a young woman who only has eyes for Nick. In other episodes, notably the entertaining "Raiders of the Lost Sub" by Mark Jones (the episode which features Geena Davis as Murray's sister Melba Bozinsky), the presence of an attractive ally causes a competitive rift between Nick and Cody which inevitably ends with the departure of the female intruder. This pattern repeats itself constantly throughout the series. In almost all these cases, the women are not at fault ... but the bond between the three male leads is constantly demonstrated to be stronger than the fleeting attractions of romance.

Friendship is a big issue in Cannell productions. Almost all of Cannell's heroes have dependable male friends with whom they can trust their lives (in Hunter's case, it's a woman). In one of many fan publications for Cannell's various series, New York fan Sue-Anne Hartwick points out that "*Hunter* is really unique I think, because for once we get to see a man and woman who can be partners and friends, and who genuinely like and care about each other without anything sexual going on between them. Is this revolutionary, or what? How many TV shows allow a man and a woman to just work together as friends, and that's it?" Fan Jean Thrower points out that, in *The Greatest American Hero* "it was refreshing to see a woman as such an equal part of the trio. Many times she was the only one to keep her head." Having portrayed masculine friendship so distinctively in *The Rockford Files* and *Riptide*, *Hunter* demonstrated that a man and a woman could work together as best friends without hopping between the sheets — yet not once could the show be accused of being coy and prudish. The opening credits exude sexual excitement, yet the good humor and banter between the duo comes not from flirtatiousness, but camaraderie.* Friendship is the subtext of all Cannell's most successful series, and when it is absent — as in *Richie Brockelman, Stingray,* or *The Last Precinct*— the show suffers for it, often failing to spark and catch on with the audience.

Other Cannell series feature ersatz father-son relationships, such as those between Ralph and Bill in *The Greatest American Hero* and the heroes of *Hardcastle and McCormick*— perhaps even Vinnie and Frank in *Wiseguy* (*Rockford Files,* of course, features a genuine father-son set-up). "Bill Maxwell reminds me a little of my dad" said scriptwriter Patrick Hasburgh of *Greatest American Hero*. "He's this guy with a lot of integrity and may be somewhat of a dinosaur, left behind. To him, right and wrong are very clear-cut. Ralph is a little bit more of the generation we've all come from, where he sees things aren't always black and white. Nothing really makes that much sense to him." But behind the conflict, there is trust; all Cannell's heroes will risk everything for their friends.†

From Batman and Robin to Starsky and Hutch, many critics, either through prejudice, trendiness, or wishful thinking, have chosen to see the male friendship in film — or the buddy movie — as a subliminal homosexual fantasy, despite the obvious and frequent evidence to the contrary. Possibly, this cliché reveals more about the mind of the critic — or perhaps the poverty of his personal life — than the characters he or she misunderstands. The homosexual subtext argument is one that dissenters can never win; if there are no women in the heroes' lives it is seen as confirmation, while if there are many, then it's a cover, or over-compensation. It took

---

*Many years into the series a one-off jump in the sheets was briefly alluded to, with the result that the chemistry just wasn't there; it had apparently happened much earlier in the series' run. While as an unnecessary revelation this was a little disappointing, it was perhaps a likely and logical development when the two had been together for so long, although it was the lack of a sexual relationship that was the more original path to take.

†In the occasional case when trust is absent, such as Rockford's love-hate relationship with Angel Martin (Stuart Margolin), a code of honor survives intact. No matter what Angel does, Rockford will stand by him, because he's that kind of guy.

a female critic — Hilary Kingsley of the London *Daily Mail* — to note that "unlike every other glossy TV crime-buster, Hunter seems to treat women as friends."

Having demystified the hero, Cannell also brought the all-powerful sneering villain down to Earth with a bump. "Heavies aren't always guys with bent noses and 42 inch necks" says Cannell staffer Patrick Hasburgh. "A lot of times they're unique, neurotic little people. I mean, Al Capone used to get up in the morning and he didn't feel well. No-one ever talks about that." "A guy who knows he's a villain is a bad character" says Cannell. "The best villains at worst think they're misunderstood!"

Cannell's villains are not Bondian gloaters. They're never happy, even when they're winning, seemingly locked into a hell-on-earth purgatory for their sins. Anguished and irritable, impotent, ignorant, and miserable, they preen and posture ineffectively between bouts of rage and whining, awash with delusions of strength, influence and grandeur, yet forever haunted and tormented by their obvious inadequacy and the painful incompetence of their dim-witted employees. Cannell's bad guys give new meaning to the word stress. To give just one of numerous examples, in the *Rockford Files* episode "The Deep Blue Sleep," James Garner blocks the car of three-time guest villain Robert Webber with his own to confront him. Even though Rockford has no hard evidence against him, can prove nothing, and two gun-toting goons are rushing through the grounds of the bad guy's luxurious home in the background of the scene to move him on, Garner leans on his car cool, calm, and collected, cheerfully smirking at the fuming, raging hoodlum whose every threat while holding the upper hand appears to be bringing him closer to a coronary.

Cannell lampoons the bullying and intimidating thugs and hoods of popular detective mythology gloriously — no-one could delight in identifying with these cretins — and pricks the pomposity of the cops, politicians and bureaucrats who have become the other bad guys of contemporary drama. Regardless of whether they menace by muscle or authority, brainless brute force or political clout, or whether they carry an arsenal of guns or lawyers, Cannell positively ridicules his bad guys into submission, exposing them relentlessly throughout his canon of work for the weak, vain, careless and stupid men they are. Often, the villains can be undone purely by the arrogant assumption that everyone else must surely be as corrupt as they are. In "The Mayor's Committee from Deerlick Falls," an episode of *The Rockford Files* written by Bill Stratton, a cowardly and jittery coven of corrupt small-town officials have no hesitation in offering Rockford a pile of money to kill someone for them, assuming that a two-bit p.i. will be only too eager to grab the small change. When Rockford refuses, they are at once mystified, terrified, and horrified, and are brought down as they hurriedly bungle their efforts to dispose of both Rockford and their original target. In *Wiseguy's* "The Gift," by Cannell and Peter Lance, smooth businessman Amado Guzman (Maximilian Schell) is so confident of Michael Santana's loyalty that he disdainfully mocks Santana's own father for the poverty he lives in because of his principles, unaware that, despite Santana's differences with his father, he is simply fanning the fires of Santana's resolve to destroy him. Even as he embraces Santana as the substitute son for the family he never had, bestowing a prized heirloom of a hand-crafted shotgun on him while sneering at the soldiers like Santana's father who went to war and experienced the horror of what real weaponry could do, he is oblivious to the strength of that love — and that inability to understand sows the seeds of his downfall.

In a Cannell series, big shots and posers are always fair game. "Steve loves to make fun of high rollers" explained *Rockford* writer and future *Sopranos* creator David Chase in a 1979 interview with *Time Out.* "He comes from a very establishment background, and he's a great satirist." But while *Rockford* and *The Greatest American Hero* might qualify, it's difficult to perceive of Cannell's early '80s work as anything quite so sophisticated as satire. Nevertheless, if sophistication on the screen has taken a back seat to Cannell's more conspicuous populism, one theme remains constant; the higher a guy rates himself, the harder the fall he is destined to take (and that goes for the heroes too, whenever they get too over-confident); media personalities, status-seekers, social climbers, and self-serving celebrities of all kinds are picked off by Cannell and his fellow marksmen like ducks in a shooting gallery. Show Cannell a fancy society function, and he'll wreck it, guns blazing, tables turning. And if there's a guy in a tuxedo to be taken down, you can be sure he'll be arrested squarely in the public eye, on the eve of his greatest triumph, in full gaze of all the people he's been trying to impress! A Call Sheet for an episode of *Sonny Spoon* lists the following requirements — Props: Fried pork rinds, cellular 'phone, actors to be bound, gagged, and chained, explosives, remote control device, checklist on clipboard, distributor cap, hors d'oeuvres, diamond case, diamond, automatic weapons, pistol for Wilson, bottle of wine, silencer equipped pistol; Art: wall plug with machine gun hits; Set Dressing: Trunk with Uzi, two automatic pistols, three ski masks; Wardrobe: Caterer uniforms change to terrorists, eye patch; Special Effects: machine gun hits; Atmosphere and stand-ins: three stand-ins, three valets (with change to guest wardrobe), one caterer, two terrorists, one uniformed guard (with change), six cops (with change), thirty five party atmos. Also, three stunt doubles (note how the bit players make up ten extra party goers). The episode was "Diamonds Aren't Forever," filmed November 1988. Just another typical day in the Cannell factory!

In his book *Wild West Movies,* Kim Newman relates the formula of the 1940s B-western, pointing out that "the B-hero is a noble drifter who comes into town, sometimes with a comical sidekick, and sometimes just with a supernaturally intelligent horse, and sorts out whatever trouble is being caused by the crooked saloon owner (or cattle baron) before getting on his way again. If there is a heroine, she is inevitably tied to the community — archetypically as a schoolmarm or the rancher's daughter — and she remains behind while the hero, for whom she has no more than a sisterly (or even maternal) affection, rides off for more fun on the trail. The villains are all big bullies who rarely need to be killed, despite all the frenetic bang-bang shoot-outs and chases, and who are motivated by no more than playground meanness and a lust for unearned profit. Geared to a pre-adolescent's fantasy of life on the range, this ideal has to do with camping out under the stars, having non-dangerous adventures, not getting involved with girls, and always being away from home, as if on an extended holiday from school and chores. The B cowboy hero was a good kid, but he was still just a kid." With the single exception of the *Dirty Harry* clone *Hunter,* the inspiration for which is self-evident, there couldn't be a more appropriate description of Cannell's output in the early 1980s. "He's able to write about what is for the most part youthful in all of us, no matter what age you are" says frequent Cannell director Rod Holcomb.

The one noticeable change to the formula has been the involvement of the women, who — while still mostly playing little sister — are today occasionally allowed a temporary romance or suggested sexual liaison, and no longer remain behind tending the hearth but actively participate in the Peter Pan escapades. Interestingly, even though it is often implied or apparent that a Cannell hero is involved sexually with a woman, Cannell's series exhibit the same boyish disinterest or mature worldly respectfulness toward what goes on between the sheets as those ancient oaters. It is rare to see as much as a kiss on a Cannell show, let alone a tell-tale rumpled sheet. There's no prudishness, no prurience. We don't know, we don't need to know. We can *assume*— if we have to.

As with Cannell's villains (and indeed the villains of the wild west), the smarter the women in Cannell's series dress, the more likely they are to be revealed as treacherous, stuffy, or duplicitous. Cannell's female visitors to the male domain are jeans and t-shirt girl-next-door types. For comical sidekick, today read Bill Maxwell, Murray Bozinsky, Howling Mad Murdock, and Jim Varney's Evan Earp in *Rousters*— maybe even Rocky Rockford and Angel Martin in *The Rockford Files*. And while supernaturally intelligent horses seem to have taken a gallop into the sunset with *Mr. Ed*, *Riptide's* Roboz, alongside *Knight Rider's* KITT 2000, *Airwolf*, and *Streethawk* of Cannell's soul-mates' vigilante shows are surely not that far removed from the tradition?

In the *Riptide* episode "Number One with a Bullet"— written and directed by Cannell— hero Cody Allen (Perry King) is confronted by a young nurse the Riptide detective agency is assisting.

"Why do you do this? I mean, be a private detective?"

"I guess I get to live life on my own terms ... indulge in a sense of romance ... still laugh at the absurdities ... and I don't have to take any orders from anybody. I take my own road now ... sometimes that's not so good, but ... at least it's never boring."

"You're a cowboy! You ride the ranges! No fences! No master!"

"What, are you making fun of me?"

"No, how could I be? We're doing the same thing, Cody. We're both trying to live a child's dream!"*

For all the critical dismay at the vigilanteism, the portrayal of a corrupt or incompetent establishment, the predominant masculine values, and ineffectual bullets and survivable car wrecks of the Cannell fantasies, the leading men — yes, even the A-Team — remain impressive role models for any male viewer. These are the good guys; they like women, hate bullies, and while the legal system, social engineers, intellectuals and politicians struggle, they, at least, have no trouble telling right from wrong. At a time when comic-book super-heroes were — and still are — psychotics and neurotics, and rock idols often egocentric ill-mannered louts, it is ironic indeed that the Cannell shows should have borne the brunt of pop culture's non-participating do-gooders and self-appointed moral guardians' wrath. In a TV environment dominated by grief-free death and duplicity in murder/mystery shows and the emotional psychological violence and unpleasantness inflicted in the prime-time soaps, Cannell makes a very big deal out of trust, friendship, and loyalty. "He brings a good-heartedness to all his work" says director Rod Holcomb. "There's hardly a bad bone in his body or in one of his lead characters. He has a very positive attitude about everything." More than any other writer or producer working in American TV, Cannell's shows demonstrate a healthy sense of values, vulnerability, and human nature. He favors sarcasm over sentiment, and straightforward moral interpretations of right and wrong over ambiguity, controversy, and realism. Despite this, one anonymous rival producer has sneered that "Cannell certainly has his finger on the pulse of the yahoo element of the nation."

Whatever the final verdict, in a sea of authoritarian, self-righteously reassuring establishment fantasies of both reactionary and liberal persuasion, Cannell and his writers were the

---

Later in Wild West Movies, *Newman points out that in "the representative late B-movie* Rider from Tucson *(1950), Tim Holt and his sidekick are appalled that a friend of theirs intends to do a fool thing like getting married, but still help him out when he is threatened by crooks, and when his spunky fiancée proves herself one of the gang."*

first in TV drama to gleefully send up the police, the military, the CIA, FBI, KGB, lawyers, rock stars, phonies, tax-men, quacks, psychologists, self-publicists ... anybody, in fact, who might have previously been taken seriously in other shows....* Indeed, a tell-tale way to spot a bad guy in a Cannell show during the 1970s and the first half of the '80s is to look for anyone who even had the audacity to wear a suit and tie, a Cannell signpost that goes all the way back to *The Rockford Files*. These are the toupeed mobsters, the all-powerful government men, the rock-faced cops, the faceless bureaucrats, the corporate raiders — the saloon owners, cattle barons, and railroad owners of the B-westerns dragged into the late 20th century.

In a Cannell show, the good guys always dress casual, with open shirt collar essential. The bad guys — unless they're redneck thugs or bullies — are always wearing a suit and tie — white shirts only! In *The Greatest American Hero*, Robert Culp's Bill Maxwell character starts out as a heavy — dressed in suit and tie. As the series progresses and he lightens up, he gradually acquires the official Cannell wardrobe of acceptance! Suddenly, he likes fishing and baseball! Of *Hardcastle and McCormick*, *TV Guide's* Robert MacKenzie wrote: "This is the kind of show in which anyone in a suit and tie is automatically a chiseler and a fink; real guys don't dress that way!" In the *A-Team* episode "The Dukes of Whispering Pines," written by Jayne Erlich, B.A. is heard to remark "She ain't so smart! She married a guy who wears ties!," and in the *Hunter* episode "Case X," written by Tom Lazarus, petty red tape is shown to be persistently getting in the way of the real work — another Cannell constant — as Fred Dryer's title character takes great delight in flouting a police dress code that stipulates a jacket and tie. Eventually — echoing a legendary Steve McQueen anecdote — he shows up with jacket and tie — but no shirt!†

This obsession with the petty regulations of the suit-and-tie guys (often represented by recurring characters, such as William Bogert's Carlyle in *Greatest American Hero* and James Whitmore, Jr.'s, Bernie Terwilliger in *Hunter*) inevitably extends to razzing the establishment in all shapes and forms. "Cannell specialises in despising institutionalised authority — the army, police commissioners, medical professionals, etc. — while celebrating tough-guy do-goodism" wrote John Leonard, reviewing *Riptide* for the *New York Herald Tribune*. "Tough guys, listening to their hearts, ignore the rules. Their muscles are sincere, their women are in peril, and they get off on machines"(!).

In fact, Cannell seems to have few qualms about the medical profession, although his characters have gone after their fair share of sinister surgeons and crooked coroners. In Rudolph Borchert's "A Different Drummer," Rockford uncovers an organ transplant ring, and the *Riptide* duo uncover a similar operation in Cannell's "Number One With a Bullet," as does Stingray in Lawrence Hertzog's "Ether," and Sonny Spoon in Jack Bernstein's "The Final Exam." In Gordon Dawson's "The Trees, the Bees, and T.T. Flowers" for *The Rockford Files*, Strother Martin plays an eccentric old man unscrupulously and unceremoniously dumped into care in order for the bad guys to get their hands on his real estate (it was Cannell who first popularized real estate fraud in detective series, another of his more popular plotlines). Rockford finds himself committed with ease in Gordon Dawson's "The Competitive Edge,"

While appearing on the British chat show Wogan in the 1980s, George Peppard — star of The A-Team — *created a brief deafening silence by likening* The A-Team *to Monty Python. In its way, this statement isn't quite so bizarre as it first sounds — both Python and Cannell productions fire numerous broadsides at establishment figures of authority and accepted television conventions. People and institutions who usually found themselves respected in the television environment, suddenly found themselves being questioned and lampooned.*
†*This sequence was apparently based on a true incident from Dryer's football days.*

and a similar predicament awaits Ken Wahl's *Wiseguy* Vinnie Terranova in the episode "White Noise," by Wahl, David Burke, and Alfonse Ruggerio.*

Generally, the targets Cannell has in his sights are not so much *of* the medical establishment, as those disdained by it — callous exploiters, the faith healers, psychics, gurus, and pop psychologists, the fakers and the frauds. Cannell saves an equal amount of poison arrows for pompous pontificating liberals, blustering hypocritical conservatives, media charlatans, and most amusingly and originally, counter-culture phonies, and *The Rockford Files* exhibits a strong disdain for such naiveté in many episodes, including the classic "Quickie Nirvana," written by David Chase, in which flighty hippie Sky Aquarian (Valerie Curtin) flits from one exploitative guru's fad to another, the eternal victim, as well as Cannell's own "Tall Woman in a Red Wagon" in which Rockford poses as a psychiatrist, Chase's "The Oracle Wore a Cashmere Suit" in which Rockford is implicated in a murder by the pronouncements of a police psychic (recurring *Rockford* guest star Robert Webber), and Juanita Bartlett's "The Deadly Maze," in which Larry Linville (Frank Burns of *M*A*S*H*) plays an emotionally barren psychologist who fabricates a phoney case in order to study Rockford's behavior patterns! In the *Riptide* episode "The Hardcase," written by Mark Jones, a psychology book which advocates reasoning with aggressive personalities (and which serves the function of steadying some crooked furniture) only comes in useful to deter three thugs when the heavy tome is employed as a weapon! In a hilarious scene in another *Riptide* episode, "Harmony and Grits," by Tom Blomquist and Babs Greyhosky, detective duo Nick and Cody turn a brotherly love seminar into a wild free-for-all ten years before Bart Simpson achieved the same thing in *The Simpsons*. In "The Circle Broken," an episode of *J.J. Starbuck* by Randall Wallace, Alan Rachins (*L.A. Law's* Douglas Brackman) plays a manipulative swami who uses the duped daughter of a congressman investigating his activ-

Rogue cop *Hunter* (Fred Dryer) — he breaks the rules but knows where to draw the line. The trick is to play the *Magnum Force* card and put the likes of him against vigilantes who aren't so morally grounded (and don't have the scriptwriters on their side).

This story idea also found its way into other non–Cannell shows, such as Lou Grant, Streets of San Francisco, *and* Harry O.

ities as a patsy to murder her troublesome father, while in "The Dwarf in the Helium Hat," another classic *Rockford,* self-deceiving rock star Jay Rockfelt (a priceless performance by John Pleshette) incurs the wrath of the mob, whose moronic goons ring up Rockford instead of Rockfelt to make their threatening ultimatums. In fact, Cannell's shows give the rock world a regular pasting throughout his series, from *Greatest American Hero's* posturing fraud in "It's Only Rock and Roll" by Babs Greyhosky to Cody's disillusionment at discovering his rock idol is a mean-minded exploiter in Tom Blomquist's *Riptide* story "Wipeout" and Cannell's own splendid "Number One With a Bullet"—also for *Riptide*—which satirizes fan adoration of often unworthy buffoons. A run of *Wiseguy* episodes is set in the rock industry with Tim Curry as unhinged rock impresario Winston Newquay (formerly Sid Fishbine of London's East End)* and in Frank Lupo's "Classical Gas," another contribution to *The Greatest American Hero,* the villain is a deranged rock concert promoter (busy Cannell regular Ed Winter). Cannell belatedly evens the score for rock impresarios to a degree with Randall Wallace's "Who's Got Tonsillitis?" in *Sonny Spoon,* where it's the agent who's being short-changed by the not-so-soulful Lamont Dupont (Leon Isaac Kennedy), a lip-synching singer.

"He always came at shows with a very odd, quirky perspective that the average person didn't step up and see," remembered Frank Lupo of his 1980s tenure with Cannell to *Variety* in 1995. "He liked to take genres that were very firmly entrenched, and bend them and twist them and come at them in a way you never expected." "Steve brought humor and sass to television drama in ways that I don't think anyone else had," agreed late-'80s colleague David Burke. "He has a wonderful way of writing dialogue that's both funny and engaging as well as storyline-conscious, and he roots around in unusual characters, especially in *Wiseguy,*" said director Rod Holcomb. "One of his best series was *Tenspeed and Brownshoe.* It was really smart and funny, had a very fast repartee and good casting."

The *Rockford Files* episode "Trouble in Chapter Seventeen," by Juanita Bartlett, ridicules anti-feminist authoress Ann Clement (Claudette Nevins), whose success as a career woman in the business of promoting serene domesticity (for other women) turns her husband into an impotent adulterer, while "A Good Clean Bust with Sequel Rights" sends up the very sort of "anti-violence" child-protecting crusaders Cannell would be confronted by himself, a decade later, during the popularity of *The A-Team.* "Who's home with the kids while you're out waving the banners?," enquires Rockford disdainfully.

One popular cliché of TV cop shows that Cannell makes good use of without subverting, is the status-seeking, self-serving investigative journalist, who turns up to give the cop heroes of both *Baretta* and *Hunter* a hard time. It took four writers to produce "Street Edition," in which Baretta's attempts to expose corruption in city hall are not helped, but hindered, by journalist Sandra Fleming (Andrea Marcovicci) who, if she would only get out of the way and stop asking difficult questions, would allow the police to get on with the job of weeding out the villains in high places! In the even more ludicrous "Saturday Night Special," an episode of *Hunter* written by Marianne Clarkson and Allison Hock, it's a journalist (Anne-Marie Johnson) who not only obstructs the open and fair-minded police from apprehending a skid-row killer, but turns out to be prolonging the story with a little bit of murder on the side herself. Both news and television reporters are the scum of the earth on TV cop shows (even the classy ones), always giving the game away when the cops are trying to keep the lid

---

*Sadly, neither the British-born Curry nor anyone else working on the series saw fit to enlighten the American and Canadian creatives on the pronunciation of "Newquay"; Fishbine is said to have taken his phoney name from the English seaside town of the same name—everyone in the show pronounces it "New-cway," but in fact it's New-key.

on something for the good of an easily-panicked public, but effortlessly manipulated into printing helpful lies when the bad guys need that extra little prod into action.* Somewhat more originally, an arrogant and magnificently offensive fashion designer played by Rene Auberjonois gets it in the neck in Rudolph Borchert's "With the French Heel Back, Can the Nehru Jacket Be Far Behind?" for *The Rockford Files,* and a vulgar and imposing family of slobs intrude on Rockford's space with their motor-home in David Chase's "The Queen of Peru" to test Rockford's liberal tolerance level to the limit.

Nevertheless, Cannell's most consistent targets are those in uniform or carrying government passes. Official government agencies such as the FBI and the CIA are frequently on Cannell's hit list, and take as tough a drubbing as the gormless, egocentric mobsters and harassed, troubled thugs Cannell pits them against. In "The Dog and Pony Show," a classic *Rockford Files* written by David Chase and directed by Reza Badiyi, George Loros, a familiar Cannell face invariably cast as a dumb hood (and with several appearances in *Rockford* to his credit) plays a mobster whose sister has married a man who is mentally ill and become a threat to his empire. Family connections forbid him to eradicate the problem with customary mob efficiency, and so the dark sheep is consequently hidden away in an L.A. laughing academy under a pseudonym. In a typically convoluted *Rockford* scenario, the hapless Rockford, already in trouble with the authorities yet again as the episode begins, is in court alongside the treacherous no-good weasel Evelyn "Angel" Martin, an unsavory hanger-on from his prison days (Rockford, in grand TV tradition, is an ex-con who was wrongly imprisoned for the famous crime he didn't commit). Martin's advantages as a conniving sneak and informer are far outweighed by his liabilities as a would-be friend; as a decoy or look-out, Angel stays around about as long as a flame on a match. The first line of the episode is Angel lamenting that "everybody steals a hotel fork now and again!" as the camera pans heartlessly past a security guard staring blandly at a beautiful silver service tea set that Angel has surreptitiously slipped into Jim Rockford's vehicle. Rockford's protestations of ignorance are to no avail, and the two of them are given suspended sentences on the condition that they attend the sessions of a well-meaning psychiatrist. There, the weary Rockford, resigned to the injustice of it all, sits patiently through endless hours of tedious therapy with the resident airheads, one of whom is an insecure woman with a history of paranoia ... something Rockford is blissfully unaware of until after he has agreed to investigate the identities of "mysterious men" who have been following her.

The concept of the investigative journalist actually getting to the truth herself (yes, herself — curiously, the real superschmuck journos are always jumped-up women who end up in jeopardy or having to apologize for the egg all over their faces at story's end), despite the efforts of the police and other authorities to keep things covered up, rarely gets an airing in American TV outside of series in which the journalists are heroes (the only two successful series of which were The Name of the Game *and* Lou Grant). *Failures have included travesties such as the late '70s* The American Girls, *in which two bimbos from the* Charlie's Angels *school of investigative journalism fluttered their way to the truth, and the farcical* Capital News, *a late-'80s MTM misfire with a thoroughly unlikable and inept cast of incompetent yuppies either stumbling onto news stories by accident or making a hash of them (one classic episode had a — girl — reporter not only leave a tape of her interview with a bad guy behind at his office, but revealed that she had recorded her conversation with the editor claiming that they were going to nail the crooks, so inviting charges — with evidence — of bias!). Male investigative journalists are invariably obnoxious louts but minus the integrity and good intentions of Robert Walden's obstreperous Joe Rossi in* Lou Grant *(Gerrit Graham, a professional meanie on TV, has played vicious journalists in such diverse shows as* My Two Dads *and* The Young Riders!), *female journalists always scatty, flighty and naive young girls who usually get what they deserve for being so hostile and pushy. Friendlier series instead plump for the more appropriately dubious tabloid hack from a thinly-disguised* National *something-or-other-but-definitely-not-the-*Enquirer; *a prime example is Tricia O'Neill's character in "Catch of the Day," a* Riptide *episode in which she plays a tabloid hack who has come to Pier 57 to exploit a slow-witted young man who claims to have seen a mermaid, or indeed the recurring character of Jack Colvin's Jack McGee in Ken Johnson's late-'70s adaptation of* The Incredible Hulk, *the model for all those who followed. Unfortunately, it's a tough profession to stick up for.*

Naturally, Rockford declines to pursue his investigation when this information is made available to him, eventually making only brief half-hearted enquiries to placate her after a tearful scene. To everyone's amazement, she really is being followed by a couple of goons in a car wearing the license plates of one of the mental hospitals she had previously been staying in. One of her fellow patients is the frightened and paranoid Joseph Bloomberg, who claims to be a CIA agent incarcerated after threatening to write a book exposing outrageous Firm activity in Chile. Having insisted that he has been dumped in the institution to stop him from blowing the whistle on his former masters, Rockford is dismayed to learn from Angel (accompanying him on a midnight escape attempt) that Bloomberg really *is* crazy, mob-connected, and exactly where he belongs. The CIA have meanwhile been spurred on to over-zealous activity by the transparent inquiries of Rockford at their office concerning the bogus Bloomberg, and — in a hilarious scene in which they postulate various "scenarios" pertaining to Rockford's motives — turn up at the estate of the mobster who put Bloomberg away just as Rockford is bargaining and blackmailing his way out of a mass termination of all concerned ... now including the unhappy CIA agents!

Cannell's prevalent anti-authority stance inevitably extends itself to the military, who are invariably portrayed as narrow-minded by-the-book hawks and fanatics. In "The November Plan," the pilot for Cannell's 1976 detective series *City of Angels*, a crazed industrialist is assembling a private army to stage a military coup. Producing the series with Cannell was Phil De Guere, who would later create the *Rockford*-inspired *Simon and Simon;* a similar covert para-military force is being formed in that series' first season episode "Tanks for the Memories." In Cannell's *Rockford Files* itself, the military mentality took a drubbing in Cannell's "Two into 5.56 Won't Go." There's no deference or flag-saluting from Rockford, just pragmatic caution and respect for individuals rather than stripes or badges.

In "Operation: Spoilsport," an episode of *The Greatest American Hero* written by Frank Lupo, an insane military man kidnaps a computer expert and forces him to reactivate a Cold War relic — a revenge system, which, in the event of a nuclear attack from Russia, will annihilate any survivors behind the Iron Curtain one day after the initial conflagration. When a nuclear strike is activated inadvertently (amid great chaos, panic and confusion in the monitoring procedure), the initial threat is quickly disarmed, but the 24 hour doomsday device is not so easily canceled.

Demented military men with half the U.S. armed forces at their beck and call to unquestioningly bring about havoc are a popular recurring theme in Cannell's series, and were quickly seized on by other series producers — virtually every action/adventure show of the 1980s featured at least one episode with a crazed colonel or gibbering general; one of the best is the second season *Airwolf* episode "Firestorm," by Calvin Clements. And of course, Cannell's ever-popular A-Team are continuously harangued by the frequently humiliated Colonel Lynch (Bill Lucking) and Commander Decker (Cannell regular Lance Le Gault), who pursue the team across the country to no avail, only to be replaced — albeit briefly — by Charles Napier as Captain Briggs (third season) and the similarly inclined General Harlan "Bull" Fulbright (fourth season), played by Jack Ging, also the highly unpleasant cop Lt. Quinlan from *Riptide!* Even Cannell's military series, the World War II–based *Black Sheep Squadron* in 1976, was a collection of tall tales adapted from *Baa Baa Black Sheep,* the somewhat suspect memoirs of the late General Pappy Boyington, and told of a maverick, authority-defying squadron of misfits and hellraisers in a curious and highly watchable cocktail of World War II movie clichés and *M*A*S*H*-style humanity and liberalism. Revealingly, the first two of Cannell's contributions have a distinctly familiar take, with titles blatantly infused with wild west imagery — "Trouble at Fort Apache" and "The Fastest Gun"! And Charles Napier — later *The A-Team's* Captain Briggs — is the enraged Major Red Buell, whom Robert Conrad's Boyington emasculates not just once — in the pilot — but again, in the first episode of the series!

Cannell gets away with all his irreverence toward the status quo because he played the TV business at its own game, and he played it very well. He never whined about network censorship for two very good reasons; he had an enviable string of successes to his credit that gained him the trust of the networks, and he never put anything into his programming that was remotely contentious to the network mentality. He worked within the medium, subverting TV conventions from the inside, providing the networks with what they wanted and expected (and expected their viewers to want) but on his own terms. But because he provided the broadcasters with the programming they wanted, rather than producing more blatantly challenging and difficult series, his achievements have been often overlooked by those who have heaped (deserved) critical acclaim onto the more daring, direct approach of such talented mavericks as MTM and their offshoots. Instead, his series were more often unfairly thrown into the same category as the Aaron Spelling/Glen Larson fantasies they sent up ... for, like Spelling, Larson and co., Cannell also dealt not in dramatic debate and social science but neat, escapist wish-fulfillment. You want rid of the corporate bullies/mobsters/thugs/drug dealers? Here's the A-Team to clean house!

But Cannell always insisted that, like his heroes, he was his own man. "I always try to be as pragmatic as I possibly can about the business we're in, and not tilt at windmills just because they're there," he told fellow producers during a transcripted roundtable for *Emmy* magazine. "It's not a matter of being a 'network producer,' it's just the opposite of that. I have only one barometer in my work, and that's the way I feel about it. If I try to produce it like a network executive, or so that anybody else will like it, then I'm guessing. Anytime I'm sitting down at the typewriter, I'm trying to please myself. I want to be able to read that script and say 'Yeah, that's a good script, I'm proud of that work.'

"Then I go to Step Two. And Step Two is I try to produce it as close to the image I have for it as I possibly can. That means I'm going to run into some people — network executives — who may disagree with some of the things that I put down on paper. They're going to say 'gee, you can't do that because we're going to program this at 8:00' or whatever it is. And I've got to deal with those problems. That is a negotiation, and in some cases, a compromise.

"The fact of the matter is, some of the greatest pictures ever produced were produced under the Hays Commission, when you couldn't have two people on a bed together. Maybe it's just the kind of work that I do, because I try to do character comedies as opposed to issue-oriented types of films. My view may be colored by that, but I have not felt that I've been hassled by Standards and Practices. There's only been a couple of times when I've said 'If you take this out of the picture I refuse to make the movie.' Most of the time I've been able to find acceptable compromises with them by understanding their problems. If I do bad work, I'm certainly not going to blame the network censor for it. I think we have some responsibilities to produce for a broad-based medium within certain guidelines. I don't always agree with the network's position on it, but usually if you sit down and work with them, you can come up with a way to write the situation so that it works for them."

Juanita Bartlett, writer on *The Rockford Files, Stone, Tenspeed and Brownshoe* and *The Greatest American Hero* reaffirmed this point of view in an interview with *Starlog* magazine. "We've had no real problems with ABC," she told interviewer James Burns, when she was working on *The Greatest American Hero*. "We have a pretty good relationship with the people that we deal with over there. Sometimes the network comes up with an idea that's even better than what we had. It's a give and take situation."

"There certainly is trust, which we also always had on *The Rockford Files*," insisted Bartlett. "On *Rockford*, there'd be certain instances with Standards and Practices where they'd say to us 'Oh dear, are you really going to do this?' We'd say 'Wait a minute, we're not in the bad taste business, it's going to be okay.' They'd believe us and let us do it."

Nevertheless, it wasn't all smooth sailing. Robert Culp related one exception—ironically concerning Bartlett's *Greatest American Hero* script "The Lost Diablo"—in another *Starlog* interview. "Some bad guys try to stop us," said Culp, relating the story. "Bill and Ralph get out of the mine, and the bad guys get buried. But because it's an 8:00 show, we can't have Maxwell bury them in the mine, or Ralph bury them in the mine. It has to be an act of God, in terms of an earthquake, and I'm really sick of that shit, but that's what we're stuck with right now."

"On American TV, at 8:00, you can't kill people," confirmed Chris Bunch and Allan Cole, two freelance writers who have contributed to various action/adventure shows, including Cannell's *Hunter* and *The A-Team*. "You can't shoot anyone. You have to miss everyone, like on *The A-Team*. In *The Incredible Hulk*, the Hulk would pick up a guy and throw him through the window, and the obligatory line in the script was 'He sits there, stunned.' And that's how you get away with it. At 8:00 you can do very little, at 9:00, you can do a bit more, at 10:00 you can start getting away with stuff."

Faced with the limitations of TV Standards and Practices, not to mention the restrictions of his budget, Cannell knew he couldn't match the effects of a *Superman* movie or get Clint Eastwood for a *Dirty Harry* series, and so did his audience. Instead, he gave them Ralph Hinckley and Rick Hunter, Hardcastle and McCormick instead of *Magnum Force* and *The Star Chamber*—and it worked. Cannell gently sends up his characters, their situations, the genre involved, and the television medium itself. A real-life Rockford or Jake Axminster would be an immoral "sleazeball" (to borrow some *A-Team* terminology) and Cannell knows that too; a genuine Judge Hardcastle, Bill Maxwell, Rick Hunter or A-Team would be a nightmare, because sooner or later they would (and do) make a mistake, and so Cannell loads the dice in their favor—he pits them against a worse mirror-image, a real vigilante or bounty hunter, a harder FBI man or band of mercenaries, a genuine renegade cop. It's a simple trick that might be termed the *Magnum Force* principle as the ploy dates back at least to one of the best examples of the gimmick in Clint Eastwood's 1973 *Dirty Harry* sequel of the same name, in which the canny Eastwood attempted to answer critics of the politics of *Dirty Harry* by pitting the moral individualist Harry Callahan—who, in the first feature, takes the law into his own hands and goes his own way—against a group of vigilante motor-cycle cops who had also taken the law into their own hands by executing pimps and dealers. Faced with the criticism that Dirty Harry Callahan is a dangerous fascist vigilante, screenwriter John Milius (later a writer/director of madly right-wing fantasies) legitimizes Callahan's actions by pitting him against a force of even worse vigilantes; while Harry is in control of his vigilanteism, able to tell simple right from wrong in the face of bureaucratic fudging, cunning lawyers and corrupt politicos, this group of helmeted, jackbooted motor-cycle cops have gone not just over the line, but over Harry's line, blowing away anybody and everybody who gets off under the guidance and supervision of frustrated cop Hal Holbrook. Thus the excesses of the vigilante hero become acceptable within the framework of the story in order to terminate the activities of those likeminded lawmen who don't share Harry's hawklike eye for the borderline. Now Eastwood's character is the good guy, a loose cannon with perfect aim going after and disposing of a group of loose cannons who have gone wildly off-target, spraying everybody with lead, and it works time and time again, justifying the questionable behavior of the hero by making the antagonists' actions even more outrageous or immoral. The premise of *Magnum Force* was lifted virtually intact for the storyline of the 1980 pilot for Cannell's short-lived *Stone.*

In *The Star Chamber,* a few years later, Hal Holbrook appears again in much the same role, as leader of a group of judges casually administering justice to the criminals who appear before them and get off on technicalities, hung juries, procedural errors and so on; compare this dark vision, which comes completely unstuck when Holbrook and his cronies inevitably start making mistakes and misjudgments of their own (and are forced to cover themselves by disposing of innocents who threaten to expose their own illegalities), with the bright and breezy premise of Cannell's *Hardcastle and McCormick,* in which hero Judge Hardcastle forces a parolee into joining him in a clean-up crusade against all the villains he saw pass through his courtroom untouched by justice. This, of course, is precisely why you don't have self-appointed rule-breakers and vigilantes running around at all, a point numerous cop and lawyer shows (such as *Hill Street Blues, L.A. Law, Law and Order, Mancuso FBI,* and many more, including *Hunter* in the memorable three-parter "City Under Siege" and others) have made on a number of occasions even as they justly savage and lampoon the failings of the authorities (and in many cases, still pander to populist emotionalism). It's the old "you'll be as bad as him"/"don't let him drag you down to his level"/"that's what separates us from him" routine.

Almost all of Cannell's series have a dark side episode in which the heroes meet their Mr. Hyde personas — in *Stone,* it's Gordon Dawson's "The Man in the Full Toledo"; in *The A-Team,* it's Richard Christian Matheson and Thomas Szollosi's "Deadly Manoeuvres" in the second season, Milt Rosen's "Showdown" in the third season, and Cannell and Lupo's "Waiting for Insane Wayne" in the fourth season; in *Hardcastle and McCormick,* it's Shel Willens' "The Georgia Street Motors"; Cannell even pits Ralph Hinckley, his *Greatest American Hero,* against an earlier recipient of the super-suit who abused the suit's powers and had it taken away from him, in Cannell's "Don't Mess Around with Jim." In *Hunter,* the *Magnum Force* principle is employed in virtually every episode of the early '80s — Hunter and McCall must do what they do because the other guys are worse! In "The Garbage Man," by Sidney Ellis, a vigilante lowlife (Ed O'Neill, still some years away from his classic portrayal of the tragic Al Bundy in the *Married—with Children* series) is killing off parolees, and "Dead or Alive," written by Lupo, offers Wings Hauser as a callous cowboy bounty hunter. In "Killer in a Hallowe'en Mask," written by *A-Team* regular Stephen Katz, McCall poses as an obnoxious cleaning lady in order to sneak a look at the confidential files of a psychiatrist who is ethically witholding legally protected information about a suspected killer. In "Rich Girl," written by Stephen Cotler, Hunter cons a flirtatious secretary into making him a photocopy of another privileged document, this time an unread will which might conceal a motive for murder. In each case, the script is written and the story developed to ensure that Hunter and McCall are justified in their suspicions, so making their unorthodox behavior approvable. The practice reaches its most extreme example in the two-parter "Rape and Revenge," written by Tom Lazarus and directed by Gary Winter and Richard Colla, in which Hunter pursues vile multiple rapist and murderer Raoul Mariano (Richard Yniguez) back to his fictional Latin country specifically to blow him away after he claims diplomatic immunity to avoid prosecution for the rape of McCall. Unlike many lesser endeavors (mostly for the wide screen), the stepping-on-eggshells script goes through the standard TV trials of making it loud and clear that Hunter and McCall have gone through all legal channels, that Hunter almost changes his mind about killing Mariano, and that the rape is presented as a permanent traumatic horror rather than a convenient plot point, and presented in a non-exploitative way. Much of this was due to the input of Stepfanie Kramer (McCall), and despite the glaring populist vigilante nature of the storyline the episode was a model example, if not of social conscience realism then at least of how to do horrific drama without being gratuitous. The producers even made sure that the event was not conveniently forgotten at episode's end by including a heavy-handed reference to McCall's healing process in the later episode "The Set Up." As "Rape and Revenge" proceeds, the atrocities of Mariano are piled on (at one point he even brazenly takes a potshot at Hunter, putting a bullet in the officer in the full knowledge he can't be touched) until Hunter finally exacts justice in a cathartic orgy of homicide that gives the audience a huge surge of relief and the guilty satisfaction of retribution in a brief respite from a real world where callous crimes of brutality go unpunished every day.

But as often as American TV shows praise the hero who steps outside the constraints of the system to take matters into his own hands, various episodes of these same series condemn this behavior in other individuals; the Cannell-created cop series *Baretta* is positively schizophrenic in this respect. In "Once More for Free," an episode of MTM's *Paris* written by ex-cop Burton Armus, Michael Conrad (Sgt. Esterhaus in *Hill Street Blues*) plays a *Dirty Harry*-type cop who, although retired, muscles in on a police operation to put a drugs dealer he could never catch while on the force out of commission ... but his vigilante actions ruin a police operation in progress. In the *Mancuso FBI* episode "Death and Taxes," a terminally ill FBI man, distressed by the idea that he will die while the mob lives on, commits the cold-blooded and calculated murder of a gangland bride to initiate a gang war ... only to find that his actions have caused the death of a deep undercover operative who was on the verge of crushing the mob family legally. The *Law and Order* episode "Subterranean Homeboy Blues" was one of a number of concerned studies into the notorious subway vigilante incident of the mid–'80s, when a white passenger on the New York underground pulled out a gun on a crowded train and shot three black youths he claimed were threatening him.

Does the end justify the means? *Hill Street Blues, L.A. Law,* and the better episodes of *Wiseguy* were among the very few shows of the 1980s to tackle the theme. As long as the democratically appointed politicians and their laws continue to fail the system, contemporary American television will continue to wrestle with the problem.

Cannell — Origins and Method

Like many producers of U.S. TV, Cannell has assembled over the years a reliable stock company of actors, writers and directors who can be sure to turn up in the credits for his shows with inevitable regularity (although none are exclusive to Cannell; all Cannell's recurring cast members and guest players do the rounds of other genre shows, of course). Scanning the episode listings in this book reveals the same familiar names appearing time and time again; as the programs are aired numerous familiar faces recur, some even appearing in several roles within the same series. There are those viewers who are irritated by this (this writer personally prefers recurring characters to different roles for the same players), but there is a pleasing feeling of comfort and amusement that comes from spotting familiar faces in Cannell shows that shouldn't be underrated; it's like a guarantee, a reassurance that you'll get exactly what you expect from a Cannell production. Faced with the prospect of only one appearance by a well-cast bad guy during the run of a series, or seeing a less charismatic villain, the regulars among Cannell's stock players are more preferable any time. A Cannell series just doesn't seem like a Cannell series without a guest appearance or two from Robert Webber, Joseph Sirola, George Loros, Richard Romanus, Dana Elcar, Ed Winter, Alan Fudge, James Luisi, Joe Santos, Jeff MacKay, Jack Ging, Red West, James Whitmore, Jr., Dennis Franz, Anthony Charnota, Michael Baseleon, Lance Le Gault, Louis Giambalvo, Ken Swofford, Dennis Lipscombe, Vincent Baggetta, Clyde Kusatsu, Luke Andreas, Paul Koslo, Gianni Russo, John Quade, Jonathan Banks, Mills Watson, Dennis Burkley, Michael Alldredge, William Windom, or Keenan Wynn!

Some of Cannell's directors go back to his days on the Jack Webb cop shows, including Arnold Laven, Dennis Donnelly, and Bruce Kessler. Others, such as Chuck Bowman, Craig Baxley and Bob Bralver are former stunt-men turned assistant director. Other contributors, mostly writers, have come aboard since Cannell formed his own company. These include Frank Lupo, Babs Greyhosky, and Patrick Hasburgh, while Juanita Bartlett arrived via *The Rockford Files* and *Nichols* (Garner's previous non–Cannell series). Already gone on to solo careers by the time Cannell became an independent were Phil DeGuere (*Simon and Simon*, the 1980s *Twilight Zone*), Donald Bellisario (*Magnum, p.i., Airwolf, Quantum Leap, JAG*), and David Chase (*Almost Grown, The Sopranos*). Cannell's *Greatest American Hero* in particular served as a training ground for many of Cannell's later arrivals, who cut their writing teeth for Cannell on the comic-book exploits of heroes Ralph and Bill; others have been with him since *Rockford*, as had almost all the other directors he bought with him. Les Sheldon came to Cannell from MTM after working on their situation comedies to produce *Hardcastle and McCormick*, and stayed to produce and direct on numerous Cannell series; he brought director Tony Mordente with him. Thomas Szollosi and Richard Christian Matheson came to Cannell to work as scriptwriters and story editors on *The A-Team, Hunter,* and *Hardcastle and McCormick* from Glen Larson, where they'd contributed to *Battlestar Galactica, CHiPs, Quincy, B.J. and the Bear* and *Knight Rider*. A whole new slew of writers, actors, and directors and producers joined up with Cannell as of *Stingray, Wiseguy, Jump Street,* and the start of his Canadian operation, about which, more later.

Cannell's fail-safe method of creating a series and getting it off on the track he intends would be to take a hand in writing the pilot himself (often with his collaborator throughout most of the 1980s, Frank Lupo), and then write the opening episode himself. Then he, and each of his regular team would go off to write an episode themselves (often drawing on themes explored in the pilot). Story ideas are talked through and handed out until a number of episodes are completed, and then the process starts again. As a writer himself, Cannell has the valuable ability, both creatively and administratively, of being able to empathize with his writers. Cannell has pointed out that his studio was one of the first to be run by a writer, and prioritizes writing over directing or producing when defining himself; indeed, his reason for walking away from *Baretta*, which he created and then departed (amicably), was the realization that Robert Blake was going to change all his dialogue.

Cannell didn't have to write, but he always did, sitting down at the typewriter every morning and tapping out scripts for all his shows, whether they were his latest babies or not. Any

Cannell series will have scripts by the boss throughout its run, even just before the close, and he'll spend just as much time, energy and inspiration on his oldest show as his newest.* And Cannell didn't just turn out the pilot and first two episodes and then leave it to a band of underlings to keep the show afloat while he barked commands. Instead, he held regular story conferences for all his series in production, batting ideas around, handing out assignments, and adding and subtracting to other peoples' scripts and ideas. "Well, I just love to write," Cannell told a TV interviewer. "You know, I was a guy who was driving a furniture truck for a while, and flunking out of school, so when I finally found this thing that I could do, it felt so good I just kept doing it and doing it, and that's why I stayed at it."

Cannell's poor track record in education is — amazingly, given his chosen profession — due to dyslexia, a condition he was unaware he suffered from as a child. "They didn't call it dyslexia in those days," Cannell explained to writer Peter Rigby, "it didn't have a fancy name. What happens is you tend to mirror-read or reverse letters or figures when you see them. And the trouble is, you're completely unaware that you're doing it." "Because of it," Cannell told journalist Dusty Saunders, "I've become an over-achiever. That's one reason I have so many projects going at once." His scripts were typed up by his secretary Grace Curcio, who was previously a secretary at Universal for Jack Laird, the producer of *Kojak* and *Night Gallery*. As the woman who deciphered, interpreted and retyped Cannell's scripts, Curcio was invaluable to the Cannell operation. She joined Cannell "...because I was so taken with his energy and enthusiasm, I suddenly realized I was incredibly bored with the job I had and that I needed to make a change." When Cannell left to start his own operation, "I was one of a handful of secretaries at Universal who had reached top seniority, and if it ever became neccesary to return, I would have had to start at the bottom again," she told interviewer Sylvia Souza. "But I loved working with Stephen, and I couldn't see myself working for anyone else, so I took the plunge and I've never been sorry."

"In six years, I never had to send back a script or complain about a scene," James Garner told Jeff Silverman of *US* magazine. "They were clean and working when I got there. Steve has a feel. He gets a character in a mood, gets in it with the character, starts writing, and it just comes out."

"I see what I'm writing," says Cannell. "I become all the characters. If I'm Hannibal Smith, I know him, I know what he's like, I know his sense of irony. I get that sort of gleam in my emotional eye. And then I become Murdock, and I get into that nut bag with him. And that's the way I go through the script. I'm pushing it sometimes, but there's always something in the back of my mind directing it, because I never get too far into the weeds. I always end up where I want to go." "And I also like television," Cannell told a reporter from Associated Press. "That's another thing. I'm not better than my audiences. I sometimes talk to people who are saying 'well, you know, they'll like this' or 'they'll like that.' I always say — what do *I* like? Then I try to *write* something I like and if I'm on target it works, and if I'm not, it doesn't."

As Cannell's shows are not computer-created contrivances, but based on this combination of his own gut impulses and the later input of his writers and actors, Cannell's series find their footing over the weeks, introducing new ideas as they are conceived, and throwing out

---

*The one exception has been Baretta, *to which Cannell did not contribute again after writing the pilot. Instead, the series was left in the capable hands of Roy Huggins and Phil DeGuere to oversee until Huggins left and DeGuere moved over to* Black Sheep Squadron, *leaving the series in the control of others at Universal. Many of those who worked on* Baretta *later went on to work for Donald Bellisario on* Airwolf.

original inclusions that have not worked, or have become over-used or redundant. In the 1980s, this approach was rare and unique, virtually unseen in the media since the creation of the Warner Brothers cartoon stable in the 1930s and '40s, and the Marvel Comics universe in the 1960s. As the episodes are being put into the can, Cannell's series are constantly evolving and growing. Cannell and his team's *modus operandi* was to throw in as many gimmicks and as much dressing as possible when the show was on the drawing board, let the cast add their own embellishments, and then throw out whatever wasn't working as the series goes on. Top heavy to start with, what remained is what worked. "A series is ongoing maintenance in a strange way," Cannell told writer Jane Lane. "You write something, you cast it, you film it. Then you watch the dailies and say 'I don't think he looks right in that leather coat.'"

Possibly the most prominent example of this process was the abandoning of Anne Francis' character Mama Jo and her boatload of escort girls after the first few episodes of *Riptide*. In fact, so strong were the three leads together that almost all the extra paraphernalia thrown into the show at the start, including the Roboz, a comical robot, faded into the background as the series progressed — as did the supporting cast for Cannell's later series, *J.J. Starbuck*. This was unfortunate for the performers involved, but Cannell had ensured they were there for the writers — and the network — in the first place, had they been needed. It's a practice almost entirely reversed by other program makers, who can often be found desperately throwing in additional attractions as the show sinks. Series such as *The A-Team, Hardcastle and McCormick* and *Hunter* were all shows that noticeably improved as the weeks went by, rather than flagging or fading — and if the show started to slip into a rut — as *The A-Team* did at one point — Cannell was not afraid to tinker with the formula for the series' fourth and fifth seasons (even though the fifth season of *The A-Team* was a horrible disaster).

Naturally Cannell added and experimented as his shows ran as well, sometimes from network suggestions, again the most prominent example being *Riptide*, which added a number of minor co-stars to the cast during the show's run, mostly for demographic effect, and also mostly to little effect. A thick-skinned, empty-headed young surfer called Dooley (Ken Olandt) was added to the recurring characters in the second season to introduce an element of trouble-making Angel/Rockford style, but offered little to the writers that they couldn't find in their less-than-flawless lead characters themselves, and the ownership of pier bar Straightaway's changed periodically, also to little avail, while a lady cop (June Chadwick as Lt. Parisi) appeared on the scene for a platonic friendship to counteract the guys' womanizing.

All these additions were almost certainly at the behest of network interference, and the characters might as well have been carrying neon placards to announce it, but it was the ideas, notions, and catch-phrases that crossed from one Cannell series to another that added the most color, as Cannell's regular team of writers re-used favorite tricks and gags in frequent in-jokes that also saved Cannell's lawyers from constantly clearing new names for characters and corporations. If something worked — or didn't work — in one series, it could often be found showing up elsewhere — much to the delight of trivia hounds. For example, the phrase "Works for me," which became a gimmick in the first two seasons of *Hunter* until lead actor Fred Dryer canned it, had originally been developed by Cannell and Lupo for Ralph Hinckley in *The Greatest American Hero*, who uses the expression constantly throughout the episode "The Shock Will Kill You." Similarly, Bill Katt and Robert Culp's "think white paper, white paper" routine from Cannell's "Don't Mess Around with Jim" episode for the same series turns up again in his "The Road to Hope" for *The A-Team*, in which Murdock uses it to clear his mind and become invisible (although Ralph has powers of invisibility for real, he uses the routine to control his telekinetic powers!). Cannell is very fond of using catch-phrase gimmicks on his series, such as Richie Brockelman's "the thing of it is" and Bill Maxwell's constant use of the word "scenario" in *The Greatest American Hero* (an FBI cliché gleefully discovered for the David Chase *Rockford* episode "The Dog and Pony Show"); Robert Blake peppered his dialogue with numerous patronizing and moralistic catch-phrases in *Baretta,* and early episodes of *The A-Team* make much of a mysterious attribute of Hannibal Smith's known as "the jazz," which is mentioned extensively in all the show's earliest publicity material, but faded into obscurity as the series went on. Surely every Cannell aficionado's favorite catch-phrase though will always be Hannibal Smith's gloriously smug and confident declaration "I love it when a plan comes together!"—invariably a portent of imminent chaos.

When a flight was taken in a Cannell series, it was frequently via Beller (Bel-Air?) Airlines, a company which figures most prominently in the 1979 unsold pilot *Boston and Kilbride* and "The Beast from the Belly of the Boeing," a first-season episode of *The A-Team,* after an initial debut in *The Rockford Files.* In "'Til Death Do Us Part," another first season episode of *The A-Team,* Murdock can be seen wearing a Captain Belly-Buster hat, an item from the burger franchise that figures prominently in the *Greatest American Hero* episode "Captain Belly-Buster and the Speed Factory," which features the good Captain himself. The gangster Crazy Tommy Todesco—sometimes Crazy Tommy T—debuts in the pilot for *The Duke,* and makes two appearances in *Tenspeed and Brownshoe* (the pilot and a series episode), only to turn up again in an episode of *The A-Team* ("The Rabbit Who Ate Las Vegas") as a corpse, be revealed as a relative of Rick Hunter, and then show up alive and kicking in *The A-Team* again for the fifth season episode "Alive at Five!"* (Crazy Tommy T is less a character than a private joke—there was apparently a musician who went by that name). This episode itself bears a striking resemblance to the plot of first season *Riptide* episode "Conflict of Interest." The Howling Mad appellation given to *The A-Team's* Murdock first makes its debut in an episode of *The Rockford Files*—"The Hawaiian Headache"—featuring Ken Swofford as Howling Mad Smith, and when Pat Corley (Phil in *Murphy Brown*) shows up in *J.J. Starbuck* as Cactus Jack Slade, he's appropriated the name from a character played by Hoyt Axton in Cannell's half-season failure *Rousters* (a Cactus Jack Slater is portrayed by John Ashton in "A Cup a'Joe," a third season episode of *The A-Team*). In a fourth season of *The A-Team,* we find the boys "Waiting for Insane Wayne," courtesy of Cannell and Lupo, but when Insane Wayne shows up again, he's David Marciano (later of *Civil Wars* and *Due South*) in Cannell's *Sonny Spoon* episode "The Story of Daring Dick Darling." The name of Joe Cadillac, the character Larry Manetti plays in *The Duke,* is re-used by Cannell for a gang boss in "Man in a Glass House," an early episode of *Hardcastle and McCormick,* a Tom Hanson turns up in *The Rockford Files* in Cannell's "A Portrait of Elizabeth" long before *21 Jump Street* swipes the name, and a mobster named Terranova makes his debut not in *Wiseguy,* but a few seasons earlier in an excellent two-part *Hunter* titled "The Snow Queen."

Greeted with a little less appreciation by the audience—albeit with a knowing wink— has been the occasional recycling of plot themes (*Hardcastle and McCormick* and *The A-Team* share several story ideas, and *J.J. Starbuck* lifts ideas generously from *The Rockford Files* and *Columbo*). In what might generously be described as wishful thinking, Cannell has stated several times that he's "never made the same show twice," but this is a little like the Captain

---

To further complicate things, a Crazy Tommy Tillis turns up in the second season A-Team *episode "Steel," and Richard Romanus—who plays Todesco in* Tenspeed *and "Alive at Five" shows up as the hood Martell in "The Rabbit Who Ate Las Vegas!"*

Belly Buster company saying they've never made the same burger twice; if there's one thing that identifies a Cannell series, it's their similarity to each other, and this has been a positive rather than a negative — it's Cannell's rare attempts to diversify from the expectations of a Cannell show that have been his greatest failures. Written by the same clique of scriptwriters, all Cannell's early '80s actioners frequently borrow from each other, as writers reminisce in story conferences about — and then re-employ — favorite themes, gags, and notions. Audiences familiar with Cannell's shows wait expectantly for the standard biker episode, the circus episode, the computer fraud episode, the movie star/hero episode, the witness protection episode, the Nazi war criminal episode (often with added buried treasure), the *Deliverance/Southern Comfort* crazy mountain men episode, the rekindled memories of Vietnam episode, the small town conspiracy episode, and of course the beloved darkside mirror-image episode. Plots like these, invariably featuring old buddies gone bad and ex-flames in trouble, poured from Cannell's writers like water from a tap, creating a huge body of work between the mid-'70s and the mid-'80s that was instantly and warmly recognizable as familiar genre product and which was distinctive enough to be more original than similar wannabe product from other sources. Interestingly, Cannell and his writers rarely plundered from the product of other studios except to parody cliché and convention.* While many plot reworkings are deliberate — perhaps even desperate — the sheer closeness of Cannell's writing team also makes duplication of ideas somewhat inevitable, but the only blatant rewrite was during the 1987 writers' strike, when the *Riptide* episode "Be True to Your School" became the *Sonny Spoon* adventure "Never Go to Your High School Reunion" — both of them by Cannell, who revised his own script in his capacity as an executive with fellow producer Jo Swerling, Jr.†

"Cannell is not especially fond of freelancers, and we are one of the few freelancers that have done a significant number of shows for Cannell series" explained freelance team Chris Bunch and Allan Cole, occasional contributors to *Hunter* and *The A-Team,* and later story editors on Frank Lupo's series *Werewolf.* "Mostly they're written in-house. Now this means that there is a certain tendency for the same story to be echoed. And this prevents any of the shows from having an individual feel to them as separate series. Like *Hunter,* for example, which was planned as a much darker show than *The A-Team; Riptide* was exactly like *The A-Team."*

"We work in total collaboration," *Rockford* writer Juanita Bartlett confirmed to *Starlog* magazine in the early 1980s, "which is a little different from the way most shows are done. (On *The Greatest American Hero*) Steve and I sat down and worked out whatever the story was. If it was a script that he was going to write, the two of us would work on it together, and then he would write it. The same held true for an episode that I would write. Later, a writer/producer named Frank Lupo and a young writer named Patrick Hasburgh joined us, so now the four of us sit down and do the same thing. Those story meetings are a lot of fun. An awful lot of laughing goes on. We get together and say 'what if such-and-such happened?' Then someone might jump in and say 'that reminds me of something that happened to me.' Then another person could add 'I like that idea, but if we turned left at the next corner, we could get here.' After an episode's completed, we can't say who came up with what, because

---

*Riptide *spoofed* Simon and Simon, Miami Vice, *and* Moonlighting *for example, while* Hunter *parodied* Murder, She Wrote *and* Wiseguy *featured a sly nod towards* Twin Peaks.

†*Also around this time, the network were preparing to dig in for a long haul by reviving failed series with the same scripts but new casts — a barrel-scraping option that was ultimately never exercised — and one of these proposed revivals was to be Cannell's late-'70s* Rockford *spin-off* Richie Brockelman — Private Eye.

the stories are done by all of us. It's not a situation where one of us has more clout than anyone else."

Working on *The Rockford Files*, David Chase told *Time Out* in 1979, "I was a little suspicious. I thought, somebody else is doing it and being allowed to get their rocks off, but will I? Because on other shows, the producer has an image of the show, and tries to keep it that way. But that's never been a problem with *Rockford*. Everybody is free to express themselves — within the basic format, obviously."

"One of the interesting things about Cannell — which, by the way, is carried over to Frank Lupo — is that his people work," said Bunch and Cole. "It's not the usual endless round of meetings. A friend of ours who really likes to work with meetings worked on a lot of Cannell shows, and he went nuts within about three and a half weeks, because all they want to do is write! (Cannell) hires all his writers on a system called write-against, where you draw x salary, right? Then you write scripts. And the script money is applied against your salary, so you're getting x amount a year, so you must write x amount of scripts before you get any additional money. Of course, the re-runs are still yours. It's a fair way of working things."

Cannell is apparently as well-liked by his actors. "It's one thing writing a scene, but it's another out in the field," William Katt, the lead in *The Greatest American Hero*, told *Starlog*, during that magazine's extensive coverage of the series. "You have to make changes, and Steve Cannell trusted us. He always seemed to go with us, let us do what we wanted to do." His co-star, Robert Culp, previously the lead in the successful 1960s secret agent series *I Spy*, had been initially reluctant to do another series, until a chance meeting with, and hearty recommendation from (of all people), Robert Blake, star of Cannell's early '70s cop show *Baretta*. Renowned for his inclination toward ad-libbing with co-star Bill Cosby in *I Spy*, Culp told *Starlog*, "Most of the guys directing episodic TV are not very imaginative. They think you are interfering with the basic simple-minded fabric of the story, which is true! I'm trying to stretch it, make it more elastic instead of less."

After working on Cannell's *Wiseguy* series, actor Ron Silver told interviewer Ed Gross, "The thing that sticks out in my mind was that the actors were treated like adults. They had contributions to make. They are encouraged to have input, and that's reflected in the show." Said Anthony Denison, who worked on the same story, "They're good writers, the whole staff. I had a great time. The whole Cannell organisation and CBS treated me like royalty, and I welcome the opportunity to work with them again."

Cannell started his TV career working at his local television station and writing at night, eventually selling story ideas to the makers of Desilu's espionage thriller *Mission: Impossible*, an immensely popular series that ran from 1966 to 1973 (none of these, if used, appear to have been acknowledged or credited). Unable to persuade the producers to let him write the scripts, he moved to Universal where, after contributing scripts to *It Takes a Thief* and *Ironside*, he joined the Jack Webb studio. A script for Webb's *Adam 12* was so well received by the cast of the show that it lead to him becoming head writer on the series. During the run of *Adam 12* (from 1968 to 1975), Cannell penned *Chase*, a pilot film for Webb's Mark VII operation which sold to NBC and resulted in a series (1973–'74). The concept was a mix of the formula cop show format of *Adam 12* with elements of *Mission: Impossible*, detailing the exploits of a special police unit that went after the more difficult targets the conventional police force couldn't reach. The future Cannell approach to creating series TV was beginning to take form.

Webb's approach to TV was strictly formula, and his much parodied *Dragnet* series, a television landmark of the 1950s and the granddaddy of all police shows, ran for nearly 400 episodes, from 1951 to '58, and then again from 1967 to '69; the 1971 pilot film for another Webb series, *O'Hara, U.S. Treasury,* starring David Janssen, is virtually a parody of itself. Nevertheless, the experience of working for Webb at Universal undoubtedly gave Cannell a first-hand education in the mechanics of plotting and writing. Unlike many would-be innovators and humorists, Cannell had the opportunity of discovering that the rules have to be understood before they can be effectively broken; *Mission: Impossible* was an ingenious, technically complex — if politically simplistic — tightly-plotted show, while the Webb productions went resolutely from A to B to C with few surprises, no sub-plots or diversions, and certainly no humor. Cannell, on the other hand, was to make humor the essential prime ingredient to his own catalog of TV successes, with concepts and attitudes that must have had Webb spinning in his grave.

Cannell's liberal use of humor on his own series many years later, and the fact that he was involved early in his career with some of the most straightforward and humorless of U.S. TV series ever made,* go a long way to explaining his own attitude to program-making since being out on his own — right-wing on the surface, but anti-authoritarian and light-hearted in execution. However, a further alliance at Universal was to play a major part in influencing the direction he was able to take, and giving him that important first step up he needed to win the considerable network influence he later enjoyed. First though, we should observe the very significant changes that American television was going through while Cannell labored in Webb's far right corner of Universal's TV output.

Universal had enjoyed great success with the ground-breaking NBC series *The Name of the Game* (1968–'72), which inaugurated several new — or nearly-new — TV practices. Firstly, the series had three different lead actors (Gene Barry, then best known for Aaron Spelling's *Burke's Law,* Robert Stack, formerly of Quinn Martin's *The Untouchables,* and relative TV newcomer Tony Franciosca), who each took turns to appear in their own separate stories, each player's segment handled by a different production team. Secondly, the series, which had sprung belatedly from the 1966 TV movie *Fame Is the Name of the Game* (with Franciosca starring and George Macready in Barry's role), was also feature-length — a 90-minute TV series with a budget to match.

This added length allowed for greater plot development outside of the constraints of 60-minute series, while the contemporary setting — a publishing empire — encouraged experimentation that the traditional formula of TV's only other 90-minute series, the long-running Universal western *The Virginian,* could not accommodate. *The Name of the Game* more closely resembled a collection of individual feature films for TV rather than a typical TV series, allowing writers, directors, and guest players the prestige and scope of a feature film or anthology series while retaining all the virtues of a continuing series' regular characters and built-in audience. Although Robert Stack's episodes were mostly grim crime dramas (and even these occasionally produced surprises), the other segments were filled with bizarre directorial flourishes (a young Steven Spielberg produced a speculative fiction concerning L.A. one hundred years into the future) and socio-political relevance mixed with the sort of eccentric character pieces and snappy wisecracks that had been absent since the demise of Barry's previous series *Burke's Law* five years earlier. The result was a light-hearted, frothy but stylish mix of jet-set adventuring and social relevance that surprisingly gelled.

---

*Both Dragnet *and* Mission: Impossible *have probably been sent up more times between them than almost any other show in the history of television, with the possible exception of* Star Trek*!*

If, while all this was going on, Cannell himself was restrained by the conservatism of Webb's Mark VII productions (still firmly entrenched in the 1950s as the '70s began), he was at least in the right place at the right time by being at Universal, who were now going full-tilt into quality TV production with a host of the Hollywood old guard. As the feature film industry turned its sights on the disenfranchised youth market almost overnight, the obvious sophistication of *The Name of the Game* (while of course dated, many episodes put Universal's later TV product to shame), the potential of the ninety minute format, and the more leisurely schedule of the "umbrella" shows (three or four series alternating under the same title) lured big-screen names such as Rock Hudson, James Stewart and Richard Widmark to the demon TV screen without losing face. At the same time, the presence of established stars with influence enhanced the quality of the scripts and budgets, as these performers had the power to demand higher standards than young hopefuls eager to land their first series. Before long, Universal had introduced the ninety minute *Mystery Movie* format that sired *Columbo* and *McCloud* (ironically, the two biggest hits under the *Mystery Movie* umbrella were fronted by TV actors Peter Falk and Dennis Weaver!). The trickle of retreating big-screen stalwarts turned into a flood, with Glenn Ford, Henry Fonda, Doris Day, Tony Randall, Burl Ives and James Garner also turning (or returning) to the small screen. After two decades of grim, wooden square-jawed cops and p.i.'s, the presence of performers of the caliber and range of Hudson and Garner ushered in the 1970s' most predominant trend of mixing humor with drama. At the same time, comedy transformed with equal suddenness, as a new breed of comedy producer injected drama and realism into humor with the three major turning-point shows *M*A*S*H*, *The Mary Tyler Moore Show*, and *All in the Family*. Before long, this brief and exhilarating period of innovation would be swallowed up by the forthcoming obsession with cop shows, the predominance of Aaron Spelling's brainless, trivial glamour fantasies, and the nostalgia craze of the late '70s. But for now, up and coming producers such as Glen Larson and Stephen Cannell were quick to spot which way the wind was blowing, and as previous boundaries blurred, or were broken down entirely, Cannell and Larson were able to carve themselves a comfortable niche that would see them through the decade and into the '80s.

Both Larson and Cannell owed their breaks partially to one of the old guard — Roy Huggins. Huggins had been involved in TV from its earliest days, having come to the infant medium as a writer of pulp mystery novels. It was a vocation that was to stand him in good stead in TV, and give the medium some of its better moments, for Huggins' expertise in the mystery field enabled him to provide those series he worked on with plots of slightly more substance than were the norm for television.

Huggins began his career at Warner Brothers, working on shows such as *Cheyenne* (Warners' first TV success, 1955–'63) and *Colt .45* (1957–'58), but it was with the legendary *Maverick* (1957–'62) starring James Garner, that Huggins' talent for lighter, cleverer plots first came to the fore, and Huggins won an Emmy award for his work on this exemplary series. He continued to produce pilot films for Warners during this period, such as those for the hit detective series *77, Sunset Strip* (1958–'64) and *Doc Holliday* (1959), before creating *The Fugitive* (1963–'67) for Quinn Martin. Prior to that, Huggins had been vice-president in charge of production at 20th Century–Fox, until — he says — he was fired for suggesting the concept of *The Fugitive* as a continuing series! "We never had a relationship after that," Huggins told *Emmy* magazine. "They lost all confidence in me!" With the exception of *The Fugitive*, which became a TV phenomenon of the '60s and created a whole new TV genre of man-on-the-run shows, the remainder of Huggins' work in the '60s and '70s was done at Universal, executive producing *The Virginian* (1962–'71), and overseeing the *Fugitive*-inspired *Run for Your Life* (1965–'68), and *The Outsider* (1968–'69), a detective drama starring Darren McGavin.

Then came the excellent series *The Bold Ones* (1969–'73), another "umbrella" series with alternating leads in the tradition of *The Name of the Game,* but of sixty minutes length, featuring teams of professionals in dramatic occupations (law, medicine, politics, police work), for which he handled the episodes featuring a team of lawyers (Burl Ives, Joseph Campanella, and James Farentino). When these were completed, Farentino moved directly over into a *Mystery Movie* slot for the short-lived millionaire-mercenary series *Cool Million* (1972–'73), which was also produced by Huggins. Huggins' wife, actress Adele Mara, co-starred, and when Farentino was cast in the lead of the lowbrow 1984 action series *Blue Thunder* at Columbia, Huggins was again producing with him.

When *The Virginian* finally ceased production, Huggins contributed numerous scripts to Glen Larson's western series *Alias Smith and Jones,* a show loosely inspired by the popularity of the feature *Butch Cassidy and the Sundance Kid,* and which set Larson off on a career turning hot movies into successful TV series. In their book *The American Vein,* writers Chris Wicking and Tise Vahimagi referred to Larson as "an enthusiastic talent, but one content to take what is to hand rather than invest dangerously in new ideas. If Larson has yet to be original, he has been prolific and ... professional. *Alias Smith and Jones*— though owing a large debt to the Roy Huggins *Maverick* sense of humor, bluff and deception — no doubt taught Larson a great deal ... while we wait for a more individual signature from Larson, we will doubtless continue to be impressed by his apparently unerring choice of which banks to rob, and which way to escape with the loot!"

Following his time with Jack Webb, Cannell next found himself allied with Huggins, and it is to this prolific TV talent that Cannell owes his greatest start-up debt. "He's my godfather in television," Cannell told *Emmy* magazine in 1988. "I still use the precepts he taught me. He's the best teacher a young man could have, and one of the best storytellers in the business." Huggins was equally glowing toward Cannell. "He was someone who couldn't write a dull scene or a dull character," Huggins told *Variety* in 1995. "I grabbed him and made him a producer almost instantly."

Together, Cannell and Huggins developed the cop show *Toma* (1973–'74) for Universal, a routine drama based on the exploits of a real-life cop in the Jack Webb taken-from-the-files tradition. Although reasonably successful, *Toma* lasted only one season when the leading man, Tony Musante, decided that the life of a TV star was not for him, and quit the show! Undaunted, the duo retooled the series the following year as the slightly more fanciful *Baretta,* which ran for three years from 1975 to 1978, with the pugnacious Robert Blake as a now fictitious undercover cop with a single-minded pursuit of mobsters, and a similarly neat line in bizarre disguises, but it was with the 1974 to 1980 series *The Rockford Files* (which sprung from an abortive and delirious mad rush to get a *Toma* episode ready to air) that the team really excelled.

Rockford began life as a one-off joke character to dominate a *Toma* episode that would be bookended by Tony Musante, who could then start work on the following episode. It was a cheat, but the clock was against them, and Huggins and Cannell were desperate. Out of their desperation came a wild and frantic spell at the typewriter, during which time *The Rockford Files* turned into a potential pilot and *Toma* missed an airdate!

For *The Rockford Files,* Huggins was reunited with his former *Maverick* star, James Garner, who brought with him to the production many of the team who had been working with him on the short-lived but critically acclaimed modern western series *Nichols* (1970–'71), including Stuart Margolin and Juanita Bartlett. Garner had left TV at the close of *Maverick* to pursue his movie career, and was not too thrilled to return to the weekly grind of a TV series, particularly after his disappointing experience with *Nichols,* which had been badly treated by the network. However, cinema trends toward more explicit sexual and violent content had dictated that his light style of feature film would be out of vogue for the foreseeable future, and perhaps the presence of Huggins, or the allure of having another shot at the themes explored in *Nichols* within a contemporary format appealed to him. Whatever the case, James Garner signed on for *The Rockford Files....*

PART ONE: BEGINNINGS

The Rockford Files
September 1974–January 1980

"This isn't Maverick*"*

James Garner was born in Norman, Oklahoma in 1928. His mother died when he was young, and a miserable childhood followed after his father remarried. Garner left home as soon as he was old enough, bookending his compulsory national service in Korea with numerous odd jobs as he drifted round the country. The story goes that Garner had no aspirations to be an actor, but looked up an old friend in Hollywood who had become a well-known producer. Stage roles and bit parts in movies followed, and Garner was off and running in a career.

Soon, Garner was vice-president of the Screen Actors Guild, while Ronald Reagan — for whom somewhat higher office would follow — was its president. "We used to tell him what to say," Garner told *Gentleman's Quarterly* in 1984. "He can talk around a subject better than anyone in the world. He's never had an original thought that I know of, and we go back a hell of a lot of years!"

In 1957, after various bit parts in several episodes of Warners' *Cheyenne*, Garner made the pilot film for the western series *Maverick*, an unusual series in that it was about a wily gambler's efforts to avoid trouble, rather than the standard ranch-hand, gunfighter, or sheriff's efforts to find it. "I had a feeling about *Maverick* from the beginning," he said, "and damned if it didn't go. Hell, it was a cult thing."

Meta Rosenberg had worked as an assistant to producer William Dozier at Warners until 1960, when she joined her husband's talent agency, later working on the medical drama *Ben Casey*. Garner was in the midst of a lengthy legal battle with Warners over his contract for *Maverick*, when Rosenberg helped him get out of it. She became his agent, and together they formed Cherokee Productions (Garner was part Cherokee), for which they created the TV western *Nichols* for the 1970–71 season. "Jim's kind of a 1930s actor," Rosenberg told writer Chris Wicking for *Time Out* in 1979, "which made it a little hard in the '60s, because a wholly different kind of star was important at that time. Even so, he had a very good career in films for many years before he went back to television. During that time, he and I got closer and closer as I saw how many different ways he could go, and we formed Cherokee."

Nichols — like *Maverick* — was another cult show, and the story behind that ill-fated series is legend. "It's the best work I've ever done," Garner told *GQ*, "(and its cancelation) about broke my heart. The show was set at the turn of the century in Arizona, and I played a sheriff who rode a belt-drive Harley-Davidson and refused to carry a gun. Wore jodphurs and cavalry boots, and Stuart (Margolin) played a variation of the character he played on *The Rockford Files*. In *Nichols* though, he really was the most back-stabbing, irritating sneak, and he was my deputy. Margot Kidder was in *Nichols* too, and she was wonderful. Anyway, we were dead the first night we showed the pilot, because some executive's wife didn't like it. She said 'Well, that's not *Maverick*.' Well of course it wasn't *Maverick*! It was better than *Maverick*, humorous with social satire. But we got pre-empted eight times out of twenty-four shows because of Nixon running for election. Then they moved us up against *Marcus Welby*, and we ran even with him, and he was the number one show in the country. Hell, the show lasted one year, and I swear to you, if they had left it on another year, it would still be running today. It was just too damned original."

"It was literate, moving, and funny," affirms Meta Rosenberg. "Jim and I absolutely loved it, it's our favorite thing. I developed it with Frank Pierson, who wrote it, produced it, directed many of the episodes. But it was before its time. It scared the hell out of NBC, and it only went for 24 shows before being canceled, and they absolutely hated it. They were under the impression at the time that you could not do comedy, you could not do humor in an hour show. There has to be all violence, shooting, hitting, and everything. If you had a hero who didn't want to get hurt, you were doing the wrong thing."

"We were so upset when the series was canceled, that we decided on an audacious act," Rosenberg told *Time Out*. "No series character is ever killed off. Columbo isn't dead, Rockford will not die ... but we killed Nichols in the opening moments of the final show, and then brought him back as his brother, looking to avenge his death ... but his brother is entirely different, straight, solid, and stern. It was like saying 'This is what you've lost'...."

Had Cannell's style of program-making been established when *Nichols* was in production, the show may very well have survived early network fears. It must have been galling for Garner and Rosenberg to see humorous adventure shows like Glen Larson's *McCloud*, Larson and Roy Huggins' *Alias Smith and Jones*, and Leonard Stern's *McMillan and Wife* take off in the following months as TV tentatively started to lighten up. But Stephen Cannell, Garner, and Rosenberg were eventually to capitalize on this new direction toward light adventure by taking the trend to its logical conclusion with *The Rockford Files*.

By 1974, the small screen was awash with cops and private eyes (including Cannell and Huggins' *Toma*). Clearly there was no percentage in bucking the trend, and Cannell's eyes were as sharply focused on the pop culture of the day as those of Larson. Amongst Garner's wide repertoire of performances and experiences with different genres were a couple of private eye movies, including the 1969 *Marlowe*, based on the Raymond Chandler novel *The Little Sister*. Meta Rosenberg had been involved in dealings with Chandler himself during that author's doomed dalliance with Hollywood; *Marlowe*, a watchable but routine detective yarn, had been directed by the appropriately named Paul Bogart, who would later work with Garner and Rosenberg on *Nichols*, and later, Garner's 1971 TV movie *The Skin Game* (perhaps an early role-model for Cannell's subsequent *Rockford* follow-up *Tenspeed and Brownshoe*). At the same time, Garner had already proven innumerable times that he was well-suited to playing comedy, both with the tongue-in-cheek *Maverick* in the '50s and such slick 1960s fare as the madcap satire *The Thrill of It All*. Who could forget Garner's expression as he drove his car into a swimming pool, unaware of this latest new fixture installed overnight in his back yard?

The mood of the times in the America of the early '70s was to debunk the popular myths of the past, whereas the predominant late '70s/early '80s trend was to rediscover them and celebrate them anew with a knowing smile. But at the beginning of the 1970s, America was not very pleased with itself after the embarrassment of Vietnam and the violence of the anti-war demonstrations, and the fall of a disgraced president was about as far as the U.S. could sink before it began the long climb upwards and rightwards again; the entire country, not yet seeking the easy platitudes of Reagan and Rambo, often seemed as though it was on the analyst's couch, reflecting on an innocent, naive youth and examining inborn, firmly-held assumptions for the first time.

This was inevitably reflected in (and perhaps even perpetuated by) early '70s Hollywood. Science-fiction was decidedly less optimistic, replacing Cold War heroics and wide-eyed wonderment for the pioneers of the Space Age with parodic symbolism and pessimistic speculation; the white hats and black hats of the western were all distinctly grey, and often interchangeable, and bullets made blood, which was visible. Contemporary comedies satirized rather than sparkled prettily, and parody replaced praise for the American Dream. Robert Altman, in particular, was a film-maker who found critical favor at the time, taking great pleasure in skillfully and perceptively debunking Americana. Altman had begun his career in TV, directing episodes of *Bonanza, Whirlybirds, Alfred Hitchcock Presents, Route 66, The Roaring Twenties,* and numerous Warners westerns and detective shows; films such as *M*A*S*H* (1970), *McCabe and Mrs. Miller* (1971), *The Long Goodbye* (1973), *Thieves Like Us* (1973), *Nashville* (1975) and *Buffalo Bill and the Indians* (1976) turned the mythology of TV on its head and no doubt exorcised some personal demons just as Cannell's later work exorcised the ghosts of *Adam 12, Ironside,* and *Toma*. Garner admired Altman (appearing for a minimal salary in his 1979 film *Health*), and — as the man behind the feature films *M*A*S*H* and *The Long Goodbye*— Altman inadvertently influenced the shape of 1970s American television ... despite holding a strong contempt for the medium that included the popular TV version of *M*A*S*H*.

Altman's 1973 film of *The Long Goodbye* was a compelling and atmospheric travesty of Chandler's original book, and featured Altman regular Elliot Gould as a shambling, incoherent p.i. in realistic L.A. surroundings deliberately opposed to the rain-soaked, neon-bathed streets of mythology. Altman's world was just as savage and dreamlike, but also stupid, and nowhere near as romantic. In place of mysterious, sharp-tongued femme fatales, Altman gave his Marlowe a group of topless, toking airheads for neighbors; Mark Rydell played a half-pint moronic gangster who, at one point, strides around *Performance*-like in his underpants, and whose callous, casual brutality is both ludicrous and horrific, while Sterling Hayden gave a masterful performance as a deluded, booze-sodden Hemingway-esque author. And the sun shined. And Marlowe had no tough, dazzling, descriptive repartee to offer, only foul-mouthed, muttered mumblings emanating from his slob-like appearance. Finally, Altman subverted even the story's end itself, by having the hero blow away his treacherous friend in the final frames, unimpressed by either his betrayal or the cleverness of his scheme. It was a shock ending that secured the film's reputation as a love-it-or-loathe-it movie, and would be purloined for TV at least four times (in episodes of *Magnum, Mike Hammer, Hunter,* and *Wiseguy*).*

---

*In Donald Bellisario's excellent Magnum *two-parter "The Sun Also Rises," Magnum does just what jaded TV viewers have been begging a TV hero to do for years — dispense with the phoney baloney morality and blow away the bad guy who swears he'll be back because the good guy is too moral to dispose of the threat he poses permanently. The* Mike Hammer *episode "Satan, Cyanide, and Murder" swipes the scene wholesale and to less convincing effect, as Hammer has already behaved in a very un–Spillane manner in the opening scenes, by calling the cops after cornering the killer of his latest in a long line of expendable ladyfriends. And in the* Wiseguy *episode "The Loose Cannon," Vinnie Terranova dispatches a leering loony threatening all manner of horrible fates for his future targets ... during which he also reveals a long line of previous atrocities and promises to blow Vinnie's cover! One of the more amusing aspects of scenes of retribution like this on television — and the famous* Hunter *two-parter "Rape and Revenge" is another glowing example — is how the producers are forced to pile on horror upon horror before the network finally allows the hero to have no option but to administer lead justice!*

From the spirit of this film — and many others that followed in its footsteps — came *The Rockford Files* (as well as Jerry Thorpe's likeminded dry and laconic, but more traditional *Harry O,* starring Garner's old buddy David Janssen). Similarly inclined films of the period included the 1972 *Hickey and Boggs,* written by Walter Hill and featuring Robert Culp (later of Cannell's *Greatest American Hero*) re-united with his 1960s *I Spy* partner Bill Cosby; the 1975 *Night Moves* by Arthur Penn, with Gene Hackman (who had already appeared in the downbeat thriller *The Conversation* and the impressively subversive *Prime Cut*) playing miserable, middle-aged Harry Moseby, a seedy p.i. with his marriage on the rocks and one last big mystery to solve as he meanders through a labyrinthine plot of constant betrayal; and the 1977 Robert Altman–produced *The Late Show,* by Alan Rudolph, with Art Carney as an ageing tough guy teamed reluctantly with Lily Tomlin's faddish modern miss. These were not the detectives of Hollywood mythology ... and the persistent appearance of such characters, and the longevity of *The Rockford Files,* would take Cannell down this path strewn with unlikely gumshoes for the next few years as, throughout the run of *Rockford,* Cannell tried in vain to duplicate his success with a series of other unlikely or fading detectives, such as *Richie Brockelman — Private Eye* (1978), *The Duke* (1979), and *Tenspeed and Brownshoe* (1980). By the end of the '70s, with considerable aid from Cannell and his contemporaries, it would be the old-style traditional tough guy who would be the oddity and the anachronism, as parodied in numerous 1980s television series that mocked the medium and the message. (Ironically, by the time everybody else on TV was following Cannell's lead in the 1980s, Cannell had diversified into new areas of spoofery...).

Born of the early '70s feature films that took private investigators out of the noir-ish shadows of Hollywood and into the sunshine, *The Rockford Files* initiated a whole new process of plotting and storytelling in television that has been continued in such series as the *Chinatown*-inspired *City of Angels, Rockford* spin-off *Richie Brockelman, Tenspeed and Brownshoe, Magnum, p.i., Simon and Simon, Riptide, Remington Steele,* and Garner's later series *Bret Maverick* (a revival of the original 1950s character, older and even more laid-back), as well as many others. Although just as contrived and unlikely as the plots of other shows, their absurdity was obscured by their complexity and ingenuity, and — in the case of the superior *Rockford Files* — married to wicked satire of sunny Californian life and character portraits of West Coast oddballs.

A discreetly quiet pioneer in the history of American television, *Rockford* was not a parody of the detective genre exactly, but it was a poke in the eye for all the fearless TV tough guys. Rockford didn't like guns, he shied away from violence, and discouraged brawls, but he could cope when the scriptwriters said he had to. He sneered at and antagonized hired muscle, in the defeatist knowledge that he was going to get his ticket punched anyway, but he was smart enough and honest enough to be scared when he knew he was in deep water. He had a policy of only taking closed cases to keep out of trouble (he was an innocent and pardoned ex-con, but now the cops hated him because he was free, and every time he solved a closed case he showed them up), but to the delight of viewers for six strong years, this precaution never worked. He greeted his trials and aggravations with wry resignation and disdain.

We have already seen, in our introductory chapter, how Cannell approached the character of Jim Rockford ("I said to myself, I'm going to break every rule about a television detective — like they never work for money! What bull! My guy wants money! Lives in a trailer, doesn't have a pretty secretary but a truck-driver father who's embarrassed by what his son does! I was laughing, sitting at the typewriter, exercising all my fantasies..."). Cannell's father, a conservative businessman, had been embarrassed by his son's chosen line of work, Cannell told *Variety,* "so when I wrote *The Rockford Files* I had Joe Rockford really embarrassed that Jim was a private eye. How do you tell your friends at the truck stop that your son's a private eye? What a joke!"

For his part, Garner invested his role as the ex-con turned detective with a world-weary cynicism and pessimism, a satisfying multi-dimensional and sympathetic portrayal drawn as much from his harassed husband roles as his tough guy credentials, and in direct contrast to his former TV persona of the card-sharp *Maverick.* Despite a number of similarities between the two, such as self-preservation and hard-learned worldly wisdom, Rockford was more likely to be one of Maverick's pigeons than allies. What remained central to both series was Garner's well-practiced portrait of the put-upon con-man, who could create any elaborate scam at the drop of a dollar bill as though his life depended on it — which the writers ensured it usually did. Rockford though, like Nichols before him, was no hero — and when he played his role of white knight it was always because he had been forced into it by a desperate friend or a desperate client.

Garner's Rockford was an easy-going, open-minded but sensible guy who lived in a trailer on the beach and — like an ordinary mortal (which was another first for the detective genre) — would win a few and lose a few. Like Joe Average rather than Joe Cool, he muddled by. Also, unlike in most other series of the day, if Rockford made a friend (or an enemy) they might well return if a later story demanded it. Rockford did not start with a clean slate every episode; although standard practice today, this was unique at the time. Return appearances included Dennis Dugan as boy detective Richie Brockelman, Isaac Hayes as ex-con and cellmate Gandy Fitch, former *Skin Game* co-star Lou Gossett as parole officer turned p.i. Marcus Hayes, Simon Oakland as seedy investigator Vern St. Cloud, James Whitmore, Jr. as sniveling fake Fred Beamer, Rita Moreno as prostitute Rita Capkovic, and many more. Rockford had done his time, been paroled, and wanted nothing now but the quiet life. His master plan was to spend as much time as possible fishing off the end of the pier and watching football on TV, while he earned the occasional crust putting his prison-taught skills to use on divorce suits and missing person cases. Unfortunately for him, but fortunately for the viewers, he frequently found himself implicated in more bizarre, unreal, once-in-a-lifetime cases than any private investigator who actively sought trouble could reasonably hope for.

James Garner as he appeared in *The Rockford Files.*

The Rockford Files established Cannell's approach to generic TV just as *Alias Smith and Jones* had established Roy Huggins' predilection for complex comedic adventure and Larson's penchant for turning cinema trends into TV series. Cannell took the Universal trademark of light-hearted humorous adventure and mixed it with subversive role-reversal and satire. He also popularized the then-innovative practice of featuring constantly recurring co-star characters (such as lady lawyer Beth Davenport, played by Gretchen Corbett, and Stuart Margolin's criminal lowlife Angel Martin) who were not obliged to appear in every single episode, but only when the story demanded it, thus creating a more believable and realistic recreation of everyday life that could still retain its television function. This same flexibility applied to Noah Beery as Rockford's dad, Joseph "Rocky" Rockford, Joe Santos as put-upon cop Dennis Becker, and Tom Atkins and later James Luisi, as not-so-friendly cops Lt. Diel and Lt. Chapman, both hard-nosed humorless by-the-book squares. The presence of these two law 'n order types also served to inaugurate the familiar Cannell trademark of lampooning bureaucracy (who, in *Rockford*, manifested themselves in all shapes and sizes, from the FBI and CIA, all the way down the evolutionary chain to parole officers, social workers, inland revenue, and city hall). Off-the-wall survivors littered *The Rockford Files,* invariably gaining more sympathy in Cannell-supervised series than the reactionary suit-and-tie men of officialdom who stomped around officiously in the more traditional and familiar Jack Webb/Quinn Martin productions of the period. In a glut of prime-time cop and detective shows, *The Rockford Files* was unique for its time, as it favored the rogue and the self-sufficient individual who went his way against the odds ... and sometimes even the letter of the law. By taking this route Cannell was almost surreptitiously taking exactly the opposite stance of series by almost every other program-maker, in which such individuals were usually perceived by the hero/es as the problem-of-the-week, the glitch in the system that had to be righted by the episode's end. This attitude would begin the trend in which almost all of Cannell's series would feature a figure of authority who would be constantly sent up for being rigid and intractable when it came to the rule-book — more prominent examples included Dana Elcar's Colonel Lard in *Black Sheep Squadron*, Robert Culp's FBI man Bill Maxwell in *Greatest American Hero* (in turn plagued by his superior, Carlyle, when the Maxwell character mellowed), Jack Ging's Lt. Quinlan in *Riptide*, Lance Le Gault's Commander Decker in *The A-Team*, and *Hunter's* numerous long-suffering co-workers, lead by James Whitmore, Jr.'s Bernie Terwilliger, Arthur Rosenberg's Captain Cain, and Bruce Davison's Captain Wyler.

Every episode of *The Rockford Files* would open with the familiar explanatory photo-montage of various California locales interspersed with images of Garner's exasperated face (the premise of every U.S. TV series is instantly defined and displayed in its opening credits, and many shows stand or fall by them — this montage, by director Reza Badiyi, who also put together the memorable opening credits of *Hawaii Five-0*, although tampered with in later seasons to its detriment, was superb), prefaced by a different message each week on Rockford's answer-phone. The fact that these calls (and often the caller) rarely had anything to do with either the forthcoming drama or detective work itself — and were often bad news or a mundane, stupid nuisance call — illustrated beautifully and immediately the irreverent and screwy tone of the series.* Rather than urgent cries for help or valuable information, each

---

*It's an interesting back-handed compliment to the series that the first season of former Cannell compatriot Phil De Guere's Simon and Simon *modeled its opening — and attitude — on the opening sequence of* The Rockford Files, *while the answer-phone idea was shamelessly purloined by the lively formula detective fantasy* Crazy Like a Fox, *as father called son each week to enquire "What could possibly go wrong?"— cue chaotic opening sequence!*

episode's intro would herald wrong numbers, debt collectors, loonies, salesmen, scroungers, irate clients, and other assorted characters borrowing money, making threats to dispose of cleaning not collected, or making final demands for unpaid bills or fines. The scene was set for another voyage into West Coast lowlife or self-centered high-life. While other series pandered to the Me Generation, Cannell and his writers mercilessly lampooned it.

Most TV p.i.'s have a friend in the department, and in this respect, *The Rockford Files* honored tradition — except that Rockford's police pal was never pleased to see him. Rockford constantly harassed the glum Dennis Becker, a character played by Joe Santos as though he had all the troubles of the world on his shoulders. Nothing was really typical in Rockford's universe, and no cliché went unturned; Becker was the antithesis of all those beaming cops who happily let the heroes of other shows trample all over the scene of the crime upstaging them. In a then-novel variation for TV detectives, Rockford — harassing Becker — was in turn harassed by Becker's vindictive superiors, who also gave Becker grief for helping him. Becker's superiors, Lt. Diel (Atkins) and later the splendidly tight-assed, tight-lipped Lt. Chapman (played masterfully by James Luisi as an icy, hateful, unhappy man) had it in for Rockford, and both wanted to see him back inside, almost as vindication for their having imprisoned him in the first place. This clever complication of a hostile police bureaucracy, pioneered in the cinema by Clint Eastwood's anti-authoritarian cop films (*Coogan's Bluff, Dirty Harry, The Enforcer,* etc.) allowed for more complex plots and characterization, injecting a healthy dose of cynicism into authorities-vs.-the-bad-guys fantasy while diluting the cozy and simplistic law-and-order right-and-wrong ambience of the more traditional cops and robbers output. This blurring of the presumed correctness of establishment morality, and acknowledgement of moral justice over official channels gave Cannell's series a simple wisdom and credibility that his predecessors did not exhibit, while at the same time exploring and exploiting the timely populism of the can of worms Eastwood had opened up in the cinema. If you couldn't trust the police and the politicians, then who were the heroes, and what were they doing to get justice?

While the ground-breaking and influential Steve McQueen thriller *Bullitt* and Clint Eastwood's *Dirty Harry* film and sequels had already provoked a trend in U.S. TV of having a morally correct police officer hampered by bosses at the beck and call of self-serving politicians (Cannell's *Baretta* would explore this, while Glen Larson's *McCloud*—itself inspired by Eastwood's *Coogan's Bluff*—had played it for laughs with the dependable J.D. Cannon as the slow-fuse burning but right-minded Chief Clifford), it was Cannell who would realize its full potential for pleasing audiences right across the board, and include a variation on the theme in almost all his subsequent TV series. However, for all its skilful thematic contrivances, *The Rockford Files* wouldn't have lasted three weeks without James Garner, who not only brought Jim Rockford to life, but fought to protect the show — and the not yet terribly influential Stephen J. Cannell — from the presumptions and safety-first mentality of the network.

"Garner is one of the best actors around," said Robert Altman. "He is often overlooked because he makes it look so easy, and that is not easy to do. I don't know anyone in the business with his charm and charisma who can act so well." "Garner looks comfortable on screen, and it's relaxing to watch him," wrote Kate Stevens in *Video Today.* "No-one could do exasperation like Garner could," said Richard Meyers in his book *TV Detectives,* "and no-one needed it as much as Rockford. All the zanies of California that the rest of the country had just heard about were right there to be seen every week on *The Rockford Files.*"

Garner has never been typecast, but whatever role he takes, it is always that of an essentially good man. "I won't do movies that glorify killers and bank robbers," Garner told *Gentleman's Quarterly*, "like *Bonnie and Clyde,* and that was a picnic compared to what's being filmed today. I've always been fortunate that I've never been that down, and I've never been that hot. I've tried to stay a commodity that's available for hire. I was never driven to be number one. I just hang in there, number six or seven, and watch 'em go up and watch 'em come down. Up and down, and I've done it for thirty years."

The deeply ingrained reluctance towards heroism in Garner's characterizations of Maverick, Nichols, and Rockford is no casual coincidence. Garner's most favorite of all his films is the 1964 light drama *The Americanisation of Emily,* directed by Arthur Hiller and written by Paddy Chayevsky from a novel by William Bradford. Chayevsky, whose feelings about television were made well-known in his heavy-handed satiric 1976 film *Network,* would later give rare praise to *The Rockford Files* as one of the few series on TV he cared for. Co-starring in *Emily* were Julie Andrews, Melvyn Douglas, James Coburn (who would later direct the *Rockford* episode "Irving the Explainer" and complain bitterly about the editing), and Edward Binns, Keenan Wynn, and William Windom (all three of whom would appear notably in Cannell productions in the years to follow). Populated by eccentric characters, the plot concerned a British war widow (Andrews) who falls in love with an American commander (Garner) who is a self-confessed "coward." Garner was singularly unimpressed with the phoney baloney heroics of the Hollywood tough guys, and consequently he found a soul-mate in the regular guy philosophy of Stephen Cannell. With these views, even putting aside the shared Roy Huggins connection between the two, it was entirely appropriate that these kindred spirits should have ended up as allies in the world of U.S. TV.

Offscreen Garner was something of a reluctant hero as well. "I was always picking up someone else's fight when they couldn't defend themselves" Garner told a reporter in 1982. "I'd jump in like a big nit. If I see someone getting stepped on, I'll still step in ... and probably get stepped on when I do. But I still hold basic values, and if I see them violated, then I'll step in."

Garner's antipathy toward all those executives not directly concerned with production, and yet calling the shots or holding the pursestrings, has been well-documented, as have his legal battles. However, one amusing anecdote deserves to be retold, and was related by Cannell to *Esquire* magazine.

Shortly after *The Rockford Files* began, CBS moved their popular police drama *Hawaii Five-0* into direct competition with *Rockford,* and the network response at that time was not to counter-program with directly opposite fare to pick up the disenfranchised audience (as is the common practice today), but to oppose with more of the same. Word came down from on high to Cannell and Rosenberg that, even though *Rockford* was already a successful show, the writers should dispense with the humor and throw in more action in a bid to attract the *Hawaii Five-0* audience and repel the threat from CBS; a similar fate had befallen the legendary TV writer Rod Serling, creator of *The Twilight Zone,* when his supernatural series *Night Gallery* opposed the dull detective drama *Mannix*—"they want *Mannix* in a shroud" he fumed, "chases through graveyards!"

"We were just punched to death," Cannell told *Esquire,* "and went to Jim and told him what was going on. Jim just sat there, and slowly said 'Okay, I'm not coming out of this trailer until those guys are here.' Jim called NBC and told them he wanted to talk to them, they could take their time, whenever it was convenient to them, but that he was not moving out of his trailer. Meanwhile, very expensive production minutes were ticking away. The guys showed up very soon. Jim told them that he agreed to do *Rockford* as originally scripted, and that he had no intention of doing *Hawaii Five-0,* and if that's what they wanted, they could hire Jack Lord's younger brother, and that if either Meta or I got one more 'phone call about this, he, James Garner, was walking. We never heard another word."*

"We're free now to do what we want to do," Meta Rosenberg told *Time Out,* after reminiscing on the fate of *Nichols.* "Nobody says you must do this, you can't do that. In the second season, NBC wanted us to change things, because they thought we were being too funny. But our ratings held, then got better, and NBC finally gave in. They don't know what makes *Rockford* work, they're not sure why we're successful, so now they have to leave us alone. We have a great deal of clout, although we use it advisedly. Anybody who is successful has a great deal of clout. It's the only way. Any show could be a *Rockford Files* if people cared enough, tried not to compromise, took the thing seriously. And if they had talent."

That afterthought is all-important ... for *The Rockford Files* did have talent. Almost all of the best episodes of *The Rockford Files* were written by just three writers, Stephen Cannell, Juanita Bartlett, and David Chase, sometimes from plots provided by Roy Huggins under his pen name of John Thomas James. When Huggins left the series to Cannell at the end of the first season, Meta Rosenberg was then sole executive producer, and brought in Chas Floyd Johnson (later of *Magnum*) and David Chase to assist her. Although Cannell, Bartlett, and Chase would continue to write the bulk of the episodes, Cannell would occasionally buy in story ideas, and sometimes even complete scripts, and other writers included Jo Swerling, Jr. (producer and writer on Cannell's *Baretta,* later Cannell's executive producer on everything), Edward J. Lakso (a Universal staffer who also contributed frequently to *Baretta*), Gordon Dawson (a former wardrobe man for Sam Peckinpah who would also write for *Lou Grant* and *Bret Maverick,* among others), and later regular on *The A-Team,* Don Carlos Dunaway. When Johnson later moved on to the staff of Donald Bellisario's *Magnum,* which began shortly after *Rockford* ended, many of the writers who had cut their teeth on *Rockford* contributed regularly to that series, and also to Bellisario's later hawkish fantasy *Airwolf.* Chase brought to *Rockford* a writer named Rudolph Borchert, with whom he had worked on Universal's supernatural series *Kolchak: the Night Stalker,* and who would later contribute a number of stories to Cannell's *Greatest American Hero.* Chase went on to write and produce on Universal's superb but short-lived ambitious 1987 show *Almost Grown,* which sadly lasted only a few episodes (his influence is strongly evident in the pilot film for that series) and then at the close of the 1990s had a huge success with *The Sopranos,* a blackly comic show about Rockfordian New Jersey mobsters. Interviewed by the BBC in 2006 (largely due to the television industry's fondness for *The Sopranos*), Chase described the guidance he had from Cannell when writing a *Rockford Files:* "What are the heavies doing?" This, when faced with the blank page in the typewriter, is Cannell's genius in five simple, obvious words.

Chase left film school in the late 1960s with a view to directing, but ended up writing for Glen Larson on a series called *Switch,* followed by a spell on the single season run of *Kolchak.* Once he saw *Rockford,* he started writing enthusiastically during the second season, joining the show on staff in 1978. "Basically, I like to write people," he told *Time Out* in 1979. "That's what the best TV's about anyway. In general, everybody on *Rockford* seems to be

---

*Proving the prejudice that networks rarely learn from experience, the fate of Phil De Guere's Rockfordian Simon and Simon, *gutted of all its quirkiness and sophisticated humor after its first season, is a sobering study of the fate that nearly befell* The Rockford Files. Simon and Simon *eventually enjoyed a lengthy run throughout the '80s in its new, lobotomized form, supported by a double-bill slot with the superior* Magnum, p.i.

interested in the kind of people who go around telling tremendous lies to each other, starting with themselves."

Interestingly, Garner confirms this in a roundabout way in his 1984 interview with *GQ* magazine. "I was raised in a place where a man's word is his bond — Oklahoma. Oh sure, we had our hustlers out there too, but for the most part, people were honest, took care of one another. If a man lied, it was usually transparent, because the norm was to tell the truth. But in L.A., people live the lie. They'll look you right in the eye and lie to you. They lie even when there's no reason to. I don't understand these people. They're too devious for me. I don't trust any of them any more."

Juanita Bartlett came to television working in a number of menial but educational jobs with tenuous show business connections before landing a job as secretary for Meta Rosenberg. She got her first writing assignment on *Nichols*, through which she met James Garner and Roy Huggins. From there, she wrote scripts for other more routine westerns, including *The Cowboys, Little House on the Prairie*, the final season of *Bonanza*, and Huggins' *Alias Smith and Jones*. This in turn lead to assignments on other Huggins series such as *Cool Million* and *Toma*, the predecessor to *Baretta*, where she met Cannell, and joined the staff of *The Rockford Files* as writer and eventually producer. Following *Rockford*, she worked on *The Greatest American Hero* and *The Quest* for Cannell, before leaving to work as an executive producer on other studios' series during the 1980s.

In *Rockford* generally," says Chase, "human nature motivates the plots. We don't have the one about the guy trying to move eight pounds of cocaine from Peru to Mexico because we've all seen that, and the character is actually doing nothing. But when you have the one about the guy who couldn't pay for the party ("The Dwarf in the Helium Hat"), or the one about the Mafia guy who'd had his hip replaced and it was done badly ("The Man Who Saw the Alligators") ... these kind of things are human nature type reactions, so you can have endlessly marvelous scenes dealing with these people, and the plot starts to drive itself because of them."

The *Rockford* pilot, titled simply *The Rockford Files*, but later re-edited with some new scenes into the two-part episode "Backlash of the Hunter," was plotted by Roy Huggins, with a script by Cannell. Directing was Richard Heffron, who had also helmed the pilot of *Toma* for Huggins and Cannell, and executive producer was — as ever — Jo Swerling, Jr. Throughout the '50s, Swerling had worked on the production side of numerous series, learning the ropes on such shows as *M Squad, Cimarron City, Wagon Train, Suspicion, Thriller,* and *87th Precinct,* before his degree in theater arts took him to the more prestigious ranks of the anthology shows of the period. In the '60s, he worked with Huggins on the award-winning series *Run for Your Life,* which starred Ben Gazarra and was loosely inspired by Huggins' previous assignment, *The Fugitive,* for Quinn Martin. Like David Janssen's character in that series, Gazarra was a wanderer from town to town, running not from the police, but the Grim Reaper himself, having been given two years to live. Despite this, the series ran for three years, from 1965 to 1968, after which Swerling worked on other series with which Huggins was associated, such as *The Bold Ones* and *Alias Smith and Jones.* Working with Huggins and Cannell on *Toma, Rockford,* and *Baretta,* Swerling joined Stephen Cannell's production company as soon as it was formed, and has been executive producer on many of Cannell's series since, later becoming senior vice-president of production for the company.

Guest starring in the *Rockford* pilot were Lindsay Wagner, later to find TV fame as *The Bionic Woman,* Cannell regular William Smith, Nita Talbot, Pat Renalia, Mike Steele, and former good-as-gold child actor Bill Mumy, now playing a slacker teen. Later regulars Joe Santos and Stuart Margolin were present, with Robert Donley playing the part of Rockford's father, the role later to go to Noah Beery, who re-filmed scenes for the two-parter that is now part of the syndicated package. The plot concerned Rockford's investigation into the death of a wino after the man's daughter (Wagner) insists he was murdered. As ever, Cannell's hero was a man defending the helpless from the impotent or unwilling authorities, who did not have the seemingly straightforward demise of a vagrant very high on their list of priorities.

Although many players returned to recreate character parts from previous episodes, *The Rockford Files* was one of those series — like *The Naked City*, *The Untouchables*, *The Invaders*, *Columbo*, and others — that had no qualms about using the same actors on two or three different occasions in different roles (thus necessitating care in scheduling re-runs). Among those who appeared in key roles more than once were Robert Webber, Scott Brady, Sharon Gless of *Cagney and Lacey*, Linda Evans of *Dynasty*, William Daniels of *St. Elsewhere*, Mary Frann of *Newhart*, Joan Van Ark of *Knots Landing*, Hector Elizondo, Ken Swofford, George Wyner, and George Loros (plus numerous bit players). Loros, who offered a superb caricature of an irritable thug in numerous Cannell series, and would later return to TV in Chase's *The Sopranos*, appeared twice in *The Rockford Files* as the hapless Anthony Boy in the Chase-scripted "To Protect and Serve" and a sequel of sorts, "The Man Who Saw the Alligators," but made several other *Rockford* appearances before, between, and after those two episodes, while his partner Syl, played by Luke Andreas, also turned up in other roles. Lindsay Wagner's character Sara Butler, from the pilot, returns in the first season episode "Aura Lee, Farewell," but in syndication the pilot turns up in the fourth season as a re-edited two-parter. James Luisi, who joined the regulars from the third season, had previously appeared in the second season episode "Joey Blue Eyes," while Garner's stand-in, Luis Delgado, and his brother Jack Garner show up in various roles throughout the entire series, Delgado usually as Officer Billings in Becker's station house.

The Rockford Files made its debut on September 13th, 1974, as part of a successful Friday night line-up consisting of the sit-coms *Sanford and Son* and *Chico and the Man* as lead-ins, and the first year of the successful — if ill-matched — *Police Woman* following, all of which it outlived. Its competition was a movie slot on CBS and the rapid MTM flop *The Texas Wheelers* on ABC, which was followed by the short-lived spook show *Kolchak: the Night Stalker*. Its initial success was also aided by the low ratings for the SF series *Planet of the Apes*, and the adventure show *Kodiak*.

When the two successful lead-in comedies were canceled in 1978, and replaced with a succession of dismal failures, *Rockford* continued to be successful, even when paired with failing series to follow it, such as Peter Fischer's *Eddie Capra Mysteries* and David Gerber's grim cop show *Eischeid*. The cynical and irreverent tone of *Rockford*, with its substantial characterizations and intelligent, complex plots were an oasis in a desert of shallow, fluffy lead-ins on the other networks, which consisted of such vacuous fare as *Donny and Marie*, *Wonder Woman*, *Fantasy Island*, and *Flying High*, a show about sexy stewardesses. Against a constant onslaught of silliness from such vapid series as these, *Rockford* couldn't help but catch on, even in a cut-throat ratings game that rewards not excellence, but clever scheduling. Shows with some semblance of quality, such as *Capra*, *Eischeid*, and *Quincy*, also paled next to the withering sarcasm of *Rockford*, which persistently failed to take similar plots seriously. But for all its style and charm, *The Rockford Files* may not have been able to withstand a low-brow smash hit from the Spelling or Larson stables. Fortunately, it didn't have to.

The Rockford Files remained in its Friday night at 9:00 slot undisturbed for its entire six season run, seeing off direct competition during that time from such series as *The Six Million Dollar Man, Hawaii Five-0, Logan's Run, The Incredible Hulk,* and *The Dukes of Hazzard.* With the exception of the humorless but then-classy cop show *Hawaii Five-0,* which opposed the show for only one season during a phenomenal eleven year run, *Rockford's* competition was composed entirely of juvenile adventure series, which undoubtedly aided it in winning over fleeing adult viewers with its wit and humor. Although, with the exception of *Logan's Run* in 1977, these juvenile series were all hit shows, none of them stayed opposite *The Rockford Files* for more than one season. *Rockford* and its audience were sitting pretty — with the teenagers out on Friday nights, and the kids watching the kidult competition on second sets, viewers could soak up the grown-up plots, dialogue and ambience unmolested.

As the series progressed, *The Rockford Files* began to pride itself on its wacky and ambiguous titles, the significance of which would often not become apparent until the episode had been viewed! During the first season, when Roy Huggins was developing the stories, *Rockford* was at its most traditional, with eloquent, pulpish titles — "The Kirkoff Case," "The Dark and Bloody Ground," "Say Goodbye to Jennifer," "Find Me If You Can," and so on — but before the first season was out, titles started turning up like "The Four Pound Brick" and "The Italian Bird Fiasco" and episode names became stranger and more obscure as the show went on! This was a tradition Cannell and his writers would carry over to many of his later series, particularly *Tenspeed and Brownshoe* — which had some spectacularly obscure gibberish on its script covers! — *Greatest American Hero, Riptide,* and *Hardcastle and McCormick.* Cannell and his writers, when titling scripts, would also frequently indulge in the most excruciating puns, and this was a habit which the MTM studios — and particularly Steven Bochco — ultimately adopted for their drama series (the episode titles for *L.A. Law,* unseen on the actual shows, have to be seen to be believed!). As *The Rockford Files* gradually moved on from the more wistful headings of the Huggins era, Cannell, Chase, and Bartlett began to conjure up such episode titles as "The Real Easy Red Dog," "Chicken Little Is a Little Chicken," "The Oracle Wore a Cashmere Suit," "Rattlers' Class of '63," "The Mayor's Committee from Deer Lick Falls," "A Three Day Affair with a Thirty Day Escrow," "A Good Clean Bust with Sequel Rights," "Local Man Eaten by Newspaper," and — deep breath — "With the French Heel Back, Can the Nehru Jacket Be Far Behind?"!

One title was mystifying in its tacky bluntness — "Hotel of Fear" could have been an episode title from any number of Quinn Martin productions, the sort of episode hook so superbly parodied by the merciless 1982 spoof cop show *Police Squad,* and the sheer unlikelihood of this being a *Rockford* title made it even more of a curiosity than usual. In fact, it turns out to be the dismal hack title of a novel to be penned by the hapless Angel, who is planning to write a best-seller based on the local mob activity he has supposedly stumbled on to. As a star witness, he is being hidden from the vengeful mob by federal agents in a succession of luxury locations ... but when it becomes apparent that the mob — thinking the melodramatic glory-hound might really know something — have decided that it might be better to be safe than sorry, the would-be celebrity's "hotel of fear" becomes an uncomfortable reality!

Of all the Cannell characters, no matter how hard done by Ralph Hinckley, Mark McCormick, or the *Riptide* boys were, Jim Rockford rivaled *City of Angels'* Jake Axminster as the all-time loser. Even his vacations were disasters.... In "The Family Hour," by Gordon Dawson, Jim and Rocky are just about to leave for a fishing trip when they stumble onto an abandoned child whose wastrel father is being pursued by corrupt cops who have already killed his partner in petty crime. In "Beamer's Last Case," written and directed by Cannell, Rockford returns from a holiday early after blowing all his money in casinos, only to find that the new owner of one of the clubs is on his tail for unpaid debts and a local loser with fantasies about becoming a p.i. (Cannell regular James Whitmore, Jr.) has adopted his identity and been running up huge bills and bad feelings under his name during his absence.

One particularly inspired episode was Cannell's own "White on White and Nearly Perfect," a classic, quintessential *Rockford* that is the perfect definition of how Cannell subverted the standard clichés of other series. A hilariously funny send-up of the super-man private eye that *Rockford* was anathema to, it was written and directed by Cannell, and features a pre–*Magnum* Tom Selleck, prophetically cast as a part-time detective and full-time wonderful human being; Lance White is a tall, handsome, and morally upright klutz who drives a flashy fast car ("You can't miss it," points out a thug, "the screwball drives a great white parade float") and keeps his gun in a fur-lined glove compartment. He was every corny TV 'tec rolled up into one satirical portrayal, and Selleck played him with all the infuriating charm he would later bring to Thomas Magnum. Unlike Magnum though, Lance could do no wrong, so experienced no difficulties or frustration. Naturally this made him a remarkably nice guy, and while poor Rockford does all the dirty work, Lance blandly receives the credit.

A wickedly accurate satire of the private investigator as seen on TV ("Things have a way of working out. They always do"), "White on White..." opens with Rocky reading a trashy paperback of the sub–Spillane tradition. Enthused by the pulp novel he has been reading ("My Gun Is Deadly," no less, by a Dan Slade), Rocky is swept up in the romance of the fantasy, and — despite everything he has ever witnessed during the course of previous episodes — is now in awe of his son's profession ("The more I read it, the more I understand what's going on around here!") ... while Rockford, just back from another night in the cooler courtesy of Angel, has now come around to his father's previous way of thinking, and is on the verge of throwing in the towel. "Things aren't like that, you know," he tells Rocky irritably, in an ominous portent of things to come, "they're never black and white. There are no heroes, they die young. See? His gun is deadly, mine's in the cookie jar." Rocky can't help but comment on the attractive woman who has just driven Jim home, quoting lines from the book about a woman "lush and lovely and ready for loving." "Lush and lovely and ready for Bellevue," snaps Rockford, having in reality endured a painful, preachy ride home with a female parole officer.

Summoned to the estate of a wealthy ailing industrialist (Bill Quinn) whose daughter (Karen Austin, later to star in Cannell's short-lived series *The Quest*) has been kidnapped, Rockford finds himself inadvertently allied with the smooth and charming White, a beloved friend of the family who chooses to moonlight as a private investigator out of the sheer goodness of his heart for the benefit of an interminable line of friends, best friends, former friends, and friends and relatives of best friends. Towering over Rockford in every respect, White is a marvelous creation perceptively and knowingly parodied by the embarrassingly good-looking Selleck, ironically then unknown, but only months away from his starring role in the super-successful *Magnum, p.i.* Selleck had been lined up for a shot at a series for years, but it wasn't until he appeared as Lance White that things began to come together for him.

Of course, *The Rockford Files* is as much of an idealized fantasy in its own way as the now familiar clichés of Spillane, Chandler, Spelling and Larson. A real-life p.i. would be fortunate indeed to experience just one of the outrageous exploits of a Jim Rockford in his entire career, and thus an episode like "White on White..." becomes a parody within a parody, cleverly legitimizing the *Rockford Files* fantasies in the process, a sort of mirror-world version of the *Magnum Force* principle. There are some splendidly inventive scenes and stinging swipes as Rockford and his cast of regulars become trapped within the absurd alternative reality inhabited by Lance White and his loyal collection of cardboard cut-out admirers, all of whom worship White after some improbable and undefined past history involving Lance as a professional (and very modest) white knight. The final indignity for the astonished Rockford is that even the acidic and highly unpleasant Lt. Chapman is a fan of the immaculate White in a delightful take on the friend of the force cliché. Indeed, Chapman's hostile and venomous attitude toward the individualist Rockford is itself a cliché of the new breed of mythological hero inaugurated by Hollywood during the '70s. While White and Chapman pal it up ("Your hunch, Lance?"), Jim and Dennis exchange weary, jaded greetings of apathy and discontent to a background chatter of mutual admiration ... even though White has typically blundered through the murder scene to the dismay of no-one. "Don't tell me — you saved his life once?" Rockford fumes, his sarcasm sliding off White like water off a duck's back. "He was wounded, I was knocked unconscious ... there were a lot of bullets flying about," White replies generously. "It's difficult to say *what* happened."

Cannell's greatest stroke of genius in this episode is that Lance White is not revealed to be a contemptible fraud or hypocrite like so many other *Rockford Files* targets, for in this case, it would totally destroy the point of the satire. White really is a lovely guy, impossibly naive but intensely likeable and good-natured at the same time, a big happy doofus ("I know you're making fun of me ... but I understand" says White graciously, in an earlier scene). Garner, never a fan of the mindless musclebound hunk variety of movie star, understands this perfectly, and gives his usual faultless performance, but it is Selleck who makes the episode work, where other actors might easily have overplayed or misunderstood. When Selleck is off the screen, the episode slips deliberately into the usual *Rockford* environment of dumb hoods, eccentric mobsters and devious corporate politics; when Lance White appears on the screen, Garner and the entire episode slip into the parody as effortlessly as one of the victims of a *Twilight Zone* yarn — suddenly Rockford is trapped in an Aaron Spelling show, and only he can see it. Our amusement comes from sharing his exasperation and disbelief, and it is the episodes of *The Rockford Files* that exploit this that signal the Cannell trademark and display *The Rockford Files* at its best.

The demise of *The Rockford Files* in the middle of the 1979–'80 season came about not because of falling ratings, but because Garner, battered and bruised by network politics and a number of painful injuries sustained during the show's six year run, suddenly walked off the show overnight in a fit of exhaustion. There was brief talk of bringing the show back in a series of ninety minute specials, and also of bringing in a younger partner for Rockford who would deal with the rougher aspects of the show and take some of the pressure off Garner. Freelance writers Chris Bunch and Allan Cole, later to contribute to a number of other Cannell shows such as *Hunter* and *The A-Team,* even went so far as to write the script introducing such a character to the series. According to Bunch and Cole, the Cannell people considered it one of the finest scripts ever written for the series, but the final word was with Garner. Ultimately — and almost certainly rightly — Garner decided it was time to call it a day.

In 1978, Garner's Cherokee Productions allied itself with Warners, the holders to the rights of *Maverick,* to produce the TV movie *The New Maverick,* which had Garner and former co-star Jack Kelly returning to their original roles of Bret and Bart Maverick. With them, cast in the title role, was the uncharismatic newcomer Charles Frank as Ben Maverick, son of the Roger Moore character Beau. Co-starring were Susan Blanchard (Frank's wife), familiar character actor Eugene Roche, and Susan Sullivan (later of *Falcon Crest*) alongside Cannell regulars George Loros and Garner's actor brother Jack (a regular bit player throughout the six years of *Rockford*). Meta Rosenberg was producing, Hy Averback was directing, and Juanita Bartlett provided the script.

Frank later went on to star in the dismal short-run series *Young Maverick* with Blanchard in 1979, before Cherokee and Garner returned to the character in 1981 for the moderately successful one season run of *Bret Maverick*. With Garner was Stuart Margolin again, recreating his *Nichols/Rockford* weasel persona one more time as incompetent bogus indian guide Philo Sandine. Producing was *Rockford* writer Gordon Dawson. The series was pleasantly diverting, co-starring Darleen Carr, Richard Hamilton, Ed Bruce, John Shearin (later Lt. Finn in *Hunter*), David Knell, and Ramon Bieri, and — unlike many recreations of old shows — was a genuine attempt to build on what had gone before, rather than simply wallow in back-patting nostalgia ... but it was nothing special, with Garner, tired and weary from his six years dominating the action on *The Rockford Files,* leaving much of the work this time to his large supporting cast. Although the smug optimism of Garner's Maverick persona had replaced Rockford's pessimism, the series inevitably seemed more of an extension of *Rockford* than the distant *Maverick,* and perhaps the greatest optimism of all was in trying to revisit the original. And while Garner was older and heavier than he was in either previous series, the show did not spoil the memory of them, it just didn't match them, despite the mass transferal of actors, writers, directors, and creative personnel from previous Garner projects, who had made the transition from '70s California to the new turn-of-the-century setting effortlessly. Certainly the pilot film was excellent, although this new format for Garner had far more limitations and restrictions than *Rockford* due to its locale and time-period. With four series (two of them smash successes) and numerous films to his credit, Garner was then in the comfortable position of being able to pick and choose his projects at whim. "I'll never retire as such," he told an interviewer in the early 1980s. "*Bret Maverick* will probably be the last series I do.* I've been working so hard for so long that when I get time off I don't know what to do with it. I used to play golf and race cars" (a pastime he picked up when he appeared in John Frankenheimer's 1966 film *Grand Prix*) "but now all my hobbies are gone. I guess I'm more or less a workaholic. If I find something else I enjoy more than work, maybe then I'll retire."

For Garner's many admirers though, the end has been far from in sight. In 1984, Garner found himself alongside Margolin, Margot Kidder, and long-time bit-player and stand-in Luis Delgado again for Margolin's film of Joseph Wambaugh's novel *The Glitter Dome*. "He's getting better and better as an actor," Margolin told *GQ* on location filming *The Glitter Dome*. "I mean, some guys are too professional, so they get slick and use the same old tricks.... But Jim is working on making it real, rougher around the edges. The next ten years should be interesting. He's turning the corner into what you call the leading character man. He's going for more experimentation, and he's brought a reality all his own to this part. You watch these scenes, and you'll see what I mean. This isn't *Maverick*."

In fact, he later appeared in the disastrous Man of the People *in 1991*. "This guy has one of the highest Q (personality) ratings in the business" *an anonymous talent agent told* Variety *in December, 1991 as the series collapsed*. "He's never failed on TV before. It took the geniuses at NBC to do him in!" "Nobody wants to see James Garner playing a nasty shyster," *said a TV exec*. "You can't just shoehorn a star into a badly executed show and expect to do well."

Episode Guide

regular cast: James Garner (Jim Rockford), Noah Beery (Joseph "Rocky" Rockford), Joe Santos (Sgt. Dennis Becker)

regular recurring cast: Tom Atkins (Lt. Alex Deihl), Gretchen Corbett (Beth Davenport), James Luisi (Lt. Doug Chapman), Stuart Margolin (Evelyn "Angel" Martin)

additional recurring cast: Luke Andreas (Syl), Luis Delgado (Officer Billings), Dennis Dugan (Richie Brockelman), Pat Finley (Peggy Becker), Lou Gossett (Marcus Hayes), Kathryn Harrold (Megan Dougherty), Isaac Hayes (Gandy Fitch), Bo Hopkins (John Cooper), George Loros (Anthony Boy), Rita Moreno (Rita Capcovich), Simon Oakland (Vern St. Cloud), Tom Selleck (Lance White), David Spielberg (Sgt. Tom Garvey), Joe E. Tata (Solly), Hunter Van Leer (Skip), Lindsay Wagner (Sara Butler), James Whitmore, Jr. (Fred Beamer)

note (1): *The Rockford Files* had the pleasing and then-innovative habit of only including supporting characters when their presence was relevant to the story, rather than shoehorning them into every episode or an obligatory number of scenes. Consequently, this listing includes the supporting players by their full names when making their first appearance, and by their surnames only on subsequent appearances. This way, readers can locate episodes with their favorite players/characters.

note (2): Some *Rockford Files* episodes were originally produced as extra-long single episodes, while others were originally prepared as two-parters. These differences are indicated, but most of the double-length single episodes have now been split into two parts for syndication (with, it has to be said, a vast amount of padding), so expect to find them in either format.

note (3): Roy Huggins' episodes are credited onscreen as being written by "John Thomas James." While the author notes that writers often have good cause for removing their real names from scripts, and makes the point again here, pen-names, where known, have been converted to the true author for academic interest; the false name on the film credit itself stands as the author's statement of intent.*

BACKLASH OF THE HUNTER
(pilot, later a two part episode)

wr. Roy Huggins, Stephen Cannell, dir. Richard Heffron

Rockford is asked to look into the death of a wino, which his daughter believes was a murder. Note: This pilot film is now split into two parts with additional scenes added; Wagner's character returns in the first season episode "Aura Lee, Farewell."

with Noah Beery, Joe Santos, Stuart Margolin, Lindsay Wagner, William Smith, Michael Lerner, Bill Quinn, Nita Talbot, Bill Mumy

First Season (1974–'75)

THE KIRKOFF CASE

wr. Roy Huggins, Stephen Cannell, dir. Lou Antonio

Rockford has qualms about investigating a murder case in which the chief suspect has hired his services ... in case the client really did it, in which case he won't get paid!

with Beery, Santos, Julie Sommars, Roger Davis, James Woods, Philip Kenneally, Abe Vigoda, Milt Kogan

THE DARK AND BLOODY GROUND

wr. Roy Huggins, Juanita Bartlett, dir. Michael Schultz

Investigating the murder of a screenwriter, Rockford becomes the target of hit-men.

with Beery, Santos, Gretchen Corbett, Patricia Smith, Nancy Malone, Walter Brooke, Linden Chiles

THE COUNTESS

wr. Roy Huggins, Stephen Cannell, dir. Russ Mayberry

A hoodlum who threatens to expose the criminal past of a minor socialite is murdered, and Rockford is the patsy.

with Santos, Corbett, Susan Strasberg, Art Lund, Dick Gautier, Harold J. Stone, Tom Atkins

---

*In the case of Roy Huggins, the habit was more likely a throwback to his days as a pulp-writer rather than any embarrassment over the finished result of his work; whereas many writers resort to pen-names if their scripts have been altered substantially by other hands in rewrites, it's doubtful Huggins was either rewritten (for Rockford he often supplied stories only, anyway) or embarrassed by his work ... on Alias Smith and Jones *and* The Rockford Files, at least.

EXIT PRENTISS CARR

wr. Roy Huggins, Juanita Bartlett, dir. Alex Grasshoff

While investigating the death of a cheating husband, Rockford uncovers a blackmail plot.

with Beery, Corinne Camacho Michaels, Stephen Bailey, Warren Kemmerling, Mills Watson, William Jordan, Roberta Collins

TALL WOMAN IN A RED WAGON

wr. Roy Huggins, Stephen Cannell, dir. Jerry London

Impersonating a salesman, a psychiatrist, and a tax man, Rockford searches for a missing woman.

with Beery, Sian Barbara Allen, George DiCenzo, Susan Damante

THIS CASE IS CLOSED (two parts)

wr. Roy Huggins, Stephen Cannell, dir. Bernard Kowalski

A powerful tycoon hires Rockford to look into the credentials of his daughter's prospective husband (this episode is an object lesson in how to pad out a thin show into two parts; many double-length *Rockfords* were too long).

with Joseph Cotten, Sharon Gless, James McEachin, Geoffrey Land, Joe Dellasorte, Fred Sadoff, Eddie Fontaine, Norman Bartold

THE BIG RIP-OFF

wr. Roy Huggins, Jo Swerling, Jr., dir. Vincent McEveety

Rockford stumbles onto an elaborate insurance fraud.

with Beery, Jill Clayburgh, Norman Burton, Nedra Deen, Fred Beir, Kelly Thorsden, Suzanne Somers

FIND ME IF YOU CAN

wr. Roy Huggins, Juanita Bartlett, dir. Lawrence Doheny

A supposedly amnesiac young woman hires Rockford to find out her real identity, but neglects to inform him that gangsters are pursuing her.

with Beery, Santos, Paul Michael Glasier, Joan Van Ark

IN PURSUIT OF CAROL THORNE

wr. Roy Huggins, Stephen Cannell, dir. Charles Dubin

Rockford is hired to follow a young woman just released from prison, in the hope that she will make her way to the missing loot.

with Lynette Mettey, Robert Symonds, Jim Antonio, Bill Fletcher, Irene Tedrow, Sandy Ward, Vince Howard, James McAlpine

THE DEXTER CRISIS

wr. Gloryette Clark, dir. Alex Grasshoff

Rockford's search for a missing girl is hindered by the presence of her room-mate and another p.i. also seeking her.

with Lee Purcell, Linda Kelsey, Ron Soble, Tim O'Connor, Joyce Jameson

CALEDONIA, IT'S WORTH A FORTUNE!

wr. Roy Huggins, Juanita Bartlett, dir. Stuart Margolin

Rockford and a convict's wife have one half of the clues to a hidden fortune, while the convict's former partners have the other.

with Shelley Fabares, Don Eitner, Richard Schaal, Ramon Bieri, William Traylor, Sid Haig, Rudy Challenger, Robert Ginty, Robert Ellenstein

PROFIT AND LOSS (two parts)

wr. Roy Huggins, Stephen Cannell, dir. Lawrence Doheny

When a potential client is kidnapped from his trailer, the head of the huge conglomerate that employed the man turns up on Rockford's doorstep and warns him to ignore the abduction.

with Beery, Corbett, Ned Beatty, Sharon Spelman, Michael Lerner, Paul Jenkins, Val Bisoglio, John Carter, Priscilla Pointer

AURA LEE, FAREWELL

wr. Roy Huggins, Edward Lakso, dir. Jackie Cooper

An investigation into the death of a young girl who is supposed to have died of a self-inflicted drugs overdose leads Rockford to suspect both a senator and a local thug.

with Lindsay Wagner, Robert Webber, Greg Mullavey, Melissa Greene, Kelly Lange

SLEIGHT OF HAND

wr. Stephen Cannell, Jo Swerling, Jr., dir. William Wiard

A girlfriend of Rockford is kidnapped, and her next door neighbor murdered by underworld mobsters.

with Beery, Santos, Atkins, Lara Parker, Allan

Miller, Howard Curtis, Pat Delaney, John Steadman, Gerald McRaney

Counter Gambit

wr. Juanita Bartlett, Howard Berk, dir. Jackie Cooper

A convict hires Rockford to locate his girlfriend, but in fact wants only the jewels she is carrying.

with Beery, Santos, Stuart Margolin, Mary Frann, Eddie Fontaine, Burr DeBenning, Ford Rainey, M. Emmet Walsh, Eric Server

Claire

wr. Edward Lakso, Stephen Cannell, dir. William Wiard

Rockford's father is put in danger by a woman who hires Rockford under false pretenses, and involves him in the search for a missing narcotics officer.

with Beery, Santos, Linda Evans, Jackie Cooper, Lane Smith, Lance Le Gault

Say Goodbye to Jennifer

wr. Roy Huggins, Juanita Bartlett, Rudolph Borchert, dir. Jackie Cooper

Rockford investigates a closed-case homicide in which an old army buddy, the lover of a young model is convinced that dental evidence was faked, and his girlfriend is alive.

with Beery, Santos, Hector Elizondo, Pamela Hensley, Regis Cordic, Kate Woodville, Thayer David, Ken Swofford

Charlie Harris at Large

wr. Roy Huggins, Zekial Marko, dir. Russ Mayberry

A playboy who once shared a jail cell with Rockford seeks a married woman he had an affair with, who can prove his innocence in the murder of his wife.

with Beery, Santos, Corbett, Tony Musante, David Speilberg, Diana Muldaur, Warner Anderson, Zekial Marko, Eddie Firestone

The Four Pound Brick

wr. Leigh Brackett, Juanita Bartlett, dir. Lawrence Doheny

Rockford investigates the death of a young police officer after the police write it off as a simple traffic accident.

with Beery, Santos, Atkins, Edith Atwater, Jess Walton, Paul Carr, William Watson, Wyatt Johnson, Jack Knight, John Furlong, John Quade, Bruce Tuthill, Frank Campanella

Just by Accident

wr. Charles Sailor, Eric Kaldor, dir. Jerry London

Rockford becomes a candidate for an "accidental death" when he uncovers an insurance scam involving traffic fatalities.

with Beery, Santos, Margolin, David Speilberg, Joey Aresco, Neva Patterson, Steven Keats, Fred Sadoff, EJ Peaker, Millie Slavin, Susan Keller

Roundabout

wr. Edward Lakso, Mitch Lindeman, dir. Lou Antonio

Rockford travels to Vegas to deliver an insurance payment to a young singer, but finds that she is helplessly involved with the mob against her will.

with Janet Margolin, Jesse Welles, Mills Watson, Ron Rifkin, Virginia Gregg, George Wyner, Joey Tata, Frank Michael Liu, Fred Lerner, Chuck Hicks

Second Season (1975–'76)

The Aaron Ironwood School for Success

wr. Stephen Cannell, dir. Lou Antonio

Rockford protects his obnoxious foster brother, now a manipulative sales guru, from the underworld.

with Beery, Santos, Margolin, Corbett, James Hampton, Jonathan Lippe, Ken Swofford, Jerome Guardino

The Farnsworth Stratagem

wr. Juanita Bartlett, dir. Lawrence Doheny

Rockford and some friends devise an elaborate scheme involving a phoney oil strike when Becker is sucked into a confidence trick involving new condominiums.

with Beery, Santos, Margolin, Corbett, Linda Evans, Pat Finley, John Crawford, H.M. Wynant, Al Hansen, Stephen Parr, Gerald McRaney

Gearjammers (two parts)

wr. Stephen Cannell, Don Carlos Dunaway, dir. William Wiard

Rockford's naive father becomes the target of mobsters after he unknowingly witnesses a pay-off.

with Beery, Santos, Scott Brady, Jack Kruschen, Terry Leonard, Bobby Hoy, Al Stevenson, Rosemary DeCamp, Reb Brown, Charles Cooper, Bucklind Beery, Ted Gehring, Peter Brocco

The Deep Blue Sleep

wr. Chas. Floyd Johnson, Juanita Bartlett, dir. William Wiard

Rockford uncovers money laundering in the fashion world after Beth receives a frantic phone call from a friend, who then turns up dead.

with Beery, Corbett, Janet MacLachlan, Robert Webber, Michael Conrad, Doria Cook, Ric Mancini, Robert Hays

The Great Blue Lake Land and Development Company

wr. Juanita Bartlett, dir. Lawrence Doheny

When he is swindled out of some money while stranded in a small town, Rockford arranges a similar scam to con the con-men.

with Beery, Richard B. Schull, Dana Elcar, Dennis Patrick, Bob Hastings, Ann Chinn

The Real Easy Red Dog

wr. Stephen Cannell, dir. Ivan Dixon

Rockford uncovers a fake suicide after he is duped into acting as a decoy by a cunning fellow investigator.

with Santos, Atkins, Stefanie Powers, Sherry Jackson, Nick Ferris, George Wyner, Bruce Kirby, Jr., Larry Cook, Wayne Grace

Resurrection in Black and White

wr. Juanita Bartlett, Stephen Cannell, dir. Russ Mayberry

Although Rockford is skeptical, he agrees to help clear a man convicted of murder when a magazine writer is convinced he is innocent. As Rockford locates a retired coroner and a senile judge, the writer's suspicions begin to look justified.

with Santos, Joan Van Ark, Milton Seltzer, Sandy Smith, John Lawlor, John Daheim, William Prince

Chicken Little Is a Little Chicken

wr. Stephen Cannell, dir. Lawrence Doheny

Angel cons Rockford into a situation that risks both their lives with the underworld, when a petty hood disappears with some money....

with Beery, Santos, Margolin, Ray Danton, Frank Campanella, Tom Williams, Angelo Gnazzo

Two into 5.56 Won't Go

wr. Stephen Cannell, dir. Jeannot Szwarc

Rockford's former army commander telephones him for help and then dies in a jeep accident, but both Rockford and the officer's daughter suspect a conspiracy that leads them into the rigid and rule-heavy environment of the military world.

with Beery, Santos, Mitchell Ryan, Charles Napier, Jesse Welles, Bill Boyett, Frank Maxwell, Carol Vogel, John Kerry, Eddie Firestone

Pastoria Prime Pick

wr. Gordon Dawson, dir. Lawrence Doheny

Beth and Rocky come to Rockford's rescue when he becomes the victim of an elaborate small-town conspiracy.

with Beery, Corbett, Warren Kemmerling, Richard Herd, William Lucking, Kathie Brown, Bill Quinn, Don Billett, Bill Zuckert

The Reincarnation of Angie

wr. Stephen Cannell, dir. Jerry London

Rockford investigates a brokerage firm to discover the whereabouts of a missing stockbroker, only to find himself implicated in a mystery that involves the underworld and federal agents.

with Beery, Elayne Heilveil, Wayne Tippit, David Huddleston, Sharon Spelman, Eugene Peterson, Charles Siebert, Dick Durock, Jenny O'Hara

The Girl in the Bay City Boy's Club

wr. Juanita Bartlett, dir. James Garner

Rockford poses as a newspaper publisher to investigate rigged gambling, but nobody else is who they are supposed to be either.

with Margolin, Blair Brown, Paul Stevens, Joel Fabiani, Stewart Moss, Stacy Keach, Sr., William Bryant, Norman Bartold

The Hammer of C Block

wr. Juanita Bartlett, Gordon Dawson, dir. Jerry London

Convict Gandy Fitch serves twenty years for killing his wife, then hires Rockford to find the real killer. The trail leads to a former hooker, who is now respectably married to a doctor, and doesn't want the past dug up.

with Santos, Isaac Hayes, James A. Watson, Jr., Annazette Chase, Lynn Hamilton, Jack Somack, Allan Rich

THE NO-CUT CONTRACT

wr. Stephen Cannell, dir. Lou Antonio
When a small-time sportsman is questioned by federal agents over some taped evidence he has on some underworld figures, he implicates Rockford to get himself out of danger.

with Santos, Margolin, Corbett, Rob Reiner, Dick Butkus, Wayne Tippit, Milt Kogan, Kathy Silva

A PORTRAIT OF ELIZABETH

wr. Stephen Cannell, dir. Meta Rosenberg
A seemingly straightforward investigation into stolen cashier money turns into an escalating nightmare for Rockford and Beth Davenport.

with Santos, Corbett, Atkins, John Saxon, Wayne Tippit, Cynthia Sikes, Kate Woodville, Robert Reisel, Chuck Winters, Angus Duncan, Ned Wilson

JOEY BLUE EYES

wr. Walter Dallenbach, dir. Lawrence Doheny
While Rockford tries to prevent an ex-con from taking more direct action, he arranges a scam to get even with gangsters who are threatening the man's restaurant business.

with Margolin, Corbett, James Luisi (not as Chapman), Michael Ansara, Suzanne Charney, Mickey Caruso, Eddie Fontaine, Robert Yuro, James Lydon, Norman Bartold, Sandy Kenyon

IN HAZARD

wr. Juanita Bartlett, dir. Jackie Cooper
Beth counsels a stockbroker and a union executive in a tax suit and finds herself in jail and under threat of a contract on her life.

with Beery, Santos, Corbett, Joseph Campanella, Richard Venture, Ben Frank, Skip Ward, Frank Campanella, Joey Tata

THE ITALIAN BIRD FIASCO

wr. Edward Lakso, Stephen Cannell, dir. Jackie Cooper
Rockford is hired to bid for, and win, a sculpture at an auction, but after outbidding the opposition finds himself pursued by some very bad losers.

with Santos, William Daniels, Camilla Sparv, William Jordan, Peter Palmer, Gerald Peters, Eric Server, Ron Silver, Ivor Barry, Dean Sontoro

WHERE'S HOUSTON?

wr. Don Carlos Dunaway, dir. Lawrence Doheny
Rockford searches for the daughter of a friend of his father who has been kidnapped, and uncovers a murderous real estate deal.

with Beery, Santos, Corbett, Lane Bradbury, Dabbs Greer, Murray MacLeod, Robert Mandan, Del Monroe, Raymond O'Keefe, Rodolfo Hoyos

FOUL ON THE FIRST PLAY

wr. Stephen Cannell, dir. Lou Antonio
Rockford is conned by a parole officer turned rival p.i., and organizes a scam of his own in retaliation.

with Lou Gossett, Dick Davalos, David White, Al Ruscio, Vincent Cobb, Pepper Martin, Chuck Bowman, James Ingersoll, John Mahon

A BAD DEAL IN THE VALLEY

wr. Donald Gold, Lester Berke, dir. Jerry London
Rockford is implicated in a counterfeit money operation by a former girlfriend and con artist.

with Beery, Santos, Corbett, Susan Strasberg, Rod Cameron, John Lupton, Veronica Hamel, Fritzi Burr, Russ McGinn, Reg Parton, Gordon Jump, David Sabin, Jack Colvin, Dudley Knight

Third Season (1976–'77)

THE FOURTH MAN

wr. Juanita Bartlett, dir. William Wiard
A casual remark to a passenger on an air-flight puts a stewardess friend of Rockford on the hit-list of a cold-blooded professional assassin.

with Beery, Santos, Margolin, Corbett, Sharon Gless, John McMartin, Michael Bell, Jack Garner, Candace Howerton, Diane Harper

THE ORACLE WORE A CASHMERE SUIT

wr. David Chase, dir. Russ Mayberry
A publicity-seeking psychic investigator leads the police to Rockford's beach trailer during the hunt for a murdered dope-peddler.

with Beery, Santos, Corbett, James Luisi (intro: as Chapman), Robert Webber, Pepe Serna, Robert Walden, John Furlong, Terry O'Connor

THE FAMILY HOUR

wr. Gordon Dawson, dir. William Wiard

Rockford is reluctantly drawn into a vicious conflict between villains when he becomes the unwilling custodian of a surly young girl whose minor-offender father is being hunted by killers.

with Beery, Santos, Margolin, Burt Young, Paul Koslo, Ken Swofford, Kim Richards, Adrian Ricard, Janice Carroll, Marge Wakeley, Fred Lerner

FEEDING FRENZY

wr. Stephen Cannell, dir. Russ Mayberry

When the statute of limitations runs out on some missing stolen money, the reformed alcoholic who stole it plans to return it, and enlists Rockford's help ... but the mob has other plans for the loot.

with Beery, Santos, Corbett, Susan Howard, Eddie Firestone, Pepper Martin, Luke Askew, Tony Epper

DROUGHT AT INDIANHEAD RIVER

wr. Stephen Cannell, dir. Lawrence Doheny

Angel suddenly becomes big in real estate, unaware that he has been set up by underworld schemers planning a tax swindle.

with Beery, Santos, Margolin, Corbett, Robert Loggia, Vincent Bagetta, Ronda Copland, Antony Carbone, Nick Dimitri

COULTER CITY WILDCAT

wr. Don Carlos Dunaway, dir., Russ Mayberry

When Rocky wins some real estate in a federal lottery, he becomes the target of vicious hoods who want the oil on the land.

with Beery, Corbett, John Anderson, Dennis Burkley, Patricia Stitch, Noble Willingham, Gordon Hurst, Norman Blankenship, Sharon Compton, Terry Leonard, Don Nagel

SO HELP ME GOD

wr. Juanita Bartlett, dir. Jeannot Szwarc

Rockford is in and out of jail for contempt during an investigation into the kidnapping of a union official.

with Beery, Santos, Margolin, Corbett, William Daniels, Jason Wingreen, Sandy Ward, Robert Ray, Lieux Dressler, John Lupton

RATTLER'S CLASS OF '63

wr. David Chase, dir. Meta Rosenberg

What appears to be the wedding of Angel Martin, with a deceived and baffled Jim Rockford as best man, is rapidly revealed to be a thoughtless scam on the part of Angel ... who is unaware that he too is being callously used by the bride's family.

with Beery, Santos, Margolin, Corbett, Luisi, Elayne Heilveil, Avery Schreiber, John Durren, James Wainwright, Rudy Ramos, Gerald Hackney

RETURN TO THE 38TH PARALLEL

wr. Walter Dallenbach, dir. Bruce Kessler

A down-and-out friend of Rockford becomes involved with one of his clients, and implicates them both in an art theft.

with Beery, Santos, Ned Beatty, Veronica Hamel, Paul Stevens, John Mahon, Chuck Winters, Michael Ebert, Jeff David

PIECE WORK

wr. Juanita Bartlett, dir. Lawrence Doheny

Rockford uncovers a gun-running operation during an accident investigation, and becomes a target for hoods and feds alike.

with Beery, Santos, Luisi, Michael Lerner, Ned Wilson, Simon Scott, Ben Frank

THE TROUBLE WITH WARREN

wr. Juanita Bartlett, dir. Chris Nyby

Beth's cousin, a brilliant genius, is being set up as the patsy for a murder, and Rockford uncovers a web of bribery and corruption at the corporation where he works.

with Beery, Santos, Corbett, Luisi, Ron Rifkin, Paul Jenkins, Joe Maross, Tom Bower, Ann Randall

THERE'S ONE IN EVERY PORT

wr. Stephen Cannell, dir. Meta Rosenberg

After being taken by a father-daughter con team, Rockford puts together a scam of his own to get back his money.

with Beery, Margolin, Joan Van Ark, John Dehner, Steve Landesberg, Jack Riley, Howard Duff, George Memmoli, Kenneth Tobey

STICKS AND STONES MAY BREAK YOUR BONES, BUT WATERBURY WILL BURY YOU

wr. David Chase, dir. Jerry London

Rockford and other small p.i.'s find they are being illegally forced out of business by the crooked practices of a large investigative organization.

with Beery, Santos, Simon Oakland, Cleavon Little, Val Bisoglio, Anthony Costello, Katherine Charles, Linda Dano

THE TREES, THE BEES, AND T.T. FLOWERS (two parts)

wr. Gordon Dawson, dir. Jerry London

An eccentric elderly friend of Rocky is the victim of a land developer and an unscrupulous brother-in-law who intend to have him declared senile to get the rights to his land.

with Beery, Santos, Corbett, Strother Martin, Karen Machon, Alex Rocco, Scott Brady, Richard Venture, Roy Jenson, Paul Sylvan, Bob Hastings

THE BECKER CONNECTION

wr. Chas. Floyd Johnson, Ted Harris, Juanita Bartlett, dir. Reza Badiyi

Becker is accused of stealing dope from the police property room, and Rockford sets out to clear his name. The search leads to a washed-up club comic, a crooked cop, and a race-car driver.

with Beery, Santos, Margolin, Luisi, Jack Kelly, Jack Carter, William Jordan, Bucklind Beery, Pat Finley

JUST ANOTHER POLISH WEDDING

wr. Stephen Cannell, dir. William Wiard

Rockford finds himself in the middle of a conflict between Gandy Fitch and Marcus Hayes, the parole officer turned p.i.

with Beery, Isaac Hayes, Lou Gossett, Pepper Martin, Anthony Charnota, Barney McFadden, Melendy Britt, Jack Collins, George Skaff, Walter Brooke

NEW LIFE, OLD DRAGONS

wr. Bernard Rollins, Leroy Robinson, David Taylor, dir. Jeannot Szwarc

Searching for a Vietnamese girl's missing brother, Rockford becomes implicated in a plot involving the CIA, three veterans, and a stolen military payroll.

with Beery, Kathleen Nolan, Irene Yah-Ling Sun, Charles Siebert, Luke Askew, James Callahan, Chris Napier, Jim Ishida

TO PROTECT AND SERVE (two parts)

wr. David Chase, dir. William Wiard

A police groupie stirs up discontent between Rockford, Becker, and Chapman, while a syndicate man has two resentful hit-men on the trail of his fleeing girlfriend.

with Beery, Santos, Luisi, Joyce Van Patten, Jon Cypher, Leslie Charleson, George Loros, Luke Andreas, Pat Finley, Lou Frizzell

CRACK-BACK

wr. Juanita Bartlett, dir. Reza Badiyi

Beth Davenport's concentration while defending a football player charged with robbery and murder is disturbed by a series of threatening sexual nuisance calls that gradually escalate into an intimidating mystery.

with Beery, Santos, Corbett, Howard McGillin, John Calvin, Joseph Mascolo, Sondra Blake

DIRTY MONEY, BLACK LIGHT

wr. David Taylor, dir. Stuart Margolin

Rocky starts receiving huge sums of money in the post, and — as Rockford sets out to investigate the cause of his father's good fortune — Angel sets his beady eyes on the loot.

with Beery, Santos, Margolin, Corbett, John P. Ryan, John Chappell, Wesley Addy, Roger E. Mosley, Joshua Bryant, Diana Ewing, Victor Argo, Michael Lane, Mary Carver, Martin Kove, Craig Wasson

Fourth Season (1977–'78)

BEAMER'S LAST CASE

wr. Booker Bradshaw, Calvin Kelly, Stephen Cannell, dir. Stephen Cannell

Rockford arrives home early from a disastrous aborted vacation to find that a local nerd and would-be p.i., enthused with the perceived "romanticism" of detective work, has taken up residence in his trailer, adopted his identity, run up huge bills, and antagonized his clients.

with Beery, Santos, James Whitmore, Jr., Jack Kelly, Robert Loggia, Bibi Besch, Howard George, Cal Bellini, Phil Hoover

TROUBLE IN CHAPTER SEVENTEEN

wr. Juanita Bartlett, dir. William Wiard

Rockford agrees to protect a best-selling author promoting femininity over feminism from enraged fanatical women's groups who oppose her dated stereotypes.

with Beery, Santos, Claudette Nevins, Ed Nelson, Arthur Roberts, Donna Bacalla

THE BATTLE OF CANOGA PARK

wr. Juanita Bartlett, dir. Ivan Dixon

Rockford's gun is stolen from his cookie jar and turns up at the scene of a murder.

with Beery, Santos, Corbett, Atkins, Nora Marlowe, Elliot Street, Adrienne Marden, John Dennis Johnston, Ted Gehring, John Perak, Brian James, Charles Hallahan, James Parks, Bruce Tuthill

The Second Chance

wr. Gordon Dawson, dir. Reza Badiyi

Working as a bouncer in a local dive, Gandy Fitch befriends and romances a singer whose ex-husband has just got out of jail.

with Santos, Margolin, Isaac Hayes, Tony Burton, Dionne Warwick, Malachi Throne

The Dog and Pony Show

wr. David Chase, dir. Reza Badiyi

Angel implicates Jim in a petty theft, and as punishment they both have to sit in on a psychiatric group, where a girl being treated for paranoia begs Rockford to protect her from men who are following her.

with Beery, Santos, Margolin, Joanne Nail, Ed Lauter, Walter Brooke, Michael Bell, George Loros, Gary Crosby, Al Ruscio, Howard Honig, Bill Quinn

Requiem for a Funny Box

wr. Burt Prelutsky, James Crocker, dir. William Wiard

A two-faced club comic who would rather let Rockford go to jail than admit he has a joke-file, bugs his embittered ex-partner to steal gags and inadvertently records details of a homosexual affair between the comedian's mobster friends.

with Beery, Santos, Corbett, Atkins, Chuck McCann, Robert Quarry, Jason Evers, Meredith MacRae, Jodean Russo, Gilbert Green

Quickie Nirvana

wr. David Chase, dir. Meta Rosenberg

A flaky fad-follower camped outside Rockford's trailer draws him into a blackmail plot into which she has naively become implicated while worshipping a devious phony guru.

with Beery, Santos, Luisi, Valerie Curtin, Kenneth Gilman, Quinn Redecker, Dick Anthony Williams, Larry Cook, Patricia Pearcy

Irving the Explainer

wr. David Chase, dir. James Coburn

Rockford becomes involved in solving a thirty year old murder mystery when he is hired by a bogus book researcher who claims to be writing about a film director who is revealed to have been a Nazi sympathizer.

with Beery, Santos, Luisi, Barbara Babcock, Maurice Marsac, Irene Tsu, Paul Stewart, Byron Morrow

The Mayor's Committee from Deer Lick Falls

wr. Bill Stratton, dir. Ivan Dixon

Pillars of a small-town community hire Rockford on the pretext of searching for a missing county vehicle, but then propose a murder plot to him. Amazed and horrified when Rockford refuses, they must now bump off Rockford as well as their original target, while Rockford must find the young girl in question before a second nominee accepts the job.

with Beery, Santos, Luisi, Edward Binns, Charles Aidman, Priscilla Barnes, Jerry Hardin, Richard O'Brien

Hotel of Fear

wr. Juanita Bartlett, dir. Russ Mayberry

Angel is living it up in luxury accommodation while planning his best-seller on how he testified against the mob ... but when the mobster gets off, the police protection automatically vanishes, and Angel manages to get Rockford onto the list for cement shoes alongside him.

with Beery, Santos, Margolin, Luisi, Frank De Kova, Madison Arnold, Vincent Bagetta, Gerald McRaney, Eugene Peterson, Barry Atwater, Fred Carney, Barbra Rose

Forced Retirement

wr. Bill Stratton, dir. Alex Singer

Angel inadvertently blows Rockford's cover wide open during an investigation into a mysterious death and theft in an up-and-coming oil company.

with Beery, Santos, Margolin, Corbett, Larry Hagman, Margaret Impert, Denny Miller, Ron Masak

The Queen of Peru

wr. David Chase, dir. Meta Rosenberg

Rockford is hired by an insurance company to negotiate for the return of an incredibly valuable diamond when it suddenly and inadvertently falls into the possession of a brainless family whose trailer was parked next to Rockford's on the beach.

with Beery, Santos, Luisi, Ken Swofford, George Wyner, Paul Cavonis, Joey Tata, Luke Andreas, Christopher Cary, Susan Davis, Jennifer Marks, Hunter Von Leer

The Deadly Maze

wr. Juanita Bartlett, dir. William Wiard

An eccentric psychologist puts Rockford through an elaborate stress test by pretending that his wife is missing ... but the experiment goes awry when unforeseen developments result in a murder.

with Beery, Santos, Larry Linville, Corinne Michaels, Lance Le Gault, Johnny Seven, J. Pat O'Malley, John McKinney, Jack Collins, Cliff Carnell, Ken Anderson

The Attractive Nuisance

wr. Stephen Cannell, dir. Dana Elcar

Rockford finds himself the target of an ambulance-chaser, while Rocky opens a trucker's diner with an old buddy, unaware that his partner has a shady mob background.

with Beery, Corbett, Ken Lynch, Victor Jory, Joe Tornatore, Dick Balducci, Jeannie Fitzsimmons, Rudy Bond, John Morgan Evans, Will Gill, Jr., Paul Sorenson, Joe Dellasorte, Hunter Von Leer, Jerome Guardino

The Gang at Don's Drive-In

wr. James Crocker, dir. Harry Falk

An alcoholic author friend of Jim's is all washed up, but hires Rockford to help on the research for a book ... but the subject matter turns out to be considerably bigger than first suspected.

with Beery, Santos, Anthony Zerbe, Arlene Golonka, Lawrence Casey, Mills Watson, Elaine Princi, Bill Fletcher

The Paper Palace

wr. Juanita Bartlett, dir. Richard Crenna

Becker is mortified when Rockford, protecting a prostitute from thugs, brings her to a dinner party that turns into a major embarrassment.

with Beery, Santos, Luisi, Rita Moreno, Bruce Kirby, Pat Finley, Patricia Donahue, David Lewis, Rene Assa, Shirley O'Hara, James Jeter, Norwood Smith, Gene Scherer

The Dwarf in the Helium Hat

wr. Stephen Cannell, David Chase, dir. Reza Badiyi

Rockford reluctantly becomes involved in the problems of an arrogant rock star who has inadvertently offended a mobster, and is oblivious to the manner in which the mob put their accounts straight.

with Beery, Luisi, John Pleshette, Rebecca Balding, Rick Springfield, Milton Seltzer, Gianni Russo, Bea Silvern, Ted Markland, Mary Nancy Burnett

South by South East

wr. Juanita Bartlett, dir. William Wiard

Jim is the victim of mistaken identity when he is whisked away to Mexico by federal agents trying to prevent the sleazy opportunist husband of a playgirl doing deals with unfriendly nations.

with Dorrie Kavenaugh, Don Chastain, Carlos Romero, Isaac Ruiz, Jr., Mark Roberts, Jim Scott, Robert Clotworthy, Don Dubbins, Jim Smith, Don Diamond, Bert Rosario, George Clifton, Eric Mason

The Competitive Edge

wr. Gordon Dawson, dir. Harry Falk

Posing as a newsman while on the trail of a missing banker, Rockford finds himself imprisoned in an insane asylum, where he must organize an escape attempt.

with Stephen Elliott, Robert Hogan, Pepper Martin, James McMullen, Neile McQueen, George Murdock, John Lupton, John Fiedler, Dennis Fimple, Sandy Newton

The Prisoner of Rosemont Hall

wr. Stephen Cannell, David Chase, dir. Ivan Dixon

When a young college boy is killed trying to reach Rockford for help, Jim teams up with a journalism teacher to uncover the mystery behind the murder.

with Beery, Santos, Frances Lee McCain, Kenneth Tobey, Buck Young, Michael Swan, Maurice Sherbanee, Danny Ades, Ric Carrott, Joyce Easton

The House on Willis Avenue
(double-length)

wr. Stephen Cannell, dir. Hy Averback

Rockford reluctantly teams up with junior detective Richie Brockelman to investigate the death of a fellow p.i. on the freeway, and discover a computerized killer with plans for their demise too. (This episode was a lead-in to the short-lived *Richie Brockelman* series)

with Beery, Santos, Dennis Dugan, Simon Oakland, Pernell Roberts, Jackie Cooper, Philip Sterling, Paul Fix, Lou Krugman

Fifth Season (1978–'79)

Heartaches of a Fool
wr. Stephen Cannell, dir. William Wiard
Rocky is an innocent pawn in a conflict between the business partners of a country-and-western singer and Chinese mobsters.

with Beery, Taylor Lacher, Lynne Marta, James Shigeta, Norman Alden, Herb Armstrong, Don Red Barry, Joey Tata, George Kee Cheung, Raymond O'Keefe, Byron Chung, and the vocals of Willie Nelson.

Rosendahl and Gilda Stern Are Dead
wr. Juanita Bartlett, dir. William Wiard
When a doctor who performed clumsy surgery on a mobster is blown away by the aggrieved party, the killing is blamed on the prostitute the doctor was with at the time, a former client of Rockford's, who begs his help again.

with Beery, Santos, Rita Moreno, William Joyce, John Karlen, Ron Gilbert, Abe Vigoda, Sharon Acker, Robin Gammell

The Jersey Bounce
wr. Juanita Bartlett, Stephen Cannell, David Chase, dir. William Wiard
Rockford becomes a target for the sniping of a grubby tabloid paper and the more permanently damaging sniping of an underworld contract when he investigates the murder of a showbiz doctor.

with Beery, Bo Hopkins, Sorrell Booke, Greg Antonacci, Eugene Davis, Luke Andreas, Walter Olkewicz

White on White and Nearly Perfect
wr. and dir. Stephen Cannell
Rockford finds himself allied with super-perfect p.i. Lance White, a too-good-to-be-true parody of a TV detective, during the hunt for a tycoon's missing daughter.

with Beery, Santos, Luisi, Tom Selleck, Karen Austin, Jason Evers, Peter Brocco, Bill Quinn, Carolyn Calcote, Eddie Fontaine, Julienne Wells

Kill the Messenger
wr. Juanita Bartlett, dir. Ivan Dixon
Bucking for promotion, and taking exams for promotion to lieutenant, Becker is mortified when he is obliged to investigate the murder of the police commissioner's wife ... with the commissioner as the prime suspect!

with Beery, Santos, Luisi, W.K. Stratton, Byron Morrow, Ed Harris, Pat Finley

A Good Clean Bust with Sequel Rights
wr. Rudolph Borchert, dir. William Wiard
Rocky is enthralled by the adventures of a TV cop based on a real-life police officer, and is even more impressed when Jim is hired to guard the renegade trouble-shooter by a toy company that wants to ensure a wholesome image for their public hero while they market related merchandise.

with Beery, Santos, Hector Elizondo, Hank Brandt, James Murtaugh, James Sikking, Jenny Sherman, Nicholas Coster, Louisa Moritz, Jerry Douglas, Joanna Lipari

A Three Day Affair with a Thirty Day Escrow
wr. David Chase, dir. Ivan Dixon
An unscrupulous real estate salesman sends a deluded gigolo into valuable properties to provoke divorces and the subsequent sale of luxury homes, but he comes unstuck when the devious duo inadvertently provoke adultery within a strict Arab family.

with Beery, Santos, Luisi, Richard Romanus, Robert Alda, Janis Paige, Maria Grimm

The Empty Frame
wr. Stephen Cannell, dir. Corey Allen
Chapman is forced to ask Rockford for help when he becomes involved with an art robbery at a party celebrating the appointment of Angel's brother-in-law to police commissioner.

with Santos, Margolin, Luisi, Richard Seff, Paul Carr, Dale Robinette, Jonathan Goldsmith, Lee Delano, Milt Kogan, Marianne Bunch

Black Mirror (two parts)
wr. David Chase, dir. Arnold Laven
A blind psychologist seeks Rockford's help when she is subjected to a string of attacks, but refuses him access to her files due to professional ethics.

with Beery, Santos, Margolin, Kathryn Harrold, John Pleshette, Leo Gordon, Brian Cutler, Julia Ann Benjamin, Alan Manson, Allan Arbus, Carl Franklin, Wallace Earl, Denny Miller

A Fast Count
wr. Gordon Dawson, dir. Reza Badiyi
When a fighter's manager is implicated in charges of bribery and murder, Rockford's investigations lead him to an elaborate fraud.

with Beery, Santos, Kenneth McMillan, Mary Frann, Lawrence Casey, Rocky Echevarria, Len Wayland, Bert Kramer

LOCAL MAN EATEN BY NEWSPAPER

wr. Juanita Bartlett, dir. Meta Rosenberg
Investigating the shooting of a doctor with show business patients, Rockford finds himself of interest to a sleazy supermarket tabloid.
with Beery, Santos, Bo Hopkins, Scott Brady, Scott Marlowe, Rose Gregorio, Joseph Hindy, Gianni Russo, Dallas Mitchell, Harlee McBride

WITH THE FRENCH HEEL BACK, CAN THE NEHRU JACKET BE FAR BEHIND?

wr. Rudolph Borchert, dir. Ivan Dixon
Rockford stumbles through the strange world of fashion when he investigates the apparent suicide of a model he once knew.
with Beery, Santos, Rene Auberjonois, Erin Gray, W.K. Stratton, Marisa Pavan, Chris Palmer, Albert Carrier, Howard Witt

THE BATTLE-AXE AND THE EXPLODING CIGAR

wr. Mann Rubin, Michael Wagner, Rogers Turrentine, dir. Ivan Dixon
Innocently driving a car that turns out to be stolen after finding himself broke in Las Vegas, Rockford is arrested for gun-running. His investigations lead him to a renegade band of U.S. spies selling defective weapons to small countries.
with Beery, Marge Redmond, Sully Boyar, Lane Smith, Glenn Corbett, Mitzi Hoag, Mary Nancy Burnett, Kirk Mee, Lindsay Jones

GUILT

wr. Juanita Bartlett, dir. William Wiard
A shooting attempt on an ex-girlfriend leads Rockford on a painful trip down memory lane when he tries to discover the reason for the attack.
with Beery, Santos, Patricia Crowley, Rita Gam, Robert Quarry, Elizabeth Brooks, James Lough, Ben Young, Eldon Quick

THE DEUCE

wr. Gordon Dawson, dir. Bernard McEveety
Called reluctantly to jury duty, Rockford attempts to clear a drunken driver of a murder charge.
with Beery, Mills Watson, Margaret Blye, Patricia Hindy, Joe Maross, Sharon Spelman, Richard Kelton, Edward Walsh

THE MAN WHO SAW THE ALLIGATORS (double-length)

wr. David Chase, dir. Corey Allen
A vengeful hit-man, convinced that Rockford turned him into the police when he was in California on a mob assignment, trails Jim to a country retreat.
with Beery, Santos, Margolin, George Loros, Luke Andreas, Sharon Acker, Joseph Sirola, Joey Aresco, Penny Santon, Marc Bentley, Joseph Perry

THE RETURN OF THE BLACK SHADOW

wr. Stephen Cannell, dir. William Wiard
Rockford's lawyer buddy John Cooper revisits his biker roots when he goes on a revenge mission against a motorcycle gang that sexually assaulted his sister while she was on a sympathy date with Rockford.
with Beery, Santos, Hopkins, Paul Koslo, Dennis Burkley, Laurie Jefferson, Paul Mace, Andy Jarrell, Jerry Ayres

A MATERIAL DIFFERENCE

wr. Rogers Turrentine, dir. William Wiard
Angel poses as a hit-man in order to pocket the first half of the fee without committing the murder, but his first customer is a Russian agent who has no intention of letting Angel renege on his contract to kill a defector.
with Beery, Santos, Margolin, Luisi, John Davey, Michael McGuire, David Tress, Rod Browning, Michael Alldredge, Donald Bishop

NEVER SEND A BOY KING TO DO A MAN'S JOB (double-length)

wr. Juanita Bartlett, dir. William Wiard
Rockford and Richie Brockelman go after an arrogant gangster who has bullied Richie's father out of his business, and the resulting scheme of retribution takes them from the race car world to ancient Egypt.
with Beery, Margolin, Robert Webber, Dennis Dugan, Trisha Noble, Pepper Martin, Gary Crosby, David Hooks, Harold Gould, Kim Hunter, Jack Collins, Stephanie Hankinson, Michele Hart, Stanley Brock, Robert Ward

A DIFFERENT DRUMMER

wr. Rudolph Borchert, dir. Reza Badiyi
Hospitalized in an accident, Rockford stumbles onto an illegal organ transplant operation, but no-one will believe him.

with Beery, Santos, John Considine, Carmen Argenziano, Dave Cass, Patrick Culliton, Anne Bellamy, Will Gill, Jr., Walter Brooke, Jesse Welles

Sixth Season (1979–'80)

PARADISE COVE

wr. and dir. Stephen Cannell

A retired sheriff has it in for Rockford, setting a court-appointed receiver onto him for damages, and trying to get him removed from the beach community.

with Beery, Santos, Margolin, Mariette Hartley, Leif Erickson, Frederick Herrick, Raymond O'Keefe, Byron Morrow, Christine Avila, John Davey, Peter Brocco, Branscombe Richmond

LIONS, TIGERS, MONKEYS, AND DOGS (double-length)

wr. Juanita Bartlett, dir. William Wiard

Rockford attends a jet-set masquerade party to protect a wealthy playgirl.

with Beery, Santos, Luisi, Lauren Bacall, Dana Wynter, Corrine Michaels, Roger Til, Michael Des Barres, Christopher Thomas, Edward Nelson, Michael Lombard, Carmine Caridi, T. Moratti, Leo Gordon

ONLY ROCK AND ROLL WILL NEVER DIE (two parts)

wr. David Chase, dir. William Wiard

Rockford is hired by a missing rock star to find his missing producer, but obstacles include a former girlfriend suing the singer for millions, mobsters bootlegging his music, and a troublesome rock journalist.

with Beery, Santos, Kristoffer Tabori, George Loros, Marcia Strassman, Lenny Baker, Stanley Brock, Fred Carney, Laurie Lea Schaeffer, Leigh Christian, Jesse Dizon, Marion Yue, Jean-Paul Vignon

LOVE IS THE WORD

wr. David Chase, dir. John Patterson

Rockford renews his romantic acquaintance with blind psychologist Megan Dougherty, but finds that his job is to locate and clear a competitor for her affections from a murder charge.

with Beery, Kathryn Harrold, Anthony Herrera, David James Carroll, Betty Kennedy, Barbara Mandrell, Richard Cox, David Cadiente

NICE GUYS FINISH DEAD

wr. Stephen Cannell, dir. John Patterson

After a murder at the Private Detective Association Awards Dinner, Lance White and Jim Rockford join forces to clear the dubious Fred Beamer of the crime. (This episode was a test drive for a non-starting vehicle to feature Lance White and Fred Beamer)

with Luisi, Tom Selleck, Larry Manetti, Simon Oakland, James Whitmore, Jr., Erica Hagen, Joe Bernard, Fritzi Burr, John Roselius, Fred Lerner, Al Berry, Larry Dunn

THE HAWAIIAN HEADACHE

wr. Stephen Cannell, dir. William Wiard

On vacation in Hawaii, Jim is conned into helping out old war buddy "Howling Mad" Smith on a dangerous spying assignment that rapidly turns into a fiasco.

with Beery, Santos, Margolin, Esmond Chung, Jake Hoopai, Daniel Kamekona, Ken Swofford, WK Stratton, James Murtaugh, Christopher Cary, Julie Blissett, Jimmy Borges

THE NO FAULT AFFAIR

wr. Juanita Bartlett, dir. Corey Allen

While Rockford tries to protect his former client and prostitute Rita Capcovich from her pimp as she attempts to quit the business, Rocky begins to detect tell-tale signs of love on the part of the girl.

with Beery, Santos, Margolin, Rita Moreno, Jerry Douglas, Corrinne Michaels, Pat Finley, William Beckley, Gloria Calomee

THE BIG CHEESE

wr. Shel Willens, dir. Joseph Pevney

While mobsters gather outside Rockford's trailer waiting for the morning post, Rockford and Chapman fruitlessly try to intercept a package of incriminating evidence that an informant has sent through the mail!

with Beery, Santos, Luisi, Constance Towers, Alan Manson, Brian Pevney, Hank Brandt, Ben Andrews, Mark Lonow, Peter Hobbs

JUST A COUPL'A GUYS

wr. David Chase, dir. Ivan Dixon

This back-door pilot has Rockford taking a back seat to the exploits of two youthful minor mobsters who turn up in town to try and make a name for themselves, but upset the balance of power between rival mob factions when they cross a gangster who has found religion.

with Greg Antonacci, Gene Davis, Gilbert Green, Lisa Donaldson, Simon Oakland, Anthony Ponzini, Doug Toby, Jr., Robin Riker, Jennifer Rhodes, Arch Johnson

DEADLOCK (aka DEADLOCK IN PARMA)

wr. Donald Gold, Lester Wm. Berke, Rudolph Borchert, dir. Winrich Kolbe

When Rockford reluctantly agrees to vote by proxy for a friend in office, he is caught between two warring factions who want control of a small town for gambling and land development.

with Sandra Kearns, Henry Beckman, Jerry Hardin, Joseph Sirola, Ben Piazza, Michael Cavenaugh

series ends

Baretta
January 1975–May 1978

Cannell's first collaboration with Roy Huggins had been *Toma,* which — like the then-current film and later tepid TV series *Serpico*— was based on the exploits of a real-life cop, in this case a dedicated undercover man renowned as a master of disguise. Co-starring in the pilot were Nicolas Colasanto (later best-known as Coach in *Cheers,* but here cast in his usual 1970s role of gang boss), a young Philip Michael Thomas (later of *Miami Vice*) as a drug addict, and the real David Toma in a bit part. Susan Strasberg played his wife Patty, and Simon Oakland — later to play a recurring role in *The Rockford Files*— was typecast in his traditional role of gruff superior following his likeable performance as same in *Bullitt.* Prior to *Toma,* Oakland had been the gruff superior of Darren McGavin on *Kolchak: The Night Stalker;* following the demise of *Toma* he became the gruff superior on Cannell's *Black Sheep Squadron!*

Toma was formulaic cop drama, and a modest success, but Tony Musante, who played the title role, decided that he didn't want to do a series regularly, and left the production. Cannell and Huggins, now finding themselves in the unprecedented position of having the successful TV series most actors dream of, and no leading man, rapidly began casting around for an actor to replace Musante.

The initial idea behind *Baretta* had been that Robert Blake should take over the role of real-life detective David Toma, but Blake's unique and very different personality rapidly dictated that a new format was conceived, and it was eventually decided to revamp the entire format with a new, more fictional series. Thus, *Toma starring Robert Blake* metamorphosized into the four year hit series *Baretta.*

Robert Blake was born Mickey Gubitosi in New Jersey in the early 1930s, and started his stage life in a family musical act with his father and sister. From there came a film contract and the popular *Our Gang* series for MGM, earning him a brief appearance in the classic 1948 film *The Treasure of Sierra Madre,* in which he sold Humphrey Bogart's character a lottery ticket. Following the army, Blake studied acting from actor Jeff Corey, but soon found that he had to content himself with stunt work. The highlight of a tempestuous and troubled childhood had been his career as a child actor in the 1940s *Red Ryder* serials, but eventually substantial movie roles followed, in Richard Brooks' *In Cold Blood,* a powerful if unconvincing anti-capital punishment film, in 1967 and the 1969 Robert Redford vehicle *Tell Them Willie Boy Is Here. Baretta*-like cop roles in the 1973 movies *Bustin'* and *Electra Glide in Blue* came along, and were almost certainly responsible for Blake's casting in *Baretta.* Blake rapidly took over *Baretta* lock, stock, and barrel, stamping his own inimitable personality on the series to highly advantageous effect. The result was one of the toughest and grittiest cop fantasies of the 1970s, far superior to the more prominent *Starsky and Hutch,* for which it operated in the schedules as lead-in during its first season. *Baretta* was high on moralizing and idealism, but it won points for portraying an environment more closely resembling something credible at a time when equally entertaining but more unlikely fantasy cops—*McMillan, McCloud, Columbo, The Mod Squad*—were all the rage. Of course the pseudo-realism of *Baretta*, realistic only in comparison to the aforementioned, was soon to be outclassed by the likes of *Kojak, Police Story, Hill Street Blues* and others, but the series undoubtedly played a part in pushing the boundaries forward, even though by today's standards the show is horribly dated.

Cannell named the new series after the small but powerful Baretta handgun, and gave the character an entirely new history and setting. Tony Baretta would not live with a patient, worried wife and two kids in suburbia, but alone with a pet cockatoo and a succession of empty-headed girlfriends in a sleazy run-down hotel. Co-starring with Blake was veteran actor Tom Ewell as Billy Truman, an ex-cop turned house detective at the hotel where Baretta resided. Playing Baretta's boss was future Cannell regular Dana Elcar as Inspector Schiller; when Elcar left after a few months—also to take a regular role in Cannell's new series *Black Sheep Squadron*—Ed Grover took over as Lt. Brubaker. Elcar appeared in the first twelve episodes, Grover in the remaining seventy; later, Elcar became known for his co-starring role in the '80s adventure series *MacGyver*.

Like most of his canon of characters, undercover cop Tony Baretta fitted in comfortably with Cannell's rapidly formulating trademarks. A champion of the underdog, he resents the fact that the little guys always get caught while the big fish invariably swim away. He is constantly at odds with his bosses (that familiar component of early '70s cop drama), who are portrayed as good men but eager to close a case to the city's cosmetic satisfaction. Instead, the rebellious and persistent Baretta digs deeper to net the sharks at the top. The excellent episode "If You Can't Pay the Price," the first to be filmed, written by Roy Huggins under his pen-name of John Thomas James and directed by Bernard Kowalski, consists almost entirely of a one-man-show by Blake, with Baretta stubbornly staked outside the palatial home of a wealthy gang boss. The gangster (reliable stone-faced character actor John Marley of *Godfather* fame) has not reached the top of his trade without connections, and soon even the police arrive to move him on, but Baretta perseveres and gets his man. The opening episode, "He'll Never See Daylight," written by Cannell and again directed by Kowalski, also manages to incorporate Cannell's noble vigilante theme, with Baretta stalking the gangster who has put out a successful contract on a girlfriend (Madlyn Rhue) who has seen too much.

A number of episode titles were based on Baretta's numerous, occasionally irritating catch-phrases, many of which were also incorporated into the series' opening theme song, a bluesy soul number performed by Sammy Davis, Jr., "The Big Hand's on Trouble," "If You Can't Pay the Price...," "Keep Your Eye on the Sparrow," "Walk Like You Talk," and "When Dues Come Down" are all first season episode titles, and typical examples of Tony Baretta's style of speech. As Baretta, Blake created almost an entirely new language, with more slogans, mottos, and ad-libbed platitudes than any other show on the air. Each week, his sing-song scolding would tell the crooks and the hoods and the misguided flotsam and jetsam that came his way that "dat's da name o' dat toon" or "dey gonna put choo where da sun don't shine no more, an' dats da truth." Baretta had a very patronizing spiel for all the "sparrows" who "strayed from the straight and narrow" and who were "gonna end up where the sun don't shine" if they didn't mend their ways, and his frowning condescension was perfectly suited to the two-fisted preacher role he would adopt ten years later for his own short-lived TV production *Hell Town*.

The bad guys in *Baretta* came strictly divided into two categories. There were the mean, vicious manipulators at the top, who callously exploited the people on the street and caused them misery, and who drove the second type — the helpless, hapless failures of society — to do their bidding. This fitted in very neatly with the authoritarian, almost paternal tone of most early/mid-'70s cop dramas, in which the likes of Kojak, Baretta, Starsky and Hutch, *Hawaii Five-0's* Steve McGarrett, Stone and Keller of *The Streets of San Francisco,* and others were all vastly superior to the sorry looking specimens they protected from themselves. These poor saps were almost longing to be arrested by their father-figure protectors, while humble citizens could hardly control their excitement at being permitted to proffer some helpful nugget of information to a smirking, condescending cop.

Also to hand were Cannell's usual gallery of goons and hoods, and a reliable steady supply of jumped-up suit-and-tie types to stand in the way of Baretta's righteous do-gooding — and perhaps even be brought down by it. That Baretta chose to go gunning for the guys at the top while looking after the cast-offs of society at the bottom was hardly surprising; not only was this consistent with Cannell's approach to TV heroism, but Blake himself had suffered a pretty hard time in his youth, with a painful childhood of well-publicized juvenile mischief behind him. Baretta's message was Blake's too. It was corny and simplistic, but he meant it, and that gave the heavy moralizing in the series a depth that had been earned the hard way, something few other TV cops could aspire to. Blake's early weaknesses were Baretta's strengths.

Blake, like his fellow Universal cop show star Telly Savalas of *Kojak,* ran a tight ship with himself as the captain, and realizing that there could be only one captain and that actors held all the power, Cannell stepped away from the series after setting it up, much to Blake's dismay. Despite Blake's protestations, Cannell knew perfectly well that there were stormy seas ahead if he stayed on board (the series subsequently went through twelve producers during one turbulent season). Both *Kojak* and *Baretta* had sympathy for the little man or ordinary Joe that went well past the point of being patronizing, but which rarely seemed to extend to their supporting casts, who stood around like lemons anxiously trying to anticipate the stars' next ad-lib while having the leading man's ego bounced off them as they tried to feed them pertinent information! Both *Baretta* and *Kojak* also shared a contempt for the organized crime and wealthy mobsters who profited from honest people's misery. They possessed a strong, grimy mean streets feel to them that was more fashionable in the movies of the period than on television. At the time it first appeared, with a lead character a little bit too good to be true, and above-average cop show action, *Baretta* provided a welcome contrast to particular trends in the television industry, even if it later became a cliché itself.

With the departure of Cannell, and later Huggins and DeGuere from the series, *Baretta* rapidly became a very schizophrenic show. While Cannell's series embraced a very specific sense of morality, *Baretta* very quickly became a show about the law according to Tony Baretta. In Cannell's pilot story, "He'll Never See Daylight," Baretta takes the law into his own hands to avenge the death of a girlfriend, and in many subsequent episodes takes it upon himself to see that justice is done; but in later stories what's good for Baretta is not acceptable for others with similar motives. In Paul Magistretti's "When Dues Come Down," a trucker murders a burglar who has crippled his wife, while in Robert Lewin's "Murder for Me" (directed by Curtis Harrington), Dallas Barnes' "Open Season" (directed by Reza Badiyi), and Larry Alexander's "The Ninja" (directed by Don Weis), fathers go after the mobsters who killed their kids. In all these cases, Baretta works to apprehend the vigilantes, while in Lewis Davidson's "Shoes," directed by Chris Robinson, it is a young boy attempting to avenge the murder of a friend who obstructs Baretta's investigations. In "Barney," written by Pat Fielder and Richard Bluel, and directed by Don Medford, a young woman investigating the death of her father is the person getting in the way of Baretta's own inquiries.

Where Baretta differs from other TV vigilantes is that he's judge and jury too; it's okay for *him* to take the law into his own hands when the system doesn't work — in one episode ("Don't Kill the Sparrows") he even resigns from the force to continue his pursuit of a crooked cop — but when anybody else steps out of line to take the law into his or her own hands and circumnavigate official channels, Baretta is first in line to lecture them on due process! Furthermore, Tony Baretta is seriously underqualified for the role of demi-god — in Peter Fischer's "The Capelli Oath," "It Goes with the Job," written by Robert Crais, and the multi-handed "Double Image," Baretta himself is the target of vengeful bereaved victims; the younger brothers of a dope-dealer and robber he has killed, and the wife of an informant who has been murdered for helping Baretta.

The series attracted a number of popular and talented performers as guest stars, including quite a few who had already made a career for themselves in film and consequently chose their TV appearances very selectively. *Baretta* was able to boast guest shots by Shelley Duvall, Burt Young, Slim Pickens and Strother Martin, not once, but several times each (Burt Young and Strother Martin also each did a *Rockford Files,* again at a time when they were not short of film work). Consequently, the better episodes had the feel of a good quality action B-movie for the drive-ins rather than the usual glossy look of a TV production, and the presence of guest stars more usually associated with the wide screen only served to heighten this impression. Strother Martin was exceptionally good in his trademark role of psychotic loony in the superior episode "On the Road" (written by Michael Butler and directed by Jeannot Szwarc), which also guest-starred Mackenzie Phillips and a young Gary Busey.

Baretta was ABC's lead-in for *Starsky and Hutch* during the 1975/76 season (placed opposite the final season of *Cannon*), and then performed the same function for Spelling's *Charlie's Angels* the following year, where it sat uncomfortably and absurdly between that series and *The Bionic Woman*. From the third season, it remained on Wednesday nights as usual, but moved to a later time-slot, exchanging places — logically — with *Charlie's Angels.* Both series opposed a movie and two flop series, *The Oregon Trail* and *Big Hawaii*, but by that time, *Baretta* was wearing thin. The following year, Spelling's glossy new action show *Vegas* took the series' vacated slot. Attempts to revive Blake's *Baretta* persona in the *Joe Dancer* TV movies of the late '70s, and as the older but still muscular star of the 1985 series *Hell Town* fell on stony ground. Like many other popular TV faces, Blake had trouble being accepted in a similar-but-different role in a new series format due to the public's reluctance to see him as anyone other than Tony Baretta (his only other regular TV work had been as a stock player on *The Richard Boone Show* in 1963/64, an anthology series in which he had the luxury of a different role every week). Nevertheless, this did not stop Blake from staging a bravura comeback performance in the mid-'80s in the faction docu-drama *Blood Feud,* as the ill-fated union boss Jimmy Hoffa. Had the 1970s/1980s era of cop shows and vigilante series not been coming to an end, Blake might have begun a new career as a TV heavy and guest bad guy, but in a twist almost too ironic to be true, at time of writing, the now elderly Blake is on trial himself, for murder.

Episode Guide

regular cast: Robert Blake (Tony Baretta), Dana Elcar (Inspector Schiller), Ed Grover (Lt. Brubaker), Michael D. Roberts (Rooster), Tom Ewell (Billy Truman)

recurring cast: Chino Williams (Fats), John Ward (Foley), Sharon Cintron (Mimi), Alyce Allyn (Alice), Titos Vandis (Mr. Nicholas), Harvey Parry (Harrigan)

First Season (1975)

He'll Never See Daylight
wr. Stephen Cannell, dir. Bernard Kowalski
An underworld figure makes a bad enemy of undercover cop Tony Baretta when he orders the loner cop's girlfriend killed for knowing too much.
with Andrew Prine, Madlyn Rhue, Timothy Carey, George Loros

The Five and a Half Pound Junkie
wr. Peter Fischer, dir. Don Medford
When a close friend is killed, Baretta must protect the man's pregnant and drug addicted wife.
with Ayn Ruymen, Gerrit Graham, Sarah Cunningham, Mario Rocuzzo, Rudolph Wilrich

Woman in the Harbor
wr. Roy Huggins, Robert Holt, Don Balluck, dir. Bernard Kowalski
Baretta pursues corrupt police officers after a friend is killed in a hit-and-run accident.
with Ed Lauter, Carole Cook, Ann Coleman, Brock Peters, Bill McKinney, Ron Soble

If You Can't Pay the Price
wr. Roy Huggins, dir. Bernard Kowalski
Baretta wages a one-man vendetta against a well-known crime kingpin whose guilt has never been proven, and now lies dying, surrounded by his wealth.
with John Marley, Val Bisoglio, Roy Jenson, Danny Goldman, Kathleen O'Malley, Marjorie Wallace

The Half Million Dollar Baby
wr. Roy Huggins, Phil De Guere, Norm Leibman, dir. Michael Schultz
Baretta is betrayed and exploited by a beautiful model.
with Ann Prentiss, Richard Ward, Marc Alaimo, Arlene Farber, Robert Nadder

Ragtime Billy Peaches
wr. Roy Huggins, Don Carlos Dunaway, Phil De Guere, dir. Bernard Kowalski
The dark past of a prominent lawyer's wife comes to light when she is discovered murdered.
with Richard Dysart, Meg Foster, Belinda Balaski

The Capelli Oath
wr. Peter Fischer, dir. Michael Butler
Baretta is the target of a vengeful younger brother when a dope-pusher is killed.
with John Friedrich, Marie Lillo, Joe di Stefano, George Di Cenzo

Walk Like You Talk
wr. L.H. Whittemore, Michael Butler, Phil De Guere, dir. Charles Dubin
Baretta's questionable working methods cause him to be investigated by a police committee, and ultimately suspected of taking pay-offs.
with Michael Parks, Lee De Broux, Julio Medina, Anita Ford

The Mansion
wr. Phil De Guere, dir. Bernard Kowalski
Baretta dons a number of disguises to investigate illegal goings-on in a palatial mansion where a policewoman has been killed.
with John Durren, Eddie Fontaine, Sondra Blake, George Loros, Frank Christie, Art Metrano, John Sylvester White, Allyn Ann McLerie

Keep Your Eye on the Sparrow
wr. Paul Magistretti, dir. Don Medford
Baretta is dismayed to suspect a simple-minded friend of numerous petty thefts in the neighborhood.
with Burt Young, Rosa Barbato, Mary Wilcox, Shepard Sanders

The Secret of Terry Lake
wr. Roy Huggins, Phil De Guere, dir. Russ Mayberry
A woman willfully implicates her lover in the murder of a gang-boss by refusing to support his

alibi that she was with him at the time of the killing.

with Margot Kidder, Joe Santos, Nicolas Colasanto, M. Emmet Walsh, Norman Cole, Don Carrarra, Allan Rich

THIS AIN'T MY BAG (a.k.a The Day the Dominoes Fell in Mount Chester)

wr. Gloryette Clark, Phil De Guere, Paul Magistretti, dir. Jerry London

Baretta is unnerved and disoriented when he is assigned to an upmarket neighborhood where the veneer of respectability is hiding a multitude of dark secrets and indiscretions that he must work to uncover.

with Granville Van Dusen, Keene Curtis, Mary Rings, Fritzi Burr

Second Season (1975–'76)

THE GOODBYE ORPHAN ANNIE BLUES

wr. Paul Williams, Paul Magistretti, dir. Bernard Kowalski

A series of drug-related deaths lead Baretta inexorably to the conclusion that the party responsible is a good friend of his.

with Paul Williams, Kim Darby, Barbara Baldavin, James Carroll Jordan

THE GLORY GAME

wr. Michael Butler, dir. Jeannot Szwarc

Baretta becomes a fugitive when he is framed for the murder of a gun-runner.

with Bill McKinney, Harris Yulin, Chuck Vennera, Joe Renteria

ON THE ROAD

wr. Michael Butler, dir. Jeannot Szwarc

Baretta and a runaway girl are handcuffed together and kidnapped by two fugitives from the law disguised as policemen.

with Strother Martin, Mackenzie Phillips, Gary Busey, Ron Rondell, Louie Elias

SHARPER THAN A SERPENT'S TOOTH

wr. Roy Huggins, Roy Dandridge, Robert Janes, dir. Charles Rondeau

A colleague is suspected of shooting a murder suspect in the back after unwelcome publicity for allegations of police brutality.

with Roger E. Mosley, Joseph Hindy, Titos Vandis, Doris Roberts, Vince Martorano, Sylvia Soares

THE FIRE MAN

wr. George Tiefer, dir. Ted Post

A severely burned retired fire investigator reluctantly assists Baretta in the pursuit of an arsonist.

with Hector Elizondo, Lincoln Kilpatrick, Bart Burns

DOUBLE IMAGE

wr. Gregory Tiefer, Michael Simpson, Jeff Spielman, dir. Jeannot Szwarc

The girlfriend of an informant who was killed helping Baretta solve a series of murders on the waterfront wants revenge on Baretta for his death.

with Susan Tyrell, Jack Colvin, Charles Napier, Giorgio Tozzi, Claude Jones, John Zee, John Kerry, Phillip Mansour

PHOTOGRAPHY BY JOHN DOE

wr. Michael Simpson, Jeff Spielman, dir. Bernard Kowalski

Billy Truman persuades Baretta to investigate a closed case in which a police officer allegedly fell to his death while drunk.

with Guillermo San Juan, Hector Elias, Brock Peters, Art Aragon, Felipe Turich

SET-UP CITY

wr. Michael Butler, dir. Curtis Harrington

Baretta trusts a disreputable safe-cracker against everyone's better judgment when he sets out to bring in a jewel robbery gang.

with Charles Durning, Larry Block, Timothy Agolia Carey, Richard Cox, Don Keefer, Harvey Parry

A BITE OF THE APPLE

wr. Robert Janes, Paul Magistretti, dir. Robert Douglas

The deceitful girlfriend of a murdered mobster causes Baretta grief from both the mob and his superiors.

with Karen Valentine, Titos Vandis, Harry Caesar, Anne Revere, Al Ferrara, Paul Stevens

WHEN DUES COME DOWN

wr. Paul Magistretti, dir. Robert Douglas

Baretta sets out to prove that a trucker has murdered the burglar who crippled his wife.

with Slim Pickens, Gloria LeRoy, Alan Feinstein, Pamela Bellwood, Don Blackman, Ron Stein, Ed Rice

THE BIG HAND'S ON TROUBLE

wr. Paul Magistretti, dir. Burt Brinkerhoff

A stubborn shopkeeper puts his life in danger when he refuses to pay out to a protection racket.

with Burt Young, Angelo Rossitto, George Loros, Ric Mancini, Richard Karron, Rick Podell

COUNT THE DAYS I'M GONE

wr. Michael Butler, dir. Bruce Kessler

A little girl disappears after witnessing a callous murder while in Baretta's care.

with Elizabeth Chesire, Meg Foster, David Downing, Alex Henteloff, Tony Burton, Judith Hanson, Ron Thompson, Lynne Holms, Angelo Rossitto

NOBODY IN A NOTHING PLACE

wr. Jack Turley, Robert Van Scoyk, dir. Arnold Laven

A witness to a murder has a dark secret reason for refusing to get involved in the process to bring the killer to justice.

with Mitchell Ryan, Terry Kiser, Janit Baldwin

THE LEFT HAND OF THE DEVIL

wr. Edward Lakso, dir. Robert Douglas

Baretta infiltrates a cycle gang offering cut-price killings for low pay.

with Bruce Boxleitner, Sally Kirkland, Billy Green Bush, J.N. Roberts, Fred Hice, John Lehne

MURDER FOR ME

wr. Robert Lewin, dir. Curtis Harrington

A distraught and grieving father goes on a killing spree of local drug pushers, starting with the drunken doctor who failed to save his son's life.

with Gregory Rozakis, Michele Marsh, Ron Thompson, Lanie Kazan, David Bennett

PAY OR DIE

wr. Michael Grais, dir. Robert Douglas

An undercover policewoman is put in jeopardy during a gangland power struggle.

with Joan Collins, Roger Robinson, Ron Thompson, Sondra Blake, Titos Vandis

THE DIPPERS

wr. T.S. Cook, dir. Douglas Heyes

Baretta investigates a murder with the aid of a professional pick-pocket.

with Whitman Mayo, William Traylor, John Dullaghan, Ron Thompson, Jeff Kanner

THE BLOOD BOND

wr. Gustave Field, dir. Vince Sherman

Baretta is accused of stealing a large amount of gangland money by gangsters, and Billy Truman is held hostage until it is returned.

with Titos Vandis, David Huffman, Pat Ast, Michael Pataki, Duffy Hambleton, Nicholas Worth, Al Scaglione

DEAD MAN OUT

wr. Mann Rubin, Earl Wallace, Robert Lewin, dir. Robert Douglas

Baretta goes undercover in prison when suspects for a jewelry heist turn up dead.

with Tommy Lee Jones, M. Emmet Walsh, Jaime Lyn Bauer, Erik Estrada, John Shay

DEATH ON THE RUN (a.k.a The Cold Breath of Death)

wr. Paul Casey, dir. Burt Brinkerhoff

Infected with a deadly disease, Baretta is caught in a race against time to locate the fleeing gun runner spreading the germs.

with Scott Hylands, Anna Capri, Alexander Courtney, Dick O'Neill, Ron Thompson, Louis Guss, Isabel Boniface, Scott Walker

AGGIE

wr. Adrian Spies, dir. Vince Sherman

A witness has her life endangered when she sees a crooked cop kill his girlfriend.

with Shelley Duvall, Richard Jaeckel, Joseph Hacker, Don Calfa, Marc Alaimo

AND DOWN WILL COME BABY

wr. Robert Holt, dir. Bruce Kessler

Baretta masquerades as a prospective customer to expose a baby-selling racket.

with Laurie Prange, Nancy Wolfe, Bill Phipps, Rudy Solari, Stanley Clements, John O'Leary, Marcia Lewis, Kay Stewart, Erica Hagen

Third Season (1976–'77)

THE NINJA

wr. Larry Alexander, dir. Don Weis

Baretta is threatened by a businessman who is using martial arts training to avenge his daughter's killing by the mob.

with John Fujioka, Helen Funai, Jeannie Linero, Pepe Serna, Henry Darrow, James Hong, Jesse Dizon, Momo Yashima

Soldier in the Jungle

wr. Gene Thompson, Norman Lessing, Lewis Davidson, dir. Sigmund Neufeld

Baretta must prevent the killing of a mobster by a hit-man who was a childhood friend.

with Burt Young, Jess Walton, Nehemiah Persoff, Rosa Barbato, Anne Revere, Jim Malinder, Jack Rader, Vince Martorano

Runaway Cowboy

wr. Milt Rosen, dir. Robert Douglas

A judge to whom Baretta is deeply indebted is being blackmailed by an extortionist.

with Geraldine Brooks, Art Hindle, David Sheiner, Jay Varela, Alan Mandell

Street Edition

wr. Robert Hamner, Robert Holt, Gene Thompson, Anthony Spinner, dir. Vince Sherman

Baretta's attempts to expose corruption in the office of a city official running for the mayor's office are hampered by the disclosures of a newspaper reporter.

with Andrea Marcovicci, Peter Mark Richman, Ellen Weston, Elisha Cook, Marc Lawrence, Gino Ardito, Virginia Gregg, Tom Bower, Howard Hesseman, Sandy Ward, Stephen Coit

They Don't Make 'Em Like They Used To

wr. S.S. Schweitzer, dir. Sutton Roley

Baretta takes an eventful bus ride in which his fellow passengers are a young jewel thief and the veteran criminal she has betrayed.

with Keenan Wynn, Laura Hippe, Michael Baseleon, Richard Lynch, Joyce Jameson, Kay Adler, Wings Hauser, William Bronder, Nanette Dannes

Under the City

wr. S.S. Schweitzer, dir. Cliff Boles

Baretta finds himself in the middle of an escape attempt by juvenile convicts, and must try to end the siege of an industrial plant before lives are lost.

with Jill Haworth, Edward Gallardo, Scott Colomby, Janit Baldwin, John Freidrich, Norman Alden, Ernest Thomas, William Traylor, Phillip Pine

Dear Tony

wr. Larry Alexander, Norman Hudis, Robert Specht, dir. Robert Douglas

When a policeman is murdered under the pretext that he died preventing a hold-up, Baretta finds himself paired with the true killer, another police officer.

with Anjanette Comer, Gil Gerard, Will Mackenzie, Ron Hayes, Edith Atwater, Rod Browning, Paul Lichtman, Michael Mancini

Crazy Annie

wr. Jeffrey Freilich, dir. Reza Badiyi

An undercover operation to capture a skid-row killer goes awry when Baretta is abducted at gunpoint by a deranged elderly woman convinced he is her son.

with Kim Hunter, James O'Connell, Richard Collier, Gilbert Green, Wayne Northrup

Nothin' for Nothin'

wr. S.S. Schweitzer, dir. Paul Stanley

A nine-year-old street kid skillfully stealing food and selling stolen property obtains valuable evidence that Baretta needs.

with Diego Gonzalez, Janet MacLachlan, Logan Ramsey, Shannon Christie

Can't Win for Losin'

wr. S.S. Schweitzer, dir. Robert Douglas

In an alcoholic stupor, a drunkard confesses to killing a drug pusher and becomes a local hero, but Baretta knows that he didn't commit the crime.

with Whitman Mayo, Lawrence Hilton, Maide Norman, Carl Crudup, Chuck Shamata, Robert Miller, DeForest Covan, Rosalind Miles, Burt Douglas, Karen Ciral, Linda McCullough

Look Back in Terror

wr. S.S. Schweitzer, dir. Vincent Sherman

Baretta's new girlfriend is in peril when her former boyfriend gets out of jail.

with Samantha Eggar, Andrew Prine, George Ranito, Douglas McGrath, Jo Lopresti, Jan Peters

Don't Kill the Sparrows

wr. Alan Godfrey, Fenton Hobart, Jr., dir. Don Medford

Convinced that a narcotics agent is on the wrong side of the law, but forbidden by his bosses to pursue the matter, Baretta resigns from the force to take matters into his own hands.

with Stephen Davies, Will Walker, Eddie Egan, Karen Glow Carr, Stacy Keach, Sr., Bennye Gattys

That Sister Ain't No Cousin

wr. S.S. Schweitzer, Mark Stirdivant, dir. Bruce Kessler

A drug pusher and former addict is murdered to prevent him from revealing details to Baretta about the next shipment.

with Edith Diaz, Timothy Carey, Jose Centano, Migdia Varela, June Smaney, Danny Mora, Judd Omen

Open Season

wr. Dallas Barnes, dir. Reza Badiyi

A prominent banker hires an elderly but lethal hit-man to dispose of the junkie who sold fatal drugs to his daughter.

with Strother Martin, Roger Robinson, Roberta Leighton, Stefan Gierasch, Will Gill, Jr.

The Reunion

wr. Don Medford, Christopher Crowe, Steve Meixell, dir. Don Medford

The trail of the murder of a famous humanitarian leads to a prostitution ring.

with Pernell Roberts, Mario Rocuzzo, Mark Vahanian, Steve Tanner, Susan Heldfond, Debi Richter, Shera Danese

Not on Our Block

wr. Steve Downing, Sean Bain, dir. Burt Brinckerhoff

Two shopkeepers witness a murder and are convinced that they will be next.

with Katy Jurado, Ross Martin, Michelle Marsh, Michael Gazzo, Joel Lombardo, Frank Bongiorno

The Runaways

wr. Richard Bluel, Pat Fielder, dir. Don Medford

Baretta stumbles onto the hideaway of three children who have run away from home after being abused by their respective parents.

with Art Metrano, Pamelyn Ferdyn, Sam Smith, Brian Andrews, Albert Salmi, Deann Mears

Everybody Pays the Fare

wr. Sidney Ellis, dir. John Ward

A dying gangster reveals the murderer of Baretta's father, now a wealthy businessman.

with Mel Ferrer, Hope Alexander Willis, Robert Lipton, Joan Caulfield, Betty Hutton

Think Mink

wr. Pat Fielder, Richard Bluel, Paul Tuckahoe, dir. Don Medford

Two foolish old men steal from the mob, and then try to sell the stolen merchandise back to them.

with Ned Glass, Joshua Shelley, Sydney Chaplin, Elisha Cook, Richard Di Angelo, Richard Libertini

Carla

wr. Pat Fielder, Richard Bluel, dir. Alex March

Baretta becomes romantically involved with a young woman living a life of misery, imprisoned by a mob family until her husband finishes his sentence.

with Adrienne La Russa, Victor Redina, Marki Bey, Jeannie Bell, George Loros, Chuck Hicks, Vera Lockwood, Lisa Moore, Duffy Hambleton

Big Bad Charlie

wr. Bernard Kowalski, Christopher Crowe, dir. Don Medford

A lovestruck news vendor is oblivious to the fact that his heroism against a brutal Chinatown gang has marked him for death.

with Slim Pickens, Sheree North, Alice Frost, Dana Lee, Frankie Liu, Mike Chan

Guns and Brothers

wr. Don Medford, Ferde Rombola, dir. Bernard Kowalski

Baretta tries to help a psychopathic criminal who is being ignored by the system.

with John Freidrich, Brad Davis, Virginia Leith, Eddie Ryder, Tom La Grue

Playin' Police

wr. Ray Hutcherson, dir. Don Medford

Baretta goes after two thugs who are impersonating police officers.

with Scoey Mitchell, Alex Rocco, Janus Blythe, Chris Mulkey

Fourth Season (1977–'78)

New Girl in Town

wr. Nick Alexander, dir. Paul Stanley

Baretta's new partner — a dope-sniffing dog with an attraction to the male of the species — has a contract out on her!

with Neville Brand, Vito Scotti, Angela Clarke

WHO KILLED COCK ROBIN? (a.k.a. Somebody Killed Cock Robin)

wr. Richard Kelbaugh, dir. Reza Badiyi

While Baretta attempts to secure evidence against the assailants of a nightclub dancer, the girl in question is abducted by one of the suspects.

with Gwen Welles, Candice Azzarra, Steve Sandor, Vincent Bagetta

ALL THAT SHATTERS

wr. Rift Fournier, Ed Waters, Sidney Ellis, dir. Don Medford

A handicapped Vietnam veteran breaks away from fellow protesters campaigning against the lack of facilities for the disabled to stage a bombing campaign to cover a bank robbery he has planned.

with Kristoffer Tabori, Toni Kalem, Anna Lee, Mary Louise Weller, Stanley Brock, Borah Silver

THE SKY IS FALLING

wr. Pat Fielder, Richard Bluel, dir. Don Medford

Baretta must find a kid who has seen a murder before the murderer can silence him permanently.

with Art Metrano, Dennis Quaid, James Ray, Barry Miller

IT'S HARD BUT IT'S FAIR

wr. Les Carter, dir. Jeannot Szwarc

Baretta goes undercover as a boxer's trainer to uncover a cocaine operation.

with Bobby Chacon, Pepe Serna, R.G. Armstrong, C.J. Hincks, Michael C. Gwynne, Val Avery, East Ismael Carlo, Michael Clark, Jan Stratton, Jack Lukes

BUDDY

wr. Richard Bluel, Pat Fielder, dir. Paul Stanley

Baretta hides a retarded youth from the authorities while he attempts to clear the boy of murdering his mother.

with Roger Kerns, J. Pat O'Malley, Ellen Geer, Norman Cole

POR NADA

wr. Chris Lucky, Miguel Pinero, dir. Reza Badiyi

When a gang leader is wounded and his girlfriend killed, Baretta works against the clock to find the killer before a gang war erupts.

with A. Martinez, Cynthia Avila, ChuChu Malave, George Cantero, Judd Omen, Bobby Chacon, Miguel Pinero, Eddie Conde, Panchito Gomez, Domingo Ambriz, Evelyn Guerrero, Abel Franco, Rita Conde

MAKE THE SUN SHINE

wr. Robert Crais, dir. Don Medford

Baretta juggles the search for the identity of an amnesiac man who returned his wallet with the task of finding a drugs-pusher preying on the preteen market.

with Sydney Lassick, Charles Wagenheim

LYMAN P. DOKKER, FED

wr. Alan J. Levitt, dir. Burt Brinckerhoff

Baretta finds himself allied with an inept federal agent when he sets out to locate a stolen necklace.

with Strother Martin, Martine Beswicke, John Harkins, Dick Sargent

IT GOES WITH THE JOB

wr. Robert Crais, dir. Reza Badiyi

Consumed with guilt over an accidental shooting, Baretta is also targeted for revenge by the brother of a dead robber.

with Tom Atkins, Cassie Yates, Shane Sinutko

HOT HORSE

wr. Joshua Shelley, Arnold Horwitt, dir. Don Medford

Sam and Leo, the two elderly men from "Think Mink," steal a racehorse and attempt to hide it in their apartment — in the same block where Baretta lives.

with Ned Glass, Joshua Shelley, Jenny Sherman, James Booth

WHY ME?

wr. Alan Godfrey, dir. Robert Douglas

After a hold-up in which her employer is killed, a young girl saved by Baretta during the incident becomes dependent on his company, and a liability during his investigations.

with Anne Schedeen, Eddie Quillan, Gerald McRaney, Jon Van Ness

I'LL TAKE YOU TO LUNCH

wr. E. Nick Alexander, dir. Don Medford

Billy Truman is taken hostage during an interrupted hold-up, and Baretta must negotiate with the robbers while hindered by a politically motivated local lawman.

with Cliff Pellow, Alan Vint, Gregory Walcott

It's a Boy
wr. Warren Worthen, Les Carter, dir. Paul Stanley

Baretta becomes engaged to a former flame, but discovers that she comes with a new-born baby and a sniper in pursuit....

with Tracy Brooks Swope, Dennis Burkley, Floyd Levine, Kenneth O'Brien

Just for Laughs
wr. Sian Barbara Allen, dir. Reza Badiyi

A fading entertainer is in the spotlight again after a series of attempts on his life.

with Ray Bolger, Dave Shelley, Sharon Cintron, Scott Edmund Lane

The Marker
wr. dir. n/a

To repay a mobster for protecting his father many years ago, a friend of Baretta's agrees to make a contract killing.

with Anthony Caruso, Susan Heldfond, Frank De Kova, Madison Arnold, Madeline Stowe, Timothy Agolia Carey, Joe Stefano, Lee Delano, Allen Joseph, Kathryn Grayson

The Stone Conspiracy
wr. Adrian Leeds, dir. Don Medford

Much against his wishes, Baretta is assigned to investigate his colleagues, some of whom are suspected of being on the take.

with Phillip R. Allen, Lara Parker, Ron Max, Ron Soble, Rockne Tarkington, Bill Fletcher, Lewis Van Bergen, Wayne Grace, Beverly Hope Atkinson

The Appointment
wr. Arthur B. Lewis, Ed Waters, Sidney Ellis, dir. Bernard Kowalski

An eyewitness has a secret reason for not volunteering descriptions of killers he can identify.

with Tom Simcox, Jerry Hardin, Robert Towers, Lorri Gay Marlow

Woman Trouble
wr. Robert Crais, dir. Bernard Kowalski

Baretta helps a twelve-year-old girl stop her father getting involved in a robbery while on parole.

with Dasha Lee Zemrus, Timothy Scott, Woodrow Parfrey, Robert Costanzo, Louie Elias

Gadgo
wr. Ray Hutcherson, dir. Don Medford

A young man is consumed by self-destructive guilt when he kills a robber revealed to be his brother.

with Robert Viharo, Claudio Martinez, Panchito Gomez, Rene Enriquez, Rudy Bond, Angela Clarke, Patricia Hyland

Barney
wr. Pat Fieldler, Richard Bluel, dir. Don Medford

Baretta poses as a truck driver to investigate the murder of a newspaper editor, but his investigations are hampered by the efforts of the man's daughter, who is also investigating.

with Sheila Larkin, Robert Symonds, Richard C. Adams, Sandy McPeak, John Quade

The Dream
wr. E. Nick Alexander, dir. Reza Badiyi

Baretta resorts to enlisting the aid of a child psychic to locate a kidnapped woman.

with Nicholas Coster, Kathryn Leigh Scott, Quinn Cummings, Bernard Behrens, Ted Markland

The Snake Chaser
wr. Richard Kelbaugh, dir. Reza Badiyi

An explosion caused by Baretta during a drug raid scars a syndicate man, who swears revenge.

with George Loros, Ron Dennis, Steve Allie Collura, Sonny Jim Gaines

The Bundle
wr. Les Carter, Leonard Stadd, Toni Van Horne, dir. Don Medford

Two out-of-work actresses come into some hot money after a local small-time gangster is murdered.

with Sheila De Windt, Roz Kelly, Frank R. Christi, Scoey Mitchill, Jack Kosslyn, Paul Pepper, Lee Delano, Gail Bonney

series ends

City of Angels
February 1976–May 1976

Wayne Rogers was born in Birmingham, Alabama in the 1930s, and became interested in acting while in the U.S. Navy, working in a number of menial jobs when he left, and sharing an apartment with another aspiring young actor, Peter Falk. After a stage career touring, he broke into the infant medium of television, playing bit parts in anthology shows. A co-starring role in the 1960–'61 western series *Stagecoach West* was followed by guest appearances on *Wanted—Dead or Alive, Gunsmoke, Johnny Ringo, Honey West,* and the Quinn Martin series *The FBI, The Invaders,* and *The Streets of San Francisco,* among others. Small movie roles followed, along with prestigious stage credits, but Rogers' big break came when he was cast in the TV version of Robert Altman's film *M*A*S*H* with Alan Alda. Irritated to see his co-starring role becoming a supporting role, Rogers left the series at the end of the third season to pursue other avenues, and promptly struck gold by securing the lead role in Stephen Cannell's and Phil De Guere's *City of Angels.*

A stylish detective series devised by Cannell and Roy Huggins, *City of Angels* was a brave and innovative series clearly capitalizing on the success of Roman Polanski's 1974 feature *Chinatown.* Rogers played Jake Axminster, a cynical idealist struggling through the L.A. (the city of angels of the title) of the '30s as a minor league private eye with a penchant for attracting major league trouble. Sharing his office with a receptionist who doubles as a liaison for callgirls (Elaine Joyce as Marsha), and situated conveniently opposite the office of friend and lawyer Michael Brimm (Philip Sterling), Axminster is exceptional in that he is one of the few TV private eyes without a friend at the police station; in fact, he has a deadly antagonist in the form of the thuggish and corrupt Lt. Quint (Clifton James) in a relationship that literally pulls no punches. This isn't the usual case of an irritating p.i. and his friendly banter with a harassed cop — Quint would like nothing more than to see Axminster six feet under, and he'd do it himself if he thought he could get away with it! Also particularly notable about the series was that — with the exception of the allegedly fact-based grand conspiracy plot of the pilot — stories invariably involved Axminster not with the glamorous fantasy scenarios of many popular detective series, but with the sleazy, sordid side of detective work ... marital infidelity. Episodes dealt with adultery, suspicion, paranoia, petty deceits, jealousies, and murders of passion.

Rogers was deeply critical of the series in the trade press, complaining about the complexity of the show's plots (many of them by former pulp detective story writer and TV veteran Roy Huggins, who had bought such depth and humor to *The Rockford Files*), but in fact he was perfectly cast in a series far superior to most one-season wonders. The stories — pulpish, violent, sometimes poignant doomed romances and illicit liaisons — and the performances, sets, and particularly the photography, were all excellent. The series was beautifully shot, with filming often taking place on location, and predictably employed the famous and stylish Bradbury Building (as indeed had the series' stylistic predecessor, the somewhat more clichéd series *Banyon* in 1972, which starred Robert Forster as a twenty-dollars-a-day detective, and lasted even less time on the air). Visually, *City of Angels* was neither as down and dirty as the appropriately Poverty Row appearance of the classic *The Untouchables,* nor as flat and uninspiring as the later 1981 mini-series *The Gangster Chronicles,* and despite being a treat for the eyes of aficionados of old automobiles, managed to avoid the mannered theme park artificiality and the look of summer day posing of most other period dramas. As unnaturally attractive as the series looked, the players seemed to be inhabiting the period, rather than playing dress-up. Only Axminster's almost weekly run-ins with the fists of the bestial Lt. Quint became repetitive.

"Rogers had plenty of chances to be the charming, cynical, raffish gumshoe beloved of popular fiction, and he carried off the role with considerable skill," wrote *Variety.* "Opposite *Switch* on CBS and *Marcus Welby* on ABC, *City of Angels* has a maximum chance of survival. If the TV public is going to buy a period private eye series, it should be this one, at least if the scripts hold up in quality." "The casting is ideal throughout," said the *Hollywood Reporter.* "Rogers, as the devil-may-care sleuth, is brash and cocky, but also genial and tender-hearted and extremely likeable. High-style '30s flavor is aided by photographer Ric Waite and art director John Corso." The *Toronto Globe and Mail* decided that Rogers was a "1934 model Rockford, an investigator who uses wide-eyed guile when he can, but resorts to break-ins, fisticuffs, and concealing clients when he must. While the debut show had a reasonable share of action, with murders, bullets, and a concluding chase, it was not devoted to violence like that of, say, the repulsive *Starsky and Hutch*." "Certainly the best new crime show," concluded reviewer Blaik Kirby, "and certainly the best new American show of any kind this season. In a year of deadly dullness, it is both a surprise and a relief.... One of the most enjoyable aspects of the show is that it sits squarely in the tradition of the '30s private detective story without embarrassment. The hero insults blockhead policemen and borrows nickels for phones as if no-one else had ever done these things before."

Some of television's most experienced directors worked on the series, with the pilot being helmed by Don Medford, a regular director on *Baretta* and an associate of Jo Swerling in the '50s. In between, the bulk of his work had been for MGM's Arena productions and Quinn Martin. Veteran writer and producer Roy Huggins, master of pulp detective fiction, provided numerous plots. The supporting players too, were skillfully cast, with interesting character actors inhabiting the period effortlessly alongside some equally well-cast leading ladies including Lara Parker and Veronica Hamel. Elaine Joyce as Marsha was a typical representation of a scatty, loveable TV-land prostitute, Philip Sterling brought some warmth and assuredness to his role of benevolent lawyer Michael Brimm, and Clifton James made a believably tough and repugnant Lt. Quint.

Unfortunately, despite having most of the ingredients of conventional TV detective dramas, the series ran for only thirteen episodes as a mid-season replacement late Tuesday nights in 1976. The pilot, although having an intriguing premise (a traitorous coup in high places to oust the U.S. President) was not the best example of the series, which worked much better in the tighter hour show format, and it may have been the splitting of the pilot film into what would become the first three episodes of the series that killed the show. Also, Axminster was one of the few Cannell creations not to be interpreted as an idealized wish-fulfillment fantasy figure with whom the viewer could enjoyably identify with or envy; no quirky, modern-day pastiche this—*City of Angels* was Cannell and Huggins' stab at producing the real thing. Unfortunately, in 1976, the timing was off. These factors, alongside a number of pre-emptions, may well have prevented the show from building a steady audience. Certainly, it did not have heavy competition in the schedules. Luckily, a healthy number of episodes were completed before cancellation to make a satisfyingly different short-run series that was a welcome addition to the ranks of high quality detective shows. Laden with affectionately knowing period references (even down to throwaway lines recalling *Amos and Andy* and Lamont Cranston), the creative team of Cannell, Huggins and De Guere ensured that the few episodes screened that Spring and Summer of '76 remain intriguing curiosities of a series that received a raw deal from the ratings game.

Episode Guide

regular and recurring cast: Wayne Rogers (Jake Axminster), Clifton James (Lt. Quint), Philip Sterling (Michael Brimm), Elaine Joyce (Marsha), Timmie Rogers (Lester)

(1976)

THE NOVEMBER PLAN (pilot)

wr. Stephen Cannell, Roy Huggins, dir. Don Medford

While working to clear a Hollywood actress of a murder charge, Axminster stumbles onto a high echelon plan to wrest power from the U.S. government in a military coup (this episode was aired as a three-part intro to the series, but is usually seen as a TV movie, often independently of the show).

with Diane Ladd, Lawrence Luckinbill, G.D. Spradlin, Dorothy Malone, Stephen Elliott, Meredith Baxter Birney, William Forrest, Paul Jenkins, Lloyd Nolan, Laurence Hugo, Rod McCary, Ross Bickell, Steve Kanaly, Pepper Martin, Ron Burke

THE PARTING SHOT

wr. Roy Huggins, Phil De Guere, dir. Sigmund Neufeld, Jr.

Unaware that Axminster has been hired by her elderly husband to investigate a possible affair with a college professor, a young wife hires him to clear the professor of a murder attempt charge.

with Corinne Michaels, Donna Mills, Joshua Bryant, Art Lund, Stefan Gierasch, Dudley Knight, Lee Bryant, Meg Wyllie, Hal Riddle

A LONELY WAY TO DIE

wr. and dir. Douglas Heyes

Crooked cops and the mentally unbalanced wife of a future potential Presidential candidate hinder Axminster's investigation of the supposed suicide of a cop.

with Belinda Montgomery, Don Porter, Martine Beswicke, Spencer Milligan, William Smith, Lynn Carlin, Karen Ericson, Robert Hoy, Francis De Sales

THE HOUSE ON ORANGE GROVE AVENUE

wr. Roy Huggins, Stephen and Elinor Karpf, dir. Robert Douglas

Axminster is hired by two elderly women to solve a murder committed eight years earlier.

with Susan Howard, Susan Sullivan, Billy Green Bush, Lara Parker, Severn Darden, Shug Fisher, George Carey, Gayle Rogers, Paul McWilliams, Robert Raymond Sutton, Ted Gehring, Don Hamner, Jerry Hardin, W.T. Zacha

THE PALM SPRINGS ANSWER

wr. Roy Huggins, Merwin Gerard, dir. Allen Reisner

Axminster searches for a missing nightclub singer who has stumbled onto a mob killing.

with Signe Hasso, Phillip Mansour, William Bronder, Heather Lowe, Christine Jones, George Gaynes, Terry Kiser, Rockne Tarkington, Pepper Martin, Milt Kogan

THE LOSERS

wr. Gloryette Clark, dir. Barry Shear

A woman Axminster is investigating to determine whether she is being unfaithful or not is discovered dead.

with Broderick Crawford, Marcia Strassman,

Brett Halsey, Priscilla Pointer, Dana Landon, Dave Cass, W.T. Zacha

A SUDDEN SILENCE

wr. and dir. Douglas Heyes

Axminster is threatened and brutalized while trying to find out why a young girl and her boyfriend are being followed by mysterious men.

with Darleen Carr, Joel Fabiani, Edward Winter, John Ragin, Rod Haase, Douglas Matthews, Todd Martin, Barbara Morrison, Harvey Gold

THE CASTLE OF DREAMS

wr. Stephen Cannell, Phil De Guere, dir. Robert Douglas

Axminster's receptionist is abducted after she tries to help a frightened friend.

with Jack Kruschen, Veronica Hamel, James Luisi, Giles Douglas, Janis Heiden, Kristine Larkin, Barry Cahill, Eugene Petersen, Pepper Martin, Michael Ebert, Laurence Haddon

SAY GOODBYE TO YESTERDAY

wr. Gloryette Clark, dir. Jerry London

Axminster's search for a missing millionaire's wife uncovers a secret past and takes him to a violent encounter in Chinatown.

with Carole Mallory, G.D. Spradlin, Beulah Quo, Jack Colvin, Bill Saito, John Durren, Cassie Yates, Chuck Winter

THE BLOODSHOT EYE

wr. Phil De Guere, dir. Hy Averback

Axminster's investigation into whether a life insurance policy has been paid out to a man who is still alive takes him to a small hick town and confrontations with a corrupt judge, a crooked sheriff, and a strange undertaker.

with John McLiam, William Phipps, Taylor Lacher, Geoffrey Lewis, Charles Tyner, Stuart Nisbet, Gene Dynarski, Lilyan McBride, Booth Colman, Robert Donner

MATCH POINT

wr. Richard Booth, dir. Ralph Senensky

Axminster attempts to clear a professional tennis star of murder.

with David Young, Renee Jarrett, Dana Wynter, William Beckley, Alan Patrick, Pepper Martin, Randolph Roberts, John Lupton

series ends

Black Sheep Squadron
September 1976–April 1978

"Just name me a hero — and I'll prove he's a bum"

*"Despite (everything), we enjoyed the war movies as much as the folks
back home — maybe more. I guess because Hollywood made the war so simple.
Everything was black and white — like the film. We were always the good guys, with steely
eyes and square jaws, fighting for freedom, mom, and apple pie. And
they were always the funny-looking guys with silly grins and weak eyes,
who wouldn't fight unless they outnumbered us by ten to one.
Yeah, we liked war films. It took our minds off the real thing...."*

Each of the 36 episodes of *Black Sheep Squadron* opened with genuine footage of the World War II propaganda newsreels of the day, over which the series' star, steely-eyed and square-jawed Robert Conrad, would add his own acerbic and world-weary observations in his role as real-life World War II maverick Colonel Greg "Pappy" Boyington. The real Boyington, still alive when the series was in production, was a larger-than-life figure who seemed made for Cannell and 1970s TV. Indeed, if he had not existed, someone would have had to invent him. In many respects, they already had, in numerous similar individualist rule-breaking mavericks of the '70s. A controversial anti-authoritarian misfit and carouser, Boyington resigned from the Marines at the outbreak of war to join up with the volunteer Flying Tigers squadron in China, outraged the authorities and the country's leader personally, returned to the U.S. and the Marines under his own steam, broke his leg, and was told by doctors that he would never fly again.

Grounding Boyington was like a red rag to a bull, and he promptly formed the notorious Black Sheep Squadron out of, according to the series, assorted fellow misfits, no-hopers, trouble-makers and rejects, and personally equaled the "kill-count" of the World War One flying ace Eddie Rickenbacker. On the same day as matching this dubious accomplishment, he was shot down, and spent the last eighteen months of the war in a Japanese prison camp. The University of Washington degree in aeronautical engineering that got him into the armed forces was topped at the close of the war with a Congressional Medal of Honor and Navy Cross, presented by President Truman. In 1958, he wrote his memoirs, under the title "Baa Baa Black Sheep." Not only did he live to see Conrad's portrayal of him in Cannell's series for Universal (and by some accounts, lived to apologize for it to his former crewmen, too!), but he even guest-starred in three episodes in a cameo as General Kenlay. He died, aged 75, in 1988.

The premise of the show, which opened with the hospitalized Boyington forming the Black Sheep, and the subsequent series telling of their exploits while based on the Pacific island of Vella La Cava, was pure Cannell, and he and star Conrad had a punchy and preposterous two years elaborating and fantasizing about the rough-edged military man's World War II exploits. How much was true, or inspired by real events, and how much was totally fabricated, may never be clear; certainly some of Boyington's men were not too thrilled with the show, and the Cannell touch is too obvious for the yarns to be that close to Cannell's requirements, whatever his affinity with the myth. The writers obviously only took their initial inspiration from Boyington's reminiscing, although many of the stories told about the Black Sheep obviously served as a springboard for various episodes even if the finished result was a fiction. The sarcastic dirge that opened each episode's credits was genuine enough — the Squadron would apparently often spend the nights singing (there was nothing else to do), and this weary lament was one of their standards:

> *We are poor little lambs who have lost our way,*
> *Baa, baa, baa.*
> *We are little Black Sheep who have gone astray,*
> *Baa, baa, baa.*
> *Gentlemen Black Sheep, off on a spree,*
> *Damned from here to Kahili,*
> *God have mercy on such as we,*
> *Baa, baa, baa.*

The real Boyington acted as the show's technical advisor, and he was also portrayed in the series in the grand tradition of the Cannell con-man, fast-talking, quick-thinking, and easy going with the facts. In the opening episode alone, he finagles himself a promotion with a phony phone call, poses as a doctor to quarantine an entire squadron, and then swipes their planes...!

In reality, the squadron was cobbled together speedily out of available, mostly untrained men to assist in an operation that urgently needed more fliers; ordinarily, squadrons prepared extensively before going on missions, but in this particular case there was no time. Amusingly, according to former Black Sheep member Fred Avey, who was interviewed by writer John Wukovits for the magazine *Aviation Heritage,* the group had originally called themselves Boyington's Bastards; in a moment reminiscent of many confrontations with military propagandists in the series, the team were asked if they wouldn't mind renaming themselves for the benefit of the press ... and (no doubt to the relief of NBC thirty years later) the Black Sheep were born.

Of the original 28 men who served in the Black Sheep (eventually 51 men served in the squadron), only three had previously seen combat. During the course of their conflict — the Squadron existed for only five months, between September 1944 and January 1945 — eleven men died in action. "When you were in the air, it was either kill or be killed," Avey told his interviewer. "We were thought to be the bravest pilots, but honestly, I was frightened often." Avey joined the Black Sheep with two other men, replacing downed fliers before them. All three had died in one raid during which the Black Sheep claimed thirty enemy planes.

Robert Conrad, a 5'8" stocky and athletic former boxer, had earlier enjoyed fame as the star of the long-running 1960s series *Hawaiian Eye* and *The Wild Wild West.* Later, he would take the lead in another Cannell series, *The Duke,* in 1979. Cannell, who also considered Conrad for the lead in *The A-Team,* told a TV interviewer, "When we did *Black Sheep,* and I started to write shows with more and more emotional content — shows where he had to cry, shows where he had to write a letter home to a dead pilot's mother — I began to see what a tremendous range as a performer this man had, and how well he had developed the ability to give you a feeling or a reaction with a very subtle expression, I just became knocked out by him."

Although bearing no physical resemblance to Boyington (who was nicknamed Pappy by his men because of his age in comparison with the young pilots), Conrad was a feisty little character himself, known in TV circles as something of a rebel. His own colorful exploits include punching out a Santa Claus at a Christmas-in-July party (an incident told in *TV Guide*), and an embarrassing debacle at a CBS press conference (related in trade paper *Variety*) to promote his new snowbound mountain-cops series *High Mountain Rangers* in the late '80s, when he snatched the microphone away from the network chief to harangue the competition to his new series. As it turned out, *High Mountain Rangers,* an acceptable time-waster panned by the critics as "Robert Conrad's home movies" due to the fact that most of Conrad's family were either in front of or behind the camera, stumbled through a single season after initial impressive ratings for the pilot. The NBC series that Conrad so vocally and prominently maligned was the long running and very successful *Golden Girls*....

Conrad had started his career at Warners in the 1950s, and friends claim that his experiences there, at a time when contract TV players were notoriously poorly rewarded for their successes, had made him a rebel and a cynic during his later dealings with the industry. He had already become renowned for vociferously promoting his series to the point of overenthusiasm before the *High Mountain Rangers* incident, having fought tooth-and-nail alongside Cannell to keep *Black Sheep Squadron* on the air. Having just suffered two rapid cancellations for his previous series, *The Men,* and *The D.A.* (the latter a Jack Webb series that had him hopelessly miscast), Conrad was not about to go under for a third time.

"I knew it was going to be a hit, it had all the right ingredients," Conrad said in a TV interview many years later. "It was a tragedy they didn't let the show stay on the air ... well, they did, but it only lasted two seasons. It shouldn't have died, and the proof is that it's been opposite *Dallas* in re-runs, and it's beaten everything it goes opposite. It has primarily male demographics — it wasn't discovered to any great extent by women, because it's airplanes, second World War, that kind of thing ... I'm very satisfied that it's done so well in syndication, and that it's a cult show." Universal's own publicity backs up Conrad's point of view (as well it might), noting that in its second season, *Black Sheep Squadron* held its own against such established hits as *Barney Miller* and *Hawaii Five-0*.

Producing the series were Cannell, his long-term partner Alex Beaton (later to supervise Universal's *Hercules* and *Xena* series in the '90s), and Phil DeGuere, a producer and writer on both this series, *City of Angels,* and *Baretta*. DeGuere was later to embark on a successful solo career in network television, with such series as the *Rockford*-inspired *Simon and Simon* and the 1980s *Twilight Zone* to his credit. Ex-Marine and flying buff Donald Bellisario joined the series — and Cannell — with the second season, and would later, flying solo, create *Magnum, p.i.* for Tom Selleck in 1980, as well as *Tales of the Gold Monkey, Airwolf, Quantum Leap,* and *JAG*.

For both Cannell and Bellisario, *Black Sheep Squadron* proved to be a series that would unite them with many of the familiar recurring names and faces who would appear and reappear throughout their subsequent projects. Boyington's squadron of wise-cracking fly-boys included James Whitmore, Jr., who has guest-starred in practically every Cannell and Bellisario series ever; Jeff MacKay, who would make numerous appearances in Cannell shows, co-star in *Tales of the Gold Monkey,* guest-star in *Airwolf,* and play a recurring role in *Magnum* (latterly as an impostor and a ghost!); Red West, former bodyguard and best buddy of Elvis Presley, who appeared in guest roles in several Cannell series and Conrad projects; and Larry Manetti, who — with fellow co-star Red West — would appear in the supporting cast of Can-

The cast of *Black Sheep Squadron* pose with series star Robert Conrad (center, hands clasped). Left to right, top: Robert Ginty, Joey Aresco, John Larroquette, Robert Conrad, Dirk Blocker, James Whitmore Jr. Left to right, bottom: Jeff Mackay, Larry Manetti, W.K. Stratton. Inset: Conrad with "Pappy's Lambs"—Navy nurses stationed at the Black Sheep's base (actresses unidentified).

nell's later series with Conrad, *The Duke*, before becoming a regular on *Magnum* as Rick. The remaining roles in the show were taken by John Larroquette (like Whitmore, Jr., in the first season only), later to become a regular on the long-running sit-com *Night Court;* Robert Ginty, later to star in the 1984 cop show *Hawaiian Heat*, but best known for his work on B-video releases such as the *Exterminator* series; Dirk Blocker, son of *Bonanza's* Dan Blocker, and noticeably so; Cannell regulars W.K. Stratton and Joey Aresco; and, as a nurse, Conrad's daughter Nancy. Also introduced in the second season, to give the series teen appeal, was Jeb Adams, son of the actor Nick Adams, another buddy of Presley, who had helped get Conrad into the acting profession. Many of the Squadron's Corsair pilots turned up some years later as futuristic fly-boys of the Viper Squadron in Glen Larson's *Battlestar Galactica,* on which Bellisario also worked.

Initially launched under the unappealing and deceptive title of *Baa Baa Black Sheep* after the title of the best-selling war memoirs it was based on, the series mixed traditional World War II heroics and buddy movie machismo with refreshing *M*A*S*H*–style cynicism and honesty that still managed to keep a respectable distance from any semblance of reality. It was as if Cannell and Conrad had made the series with P.J. O'Rourke sitting in a devil suit on one shoulder, and Alan Alda sporting a halo on the other. On the one hand, the series was as gung-ho and heroic as any World War II movie ("as phoney as a three dollar bill," said another former member of the original Black Sheep), while on the other hand it showed the U.S. servicemen as flawed, vulnerable young men, Conrad as a commander who could cry over the deaths of his men (no "you wanna live forever?" crap), and in many ways helped set a precedent on TV for later classy Vietnam-based series such as *Tour of Duty* and *China Beach*. Certainly the series demonstrated a very healthy and typical 1970s suspicion of bureaucracy, administrative incompetence and bloody-minded superiors at odds with the personnel in the thick of the action, attitudes of the day fostered in part by the effects of the Vietnam war on the American psyche, and which were by now an established Cannell trademark. *Black Sheep Squadron* carefully and cleverly redefined the war movie for 1970s consumption, retaining the tried and tested elements of the war film while simultaneously introducing a streak of cynicism for contemporary sensibilities. It was either brave or foolhardy to introduce a war series to U.S. TV so soon after Vietnam, but on the other hand it may have anticipated the need of certain segments of America to rewrite that period within an acceptable framework that defied historical fact. If Vietnam had been a disgrace and a disaster, World War II was perceived as a just and unavoidable conflict.

Black Sheep Squadron cautiously covered all the bases to make the genre acceptable for all but the most blinkered and politically dogmatic. While slyly employing all the clichés of the Hollywood war movie and lifting familiar plots from every war film, western and spy show ever made, Cannell and his writers quietly nudged the more reactionary sentiments that usually accompanied them into the dustbin. The series cleverly puts forward the other side's perspective on things, while defending the home position; the hawks are exposed to the perspective of the formerly faceless enemy while the doves get to take in the views of the American soldier. War is neither condoned or justified in *Black Sheep Squadron;* as opposed to the propaganda produced when a war is in full flow (such as John Wayne's 1968 travesty *The Green Berets,* for example, vilified at home and by the troops alike), peacetime productions tend to elaborate and enlighten from a neutral political perspective.

Playing Boyington's superiors were Simon Oakland as the stern but sympathetic General Moore, and Dana Elcar as the somewhat less amenable Colonel Lard (note how the Aunt Sally figures always have names that just invite abuse even before the character's even opened his mouth!). Oakland was a heavy, thick-set character actor of numerous film and TV appearances who had appeared several times on *The Rockford Files* and was a regular on Cannell's *Toma* and the David Chase–scripted cult series *Kolchak—the Night Stalker.* Dana Elcar was another familiar TV face and Cannell regular formerly in the supporting cast of Cannell's cop show *Baretta.* He made numerous guest-appearances in Cannell shows, but was best known during the '80s for his co-starring role in the adventure series *MacGyver.* He had also appeared in the 1969 Jack Webb pilot *The D.A.: Murder One* alongside Conrad.

Elcar brought three dimensions to the two dimensional character of Colonel Lard, most notably in "Forbidden Fruit," written by Cannell and Bellisario, and "The Iceman," written by Bellisario, and would later—along with Conrad himself—direct a number of episodes (including "The Iceman"). Numerous TV roles included a corporate polluter in "Arriverderci, Baby" for *Riptide* and a judge threatened by bad guys in "Judgement Day," a double-length episode of *The A-Team*. In actual fact, there was an intelligence officer — a former police sergeant named Walton — whose job it was to watch over Boyington, who was prone to drinking sprees.

After a haggle with Universal about money, NBC gave Cannell and Conrad a second season order for a half-season of thirteen episodes as a mid-season back-up. There were two conditions: in the bookshops, the title "Baa Baa Black Sheep" had posed no problems of identification when represented on a book jacket in the appropriate section of the store, but as a title listed in *TV Guide* it was obtuse and unattractive, with NBC belatedly, if a little obviously, discovering that when tested, the title was generally assumed to be that of a children's nursery series. Now, the title was to be changed to the more accessible *Black Sheep Squadron*, and somehow, Cannell had to bring some women into the cast. Having survived the first season time-slot against the indomitable double-bill of nostalgia sit-coms *Happy Days* and *Laverne and Shirley*, the Black Sheep were now sent into combat against another smash-hit of the period, the infamous *Charlie's Angels*. Many producers might have glumly folded their tents and disappeared into the night at this point, but Cannell and his people confronted the challenge head-on and with good humor, by conceding to network requests and introducing a squad of attractive nurses to the island (Denise DuBarry, Kathy McCullem, Brianne Leary, and others) and nicknaming them Pappy's Lambs! As these characters were never quite as well-developed as their bodies, they might have been more accurately labeled the Black Sheep Bimbos; arriving beauty queens in the episode "Sheep in the Limelight," were in actuality not quite so alluring as the nurses who were so distressed by their arrival! Taking no chances, producers Cannell and Bellisario wrote the episode introducing the girls — "Forbidden Fruit" — and Conrad directed, but a grotesquely sexist press release from NBC did them no favors ("Brianne Leary is a long-haired brunette with a well-packed uniform; Kathy McCullem is a perky blonde with no-no on her lips and yes-yes in her eyes...!"). Happily, the series survived such helpful efforts (the move was indicative of the coy sexism of late-'70s U.S. TV in the wake of *Charlie's Angels* and the inane sit-com *Three's Company*) and gradually crept up in the ratings. The reasoning behind the cancellation of a show that had delivered respectable alternative audiences against three of the biggest hit series of the late '70s will remain one of life's little mysteries.

Episode Guide

regular and recurring cast: Robert Conrad (Major Gregory "Pappy" Boyington), Simon Oakland (General Moore), Dana Elcar (Colonel Lard), James Whitmore, Jr. (Capt. Jim Gutterman), W.K. Stratton (Lt. Lawrence Casey), Jeff Mackay (Lt. Don French), Dirk Blocker (Lt. Jerry Bragg), Robert Ginty (Lt. T.J. Wiley), Larry Manetti (Lt. Bob Boyle), John Larroquette (Lt. Bob Anderson), Red West (Sgt. Andy Micklin), Joey Aresco (Hutch), Jeb Adams (Lt. Jeb Pruitt), Steve Richmond (Cpl. Stan Richards), Katherine Cannon (Capt. Dottie Dixon), Denise DuBarry (Samantha Green), Nancy Conrad (Nancy Gilmore), Kathy McCullen (Ellie), Brianne Leary (Susan), Byron Chung (Harachi)

First Season (1976–'77)

BAA BAA BLACK SHEEP (pilot, a.k.a. The Flying Misfits)

wr. Stephen Cannell, dir. Russ Mayberry

Flying ace Gregory Boyington tricks himself a promotion to major, and then forms a crew of fighter pilot's out of the military's "black sheep," young pilots awaiting court martial. After conning an entire squadron of planes out of another squad, Boyington (nicknamed Pappy by his youthful charges) realizes that he can only save his own hide by winning such a spectacular air victory that the higher-ups will be forced to overlook the liberties he has taken.

with George Gaynes, John Durren, Peter Donat, Sharon Gless, Charles Napier, John Lawlor, Jake Mitchell, Anthony Charnota, Lance Le Gault, Sandra Kearns, Janice Carroll

Best Three Out of Five

wr. Stephen Cannell, dir. Larry Doheny

Boyington has found a grudging ally in the form of General Moore, quietly amused while officially expressing his displeasure at the Black Sheep's flagrant abuse of authority. While Moore is absent, Boyington goes into hiding at an R&R camp to avoid the attentions of Colonel Lard, who despises his undisciplined behavior, and Major Red Buell, the original owner of the Black Sheep planes, who has every intention of reclaiming his property.

with Charles Napier, Noel Conlon, Dave Ray Chandler, Richard Doughty, Robin Riker, Curtis Credel, Patrick Skelton

One Small War

wr. Phil De Guere, dir. Walter Doniger

After Boyington is accidentally shot down by one of his own planes, he is marooned on an island being used by the Japanese as an air base, where he finds an Australian pilot who has no intention of returning to the war, or allowing Boyington to betray his hideout.

with Rene Auberjonois, Lloyd Kino, Dale Ishimoto, Hatsuo Uda

High Jinx

wr. Ken Pettus, dir. John Peyser

The morale of the Black Sheep is threatened when Gutterman develops psychological problems over the presence of a young pilot who was considered a jinx by his previous squadron.

with Donald Petrie

Prisoners of War

wr. Ken Pettus, dir. Jackie Cooper

With an impending table-tennis tournament threatening to be a major embarrassment for the flyers, the Black Sheep draft an enemy prisoner onto their team.

with Clyde Kusatsu, Robert Clotworthy, Jerry Hardin

Presumed Dead

wr. Milt Rosen, dir. Larry Doheny

Mystified by the presence of a large number of Japanese bombers, Boyington discovers that a visiting Navy man is a brainwashed sleeper agent, primed as a human weapon against a top-level meeting where some of the top military strategists will be present.

with Kent McCord, James Hong, Norman Burton, Eric Server

Meatball Circus

wr. Stephen Cannell, dir. John Peyser

Refusing to take his pilots on a certain suicide mission, Boyington instead proposes that they fly captured Japanese aircraft against an enemy carrier.

with Bill Fletcher, John Kerry, Stewart Moss, Robert Clark, James Ingersoll, Dan Ferrone, Dudley Knight, Fil Formicola, Richard Sarradet

Up for Grabs

wr. Phil De Guere, dir. Ivan Dixon

T.J. and Casey fortuitously decide to go on an early morning fishing trip on the morning the island is invaded by Japanese soldiers who take everybody else hostage.

with George Takei, Yuki Shimoda, Harry Fleer, Marcus Mukai, Jim Ishida, James Saito

Anyone for Suicide?

wr. Ken Pettus, dir. Jackie Cooper

Refusing to be grounded during an illness, Boyington leads his pilots on a dangerous mission, only to be taken ill during the assignment.

with Dale Ishimoto, Edmund Gilbert

New Georgia on My Mind

wr. Ken Pettus, dir. Jeannot Szwarc

Boyington comes into conflict with a powerful Marine colonel who wants to take command of his men to assist his own.

with James Luisi, Bill Lucking, Muni Zano

The Cat's Whiskers

wr. Milt Rosen, dir. Russ Mayberry

Faced with yet another impending court martial, Boyington seeks the usual sugar pill to appease his superiors, and finds it in the notion of destroying an enemy radar base.

with Jill Jaress-Brennan

LOVE AND WAR

wr. Phil De Guere, dir. William Wiard

Reunited unexpectedly with a former college sweetheart, Bragg clashes with Casey when she takes a shine to him instead.

with Leslie Charleson, Sharon Ullrick

WAR BIZ WARRIOR

wr. Gordon Dawson, dir. Lawrence Doheny

A movie star is sent to the base as a morale-boosting publicity stunt, but things get out of hand when the actor is encouraged to lead a relatively simple mission.

with James Darren, Robert Gooden, Ford Rainey, John Haymer

THE DEADLIEST ENEMY OF ALL (two parts)

wr. Phil De Guere, dir. Barry Shear

After pulling French from a blazing plane, Boyington falls in love with the nurse who is tending to him.

with Anne Francis, Linda Scruggs Bogart

DEVIL IN THE SLOT

wr. Phil De Guere, dir. Barry Shear

Gutterman is grounded after being shot down by a Japanese "ace," and tough sergeant Andy Micklin, his replacement, turns out to be an overbearing ogre (this episode introduces Conrad's old buddy Red West to the cast as Micklin, following his infamous firing by Vernon Presley from the Elvis entourage).

with Byron Chung

FIVE THE HARD WAY

wr. Ken Pettus, dir. Jackie Cooper

French is pressured by his overbearing father and some visiting reporters to risk his life getting the fifth kill he needs to become an "ace."

with Kenneth Mars, Doug Dirkson, Jim Gallanti

LAST MISSION OVER SENGAI

wr. Phil De Guere, dir. Jackie Cooper

Boyington is set up to take the fall for the cowardly lies and incompetence of the unstable son of a famous general after U.S. troops are fired on during a mission.

with Frederick Herrick, Booth Colman, Alex Henteloff, Dennis Fimple, Mills Watson, Fred Sadoff, Hal Bokar

TROUBLE AT FORT APACHE

wr. Stephen Cannell, dir. Edward Dien

A visiting glory-seeking general countermands Boyington's orders from Moore to fly cover for a new bomber's test flights.

with Joel Fabiani, James Keach, Les Lannom, Ron Kuhlman, Tim Haldeman

POOR LITTLE LAMBS

wr. Ken Pettus, dir. Jackie Cooper

Shot down over an island occupied by the Japanese, Boyington, Anderson, and Boyle encounter a contrary and antagonistic nun looking after some orphans at their church.

with Lilyan Chauvin, Sorrell Booke, Soon-Teck Oh, Jesse Dizon, Jim Ishida, Bob Neill, George Cheung

WASPS

wr. Phil De Guere, dir. Dana Elcar

Boyington crosses swords with a tough female squadron leader who wants to keep her flyers well clear of any distractions from the Black Sheep's attentions.

with Andi Garrett, Laurie Prange, Melinda Naud

LAST ONE FOR HUTCH

wr. Glen Olson, Rod Baker, James Crocker, dir. Lawrence Doheny

The Black Sheep are disbanded after a particularly destructive attack on their island, but the squadron are determined to avenge the death of their mechanic Hutch, killed during the attack.

with Vince Cannon, Gordon Jump, Philip Charles MacKenzie

THE FASTEST GUN

wr. Stephen Cannell, Phil De Guere, dir. Phil De Guere

Unwilling to shoot down Boyington's disabled plane, the Japanese air ace who previously shot down Gutterman challenges Boyington to a duel in the sky the next day.

with Byron Chung, Paul Lichtman

Second Season (1977–'78)

DIVINE WIND

wr. Donald Bellisario, dir. Lawrence Doheny

Having been erroneously listed as killed in action, pilot Anderson is convinced that he has been the recipient of a bad omen (this episode introduces Katherine Cannon as Captain Dottie Dixon).

with Scott Hylands, Soon-Teck Oh, James Saito, Lloyd Kino, Sab Shimono, J. Kenneth Campbell

THE 200 POUND GORILLA

wr. Stephen Cannell, dir. Dana Elcar

Micklin, faced with the prospect of a promotion that will force him into the ranks of the officers he so despises, goes on a drunken rampage.

with Craig Wasson

THE HAWK FLIES ON SUNDAY

wr. Frank Abatemarco, dir. Robert Conrad

A romance with T.J. and one of the local girls involved with the black market endangers the integrity of a vital mission.

with Victoria Racimo, Byron Chung, Sean Garrison

WOLVES IN THE SHEEP PEN

wr. Donald Bellisario, dir. Edward Dein

A green navy officer is assigned to liaise with Boyington in the destruction of an enemy radar ship ... but Boyington suspects that their task has been accomplished easier than it should.

with Tim Matheson, Darrell Larson, Sean Roche

OPERATION: STAND-DOWN

wr. Glen Olson, Rod Baker, Donald Bellisario, dir. Phil De Guere

Grounded after dismal exam results, the flyers get a second chance to prove their mettle in the air, only to be confronted by their nemesis, Japanese air ace Harachi.

with Byron Chung, Michael Durrell, Tom Ligon, John Durren, John Fujioka, Marcus Mukai

TEN'LL GET YOU FIVE

wr. Peter Lefcourt, Phil De Guere, dir. Robert Conrad

Boyington and his men get taken by con-men even more devious than themselves, losing all their drink for bad engine oil.

with Scott Colomby, Morgan Paull, Barry Cahill

FORBIDDEN FRUIT

wr. Stephen Cannell, Donald Bellisario, dir. Robert Conrad

A new nurse on the base turns out to be not only the general's daughter, but an old flame of Boyington's, while the only pilot on the base who can fly a new type of plane is suspected to be underage (this episode introduces "Pappy's Lambs" and Jeb Adams as Jeb Pruitt).

with Phillip Allen, Diane Lewis, Jon Van Ness

FIGHTING ANGELS

wr. Stephen Cannell, dir. Lawrence Doheny

With the Black Sheep airborne to defend the island, the camp must be defended by the officers and the nurses.

with Sam Gilman, Steve Tannen

THE ICEMAN

wr. Donald Bellisario, dir. Dana Elcar

Boyington is relieved of his command and replaced by a by-the-book officer, a move which immediately antagonizes both Boyington and his men.

with Richard Jaeckel, Richard Narita, Harry Moses, Marcus Mukai

HOTSHOT

wr. Donald Bellisario, dir. Lawrence Doheny

Junior pilot Jeb is endangered by the reckless actions of a competitive officer who wants to rival Boyington's military record.

with Frank Converse, Richard Stanley, James Crittenden

THE SHOW MUST GO ON ... SOMETIMES

wr. Lester Berke, Don Gold, James Crocker, dir. Dana Elcar

In order to get the airstrip repaired, Boyington bribes the workers with a girl-packed variety show. As the men diligently work at the landing strip, the girls are taken ill.

with Joe Santos, Loren Ewing, Betsy Slade

SHEEP IN THE LIMELIGHT

wr. Frank Abatemarco, dir. Lawrence Doheny

Having unknowingly saved the life of Eleanor Roosevelt while on a mission, the Black Sheep find that their new-found fame as super-heroes has earned them a dangerous and near-impossible mission for their deeds.

with James Callahan, James Lydon, Bob Hastings, Dana Gladstone, J.P. Bumstead, Michael Boyle

A Little Bit of England
   wr. and dir. Donald Bellisario
   A tiny island nicknamed England by the flyers due to the presence of a couple of English officers as the sole occupants, is put at risk after visits from the Black Sheep inadvertently cause their location to be betrayed.
   with Peter Frampton, Ernie Hudson, Sheryl Lee Ralph, Tak Kubota, Michael Yama
      series ends

Richie Brockelman, Private Eye
March 1978–April 1978

"Uh ... the thing of it is...."

The *Richie Brockelman* series was something of an oddity, in as much as it's the closest Stephen Cannell came to producing a spin-off series until *Booker* ten years later. Brockelman was a young kid from a suburban neighborhood who fancied himself as a private eye in the Bogart tradition, dreaming naively of the kind of life lived by the likes of the Jake Axminster character in *City of Angels* ... with all the rough bits taken out. The thing of it was, that with the rough bits taken out, there wasn't that much to be left in.

Coming in at a paltry five episodes, *Richie Brockelman, Private Eye* ran as an end-of-season replacement for *The Rockford Files,* the series it spun off from. In the pilot film, Brockelman (Dennis Dugan) sets himself up in an office and waits patiently to be implicated in a Chandleresque mystery, until Elizabeth Morton (Suzanne Pleshette) enters to (partly) fulfill his wishes. The woman has lost her memory, but has a vague recollection of being involved in a murder, and is being pursued by a gunman. Also guesting in the pilot is familiar screen villain smoothie Lloyd Bochner, the reliable William Windom, and the then-unknown Sharon Gless of *Cagney and Lacey,* a two-time guest player in *The Rockford Files.*

Despite the presence of Stephen Cannell and co-creator Steven Bochco (who was only a few months away from striking gold with *Hill Street Blues,* and had already proven himself as the story editor on the exemplary *Columbo*), the concept just did not work. The problem was not with the creative talents—William Phillips had produced the pilot, and had (and would) act as producer on a number of Cannell projects, and Hy Averback, a TV pilot veteran, directed. The subsequent series was produced by Peter Fischer, known to Bochco from *Columbo,* and a producer who had gone on to helm other detective series such as *The Adventures of Ellery Queen* (1975–'76), and *The Eddie Capra Mysteries* (1978–'79), and would spend the 1980s producing *Murder She Wrote.* Writing the scripts were Cannell, Bochco, Fischer, Robert Swanson (a regular co-worker with Fischer), and Michael Kozoll (later co-creator of *Hill Street Blues*), and directors were Cannell regulars Ivan Dixon, Arnold Laven, and David Moessinger.

Dennis Dugan was a talented young actor who specialized in playing wimps, which was exactly what Brockelman was supposed to be, and therein lie the joke. Unfortunately, this also made him a very poor identification figure to sympathize with in the lead role. In *Columbo,* the viewer enjoyed seeing the smug, arrogant villain squirm on the hook, beaten by this shabby, respectful man in a raincoat; in *Richie Brockelman,* the viewer was as aggravated by the little chump as the bad guy, and the audience was most likely to end up sympathizing with the criminals! As the archetypal nerd, Brockelman had a hard time convincing either his family, friends, clients, or the Cannell-esque army of killers, crooks and heavies he confronted each week that he was a detective at all, let alone a good one ... and yet, each week the deluded youth would find himself dropped into one of Cannell's standard outrageous plots to a deliberately incongruous background of West Coast surfing music and brightly-lit, sunshine-smothered Californian locales ... hardly conducive to the dirty, wet pulp fantasies of puddles and neon lights that Brockelman longed for.

Dugan was not a very charismatic leading man, working much better in ensemble casts (as in the excellent early cancellation comedy *Empire* in 1984), and the Brockelman character stood alone in every sense; he was neither funny enough, or heroic enough to sustain an hour show. Instead, he came across as a lucky idiot, despite his *Rockford*-like resourcefulness, and although this was entirely intentional, the character was not as outrageously comical or sympathetic as Ralph Hinckley or Murray Bozinsky in Cannell's later series *The Greatest American Hero* and *Riptide*.

The intention may have originally been to introduce the aggravating Brockelman into *The Rockford Files* as a semi-regular partner for Rockford (to take some of the pressure off James Garner's aching back). Fortunately, reason prevailed, and the character was instead written into the 1976 pilot film before resurfacing in a double-length 1978 episode of *Rockford* entitled "The House on Willis Avenue," which served to introduce the doomed five-week run of *Richie Brockelman*. Written by Cannell, and again directed by Averback, the guest players were Simon Oakland (of *Black Sheep Squadron*) as obnoxious p.i. Vern St. Cloud (a recurring character in *Rockford*), Philip Sterling (of *City of Angels*), Pernell Roberts (of *Bonanza* and *Trapper John*) and actor-director Jackie Cooper. When *The Rockford Files* paused for its summer break early in '78, the *Richie Brockelman* series had the unenviable task of filling the timeslot. As the stories were basically *Rockford* yarns filmed without Rockford, this little innovation didn't go down too well with the audience. It ran for five weeks in March and April of that year and flopped disastrously. Curiously, Brockelman then returned for his swan song appearance in a two-part *Rockford Files* titled "Never Send a Boy King to Do a Man's Job"; the title suggests a *Brockelman* script, and one wonders whether it was a left-over script put to good use, a *Brockelman* episode guest-starring Garner to belatedly boost the show before the axe fell, or a *Rockford* episode to, again belatedly, save the spin-off.

Part of the problem with the series was that private-eye send-ups with unlikely or laughable heroes were by now nothing new. In fact, there were more spoofy, mock detectives on TV and in the movies by now than there were traditional types; Mannix and McGarrett were positively outnumbered. Aging, unlikely investigators who were either shabby, shambling Spillane parodies or highly dubious candidates for the profession were quite prolific in the '70s, and would become even more so in the 1980s. As American television was going through one of its periodic sackcloth-and-ashes periods over the interminable issue of violence on TV (panic, clean-up, plummeting ratings, another panic, and a new rash of no-holds-barred actioners), *Richie Brockelman* was a perfect candidate for the watered-down "family hour" type of TV series that were dropping like flies in '77 and '78, but like those other series, the public was not buying.

Playing Richie's secretary was Barbara Bosson, co-creator Steven Bochco's wife, and later Fay Furillo on *Hill Street Blues*. Every show that Bochco went, his wife was sure to follow, and as well as guesting in both *L.A. Law* and *Doogie Howser,* she also had regular roles in *Hooperman* and *Cop Rock*. Dugan himself would guest-star memorably on *Hill Street Blues* in 1981, as Captain Freedom, a send-up super-hero of the Walter Mitty/Richie Brockelman persuasion, but with several extra screws loose as a character created by writer Michael Wagner and quite possibly inspired by Cannell's then brand-new series *The Greatest American Hero.* Robert Hogan, also to make a memorable guest-appearance in *Hill Street Blues,* played the inevitable — and here, rather dull — police buddy, Sgt. Ted Coopersmith, with Norman Fell (in the pilot) and John Randolph (in the series) as Richie's father, and Helen Page Camp as his mother. Dugan went on to co-star in the rapidly canceled spook show *Shadow Chasers,* but later turned to directing, on series such as *Moonlighting* (on which he also guested), Bochco's *Hooperman,* and Cannell's *Wiseguy.*

Episode Guide

regular and recurring cast: Dennis Dugan (Richie Brockelman), Robert Hogan (Sgt. Ted Coopersmith), Barbara Bosson (Sharon Deterson), Norman Fell/John Randolph (Mr. Brockelman), Helen Page Camp (Mrs. Brockelman)

(1978)

RICHIE BROCKELMAN, PRIVATE EYE (pilot)

wr. Stephen Cannell, Steven Bochco, dir. Hy Averback

Expecting to find a seasoned veteran behind the door of Richie Brockelman's detective agency, Elizabeth Morton instead finds an eager young teenager yet to take on his first case.

with Suzanne Pleshette, Sharon Gless, Lloyd Bochner, William Windom, Ned Wilson, W.T. Zacha, Tom Falk, George Fisher, Harold Sylvester, Gloria LeRoy

A TITLE ON THE DOOR, AND A CARPET ON THE FLOOR

wr. Steven Bochco, dir. Arnold Laven

Richie's tiny operation is bought out by a larger, established organization, who ask him to join them ... but it's all a ruse to obtain access to one of his files.

with Carol Lynley, John Holland, Herb Voland, Rene Auberjonois, Amanda Harley, Charles Seibert, Jim McKrell, Virginia Gregg

ESCAPE FROM CAINE ABEL

wr. Peter Fischer, dir. David Moessinger

Richie rescues an accident victim and takes him to the hospital, but then his wife announces that the man was killed years ago in a plane crash, and the hospital staff deny that he was ever bought in.

with Howard Witt, Joanna DeWinter, Ayn Ruymen, Ward Costello

THE FRAMING OF PERFECT SYDNEY

wr. Michael Kozoll, dir. Arnold Laven

Attempting to clear his brother of a charge of embezzling, Richie promptly gets both himself and his brother accused of murder, and they are forced to go on the run.

with David Spielberg, Rosanna Huffman, Jerry Douglas, Tasha Martel

JUNK IT TO ME, BABY

wr. Robert Swanson, dir. Ivan Dixon

Richie is hired to bid for an old automobile at an auction, but two heavies get rather annoyed when Richie outbids them for it.

with Stanley Brock, Robert Phalen, Lisa Eilbacher, Nehemiah Persoff, Danny Dayton, Jake Mitchell, Gianni Russo

A PIGEON RIPE FOR THE PLUCKING

wr. Peter Fischer, dir. Ivan Dixon

Richie searches for his friend, a compulsive gambler, when his young daughter turns up at the office to announce he's gone missing.

with James Whitmore, Jr., Caroline McWilliams, Michele Stacy, Carole Shelyne, Lonny Chapman, John Perak

series ends

The Duke
April 1979–May 1979

Conrad Robert Salk was the son of a Chicago tough guy, and became a boxer. He arrived in Hollywood when he was 22 years old. Guest appearances in such early Warners television series as *77, Sunset Strip, Colt .45* and *Maverick* resulted in his securing the lead role in another Warners series, *Hawaiian Eye* (1959–1963). It was the first of many TV series in which Robert Conrad would star. Next came *The Wild Wild West* (1965–1970), followed by *The D.A.* (1971–'72), *The Men* (1972–'73), and later the role of Pasquinel in the mini-series *Centennial* (1978). Prior to *Centennial,* he had starred in Cannell's *Black Sheep Squadron.*

Set and filmed on location in Chicago, *The Duke* was Cannell's second series to star Robert Conrad, casting him to type as an ex-boxer from Chicago turned — yes — private detective. Having featured Conrad in a series based on someone else's life story, it was perhaps appropriate that Conrad's own colorful early years should form the background for *The Duke,* which was to run for only five episodes at the close of the 1978–'79 season.*

Co-starring with Conrad were former *Black Sheep Squadron* co-stars Red West as Sgt. Mick O'Brien, and Larry Manetti as the sharp and shifty Joe Cadillac, playing the life he would later fantasize about as Orville "Rick" Wright in *Magnum.* Patricia Conwell played socialite Dedra Smith. If the characters sounded as if they had just stepped out of a bad pulp novel, then that was no doubt intentional, but it was also perhaps the series' greatest problem. Whereas *The Rockford Files* sustained itself on characterization, and Garner parodied the tough guy image that *The Duke* represented, Conrad's Duke Ramsey really was a tough guy, and once past the initial introduction of the rather one-dimensional cast of players, there was little to sustain the show further. Ironically, if *Richie Brockelman* failed for being too unlike a traditional detective formula and offering viewers a nerdy hero, *The Duke* failed for being too typical of the genre; audiences had seen this once too often.

Conrad left *The Duke*—tentatively renewed, it was rumored—to take the lead in a now renowned turkey which the network had apparently assured him was a better long-term bet—the dismal *A Man Called Sloane,* a recreation of his *Wild Wild West* persona in a dated and low-rent *Man from UNCLE* environment. A pathetically misguided shadow of its inspiration, it bombed instantly, and is rapidly dismissed by Conrad and those who contributed to it. Conrad added another series to his resume in 1988, the snow-bound adventure series *High Mountain Rangers,* which scored high in the ratings as a pilot, but low as a series. A revamp, taking Conrad's character into the city streets, and named after his character *Jesse Hawkes,* died even quicker.

**Another series called* The Duke, *a sit-com in which the hero was also a boxer, had been on the air briefly in 1954.*

Episode Guide

regular and recurring cast: Robert Conrad (Oscar "Duke" Ramsey), Larry Manetti (Joe Cadillac), Red West (Sgt. Mick O'Brien), Patricia Conwell (Dedra Smith), Daphne Maxwell (Barbara Lyle)

(1979)

THE DUKE (pilot)

wr. Stephen Cannell, dir. Lawrence Doheny
After Oscar "Duke" Ramsey's final bout in the ring, his manager is murdered during an apparent robbery. Duke sets out to bring the killer to justice.
with Joey Green, Percy Rodriguez, Peter Haskell, Michael Baseleon, Frederick Herrick, Burton Collins, Lynwood Jones, Thom Huge

BLUES FOR THE DUKE

wr. Shel Willens, dir. Tony LoBianco
Two heavies posing as cops come looking for a cleaner at Duke's bar.
with Arnold Johnson, Frankie Hill, Byrne Piven, Mike Arcesi, Taylor Williams, Jean Davidson, Jack Owen, Barry Cullison, Ira Rogers, DeeDee Dolan

THE ZOO UNDER THE WACKER STREET BRIDGE

wr. Frank Abatemarco, dir. Dana Elcar
The Duke tries to help out a delinquent youngster pursued by mobsters.
with George Parry, Burton Collins, Felix Schuman, Jack Wallace, Ron Dean, Ben Rawnsley, Frank Howard, Gary Sinise, Tony Mockus, Robert Doyle

LONG AND THIN, LORNA LYNN

wr. Don Carlos Dunaway, dir. Lawrence Doheny
The Duke is harassed by a jealous boyfriend before he's even had the chance to meet the lady in question. Then, she enters his life.
with Brioni Farrell, Frank Miller, Don Manning, Steve Vujovic, Robert Swan, Wilbert Bradley, Dean Hill, Clair Nelson

NOTHING 'CEPT NOISE

wr. Stephen Cannell, dir. Robert Conrad
The Duke becomes involved in a moonshine war while searching for a missing girl.
with Roy Hine, LaVelda Fann, Jeff Mackay, Richard Henzel, Lance Kinsey, Dana Halsted, Dawn Davis, Wayne Cochran
series ends

Stone
January 1980–March 1980

After the veritable deluge of cop shows, good, bad and indifferent, during the 1970s, *Stone* came in with a lot to follow and very little to add. On the one hand, the public had seen it all before, and on the other, there was very little left to do with the cop show; it was Steven Bochco and Michael Kozoll with *Hill Street Blues* who would ring in the changes for the 1980s.

The cop shows of the '70s had been inspired and influenced mostly by Peter Yates' 1968 film *Bullitt*, written by Harry Kleiner and Alan Trustman (from Robert Pike's novel "Mute Witness") and Clint Eastwood's first three *Dirty Harry* films (*Dirty Harry, Magnum Force,* and *The Enforcer*, 1971, 1973, and 1976), directed by Don Seigel, Ted Post and James Fargo, and written by Dean Reisner, Harry and Rita Fink, John Milius and Stirling Silliphant; Cannell in particular had taken his cue from the anti-authority rebel/vigilante stance promoted by many of Eastwood's phenomenally successful movies. *Stone*, co-created by Richard Levinson and William Link, the team behind *Mannix* and *Columbo* among others, cast the popular television actor Dennis Weaver—formerly of Glen Larson's enjoyable *McCloud* (1970–'77)—in his second TV cop role, here playing a police officer who had become a best-selling author. The Eastwood factor came into play with the revelation that the authorities are not impressed with Stone's high public profile as a personality (the show's working title had been *Celebrity Cop*), and this puts him, like almost every other solo TV hero of the 1970s (including Weaver's own previous cop character *McCloud,* a series itself directly inspired by Eastwood's 1968 cop film, *Coogan's Bluff*) firmly up against suit-and-tie authority and official displeasure against "unorthodox behavior." The influence of Eastwood on the TV cop shows of this period, already mentioned elsewhere in chapters of this book, cannot be over-emphasized; indeed, the pilot story for *Stone* is a shameless swipe of the premise of the second *Dirty Harry* film, *Magnum Force*.

The character of Stone was quite plainly inspired by the career of real-life cop-turned-author Joseph Wambaugh, whose work had been a key factor in defining the cop shows of 1970s and early '80s. Numerous novels by Wambaugh had been turned into films with varying degrees of success, and TV had spawned *Police Story,* a strong but now-dated anthology series that ran from 1973 to 1977. Wambaugh's transition from printed page to wide screen had not been an entirely happy one, with the author taking full-page ads in *Variety* to disown and condemn the 1978 Robert Aldrich interpretation of his book *The Choirboys,* and ensuring that the rights to his novels thereafter remained in his control.* Wambaugh's role as a name advisor on David Gerber's *Police Story* was also, he claimed, an uphill struggle with

---

*One of those he ultimately trusted to film his work was Stuart Margolin (Angel on The Rockford Files). Margolin was a long-time friend of Rockford star James Garner, and—with Garner starring—they turned in an excellent adaptation of Wambaugh's The Glitter Dome with an army of old buddies from their past work together, including Margot Kidder of Nichols.

creative staff and network alike, and a spin-off series—*Police Woman* (1974–'78), starring Angie Dickinson—was made without any input from Wambaugh, and, as writer Richard Meyers pointed out in his excellent book *TV Detectives*, would "fly in the face of everything Wambaugh had attempted to achieve with *Police Story*."*

The twist in Cannell's fictionalization was that whereas Wambaugh had been inclined to leave the force after turning his experiences into fiction, Weaver's character stayed on as a cop. Had the show continued, it would have been interesting for the writers to play with the idea of having Stone's books turned into TV or films!† Sadly, the *Stone* series was notably undistinguished, and did not last long enough.

Cast as Stone's mean and unpleasant superior was the dependable character actor Pat Hingle, a performer with many fine characterizations behind him as a villain or a loveable old buddy. Two of those performances include supporting roles in the Clint Eastwood films *Hang 'em High* in 1967 and *The Gauntlet* in 1977. Barbara Rhoades was introduced rather half-heartedly as Stone's "love interest," and Nancy McKeon (later of the sit-com *The Facts of Life*) played Stone's daughter. For supporting players like Carmen Argenziano (later in Cannell's *Booker*), Eddie Barth (later in De Guere's *Simon and Simon*), and David Spielberg (later in *Wiseguy*), cast in bland and unchallenging paint-by-numbers roles, it was business as usual.

Compared with Weaver's previous series *McCloud*, a popular long-running success that had secured Weaver's future as a leading man, *Stone* was a remarkably routine series, and its failure to catch on was no great surprise. Although played by the same performer, the carefree and optimistic *McCloud* was a far more likeable and personable character than the troubled *Stone*, and Larson's series had a popular and likeable cast. Furthermore, *McCloud* had enjoyed a seven year run with healthy ratings, closing in 1977—it was hardly a fading memory with the audience. Clearly the network assumed that just dropping Weaver into a new cop show was a guarantee of success, but both he and Cannell had done better and everybody knew it. In fact, the colorful *McCloud* resembled the usual light-hearted Cannell approach far more than the dour *Stone*, with the same wry humor, camaraderie, absurd action and station-house politics that would later become synonymous with the Cannell signature. Audiences no doubt preferred to see the breezy Sam McCloud baiting J.D. Cannon's Chief Clifford and driving his colleagues crazy with mad stunts and improbable hunches than the troubled, grim and harassed Dan Stone; in the episode "What Do You People Want from Me?," Cannell devotes an entire story to the twin pressures of being a competent police officer and a best-selling author with deadlines to meet. Cannell has produced other episodes in which his heroes were under pressure (it was a recurring theme in both *The Rockford Files* and *The Greatest American Hero*), but again, in *Stone*, it was done straight. Trapped by his previous persona of McCloud (when all said and done, only a wiser and older version of Chester from *Gunsmoke*), nobody wanted to see Sam McCloud come unraveled, and although the series had a running joke about Weaver's partner (played by Robby Weaver, his real-life son) being named Buck Rogers, the rest of the series was resolutely hard-going.

This is not to say the series didn't have its moments. Juanita Bartlett turned in an episode

---

**Later,* Police Woman *would be parodied mercilessly in the 1977 MTM series* The Betty White Show *for CBS. Not entirely uncoincidentally perhaps,* Police Woman *aired opposite MTM's superlative* Lou Grant*, also on CBS!*

†*A slight hint of how this might have turned out is provided some years later by "Killer in a Hallowe'en Mask," an enjoyable episode of Cannell and Lupo's* Hunter *written by Stephen Katz and directed by Sidney Hayers, in which Hunter and McCall are ordered to serve as technical advisors on a fictional cop show in another doomed attempt by their superiors to get them out of the way. This was a theme also explored in episodes of* Hill Street Blues, Cagney and Lacey, *and Lupo's* Hardball *with similar sly humor.*

titled "But Can She Type?," in which the appointment of a woman cop in the precinct provokes an outbreak of chauvinism, and Gordon Dawson, another *Rockford Files* regular, wrote an episode featuring Mary Frann (used twice in *Rockford* and later of *Newhart*) as a psychic called in to help the police, drawing parallels between her self-promoting publicity seeking and Stone's determinedly low-key celebrity status. Richard Christian Matheson and Thomas Szollosi, future story editors of *The A-Team*, had Stone investigating the unpleasant colleague of a dead officer in "The Partner," and Donald Bellisario, ex–*Black Sheep Squadron* and later creator of *Magnum, Airwolf* and *Quantum Leap,* wrote "Death Run," in which the city is plagued by copycat killings from an unpublished manuscript of Stone's. Phil DeGuere, ex–*Black Sheep, Baretta* and *City of Angels,* and later creator of *Simon and Simon,* teamed up with Stephen McPherson to come up with an episode about nuclear blackmail. In surprising contrast, Cannell's own contributions, the pilot and three other episodes, all had a more typical, ordinary and obvious premise. "Homicide," written and directed by Cannell, was particularly farcical. Here we were in typical Cannell territory, with a defiant Stone relentlessly tailing and staking out the residence of a psychopathic killer (Chuck Connors), who has been released by the liberal folly of a soft judge. Convinced that it is only a matter of time before the killer strikes again, Stone is determined to ensure that he provides the protection for the public where the authorities have failed. Not only does the episode take itself desperately seriously, lacking the all-important light touch of Cannell's later populist vigilante yarns, but far from being a serious study of judiciary incompetence, "Homicide" is quite hysterical in all senses of the word, as Connors' Thomas Littleman (his name being Cannell's sole stab at humor in this episode) — a huge, towering, bedraggled, bear-like figure — leers and drools and gloats with an eye-swiveling venom and insanity that he would not have the chance to repeat for almost another decade, until becoming the scenery-chewing, cast-munching wolfman Janos Skorzeny, highlight of Frank Lupo's 1987 series *Werewolf.* As the demented Littleman, this crazed killer is so obviously raving mad that even the daftest judge in the country would think twice about letting him loose!

Stone failed in a time-slot on ABC that offered no significant or similar series scheduled against it (although it did have to compete with the politically opposite but popular *M*A*S*H*), laying the blame squarely on the shoulders of the show. The series' failure did no noticeable harm to the reputations of either Cannell or Weaver; in fact, when Cannell left Universal after *Stone* to form his own company, ABC bankrolled Cannell's first efforts, and bailed him out of financial difficulty in the early days. Robby Weaver went on to play a small recurring role in Cannell's later ABC series *The Greatest American Hero,* and the entire Weaver clan turned up some years later in a 1985 episode of Bellisario's *Magnum,* "Let Me Hear the Music," written by Jay Huguely and directed by David Hemmings. Not surprisingly, Weaver, Jr. also guested in *Gunsmoke* and *McCloud,* and again with his dad in the superb mini-series *Centennial.* Weaver Sr., followed *Stone* with the pacifist mini-series *Pearl,* an anti-war World War II melodrama based on events at Pearl Harbor, which ironically took him into the cast of the short-lived military soap *Emerald Point* in 1983. In 1987 he played a rancher/medic in the absurd *Buck James,* which lasted half a season. With three hit series under his belt — *Gunsmoke* (1955–1975; Weaver left after nine seasons in 1964), *Gentle Ben* (1967–1969) and *McCloud*— the Missouri-born former athlete and air force man turned actor was perfectly able to survive his occasional failures,* and continued to work extensively in TV movies until his

---

*The short-lived Kentucky Jones *(1964–65) was Weaver's first and only failure before* Stone.

death in 2006 ... including *The Return of Sam McCloud* (1989)! Levinson and Link, who had proposed the show to Cannell and asked him to show-run for them, moved on to the more demure author/investigator exploits of *Murder She Wrote,* a cynical post–*Columbo* sell-out. And Cannell, producer Alex Beaton, and secretary Grace Curcio moved out of their comfortable Universal offices and into the more modest headquarters of Stephen J. Cannell Productions....

Episode Guide

regular and recurring cast: Dennis Weaver (Det. Sgt. Dan Stone), Pat Hingle (Chief Paulton), Robby Weaver (Det. Buck Rogers), Joby Baker (Murray Weinstock), Nancy McKeon (Jill Stone), Barbara Rhoades (Britt Bickle), Mel Stewart (Captain Patchett), Carmen Argenziano (Det. Guttardo), Eddie Barth (Sgt. Vandis), David Spielberg (Lt. Roth)

(1980)

STONE (pilot)

wr. Stephen Cannell, Richard Levinson, dir. Corey Allen

Divorced by his wife, who is seeing a fellow cop, and despised by his boss for becoming a successful author of police fiction, Dan Stone must investigate fellow officers who are taking the law into their own hands as vigilante judge-and-jury killers.

with Roy Thinnes, Mariette Hartley, Vic Morrow, Tara Buckman, Colby Chester, Alvin Ing, Michael Vandever, Gregory Michaels, Jack Kutcher, Paul Sorensen, Joey Forman, Kim Hamilton, Tom Pedi, Mel Stewart, Steve Allen, William Bronder, Phil Pine

DEEP SLEEPER

wr. Don Carlos Dunaway, dir. Winrich Kolbe

Stone is assigned the task of returning a sleeper agent who has infiltrated the mob safely back to the force after the only other officer besides his boss aware of his double identity is found dead.

with Robert Hogan, Sharon Acker, Paul Lambert, Priscilla Pointer, Granville Van Dusen, Shannon Terhune

BUT CAN SHE TYPE?

wr. Juanita Bartlett, dir. Corey Allen

Stone defends the appointment of a woman cop, and together they investigate the suicide of a construction worker whose latest project has collapsed with fatal results.

with Trisha Noble, Karen MacMahon, Denny Miller, Luke Andreas

HOMICIDE

wr. and dir. Stephen Cannell

Stone keeps a homicidal killer under observation after a soft judge has given him bail.

with Chuck Connors, Alex Henteloff, Eddie Fontaine, Taylor Lacher

THE MAN IN THE FULL TOLEDO

wr. Gordon Dawson, dir. Paul Stanley

Stone finds himself allied with a fellow celebrity — a psychic!

with Mary Frann, Richard McKenzie, Dolph Sweet, Norman Burton, Alexandra Stoddart, Mario Rocuzzo, Robert Phillips

JUST A LITTLE BLOW BETWEEN FRIENDS

wr. Stephen Cannell, dir. Corey Allen

Stone's daughter is arrested at the airport for drug smuggling.

with Beth Brickell, Richard Cox, Tammy Taylor, Denice Kumagai, Fernando Roca, Ben Frank, Ray Girardin, Charles Weldon

DEATH RUN

wr. Donald Bellisario, dir. Harry Winer

Copycat killings terrorize the city based on Stone's new book. The kicker — it hasn't been published yet.

with Jonathan Goldsmith, Dennis Howard, Clare Nono, Luke Andreas, Robert Clotworthy

67 HOURS, 24 MINUTES AND COUNTING

wr. Phil De Guere, Stephen McPherson, dir. Winrich Kolbe

Stone receives a delivery of plutonium ... and a blackmail threat.

with Michael Cavenaugh, Antony Carbone, Nicholas Hormann, Michael Prince, Lisa Figus, James Blendick, Lew Brown

What Do You People Want from Me?

wr. Stephen Cannell, dir. Rod Holcomb

Stone comes under dual pressure from police and publishing duties.

with Roger E. Mosley, Amanda McBroom

The Partner

wr. Richard Christian Matheson, Thomas Szollosi, dir. Guy Magar

When a cop is killed, Stone is assigned his dislikeable young partner.

with W.K. Stratton, Jorge Cervera, Jr., Diane Shalet

series ends

Unsold Pilots (1)

Like all television producers, Cannell has had his fair share of pilots that did not go to series. While *Rockford, Baretta,* and *Black Sheep Squadron* were all flying high in the '70s, Cannell was wasting no time in preparing pilot formats for further potential hit series. Some, like "The November Plan" for *City of Angels, The Duke,* and *Stone,* did indeed go to series, but others either didn't work, didn't sell, or both.

Scott Free (1976) starred Michael Brandon in the lead, and was made by Meta Rosenberg's and James Garner's Cherokee company; it covered typical *Maverick/Rockford* territory, but lacked a star with Garner's easy-going ambience to front it. Brandon was Tony Scott, a professional gambler being pursued by numerous interested parties who wanted a piece of land he had won, and a piece of his hide to go with it. Co-starring were Susan St. James, Robert Loggia, Stephen Nathan, Allan Rich, Cal Bellini, Dehl Berti, and Cannell regulars Ken Swofford and Paul Koslo. Most of Cannell's regular collaborators of the period were on hand, including Jacques Marquette on photography, Mike Post and Pete Carpenter on music, Alex Beaton producing, and *Rockford* regular William Wiard directing. It was not the stuff of series, with *Variety* concluding that it was "such a remarkably consistent portrayal of an unsympathetic character that it is likely that weekly viewers would find the cynicism too hard to take on a regular basis."

Three pilots failed to take off in 1978, *Doctor Scorpion* (first called *Shack*), *The Jordan Chance,* and *The Gypsy Warriors. Doctor Scorpion* starred Nick Mancuso, later to go to series for Cannell in *Stingray,* and was Cannell's first attempt to dabble in comic-strip fantasy. A hopelessly bungled and confusing secret agent thriller, it starred Mancuso as Jonathan Shackleford, a cynical, weary and retired former spy called back into service by his shifty and unscrupulous bosses for one more mission to avenge the death of a friend. Co-starring were Christine Lahti, Sandra Kearns, Richard Herd (later in the *Greatest American Hero* pilot), Denny Miller, Roscoe Lee Browne, Granville Van Dusen, Philip Sterling (of *City Of Angels*), Lincoln Kilpatrick, Joseph Ruskin, and Bill Lucking (Colonel Lynch on *The A-Team*) as the unfortunate friend. The Doctor Scorpion of the title referred to villain Roscoe Lee Browne as the evil Doctor Cresus.

The Jordan Chance was typical Cannell fare, and was an attempt to find a new series format for Raymond Burr, formerly of *Perry Mason* and *Ironside*. Another collaboration between Cannell and Roy Huggins, Burr would play lawyer Frank Jordan who'd been — all together now — imprisoned for a crime he didn't commit. As a result, he now worked on suspect cases to free other poor folk who'd been unjustly imprisoned. Thus they were the lucky recipients of — *The Jordan Chance.*

The last of 1978's no-go projects was the slow and dreary adventure drama *The Gypsy Warriors,* the first of two attempts by Cannell to launch Tom Selleck's TV career before Glen Larson and Donald Bellisario hit pay dirt with *Magnum, p.i.* The pilot was also another attempt by Cannell to do a World War II series after the unfortunate early demise of *Black Sheep Squadron*. Here, he was partnered with Cannell regular James Whitmore, Jr., with guest players Kathryn Leigh Scott, Lina Raymond, Michael Lane, Albert Paulsen, Kenneth Tigar, William Westley, and Hubert Noel. Selleck and Whitmore were freedom fighting spies who posed as traveling gypsies — probably not that smart a move in Germany and occupied France at the time.

The second attempt to launch Selleck in a series was pure Cannell through and through. *Boston and Kilbride* (1979), also known as *The Chinese Typewriter,* again starred Tom Selleck with James Whitmore, Jr., this time as private detectives Tom Boston and Jim Kilbride. "We'll do anything as long as it doesn't land us in jail," they announce rather optimistically, and the stage is set for some inevitable convoluted Cannell chaos.

Boston and Kilbride were really Magnum and Beamer, with a typically clever Cannell plot. Selleck is the muscle of the team, bright and breezy, Whitmore is the brains, precise and methodical, divorced, employed by a think-tank, and father to a smart son. Selleck's Boston is — surprise — an ex–Vietnam vet (compulsory for a TV hero in 1979), a former paratrooper and a weapons expert, and — surprise again — has written several "cheap detective novels." The villain of the piece is embezzler Donald Devlin, played by William Daniels, who had already appeared in *The Rockford Files* and would later play the wonderful creation Dr. Mark Craig in the series *St. Elsewhere*. Also in the cast were Don Ameche, Jaime Lyn Bauer, Lane Bradbury, and Kathryn Leigh Scott. The story opens with the ubiquitous Beller Airlines losing a ten million dollar aircraft, and Boston and Kilbride's subsequent investigations take place in Hawaii, at numerous locations later to be used for *Magnum* the following year, including Robin's Nest. Indeed, Selleck's Boston is so like Magnum the character, and the locations and plot so like *Magnum* the series, that any uninformed viewer is likely to get very confused indeed should they stumble onto an airing of the film midway! After Selleck's smash-and-grab approach to the assignment fails, Whitmore develops an elaborate scam that not only foils Devlin, but the FBI and CIA as well. And what Cannell-conceived scam wouldn't?

Night Rider (1979, and no relation to Glen Larson's successful *Knight Rider* of 1982) was Cannell's second foray into the land of the comic-strip hero before striking gold with *The Greatest American Hero*. Here, David Selby (formerly of *Dark Shadows,* later of *Falcon Crest*), played Lord Thomas Earl, a masked avenger-type who was a cross between the Scarlet Pimpernel and Zorro (as we have observed, the Cannell house of ideas was no stranger to Republic serials). Also in the cast were Percy Rodriguez, Kim Cattrall, George Grizzard, Anthony Herrera, Pernell Roberts, Harris Yulin, and Whit Bissell, as well as another former masked avenger, Van Williams, formerly TV's *Green Hornet* in the 1960s.

Cannell's final unsold pilot for Universal was *Nightside* in 1980, produced the year *Stone* went to series. It was a collaboration with Glen Larson, and would appear to have been completed by Larson after Cannell started it. The premise of the pilot was one that Cannell would return to twice in later years — crazy cops — with *The Last Precinct* in 1987 and *Broken Badges* in 1990. However, the finished product stars Larson regular Doug McClure and has the visual look of Larson's Universal series, right down to the opening titles. McClure plays Danny Dandoy, a rule-bending wiseguy cop, with Michael D. Roberts of *Baretta* doing his usual hip jivin' dude routine as "Greenlight" (shades of *The Last Precinct*), an equally outrageous ambulance driver. The pair of them work nights as the title suggests, and so the inevitable comical authority figure pairs McClure with a freshly trained sergeant as a partner in the hope that he can be a calming influence, only to find that the two of them get on famously (shades of *Hunter* and *Sledge Hammer*) — the raw recruit is a naive bespectacled computer nerd, easily manipulated and as green as a berry (shades of Bozinsky in *Riptide*). "There is no manual when you're working on nights," McClure tells his partner somewhat erroneously as they patrol Cliche City populated by TV stereotypes. "People act like there's a perpetual full moon. It's not like in the movies." No, it's like on TV, but Cannell's rebel-within-the-system m.o. doesn't work here because the characters aren't noble or deep-down responsible, they're dangerous jokers entrusted with an important job. Unlike the oafs from the teen-targeted *Police Academy* films, these guys are out there on the streets. This one tries to be *Police Story* played for laughs, but it doesn't quite come off. For Cannell and Larson, it's a rather clumsy misfire, and careless, cynical thinking on their part. It's easy to be smart with hindsight, but cops partying with hookers when they should be on duty, and ambulance drivers chasing around for cab fares like maniacs just isn't that amusing to a general public surrounded by police corruption, unsafe streets, inefficiency, tragedy, and incompetence, and Cannell should perhaps have figured that out; even the foul mess the movies made of Joseph Wambaugh's novel *The Choirboys,* an obvious source of inspiration here, wasn't playing for laughs. Other cast members included Michael Cornelison, John De Lancie, Roy Jenson, Melinda Naud, Janice Lynde, Danny Wells as a reporter hanging around the station for a story, Michael Winslow (of the *Police Academy* films) and Jason Kincaid.

Part Two: The Golden Years

Tenspeed and Brownshoe
January 1980–June 1980

> *"Wait a minute — you said that because we gave back the money, and we did end up catching a German war criminal and ten mobsters and neo-Nazis, that the judge might go easy!"*

Tenspeed and Brownshoe was the first production that Cannell created for his own studio, and the critics hailed it as the new *Rockford Files*. Broadcast by ABC in the first half of 1980 as a mid-season replacement, the series bombed rapidly, although Cannell completed the standard thirteen episode half-season run. "I'm proud of the fact that I did (*The Rockford Files*)" said Cannell in a 1983 interview for *Emmy* magazine, "but I'm just as proud of *Tenspeed and Brownshoe*, which will never be seen again. I took just as much joy from the manufacturing of those thirteen hours, which I really loved, as I did from *The Rockford Files*." Cannell's commitment is profoundly evident in the episode credits; he wrote the pilot and wrote or co-wrote eight of the twelve episodes, even directing one of his scripts himself, farming the other writing chores out to reliable *Rockford* veterans.

Song and dance man Ben Vereen was con-man E.L. "Tenspeed" Turner, and Jeff Goldblum, later to enjoy a successful film career, was former stockbroker and aspiring private eye Lionel "Brownshoe" Whitney. Whitney just happened to be an avid reader of pulp detective novels (he favored the Mark Savage brand, which also just happened to be decorated with Cannell's name and photograph as author!). He was clearly modeled on Richie Brockelman, a character Cannell could quite conspicuously not let go of, and like Rockford's dad in "White on White and Nearly Perfect," Lionel has his nose buried in a bad pulp novel when we first meet him. When we first encounter Tenspeed Turner, he is rapidly switching stories and identities (some of Tenspeed's scams in the pilot were re-used in the pilot for *The Quest*) as he thinks on his feet to avoid the usual army of Cannell's typical gun-toting thugs who have turned up at their bank deposit boxes on the very same day Turner has decided to rip them off. (This being TV, Turner is not stealing the mob money for himself, but avenging a victimized friend brutalized by the gangster's loan sharks). After continuously crossing paths with the gormless Whitney, who is on the verge of a suit-and-tie job and a ball-and-chain marriage, the two of them abscond together, in deeper than they ever dreamed, caught between two warring factions of gangsters and Nazis! Indeed, we're not ten minutes into the pilot before we've seen a variety of Cannell trademarks — a scam, flying cars, cops, and mobsters. Enthused with their success, and exhilarated by the adventure, Whitney cajoles Turner into taking a semi-straight path and joining him as a detective team.

For all its similarities to the oddball characters, comic-book gangsters and unlikely detectives of *The Rockford Files*, *Tenspeed and Brownshoe* was very much a predecessor of the body of work that would make up Cannell's early '80s output, his most popular and successful period.

Having come to the end of his eight year contract with Universal, Cannell had the option of signing on for another few years (during which, he reasoned, he would be sitting at the same desk, doing the same sort of shows, and getting just a little bit richer) or taking the plunge and breaking out on his own as an independent. Mostly this was so that he could work on the projects he chose to and be answerable only to himself, even though he had never been particularly dissatisfied during his time at Universal, calling them "the best years of my life." Paralleling Whitney's boredom with the specter of safe security he saw looming ahead for him, Cannell struck out on his own, forming his own small company, and making a deal with the ABC network for three pilots (*Tenspeed and Brownshoe, Greatest American Hero*, and *The Quest*). Not surprisingly, given Cannell's frame of mind, all three series concerned very ordinary people living safe, mundane, comfortable lives who are suddenly thrown into chaotic and unpredictable adventure as they nervously live out their fantasies. As Lionel's astonishingly rude future mother-in-law (Jayne Meadows) and her overbearing husband (three-time *Rockford* guest Robert Webber) organize his future life of married bliss and a pre-arranged boost up the social ladder en route to the airport, Lionel laments to his fiancé, "I don't like him making decisions about my career without asking me! I'm bored with the stock market, I don't want to live in University Park! I don't like it there! I told you that, and I told your father that! He's gonna come over there and tell me that the lawn needs cutting and that I should paint the front door, and that's not the way I want to live!"

Ironically, in leaving the safe confines of Universal and making *Tenspeed and Brownshoe* for himself, Cannell was in danger of losing the very same things Lionel Whitney was rejecting for his fantasy life as a detective. As Cannell told *Electronic Media* in 1986, it was like "sailing a ship with no rudder. It was much worse than I ever thought it would be. I realized that I was running a company that was literally going to end up taking my car, my house, and everything else."

Fortunately for the newly-formed Stephen J. Cannell Productions, ABC came through with more money, and sent all three pilots to series, although only *Greatest American Hero* stayed on the air for any length of time. On *Tenspeed*, and particularly *The Quest*, which would be filmed in the South of France, Cannell took an expensive bath. Even with *Riptide* and *Hardcastle and McCormick* joining *Greatest American Hero* as modest hits a couple of years later, it was quite a few years before any of the shows went into profit, and it wasn't until Cannell's success with *The A-Team* (ironically, made in partnership with Universal!) that his bold venture started to see light at the end of the tunnel. Cannell quickly learned, he said, to hire as large an accounting department as he had a writing department, as he wasn't getting the daily budget reports he had grown accustomed to while at Universal.

The pilot film for *Tenspeed and Brownshoe* had feature film production values. *Variety* maintained that elements of the *Tenspeed* pilot resembled sequences to be found in the feature films *What's Up, Doc?* and *The In-Laws*, while *Hollywood Reporter* noted that "like Cannell's earlier detective series *Richie Brockelman*, the fun comes from watching two basically nice but inept guys bungle their way to success."

The premise around which the series was based was that Whitney was naive and gullible, and all Tenspeed's skills as a consummate con-man were needed to bail him out. Consequently, the series was littered with *Rockford*-isms, including wacky characters, complicated scams, stressed-out villains, and gormless thugs. Lionel Whitney, nicknamed Brownshoe by Turner ("You're a three-piece suit, you know that?") has everything safely mapped out for him in life, and he is indeed one of Cannell's amiable losers, the sort of flotsam who would drift into Jim Rockford's life just as he was about to go fishing.... As he feels the dog collar and leash tightening around his neck, a differently dog-collared phony Reverend Tenspeed finds a net closing in on him, and an unlikely partnership is born....

It was a partnership that very nearly didn't happen. Following the enormous success of the mini-series *Roots,* in which veteran performer Vereen participated, ABC were very keen to have him for *Tenspeed and Brownshoe.* Despite ABC's interest, Cannell was doubtful; Vereen had turned down a very high offer to reprise his role in *Roots II,* but ABC insisted he be approached, and Cannell went through the formality of offering it to him. To everyone's surprise, Vereen liked the role, and the idea of a TV series. For Brownshoe, Cannell was looking for a Ryan O'Neal type (wonder of wonders, O'Neal had starred in *What's Up, Doc?*), and had to be talked round to seeing Jeff Goldblum in the role.

If Goldblum was Brockelman reincarnated, then Vereen's character was composed of all the *Rockford* driftwood — Angel Martin or Gandolph Fitch with a conscience. But it seemed as though Cannell's odd couple were a little too odd for the viewing public to warm to. The series closed at the end of the season.

Guesting in the pilot, and sadly under-used as gangster Tommy Todesco, was Richard Romanus, regularly cast in action/adventure shows as a hood after his memorable supporting role in Martin Scorsese's superb 1973 feature *Mean Streets.* Both Romanus, as Todesco, and Larry Manetti (of *Black Sheep Squadron, The Duke,* and *Magnum*) as hood Chip Vincent would reappear in a later episode. Cannell even indulged in a cameo appearance himself; after all, it was fantasy time — time to live the dream.

Episode Guide

regular cast: Jeff Goldblum (Lionel "Brownshoe" Whitney), Ben Vereen (E.L. "Tenspeed" Turner)

(1980)

TENSPEED AND BROWNSHOE (pilot)

wr. Stephen Cannell, dir. E.W. Swackhamer

Despairing dreamer Lionel Whitney is a stockbroker heading reluctantly towards marriage and security when Early Leroy Turner, a hustler and ex-con, barges into his life, pursued by both mobsters and the American Nazi Party.

with Robyn Douglass, Richard Romanus, Robert Webber, Jayne Meadows, John Harkins, Simone Griffeths, Larry Manetti, Luke Andreas, A.C. Weary, Peter Brocco, Edwin Owens, Nicholas Worth, John Zee, Peter MacLean, Frank Farmer, Argentina Brunetti, Bill Capizzi, Robert Casper

THE ROBIN TUCKER'S ROSELAND ROOF AND BALLROOM MURDER

wr. Stephen Cannell, dir. Arnold Laven

Having formed their own detective agency together, Lionel is promptly kidnapped by his own client.

with Elayne Heilveil, John Pleshette, Leo Gordon, Mark Giardino, Lee V. Paul, Bruce Fisher

SAVAGE SAYS THERE'S NO FREE LUNCH

wr. Stephen Cannell, dir. John Patterson

Lionel becomes infatuated with a young woman who claims that business executives where she works are trying to kill her.

with Janice Heiden, Denny Miller, Tony Burton, Edward Bell, Michael Fairman, Darrell Zwerling

SAVAGE SAYS THAT'S WHAT FRIENDS ARE FOR

wr. Shel Willens, dir. Reza Badiyi

Lionel is hired by an old friend for an investigation to clear his name, but his wife, who Lionel desires, maintains that his friend is suffering from paranoia.

with Cassie Yates, James Murtaugh, John Zenda, Tom Stechulte, Sandy Ward, Martin Kove, Deborah Shelton, Dave Shelley

The Sixteen Byte Data Chip and the Brown-Eyed Fox

wr. Rudolph Borchert, dir. Arnold Laven

The kidnapping of a computer wizard leads Whitney and Turner into a web of abduction and embezzlement.

with Lynne Moody, Dennis Burkley, Laurence Haddon, Harry Basch, Richard Dix, Lewis Arquette, Stanley Brock, Michael Ensign, Tom Reason

The Millionaire's Life

wr. Stephen Cannell, dir. Georg Stanford Brown

Turner makes the serious mistake of conning money from a crooked millionaire.

with James Sloyan, Ben Hammer, Floyd Levine, Sheldon Feldner, Meeno Peluce, Alan Braunstein

Savage Says the Most Dangerous Bird Is the Jailbird

wr. Stephen Cannell, dir. Reza Badiyi

Whitney and Turner have the misfortune to run into Crazy Tommy Todesco again.

with Richard Romanus, Shelley Smith, Richard Dimitri, Larry Manetti, Woody Eney, Luke Andreas, Bill Capizzi

It's Easier to Pass an Elephant Through the Eye of a Needle Than to Pass a Bad Check in Bel-Air

wr. Stephen Cannell, Juanita Bartlett, dir. Ivan Dixon

One of Turner's scams is interrupted by the arrival of his nephew and a mobster who is convinced that Turner has something of his.

with James Bond III, Dick Anthony Williams, Robert Alda, Rockne Tarkington, Henry G. Sanders

Loose Larry's List of Losers

wr. Stephen Cannell, dir. Rod Holcomb

Turner has a new hard-nosed parole officer.... Unfortunately, he's just given Lionel a stolen watch as a birthday present.

with Nicolas Coster, Candice Azzarra, Robert Hirschfield

This One's Gonna Kill Ya

wr. and dir. Stephen Cannell

Bored by a lack of cases, Lionel drops the duo into trouble when he begins investigating a forty-year-old murder mystery.

with James Whitmore, Jr., John Anderson, James Parkes, Patricia Gaul, Lynn Ferring, Bruce Tuthill, Fred Stuthman, Stephen Cannell

Untitled

wr. Juanita Bartlett, Stephen Cannell, dir. Rod Holcomb

A Hollywood talent scout is about to get himself a title by marrying a cleaning lady whom he has discovered is actually a Russian countess ... but the wedding is about to be hindered by the attentions of a crooked history professor pursuing a valuable heirloom.

with Rene Auberjonois, Claude Earl Jones, Lesley Woods, Mario Rocuzzo, James Gosa, Harvey Gold, Derek Murcott, Jeff Mackay

The Treasure of Sierra Madre Street

wr. Gordon Dawson, dir. Harry Winer

Turner is secretly steering the duo out of trouble by sending the more potentially dangerous cases to Lionel's rival, but he's not so quick to unload an investigation into a hired killer now residing in an asylum under the impression that he's a visitor from outer space...!

with Lynn Carlin, Pamela Brull, Bart Burns, Red West, Maddy McGuire, Bert Conway, Don Pedro Colley, David Chow, Ted Lehmann, John Volstadt, Kendall Carly Brown, James Whitworth, Michael C. Gwynne, Sondra Blake, Timothy Agolia Carey

Diamonds Aren't Forever

wr. Juanita Bartlett, dir. Chuck Bowman

Turner attempts to impress Lionel's visiting parents, still smarting over Lionel's flight from wedded bliss, by borrowing a flashy office and car.

with John Hillerman, Dana Wynter, Camilla Sparv, Simone Griffeths, Thaao Penghlis, Kurt Grayson, Dick Yarmy

series ends

The Greatest American Hero
March 1981–February 1983

The Greatest American Hero was a genuine curiosity, and marked a radical departure for Cannell from his standard detective-oriented fare. Setting the scene for the more frivolous, light-hearted and easy-going direction his series would take during the course of the 1980s, it was a sort of Superman-meets-Spider-Man spoof with a pleasing naive charm and a dash of then-fashionable *Close Encounters* influence thrown in for good measure. Starring the personable young newcomer William Katt, it concerned the exploits of schoolteacher Ralph Hinckley,* who inadvertently becomes the Billy Batson–like recipient of a powerful super-suit bestowed upon him by benevolent aliens in a Spielbergian saucer. Ralph doesn't particularly want the ill-fitting item, but he's got it — as well as FBI agent Bill Maxwell (Robert Culp), a hard-as-nails, straight-as-an-arrow gung-ho tough guy, to make sure he uses it for truth, justice and the American Way! There's only one catch ... Ralph's lost the instruction book. His powers, as he gradually discovers them in a series of comic incidents, include teleportation, flying, extra strength, invulnerability, ESP, and anything else the writers could dream up. It just makes him a generally pretty souped-up super-guy. But Ralph doesn't want the difficulties and embarrassment of being a super-hero in a world where there are none except in the funny books. He teaches a class of juvenile under-achievers, and he enjoys his work too much to become a full-time flake. Unfortunately, these crises just keep on coming up....

The premise of the pilot film, written by Cannell and directed by Rod Holcomb, is one of Cannell's most imaginative, with a puppet politician of the far right — a reactionary Vice-President with few original thoughts in his head — being groomed for the presidency after a coup to be instigated by a Moral Majority millionaire and his bogus born-again religious fanatic followers. The pilot's opening scene is intriguingly bizarre, with evangelist Nelson Corey's mini-army of shaven-headed thugs pursuing an FBI man (stunt director Bob Minor) through the desert in dune-buggy contraptions and then, having halted his escape, surrounding him and bursting into a rousing chorus of "Onward, Christian Soldiers!"† When our heroes Ralph and Bill encounter the poor man, his lifeless body has been retrieved by the aliens; he descends from the alien saucer as a zombie messenger, dead but happy, to present Ralph with the super-suit, while the car radio ominously hammers the point home by mysteriously broadcasting the unmistakable sounds of one of Hitler's Nazi rallies. Ralph and Bill have their first assignment.

---

*Later briefly renamed Hanley or "Mr. H" in the series for a while after a real-life Hinckley took some pot shots at then–President Reagan.

†*The very first shot, which shows desert life scuttling around in the sand, the silence suddenly shattered by the arrival of the dune-buggies hurtling over the hilly terrain into shot, was lifted wholesale a couple of years later for the opening of Donald Bellisario's pilot for* Airwolf, *with the super-powered helicopter shattering the silence.*

Highlights of the pilot included a little kid instructing Ralph on how to take off into flight comic-book style ("You see, it's my first time" Ralph explains sheepishly to the boy), and Ralph, reluctantly and with great embarrassment trying on the suit in the privacy of his bedroom while the sonorous tones of Ted Knight narrating the *Super-Friends* TV cartoon series echo through the house courtesy of his young son — serving only to heighten Ralph's misery.

Ralph's first flight is a disaster — he flies screaming into a brick wall with a horrible thud — and while he's unconscious in the alleyway where he's fallen, a vagrant has helped himself to his clothes and a private detective hired by his shallow ex-wife to accumulate evidence for a custody case takes incriminating pictures to show the court what a nut he is. To make matters worse, Ralph had only dared to use the suit that first time because he was late for the hearing! Unavoidably delayed, Ralph is forced to change into fresh clothes in a shabby toilet where, inevitably, someone else enters with his young boy to use the facilities for somewhat more conventional purposes. Ralph is immediately branded a weirdo and hauled off to the nearest funny farm ... still in his suit, where his heartbroken girlfriend/lawyer Pam Davidson (a well-cast Connie Sellecca) discovers him. FBI man Bill Maxwell is not faring much better — following his own nerve-racking experiences with the saucer, he has taken off on a drinking binge, and then — when he recovers — finds that Ralph won't take his orders and Pam won't play ball as his obedient Girl Friday. As the story proceeds, Ralph rescues Bill from the bad guys and the President from an assassination, and the duo reveal their secret to a skeptical, and then rather faint, Pam Davidson.

William Katt, starring in the show, was then probably best known for his role as Sissy Spacek's prom date in the influential 1976 shocker *Carrie,* a feature film that deservedly made a star out of Spacek for her *tour-de-force* portrayal of the title character. A major influence on the horror genre during the late '70s and early '80s, Brian De Palma's film also starred then-unknowns Nancy Allen and John Travolta, but for Katt, the big breaks remained elusive. The highly touted *Butch and Sundance: the Early Years* (1979) failed to take off as expected, and the gentle, witty romance *First Love* (1978), with Susan Dey in between roles in *The Partridge Family* and *L.A. Law,* also sank without trace. Later films following his stint on *The Greatest American Hero* (many in the fantasy genre, such as Disney's dino-turkey *Baby* and the horror film *House*) also failed to establish him on the wide screen, and Katt later returned to TV. Having grown up playing on the set of the 1960s courtroom drama *Perry Mason,* in which his actress mother Barbara Hale co-starred (and who portrayed his mother in the *Greatest American Hero* episode "Who's Woo in America"), he was a natural for the role of youthful investigator Paul Drake when Hale and series star Raymond Burr returned to their roles in the late '80s for a series of successful *Perry Mason* TV movies. Katt doesn't appear in all of these; he later took the lead in a second series for Cannell, the disappointing *Top of the Hill,* only to return to the *Perry Mason* series after the show was junked.

Playing the lawyer Pam Davidson, Ralph's girlfriend and later wife in *Greatest American Hero,* was the bright and attractive Connie Sellecca, a former model and TV actress who had experienced a similar uphill climb of false starts and dashed hopes. An earlier fantasy series the previous year, *Beyond Westworld* (inspired by the features *Westworld* and *Futureworld,* but which owed more to the 1960s series *The Invaders*) in which she had co-starred, was canned by CBS, who pulled the plug after only a single episode was aired. Sellecca had not been much luckier with her 1978 series, a dim candy floss show about stewardesses called *Flying High,* which didn't. Sellecca also appeared in the second pilot for the aborted *Captain America* TV series, and later kept the comic-book/serials connection alive by marrying actor Gil Gerard

Connie Sellecca (left) and Robert Culp (right) pose with *Greatest American Hero* William Katt (center, in "the jammies") in this early publicity shot.

just as he commenced work on the Glen Larson series *Buck Rogers in the 25th Century*. She was absent from a handful of *Greatest American Hero* episodes while pregnant, making brief phone call appearances to advance the plots. Following *The Greatest American Hero*, she finally found herself cast in Aaron Spelling's dull but successful *Hotel* (1983–'89). Later, she took the lead in the sit-com *Baby Talk*, which she dropped out of in pre-production, and then the Glen Larson detective show *P.S. I Luv You* (1991–92). Her marriage to Gerard failed, and she later married musician John Tesh.

Robert Culp was born in Berkeley, California in 1930. Enthralled with acting from an early age, he joined local theater groups, doing menial jobs to earn money between performances. Later, he became a cartoonist, and — following university — worked in a bank while waiting for his big break. He hated the bank, and eagerly snapped up his first role when it was offered, but despite later success on Broadway, Hollywood beckoned. His first series was *Trackdown,* which ran for two years between 1957 and 1959, for which Culp wrote episodes and learned — painfully — to twirl six-guns and ride horses as Texas Ranger Hoby Gilman.

Later, Culp produced the first independently made TV documentary to air in primetime (on poverty) and, when he went to producer Sheldon Leonard (whose credits included *The Dick Van Dyke Show, Gomer Pyle, My World and Welcome To It*) with an idea for a new series, Leonard passed on it, but cast him in *I Spy,* a three year hit (1965–1968) that made stars out of Culp and co-star Bill Cosby.

Despite appearing in many feature films, including the swingin' '60s critique *Bob and Carol and Ted and Alice* (1969), the tough, stylish revenge western *Hannie Caulder* (1971), and the populist Cannell-esque fantasy *Turk 182* (1985), his best work has been done for TV, rather than the occasional film — appearances three times in the legendary science-fiction horror series *The Outer Limits,* a remarkable and mostly intelligent anthology series of extra-terrestrial contacts, and the equally impressive *Columbo,* perhaps the finest murder/mystery series ever made. His roles in the excellent *Columbo* episode "Death Lends a Hand" (written by *Columbo* creators Richard Levinson and William Link, and directed by Bernard Kowalski) as the head of a super-sophisticated detective agency, and in Cannell's only *Columbo* episode "Double Negative," directed by Richard Quine, are wonderful (note Culp's sheepish beaming grin as he's caught red-handed in the latter), as is Culp's third and final *Columbo,* "The Most Crucial Game," written by John Dugan and directed by Jeremy Kagan. A scene that only Culp could pull off occurs in the latter at a golf club; as Peter Falk's genial sleuth corners his suspect in the rough, Culp's villain declares his colors, picking up the ball and tossing it gently onto the green, with the words "Here it is — I'll just toss it right back out there, and no-one will *ever know!*" That one single, silly line brazenly spoken full in Columbo's face, sums up the entire premise of the *Columbo* series in all its glory — he knows, I know he knows, he knows I know he knows.

Each of these performances are all quite different from one another, as are his three roles in *The Outer Limits,* even though all three stories concern themselves with the theme of paranoia. An early appearance as a weary gunslinger in the western series *Johnny Ringo* neatly paves the way for his role in the later *Hannie Caulder,* in which he plays an almost identical role some ten years later, again quite differently (another western role is that of Wild Bill Hickok in the 1964 feature *The Raiders*), and an early episode of *The Man from UNCLE,* "The Shark Affair," in which Culp plays a bizarre misguided Captain Nemo type, gives audiences the rare spectacle of the future star of *I Spy* confronting fellow 1960s super-agent Napoleon Solo, and an interesting clash of acting styles between Culp and the equally appealing performance of Robert Vaughn. The role doesn't offer Culp much, but he makes the best of his opportunities, including one of his familiar two-beat slow burns as Solo parries quips. Later he faced '60s spy and Cannell regular Robert Conrad — not in *The Wild Wild West,* but the pilot for Conrad's disastrous *A Man Called Sloane.* It has been suggested more than once that Bill Maxwell is *I Spy's* Kelly Robinson, but older, but this is nonsense, and gives Culp no credit for creating two entirely different characters from the same piece of cloth.

In minor supporting roles were June Lockhart (of *Lassie* and *Lost in Space* fame) as Pam's mother, and Barbara Hale as Ralph's mother. Faye Grant, who has guest-starred in the pilots for *Voyagers, Hardcastle and McCormick,* and *Private Eye,* but is best known for her role as the heroic Julie Parrish in the sci-fi series *V,* and Michael Pare, later to star in the dull cop series *Houston Knights* (1987–'88) and the movies *The Philadelphia Experiment* and *Streets of Fire* (both 1984), played two of Ralph's no-hoper students, Rhonda Blake and Tony Villicana. Other pupils who appeared semi-regularly were Jesse D. Goins as Cyler and Don Cervantes as Paco Rodriguez, but as the chemistry between the three leads began to fizz beyond anybody's wildest hopes and dreams, all the students gradually receded into the background, eventually even disappearing from the credits. Robby Weaver, previously co-star of Cannell's cop show *Stone,* was Ralph's gym teacher colleague Ray Buck, and William Bogert appeared occasionally as Maxwell's superior Carlyle. Brandon Williams appeared fleetingly as Ralph's son Kevin, and Simone Griffeths, nearly Lionel Whitney's bride in *Tenspeed and Brownshoe,* was Ralph's shallow and self-centered ex-wife Alicia. These last two characters and the sub-plot dealing with Ralph's attempts to get custody of his child, were abandoned very quickly after the pilot as extraneous additions. Again, Cannell was throwing in more than he later found he needed.

Without Culp as the super-straight Bill Maxwell, *The Greatest American Hero* would have had nothing special, and been nothing special, despite the estimable talents of Katt and Sellecca. Those critics who refer to Bill Maxwell as a middle-aged extension of Culp's Kelly Robinson persona from *I Spy* are doing Culp an injustice; although both are government agents, they are as alike as chalk and cheese, and yet in every role he takes, the unmistakable Culp personality shines through. He is always Robert Culp, and yet he never plays the same part twice. "I wouldn't leave after wrapping our scenes" said Faye Grant. "I learned all the technical stuff that I needed to know because I didn't have much to do. I would stay and watch Bob Culp work. He's *really* good."

The special effects on the series were acceptably done, if not particularly special, consisting mostly of the same footage of poor Ralph hurtling through the air against various backdrops, with the blue matte screen process being used for the technically shaky but always funny flying sequences. In many ways, the cheesy effects added to the absurdity of Ralph's situation. In the earliest episodes, Ralph launches himself reluctantly into the air screaming maniacally, and on one memorable occasion prefers to walk the long way home rather than suffer another landing! So this is what it's like as a super-hero — so much for the exhilaration of flying through the wild blue yonder. Suffice it to say that the bushes around California took as much of a beating as Ralph....

Running around in his conspicuous red suit ("the jammies" as Bill Maxwell sensitively refers to the outfit), Ralph Hinckley is inevitably assumed to be a crank, pervert, or worse! Unlike the super-heroes of the comics, who run around in a world more accustomed to the presence of colorful, costumed characters cavorting around the streets (witness the studied disinterest of the citizens of Gotham City in William Dozier's splendid 1966–'68 TV incarnation of *Batman*), poor Ralph exists in the "real" world, where crime-busting vigilantes exist only in the comics. The pilot film in particular makes much of this, making a mockery of such time-honored clichés as the worshipful girlfriend figure, the dashing flight through the air, the thunderous arrival through brick wall or window (Ralph just dents the wall rather badly, and showers innocent home-dwellers with glass) and particularly the speedy change into costume (a lot can be happening while Ralph struggles to get his pants off in the back seat of the car!). Not for Cannell is the steely-eyed play-it-straight approach of the superb Richard Donner *Superman* movie of '78 (although both have their fair share of telephone booth gags!). This is not a world where fantasy is the norm, although Cannell's worlds are often no more reality-based than those of the comic-books.

Having lost the instruction book from the aliens, Ralph must play super-hero by the comic-book ... and is failing as miserably at being a square-jawed super-hero as his predecessors Beamer, Brockelman, and Whitney et al did at replicating the Chandler/Spillane image ... even if the bad guys do end up in the slammer at story's end. Some episodes were inevitably better than others, but they all possessed a wicked sense of humor that the super-hero TV shows of the '70s (*Six Million Dollar Man, The Bionic Woman, The Incredible Hulk, Wonder Woman, Man from Atlantis, Amazing Spider-Man,* etc.) didn't have, and the same self-deprecating lightheartedness and mocking wise-cracking that has made so many of Cannell's other suspect super-heroes so enjoyable. Where Wonder Woman spun earnestly into action, and the bionic agents went to work with swift, grim-faced competence and urgency, reluctant Ralph Hinckley was more likely to stumble over his own feet, or crash into a criminal hideaway without stopping; Ralph's flights came to a halt more in the manner of Wile E. Coyote than Superman. He was to TV super-heroes what Rockford and Richie Brockelman had been to TV detectives, and future Cannell heroes, particularly the characters in *Riptide* and *Hardcastle and McCormick,* would follow the same appealing path, adding to Cannell's canon of hard-done-by heroes.

In "Operation: Spoilsport," written by Frank Lupo and directed by Rod Holcomb, Ralph embarrassingly ploughs into the home of a missing computer expert to locate him by using his power to see images from the "vibes" of that person's possessions. After humbly handing the stunned woman her front door (he hasn't time to explain — the world is doomed in 24 hours and she, quite understandably, won't let him in), a scene of magnificent absurdity ensues, as Ralph dons the professor's clothes over his suit ("actually that hat isn't his, it's mine"), while the horrified woman (Robin Riker), having read all the relevant literature about how to psychologically handle a situation like this, looks on in disbelief while desperately trying to humor the boy. In "My Heroes Have Always Been Cowboys," written by Cannell and directed by Arnold Laven, a red-suited Ralph in pursuit of villains foolishly attempts to alert the police while in his full regalia, and rapidly finds himself pursued around the neighborhood by the cops instead. All attempts to fly to safety result in frustrating collisions with trees and bushes. Worse damage is done in the desert during the course of "The Best Desk Scenario," written by Cannell and Juanita Bartlett (note again Cannell's use of absurd law agency vocabulary), when an attempt to set a bush on fire with newly-discovered psychic powers results in Bill's car being blown sky-high instead (Cannell also loves to revel in the later official consequences of the mass destruction his series wreak on automobiles, as this and the running joke in numerous early episodes of *Hunter* concerning an abundance of wrecked vehicles demonstrate!).*

The regular directors on the series were contacts Cannell had made during his days with Jack Webb's operation, or while working on *The Rockford Files* and his other detective series at Universal; of the writers, Juanita Bartlett and Rudolph Borchert had also come to Cannell via *The Rockford Files.* Frank Lupo, whose first scripts for Cannell were "Operation: Spoilsport" and "Classical Gas," rapidly became Cannell's right hand man during the 1980s, lend-

---

The Greatest American Hero is hardly the only television series to parody comic-book heroes, but it is still the best. Two very poor sit-coms —Captain Nice and Mr. Terrific— had hastily appeared, both in 1966, to milk the Batman TV craze, and disappeared equally as quickly, a British series of the early '80's called Whoops Apocalypse, which featured Peter Jones as a British prime minister who thinks he has super-powers, a syndicated series called My Secret Identity ran in the late '80s, and the short-lived 1987 series Once a Hero was uncertain whether it wanted to honor the innocence of the costumed crime-busters of bygone days or ridicule it, finishing absolute last in the ratings for that season. Movie pastiches had included The Projectionist (1971), starring Chuck McCann (Greatest American Hero's very own Captain Bellybuster!) as Captain Flash, Hero at Large (1980), with John Ritter (of Three's Company and Hooperman) as Captain Avenger, and The Return of Captain Invincible (1982) starring Adam Arkin.

ing his dark, idiosyncratic humor and talent for snappy, humorous dialogue to some of the best episodes of *Riptide* and *The A-Team,* creating *Hunter,* and co-creating *The A-Team* and *The Last Precinct.* Although he eventually left Cannell in the late '80s to work on projects of his own (they both worked better together), including the series *Werewolf, Something is Out There, Hardball,* and *Raven,* it was Lupo who gave Cannell the missing piece of the jigsaw that made *Wiseguy* as good it was — the show, he said, should be about the hero and adversary, not hero and girl.

As another new addition to the team, Babs Greyhosky, who — like Lupo — had first attracted attention writing scripts for the first season of Donald Bellisario's much-admired *Magnum,* produced episodes of *The Greatest American Hero* that showed great promise for the future, joining the series during its third season with the wedding episodes "This Is the One the Suit Was Made For" and "The Newlywed Game." She contributed extensively to *Rousters* and *The A-Team,* and so impressed Cannell with her handle on *Riptide* that he put her in charge of the whole series.

Patrick Hasburgh, who came in on the second season with "Now You See It..." and "It's All Downhill from Here," eventually became the series' story editor. Hasburgh went on to serve on Cannell's *Hardcastle and McCormick* as a writer/producer, a series on which the relationship between the two leads owed much to Culp and Katt's ad-libs; both *The Greatest American Hero* and *Hardcastle and McCormick* demonstrated how the weaker scripts and flimsier ideas could often be saved on set by the chemistry and interaction between the lead performers.

"Bob and I relied on our own sense of truth" William Katt told *Starlog* magazine. "If the writers had written a scene which had us playing the fools in the wrong situation, we just wouldn't do it. Bob and I did a lot of rewriting, not so much the story or form, but our own dialogue. We would rewrite quite often, changing a line here or there to make it suit how we felt about the scene."

After a wonderful first season of seven episodes and pilot, the second year of *Greatest American Hero* (which consists of the bulk of the series) began well, opening with Cannell's "The 200-Mile-an-Hour Fastball," in which Bill finds himself transforming into a greedy but incompetent manager for super-powered ball player Ralph, who is undercover to investigate dirty doings in a baseball team. Ralph is mortified that he's using the suit's powers to cheat in order to get into the games, while Bill is appalled that such an All-American institution as baseball could be corrupted by "the bad guys." Markie Post, a fine actress under-used here (a regular in Glen Larson's *The Fall Guy* and the sit-com *Night Court,* but seen to best advantage in the "Just Good Friends" episode of *Cheers*), appears as the owner of the team, with familiar cop show regular Bruce Kirby as the crooked Coach. The outrageous and simplistic plot is enhanced masterfully by Robert Culp's persistent hamming as Bill Maxwell, a feat he also performs to give "Classical Gas" — an even more absurd plot — a considerable helping hand. Here, in the closing scenes, Bill is congratulated by Ralph and Pam for saving a rock concert, "even though you don't like rock and roll!"; "I don't even like music!" snaps the philistine fed, but a few seconds later as the kids perform on stage, Maxwell is furtively removing his earplugs to covertly boogie on down in shameless mimicry of all those elderly converts in the last reel of every 1950s rock and roll movie ever made! No matter how fantastic or incredible the stories get (or how lame, toward the end of the series), Culp and Katt manage to invest the proceedings with enough humor and bits of business to keep the plots afloat.

Some episodes though were good enough not to need any help other than the cast's reliably excellent performances. Juanita Bartlett's "The Beast in the Black" was a dark horror in which Bill is possessed by a ghostly force from another dimension, while Cannell's inspired "Don't Mess Around with Jim" has veteran actor Joseph Wiseman (Bond's *Dr. No* and the elderly and powerful mob czar in *Crime Story*) as a former recipient of the suit, who — many years earlier — had abused the powers of the suit and had the gift reclaimed by the aliens. Now wheelchair-bound and fading fast, he enlists the aid of Ralph and Bill to give his ill-gotten gains to charity, a move that hasn't much thrilled his former partners-in-crime, who intend to change his mind.

Yet another triumph was "The Hand-Painted Thai" (ouch!!), by Cannell, Lupo, and new arrival Patrick Hasburgh (later to helm *21 Jump Street* and *seaQuest*), which featured an extraordinary Rockfordian collection of characters with James Shigeta leading the parade as a Red Chinese sleeper agent who has grown accustomed to his capitalist cover while awaiting the call to duty, and John Fujioka, regular TV villain, as his fiercely loyal-to-the-cause superior, a fearsome monster who at one point threatens the distraught successful businessman with a bare-handed throttling if he has "turned soft!" This is also the memorable episode in which the skeptical Bill is unknowingly hypnotized to fall asleep every time he hears the word "scenario," which — as one of Cannell's parodic FBI men — is one of the most prominent in his vocabulary (Bill's catch-phrase "Here's the scenario" was first mercilessly pilloried in Cannell's *Rockford* episode "The Dog and Pony Show!"). In "It's All Downhill from Here," Hasburgh offers some Rockfordian sarcasm from Bill toward a counter-culture leftover from the '60s, when Ralph encounters an old friend (Sandra Kearns as Samantha) on a skiing holiday, a save-the-whaler ecologist put through her paces by the caustic and resentful reactionary Maxwell. Hasburgh's most notable move on the series though was to introduce the stronger sci-fi elements of certain episodes. He and Cannell produced "The Shock Will Kill You," about an electrical being that arrives on Earth via a returning space probe, for the second season, and in the third season opener, the touching "Divorce, Venusian Style," in which Ralph and Bill board the alien saucer that delivered the super-suit to them, and confront some absurdly low-budget trick-or-treat style aliens.

In many ways, Stephen Cannell is to TV what Stan Lee was to the comic-book industry — both present us with heroes who are vigilantes, Robin Hoods, and anti-heroes, flawed, vulnerable tongue-in-cheek parodies of harder, straighter fare. Like Lee's 1960s Marvel super-heroes, Cannell's TV heroes — particularly those of the early '80s (*Greatest American Hero, Hardcastle and McCormick, The A-Team, Riptide, Hunter*) — are living in a half-way world too real to be as phoney as the fantasy environments of more straight-faced entries in their chosen *genres*, too fake to be confused with grim reality. Stan Lee took super-heroes out of impossibly pure characterizations and make-believe locales, and dropped them squarely in an equally fictional environment that more closely resembled reality — Spider-Man swings over the streets of New York while Batman patrols the non-existent Gotham City, and so the character is elevated one higher plane nearer to the real world — and yet Stan Lee's New York no more exists than Metropolis or Gotham City. Cannell has played the same trick with the TV hero; television does it all the time, replacing one fictional fantasy world with another, more credible environment — and so we move through the television landscape from *Mike Hammer* to *Mannix* to *The Rockford Files*, from *Dragnet* to *Kojak* to *Hill Street Blues*, from *Dr. Kildare* to *St. Elsewhere*, from *Space Patrol* to *Star Trek* to *Alien Nation*, each world more credible than the last, each one as bogus and contrived as the one before it, each more deviously sophisticated in its allure and deception.

Hill Street Blues or *St. Elsewhere* reality? Hardly — but more complex, more credible in presentation when compared with *Dragnet* or *Marcus Welby,* and consequently more convincing for the moment. Having read *Superman*, we turn to Stan Lee's equally implausible *Spider-Man* or Stephen Cannell's *Greatest American Hero*, and tell ourselves that this is how it would *really* be if a super-hero did exist. In the process, we have now accepted the notion of the super-powered hero. Add a dash of populism and a good helping of humor and parody so that we know we're kidding ourselves, and the adult can now safely unleash the juvenile within him. "This is like *I Spy* in a lot of ways," reasoned Robert Culp to the science-fiction magazine *Starlog*. "You take two really human, ordinary people and you drop them into remarkable situations. There is no camp involved in this. It has to do with two real people trying to deal with the impossibility of the situation they've been dropped into."

There have been many stumbling blocks in making super-hero TV shows work on television — financial restrictions on what can be done, of course, and an unfamiliarity either with the original source material and/or the passion and pedantry of the fans, often coupled with an often outright disdain for the material. For reasons which may never be determined, creative talents, film producers and networks, having bought into a successful guaranteed concept, then often go out of their way to remove all those elements that made the original such a proven success (the 1970s versions of Marvel's *Amazing Spider-Man* and *Incredible Hulk* being obvious examples),* but Cannell, with the same air of nonchalance and affection for TV as Stan Lee had for his chosen medium, was the perfect person to bring off a series of this nature—and it was a personal creation, rather than a pre-sold package that had been assigned to a cynic.

The success of the pilot and the first seven episodes had resulted in two Emmy nominations and an order for a full second season. The series nudged into a third half-season, and might well have run longer had it not been dealt the double death blow of being scheduled against *Dallas* on CBS and the debut of *Knight Rider* on NBC for that third fateful year. Most of the series' stinkers, still more entertaining than much prime-time adventure of the period, appeared in this third season, but perhaps the only real regrets where *The Greatest American Hero* is concerned are the episodes that didn't get made, particularly those conceived and planned by Robert Culp, who also wrote for his previous series *Trackdown* and *I Spy*. Culp had an intriguing two-parter planned in which Ralph and a reluctant Bill set out to "save the whales" by changing their migratory habits.†

Ideas of Ralph using the suit for purposes other than roughing up mobsters had already been hinted at in episodes such as "Dreams" by Cannell and "The Good Samaritan" by Rudolph Borchert, but Culp's premise for this story and others sounds fascinating.§ Certain plans for episodes that were originally produced, such as Culp's written and directed "Lilacs, Mr. Maxwell" and the dismally edited "Vanity, Says the Preacher" indicate that these episodes did perhaps not turn out as well as hoped; they are certainly no match for Culp's masterful *I Spy* work, notably "Home to Judgement" and "The Magic Mirror," which are fabulous television.

The ratings plummeted from the dual assault of *Dallas* and *Knight Rider,* and four episodes already in the can were never broadcast by the network, although they have been shown since in syndication. These are "Wizards and Warlocks," "Desperado," "It's Only Rock

---

*Stan Lee, upon enquiring why the producers of the 1990 movie version of Marvel's The Punisher *were not using the character's familiar and striking skull's head shirt, plumping instead for an ordinary leather outfit, was told that it would make the character "look too comic-bookish!"*
†This idea later resurfaced as the plot for a revival of the series with a young girl taking over the suit under Maxwell's guidance, titled The Greatest American Heroine.
§Culp gives an in-depth interview detailing his history and hopes for The Greatest American Hero *in issues 54 and 55 of the fantasy media magazine* Starlog *during that publication's extensive coverage of the show which is essential reading for all fans of Culp, Cannell, and/or* Greatest American Hero.

and Roll," and "Vanity, Says the Preacher." None of these episodes worked particularly well, and to be blunt, the series had probably run its course. Everyone was looking very tired, co-stars Grant and Pare had moved on, and everyone seemed to be simply going through the motions. Although the partnership of Katt, Culp, and Sellecca, by now running on auto-pilot, continued to spice up the series with some marvelous visual humor and comic exchanges ("The Price is Right" and the otherwise mundane "Wizards and Warlocks" offer particularly good examples of the life they brought to the series), the series was rapidly running the risk of becoming a one-joke show. The vitality of those early episodes had gone; the parodic elements had been played out and the point had been made. With the absurd figure of Ralph now accepted by the viewers, the series was in danger of slipping into a straight adventure format, and only the trio's sparkling play-acting was providing the necessary satirical input.

Although curiously defeatist on the part of ABC given the show's record and the strength of the competition, the cancellation notice probably came at just the right time — Ralph and Bill had been aboard the saucer and discovered the origins of the suit (Hasburgh's "Divorce, Venusian Style"), they had saved the world and each other on numerous occasions, and Ralph and Pam had married. Even Cannell's own final contribution, the interesting "Desperado," was below par, despite boasting a guest appearance from the always excellent screen villain John Vernon. The team Cannell had gradually assembled had between them produced 42 episodes after the pilot, and at least 30 of them had been excellent, a dozen of those, marvelous. As for the remaining twelve ... well, they passed the time. For his part, Cannell had proven that he could do something other than cops and detectives, and a formula and philosophy for the future was forming. While he had lost some of the writers from his *Rockford*/Universal period to other projects, a new like-minded family of writers had been assembled. Phase II was just beginning....

Episode Guide

regular cast: William Katt (Ralph Hinckley), Robert Culp (Bill Maxwell), Connie Sellecca (Pam Davidson)

recurring cast: Michael Pare (Tony Villicana), Faye Grant (Rhonda Blake), Jesse D. Goins (Cyler), Don Cervantes (Rodriguez), William Bogert (Carlyle), Robby Weaver (Buck)

First Season (1981)

THE GREATEST AMERICAN HERO (pilot)

wr. Stephen Cannell, dir. Rod Holcomb

An idealistic teacher on a field trip with some problem kids and a moody FBI agent trying to trace his colleague, have a close encounter with aliens from space in the desert. It's all part of a plan of the aliens to protect the Earth by making various individuals into secret super-heroes. The teacher is their latest candidate, and his first job is to prevent a fascist religious sect from doing away with the U.S. President...!

with Richard Herd, G.D. Spradlin, Bob Minor, Ned Wilson, Edward Bell, Jeff MacKay, Brandon Williams, Simone Griffeth

THE HIT CAR

wr. Stephen Cannell, dir. Rod Holcomb

A scatty none-too-bright actress agrees to testify against her mobster boyfriend, but insists that her horoscope demands she take the trip to the courthouse by road, a condition the authorities are hardly in a position to refuse. With Bill assigned as her escort, they are pursued by an armored arsenal of a car.

with Gwen Humble, Gianni Russo, Kene Holliday, Anthony Charnota, W.T. Zacha, Ernie Orsatti

HERE'S LOOKING AT YOU, KID

wr. Juanita Bartlett, dir. Robert Thompson

Ralph's first meeting with Pam's parents is delayed when a valuable prototype aircraft is stolen, and further complicated when the super-suit develops invisibility powers that Ralph can't control.

with James Whitmore, Jr., June Lockhart, Bob Hastings, Red West, Thomas Babson, Zitto Kazann, F.J. O'Neil, Laurence Haddon, Roger Etienne, Denise Halma, Benny Medina

SATURDAY ON SUNSET BOULEVARDE
wr. Stephen Cannell, dir. Rod Holcomb
Bill has to race Russian spies and fellow FBI agents to a wealthy heiress after failing a lie detector test for the FBI during which he was unable to reveal his story of the alien encounter in the desert and the existence of the super-suit.
with Alexa Hamilton, Kai Wulff, David Tress, Mel Stewart, Joseph Warren, Will MacMillan, Christopher Thomas, Lawrence Benedict, Ion Teodorescu, Lev Mailer, Glenn Wilder

RESEDA ROSE
wr. Juanita Bartlett, dir. Gabrielle Beaumont
When Rhonda's mother goes missing, it turns out that she's been prying into top secret files at her cleaning job, and uncovered a spy network.
with E.J. Peaker, Peter White, Dave Shelley, Nicholas Worth, Kurt Grayson, Stephen Kahan, Al White

MY HEROES HAVE ALWAYS BEEN COWBOYS
wr. Stephen Cannell, dir. Arnold Laven
When Ralph accidentally endangers lives while wearing the super-suit, he starts to contemplate giving up his super-hero activities ... just as Bil Maxwell endures his own crisis of confidence when a hero from his past looks as though he's turning bad.
with Jack Ging, John Hart, Ferdy Mayne, Frank McCarthy, Joseph Chapman, Robert Gooden, Bruce Tuthill, William Woodson, Charles Walker, Glenn Wilder

FIRE MAN
wr. Les Sheldon, dir. Gabrielle Beaumont
Ralph gets Tony a job repossessing cars, but the job leads to an accusation of arson, and Ralph must use the suit to clear his pupil's already dubious name of the crime.
with Mark Withers, Raymond Singer, Steven Hirsch, Woody Eney, Timothy Carey, Sandy Ward, Paul Cavonis, Danny Glover

THE BEST DESK SCENARIO
wr. Juanita Bartlett, Stephen Cannell, dir. Robert Thompson
Bill is intimidated by the success of Ralph and Pam in their respective jobs and the arrival of a young go-getter in his FBI office, but neither Ralph or Pam find their new career opportunities quite what they expected.
with Eugene Peterson, Duncan Regehr, Michael Ensign, Tom Pletts, Eric Server, Rod Colbin, William Frankfather

Second Season (1981–1982)

THE 200MPH FAST BALL
wr. Stephen Cannell, dir. Georg Stanford Brown
Bill gets carried away by his role as Ralph's manager when they use the suit to join a baseball team that arms dealers are planning to use as a cover during the World Series.
with Markie Post, Carmen Argenziano, Bruce Kirby, Michael J. London, Richard Gjonola, Hector Elias, William Marquez, Stanley Brock, Ralph Maura

OPERATION: SPOILSPORT
wr. Frank Lupo, dir. Rod Holcomb
A nuclear attack revenge system is deliberately activated by an insane military man.
with John Anderson, Dudley Knight, Robin Riker, James Burr Johnson, John Di Fusco, John Brandon, Al White

DON'T MESS AROUND WITH JIM
wr. Stephen Cannell, dir. Robert Thompson
Ralph and Bill encounter an elderly millionaire who knows about the super-suit because he and his partner had been previous beneficiaries of the aliens, but had abused their powers.
with Joseph Wiseman, Byron Morrow, Stan Lachow, Bernard Behrens, Michael Alldredge, W.T. Zacha, Barry Cutler, Luke Andreas, Fred Lerner, Jerry Dunphy

HOG WILD
wr. Stephen Cannell, dir. Ivan Dixon
Ralph's suit is stolen by a motorcycle gang, who then terrorize a small town while Ralph and Bill are helpless.
with Dennis Burkley, Paul Koslo (Burkley and Koslo previously ran a cycle gang in the grim *Rockford* episode "The Return of the Black Shadow"), Gregory Sierra, Marrianne Muellerleile, Tony Burton, Dennis Fimple, Hoke Howell

CLASSICAL GAS
wr. Frank Lupo, dir. Bruce Kessler

A rock concert promoter plans a deliberate "accident" with nerve gas at an event where Ralph's students will be playing.

with Edward Winter, George Loros, Garnett Smith, Blake Clark

THE BEAST IN THE BLACK

wr. Juanita Bartlett, dir. Arnold Laven

Ralph and Bill explore a haunted house which conceals a doorway to another dimension, where Bill becomes possessed by the ghost of a dead woman and a powerless Ralph is attacked by the monstrous guardian of the doorway.

with Christine Belford, Rae Allen, Jane Merrow, Jeff MacKay

THE LOST DIABLO

wr. Juanita Bartlett, dir. Lawrence Doheny

Bill tricks Ralph and the kids into going on an impromptu field trip that turns out to be a gold rush.

with John Miranda, Gary Grubbs, Fred Downs, Bill Quinn, Joseph Whipp

THE PLAGUE

wr. Rudolph Borchert, dir. Arnold Laven

Bill is remarkably confident about the supersuit's immunity to deadly germs when he accepts an FBI mission to prevent a group of terrorists from putting lethal bacteria into the water supply of a Middle East country.

with Ed Grover, Arthur Rosenberg, Jeff Cooper, Glenn Wilder

TRAIN OF THOUGHT

wr. Frank Lupo, dir. Lawrence Doheny

When Ralph hits his head after stopping a runaway train the hard way, he develops amnesia and forgets about Bill, the suit, and his powers.

with Jean Le Clerc, David Tress, Dave Shelley, Frank McCarthy, F. William Parker, Sonia Petrovna, Judd Omen, Robert Alan Browne, Milt Kogan, James Lydon, Dabbs Greer, Nick Shields, Nick Cinardo, Arnie More, Ari Barak, Warren Munson

NOW YOU SEE IT ...

wr. Patrick Hasburgh, dir. Robert Thompson

Ralph has a premonition of a plane crash on a flight with Pam on board, but it's an experimental plane invisible to radar.

with Jon Cypher, Christopher Lofton, Charles Bateman, Lawrence Haddon, Richard Beauchamp, Matthew Faison, Joe Mantegna

THE HAND-PAINTED THAI

wr. Frank Lupo, Stephen Cannell, Patrick Hasburgh, dir. Bruce Kessler

A Red Chinese undercover agent who has been seduced by the capitalist way of life is brutally jolted back into his old ways when suddenly ordered to activate four sleeper agents for a suicide mission.

with James Shigeta, John Fujioka, Kurt Grayson, Terrence O'Hara, Charles Lanyer, Hilary Labow, Terrence Evans, Michael Cornelison, J.P. Bumstead

JUST ANOTHER THREE RING CIRCUS

wr. Stephen Cannell, dir. Chuck Bowman

Bill is assigned to find a missing circus clown, and Ralph becomes a human cannonball.

with Catherine Campbell, Kai Wulff, David Winn, Alex Rodine

THE SHOCK WILL KILL YOU

wr. Patrick Hasburgh, Stephen Cannell, Frank Lupo, dir. Rod Holcomb

Ralph is magnetized when he confronts an electrical creature that has arrived on Earth via a damaged space shuttle.

with Rod Colbin, Don Starr, Leonard Lightfoot, Ray Girardin, Doug Hale

A CHICKEN IN EVERY PLOT

wr. Danny Lee Cole, Jeff Ray, dir. Rod Holcomb

Ralph, Pam, and the schoolkids become implicated in a plot to unseat a foreign government when they take a vacation with Bill in the Caribbean.

with Thalmus Rasulala, Ron O'Neal, Lincoln Kilpatrick, John Hancock, Todd Armstrong

THE DEVIL IN THE DEEP BLUE SEA

wr. Frank Lupo, dir. Sidney Hayers

Bill's turn to be duped into an assignment, when Ralph becomes convinced that the unexplained disappearance of several ships in the notorious Devil's Triangle is due to the presence of a sea monster.

with Glynn Turman, Jeremy Kemp, Michael Halsey, Anne Bloom, Will Hare

IT'S ALL DOWNHILL FROM HERE

wr. Patrick Hasburgh, dir. Sidney Hayers

Third vacation story in a row as Ralph and Pam reluctantly call Bill to their ski resort where a defection and a CIA operation result in the death of a skier.

with Sandra Kearns, Red West, Bill Lucking, Michael Billington, Stefan Gierasch, Norbert Weisser, Sara Torgov, Craig Schaeffer

DREAMS

wr. Stephen Cannell, dir. Bruce Kessler

Ralph learns a bitter lesson when he uses the suit for the personal gain of his colleagues, and unleashes a domino effect of disasters on them. Meanwhile, a crazy gangster feigns religious conversion to escape from the psycho ward and pursue the "flying man" who put him away.

with Michael Baseleon, Fred Stuthman, Nick Pellegrino, Nicholas Worth, Edward Bell, Elizabeth Hoffman, Milt Kogan

THERE'S JUST NO ACCOUNTING

wr. Frank Lupo, dir. Ivan Dixon

A zealous agent of the IRS discovers a suitcase of money in the possession of Ralph and Bill, who need it to solve a kidnap case ... but Bill's lost his receipts.

with James Whitmore, Jr., Jerry Douglas, Marc Alaimo, Emily Moultrie, Carole Mallory, Eugene Peterson, Ted Gehring

THE GOOD SAMARITAN

wr. Rudolph Borchert, dir. Bruce Kessler

Ralph and Pam coerce Bill into a series of exploits in which they will use the suit not to chase bad guys but do good deeds instead, and the trio set out to find some people in need.

with Keenan Wynn, Dennis Lipscomb, Carmen Argenziano, Bill Quinn, Harry Grant, Ron Thompson, Will MacMillan, Sandra McCulley, Wendy Wessburg, Pat Wilson, Joshua Miller

CAPTAIN BELLYBUSTER AND THE SPEED FACTORY

wr. Stephen Cannell, Frank Lupo, dir. Arnold Laven

The super-hero mascot of Hamburger Heaven calls in the FBI when his image is tarnished by a secret drugs operation within the fast food chain ... but only succeeds in exposing Ralph's powers.

with Chuck McCann, Anthony Charnota, Stanley Grover, Danny Wells, Colin Hamilton, Rex Ryon, Jim Greenleaf

WHO'S WOO IN AMERICA

wr. Patrick Hasburgh, dir. Bob Bender

Ralph must discover the secret of a smooth-talking charmer who has seduced his mother and is being pursued by a variety of suspicious characters.

with Barbara Hale, Tom Hallick, Michael Prince, Jon Cedar, Hugh Gillin, Dave Cass, Daniel Chodos

LILACS, MR. MAXWELL

wr. and dir. Robert Culp

Hunting for unsolved cases for the suit to solve in the basement of the FBI building, Bill finds an efficiency expert in exile for criticizing the boss' office decor, and falls head over heels in love.

with Dixie Carter, Adam Gregor, Ted Flicker, Arnold Turner

Third Season (1982–1983)

DIVORCE, VENUSIAN STYLE

wr. Patrick Hasburgh, dir. Ivan Dixon

Ralph takes the suit off, and is seriously injured after falling out with Bill during an assignment. Whisked aboard the alien spaceship again, Ralph is repaired by their super-science, and they finally meet the saucer's occupants and find out why they were given the suit.

with Jeremy Kemp, Dean Santoro, James McIntire, Kurt Grayson, Jason Bernard, Robert Gray, Al Koss, Joe Clark, Frank Doubleday, Eugene Brezany

THE PRICE IS RIGHT

wr. Stephen Cannell, dir. Ivan Dixon

A football star Bill idolizes and Ralph once knew is implicated in a mob scheme to throw the game (Ralph attends his high-school reunion in this one, a popular Cannell plot device).

with Stephen Shortridge, Dick Butkus, Claude Jones, Patrick Collins, Heather Lowe, Chip Johnson, Martin Speer, Anthony Davis, Edith Fields, Jack Andreozzi, Ben Powers, Tom Harmon, Ted Dawson, Doug France, Bob Hastings

THIS IS THE ONE THE SUIT WAS MADE FOR

wr. Babs Greyhosky, dir. Ivan Dixon

Ralph and Pam's relationship is put to the test when a vacation to escape the suit turns out to be a ruse by Bill Maxwell to lure Ralph on a mission to locate a stolen plane (this is the episode in which Ralph and Pam get engaged).

with Bo Brundin, Pepe Serna, Loyita Chapel, Jay Varela, Randall Nazarian, Bob Basso

THE NEWLYWED GAME

wr. Babs Greyhosky, dir. Chuck Bowman

While Bill prepares a surprise stag party for

Ralph on the eve of his wedding, the former Secretary of State appears to have a different kind of surprise for him — he knows about the supersuit.

with Hansford Rowe, Woody Eney, Norman Alden, June Lockhart, Alice Backes, Terrence McNally, Cynthia Steele, Pamela Bowman

HEAVEN IS IN YOUR GENES

wr. Patrick Hasburgh, dir. Chris Nyby, Jr.

Ralph and Pam despondently attend the funeral of Bill Maxwell when his car is run off the road to an explosive end ... but then Ralph begins to receive telepathic messages from him.

with William Prince, George McDaniel, Dennis Lipscombe, Carolyn Seymour, Andre the Giant, Rick Barker, Ted Gehring

LIVE AT ELEVEN

wr. Babs Greyhosky, dir. Arnold Laven

A demented TV newsreader intends to run for office after his retirement, and engineers a nuclear terrorist disaster to give substance to his campaign by signing off with a major story that supports his platform.

with William Windom, Alan Fudge, Eugene Peterson, Miguel Fernandes, Will MacMillan

SPACE RANGER

wr. Rudolph Borchert, dir. Ivan Dixon

A student in Ralph's class is a technological whizkid whose computer know-how attracts the attention of both the CIA and the KGB when he starts decoding their satellite transmissions.

with Joe Santos, Doug Warhit, Kene Holliday, Edward Bell, James Beach, Alex Rodine, Jan-Ivan Dorin, Benny Medina, Deborah Mays, Jay Gerber, Paul Carafotes

THIRTY SECONDS OVER LITTLE TOKYO

wr. Danny Lee Cole, Jeff Ray, dir. Arnold Laven

A blind date for Bill results in a battle with teenage gangs and Ninja warriors and a confrontation with a deadly ray-gun for Ralph and the suit.

with Soon-Teck Oh, Mako, Lloyd Kino, Christine Belford

THE RESURRECTION OF CARLINI

wr. Frank Lupo, dir. Arnold Laven

A number of magicians find their lives endangered by acts of sabotage when they try and perform tricks worked only by the late, great Carlini.

with Andrew Robinson, Jack Magee, Timothy Carey, Ferdy Mayne, Randi Brooks, Wiley Harker, Ken Lerner, Melanie Vincz, Tawny Little

WIZARDS AND WARLOCKS

wr. Shel Willens, dir. Bruce Kessler

A group of college kids who take their role-playing games a little too seriously are implicated in a kidnap plot when one of their number is revealed as a foreign prince.

with James Whitmore, Jr., Steven Peterman, Michael Huddleston, Nico Minardos, David Paymer, Harvey Solin, Toni Hudson, Bob Saget, Shunil Borpujari

DESPERADO

wr. Stephen Cannell, Frank Lupo, dir. Christopher Nelson

"Oh boy — the two of you out here communing with the fleas and the flies for five minutes, and all of a sudden we're the Sons of the Pioneers!" Bill Maxwell hits the trail when Ralph and Pam stumble onto a horse-rustling ring and a Captain Ahab figure looking for revenge on one particular horse ("I tried to break that horse — but instead, he broke me!").

with John Vernon, James Hampton, Red West, Luke Askew, Rick Lenz, Conlan Carter, Linda Hoy, Beach Dickerson

IT'S ONLY ROCK 'N ROLL

wr. Babs Greyhosky, dir. Chris Nyby, Jr.

Bill is reluctantly assigned to guard the life of a rock star after he and Ralph save his flight from a bomb attack.

with Judson Scott, Anthony Charnota, Robert Dryer, George Dickerson, Lesley Woods, Paul Carafotes, Deborah Mays, Dennis Stewart, Andy Wood, Michael Mancini, Sheila Frazier, Rick Dees

VANITY, SAYS THE PREACHER

wr. and dir. Robert Culp

The aliens intervene when Bill returns to a troubled country where he had been a hero in his youth and becomes involved in the changing political structure. In the meantime, Ralph has been seen and mistaken for a national comic-book hero come to life in their time of peril.

with Isela Vega, Julio Medina, Dehl Berti, Joseph Culp, Jason Culp, Luis Moreno

series ends

The Quest
October 1982–November 1982

Although a Cannell series through and through, *The Quest* was created by Juanita Bartlett, who had been with Cannell since *The Rockford Files*, to which she had contributed substantially. Prior to that, she had worked on James Garner's pre–*Rockford* series *Nichols* and had since contributed scripts to many Cannell series, including *Toma, Stone, Tenspeed and Brownshoe*, and *The Greatest American Hero*. Her other writing credits included the *Buck Rogers*–style pilot film *Planet Earth* for Gene Roddenberry of *Star Trek* fame, and episodes of the series *Bonanza, The Cowboys, Little House on the Prairie, Cool Million, Paper Moon, The Magician*, and *Scarecrow and Mrs. King*. Producing was John Ashley, a former actor in 1960s beach movies and Z-grade horror who would enjoy a somewhat longer relationship with the Cannell organization performing the same duties on Cannell and Lupo's *The A-Team*, before leaving to produce Lupo's solo series *Werewolf, Something Is Out There* and *Hardball*. Supervising producers on *The Quest* were Lupo and Jo Swerling, Jr., with Bartlett exec. producing.

The Quest was one of three series that season that quite plainly had an eye or two on the *Indiana Jones* trend in the cinema. The other two were *Bring 'Em Back Alive*, by Frank Cardea and George Schenk (who would have more success a couple of years later with *Crazy Like a Fox*) and *Tales of the Gold Monkey*, the most direct of the swipes, by Cannell's former collaborator on *Black Sheep Squadron, The Duke*, and *Stone*, Donald Bellisario (who would have better luck with *Airwolf* and *Quantum Leap*); there was even a parodic *Indiana Jones* produced in pilot form only, the mildly amusing but threadbare *Callahan*. *The Quest* did at least have a little more individuality than the others, in that it attempted to capture the spirit of *Indiana Jones* without so obviously imitating the character, although *Tales of the Gold Monkey* was probably the most interesting of the three by default.

In the pilot film for *The Quest* we learn that an obscure and ancient agreement dictates that without a direct descendant to the throne, the small Mediterranean kingdom of Glendora will revert to being part of France. Desperate to save the monarchy and preserve their independence, the king and his ministers track down four American citizens who are descendants of the Royal bloodline. Knighted by the king, the foursome must compete for the throne in a series of challenges to test their worthiness to rule. The Cannell factor comes into play by having all four questers turn out to be completely ordinary folk and quintessential Cannell heroes — mundane survivors who will be permitted to use any method, from muscle to mental agility, to get where they're going and complete whatever task they have been set. It was a weak concept, with little chance of providing one hundred storylines for a five year run, but it was off and limping for the 1982–'83 season.

Naturally there were opponents to the proposition put forward by the monarchy, the most dangerous being the evil Count Dardinay, in whose interests it was for the royal line to be discontinued. As the questers flit around the world (the pilot was filmed in the South of

France), the various members fall into (or would have fallen into) a variety of adventures ranging from robbery to romance.

"I went to the South of France for the first time on my vacation this year, and loved it," Bartlett told *Starlog* magazine in 1981. "It's calling to me. Stephen and I joke about how we can figure out a way to base an episode of *Greatest American Hero,* or an entire series in the South of France. Unfortunately, economics prohibit that."

Starring in *The Quest* were Perry King, who would later take the lead in Cannell's successful *Riptide* series in the 1984/85 season, Noah Beery, Jr., who had played Joseph Rockford in *The Rockford Files,* and newcomers Ray Vitte and Karen Austin. Austin, who guested regularly in various series and B-movies, had been seen previously in a small but memorable part as a lonely, despairing housewife in *Hill Street Blues,* and in the *Rockford Files* episode "White on White and Nearly Perfect" as Lance White's bride-to-be.

King played Dan Underwood, a photo-journalist whose little-boy-lost manner made him a big hit with the women who went for the shy, innocent approach. Austin was Carrie Welby, a department store buyer in the shoe department, and Noah Beery was Art Henley, a retired cop from Kansas. Vitte was Cody Johnson, a con-man type well on the way to becoming a stereotypical cliché even then.

King's glamorous career choice was offset by the regular guy qualities he would eventually bring to *Riptide,* while Austin's shop-girl was a character as dull as her job. Noah Beery resurrected his "Rocky," but with a little less naiveté and a little more guile, while Vitte's trickster had apparently just sold some poor sap the Brooklyn Bridge in time-honored tradition (most of his shtick in the pilot for *The Quest* bore a remarkable similarity to that of Tenspeed Turner in the *Tenspeed and Brownshoe* pilot). These reality-based characters (although Vitte was way over the top in his attempts to cartoon a Richard Pryor identity) were promptly dropped into a storybook world inhabited by Disney-esque loons straight out of a traditional fairytale. The king is a kindly, wise old fellow (played by Ralph Michael), but slightly daffy, with British actor John Rhys-Davies (who had recently played a role in *Raiders of the Lost Ark*) as his devoted and equally dotty advisor, Sir Edward. As the villainous Dardinay, whose desire was to see the questers come to a sticky end, was Michael Billington, another Britisher who had turned to America for work on the strength of a number of roles in ITC exports from Britain (he co-starred in Gerry Anderson's *UFO*).

In theory, it might have sounded an original and winning formula. In practice, there wasn't one character a viewer might have wanted to come back next week and see again. It was difficult to care whether the fictional and bland Glendora retained its monarchy, and obvious that as long as the series was on the air, the quest would never come to an end, and a monarch never be selected from these four. Audiences were sharp enough to know by now that even after a healthy run, a final episode resolving things would be unlikely. Bartlett cleverly mixed olde worlde tourist pageantry with typical Cannell plots and stunts, with none of the players taking their situation any too seriously. There was never any sense that these people were particularly eager to become Glendora's monarch. The pilot, directed by TV pilot veteran Rod Holcomb was a fun diversion, and set the scene for what was to be a very short-lived series and an expensive flop.*

---

*The series was almost certainly not helped by the fact that there had only recently been another series with the same name back in the 1976–'77 season, a western series called The Quest *which had fallen prey to the phenomenal popularity of* Charlie's Angels. *There had been series with identical titles before (including a* Riptide *in 1965, a* Hunter *in 1977, and a* The Hunter *in 1952), but these were also instances when the originals had disappeared long ago in the dim and distant past. The western series* The Quest *was not even ten years old, and although it had been quickly forgotten, it may have rung bells of confusion in some viewers' heads.*

The Quest made its debut scheduled after *The Greatest American Hero,* which was in its third and final season and about to fall to the twin onslaughts of *Dallas* and Glen Larson's new show, *Knight Rider,* a slot which must have dismayed Cannell. Although it was twinned with an established and popular Cannell show as a lead-in, it did not take a genius to see that *Dallas* was now unstoppable and that *Knight Rider* was a sure-fire hit. *The Quest* would surely lose its suitable supporting act, and even with it was in a hopelessly unwinnable time-period at 10:00 on a Friday night; this was a show-killing slot that had even taken down *Star Trek.* Now, thanks to ABC's scheduling, Cannell was almost certain to lose not only his first successful show made under his own banner, but his newest and most expensive series as well, and his fears were almost immediately realized. Not only was *The Quest* not really a 10:00 show in the first place, but the two lead-ins were the sit-coms *Benson,* now in its fourth year, and *The New Odd Couple,* a black version of the original hit show, and an instant failure. Ultimately, so unloved was *The Quest,* when *The New Odd Couple* and *The Greatest American Hero* went down in February 1983, *The Quest* had already been terminated, having also had to compete directly with the second year of *Falcon Crest* and the debut of *Remington Steele.*

There were over thirty cancellations that year, and *The Quest* was one of the first to go. It was not the year for fantasy series; other shows lost included both the other *Indiana Jones* cash-ins, and — as well as *The Greatest American Hero*— three other magical fantasy formats, *The Powers of Matthew Star, Tucker's Witch,* and *Voyagers.*

Episode Guide

regular and recurring cast: Perry King (Dan Underwood), Noah Beery (Art Henley), Karen Austin (Carrie Welby), Ray Vitte (Cody Johnson), John Rhys Davies (Sir Edward), Ralph Michael (King Charles), Michael Billington (Count Dardinay)

(1982)

THE QUEST (pilot)

wr. Juanita Bartlett, dir. Rod Holcomb

Four ordinary and unassuming people are summoned to the court of the King of Glendora by deceit, in order to participate in a challenge that will determine the next ruler of the tiny kingdom.

with James Sloyan, Bill Lucking, Ray Girardin, Rod Colbin, Stephanie Blackmore, Richard Beale, Ryan Michael, Marsha Wolf, Patrick Cameron, Leah Cates, Fritzi Burr, Jack Garner, Jean-Celeste Aherne, Shirley Anthony, Robert Alan Brown

LAST ONE THERE IS A ROTTEN HEIR

wr. Frank Lupo, dir. William Wiard

Cody's shifty past catches up with him when an old buddy turns up in his closet with plans to heist the crown of Glendora!

with Danny Wells, Tracy Reed, Michael Halsey, Lucille Benson, Brad Savage, David Sage

HE STOLE-A MY ART

wr. Juanita Bartlett, dir. Bruce Kessler

Having rescued some Italian children from going over a cliff in their school bus, Cody is more than a little surprised to find himself the target for machine-gun bullets shortly afterwards ... and nobody wants to know him any more!

with Michael Gazzo, Dominique Dunne, Rhonda Gemignani, Titos Vandis

HIS MAJESTY, I PRESUME

wr. Frank Lupo, dir. William Wiard

The questers suspect foul play when an attempt is made to persuade them that the king has died on safari without naming a successor, and the team set off to the jungle to determine the truth.

with Barrie Ingham, Kathryn Leigh-Scott, Ji-Tu Cumbuka, John Hancock

Escape from a Velvet Box
wr. Stephen Cannell, dir. William Wiard
Cody goes to the aid of a modern-day damsel in distress, only to have her turn on him when he follows up her plea for help.
with Alexa Hamilton, Byron Morrow, Charles Cypher, Derek Partridge

Hunt for the White Tiger
wr. dir. n/a
Carrie is seduced by a handsome millionaire, and it seems as though she is about to drop out of the quest ... until the rest of the team start to investigate a series of suspicious diamond thefts committed by the mysterious White Tiger.
with Ian McShane
series ends

The A-Team
January 1983–December 1986

"I love it when a plan comes together!"

At first glance, it might seem as though the 1982–'83 season had been a bad one for Stephen J. Cannell Productions ... but only at first glance. Although *The Quest* had come to an end in November 1982, and *The Greatest American Hero* would close in February 1983, a new Cannell venture had made its debut in January '83 that would change the fortunes of the company for the better irrevocably. That series was Cannell's final commitment to Universal — a pilot and distribution deal for any subsequent series apparently in exchange for letting producer Alex Beaton out of his contract to join Cannell Productions. Universal could have got *Tenspeed and Brownshoe* or *The Quest* ... but they got lucky. They got the mid-season replacement *The A-Team*.

The A-Team were a group of cuddly, good-natured soldiers of fortune who, in the grand TV tradition pioneered in *The Fugitive* (and revived almost every season in one form or another), were on the run for a "crime they didn't commit." In this case, the crime was the robbery of the Bank of Hanoi during the last days of the Vietnam war, a mission authorized by their commanding officer who had then inconsiderately got himself missing in action before he could clear the team's reputation. Over a decade later, they're still on the run, despite being rather flamboyant characters and traveling around L.A. and the rest of the country in broad daylight in a distinctive black and red van. Pursued by the military at every turn (who couldn't catch a cold), the audacious threesome — accompanied by a tenacious girl reporter and a loony pilot who regularly absconds from the veterans' hospital — survive by building themselves an enviable reputation as heroes-for-hire, a vigilante theme that was taken aboard by numerous other series of the early '80s including Glen Larson's *The Fall Guy* and *Knight Rider*, Donald Bellisario's *Airwolf,* Michael Sloan's *The Equalizer,* and Cannell's own *Hardcastle and McCormick* and *Stingray,* among others.

A connection between the man who gave us a sophisticated series like *The Rockford Files* in 1974, and such a simplistic one as *The A-Team* nearly a decade later may at first seem an unlikely and dubious one ... but when the dots are connected between these two series and Cannell's other creations, the comparisons become more obvious. True, *Rockford* is Cannell's classiest, most intelligent, multi-layered show (at least until the grimmer, darker *Wiseguy* came along to give it a run for the accolade in 1987), and *The A-Team* his most blatantly juvenile (seven million of the 42 million audience in the U.S. were estimated to be under twelve years of age, with an even greater percentage in European markets), but the theme of both *The Rockford Files* and *The A-Team* (and indeed, the common denominator in all his series) is Cannell's most labored and consistent — the underdog as unlikely hero, the wrongly-accused white knight up against the suit-and-tie authority of the system, the defender of the helpless and hopeless. And, as Cannell's upright, moral heroes — Baretta, Jake Axminster of *City of Angels,* Pappy Boyington of *Black Sheep Squadron,* Ralph and Bill of *Greatest American Hero,* Hardcastle and McCormick, Hunter and McCall, and all the others — come up against their various authoritarian antagonists, Cannell subverts the genre he is exploiting from the inside; Rockford and Axminster are hassled by the cops, as are the *Riptide* detectives, and Baretta, Boyington, Bill Maxwell and Hunter by their superiors, all for operating over the fine line of the law to achieve what the law itself cannot. The A-Team manage to go one better. Not only do they ignore the troublesome procedural technicalities of the law with spectacular abandon and successful results, not only are they on the run for that ol' crime they didn't commit (or rather, did commit, but thought they were doing right), but they're pursued by the massed forces of the military police.

Cast as Colonel John "Hannibal" Smith was actor George Peppard, returning to prime-time TV after a number of years consigned to the purgatory of a daytime medical soap, following a lost battle over his previous successful show, the *Mystery Movie* series *Banacek.* The wily Smith masquerades as a B-movie monster — the Aqua-Maniac — when he's not in some fanciful disguise to check out potential clients for the services of the team. Bright-eyed and bushy-tailed Dirk Benedict, previously co-star of the 1974 flying cops series *Chopper One* and then Lt. Starbuck in Glen Larson's *Battlestar Galactica* during 1978 and '79, played Templeton "the Faceman" Peck, a cheerful con-man in the tried-and-true Cannell tradition.* Media star of the show was the colossal former military policeman and bodyguard to the stars Mr. T (formerly Laurence Tureaud until he legally changed his name to his stage identity), a giant of a man bedecked in gold chains. Formerly the musclebound protector of Muhammed Ali, Leon Spinks, Michael Jackson, and LeVar Burton (of *Roots* and *Star Trek — the Next Generation* fame) he had begun an acting career of sorts in *Rocky II* (1979). Tureaud, now T, didn't have to do much but fume and look fearsome, but he did it well, and Cannell tempered the monster for TV by having his character, B.A. ("Bad Attitude") Baracus, have a soft spot for kids and a soft stomach for flying. A highlight of each adventure taking place over a wide expanse of ground was to see how Smith and Peck would dupe the hapless giant into boarding a plane — usually, it involved furtively doping the poor dope. By far the strangest and most bizarre member of the group was "Howling Mad" Murdock, a veteran pilot who was hospitalized in a variety of veterans' hospitals that seemed curiously unable to hold him when he was required by the team for a mission. Even funnier than the scenes getting B.A. Baracus on an airplane were those getting the mental mimic Murdock out of the well-intentioned clutches of his doctors and numerous psychiatrists, and needless to say, Murdock drives the short-fused B.A. almost as crazy as he is. Dwight Schultz played Murdock.

Series creators Cannell and Frank Lupo toyed with putting a woman into the show, but the format (and, by his own admission, George Peppard) fought against it. In the exploits of the A-Team there was little for a woman to do that wasn't demeaning; intentionally or otherwise, the women in other similar shows (such as *Mission: Impossible,* one of many sources of reference for *The A-Team*) often came across as little more than decoys at best and prostitutes at worst. Little wonder then, that Melinda Culea, as reporter Amy Allen (who hires, and then joins up with the A-Team in the pilot) left after the first season, and Marla Heasley,

---

Early episodes' opening credits include a shot of Benedict in the Universal theme park giving a "haven't I seen you somewhere before?"—style double-take as one of the Cylon robots from Battlestar Galactica *marches past!*

Breaking the rules for TV heroes ... the *A-Team* pose for a first season publicity shot. Clockwise from top left, con man Face (Dirk Benedict), angry "Bad Attitude" Baracus (Mr. T), deranged pilot Murdock (Dwight Schultz), short-lived token girl Amy (Melinda Culea), and lead mercenary John "Hannibal" Smith (George Peppard).

as her replacement Tawnia Baker,* left shortly after that.† When actress Judith Ledford joined the cast for the final few weeks in 1986, she joked to a fan magazine "I'm the only woman (on the set) besides the wardrobe lady, the lady in hair, and the lady in make-up! But the guys have been wonderful." Also absent from the team after just the pilot was the original "Faceman," Tim Dunigan, who was ultimately considered too young for the role; Dunigan went on to star in the lame sit-com *Mr. Smith,* and as the heroic lead in two later series, Disney's short-lived revival of *Davy Crockett,* and the syndicated series *Captain Power.*

*This name has an interesting history; Cannell first uses the name, or an approximation of it, in his Columbo *episode "The Most Crucial Game," which features an unseen character by the name of Tanya Baker. Later, in Cannell's "The Kirkoff Case," the first episode of* The Rockford Files, *Julie Sommars plays a Tawnia Baker. And Cannell has a daughter named Tawnia.*
†Interestingly, this hasn't harmed the show's popularity with female fans; indeed, many of the most popular TV series with women are those without female co-stars or leads — examples would include Laredo, Laramie, Voyage to the Bottom of the Sea, Garrison's Gorillas, The High Chaparral, *and Cannell's* Riptide, Hardcastle and McCormick, *and* Wiseguy.

Pursuing the A-Team on behalf of the U.S. government was the blustering Aunt Sally figure Colonel Lynch, played by veteran TV tough guy and Cannell regular Bill Lucking. In the excellent two-parter "When You Comin' Back, Red Ryder?," written by Frank Lupo and directed by Chris Nyby, the Lynch character is replaced by Commander Roderick Decker, a grim, hard-nosed hawk played by former stunt-man and stand-in for Elvis Presley, Lance Le Gault. Among Le Gault's earliest TV parts were a couple of minor roles in *The Rockford Files,* and either side of his role on *The A-Team* he had played the similarly hawkish military man Buck Greene in several episodes of *Magnum*. Later, Lupo would hire him to go in pursuit again, this time as the obsessed indian scout and bounty-hunter Alamo Joe in his late–'80s horror series *Werewolf.* Assisting Decker in his cross-country pursuit of the A-Team was Carl Franklin, formerly of the short-lived 1977 SF series *Fantastic Journey,* later a successful film director. In the third season, another familiar TV heavy and Cannell regular, Charles Napier (who had already previously guested in an *A-Team* episode—"Labor Pains"—in a different role) shows up as Colonel Briggs in the episode "Fire." As another military man, Major "Red" Buell, Napier had also had the honor of being humiliated by the Black Sheep Squadron as the guy whose planes are stolen in the pilot and first episode of that series. Both Briggs and Decker pursue the A-Team throughout the third season.*

During the fourth season of *The A-Team,* Decker was replaced by another Cannell regular, Jack Ging, who had also appeared in the series twice earlier as a bad guy (in the episodes "A Small and Deadly War" and "Bad Time at the Border"), and whose character of Lt. Quinlan in Cannell's *Riptide* had just been killed off during that series' third season (apparently by NBC, who wanted a regular female character in the *Riptide* cast). Ging moved lock, stock and barrel from *Riptide* over to *The A-Team,* making his first appearance as General Harlan "Bull" Fulbright in the episode "Mind Games," written by Cannell and directed by Michael O'Herlihy. A few months later, O'Herlihy was back to direct Fulbright's swan song in the final episode of the fourth season, "The Sound of Thunder" by Frank Lupo, one of the best—and darkest—episodes of the series, in which Fulbright dies in the company of the A-Team when the group return to Vietnam.

Like all the best heroes, Cannell's characters of the early '80s never had to deal with blurred, hazy realities. His comic-book style series were colorful (the opening credits of *The A-Team* were even colored in comic-book primary colors, with bright red backgrounds and yellow skies), but the two sides of the argument were always in glorious black and white. Rednecks and intellectuals alike could enjoy Cannell's escapist fantasies, simply because no-one could argue with the basic tenets of right and wrong[†] (although, of course, one shouldn't underestimate the critics, about whom, more later). Thus, an *A-Team* episode such as "Bad Time at the Border," the first to be written by Thomas Szollosi and Richard Christian Matheson (who joined the series during the second season—having previously contributed a script to *Stone*—and became story editors) had to confront none of the complexities faced by, say, the *Lou Grant* episode "Immigrants," with its similar illegal aliens theme; the focal point of that episode is the greyness of the issue, whereas in "Bad Time...," it's a simple matter of round-

---

*Both Bill Lucking and Charles Napier went on to co-star in the 1987 Rod Taylor series from Universal, Outlaws, a short-lived cowboy/detective fantasy.
†Only two episodes touched on vaguely political themes, and these two storylines contradicted each other, balancing out; "Labor Pains," by Matheson and Szollosi in the second season has the A-Team helping exploited farmworkers form a union against the efforts of the boss, while Jeff Ray's "Timber" in the third season has them helping lumber-workers avoid a crooked one.

ing up the border patrol agents between Mexico and America who are *themselves* smuggling in illegal workers. Neither series condones or condemns this unhappy situation of circumstance, and neither can offer any answers or tries to glibly find any ... but while a series like *Lou Grant* confronts the problem, *The A-Team* tactfully avoids the issue. It becomes a backdrop for a straightforward heroes and villains conflict, which can be comfortably resolved at story's end.

During the early part of the 1980s, before later Cannell series such as *Wiseguy, 21 Jump Street* and *Top of the Hill* tried to acknowledge and confront these greater issues, Cannell's *modus operandi* for such smash-and-crash series as *Greatest American Hero, The A-Team, Rousters, Riptide, Hunter,* and *Hardcastle and McCormick* was to use the premise of his stories simply as hooks on which to hang the various jokes, stunts, wacky characters and bits of business that make up a Cannell hour and make his shows so superior to those lesser attempts in the genre by other producers. No in-depth character development or sub-plots were allowed to slow down the action, and personality took precedence over emotional content to hold the characters together as something more than the cardboard cut-outs that inhabited other action/adventure shows. Nowhere was this tendency more in evidence than on *The A-Team*, where the hammy heavy-handed larger-than-life comic strip performances of the cast made the reliance on stunts and comedy over drama essential.

This is not to underestimate the talents that the cast did possess, all of whom were perfectly suited to the antics and mayhem of *The A-Team*. Mr. T had to do little but stand there to fill up the screen, while some of Dwight Schultz's wildly over-the-top impersonations were often the highlights of the show, even more so than the exploding buildings and catapulting vehicles.* For his part, Benedict was more than able to deliver a good line, particularly when written by the masters of the one-liner, Cannell and Lupo. During one particularly frantic car chase, Peppard is lighting up one of his huge trademark cigars while driving erratically down the street. As the vehicle careens wildly from side to side, Benedict leans over to the insanely grinning Peppard, and asks nervously "Can I get that for you?" It's moments like that which separate a Cannell production from his would-be rivals in the genre.

Early episodes of *The A-Team* (and many later ones) had a popular formula plot. Each story would open with a scene-setting menace, and then switch to the A-Team's client (often the pretty daughter of the downtrodden victim) who would seek out the group's rather unorthodox services, first enduring a frustrating paper chase while Hannibal verified the integrity of their customer in a variety of disguises. Once hired, the A-Team would make their first provocative appearance in the bad guys' territory to assess the situation and noisily announce their arrival in the most aggravating way possible. Soon, bullets, bodies, and automobiles would be flying about as incidents escalated. There would be a brief setback as the foolish villains attempted to fight back with their own show of power, and after some juvenile *Mission: Impossible*–style antics sprinkled with Rockfordian confidence tricks and assorted impersonations, the team would ultimately build some makeshift weapon, or organize an elaborate offensive to end the conflict in a final showdown.

When *The A-Team* first appeared in January 1983, it was quickly acknowledged by most observers to be the 1980s equivalent of William Dozier's *Batman* series of the '60s, or Sam Rolfe's *The Man from UNCLE* — a live-action comic-book played out by real people as larger-

---

*In all fairness, it should be pointed out that Dwight Schultz has since escaped his Murdock nut-bag to offer less over-the-top performances elsewhere.

than-life characters in absurd situations. Kids could enjoy it on its surface level, while adults could view it as a knowing parody (the pilot film sends up westerns like *The Magnificent Seven* and *The Wild Bunch*). Although the premise of *The A-Team* was new, the formula was all-too-familiar, and critics were quick to pick up on the myriad obvious influences of the series. "A sort of raunchy *Mission: Impossible*" said *Variety*. "A revved-up version of *Mission: Impossible*" echoed *New York*. But "...they pursue their own brand of law and order. This fits nicely within the overall vigilante concept that television seems to favor so strongly these days. For instance, another NBC series, *Knight Rider,* offers a hero and a talking car who 'champion the innocent and the powerless in a world of criminals who live above the law!'" In many of Cannell's series, it was often those who were supposed to be representing the law who *were* the bad guys. "*The Dirty Dozen, The Magnificent Seven, The Road Warrior,* and *Mission: Impossible*" admitted NBC president Brandon Tartikoff, while Leslie Halliwell, who bought the series for Britain's ITV network described the series as "a hybrid of *The Dirty Dozen, Garrison's Gorillas,* and *The Four Just Men*." Mary Harron in the U.K.'s *New Statesman*, the left-wing political journal that notoriously sneered at 9/11, was less specific. "The first episode was a 90 minute special which combined (with that lurid enthusiasm only the Americans can muster) every blockbuster movie and TV adventure series in living memory into a single package. And it did so brilliantly; the politics that underlie this story of a group of Vietnam veterans turned desperadoes may be dangerous, but it's an exhilarating show to watch. The gradual assimilation of Vietnam into popular American mythology, which began solemnly with *The Deer Hunter,* has reached its culmination with *The A-Team*— no longer a memory to be brushed aside, but heroes of a network adventure show. Their enemy is a comic army officer ... whose pursuit of our heroes is doomed to slapstick failure. This is classic right-wing American populism — patriotic, macho, anti-authority — and is unlikely to be understood in Britain, where to be right-wing implies an obsequiousness towards officers and the status quo ... America sailed to Vietnam on a sea of comic-book fantasies, and this is how she wishes it had turned out. The saddest thing is that America encourages her people to go to war by playing on their better instincts: heroism, rescuing the down-trodden, being Errol Flynn ... *The A-Team* is a significant fantasy ... there's a new generation of young men watching television now...."

"I can think of ten ways in which this nonsense was depressing or offensive, and that's not counting the rotten acting or the soppy plotting," snapped Patrick Stoddart in the U.K. trade paper *Broadcast,* reviewing the pilot. "It is offensive in these days of instant war reporting to see jeeps blown apart and watch the occupants crawl out covered in nothing but dust. It is depressing to see violence and illegality made glamorous, and it is insulting to anyone with the IQ of a horse watching the awful problems of Central America laughed off with a smile, a joke, and a hand grenade. 'Yes' says my American friend, 'but nobody gets killed.' Tell 'em that in El Salvador, buddy."

Both the above critics, who — like myself and indeed many Americans — have issues about certain aspects of American foreign policy, appear to be using *The A-Team* as a springboard with which to leap into an opportunity to air their prejudices rather than reviewing the TV show aired by NBC. Although the pilot took place across the border, the vast majority of *A-Team* episodes were set within the United States and had nothing to do with the American government's activities elsewhere. Commentators and the creative media had dealt with the aftermath of Vietnam in two very different ways. In the 1970s, with events and the result fresh in everyones' minds, film and TV had reflected a collective guilt and confusion. By the 1980s, America had pulled itself together but was now rewriting and revising history selectively. It was now about finding someone to blame, and the obvious easy-to-spot culprits were the people in positions of power, people who had failed the common man.

Prior to *Magnum* and *The A-Team,* Vietnam veterans on TV had been either shell-shocked psychos, gung-ho reactionary loons, or objects of pity or contempt — now, almost every TV tough guy, from *Knight Rider,* to CBS' reincarnated *Mike Hammer,* to *Hill Street Blues'* Joe Coffey and *Airwolf's* Stringfellow Hawke, had been in that fearsome conflagration. It was almost a prerequisite to becoming a 1980s TV hero — no tour of duty on your CV, no TV show! Although the glorification of Vietnam veterans was a novelty, the most significant factor about the success of *The A-Team* and many other hit shows of the 1980s was the preponderance of vigilante loners and outsiders over agents of officialdom; the audience for American action shows appeared to have taken aboard the sentiments of betrayal voiced by Stallone's John Rambo *en masse.* With relentless and assured predictability, all those shows that succeeded during the 1980s were those that dealt with characters outside the system, while almost every series that offered heroes working for a police department or some other authorized agency dropped like a stone. It may have been chance, but while *Manimal, Blue Thunder, Automan, Hawaiian Heat, Masquerade, Cover-Up, Codename: Foxfire, Hollywood Beat,* and *The Highwayman* all failed during their first year, *Magnum, Hunter, Mike Hammer, The Fall Guy, Airwolf, The Equalizer, Hardcastle and McCormick, Riptide,* even *T.J. Hooker,* whose cop hero quit his desk job to clean up the streets, took off like a sky-rocket. If your hero was critical of the way the system worked, he was in. If he believed in working within the accepted bureaucracy, he was out. With only a few exceptions, planning a 1980s action/adventure show or cop series really was that simple. Even the TV cops who stuck around endured endless confrontations with red tape desk jockeys or corrupt superiors, as in *Hill Street Blues* and *Cagney and Lacey,* or Michael Mann's *Miami Vice* and *Crime Story.*

A number of commentators condemned the series for its "violence" while missing the more genuine heroic content. Certainly the spoils went not only to those whose hearts were noble and true, but also to those who were wielding the biggest stick, but the show was also a very moral one, teaching what were otherwise very positive attitudes — getting involved and helping, and defending the weak as opposed to just standing by in the face of unfairness, injustice or intimidation. Beyond all the academic analysis, personal prejudices and political posturing, one thing was undeniable — the A-Team *were* heroes. Oddly, this one solitary nod to reality in the show (that bullies, great or small, whether running a country or a neighborhood protection racket, only respond to a bigger stick, and will then run like the cowards they are) was the major bone of contention with those who objected to the fantasy. *The A-Team* was the classic myth of getting even with the bullies by calling in your big brother and his friends. It may not have been kiss-and-make-up, but it was an instantly identifiable and universal fantasy.

The A-Team was not only a phenomenal success (it remains Cannell's biggest hit by far), but also helped to reverse the fortunes of the ailing NBC in the annual ratings game. Ironically, NBC's ratings triumph in the early 1980s — a status they maintained throughout the decade with the likes of *Cheers, The Cosby Show,* and *L.A. Law*— could be credited not only to the likes of *Knight Rider* and *The A-Team,* but their commitment to a string of critically acclaimed series of sophistication, including *Taxi* (picked up from ABC after cancellation), *Cheers, St. Elsewhere,* and *Hill Street Blues.* If the gut-level simplicity of *The A-Team* represented the other end of the spectrum, it was at least not as morally reprehensible as the psychological and emotional violence being meted out to the miserable characters in the glossy soaps so beloved in the '80s, or the extraordinary dismissive insensitivity towards the former living, breathing human beings that lay sprawled or slumped before the merry and unmoved leads of innumerable bland murder/mysteries like *Hart to Hart* and *Murder She Wrote* and its clones, where a sort of *Cluedo* mentality prevailed, and the death of a former friend or new acquaintance was regarded as nothing more than a simple springboard into a zany caper. Neither were Cannell's populist concoctions as foolish and as empty of truth or feeling as some other producers' cynical second guessing of popular trends. While the concept of *The A-Team*, with its mercenary soldiers of fortune as heroes and its "law of the gun" frontier justice might have been contentious, Cannell had a way of disarming his more perceptive critics by refusing to take his material seriously, something which many other outlandish adventure series seemed unable to do. It is telling that there were no successful imitations of *The A-Team* from copycat producers, despite the series' enormous success.

Indeed, Cannell's tongue-in-cheek approach was something conspicuously missing from his fellow producers' product. The fear that Edward Woodward's middle-aged vigilante provoked among people who could have mopped the floor with him in *The Equalizer* rendered the series laughable, while the heroes of *Airwolf* simply blasted the bad guys into oblivion with missiles every episode. Cannell parodied such macho posturing, just as Bill Dozier's *Batman* had been sending up the grim earnestness of the super-hero comics, and he was extremely careful to ensure that the bad guys deserved the bashing they were going to get; if they didn't, then the A-Team became the bullies. Robert Thompson relates in his book *Adventures on Prime-Time,* with apparent bafflement, how Cannell announced he was beefing up the dialogue of the villains because it "wasn't tough enough for an appropriate A-Team response." "Often a writer would get this part of the equation wrong, and Cannell, like a maths teacher, would have to correct it" he wrote in 1990. It "sounds more like the parlance of the chemistry lab than the writers' meeting." But Cannell understood, crucially, that it was because *The A-Team* lacked gray areas and moral ambiguity in its characters, that it had to be absolutely right — and, as Thompson suggests, Cannell's productions were meticulously crafted. Early episodes, such as "Children of Jamestown" (the Jonestown massacre), "Pros and Cons" (prison brutality) and "A Small and Deadly War" (cops as hired killers) were quickly and correctly perceived to have been too dark in premise; Cannell swiftly fixed this and lightened the show up. "It's the best comedy show on the air," Cannell insisted defensively to his critics in numerous interviews. Many of them smiled and had to agree, if not with the statement then the sentiment, leaving the more humorless, straight-faced critiques to the detached sociologists and the morally superior who never watched such series either for research or for pleasure, and could thus judge them in blissful ignorance.

"The fun comes in the action scenes" wrote Walter Goodman in the *New York Times,* "which are innocently bloodless. Lots of crashes, explosions and acrobatics from which nobody comes out dismembered. Most of the bullets splatter in the dirt. (In one episode) there is a particularly lively chase through a movie lot, with Mr. Peppard in a dragon costume!"

"The exploits of *The A-Team* (are) so outrageous that it is impossible to take them seriously," wrote John J. O'Connor, seriously underestimating the witlessness of not just a panicky, pernicious press or publicity hungry pressure groups, but often the broadcasters themselves! "At one point," he adds, "Hannibal and Murdock escape from prison by tying themselves to inflated plastic garbage bags that waft out over the walls. And ... before taking a swing at a prison deputy, Hannibal, impersonating a hair-stylist, insists affectedly 'Oh, damn, I hate violence, I really hate it!'"

"The stars of *The A-Team* keep throwing us a wink to let us know that they're in on the mischief," wrote another critic in *New York*, "but their comic style is too broad and raggedy to have a satiric gloss. Dirk Benedict is the worst offender. A former glamor boy on *Battlestar Galactica*, he acts with his dimples and overdoes every effect. As his co-stars camp it up, Mr. T just stands there and glowers...."

The episode "The Rabbit That Ate Las Vegas," written by Frank Lupo and directed by Bruce Kessler "climaxed with a car chase that was the funniest thing I've seen on TV in a while," wrote Tom Carson in *The Village Voice*. "When the hit-men start firing pistols at the heroes' stolen limousine, they fire back with a machine-gun, but all the other cars they're weaving through, at not very high speed, don't falter or change direction a bit. When the chasing car goes into a wildly extended, careening crash, the camera holds on the overturned wreck for a second, while one voice from inside grunts 'You okay, Al?' and another answers bemusedly 'Yeah, I'm alright.'"

Moments like those were a self-parodic bit of lunacy often imposed by the networks themselves, as Chris Bunch and Allan Cole, two freelance scriptwriters for shows such as *The A-Team, Hunter,* and *The Incredible Hulk* confirmed, due to the series' early time-slot. "When the Hulk throws a man through a plate-glass window" they laughed, "it actually has to be written into the script that 'dazed, he gets up, shaken but unharmed!'"

"*The A-Team* doesn't seem to me to be nearly as 'mindless' as many critics find it," observed John Leonard in *New York*. "It is funnier than most situation comedies (and) better written than anything yet to be dreamed up by the bats in Aaron Spelling's attic ... what they embody so perfectly is the macho rubbish of American pop culture. We are laughing at a rear-view mirror." *Variety* echoed these sentiments. "As showcased in the pilot, *The A-Team* looms as escapist action adventure, to be played all stops out for the action trade, with little attempt at credibility. Credulity goes by the board in Cannell's highly innovative plots."

Naturally this critical acceptance from some quarters did not stop the lower levels of the hypocritical, hyper-critical media from filling its pages with venom, always lovingly illustrated with large eye-catching publicity stills of the shows they profess to despise. The familiarity and popularity of the images having attracted the attention of the readers, these pictures are then used to sell the usual tired tirade of scaremongering clichés of that convenient old bogeyman for the world's failings, "violence on TV." *The A-Team,* in which bullets are fired, grenades are thrown, and large numbers of vehicles sent flying, was a series sent from heaven for those who cared to resurrect the old arguments of TV trivializing violence.

Can these critics have it both ways? Apparently so. Film makers who find it either artistically necessary or commercially advantageous to show violent action in all its bloody glory are caught between the metaphorical rock and the hard place. If they show blood and bodies being blown to smithereens, they are condemned by the moral guardians, yet the sociologists argue with equal conviction that less realistic, comic-book violence is equally dangerous for failing to show the consequences. If audiences see people using guns and bombs, but there is no blood and death, they reason, then they will expect the same results in real life. Not only is this assumption patently absurd, but ordinary everyday life proves this point of view wrong almost daily. In fact, with real-life atrocities being broadcast repeatedly and often quite gratuitously under the argument that it is reality, it's difficult to imagine any television viewer being unable to tell the difference between *The A-Team* and the nightly news, even the children in whose name most acts of casual, sweeping censorship are usually performed. Unfortunately, the attitude all the campaigners seem to have in common is to presume that only *they* have the intellect to make these distinctions. They, in their infinite wisdom, can see the various issues of the debate in all their complexity, while the rest of us must be naive and impressionable dunces, waiting like sleeper agents to be triggered into an orgy of madness and destruction by the new season's television. In truth, the general mass audience is probably way ahead of them in perceiving the nature of fact and fiction on TV; for a start, they can usually see right through the professional complainers to the sad, lonely time-wasters they are, an attribute sadly lacking in the upper echelons of much television management.*

Common sense dictates that contrary to the ingenious imaginations of barrel-scraping defense lawyers and their cunning clients, an unhinged, mentally dangerous or exceptionally stupid person is prone to performing anti-socially whether they watch TV or not. Anti-social behavior was not invented by the television industry, and — of course — if we sanitize and censor innocuous forms of popular entertainment such as television (or music, or cinema, or comic-books) then the equally powerful classics of fine art forms such as literature and painting must follow, each of which have their fair share of intense violence and horror ... or the argument falls apart for the pompous anti-popular entertainment posturing and easy-answer blame-shifting that it undoubtedly is. As for the political arguments against programming such as *The A-Team* (or, for that matter, other juvenile right-wing fantasies such as *Mission: Impossible, Blue Thunder, Masquerade, Cover-Up,* or *Airwolf*), it would seem futile wasting words and energy on the politics of pop culture, which is surely more a result of society than an influence on it.

In 1985, the National Coalition on Television Violence (!) maintained that *The A-Team* offered 39 "violent acts" an hour, thus beating the previous season's holder of this dubious honor, Glen Larson's asinine *The Fall Guy*. The following year, a similar pressure group (or perhaps the same one with a new name), calling themselves the International Coalition Against Violent Entertainment upped the figure to 49 ... but David Gerber's short-lived *Lady Blue* had pipped it at the post with 50! Cannell's *Hunter* came third on their list with a figure of 48, while Michael Mann's *Miami Vice* followed, clocking up a mere 38. Their other figures claimed that the U.S.A. is "responsible" for 70 percent of all violent TV shows in the world (and probably 70 percent of all TV shows of any kind, I suspect), that TV cops shoot their guns 800 times more often than real-life police in the U.S., and that 54 percent of evening TV shows in the U.S. offer "violent themes!" However, few of these meticulous and humorless public watchdogs take into consideration the format that these heinous acts are occurring in, or the context in which they are being presented. Number-crunching offers no analysis of program approach and content, beyond totting up figures on notepads.† It is not reported whether being exposed to all this violence and becoming so obsessive about it, has yet transformed any of them into homicidal maniacs unable to tell the difference between a real car wreck and a stunt trick. "The show isn't working because we're flipping jeeps over," insists Cannell. "People are getting a kick out of the characters; we have specific things that make them funny." "It has a much broader appeal than we thought it would" said an NBC researcher.

Media professor Jib Fowles, in his 1983 book Television Viewers vs. Media Snobs, *suggests that "What the American people have freely selected for their after-hours diversion are fantasies laden with sex and violence. Other content they have largely spurned, but these myths and fantasies, coming first in one guise and then another, have proved to be thoroughly therapeutic for weary minds. It is a therapy that virtually everyone needs. One of the findings of the NBC/Roper poll was that those who ... expressed the most concern about sex and violence, then viewed as much television, and the same sorts of programs, as everyone else!"*

†*My favorite violence-on-TV survey comes from New Zealand, where the Mental Health Foundation (!) listed the ten most violent shows they could find on the air;* Wiseguy, Magnum, *and* Mannix *came in at numbers 7, 9, and 10 — but were ignominiously pipped at the post by* Huckleberry Hound *at no. 3 and* Duck Tales *at no. 5!*

Pop culture is by definition, popular; if the public rejects it, it ceases to be a commercial proposition and is no longer produced in that form. As one of America's most watched programs, *The A-Team* was the only runaway hit out of 45 new series in the 1983–'84 season; the professional complainers would do the society they fret for a far greater service by analyzing the grievances against officialdom and the failings of the system that caused the American public to turn so conclusively to *Lone Ranger* fantasies rather than the law, instead of trying to sweep America's rewriting of the Vietnam war and disenchantment with the proper channels of justice under the carpet as some sort of media conspiracy — but then, that would require a greater intellectual effort than simply taking pot shots at popular culture. "These are crazy times" explained then–NBC president Brandon Tartikoff, who claimed to have had a hand in devising the concept. "These (the A-Team) are underdogs, outcasts of society at a time when there are a lot of disenfranchised people. The show is escapist, and fun to watch. ... We are not looking for Emmy award nominations," said Tartikoff, "but to get the blood pumping at the network. In that, *The A-Team* has exceeded my expectations. As long as 42 million people keep watching, I don't see any reason to change."

"There is always going to be a section of the audience which has natural concern over particular programmes," the then-director general of Britain's Independent Broadcast Authority, John Whitney, diplomatically told the trade paper *Broadcast* in 1986. "It would be odd if people didn't voice their concerns. We have had surveys which have shown that a very substantial group of parents feel that *The A-Team* is make-believe. It is entertainment, it doesn't bring the three-dimensional realism of violence into the home, and they are happy with its content."*

In an interview on British television, George Peppard told his audience, "I think the A-Team are either the *worst* shots in the world...! But it *is* good, because it tells everybody we're out for fun, there's going to be no blood, there's going to be no horror, you *know* what we intend, you know we don't like the bad guys, and we *do* defeat them. It also gave us some leeway into farce, because basically, the best thing about *The A-Team* to me is when you have something utterly ridiculous that's treated with absolute seriousness, and when we did that well, I thought we were very funny."

Certainly Cannell has succeeded, and continued to succeed, where imitators have failed, and *A-Team* clones have been few and far between considering the series' phenomenal popularity. Those that have appeared, such as *Command Five* and the "adult's *A-Team*" *CAT Squad*, existed in pilot or TV movie form only before disappearing so fast as to be barely noticed.

As for *The A-Team* itself, the series went through a number of phases. After an excellent first season (which, as a mid-season replacement, consisted of only twelve episodes and the pilot), and a reasonable second season, the third year started to show the limitations of the narrow premise, and was rather dull. Part of the problem was that some of Cannell's stronger writers were being siphoned off *The A-Team* to write for other Cannell productions, such as *Riptide, Rousters, Hunter,* and *Hardcastle and McCormick*. The more successful *The A-Team* was, the more product the networks wanted from him ... and with *The A-Team* already working, and a winning formula already discovered, Cannell's better writers tended to be assigned

---

**Sadly, the opinion of the director general did not filter down to his minions within the ITV network that broadcast* The *A-Team* to huge audiences throughout the 1980s, and considerable chunks of action were frequently hacked out of the episodes — thus maintaining a tradition of double standards and hypocrisy that mutilates films and TV on Britain's television to this day.

to the other series. Although certain episodes stood out, as the second season drew to a close, *The A-Team* was starting to get a little stale and repetitive, simply going through the motions. Fortunately, Cannell had the ability to see it, and the courage to do something about it. By this time, with the tougher, grimmer episodes with strong themes such as the first two in the series (Cannell's "Pros and Cons" and "Children of Jamestown") generally agreed to have missed the mark conceptually, Cannell and his writers had settled in very quickly to the notion of *The A-Team* as comic-strip.* Very early on in the series it was decided that people would not get killed and there would be no high drama†; Cannell and Lupo started having fun with the series, and encouraged their growing team of writers to do the same. As the excellent and vastly improved fourth season began, *The A-Team* was back to its old self—or rather, it had moved on beyond the formulaic structure of the series (innocents are menaced, innocents contact the A-Team, A-Team roust the bad guys, bad guys retaliate, A-Team utilize useful junk to construct outrageous escape-and-destroy device). The constraints were loosened to produce a series of somewhat less predictable and more original escapades that still retained the spirit and traditions of the first three seasons. As with all experimentation, some of these episodes were among the best yet, others among the worst.

This very early promotional leaflet shows the *A-Team* cast before suiting up in character ... top to bottom, Mr. T, George Peppard, Dirk Benedict, Melinda Culea, Dwight Schultz.

One peculiarity of the fourth season was the extraordinary choices of guest stars, as the series searched for new angles through stunt-casting. Some of the more creative choices included wrestlers Hulk Hogan (who appeared twice) and William "the Fridge" Perry, rock stars Rick James and Boy George as themselves, Isaac Hayes (playing a role very similar to his Gandy Fitch in *The Rockford Files*), game-show hosts Pat Sajak and Vanna White,§ and comedians Sheckey Greene and Arte Johnson. Easily one of the most bizarre episodes was "Uncle Buckle-Up," credited to Danny Lee Cole, which

---

*Indeed, this author enjoyed the pleasure of writing the comic-strip version of *The A-Team* in Britain's TV Comic!
†Later comic-strip series of the period, such as Blue Thunder, Airwolf, Manimal *and* Automan *etc. had no such qualms—and curiously attracted less criticism!; in an episode of* Automan, *screened in Britain by the BBC in the same time-slot ITV aired* The A-Team, *we see a man thrown bodily out of a plane in flight!*
§*White, a popular celebrity of the '80s, also appears in her game-show hostess persona during the fifth season of the series* L.A. Law.

featured Johnson as a *Sesame Street*–style kiddie host, complete with furry animal suit, being intimidated by thugs who want his merchandising rights!* The A-Team foil the dastardly plan to fill shoddy Buckle-Up products with smuggled drugs in an outrageous battle with improvised toys!

Several other efforts were made during the fourth season to diversify from the rigid plot development formula established during the first season and then slavishly followed since. In "Lease with an Option to Die," a corny title if ever there was for an episode written by newcomer Bill Nuss, the A-Team go to the aid of B.A.'s mother (Della Reese), whose apartment block is being terrorized by thugs trying to evict the tenants; in "Members Only," also by Nuss, it's *Caddyshack* revisited as Face cons his way into an exclusive country club and discovers a counterfeiting operation overseen by villainous Kevin McCarthy. In "There Goes the Neighborhood," another from Nuss, the A-Team are guarding a rock singer and discover that the supposedly sedate suburbs are teeming with crooks and loons. Cannell himself breaks away from the established formula pattern with the superb "The Road to Hope," directed by David Hemmings, an unusual and genuinely gripping episode which begins as a standard yarn and then gradually unravels.

In this, a meet for an assignment goes awry when a decoy client sent by Colonel Decker, who has been told by Hannibal to meet a vagrant (Hannibal in disguise) in an alley, gives the A-Team's advance fee to the wrong person, a real wino. While the A-Team, watching safely from a distance, are also fooled, the disguised Hannibal is being abducted by a secret criminal organization that provides fake i.d.s from deceased drunkards! When the A-Team rescue Hannibal from Decker, they are mortified to discover that they have a real vagrant, while the bad guys—who wanted an anonymous nobody—are equally distraught to find out they've abducted Hannibal, who clearly isn't what he seems, and claims to be a journalist researching a story on street life. Unconvinced by Hannibal's story, and rattled by some beautifully scripted and performed bravado ("You don't like journalist? How about farmer?"), the hoods make Hannibal dig his own grave at the locale where the remains of several other previously abducted hobos have been hidden. Escaping in a burst of ingenuity and dumb luck, Hannibal vows to use Decker's decoy money to expose and dispose of the racket he's stumbled onto. Excellent action scenes in this episode feature a trampoline thrown over a wall so that Face can make a rapid exit during gunplay, while the scam of the week includes Face as a building inspector, with Murdock becoming an invisible evangelist to lead an army of reformed drunks into battle for the usual fireworks finale!

In Cannell's "Where Is the Monster When You Need Him?," directed by Michael O'Herlihy, Hannibal is appearing as "the Aqua-Maniac" in a South American–filmed B-movie when he stumbles onto the hiding place of a Nazi war criminal (Walter Gotell, who made a career out of such roles; he plays a similar part in the *Greatest American Hero* episode "Heaven Is in Your Genes")†; in Cannell and Lupo's "Waiting for Insane Wayne" the A-Team are mistaken for the bad guys by a group of ranchers who have hired a band of unscrupulous mercenaries to run an elderly man off his land. Writers Richard Christian Matheson and Thomas Szollosi came up with a further variation on the series' formula in "The Doctor Is Out," another

---

*Ironically, lawsuits were later flying around from cast members of The A-Team, *who—according to a report in* Variety—*were suing Cannell Productions for allegedly unpaid merchandising fees.*
†*Nazi war criminals lurk everywhere in Cannell shows—others include "Irving the Explainer" and "Paradise Cove" in* The Rockford Files, *"Raiders of the Lost Sub" in* Riptide, *"Surprise on Seagull Beach" in* Hardcastle and McCormick, *and "The Final Exam" in* Sonny Spoon.

superior episode again directed by David Hemmings, who worked extensively on Cannell, Bellisario, Larson, and Lupo productions. In this, Geoffrey Lewis, a familiar TV face and supporting player in many a Clint Eastwood movie, plays a demented military man who abducts his psychiatrist (Richard Anderson of *The Six Million Dollar Man* and *The Bionic Woman*), who is about to spill the beans on his mental condition! The doctor also has Murdock as a patient, and when Murdock witnesses the abduction, the A-Team are inevitably drawn into the fray, and a rescue mission is undertaken in a troubled foreign country alongside a mysterious young woman whose identity seems to change almost every five minutes! In "Mind Games," also written by Cannell, a renegade band of CIA operatives headed by David Hedison (formerly the hero of the 1960s series *Voyage to the Bottom of the Sea*, but later more frequently a guest villain in various series) splits the A-Team by fooling Face into thinking he has been granted a pardon by the government. In fact, they only want to use the Faceman — who is now completely intoxicated by images of impending stardom as a media celebrity — for their own ends. A similar scheme unfolds in "Wheel of Fortune" by Bill Nuss, in which Murdock wins a holiday on the celebrated game show with the assistance of Face, and then seemingly disappears on vacation with one of his fellow inmates instead of the furious Faceman. In fact, he has been kidnapped by a group of gangsters who need his skills as a helicopter pilot for a Vegas rip-off. Again, nobody is who they appear to be, and Dwight Schultz gives a fine performance in the game-show sequences.

While the fourth season went out of its way to supply the audience with novelty guest stars and made a conscious effort to break free of the traditional formula, the first three seasons had provided regular Cannell aficionados with a host of familiar faces, most of them portraying that specific breed of Cannell bad guy we'd come to know and love — stressed out thugs! In the first season, we'd seen John Saxon, Clifton James, Red West, Paul Koslo, Jack Ging, Dean Stockwell, Richard Romanus, Charles Cioffi, Ed Winter, Bill McKinney, Yaphet Kotto, Albert Popwell, Stuart Whitman, Alan Fudge, Andy Robinson, and Don Stroud; Clifton James, Jack Ging, Alan Fudge and Andy Robinson were back for a second shot at the boys the following year, along with Albert Salmi, Michael Halsey, Marjoe Gortner, John Fujioka, Don Knight, Dennis Lipscombe, Morgan Woodward, Mills Watson, Michael Ironside, John Vernon, John Quade, Michael Baseleon, Anthony Charnota, Michael Fairman, Kurtwood Smith, Bo Hopkins, Dennis Franz, Steven Keats, Michael Cavenaugh, and Geoffrey Lewis.*

The third season opened with an obvious network suck-up, "Bullets and Bikinis," a bimbo-laden saga that was obviously NBC's idea of a good hook to pull in the undecided for the new season (the second year of *Riptide* started in exactly the same way, with the dismal "Where the Girls Are," a similar sop to network presumptions, while *Hunter* began *its* second season with the porno investigation "Case X"). With duty done, Cannell could get down to business with his and Lupo's "The Bend in the River," a double-length episode directed by Michael O'Herlihy, which wrote out the Tawnia Baker character; Marla Heasley, who — in keeping with tradition for later cast additions — had previously appeared in an earlier episode in a different role ("Bad Time at the Border") had made her debut as Tawnia midway through the second season in "The Battle of Bel-Air," and been told bluntly to her face by Peppard that she wasn't welcome or wanted. For the next two seasons, the A-Team would

---

Some nice continuity was spoiled when Tricia O'Neill returned in Matheson and Szollosi's second season episode "Deadly Manoeuvres" as Dr. Maggie Sullivan, after first appearing in Patrick Hasburgh's first season story "Black Day at Bad Rock" ... only to have fellow guest-star from that episode Ed Lauter show up in the second season story in a completely different role!

consist of only the four guys, but the third season was interesting primarily for its guest stars. In Mark Jones' "Trouble on Wheels," James Luisi and Joe Santos were reunited from *The Rockford Files;* Santos played a motor works foreman with a shady past who was being intimidated by bad guy Luisi, who is ripping off auto parts. In "Fire," written by Stephen Katz, Stepfanie Kramer guested, undoubtedly to help NBC promote the ailing *Hunter,* playing a feisty fire chief, and Dana Elcar of *Baretta* and *Black Sheep Squadron* made the first of two appearances in the series in "Double Heat,"* an episode that also featured Steven Williams, later of *21 Jump Street,* as a warring mobster. Robert Davi and Elsa Raven of *Wiseguy* both appear in Mark Jones' "Sheriffs of Rivertown," and Dennis Franz of *Hill Street Blues* and *NYPD Blue,* a regular fixture as a Cannell sleazeball, returned to guest alongside professional villainous smoothie Lloyd Bochner in Paul Bernbaum's enjoyable *"Beverly Hills Assault."* Other returning villains included Alan Fudge, Michael Baseleon, Morgan Woodward, John Quade, John Saxon, Ed Winter, Don Stroud, Bill McKinney, and Paul Koslo; new villains were played by Robert Desiderio, Richard Lynch, Wings Hauser, Joe Sirola, Al Ruscio, Alex Rocco, John Calvin, Ken Swofford and Louis Giambalvo. Given the predominance of returning performers, it was perhaps a shame Cannell never brought back some of the same characters for another go-round. Notable storylines included "Breakout," written jointly by Mark Jones and Stephen Katz, in which B.A. and Murdock are handcuffed together in a chain-gang, and Stephen Katz' Murdock episode "Bounty," co-starring Wendy Fulton, Dwight Schultz's real-life wife, in which Murdock is used as bait by bounty hunters looking to capture Hannibal, Face, and B.A.†

Among the more conventional guest stars of the fourth season were the aforementioned Kevin McCarthy, David Hedison and Richard Anderson, and Daryl Anderson (who, following the demise of *Lou Grant* and his role of "Animal," became a clean-shaven heavy for a number of series during the '80s, including Cannell's); Wings Hauser, Stuart Whitman, Jason Evers, John Hancock, Red West, Warren Berlinger, and Geoffrey Lewis were among the returnees.§

For the fifth season, Cannell drastically altered the format of the show in a last-ditch attempt to boost the series' flagging ratings, even to the point of having Mike Post and Pete Carpenter re-score the familiar theme. Although it was a bold attempt to keep afloat a series that had run its course, the result was a weaker show and a poorer concept. As well as introducing Eddie Velez into the cast as Frankie Santana, a gadget-crazy special effects man encountered during one of Hannibal's movie assignments, Cannell brought in the splendid character actor Robert Vaughn as General Hunt Stockwell, a calculating and manipulative mystery man and now employer of the A-Team. The role of devious representative of power and officialdom was one that Vaughn had played to perfection over the years in numerous series guest shots, mini-series (including *Washington: Behind Closed Doors, Centennial,* and the three-part *Hunter* story "City Under Seige"), and TV movies. Although best-known for his starring role as suave '60s super-spy Napoleon Solo in the cult series *The Man from UNCLE* (1964–'68), Vaughn had broken free from being typecast as a hero by appearing as a crooked and con-

---

**His other appearance, in the double length fourth season opener* "Judgement Day" *by Frank Lupo, has a remarkably similar plot!*

†*Dirk Benedict's wife, Toni Hudson, appears in the fourth season episode "Blood, Sweat and Cheers."*

§*Of the fifth season's guest players, it is perhaps only worth noting that "Alive at Five," written by Bill Nuss, and directed by A-Team director, second unit director and stunt co-ordinator Craig Baxley featured Richard Romanus, making a return appearance as gangster Tommy Todesco; further details of Mr. Todesco's illustrious career can be found in the introductory chapter!*

niving politician in the 1969 film *Bullitt,* only to be ironically stereotyped from that moment on in powerful and corrupt roles; if you wanted a sly, untrustworthy senator, general, or police chief, there was Robert Vaughn, apparently at the top of most people's list — and he has been playing that part to perfection ever since! Despite a brief run in Gerry Anderson's dreadful Euro-series *The Protectors* (which he maintains he accepted for the opportunity to travel), and a return bow as Solo in the 1981 TV movie *Return of the Man from UNCLE,* the role of factional Watergate conspirator Frank Flaherty in *Washington*— in which he was superb — finally and irrevocably cast him as a smooth heavy. Having been brought in belatedly to give a boost to the failed 1983 soap *Emerald Point,* Cannell now hoped to employ his talents in a similar way to bolster *The A-Team.*

Unfortunately, despite Vaughn giving his usual fine and well-practiced performance, his inclusion (as well as that of Velez as Frankie Santana* and Judith Ledford as Stockwell's assistant Carla) was a disastrous ploy that completely destroyed the appealing elements of the series. The acting style of Vaughn clashed horribly with Peppard and the A-Team — Vaughn looked like he'd walked into the wrong show[†] — and it was awful to see the freewheeling A-Team coerced against their wishes into cowed subservience to the military (albeit a renegade military man clearly going his own way), and taking orders from a superior in uniformed authority (an ill-advised digression from the usual Cannell m.o., and totally out of character for the A-Team). To make things worse, this was not a situation that would be resolved at the episode's end, but a new format for the show; audiences knew that the A-Team would never discover exactly who Stockwell was and what he was up to ... which meant that Vaughn, perceived as a villain, would never get his comeuppance. The A-Team were now seen to be in the same no-win position of pressure that they were more accustomed to applying to their adversaries.

Although this was a serious misjudgment on Cannell's part, the low ratings had meant that it was a case of change or die. When a popular series finally hits the skids, there are only two options; you either call it a day and get off before the network throws you off, or you make a last-ditch attempt to stay on the air by completely revamping the show. Cannell made a calculated gamble, but the fact that the ratings were not helped by a laborious introductory three-parter including the dramatic development of having the A-Team captured and put on trial for their "crime" seemed to indicate that the novelty of the show had worn off. While it prospers in re-runs, particularly in European markets, *The A-Team*— like *UNCLE* twenty years earlier — was unceremoniously ditched mid-season in 1986. However, it may turn out to be Cannell's most timeless creation.

Episode Guide

regular and recurring cast: George Peppard (Colonel John "Hannibal" Smith), Dirk Benedict (Templeton "Faceman" Peck), Mr. T. (B.A. "Bad Attitude" Baracus), Dwight Schultz ("Howling Mad" Murdock), Melinda Culea (Amy Allen), Marla Heasley (Tawnia Baker), Eddie Velez (Frankie Santana), Bill Lucking (Colonel Lynch), Lance Le Gault (Colonel Roderick Decker), Charles Napier

---

*A Michael Santana, played by Steven Bauer, replaced Ken Wahl's Vinnie Terranova in the final season of *Wiseguy.*
[†]On one notable occasion, it was another player who appeared to wander into the wrong show; Vaughn's old partner from The Man from UNCLE, David McCallum, guest-starred in a knowing nod to Vaughn's own former cult series in "The Say Uncle Affair," a deliberate tribute to the UNCLE phenomenon complete with that series' affectations (color flashes between scenes and the UNCLE episode titling format— all UNCLE episodes were "affairs") written by Hunter stunt director Terry Nelson and directed by Michael O'Herlihy.

(Colonel Briggs), Jack Ging (General Harlan "Bull" Fulbright), Robert Vaughn (General Hunt Stockwell), Carl Franklin (Captain Crane), Judith Ledford (Carla)

First Season (1983)

THE A-TEAM (pilot)

wr. Stephen Cannell, Frank Lupo, dir. Rod Holcomb

Reporter Amy Allen seeks out the A-Team, a band of near-mythological fugitive mercenaries, to hire them to find and rescue her editor, who is in the clutches of a small band of Mexican bandits who are terrorizing a small, cowed village.

with Tim Dunigan (as "Faceman"), Sergio Calderon, William Windom, Jorge Zepeda, Felix Gonzales, Enrico Lucero, Ron Palillo

CHILDREN OF JAMESTOWN

wr. Stephen Cannell, dir. Christian Nyby, Jr.

The A-Team are captured by a fanatical religious cult when they are hired to free one of the group's brainwashed members.

with John Saxon, Gerrit Graham, Carol Jones, John Carter, Fred Lerner, Ron Hayes, Sherilyn Walter

PROS AND CONS

wr. Stephen Cannell, dir. Ron Satlof

The A-Team break *into* prison, where guards are making convicts fight to the death for gladiatorial sport.

with Clifton James, Red West, Bill Smith, Meeno Peluce, Ken Norton, Paul Koslo

A SMALL AND DEADLY WAR

wr. Frank Lupo, dir. Ron Satlof

The A-Team pursue a group of renegade cops who are hiring themselves out as hit-men.

with Jack Ging, Norman Alden, Dean Stockwell, Al White, Lew Palter, Fil Formicola

BLACK DAY AT BAD ROCK

wr. Patrick Hasburgh, dir. Christian Nyby, Jr.

Although the A-Team are able to escape from a small-town sheriff who has discovered their identities after B.A. sustains a bullet wound, the group return when they discover that a vicious motorcycle gang, the Road Warriors, are planning to terrorize the town.

with Ed Lauter, Ted Gehring, Sid Haig, Tricia O'Neill, John Dennis Johnston

THE RABBIT WHO ATE LAS VEGAS

wr. Frank Lupo, dir. Bruce Kessler

The A-Team are hired by two college girls to protect their professor from the mob, who are more than a little peeved that he has conceived a method of breaking the bank at Vegas.

with Richard Romanus, Charles Cioffi, Terrence McGovern, Kitty Moffat, Michele Avonne, Tracy Scoggins, Luke Andreas

HOLIDAY IN THE HILLS

wr. Babs Greyhosky, dir. Arnold Laven

The A-Team attempt to hang-glide to freedom when they are pursued by crazy mountain-men after their plane crash-lands in the hills.

with Ed Winter, Philip Sterling, Bill McKinney, John Perak, Denise Galik

THE OUT-OF-TOWNERS

wr. Frank Lupo, dir. Chuck Bowman

The A-Team arrange an elaborate array of stunts and disguises to put an end to the intimidation of local shop-keepers by gangsters running a local protection racket.

with Yaphet Kotto, Robert Tessier, Albert Popwell, Wendy Hoffman

WEST COAST TURNAROUND

wr. Babs Greyhosky, Stephen Cannell, Patrick Hasburgh, dir. Guy Magar

The A-Team protect a farmer from the bullying tactics of a rival.

with Stuart Whitman, Robert Sampson, Devon Ericson, Tom McFadden, Michael Alldredge, Tim Rossovich

ONE MORE TIME

wr. Babs Greyhosky, Frank Lupo, Patrick Hasburgh, dir. Arnold Laven

Captured by the military, the A-Team are coerced into aiding a captive general and his daughter.

with Ed Grover, Warren Kemmerling, Alan Fudge, Nico Minardos, Barbra Horan, Amy Steel

'TIL DEATH DO US PART

wr. Babs Greyhosky, Frank Lupo, dir. Guy Magar

The A-Team masquerade as caterers to save a young socialite from a high society shotgun wedding.

with Janice Heiden, John Ericson, Jim Antonio, Tony Dale, Jenny Neumann

THE BEAST FROM THE BELLY OF THE BOEING

wr. Patrick Hasburgh, dir. Ron Satlof

Hannibal masquerades as the head of Beller Airways when one of the company jets is hijacked by terrorists. When the rest of the team get on board and disarm them, they discover that Hannibal will have to land the plane.

with Andrew Robinson, Alan Stock, Xander Berkeley, Tony Brubaker, Steve Chambers, Jesse D. Goins, Scott Lincoln, Jim McKrell, Michael Swan, Mary Kate McGeehan

A NICE PLACE TO VISIT

wr. Frank Lupo, dir. Bernard McEveety

Attending the small-town funeral of a friend, the A-Team discover that he was murdered by a family of brothers who are terrorizing the town, and intend his pregnant widow to be their next victim.

with Joanna Kerns, Don Stroud, Robert F. Lyons, Ted Markland, M.C. Gainey, Tony Epper, Sandy Ward, Kelbe Nugent, Burton Gilliam

Second Season (1983–'84)

DIAMONDS AND DUST

wr. Patrick Hasburgh, dir. Ron Satlof

The A-Team coerce a trader out of his entire dynamite supply in order to return to a diamond mine to its rightful owner.

with Kristen Meadows, Michael Halsey, Albert Salmi, Sam Scarber, Brian Libby

RECIPE FOR HEAVY BREAD

wr. Stephen Cannell, dir. Bernard McEveety

The A-Team run into an old friend and an American traitor from the Vietnam war when they stumble onto a heroin smuggling operation.

with Mako, Marjoe Gortner, John Fujioka, Nick Dimitri, Rudy Chromchak, Michael Alldredge

THE ONLY CHURCH IN TOWN

wr. Babs Greyhosky, dir. Christian Nyby, Jr.

The A-Team swipe a military jet to go to the aid of one of Peck's former girlfriends, now a nun whose orphanage in South America is being terrorized by local thugs.

with Markie Post, Elizabeth Hoffman, Don Knight, Judd Omen, Beau Starr, East Ismael Carlo

BAD TIME ON THE BORDER

wr. Richard Christian Matheson, Thomas Szollosi, dir. Bruce Kessler

B.A. befriends a little Mexican girl and the team uncover a group of corrupt border guards who are smuggling in illegal workers to an L.A. sweatshop (both Jack Ging and Marla Heasley are playing different parts to their later featured roles in the series).

with Jack Ging, Dennis Lipscomb, Edie Marie Rubio, Marla Heasley, David Graf, Jeffrey Josephson, Joey Aresco, Carlos LaCamara, Bert Santos

WHEN YOU COMIN' BACK, RANGE RIDER?

wr. Frank Lupo, dir. Christian Nyby, Jr.

Murdock adopts the identity of the famous Range Rider when a Native American discovers a plan to make dog food out of some Arizona wild mustangs (this episode introduces Lance Le Gault as Colonel Decker and Carl Franklin as Captain Crane—but see "The White Ballot" below).

with Richard Yniguez, Morgan Woodward, Philip Gordon, Dana Kimmel, Mills Watson, Bobby Bass, Jack Verbois

THE TAXI-CAB WARS

wr. Stephen Cannell, dir. Gilbert Shelton

The A-Team help out a small cab company that is being victimized by a larger rival destroying their cabs and assaulting their drivers.

with Michael Ironside, Ed Lynch, Michael Crabtree, Liz Sheridan, Ernie Hudson

LABOR PAINS

wr. Richard Christian Matheson, Thomas Szollosi, dir. Arnold Laven

The A-Team are hiding out in a small farming community when they become involved in a local land-owner's attempts to stop the workers from forming a union.

with John Vernon, Alan Autry, Penny Peyser, Charles Napier (not as Briggs), Ted Markland

THERE'S ALWAYS A CATCH

wr. Richard Christian Matheson, Thomas Szollosi, dir. Ron Satlof

The A-Team attempt to preserve the ecology of

a small fishing town from the selfish activities of a greedy bully.

with John Quade, Len Wayland, Tracy Scoggins, Robin Strand, Rebecca Stanley

WATER, WATER, EVERYWHERE

wr. Sidney Ellis, Jo Swerling, Jr., dir. Arnold Laven

The A-Team go to the aid of three handicapped Vietnam veterans who have been threatened and beaten up by a businessman who wants their land.

with Alan Fudge, Robin Riker, Jim Knaub, Jon Feather, R. David Smith, Michael Rider

STEEL

wr. Frank Lupo, dir. Gilbert Shilton

The demolition of an old warehouse is hampered by the terror tactics of a larger demolition company with mob connections.

with Michael Baseleon, Ray Girardin, Norman Alden, Mary Margaret Humes, Tim Rossovich

THE WHITE BALLOT

wr. Jeff Ray, dir. Dennis Donnelly

Face opposes a crooked sheriff in a small-town local election (note: this is the episode which actually introduces Colonel Decker and Crane to the series, although the first episode to feature Decker on-air was "When You Comin' Back, Range Rider?"; this is also the last episode to feature Melinda Culea as Amy Allen, although she was already absent in the previous episode, "Steel," and she appeared in "When You Comin' Back, Range Rider?" which should therefore follow it. These discrepancies are caused by the network changing the running order of the series from the order of production; however, the production numbers of the episodes do not correspond with continuity either, suggesting that some episodes were started earlier, but completed later than others given production numbers in between. For this reason, all episode guides in this book are given in the sequence of U.S. transmission).

with Clifton James, Joshua Bryant, Andy Robinson, Martin Azarow

THE MALTESE COW

wr. Richard Christian Matheson, Thomas Szollosi, dir. Dennis Donnelly

The A-Team go to the aid of an old friend from Saigon, whose restaurant business in Chinatown is being threatened by drug smugglers.

with Keye Luke, Lydia Lei, James Hong, Paul Mantee, Peter Kwong, John Milford, Richard Kuhlman

IN PLANE SIGHT

wr. Babs Greyhosky, dir. Tony Mordente

The A-Team fly to South America to clear the name of a young man framed for smuggling cocaine.

with Judy Strangis, Grainger Hines, Anthony Charnota, Rod Colbin, Lesley Woods, Bruce French, Lance Henriksen, Carmen Argenziano

THE BATTLE OF BEL-AIR

wr. Frank Lupo, dir. Gilbert Shilton

The A-Team discover a plot to kidnap a visiting VIP after a security firm abducts one of its own employees (this episode introduces Marla Heasley as Tawnia Baker ... and special congratulations to Frank Lupo for getting "Sheik Fatasi" past Network Standards and Practices...!)

with Michael Fairman, Kurtwood Smith, Randolph Roberts, Ronald Meszaros, Charles Walker, Edward Ansara

SAY IT WITH BULLETS

wr. Richard Christian Matheson, Thomas Szollosi, dir. Dennis Donnelly

The A-Team investigate arms trafficking from an army base, and come close to being captured by Colonel Decker.

with Lauren Chase, Monte Markham, Sam Melville, Miguel Fernandez, Patrick Brady

PURE-DEE POISON

wr. Chris Bunch, Allan Cole, dir. Dennis Donnelly

The A-Team set out to destroy the contaminated still of some thugs producing poisoned moonshine.

with Bo Hopkins, Tracy Reed, John Amos, Steve Sandor, Tony O'Neil

IT'S A DESERT OUT THERE

wr. Bruce Cervi, dir. Arnold Laven

A group of outlaws riding dune buggies are the targets of The A-Team after they steal from elderly tourists.

with Jeannie Wilson, Robert Dryer, Parley Baer, Tony Burton, Anthony James

CHOPPING SPREE

wr. Stephen Katz, dir. Michael O'Herlihy

B.A. becomes a trifle perturbed when his distinctive van is stolen by a car theft ring to be broken down for spare parts.

with Dennis Franz, Joe Colligan, Lee Patterson, Nick Shields, Liberty Godshall

Harder Than It Looks

wr. Frank Lupo, dir. Ivan Dixon

The A-Team discover a terrorist plot to blow up the Hanson Dam while on a mission to rescue a millionaire's daughter from the terrorists' ranks.

with Lori Lethin, Michael Prince, Steven Keats, Kevyn Major Howard, Cherie Michan, Suzanne Albert, Frank Annese

Deadly Manoeuvres

wr. Richard Christian Matheson, Thomas Szollosi, dir. Mike Vejar

A group of vengeful victims of the A-Team's do-gooding hire their own band of mercenaries — a sort of darkside A-Team — to eliminate the group. Soon, only Hannibal and Tawnia remain free to rescue the rest of the team.

with Tricia O'Neill, Ed Lauter, Michael Cavenaugh, John Scanlon, Ed Johnson, Richard Kuss

Semi-Friendly Persuasion

wr. Danny Lee Cole, dir. Craig Baxley

The A-Team attempt to protect an Amish-style community from being bullied out of the area ... but they are asked to do the job without resorting to force...!

with Tim O'Connor, Geoffrey Lewis, Sam Jones, Robby Kiger

Curtain Call

wr. Stephen Katz, dir. Dennis Donnelly

A "cheater" episode, using clips from previous episodes within a framework concerning the A-Team pinned down in a cabin by Decker with a seriously wounded Murdock in tow.

with Danny Wells, Nik Celozzi, Steve Tannen, George Wyner

Third Season (1984–'85)

Bullets and Bikinis

wr. Mark Jones, dir. Dennis Donnelly

Two beautiful girls hire the A-Team to protect their Fort Lauderdale hotel from local mobster Joey Epic.

with Betsy Russell, Kimberly Ross, Vincent Bagetta, Ben Piazza, Jeana Tomasina

The Bend in the River (double-length episode)

wr. Frank Lupo, Stephen Cannell, dir. Michael O'Herlihy

When Tawnia gets word that her fiancé is alive but in danger in Brazil after setting out on a quest for the Lost City Of Del Rio along the Amazon river, the A-Team discover a nuclear reactor in the jungle, complete with Nazi war criminal in charge of it ... (this double-length episode writes out the Tawnia Baker character introduced to replace Amy Allen during the second season; in fact, she is already absent from the previous episode).

with Sergio Calderone, Marta Dubois, Mike Preston, Don Pedro Colley, Barry Van Dyke, Erik Holland

Fire

wr. Stephen Katz, dir. Tony Mordente

The A-Team are pursued by a new adversary — Colonel Briggs — while they attempt to prevent the harassment of a small fire-fighting service.

with Stepfanie Kramer, Buddy Garion, Alan Fudge, Paul Gleason, W.K. Stratton, Brad English, Terrence Evans, Christopher Pennock

Timber

wr. Jeff Ray, dir. David Hemmings

Previously, the A-Team helped farm workers form a union; here, they're helping out loggers who want no part of a crooked one.

with Joe Lambie, Tracy Brooks Swope, Beau Starr, Wiley Harker, Ray Bickel, Jon Andre Gower, Shirley Slater, Cindy Roberts, Art LaFleur

Double Heat

wr. Stephen Katz, dir. Craig Baxley

An accountant about to testify against the mob hires the A-Team when they kidnap his daughter.

with Michael Baseleon, Dana Elcar, Leah Ayres, Daniel Green, Steven Williams, Christine DeLisle, Reid Cruikshanks, Sal Landi

Trouble on Wheels

wr. Mark Jones, dir. Michael O'Herlihy

A foreman with a shady past is intimidated by bad guys into supplying them with stolen auto parts ... so he contacts the A-Team.

with Joe Santos, James Luisi, Melinda Moreno, Michelle Rosas, Mills Watson, Dennis Pratt

THE ISLAND

wr. Mark Jones, dir. Michael O'Herlihy

A small isolated fishing village is invaded by heroin smugglers.

with James Callahan, Paul Drake, Sonny Landham, Carole Davis, Alejandra Garray

SHOWDOWN

wr. Milt Rosen, dir. James Fargo

A bogus A-Team attempt to intimidate the members of a traveling Wild West show into transporting drugs for them (for reasons presumably connected with actor availability, Bill Lucking returns as Colonel Lynch to pursue the A-Team in this single episode).

with Morgan Woodward, D.D. Howard, Michael DeLano, John Carter, W.K. Stratton, Ben Hamner, Xander Berkeley, Joseph Di Reda, K.C. Winkler

SHERIFFS OF RIVERTOWN

wr. Mark Jones, dir. Dennis Donnelly

The A-Team are hired by a group of businessmen to bring law and order to a corrupt town that houses their workers.

with Robert Davi, Wendy Kilbourne, Edmund Gilbert, East Ismael Carlo, Chip Johnson, Will MacMillan, Bryan McGuire, James Lough, Curtis Taylor, Elsa Raven

THE BELLES OF ST. MARY'S

wr. Stephen Cannell, dir. Dennis Donnelly

The A-Team protect a singing group from the attentions of their unscrupulous manager when their unfair contract is up for renewal.

with Robert Desiderio, Joseph Wiseman, Michael Alldredge, Reginald Dorsey, Deborah Lacey, Kathleen O'Malley, Dawn Mangrum, Karl Johnson, Leslie Kawai, Lisa Antille

HOT STYLES

wr. Stephen Katz, dir. Tony Mordente

A beautiful fashion model is being coerced into betraying her employer's designs.

with Markie Post, Richard Lynch, John Moschitta, Jr., Andy Romano, Arthur Taxier, Stephen Liska, Liam Sullivan

BREAKOUT

wr. Mark Jones, Stephen Katz, dir. Dennis Donnelly

B.A. and Murdock find themselves chained together in a work farm after being framed of participating in a robbery.

with Steve Sandor, Jeff Doucette, Robert Donner, Lenore Kasdorf, Bruce Fischer, Tawny Moyer, Melanie Wilson, Joe La Due, Joe Unger

A CUP A'JOE

wr. Dennis O'Keefe, dir. Craig Baxley

Developers who want a piece of land for a shopping mall must first dispose of a family diner, and terrorize them into a sale.

with Claude Earl Jones, John Ashton, Dave Shelley, Toni Sawyer, Lisa Denton, Gary Lee Davis, Shawn Southwick, Herb Mitchell, Jim Boeke

THE BIG SQUEEZE

wr. Stephen Cannell, dir. Arnold Laven

The A-Team open a bar in order to attract the attention of local loan sharks they intend to close down.

with Wings Hauser, Joe Sirola, Al Ruscio, Janine Turner, Marshall Teague, Victoria Bass

CHAMP

wr. Stephen Katz, dir. Michael O'Herlihy

The A-Team assist a boxer who is under pressure to throw a fight.

with Greg Collins, Alex Rocco, Joey Tata, Holly Gagnier, Daniel Faraldo, Dick Balduzzi, Herman Poppe, Lana Clarkson, Jimmy Lennon

SKINS

wr. Mark Jones, dir. Dennis Donnelly

The A-Team go after poachers who are killing protected species.

with John Quade, John Calvin, Daphne Maxwell, Jesse Lawrence Ferguson, Darin Taylor

ROAD GAMES

wr. Stephen Katz, dir. Nicholas Sgarro

The A-Team set out to break the bank of a traveling casino that has stolen the mortgage money for a foster home.

with Ed Winter, Jason Evers, Daphne Ashbrook, Kaz Garas, Frank Marth, Don Maxwell, Read Morgan, Katy Baldwin

MOVING TARGETS (a.k.a. Prey)

wr. Mark Jones, dir. Dennis Donnelly

The A-Team find themselves stranded in the desert with a reluctant bride.

with Sue Kiel, John Saxon, Jack Heller, Frank Annese, Maurice Sherbanee, Kavi Raz, Ava Lazar, Adam Ageli

KNIGHTS OF THE ROAD (a.k.a. Tow)

wr. Steven Sears, Burt Pearl, dir. Michael O'Herlihy

An auto-mechanic hires the A-Team when a bigger rival attempts to force him out of business.

with Jim McMullan, Deborah Goodrich, Don Stroud, Carlos Romero, Ji-Tu Cumbuka, Jimmie Skaggs, Ricardo Lopez

WASTE 'EM

wr. Stephen Katz, Mark Jones, dir. Sidney Hayers

A brother and sister running a delivery service are intimidated by a chemical company secretly dumping toxic waste near their site.

with Joseph Hacker, Stacy Nelkin, Mitchell Ryan, John Dennis Johnston

BOUNTY

wr. Stephen Katz, dir. Michael O'Herlihy

Murdock is abducted by bounty hunters intent on bringing in the A-Team.

with Bill McKinney, Paul Koslo, Wendy Fulton, Gene Evans, Mickey Jones, Joan Roberts

BEVERLY HILLS ASSAULT

wr. Paul Bernbaum, dir. Craig Baxley

Face masquerades as an art critic and Murdock as a painter when the A-Team go to the aid of a talented artist being forced to produce forgeries.

with Lloyd Bochner, Maylo McCaslin, Dennis Franz, Branscombe Richmond, Bruce Glover, Kathy Witt, Garnett Smith, Cherie Michan, Michael Young Evans

INCIDENT AT CRYSTAL LAKE

wr. Frank Lupo, dir. Tony Mordente

Three armed robbers who have heisted an empty van stumble onto the A-Team while they are treating themselves to a fishing vacation.

with Kristen Meadows, Christopher Stone, Ken Swofford, Robert Gray, Robert Tessier, Judson Scott

TROUBLE BREWING

wr. Steven Sears, Burt Pearl, dir. Michael O'Herlihy

Two sisters running a soda-pop factory are threatened by an unscrupulous bigger rival trying to muscle in.

with Louis Giambalvo, Claudia Christian, Suzanne Barnes, Robert Dryer, Anthony James, Walter Mathews, Jack Hogan, Cal Gibson

Fourth Season (1985–'86)

JUDGEMENT DAY

wr. Frank Lupo, dir. David Hemmings

The A-Team follow the kidnapped daughter of a judge to Italy, where the mobsters have absconded with her in the hope that her father will throw a trial.

with Dana Elcar, LaGena Hart, Zack Norman, Robert Miranda, James Kelly, Carl Strano, Ann Obregon, Michael DeLano, Christie Claridge, June Chadwick

WHERE IS THE MONSTER WHEN YOU NEED HIM?

wr. Stephen Cannell, dir. Michael O'Herlihy

While making a difficult B-movie (in his cover as a monster movie stunt-man) with an arrogant leading man and an irresponsible co-star, Hannibal stumbles onto a South American town where a war criminal is hiding out.

with Michael Lerner, Dennis Cole, Judy Landers, Mike Preston, Walter Gotell, James Victor

BLOOD, SWEAT, AND CHEERS

wr. Tom Blomquist, dir. Sidney Hayers

A powerful Chicago underworld boss muscles in on a young race-car driver so that the spoils of victory will go to his undeserving and unpleasant nephew.

with Ken Olandt, Wings Hauser, Stuart Whitman, Toni Hudson, Arthur Taxier

LEASE WITH AN OPTION TO DIE

wr. Bill Nuss, dir. David Hemmings

The A-Team rush to the aid of B.A.'s mother, whose apartment block is being terrorized by thugs in the employ of a powerful estate agent.

with Della Reese, Ray Wise, Wendy Schaal, John Vargas, East Ismael Carlo, Brion James, Liz Sheridan, Wiley Harker

The Road to Hope

wr. Stephen Cannell, dir. David Hemmings

A trap arranged by Colonel Decker causes Hannibal, posing as a wino, to stumble onto a scheme involving the abduction and murder of vagrants.

with Warren Berlinger, Christopher Neame, Elisha Cook, Rick Garcia, Bill Marcus, Gloria Charles

The Heart of Rock and Roll

wr. Frank Lupo, dir. Tony Mordente

The A-Team uncover a plot in which a prison warden is using convicts to commit crimes for him while released from prison.

with Rick James, Isaac Hayes, Peter Haskell, Eileen Barnett, Beau Starr, Ji-Tu Cumbuka, James Avery

Body Slam

wr. Bill Nuss, dir. Craig Baxley

Wrestler Hulk Hogan enlists the aid of the A-Team when hoods attempt to close down a local boys' club.

with Hulk Hogan (Terry Bollea), Titos Vandis, Michael Gregory, Deborah Wakeham, Sam Melville, James Bartz, Preston Hanson

Mind Games

wr. Stephen Cannell, dir. Michael O'Herlihy

Face is granted a pardon as a ruse by a renegade CIA agent to attract the attention of a Vietnamese general with a fierce hatred of Face since the Vietnam war (this episode introduces Jack Ging as General Harlan "Bull" Fulbright, latest nemesis of the A-Team).

with David Hedison, Barney McFadden, James Hong, Shelagh McLeod, Ping Wu

There Goes the Neighborhood (a.k.a. The Battle of Canoga Park)

wr. Bill Nuss, dir. Dennis Donnelly

A supposedly quiet suburb where the A-Team are hiding out with a rock star whose life has been threatened turns out to be a den of drug smugglers, lunatic neighborhood watchers, and teenage delinquents.

with Valerie Stevenson, John Aprea, Walter Olkewicz, Victor Campos, Julius Carry III, Richard McGonagle, Steve Eastin

The Doctor Is Out

wr. Richard Christian Matheson, Thomas Szollosi, dir. David Hemmings

Murdock is in the middle of one of his therapy sessions when gun-toting mercenaries burst in and kidnap his psychiatrist.... Clearly a job for the A-Team, who follow his trail to a small South American dictatorship.

with Richard Anderson, Geoffrey Lewis, Jeanetta Arnette, Daniel Davis, Danny Mora, Richard Duran

Uncle Buckle-Up

wr. Danny Lee Cole, dir. Michael O'Herlihy

When Hannibal auditions to play a teddy bear on a childrens' TV show, he discovers that the star of the show — Uncle Buckle-Up — is under pressure from gangsters who want to exploit his toy franchise for criminal purposes.

with Arte Johnson, Jonathan Goldsmith, Art Metrano, Susan Scannell, Bruce Solomon, Eric Lawson, Toni Attell, S. Marc Jordan

Wheel of Fortune

wr. Bill Nuss, dir. David Hemmings

More antics in the world of television, as Murdock wins a trip to Hawaii on a game show, but then disappears mysteriously on the morning he's supposed to leave.

with Lydia Cornell, George McDaniel, Pat Sajak, Vanna White, Judd Omen, Richard Evans, Bernie Pock, Gregory Itzin, Kerry Michaels

The A-Team Is Coming, The A-Team Is Coming

wr. Steve Beers, dir. David Hemmings

A mission to assist a Russian ballerina in her defection to the U.S. is revealed to be a ploy to prevent the heist of a powerful satellite that could provoke a nuclear holocaust.

with William Smith, Raissa Danilov, Gene Scherer, John Considine, Daryl Anderson, David Kagen, Curt Lowens, Jay Scorpio

Members Only

wr. Bill Nuss, dir. Tony Mordente

Face cons his way into a fashionable country club to meet girls, but instead uncovers a counterfeit money operation.

with Kevin McCarthy, Betsy Russell, Scott Colomby, Carole Cook, Barrie Ingham, Sheckey Greene, Steve Tannen, Paul Tinder, Rod Stryker

Cowboy George

wr. Stephen Cannell, dir. Tony Mordente

Face fears he's heading for a lynching when —

working a scam as a theatrical agent — he books an effeminate British pop singer into a Wild West club instead of a country and western performer ... which doesn't go down too well with the crooks who planned to rip off a full house, either.

with Boy George (George O'Dowd), L.Q. Jones, Taylor Lacher, Ben Slack, Jim Boeke, London Donfield, Johnny Lee

WAITING FOR INSANE WAYNE

wr. Stephen Cannell, Frank Lupo, dir. Craig Baxley

The A-Team are mistaken for a group of mercenaries who have been hired by a rancher to run an old man and his son off a valuable piece of land.

with Barry Corbin, Gillian Grant, Moosie Drier, Red West, Jesse Vint, Anthony James, Dennis Stewart, Gary Clarke

THE DUKE OF WHISPERING PINES

wr. Jayne Erlichh, dir. Sidney Hayers

The A-Team discover a bogus gold mine when they go to the aid of an old friend of B.A.'s, whose husband has gone missing.

with Sheila DeWindt, Rick Fitts, Jack Starrett, Don Hood, Gary Grubbs, Michael Bowen, David Dunard, Bobby Jacoby, Suzanne Dunn

BENEATH THE SURFACE

wr. Danny Lee Cole, Lloyd Schwartz, dir. Michael O'Herlihy

Attending a high-school reunion, Face is betrayed by one former classmate, and sent on a treasure hunt for a sunken galleon with another.

with Kim Ulrich, Tom Villard, Paxton Whitehead, Nancy Everhard, MacKenzie Allen, Carol Francis, Archie Lang, Wayne Heffley

MISSION OF PEACE

wr. Steven Sears, Burt Pearl, dir. Craig Baxley

The A-Team go to the aid of a group of elderly people whose mission is in danger of being closed down by a Texan tycoon who wants their land.

with Ann Doran, David White, Jason Evers, Nedra Volz, Ric Mancini, Eric Server, Iron Eyes Cody, Michael Lally, Nora Ball

THE TROUBLE WITH HARRY

wr. Bill Nuss, dir. David Hemmings

The A-Team join forces with Hulk Hogan again to protect a young boy's father and capture some arms dealers.

with Hulk Hogan (Terry Bollea), Paul Gleason, Billy Jacoby, John Hancock, Carl Strano, William "the Fridge" Perry, Vic Polizos, Clare Peck, Denise Gallup, Dian Gallup

A LITTLE TOWN WITH AN ACCENT

wr. Richard Christian Matheson, Thomas Szollosi, dir. Michael O'Herlihy

The A-Team find themselves arrested when they go to the aid of a small town being infiltrated by mobsters.

with Noble Willingham, Kathryn Leigh-Scott, Robert Viharo, Joseph Burke, Rex Ryon, Mark Lawrence, Alex Colon, Corinne Wahl, Michael O'Keefe

THE SOUND OF THUNDER

wr. Frank Lupo, dir. Michael O'Herlihy

General Fulbright tricks the A-Team into helping him locate his daughter in Vietnam, who has rejected him (this final episode of the fourth season writes out Jack Ging as General Fulbright).

with Tia Carrere, George Kee Cheung, Haunani Minn, Lena Pousette, Sol Trager, Peter MacLean

Fifth Season (1986–'87)

DISHPAN MAN (1/3)

wr. Stephen Cannell, dir. Tony Mordente

General Hunt Stockwell persuades the A-Team to rescue the passengers of a hijacked plane with the information that the one man who can clear them of the criminal charges brought against them is on board. The A-Team join up with special effects wizard Frankie Santana, met on the set of Hannibal's most recent film, to effect the rescue (this episode introduces Eddie Velez, Robert Vaughn, and Judith Ledford to the cast).

with Sandy McPeak, David Hess, Fernando Escandon, Stanley Brock, Marc Tubert, Hector Jaime Mercado, Andrew Divoff

TRIAL BY FIRE (2/3)

wr. Tom Blomquist, dir. Les Sheldon

After the successful completion of their rescue of the hijack victims, the A-Team fail to make their usual escape, and Murdock and Santana are forced to watch helplessly as their colleagues are about to finally stand trial.

with David Ackroyd, Byrne Piven, J.A. Preston, Sandy McPeak, Dana Lee, Robert Darnell, Adam Gregor, Richard Newton, Tiiu Leek

Firing Line (3/3)

wr. Frank Lupo, dir. Michael O'Herlihy

Murdock and Santana are forced to ally themselves with General Stockwell in order to save the team from the firing squad.

with Frank McCarthy, Rodney Saulsberry, John Durbin, Dan Tullis, Andrew Divoff, Tiiu Leek

Quarterback Sneak

wr. Paul Bernbaum, dir. Craig Baxley

The A-Team head for East Berlin to get a biochemist out of the country, and set up a football game as a diversionary cover.

with Joe Namath, Alan Autry, Jim Brown, Bo Brundin, Judy Geeson, John Matuszak, Ray Reinhardt, Lyman Ward

The Theory of Revolution

wr. Steven Sears, Burt Pearl, dir. Sidney Hayers

The A-Team travel to a Central American island to free three American agents from a dictatorship where a civil war is in progress.

with Castulo Guerra, Alejandro Rey, Pepe Serna, Gino Silva, Vladimir Skomarovsky, Peter Brown, Tasia Valenza, Blake Conway, Carlos Cervantes, Damon Clark, Charles Howerton

The Say Uncle Affair

wr. Terry Nelson, dir. Michael O'Herlihy

The A-Team steal a Russian jet on the orders of Stockwell, who is promptly kidnapped by a Russian agent (this episode is a stylish tribute to Robert Vaughn's 1960s cult show *The Man from UNCLE*, even bigger than *The A-Team* in its day, in which guest star McCallum co-starred with him).

with David McCallum, James Saito, Toni Attell, Eric Goldner

Alive at Five

wr. Bill Nuss, dir. Craig Baxley

An undercover reporter, masquerading as dangerous gangster Tommy Todesco's girlfriend, is imprisoned by him at his mansion.

with Richard Romanus, Red West, Valerie Wildman, Linden Chiles, Dennis Fimple, Paul Sylvan, Hope North, Lora Staley, Michael Lally, Robert Miano

Family Reunion

wr. Steven Sears, dir. James Darren

The A-Team protect a dying criminal who plans to give Stockwell his valuable diaries, while Stockwell pursues Murdock's suspicions that the gangster might actually be the orphan Face's father.

with Jeff Corey, Clare Kirkconnell, John Carter, Terri Treas, Beau Billingsley, Lou Felder, Anna Rapagna

Point of No Return

wr. Burt Pearl, dir. Bob Bralver

Hannibal goes missing while on the trail of some stolen plutonium.

with Nancy Kwan, Rosalind Chao, Soon-Teck Oh, Dustin Nguyen, Nathan Jung, Clive Rosengren, Dale Ishimoto

The Crystal Skull

wr. Bill Nuss, dir. Michael O'Herlihy

Natives make Murdock their god when the A-Team travel to a primitive island where mercenaries are stealing diamonds.

with Sam Hiona, Manu Tupou, Rochelle Ahsana, Art Tizon, Jack Verbois, Peter Iacangelo, Barry Pierce, Jeffrey Alan Chandler, Aki Aleong, Charles Hyman

The Spy Who Mugged Me

wr. Paul Bernbaum, dir. Michael O'Herlihy

Murdock becomes a Bond-like secret agent to discover the identity of the Jaguar, a mysterious assassin.

with Karen Kopins, Roy Dotrice, Kai Wulff, Marianne Marks, Nick Faltas, Maurice Marsac, Prof. Toru Tanaka, Ronan O'Casey, Marius Mazmanian

The Grey Team

wr. Tom Blomquist, dir. Michael O'Herlihy

A young girl stumbles into her father's plot to uncover a spy ring for government defense secrets.

with Lew Ayres, Moya Kordick, Michael Shannon, John McLiam, Tony Steedman, Paula Victor, Lynn Longos, Nick Angotti, Paul Petersen

Without Reservations

wr. Bill Nuss, dir. John Peter Kousakis

Murdock and Face are taken hostage with others when they accidentally stumble onto an assassination attempt.

with Mills Watson, Marc Alaimo, Edward Bell, Lonny Chapman, Alfred Dennis, Bobby Di Cicco, Terence O'Connor, Ely Pouget

series ends

Hardcastle and McCormick
September 1983–May 1986

"You didn't see Billy the Kid gettin' off on a technicality!"

Following the demise of *The Greatest American Hero*, Patrick Hasburgh had joined the writing team on *The A-Team*, but departed to co-create *Hardcastle and McCormick* with Cannell for the ABC network. The sudden and surprise success of *The A-Team* on NBC had put Cannell and his company much in demand, and naturally ABC, who had initially bankrolled the Cannell organization with orders for his first three pilots, were eager to benefit; already, NBC had the *A-Team* clone *Rousters* ready to roll, and Cannell was talking to them about a back-up series for *The A-Team*, which would ultimately become *Riptide*. The following season, NBC would take *Hunter*. Having made a hash of the scheduling of their last two Cannell productions, practically killing off the successful *Greatest American Hero* themselves by placing it opposite *Dallas*, and sabotaging the admittedly poor *The Quest* with a wildly inappropriate time-slot, ABC could only stand and watch as NBC's ratings for *The A-Team* rocketed.

Hardcastle and McCormick offered the same kind of opposites attract relationship as that between Ralph and Bill in *The Greatest American Hero*, and would feature the same good-natured banter, zany gags, preposterous plots, highly-strung gangsters, questionable politics and spectacular mayhem as all Cannell's other shows of the early '80s. This time, the buddy relationship was between Brian Keith (playing a middle-aged tough guy and father figure) and Daniel Hugh-Kelly (amiable-but-tough nice guy).

Keith was Milton C. Hardcastle (convicts and colleagues alike called him "Hardcase"), a hard-line hanging judge who coerces unwilling parolee Mark McCormick (Daniel Hugh-Kelly) into joining him in his retirement in a bid to round up some of the assorted criminal flotsam and jetsom that escaped his hammer on a technicality.* Fortunately for humankind (and conveniently for television-land), underneath Hardcastle's uncompromising gruff, tough exterior is a fair-minded individual — while underneath his judge's robes are jockey shorts, tennis shoes, a Hawaiian shirt, and invariably a couple of *Lone Ranger* comics for when a trial gets "dull!" In short, not the kind of guy you'd like to have judging *your* case.

With the TV screen awash with unquestioning, flawless authority figures, and with plenty of other TV craftsmen more than ready and willing to handle the more ambiguous, analytical side of American TV drama, Cannell and his colleagues had found their niche, filling the gaping void between the traditionally conservative and the fashionably liberal with age-old

---

*It was a similar format to that of the 1961–'62 series Cain's Hundred, *a sort of combination of* Hardcastle and McCormick *and* Wiseguy, *with Peter Mark Richman as Nick Cain, a former gangland lawyer now using his inside knowledge of the mob and his legal expertise to bring down the mobsters the law had so far failed to touch.*

but brand-new wish-fulfillment fantasies that displayed a parodic self-awareness exclusively associated with Cannell's populist creations. The strength of the series came not from the routine and often quite familiar plots, which were simply hooks on which to hang the stunts, humor, and villainy, but the bantering love-hate relationship of the two ill-matched leads. McCormick's distress at having to ally himself with the judge is not too dissimilar to Rockford's despair at Angel Martin's antics, or Hunter's initial dismay at being saddled with female officer McCall in the later *Hunter* pilot.

"You really read this junk, don't you?" asks McCormick incredulously as he meets Hardcastle in the pilot.

"Sure" says the human brick wall, "Tonto and the Lone Ranger ridin' the plains dispensin' justice! You didn't see Billy the Kid gettin' off on a technicality! Hunt 'em, hear 'em, and hang 'em, that's the way!"

Wildly over the top to no doubt disarm the inevitable criticisms (as with *The A-Team*), this loveable old lunatic (designated bad guy in any other film) is offered up as the acceptable face of vigilantism, cleaned up and whitewashed for public consumption as a fantasy figure who deals with the public's growing frustrations with whiz-kid lawyers, corrupt officialdom, and lenient, liberal judges. Would that life and law 'n order were so cut and dried, but this was a series for those who couldn't or wouldn't understand that they weren't ... or would like to pretend for an hour each week that they were. Cannell, along with a slew of far less reputable, thoughtful, or cautious film-makers, had lucked on to a popular hobby horse and sore subject with the general public first explored and exploited by the Clint Eastwood *Dirty Harry* films, and a staple ingredient of 1980s TV and cinema — a very real and genuine grievance and disillusionment with a legal system driven by plea-bargaining and over-

No, it's not Popeye, but the acceptable face of vigilanteism ... Brian Keith and Daniel Hugh Kelly as *Hardcastle and McCormick*.

crowded prisons and riddled with bureaucratic heartlessness, naiveté, stupidity and incompetence (Hardcastle wears a t-shirt that reads "No Plea-Bargaining in Heaven!").

Although a character named Judge Hardcastle had previously appeared in the 1977 series *Rosetti and Ryan* (played by busy TV face Dick O'Neill of *Cagney and Lacey* and later Cannell's *Top of the Hill*), the part seemed more obviously inspired by Buford Pusser, the baseball bat-wielding real-life Southern sheriff who had already been satirized in the comedy series *Soap* (1977–'81), and portrayed in earnest by Joe Don Baker in the 1973 movie *Walking Tall* (and subsequent failed 1981 TV series of the same name starring Bo Svenson). These antics had been hailed strictly by the pin-heads, but if anyone could make such behavior workable for a mass audience, it was Cannell, who jammed his tongue even further into his cheek for this one. Conveniently, the pressganged McCormick just happens to be a former race-car driver, giving the series the opportunity for numerous magnificently shot car chases which—unlike the dreary repetition of many similar shows—are often genuinely thrilling and spectacular. Indeed, as was often the case with the early episodes of Cannell's later vigilante show *Hunter*, which started life as two rebel cops without a rule-book, the stunts were often more substantial than some of the plots! Nevertheless, co-creator Hasburgh told *USA Today*, "I never wanted to do a car chase show. That's what ABC wanted, and we were willing to give it to them in the beginning because we were willing to do whatever they wanted just to get the show on the air." At this point, however, it's doubtful that ABC or any other network would have rejected anything from Cannell in the wake of *The A-Team*.

Hardcastle and McCormick, so extreme they parodied the genre, but in reality pandering to the wishful fantasies of the put-upon public just as much as the movies and like-minded TV series, effortlessly joined Cannell's rapidly growing number of anti-heroes, chalking up an impressive three years on the air.

Unlike many of the straight-faced entries in revenge movie cinema, Cannell's previous work, in particular *The Rockford Files, City of Angels,* and *The A-Team,* had demonstrated quite plainly that Cannell didn't really believe in the message of the vigilante law 'n order genre. Furthermore—this being a Cannell show after all—several episodes demonstrated the folly of Hardcastle's simplistic outlook on right and wrong. Of the 22 episodes in the first season, ten deal directly with corrupt law officials, cops, judges, or prison wardens, and/or flaws in the system.

Stephen Katz's "The Crystal Duck" and Tom Blomquist's "Scared Stiff" have a parole officer and a prison warden respectively forcing cons to commit further crimes.* Shel Willens' "The Georgia Street Motors" is essentially a reworking of the feature *The Star Chamber,* and *Hardcastle and McCormick*'s contribution to the darkside plot, or *Magnum Force* principle; the second season episode "Undercover McCormick," by Marianne Clarkson, even has cops hiring themselves out as hit-men, a favorite plot-line that also turns up in other Cannell shows, such as Cannell's pilot for *Stone*, Lupo's first season *A-Team* "A Small and Deadly War," and Cannell and Lupo's first season *Hunter*, "Hard Contract," while Cannell's "One of the Girls from Accounting" has cops bumping up their pay by computer. Hardcastle himself

---

*The plot of the latter, again directed by Tony Mordente, but this time penned by Frank Lupo, is resurrected in the fourth season A-Team *episode "The Heart of Rock and Roll," although this time the plot is simply a device to showcase the talents of former* Rockford *recurring player and singer/songwriter Isaac Hayes and fellow performer Rick James, both of whom get to strut their stuff during the program, while a second evil parole officer, played by* Married—with Children*'s Ed O'Neill, is employed in another old chestnut, our old friend the Magnum Force principle, in Sidney Ellis' "The Garbage Man," a first season* Hunter.

is humbled by Evan Lawrence's "Third Down and Twenty Years to Life," which suggests that one of his judgments has caused him to send the wrong man to jail, and in the second season, in Hasburgh's "The Games You Learn from Your Father," another judge admits a phoney conviction on his death-bed. There are further ambiguities about a conviction in Hertzog's third season yarn "Duet for Two Wind Instruments," while Cannell is on familiar territory with "The Career Breaker," which bears a striking resemblance in theme to his earlier first season *Hunter* story "The Hot Grounder," and Juanita Bartlett's *Rockford Files* offering "Kill the Messenger," except that here events take place in a hick town with a redneck sheriff as the untouchable killer — all of which takes us right back to *Hunter* and Frank Lupo's first season story "A Long Way from L.A."

There are numerous frames and double-crosses that put Hardcastle and/or McCormick into jail cells throughout the series' run, plus the usual welcome array of wicked establishment figures, including a gun-running CIA agent, an unscrupulous newspaper publisher, a toxic chemical dumping industrialist, and various other killer judges, crooked cops, deranged military men, corrupt lawyers, whitewashing politicos and murderous businessmen. None of this sits particularly well alongside Hardcastle's intractable attitude toward the guilt of those who come before him, but it does reflect more than adequately his disillusionment with the system!

As is apparent from the above, of all Cannell's series, the plot ideas in *Hardcastle and McCormick* were the most derivative. The premise of Stephen Katz' "The Crystal Duck" was lifted in part from an earlier *Tenspeed and Brownshoe* story "Loose Larry's List of Losers," while another *Tenspeed* routine had been utilized in the *Hardcastle* pilot film "Rolling Thunder"; knowing full well that the thirteen episodes of *Tenspeed* would for the most part remain in TV limbo-land in the U.S., Cannell and his team had no qualms about giving their ideas wider exposure in later series. "Did You See the One That Got Away?" was a replay of the old man-who-doesn't-exist storyline, played to best effect in the short-lived *Richie Brockelman* series in Peter Fischer's "Escape from Caine Abel," and appearing again in Jo Montgomery's "Burned" for *Hunter,* when DeeDee McCall sees a villain who should be dead. Hasburgh's "Just Another Round of That Old Song" is indeed another chorus of Cannell's "In Pursuit of Carole Thorne" for *The Rockford Files,* and hidden loot stories proliferate as motivation for dark deeds and intimidation in numerous Cannell yarns, including Jeff Ray's "McCormick's Bar and Grill," which is itself reminiscent of Cannell's *Rockford* yarn "The Attractive Nuisance!"

Hasburgh's "Outlaw Champion" is a replay of the hero-who-wasn't yarn, in which a hero best worshipped from afar, or a valued old buddy or mentor, is revealed to be a corrupted disappointment, pathetic has-been, or overblown braggart, a familiar Cannell theme best represented by Cannell's "My Heroes Have Always Been Cowboys" for *Greatest American Hero* and Tom Blomquist's "Wipe Out" for *Riptide.* "Wipe Out" itself echoes Cannell's earlier "Number One with a Bullet" for *Riptide,* which itself owed a debt to Rudolph Borchert's "A Different Drummer" for *Rockford,* and had no sooner aired in *Riptide,* than the same theme turned up later in the year on *Hardcastle and McCormick* as Marianne Clarkson's "Pennies on a Dead Man's Eyes!"

Hertzog's "Hardcastle, Hardcastle, Hardcastle and McCormick" echoes Juanita Bartlett's *Rockford* episode "The Fourth Man," "Surprise on Seagull Beach" bears a resemblance to Cannell's "Paradise Cove," Marianne Clarkson's "Mirage a Trois" recalls Cannell's "Three Day Affair and a Thirty Day Escrow" (not to mention *Riptide's* jus' plain "Mirage"), and Carol

Mendelsohn's "If You Could See What I See" borrows the psychic theme of David Chase's "The Oracle Wore a Cashmere Suit" and Gordon Dawson's "The Man in the Full Toledo" for *Stone* (and indeed crops up in Paul Bernbaum's *Riptide*, "Fuzzy Vision"). Another *Stone* story, Richard C. Matheson's and Thomas Szollosi's "The Partner," is rehashed in Cannell's "The Birthday Present," and reappears in several forms during the lengthy run of *Hunter*. In the second season *Riptide* episode "Catch of the Day," by Edward Dectar and Frank Lupo, a local lad swears he's seen a mermaid, while in Daniel Hugh Kelly's "In the Eye of the Beholder," McCormick thinks he's seen leprechauns digging in the garden.*

In fairness to the series, it should be pointed out that the plots were traveling down a two-way street; Lawrence Hertzog's "There Goes the Neighborhood" becomes the second *Hardcastle and McCormick* episode (after "Scared Stiff") to be blatantly rehashed for *The A-Team* (by Bill Nuss), not only in the very same year, but with the same title!† It was rapidly followed by Nuss' "Wheel of Fortune," in which Murdock goes on a game show only weeks after McCormick's fifteen minutes of fame in "Games People Play," a *Hardcastle and McCormick* yarn compiled by four different writers, and Murray Bozinsky's appearance on the fictional "Beat the Brain" show in Terry Nelson's "Still Goin' Steady" for *Riptide*. It should be pointed out also, for what it's worth, that Cannell rarely rewrote entire stories, but rather borrowed bits of them, so that many early '80s yarns are in effect composites of a variety of familiar themes.§

As well as recurring plots, the series enjoyed recurring cops, with three different players filling the obligatory role of station-house buddy. From the second season on, John Hancock appeared as Lt. Mike Delaney, Ed Bernard (formerly of the late '70s cop show *Police Woman*) was Lt. Bill Giles, and the dependable Joe Santos was Lt. Frank Harper. By the third season, Santos as Harper dominated.

Formerly Dennis Becker in *The Rockford Files*, Santos had subsequently enjoyed a positively schizophrenic career in hour dramas, switching effortlessly between weary benevolent cop, sadistic leering villain, and troubled blue-collar working-class stiff. As a cop buddy, he had appeared in a couple of episodes of the now-dated but then-classy *Police Story*, a single episode of *Hunter* (a hilarious scene in Cannell's "The Hot Grounder"), and the final season of *Magnum* in the late–'80s. Glen Larson chose to employ him as an El Generale–type ethnic villain in the laughable likes of *Masquerade*, *Automan*, and *Cover-Up*, but it was his triumphant portrayal of a brutal psychotic homosexual gangster in a string of *Hill Street Blues* episodes that finally showed exactly what Santos was capable of given the chance, and should have blown away his tired cop persona forever. His charismatic, shocking, and high-energy performance was a revelation, and Santos seized the opportunity to transcend his co-star status and ran like a demon with it; it's quite extraordinary that this memorable and exciting performance didn't lead to further assignments and create a new typecasting cliché for him (although early episodes of *NYPD Blue* found him in another well-realized gangster role). During the first season, a Lt. Carlton played by Robert Hooks made fleeting appearances,

---

*Some plots were a little older. Hertzog's "Something's Going On on This Train" has the passengers being bumped off one by one, while in Hasburgh's "Do Not Go Gentle..." Hardcastle erroneously believes he's got just a few months to live...!

†This was also the working title for the first season *Riptide* that had a different storyline, and ultimately became "The Hardcase." Interestingly, the *A-Team* episode had first been titled "The Battle of Canoga Park"... but that that had been used on *The Rockford Files*!

§The one exception to this, as mentioned in the introduction to this book, was Cannell's *Riptide* episode "Be True to Your School," which was rewritten as "Never Go to Your High School Reunion" for *Sonny Spoon* during the Writers' Strike of '87. And, it hardly needs to be said, high-school reunion stories were also a popular Cannell standby.

and a housekeeper character, Sara Wilkes, played by Mary Jackson, was quickly deemed superfluous and fell victim to Cannell's "overloading" approach to formatting.

As it turned out, *Hardcastle and McCormick* swiftly drifted away from its initial premise of nailing the ones that got away to become a rootless buddy show. Apart from the inevitable parade of old pals and former girlfriends in peril familiar to all action/adventure shows (one lost love for Hardcastle in Cannell's "The Long Ago Girl," two for McCormick in "Never My Love" by Thomas Szollosi and Richard Christian Matheson, and "Faster Heart" by Hasburgh), the second season was for some reason awash with visiting relatives; McCormick's father (in "Ties My Father Sold Me" from Hasburgh), Hardcastle's sister-in-law ("D-Day" from Lawrence Hertzog), niece and two aunts ("It Could'a Been Worse, She Could'a Been a Welder" and "Hardcastle, Hardcastle, Hardcastle, and McCormick," also both from Hertzog), and—in the third season—his brother ("Brother Can You Spare a Crime," by Donald Ross) all turned up on the doorstep to inconvenience and delay the dynamic duo in their quest for retroactive justice. "Hot Shoes," "Outlaw Champion" and "Faster Heart," all by Hasburgh, took McCormick back to the racetrack, and on several occasions ("The Homecoming" by Hasburgh, Hertzog's "You're Sixteen, You're Beautiful, and You're His," and Burt Pearl and Steven Sears' "Conventional Warfare") disaster strikes while Hardcastle attends a function or convention. The boys also spent quite a few episodes trying to complete vacations; Stephen Katz' "Flying Down to Rio," Hertzog's "You Would Cry Too if it Happened to You," Hasburgh's "She Ain't Deep But She Sure Runs Fast" and "Do Not Go Gentle...," and Blomquist's "The Day the Music Died" all involve vacations either starting or ending that turn into mysteries or nightmares. Initially, the premise had been that Hardcastle, now retired, had a caseload of unfinished business, and that he was going to work his way through them with the unlucky McCormick—however, once the series got underway, very few of the dilemmas the team found themselves in were actually provoked by their investigations. Like Ralph and Bill in *The Greatest American*

Suited up for action. Well, one of them is ... Daniel Hugh Kelly loosens his tie to show he's one of the good guys while Brian Keith overdoes the Cannell casualwear look.

Hero, the carnival in *Rousters,* and later episodes of *The A-Team,* our heroes would often stumble onto a fantastic plot or dangerous situation just by chance; the writers were all so busy coming up with character comedies or diversions from the format that nobody remembered to write any conventional episodes based around the original premise! As Gail Williams perceptively observed in *Hollywood Reporter,* "There's nothing logical about the cases that come their way. Trouble just sort of tracks them down every week!"

Of course, this contrivance was hardly exclusive to Cannell's series, but the difference here was that the pure chance factor was often stretched to breaking point — by the time the duo were discovering white slave rings in the world of womens' wrestling (Marianne Clarkson's "Strangle Hold"), being mistaken for hit-men and handed weapons for a killing (Sears' and Pearl's "Conventional Warfare"), and spotting leprechauns in the back garden (Daniel Hugh Kelly's "In the Eye of the Beholder"), the plots were matching 1960s science-fiction shows for insanity! The series was only a few episodes in when Cannell and company saw which way the wind was blowing, wisely decided *not* to go into reverse gear, and dropped the explanatory narration on the opening credits detailing Hardcastle's obsession with escapees from justice. Appropriately enough for such a wild premise, the show eventually took on the ambience of a super-hero comic, where a gaggle of villains and a preposterous plot lurked around every corner just waiting to jump our leading characters; a similar situation developed during the fourth season of *The A-Team* (which ran simultaneously with *Hardcastle and McCormick*), and it was to the benefit of both series that Cannell was bold enough to break from the formula and avoid falling into a rut.

Cannell and his writers used a series premise not as a ball and chain but as a springboard from which to jump head first into the rapid currents of weekly series production. In the case of the fourth season of *The A-Team,* this procedure pulled an already dangerously rigid formulaic show out of its *Mission: Impossible*-for-kids corner with some fresh and inventive storylines; for *Hardcastle and McCormick,* it blurred and blunted any accusations of vigilantism, but in so doing stretched the credibility of the series even further! In terms of entertainment value though, it did the series no harm at all. By the time the series closed after three seasons, Hardcastle was no closer to wrapping up his one hundred cases than he had been in the pilot!

The greatest contribution toward making Hardcastle barely humanoid came from Brian Keith, who was a natural for the role of Hardcastle and, like James Garner and Robert Culp before him, understood perfectly the audience that Cannell was playing to. The New Jersey son of a show business family, Keith was a former U.S. Marine and Broadway performer raised in New York, who was in television from its earliest days. His drama series included the Red-bashing *Crusader* in 1955, Sam Peckinpah's legendary *The Westerner* in 1960, and *Archer,* a 1975 detective series, as well as a short but powerful contribution to the pilot for the western series *The Quest* in 1976, but his longest running TV work was playing comedy in the bland but successful sit-com *Family Affair* (1966–'71). Ventures into that arena with less longevity have included *The Brian Keith Show* in 1972, *Pursuit of Happiness* in 1987, *Heartland* in 1989, and *Walter and Emily* in 1991. Having spent many years previously alternating between sit-com vehicles as a tough guy with a soft heart (*Family Affair, The Brian Keith Show*), and grim western or detective roles as a tough guy with a hard heart (*Crusader, The Westerner*) it was a simple matter to combine the two for Cannell. His role in the well-received 1978–'80 mini-series *Centennial,* based on the doorstep novel of the same name, in which he had played a strong, hard-headed and persistent sheriff, and the role of Judge Hardcastle tie for first place as the most striking and memorable use of his talents in either TV or film (the latter of which he was particularly ill-served by).

Co-star Daniel Hugh-Kelly, as Mark McCormick, was equally well-cast, previously a player in the daytime soap *Ryan's Hope,* and fresh from a prime-time role in the ill-fated *Chicago Story,* a brave and likeable attempt at combining sub-MTM dramatics with the spirit of *The Naked City* and *The Bold Ones,* which starred, among others, recurring Cannell villains Vincent Bagetta and Dennis Franz in rare good guy roles. The son of a cop and a social worker, his most prolific and successful arena was the stage. Later, Hugh-Kelly starred in the short-lived 1991 Cannell series *The 100 Lives of Black Jack Savage* alongside *21 Jump Street's* Steven Williams. In *Hardcastle and McCormick* the duo clicked perfectly, and the series became a modest success despite being scheduled against a powerhouse combination of *Murder She Wrote* and *Knight Rider.* While the CBS murder mystery was no great threat, appealing to an entirely different sort of audience, NBC's *Knight Rider* had already clobbered *The Greatest American Hero,* was a proven hit, and worse yet, was another vigilante/fast car show, one of the rare incidents in the 1980s when networks scheduled like against like.

Odder still than the series' survival that first season, was the threat it faced during its second year. Incredibly, *Hardcastle and McCormick* was being consistently outrated by the dreary spy fantasy *Scarecrow and Mrs. King.** Although *Hardcastle and McCormick* had attracted the usual heavy female following that Cannell shows were renowned for, *Scarecrow and Mrs. King* was squarely aimed at female viewers fleeing the Monday night football that *Hardcastle and McCormick* shared the night with, and surprisingly, this audience didn't outnumber the women swooning over the bland leading man of its rival—or perhaps identifying with the frilly Mrs. King. Having stood its ground against the hit shows *Knight Rider* and *Murder She Wrote, Hardcastle and McCormick* was gradually run off the schedule by one of the drabbest, most mediocre adventure series of the decade!

Episode Guide

regular and recurring cast: Brian Keith (Judge Milton C. Hardcastle), Daniel Hugh-Kelly ("Skid" Mark McCormick), Mary Jackson (Sarah Wicks), John Hancock (Lt. Delaney), Joe Santos (Lt. Harper), Ed Bernard (Lt. Bill Giles)

First Season (1983–1984)

ROLLING THUNDER (pilot)

wr. Stephen Cannell, Patrick Hasburgh, dir. Robert Young

Retiring Judge Milton "Hardcase" Hardcastle coerces racing car driver "Skid" Mark McCormick — charged with the theft of a vehicle he thought he was repossessing — into joining him as a parolee in his charge to bring two hundred guilty offenders that got away on technicalities to justice. McCormick reluctantly agrees, on the condition that the first case they pursue is the murder of his business partner, designer of a new car named the Coyote.

with John Saxon, Faye Grant, Ed Lauter

MAN IN A GLASS HOUSE

wr. Stephen Cannell, dir. Guy Magar

Retired Mafia mobster Joe Cadillac intends to expose his former partners in crime in a book which also libels Judge Hardcastle, but then has to seek Hardcastle's help when the mob abduct his son.

with John Marley, Lance Hendriksen, Michael Hawkins

Ironically, the first of many TV movie assignments for Daniel Hugh-Kelly had been Thin Ice, *a TV movie with Kate Jackson—star of* Scarecrow and Mrs. King.

THE CRYSTAL DUCK

wr. Stephen Katz, dir. Guy Magar
A parole officer is blackmailing ex-cons into stealing for him.
with Joe Pantoliano, Nicholas Coster, Allan Rich

GOING NOWHERE FAST

wr. Patrick Hasburgh, dir. Guy Magar
A prison warden's wife aids the escape of a devious ex-con who has a grudge against Hardcastle.
with Robert Desiderio, Caren Kaye, Antony Ponzini

THE BLACK WIDOW

wr. Stephen Cannell, dir. Richard Compton
McCormick is set up as a fall guy by a prostitute working undercover for the police setting up mobsters.
with Marta Dubois, Richard Kuss, Robert Viharo, Robert Pastorelli, Frank Annese, Arthur Burghardt, Joe Horvath

THE BOXER

wr. Patrick Hasburgh, dir. Guy Magar
The father of an up and coming young boxer is kidnapped by mobsters.
with Richard Lawson, Richard Romanus, Hank Rolike

ONCE MORE WITH VIGORISH

wr. Patrick Hasburgh, dir. Arnold Laven
A lady D.A. cajoles Hardcastle and McCormick into helping her entrap a loan shark dealing in stolen goods.
with Tricia O'Neill, Michael Callan, Antonio Fargas

KILLER B'S

wr. Stephen Katz, dir. Ron Satlof
Hardcastle and McCormick investigate a low-budget film-maker who is importing drugs from Mexico in his stunt cars.
with Edward Winter, Buddy Ebsen, Tracy Scoggins, John Sanderford

PRINCE OF FAT CITY

wr. Patrick Hasburgh, dir. Tony Mordente
A youthful gang leader in possession of some incriminating tapes is the target of both his former gang members and a crooked judge.
with Stoney Jackson, Victor Arnold, Reginald Dorsey

HOT SHOES

wr. Patrick Hasburgh, dir. Richard Compton
When McCormick discovers that his sponsor in a motor race is running a stolen car operation, his vehicle is sabotaged after he informs Hardcastle.
with Joe LaDue, Terry Kiser

FLYING DOWN TO RIO

wr. Stephen Katz, dir. Tony Mordente
Hardcastle and McCormick travel to the Caribbean in pursuit of a CIA agent turned arms dealer.
with Alan Feinstein, Gail Strickland, Bruce French, Victor Mohica

JUST ANOTHER ROUND OF THAT OLD SONG

wr. Patrick Hasburgh, dir. Allen Reisner
An elderly crook leaves jail only to discover that the city has changed so much that he can't locate his hidden loot, and that the crooked cop who arrested him is also after the haul.
with Keenan Wynn, Jack Ging

THIRD DOWN AND TWENTY YEARS TO LIFE

wr. Evan Lawrence, dir. Georg Stanford Brown
Hardcastle grudgingly reopens investigations into the case of a football player he sentenced when the boy's sister, a law student in his class, humiliates him in front of his other pupils.
with Corinne Bohrer, Garry Walberg, Liberty Godshall, James Karen, Robert O'Reilly

WHISTLER'S PRIDE

wr. Stephen Katz, dir. Tony Mordente
Hardcastle investigates fixed horse racing after being lumbered with a useless nag in a bookie's will.
with Ann Dusenberry, Kathryn Leigh-Scott, Timothy Scott, Peter MacLean

MR. HARDCASTLE GOES TO WASHINGTON

wr. Patrick Hasburgh, dir. Arnold Laven
Hardcastle becomes the victim of political intrigue when a newspaper publisher attempts to keep him out of the Supreme Court.
with Richard Herd, James Whitmore, Jr., Jack Rader

CRIME SCHOOL

wr. Tom Blomquist, dir. Tony Mordente
McCormick enrolls in a smooth ex-con's school

for criminals, but is set up when his identity is uncovered.
with Robert Culp, Doug McClure, Randi Brooks, Charles Cooper

THE GEORGIA STREET MOTORS

wr. Shel Willens, dir. Joe Manduke
Hardcastle infiltrates a secret society of three fellow retired judges who are bumping off killers on parole.
with Efrem Zimbalist, Jr., Dana Elcar, Andrew Duggan

THE HOMECOMING (two parts)

wr. Patrick Hasburgh, dir. Tony Mordente, Bruce Kessler
When an old friend is killed in suspicious circumstances while Hardcastle attends an awards ceremony in his honor, McCormick and the man's daughter become the next targets of the murderer.
with Cathy Lee Crosby, Cameron Mitchell, Mitchell Ryan, John Amos, John Ireland

DID YOU SEE THE ONE THAT GOT AWAY?

wr. Lawrence Hertzog, dir. Ron Satlof
Hardcastle hunts down a lifer that he has seen walking around free, but then discovers that there is no record of the man he sent to prison ever existed.
with James Wainwright, Dennis Franz, Victoria Young, Gene Dynarski

REALLY NEAT CARS AND GUYS WITH A SENSE OF HUMOR

wr. Lawrence Hertzog, dir. Ron Satlof
McCormick discovers the horrors of car insurance while the thrill-seeking and girl-hungry car maintenance engineer makes off with the Coyote to impress the girl he desires ... unaware that she is implicated in a murderous dating agency scam.
with Patrick Collins, Marilyn Jones

SCARED STIFF

wr. Tom Blomquist, dir. Tony Mordente
Hardcastle, McCormick, and a group of juvenile delinquents in their care are taken hostage by prisoners desperate to reveal the activities of their crooked warden, who is bribing men into acting as hit-men for mob contracts.
with Alan Fudge, Red West, Michael MacRae

Second Season (1984–1985)

OUTLAW CHAMPION

wr. Patrick Hasburgh, dir. Leo Penn
McCormick must curb feelings of resentment when he and the judge go to the aid of a racing car driver who constantly succeeded where he failed. Now he discovers that this hero has feet of clay.
with Larry Wilcox, Jonathan Banks, Ray Girardin

TIES MY FATHER SOLD ME

wr. Patrick Hasburgh, dir. Ron Satlof
McCormick hunts down his long-lost father, only to discover that he's a sleazy cabaret singer in a seedy Atlantic City dive, with little loyalty, love, or concern for his offspring.
with Steve Lawrence, Alex Rocco, Michael DeLano, Michael Swan, John Brandon

YOU WOULD CRY TOO IF IT HAPPENED TO YOU

wr. Lawrence Hertzog, dir. Tony Mordente
With Hardcastle in Hawaii for a convention, McCormick is conned into open house for a wild party, during which the judge's files are stolen and the contents of Gulls Way completely ripped off.
with Paul Gleason, Andrew Rubin, Mark Adams, Debi Richter, Victoria Young, Betty McGuire, Paul Willson, Bill Handy, Mickey Jones, Renee Jones, Chester Grimes

D-DAY

wr. Lawrence Hertzog, dir. Bruce Kessler
When Hardcastle's sister-in-law turns up on the doorstep with mobsters close behind her, he and McCormick can't get rid of her quick enough.
with Trish Van DeVere, Greg Mullavey, David Opatoshu, Jonathan Goldsmith

NEVER MY LOVE

wr. Thomas Szollosi, Richard Christian Matheson, dir. Bruce Kessler
A girlfriend of McCormick's from his schooldays turns up at Gulls Way after being presumed dead, and hunted by a politician trying to cover up the hit-and-run accident she witnessed.
with Molly Cheek, Peter White, Lance Henriksen, Raymond Singer

WHATEVER HAPPENED TO GUTS?

wr. Thomas Szollosi, Richard Christian Matheson, dir. Michael Hiatt

Hardcastle becomes an instant TV celebrity when he fills in on a TV courtroom show, and also the intended victim of an obsessive woman.

with Marilyn Jones, Patricia Barry, John Carter, Bill Morey, Jim McKrell, Sydney Lassick

YOU AND THE HORSE YOU RODE IN ON

wr. and dir. Patrick Hasburgh

McCormick is humiliated when he storms out of Gull's Way in a temper tantrum and becomes implicated in a criminal fraud that Hardcastle must rescue him from.

with Ray Buktenika, Steve Leavitt, Michael Ensign

ONE OF THE GIRLS FROM ACCOUNTING

wr. Stephen Cannell, dir. Bruce Kessler

McCormick is attracted to a young payroll clerk whose life is in danger when she discovers a fraud in the police pay for ten men.

with Bonnie Urseth, Edmund Gilbert, Marc Alaimo, Robert Dryer, David Gateaux, Charlie Dell

IT COULD'A BEEN WORSE, SHE COULD'A BEEN A WELDER

wr. Lawrence Hertzog, dir. Tony Mordente

Hardcastle's niece angers her uncle, but inadvertently uncovers a scam, when she leads a controversial protest against replacing a students' dive with a law library.

with Maylo McCaslin, Joe Dorsey, Val Avery, Arthur Taxier

HATE THE PICTURE, LOVE THE FRAME

wr. Erica Byrne, dir. Dennis Donnelly

Hardcastle is framed on Christmas Eve while investigating a gun-running operation.

with Jon Cedar, Fil Formicola, Lisa Rafel, Michael Gregory

PENNIES FROM A DEAD MAN'S EYES

wr. Marianne Clarkson, dir. Tony Mordente

When a record company executive discovers that the long-dead singer he intends to release a memorial album for is actually still alive, he intends to correct the situation to protect his investment!

with Larry Gatlin, Steven Keats, Joan Sweeney, Norman Alden, Hugh Gillin, Gary Lee Davis

THERE GOES THE NEIGHBORHOOD

wr. Lawrence Hertzog, dir. Ron Satlof

When Hardcastle forms a neighborhood watch committee after a spate of robberies, he uncovers mobsters and spies on the block...!

with Kenneth Kimmins, Dennis Franz, Jed Allan, Frank McCarthy, Joan Freeman, Tony Longo, Kai Wulff, Jimmie Skaggs, Lesley Woods

TOO RICH AND TOO THIN

wr. Thomas Szollosi, Richard Christian Matheson, dir. Michael Kane

When a friend of Hardcastle dies at a health farm, he poses as a fellow client to investigate, uncovering a murderous criminal operation.

with David Spielberg, Kenneth Mars, Lynda Day George, Tracy Brooks Swope, Sam Jones, Charles Stewart, Stephanie Hagen, Valerie Stanton

WHAT'S SO FUNNY?

wr. Patrick Hasburgh, dir. Tony Mordente

Mark McCormick poses as a stand-up comic after an ex-con turned comedian is murdered following a set ridiculing Hardcastle...!

with Patrick Collins, Jan Murray, James Sutorius, Joey Bishop, Mary Margaret Humes, John Aprea

HARDCASTLE, HARDCASTLE, HARDCASTLE, AND MCCORMICK

wr. Lawrence Hertzog, dir. Kim Manners

Hardcastle is visited by his two aunts, who cajole McCormick into joining them on a murder mystery investigation based on a conversation they overheard at the airport.

with Mary Martin, Mildred Natwick, Jim McMullan, Wolf Muser

THE LONG AGO GIRL

wr. Stephen Cannell, dir. Richard Colla

Hardcastle pursues an embezzler who married a woman he once loved.

with Anne Lloyd Francis, Lou Felder, Ed Bernard

YOU DON'T HEAR THE ONE THAT GETS YOU

wr. Lawrence Hertzog, dir. Tony Mordente

Hardcastle and McCormick are ambushed by a Bonnie and Clyde–style duo, who shoot Mark and steal the Coyote.

with Wings Hauser, Karlene Crockett, Sonny Landham, Christopher Roland, Billy Drago, Emily Banks, Bill Gratton, Stanley Brock, Gary Lee Davis

THE BIRTHDAY PRESENT
wr. Stephen Cannell, dir. Tony Mordente
McCormick allies himself with a young cop he despises to bring a psychopathic killer to justice after Hardcastle is shot in court.
with Stephen Shortridge, Jonathan Banks, Steve Sandor, Vincent Schiavelli, Angel Tompkins, Vernon Weddle, Rosemarie Thomas

SURPRISE ON SEAGULL BEACH
wr. Patrick Hasburgh, dir. Michael O'Herlihy
Surfers and a Nazi war criminal figure in this plot concerning missing gold bullion buried on the beach where Hardcastle proposed to his wife.
with William Windom, John Dehner, Stanley Kamel, Ken Stovitz, Fran Parrish, Jim Boyle, Michael Cornelison, Ed Bernard, Erik Holland

UNDERCOVER MCCORMICK
wr. Marianne Clarkson, dir. Les Sheldon
McCormick poses as a rookie cop to flush out some officers who are moonlighting as mercenaries.
with David Ackroyd, James Cromwell, John Calvin, Raymond St. Jacques, Keith Charles

THE GAMES YOU LEARN FROM YOUR FATHER
wr. Patrick Hasburgh, dir. Kim Manners
Hardcastle aids an embittered con, freed after a judge admits to the man's innocence on his deathbed.
with Tim Thomerson, Jeff MacKay, Sandy Ward, Ray Girardin, Ken Swofford, John Dennis Johnston

ANGIE'S CHOICE
wr. Thomas Szollosi, Richard Christian Matheson, dir. Bruce Kessler
Hardcastle babysits for the sassy kids of a witness to a mob killing.
with Lynne Topping, Bobby Jacoby, Anne Marie McEvoy, Robert Desiderio, Beau Starr

Third Season (1985–1986)

SHE AIN'T DEEP BUT SHE SURE RUNS FAST
wr. Patrick Hasburgh, dir. Tony Mordente
Stranded in the wilderness after a plane crash, Hardcastle and McCormick's vacation plans take another turn for the worse when they stumble onto a murder scene.
with Pat Corley, Jonathan Banks, James Whitmore, Jr., Terry Bradshaw, Richard Lineback, Lee DeBroux, Patrick Brady

FASTER HEART
wr. Patrick Hasburgh, dir. Charles Picerni
A racing car driver who stole McCormick's girlfriend from him and married her, now plans her murder to cover up some shady dealings.
with Barbra Horan, John Sanderford, Robert Sampson, Judd Omen, Peter Van Norden, Paul Picerni, Bob Delegall, James Crittenden, Linda Hoy

THE YANKEE CLIPPER
wr. Patrick Hasburgh, dir. Sigmund Nufeld, Jr.
After attending the funeral of a long-lost friend, formerly missing in action in Vietnam, Mark discovers his old pal is still alive and well.
with Charles Rocket, Richard Herd, Joe Regalbuto, David Paymer, Vincent Guastaferro, Bennett Ohta, Dana Lee, Albert Leong, Charles Parks, Paul Eiding, Arsenio Sonny Trinidad

SOMETHING'S GOING ON ON THIS TRAIN
wr. Lawrence Hertzog, dir. Tony Mordente
Mark McCormick is trapped on a train with passenger Judge Hardcastle while an old Agatha Christie plot seems to be playing itself out through a series of murders.
with Eugene Roche, Joseph Hacker, P.J. Soles, Nancy Parsons, Richard Schaal, Raye Birk, David Wiley, Michael Rider, John Allen

THE CAREER BREAKER
wr. Stephen Cannell, dir. Kim Manners
McCormick has to engineer a jail-break for the judge when Hardcastle becomes the victim of some redneck justice in a hick town.
with Randall "Tex" Cobb, Matt Clark, Benjamin Slack, Faith Ford, Bruce Wright, Rance Howard, Kathryn Daley, Mark Burke

DO NOT GO GENTLE ...
wr. Patrick Hasburgh, dir. Bruce Kessler
Believing that he only has six months to live, Hardcastle sets off on a world cruise courtesy of a sympathetic Mark McCormick, only to have their huge boat hijacked.
with Allan Arbus, Sam Freed, Rand Holland, David Selburg

Games People Play

wr. Tony Michelman, Scott Schneider, Carol Mendelsohn, Larry Forrester, dir. Peter Hewitt

McCormick becomes a successful contestant in a rigged TV game show that leads to murder.

with Herb Edelman, Bill Macy, Tom Kennedy, Molly Cheek

Strangle Hold

wr. Marianne Clarkson, dir. Michael Switzer

As the storylines get stranger and stranger, McCormick uncovers a white slavery ring operating in the world of women's wrestling!

with Tom Bower, Sharon Barr, Ernie Sabella, Kit Fredericks, Dar Langlois, Deborah Rennard, John Considine, Faith Minton

You're Sixteen, You're Beautiful, and You're His

wr. Lawrence Hertzog, dir. Kim Manners

Hardcastle becomes a judge of a different sort, when he becomes a member of the panel for a beauty contest, but before long, he and McCormick are busy with an investigation involving illegal immigrants.

with Gary Bayer, Jonna Lee, Dean Devlin, Reni Santoni, Rebecca Street, Jeff Austin, Earl Bullock, Jay Varela, Mike Robelo, Chip Heller, Lisa Wilcox, Erica Zeitlin

Mirage a Trois

wr. Marianne Clarkson, dir. Sidney Hayers

When Mark gives an Arab girl a friendly peck on the cheek, he suddenly finds himself pursued by a small army of vengeful males.

with Michael Ansara, Lycia Naff, Grant Alexander, Ari Barak, Kavi Raz, Bruce French, John Shearin, Barry Sattels, Ben Rawnsley

Conventional Warfare

wr. Steven Sears, Burt Pearl, dir. Sigmund Neufeld, Jr.

Hardcastle and McCormick are mistaken for a pair of hit-men while attending a judges' convention, and soon become additional targets.

with Tim O'Connor, Ray Reinhardt, Jason Bernard, Antony Ponzini, Gerry Gibson, Dan Lauria, Arthur Taxier

Duet for Two Wind Instruments

wr. Lawrence Hertzog, dir. Bob Bralver

When a former conviction is quashed due to legal incompetence, Hardcastle and McCormick disagree on the subject of the ex-con's guilt.

with Cotter Smith, Laurie Prange, Louise Claire Clark, Jeff Donnell, Samantha Harper, K.T. Sullivan, Peggy Walton-Walker, Garry Goodrow

If You Could See What I See

wr. Carol Mendelsohn, dir. Kim Manners

Hardcastle makes use of the abilities of his new maid's psychic powers when McCormick goes missing on a case.

with Rosemary Clooney, Jonathan Goldsmith, Teresa Ganzel, Lyle Waggoner

Hardcastle for Mayor

wr. Alan Cassidy, dir. Kim Manners

An industrialist has an ulterior motive for nominating Hardcastle as a mayoral candidate.

with Richard Anderson, J.A. Preston, Andy Romano, Alvy Moore, Edward Bell, Stacy Keach, Sr., Diana Douglas, Stanley Grover, Richard Kuss

When I Look Back on All the Things

wr. Lawrence Hertzog, dir. Steve Beers

The Coyote is destroyed when ghosts from the past return to haunt McCormick.

with Jeanetta Arnette, Vincent Bagetta, Paul Carr, Fred McCarren, Dick Bakalyan

Brother Can You Spare a Crime

wr. Donald Ross, dir. James Conway

Hardcastle's no-good gambling brother turns up, with angry bookies hot on his trail.

with Kenneth Mars, Robert Picardo, Claudette Nevins, Andrew Masset, Leslie Bevis, Phil Rubenstein, Wanda Richert, S. Marc Jordan, Clare Nono, Charles Walker

Round Up the Old Gang

wr. Stephen Katz, dir. Tony Mordente

The discovery of a basketball trophy in his garage leads Hardcastle to track down an old friend in the nick of time to help him out.

with Stuart Whitman, Peter Mark Richman, Abby Dalton, Beau Starr, Sam Scarber, John Crawford

McCormick's Bar and Grill

wr. Jeff Ray, dir. James Giritlian

McCormick goes into business with his father and Hardcastle after they acquire a bar and grill ...

but mobsters have their own reasons for wanting the joint closed.

with Steve Lawrence, Michael Callan, Denny Miller, Sam Anderson, Teddy Wilson

Poker Night

wr. Marianne Clarkson, dir. Michael Kane

McCormick is out on the town and Hardcastle and Lt. Harper are among the hostages when panicky hold-up men barge in on the judge's poker night.

with Gregg Henry, Marlyn Mason, Paul Drake, Al Ruscio, Lou Richards

In the Eye of the Beholder

wr. and dir. Daniel Hugh Kelly

Hardcastle is convinced that McCormick has flipped after he claims to have seen a group of leprechauns digging in the garden...! (The Coyote returns in this episode).

with David Rappaport, Leo Rossi, Walter Olkewicz, Fran Ryan, Steve Levitt, James Moriarty

The Day the Music Died

wr. Tom Blomquist, dir. Charles Picerni

McCormick helps out a former d.j. who inspired him in his youth, but has fallen on hard times.

with Louis Giambalvo, Patricia Harty, Daniel Davis, Michael David Lally, Georgeann Johnson

A Chip Off the Ol' Milt

wr. Carol Mendelsohn, Marianne Clarkson, dir. Les Sheldon

McCormick's parole period is over, and he decides to take up an offer of employment at a law firm, where his discovery of illegal activities soon puts both him and Hardcastle in the slammer.

with Billie Bird, Walter Brooke, John Ashton, Camilla Ashland, Frank Hamilton, Dub Taylor
series ends

Rousters
October 1983, June 1984–July 1984

Rousters ran for only thirteen weeks (a pilot and twelve episodes) and concerned the exploits of a family of typical Cannell zanies all descended from the famous western hero Wyatt Earp. In his later years the legendary lawman had become a showman and a stunt-player during the earliest days of Hollywood and was immortalized in his own TV series — *The Life and Legend of Wyatt Earp,* starring Hugh O'Brien — from 1955 to 1961.*

The *Wyatt Earp* TV series of the '50s was a cut above most other TV incarnations of real-life icons of legend, in that it progressed methodically through a chronological, if not entirely accurate history of Earp's career as a frontier lawman, starting in 1955 with him becoming marshal of Ellsworth, Kansas, moving him on to Dodge City in the second season, and later to Tombstone, where the final five episodes neatly packaged the story of the gunfight at the OK Corral. Earp's ultimate resting place in Hollywood however was not entirely inappropriate, since it is generally acknowledged that he could be as colorful with the facts and economical with the truth as any of the dime-store novelists of the nineteenth century or filmmakers of the twentieth century who created the western myths around genuine figures that have endured in fiction.† According to many historians, Earp and his cronies only got into lawkeeping in the first place to maintain their stranglehold on the profitable saloons, casinos and whorehouses in the towns they policed, making them no better than the Clantons they feuded with, and more suitable for taking down by the A-Team than canonization as western heroes!

Although he had been far more than a simple showman like Buffalo Bill, Earp owes much of his heroic stature to what Kim Newman, in his book *Wild West Movies,* calls "the pack of lies Earp told writer Stuart Lake" as he neared the end of his life in Tinseltown (born in 1848, Earp died in 1928). "Earp's secret," wrote Newman, "was that, unlike many Old West characters, he lived long enough to cash in on his own legend ... omitting any mention of the days when he robbed stagecoaches, ran whores, cheated at cards, and drove his wife Mattie to prostitution and suicide by abandoning her for a singer named Sadie!" Thus Earp ensured his immortality in numerous cinematic endeavors, and while Hugh O'Brian's Wyatt Earp was cleaning up Dodge *and* Earp's image in *The Life and Legend of Wyatt Earp,* James Arness was commencing a twenty year stint in Dodge City himself, as Marshal Matt Dillon in *Gunsmoke*.

Like the great film-makers of westerns and detective fantasies, Cannell was in the business of manufacturing mythology rather than documentary, and in *Rousters,* the legendary

---

*In 1988, James Garner would portray the elderly Earp in the feature film Sunset, *a fiction based on his Hollywood years and co-starring Bruce Willis of* Moonlighting *as early western movie star Tom Mix.*

†Cannell himself acknowledges this in the Rousters *pilot, "The Marshal of Sladetown," when a lecture on Earp being given by his grandson Wyatt Earp III is taken over by Amanda, who proceeds to spin a yarn of obvious fiction to her captive audience.*

gunfighter's great grandson, Wyatt Earp III, continues the showbusiness tradition in a traveling carnival, Sladetown, for which he is the head trouble-shooter and sometimes, against his better judgment, a part-time bounty-hunter. Unfortunately for Earp III, his family are a bunch of wackos with delusions of Old West grandeur, and see him as a modern-day model hero, but Earp wants only the quiet life, and is another of Cannell's decidedly reluctant heroes. Also, like his predecessors in Cannell vehicles, trouble invariably found him, mostly thanks

The cast of *Rousters,* the *A-Team* follow-up that wasn't. Clockwise from top left, Hoyt Axton, Mimi Rogers, Chad Everett, Maxine Stuart, Jim Varney, Timothy Gibbs.

to the efforts of his friends and family — not to mention the efforts of such reliable Cannell writers as Frank Lupo, Babs Greyhosky, Mark Jones, and the man himself, among others. Just as Angel Martin would turn up out of the blue to drop Jim Rockford in hot water, just as Bill Maxwell would appear at the most inconvenient of times to utilize the talents of Ralph, and just as the retired Hardcastle made life a misery for Mark McCormick, so did Earp's family regularly raid the wanted poster displays at the local jailhouses to keep Wyatt Earp III occupied.

Chad Everett, former beefcake star of the popular *Medical Center* series (1969–1976) and later lead in Cannell's unsold pilot *Thunderboat Row* (1989) starred as Wyatt Earp III, with burly country and western star Hoyt Axton as "Cactus Jack" Slade, the owner of the carnival. Co-starring was Jim Varney (later to find fame in the thickear *Ernest* films) as a "Howling Mad" Murdock type, Wyatt's shifty and scheme-laden brother Evan Earp, the inevitable con-man character of the show. Maxine Stuart was their dotty Granny Clampett of a mother, Timothy Gibbs played Earp's young son Michael, and Mimi Rogers appeared as Ellen Slade, Earp's long-suffering girlfriend and Jack's daughter, a schoolteacher for the carnival's kids in the grand tradition of the western. Producing were Babs Greyhosky, formerly of *Greatest American Hero* and later of *Riptide,* and Chuck Bowman, later of *The A-Team.* Associate producer was Alan Cassidy, later assigned to *Hunter* and *Wiseguy,* and — as usual — Mike Post and Pete Carpenter provided the music and Jo Swerling, Jr. was executive producer.

Most of Cannell's regular array of stock players put in guest appearances during the series' short run, including Jeff MacKay and James Whitmore, Jr., as well as Chuck McCann, Ed Winter, Dick O'Neill, Michael Delano, Phillip Sterling, Joey Aresco, John Dennis Johnston, Ken Swofford, and Randi Brooks. In the pilot, Earp's biggest problem comes from the Clayton Brothers (as opposed to the Clantons!), played by no less a formidable duo than Fred Dryer and Robert Davi, who are ultimately seen off by the original Earp's famous Buntline rifle! Cannell wrote the pilot and opening episode, and then turned the format over to the reliable hands of his regular *A-Team* contributors, including Greyhosky, Lupo, Jones, Jeff Ray, and Jim Carlson and Terrence McDonnell. Directors included Cannell regulars Arnold Laven, Dennis Donnelly, Ron Satlof, Guy Magar, and Bruce Kessler, all *A-Team* stalwarts, as well as veterans Joe Pevney, Sigmund Neufeld, Jr., Barry Crane, and Georg Stanford Brown.

The plots were as outrageous as Earp's family, and featured the usual array of spies, enemy agents, hoods, assassins, mobsters and charlatans that Cannell and Greyhosky had brought to *The Greatest American Hero, The A-Team, Hardcastle and McCormick,* and — in the months to come — *Riptide.* However, had the series continued, the writers would have been faced with increasing credibility problems in getting the bad guys within the vicinity of the Sladetown carnival (although it has to be said that it was done easily enough for the first twelve!). Perhaps it's a foolish concern where a preposterous premise such as those of Cannell's series are concerned, but whereas Bill Maxwell — and, once in a while, the "green guys" themselves — sought out adversaries for Ralph in *Greatest American Hero,* Earp's chief source of trouble was his family. Just how many enemy agents, hit-men, and spies could Earp conceivably run into, without stepping over even Stephen Cannell's thin red line of possibility?

As it happened, the problem never arose. *Rousters,* which had made its debut in early October of 1983, was canceled almost immediately, with the remaining episodes being aired in the mid-summer of '84. Given a time-slot perhaps an hour too late for the sort of show it was, and on the notoriously difficult Saturday night slate where *Hunter* would flourish a few seasons later, its lead-ins were the two popular sit-coms *Diff'rent Strokes* and *Silver Spoons,* and it preceded the *Dallas*-inspired ranch series *The Yellow Rose*, a series that suffered conceptual indecision and failed. Opposing this line-up were a trio of established and successful Aaron Spelling stinkers on ABC, and a film and the low-rated medical drama *Cutter to Houston* on CBS.

Although its scheduling had been unhelpful, *Rousters* could not blame its failure on competition with any conviction. The audience simply chose not to tune in—and yet the popularity of the very similar *A-Team* was going through the roof! For whatever reason, *The A-Team* took off like a rocket, and *Rousters* like a damp squib. It was the sort of audience idiosyncrasy that makes program planners and buyers tear their hair out; *The Beverly Hillbillies* as *The A-Team* sounds like a no-brainer in every sense of the expression. Clearly NBC thought they had a second *A-Team* on their hands that year, and it certainly must have looked that way to all but the fickle audience; perhaps somewhere, in a parallel universe, *Rousters* has run for five years and *The A-Team* died in two months.

Of 22 new productions introduced at the start of the 1983/84 season, only five took off with any degree of success—*AfterM*A*S*H*, which started off well and then dropped off dramatically, the *Diff'rent Strokes* rip-off *Webster*, Aaron Spelling's *Hotel* (which offered Connie Sellecca of *Greatest American Hero* fresh employment), and two action/adventure series, *Scarecrow and Mrs. King*, a drab secret agent adventure show on which Juanita Bartlett, Cannell's associate from *The Rockford Files* and *Greatest American Hero* would later work, and Cannell's own *Hardcastle and McCormick*. Some of the blame might conceivably be laid at the feet of NBC's advertising department, who ran an arrogant and negative promotional campaign presuming success and specifically badmouthing Aaron Spelling's *Love Boat*, scheduled directly opposite. Or possibly, the television audience simply didn't need a new A-Team populated with Beverly Hillbillies.

Episode Guide

regular and recurring cast: Chad Everett (Wyatt Earp III), Jim Varney (Evan Earp), Timothy Gibbs (Michael Earp), Maxine Stuart (Amanda Earp), Mimi Rogers (Ellen Slade), Hoyt Axton ("Cactus Jack" Slade)

(1983)

ROUSTERS (pilot, a.k.a.
The Marshal of Sladetown)

wr. Stephen Cannell, dir. E.W. Swackhamer

It's the Earps who are in danger of being run out of town when the Clayton brothers plan an armored car hold-up. In the meantime, Wyatt must deal with a runaway girl and a phoney lawsuit.

with Fred Dryer, Robert Davi, Allan Stock, Danny Wells, Lisa Trusel, Pamela Susan Shoop

THE CARNIVAL THAT ATE SLADETOWN

wr. Stephen Cannell, dir. Joseph Pevney

While Earp's Sladetown carnival is involved in a bitter conflict with rivals over territorial rights, Earp must deal with a murderer who is stalking a handyman who witnessed his crime.

with Chuck McCann, Terry Kiser, Robert Pierce, Jack Starrett

FINDERS KEEPERS

wr. Mark Jones, dir. Dennis Donnelly

While Evan's Policemens' Day at the carnival turns into a riotous fiasco, Earp confronts a ruthless bounty hunter who is pursuing an innocent man.

with Dick O'Neill, Don Stroud, Ken Swofford, Robin Evans

A PICTURE'S WORTH A THOUSAND DOLLARS

wr. Babs Greyhosky, dir. Arnold Laven

Evan takes a photograph of a famous actress leaving a restaurant with mobsters, and Amanda and Michael are kidnapped in an effort to retrieve it.

with Sam Jones, Michael De Lano, Ken Swofford, Peter Lownds

EYEWITNESS BLUES

wr. Babs Greyhosky, dir. Ron Satlof
Earp becomes the target of three crooks whose identities he has exposed.

with Andrew Robinson, Joey Aresco, John Dennis Johnston, Kelly Parsons

EVERYBODY LOVES A CLOWN

wr. Frank Lupo, dir. Guy Magar
Russian agents hunting a fugitive dressed as a clown and carrying valuable microfilm kidnap Evan while he is in costume by mistake.

with Jeff MacKay, Robert Tessier, Jeffrey Josephson, Herman Poppe

THIS TOWN AIN'T BIG ENOUGH FOR THE TWELVE OF US

wr. Mark Jones, dir. Guy Magar
A motorcycle gang waiting for the escape of a prison worker hiding out in Sladetown hold the occupants of a farmhouse hostage.

with Dennis Burkley, Diane Robin, Nadine Van Der Velde, Mary Margaret Humes

TWO AND A HALF DAYS OF THE CONDOR

wr. Mark Jones, Babs Greyhosky, dir. Bruce Kessler
Evan is convinced that a mental patient on a day trip to the carnival is in fact a U.S. spy who has been put away by a treacherous colleague.

with Ed Winter, Philip Sterling

SLADE VS. SLADE

wr. Babs Greyhosky, dir. Guy Magar
Slade's wife, who walked out on Jack and Ellen years earlier, suddenly turns up at the carnival asking for half the assets and a divorce ... while Wyatt goes to the aid of a young woman whose mobster husband is trying to bump her off.

with Barbra Horan, Kevin McCarthy, Ruta Lee, Bruce Tuthill

SNAKE EYES

wr. Mark Jones, dir. Sigmund Neufeld, Jr.
While Wyatt is in Vegas for an absurd Bounty Hunter of the Year ceremony, Evan wins the jackpot from a slot machine in Vegas, unaware that it was intended as a mob pay-off.

with Rita Wilson, John Fujioka, Randi Brooks, James Sutorius

COLD STREAK

wr. Jim Carlson, Terrence McDonnell, dir. Georg Stanford Brown
An uncontrollable ostrich and a prize racehorse cause problems for Earp and the carnival when a self-made millionaire friend of Earp's turns up asking for help.

with Dale Robinette, Angel Tompkins, Robert Dryer

NEVER TRUST A CRYSTAL BALL

wr. Mark Jones, dir. Barry Crane
While Wyatt searches for a thief of video-game secrets operating in Sladetown, Evan is convinced that he has had a gypsy curse placed on him.

with Claude Earl Jones, Reuven Bar-Yotem, Michael Cavenaugh, Dawn Jeffory

WYATT EARP TO THE RESCUE

wr. Jeff Ray, dir. Arnold Laven
A rodeo star is blackmailed and threatened into working for dope dealers, but the drugs are lost, and the lives of his wife and child are on the line.

with James Whitmore, Jr., Christopher Pennock, George McDaniel, Kathleen Cody

series ends

Riptide
January 1984–April 1986

"Well, well, if it isn't the B-Team!"

Reviewing *Riptide* in *TV Guide*, columnist Robert MacKenzie tapped into the true secret of Cannell's post–Universal series (*Greatest American Hero, Hardcastle and McCormick, The A-Team, Rousters,* and *The Quest*) with amusing wit and accuracy.

"Lately I have been reading about the Peter Pan syndrome," he wrote, "a psychological condition of men who refuse to grow up. The disease is said to be widespread. Television may have something to do with it. In videoland, growing up means mortgages and tight collars; staying a boy means girls, cars, and adventure. Who would choose to grow up?"*

Who indeed? In Cannell's series, investigating and adventuring are fun. In each subsequent Cannell production up until *Wiseguy*, fewer and fewer people get hurt or killed, and life is one long adventure holiday. There is as little as possible of the casual, careless killing of the Quinn Martin, Aaron Spelling, or Glen Larson shows — bullets fly fast, but Cannell's bad guys are all lousy shots. Murders occur, but invariably offscreen.

By the early 1980s, Cannell's characters were all enjoying the easy life Jim Rockford had so diligently pursued. Mark McCormick may have had to do the chores, but at least he didn't go to jail for "the crime he didn't commit"; Rockford did, which accounted for his rather sour and cynical attitude. *Rousters* was every boy's dream of running away with the circus; Hardcastle and McCormick were perpetually going on vacations, albeit pursued by, or heading for, trouble; the A-Team and the *Riptide* boys were frequently to be found lolling around in hotels or on boats. Even Ralph, Bill, and the delinquent schoolkids enjoyed frequent holidays in the sun ("The Devil and the Deep Blue Sea") or the snow ("It's All Downhill from Here"), and got to live out their rock and roll fantasies ("Classical Gas"). Poor Rockford's vacations were usually messed up by lunatics, bores, runaways, or airheads! Still, he managed to live an idyllic life on the seashore, independent, yet surrounded by friends, family, and girlfriends. It must have seemed a good idea to combine Cannell's two greatest hits — *The Rockford Files* and *The A-Team* — into a new series, and it was.

Riptide was a sunny and cheerful detective fantasy set around Pier 56 at King Harbor in California's Redondo Beach. Perry King and Joe Penny played Cody Allen and Nick Ryder, two California beach bums who had started up a private detective operation from their homebase — the cruiser *Riptide* — with their old army buddy Murray "Boz" Bozinsky, a scrawny, pale and bespectacled computer wizard who, for all his abundant naiveté and lack of muscle

---

Cannell and Babs Greyhosky returned the compliment by titling a second season episode "Peter Pan is Alive and Well!" Peter Pan syndrome gets another mention in the late-'80s sit-com My Two Dads, *in an episode titled "Stupid Macho Guy Time!"*

power and social skills was — Cannell subverting TV tradition again — smarter than both Nick and Cody put together. The team are victimized by fate (courtesy of Cannell and Lupo's wicked humor) and the local yahoo cop, Lt. Ted Quinlan (Jack Ging), a loutish, reactionary brute vaguely reminiscent of Lt. Quint in *City of Angels,* although less physically brutal — just as dumb, but mostly harmless. Quinlan, bitter and twisted from an earlier altercation with Ryder, bears a grudge against the trio, and harasses them in the grand tradition of all Cannell's brainless authority figures (Deil and Chapman in *Rockford,* Lard and Schiller in *Black Sheep Squadron* and *Baretta,* and so on) until getting unceremoniously bumped off during the

The boys in their red Corvette, virtually a co-star. Thom Bray as Murray (in hat), Perry King as Cody, Joe Penny (in driving seat) as Nick.

third season.* In his place, the character of Lt. Joanna Parisi was introduced, a likeable, friendly and pleasant young woman played by June Chadwick, later the lizard-queen Lydia on *V!*[†] Parisi makes her first appearance as platonic relationship and new police liaison with the guys midway through the third and final season in the episode "Lady Killer," written by Babs Greyhosky and Tom Blomquist and directed by Michael Lange, although the part never came to much in the limited time Chadwick was there. To accommodate Parisi into the storyline, Quinlan had to go, and so he did — almost as an afterthought — under the wheels of a would-be hit-and-run driver in "Requiem for Icarus," by *A-Team* alumni Burt Pearl, Steven Sears, and Chuck Bowman. As all this happens in the last few moments of the episode, it's likely that this was a quick rewrite to lose the character swiftly; when the networks decide to change something, they don't waste much time!

Perry King, who had previously been in the cast of Cannell's ill-fated *The Quest*, graduated from Yale with a B.A. in drama and studied under actor John Houseman at Juilliard. Despite Broadway and a Golden Globe award, King's celluloid career has demonstrated an unerring aim for film material that has managed to be contentious without being worthwhile! With the exception of the 1972 cult film *The Lords of Flatbush*, in which King starred as one of a group of '50s rock and roll delinquents alongside fellow unknowns Sylvester Stallone and Henry Winkler, his films have been either minor outrages (*Slaughterhouse Five, Mandingo, The Wild Party, Lipstick, Andy Warhol's Bad, The Choirboys*, etc.) or routine TV movies and mini-series. *Riptide* remains the best use to date of this likeable leading man.

Joe Penny's dark, brooding and heavy-lidded Italian looks have often lead to him being cast in mobster roles (such as his starring role in *The Gangster Chronicles*, a bland 1981 series),[§] but in actual fact, Penny was born in London, England, moving to the U.S. with his parents while still very young. He studied acting under Lee Strasberg and others, while appearing in local L.A. theatre groups. TV guest shots have been a diverse collection of genres, roles, and quality, including *Nancy Drew, Lou Grant, Vegas, Flamingo Road, Archie Bunker's Place, T.J. Hooker, Tucker's Witch* and the '80s *Twilight Zone*, a mostly undistinguished string of credits but for "Cop" in *Lou Grant*, and his courageous portrayal of a tough homosexual officer who dares not come out of the closet in his resolutely macho profession for (ultimately justified) fear of the reactions of his mostly bigoted fellow cops (led by one of TV's — and Cannell's — favorite sleaze merchants, Ed Winter!).

Thom Bray earned a B.A. in music and theater in New York, and did a considerable number of stage plays and TV commercials there before moving out to Hollywood and guest spots in *Quincy, Lou Grant, Murder She Wrote,* and *Remington Steele*. Either side of *Riptide* he had supporting roles in two brief series, *Breaking Away* and *Harry,* but perhaps his most interesting TV work since *Riptide* has been his role as a politically dubious intellectual in an above-average episode of *Mancuso, FBI;* as Daryl Ross in the episode "Daryl Ross and the Supremes"(!), he plays a grimmer, darker Mr. Hyde version of his *Riptide* persona.

Although Jack Ging's career began with the western series *Tales of the Wells Fargo* in 1961,

---

*From *Riptide* Ging moved back an hour in the NBC Tuesday night schedule to harass the A-Team for a season as General Harlan "Bull" Fulbright, until he got bumped off in that series as well!

[†]Parisi is not antagonistic to the boys at all, but quite helpful; by the late 1980s the hostile superior had become such a cliché that the breed was virtually dead as a species; antagonistic bosses were out — compromise and co-operation were now the name of the game. Shame, really — in the previous episode to Quinlan's demise — Paul Bernbaum's "Robin and Marian"— Quinlan was mellowing ... almost helpful, almost human!

[§]The Gangster Chronicles *featured Joe Penny as Bugsy Seigel, Jonathan Banks as Dutch Schultz, Robert Davi as Vito Genovese, and Louis Giambalvo as Al Capone; what it lacked in style or drama it gained in trivia value...!*

and then the medical drama *The Eleventh Hour* in 1962, he appears to have been playing cops and bad guys ever since, with numerous guest roles interspersed with semi-regular cop parts in the series *Mannix* (1967–'75) and *Dear Detective* (1979). Many times the guest villain on Cannell productions, he even made two separate appearances as a bad guy on *The A-Team* before briefly joining the regular cast in the fourth season after Quinlan's demise. He makes brief cameo appearances in the pilots for *The Highwayman* and *Wiseguy.*

Anne Francis, who appeared briefly in the first few episodes — and opening credits — as Mama Jo, a crusty, middle-aged harridan running a floating "escort agency" at the pier, has made numerous appearances in many television series, most memorably in "The After Hours," a famous episode of *The Twilight Zone,* and as the lead in the mid-'60s detective series *Honey West.* She is probably best known for her role as Althea in the classic 1950s science-fiction film *Forbidden Planet.* The owner of Pier bar and Riptide agency hang-out Straightaways was — naturally enough — nicknamed Straightaway, and portrayed by Gianni Russo. It was a nothing part for one of Cannell's best resident gangsters, his most conspicuous mob role being that of Dave Steelgrave in the *Wiseguy* pilot. Later, stand-up comic Marsha Warfield, who went on to join the cast of sit-com *Night Court,* puts in some hopelessly incongruous and out-of-place cameos as Mama Max, the new owner of the bar, which appears to change hands with some regularity!

June Chadwick, cast as Lt. Parisi, will forever be etched in the minds of TV viewers as the lizard queen Lydia of *V!* Another British emigree, her first film in the U.S. was the SF cheapie *Forbidden World.* Most of her other roles have been bland nondescript guest appearances in various action adventure series, including two episodes of *Magnum, p.i.,* although she shone in Rob Reiner's vicious rock 'n roll band spoof *This Is Spinal Tap* (1983), as the sulky and self-important girlfriend of one of the equally sulky and self-important band members. Ken Olandt, who plays surfer Dooley in the series, is a former male model with numerous TV and teen-pic credits including the lead in the syndicated 1990s series *Super Force.*

Riptide was a computer-contrived confection of all the recent successes not only of Cannell himself, but those former colleagues and fellow producers who had taken their lead from him. It was almost as if Cannell was saying good-naturedly, okay guys, now I'll take from *you* ... it's payback time! Whatever the reasoning, and network TV is notoriously and shamelessly parasitic with what works, there was a dash of Donald Bellisario's *Magnum* in *Riptide,* and more than a little of Phil De Guere's own *Magnum* clone *Simon and Simon* (What could be better than one Magnum? *Two* Magnums!!).

If the ambience and attitude of *Magnum* owed a debt to *The Rockford Files,* and *Simon and Simon* owed no small debt to both *The Rockford Files* and *Magnum,* then *Riptide* owed a debt to all of them, and this little pocket of early '80s post–*Rockford* detective series virtually created a whole new strand of programming by themselves, so incestuous was their relationship with each other.* However, Cannell, Bellisario, and De Guere had all worked together in the past, all utilized the same pocket of performers and creative talents, and consequently all created good shows; both Frank Lupo and Babs Greyhosky had contributed scripts to the early episodes of *Magnum,* and Tom Selleck and Gerald McRaney (one half of the *Simon* brothers) had worked extensively with Cannell in the past — indeed, Cannell had produced two

---

*The ailing Simon and Simon *was saved by twinning it with* Magnum; *CBS seemed to take a belated revenge on* The Rockford Files *by removing the more blatant and satirical humor from* Simon and Simon *when it went into decline, as they had tried with* Rockford *nearly a decade earlier — the series was robbed of its more bizarre, off-center elements and was never as good again as it was during a wonderful first season.*

unsold pilots for Selleck, *The Gypsy Warriors* and *Boston and Kilbride*—before Bellisario had struck gold revising Glen Larson's outline for *Magnum*. It was only when outsiders tried to emulate the formula, with rubbish like *Legmen* and *Matt Houston,* that, bereft of Cannell's unique outlook, and seduced by a formula that looked deceptively easy, they got it all horribly wrong.

Riptide made its debut on NBC in January 1984, exactly a year after *The A-Team* barreled into prime-time on Tuesday nights, and followed that series in the schedule. This was entirely deliberate, for—as many industry observers pointed out—NBC had specifically requested a series from Cannell to hold the *A-Team* audience. As this audience was made up of young boys, Cannell created a fantasy that could be enjoyed by Peter Pan adults too. The idea was that if *The A-Team* was essentially a kids' show that adults enjoyed, then *Riptide* would be aimed at adults but with access to the kids.

Adopting his usual everything-but-the-kitchen-sink policy, and throwing in numerous gimmicks that could be dropped or retained depending on their popularity, Cannell gave *Riptide* the Roboz, an inept little robot created by Boz which was supposed to perform menial tasks and flash messages, but rarely performed either properly. As with some of the extraneous gimmicks in *The A-Team* when it began, Roboz faded into the background as Cannell and his writers became more confident about their performers and their material, although in one memorable early episode, ("Four Eyes" by Babs Greyhosky), a sneaky back-door pilot for Stepfanie Kramer and D.D. Howard as two lady p.i.'s (Kramer's catch-phrase—a disbelieving "Get outta town!"), Roboz doubles as a vacuum cleaner when Nick and Cody pose as salesmen.

The duo also possessed a speedboat, the *Ebbtide,* and a battered, broken-down and temperamental helicopter from Nick's Vietnam days, the Screaming Mimi, a pink-painted monstrosity with bug eyes and gaping mouth painted on the nose! Helicopters were a must-have accessory at this point in American prime-time—*Magnum* had T.C.'s Island Hoppers service (characters with initials for names were also *de rigeur* in the early '80s), and two super-chopper shows, Roy Huggins' TV version of the movie *Blue Thunder,* and Donald Bellisario's hawkish and macho *Airwolf,* made their appearance that same season.

Prior to the introduction of *Riptide* to the schedule mid-way through the 1983–'84 season, *The A-Team* had begun its first full season as lead-in for MTM's *Remington Steele,* which was followed by another MTM show, the expensive and opportunistic flop *Bay City Blues*. An obvious attempt to transpose the successful *Hill Street Blues* formula to baseball, audiences saw through this crass ploy immediately, and *Bay City Blues* became an early casualty of the new season. *Remington Steele* and *The A-Team* were about as alike as chalk and cheese, and NBC bumped *Remington Steele* up to the *Bay City Blues* 10:00 slot and introduced *Riptide,* which wasn't particularly compatible with the MTM detective show, but twinned superbly with *The A-Team*. Unlike the doomed *Greatest American Hero/The Quest* double-bill, preordained to fail, the *A-Team/Riptide* team-up was charmed enough by the fates to catch on, slaughtering some already pretty lame opposition on the other networks.

Also unlike the *Greatest American Hero/The Quest* double-bill, which had received relatively positive notices, *Riptide* was met with almost universal critical sarcasm. Typical of many of the comments made were those of TV enthusiast and *A-Team* fan Cynthia Broadwater in the short-lived *Daredevils* magazine, who wrote bluntly, "If you are male, well-built, and a good guy, you are dumb but determined. If you are male, intellectual, and a good guy, you are a wimp, able to understand microchips but not people. You need the dumb guys of the world to protect you. If you are a policeman, you hate private detectives, and will do anything to get them into trouble, even if they are trying to save your life. If you are a girl with a name like Tina, Brandy, or Crystal, you look terrific in a bikini, but are easily taken in by the bad guys of the world.... The beautiful women keep coming in with names that sound like something out of an Ian Fleming novel. Lt. Quinlan appears and promises to throw our heroes in jail. And Roboz spends its time shooing away pelicans and spilling water on everybody."

Other reviews were in the same vein. This was a crass over-simplification of a simple series, but it does illustrate the spirit of the show, if not the heart and soul. As criticism goes, some of the best series on TV could be condensed in the same manner, including *M*A*S*H* and *Hill Street Blues;* for all the criticisms of American TV as being heavy-handed and obvious, it is always those paid to do so who are the last to spot the subtleties and double edges in TV series—particularly Cannell's.*

Although *Riptide* strongly emulated *The Rockford Files,* particularly in its first and best season (as did *Magnum* and *Simon and Simon* before each developed their own styles), the series inevitably lacked the all-important wry, cynical presence of James Garner, but what King and Penny's characters lacked in wit, they more than made up for in lively and exciting stunt action. Despite its failings to live up to the complexities of *The Rockford Files* (not its reason for being anyway), its appearance was fortuitously timed to coincide with a rash of programming in a TV season that was finally beginning to focus on giving women equal time on TV after more than three decades as dummies, housewives, victims or decoration — series such as *Remington Steele, Scarecrow and Mrs. King, Cagney and Lacey, Kate and Allie, Codename: Foxfire, Mary, Foley Square,* and others, including the female co-stars of Cannell's own *Greatest American Hero* and *Hunter.* Indeed, the only exclusively masculine shows on the air during *Riptide*'s run were *Blue Thunder* and *Airwolf,* Jay Bernstein's *Mike Hammer,* and Cannell's *Hardcastle and McCormick* and *The A-Team,* and in all but the two helicopter shows, the machismo was decidedly self-parodic.

Riptide was neither as laughably deadly serious as *Airwolf's* machismo nor as heavy-handed as the high camp interpretation of Mickey Spillane's *Mike Hammer.* It was joyously celebratory in its unabashed espousal of masculine camaraderie, and the focus of attention was on male friendship with the same idealized exclusivity as the female-orientated shows such as *Cagney and Lacey* and *Kate and Allie.* However, Cannell was careful where it counted.

In some episodes, the girls were indeed the traditionally sparsely clad beach bunnies in need of assistance, and the opening credits of the first season feature a particularly striking woman striding along the deck of a boat who is difficult for men to ignore. However Cannell was neither so reactionary nor so commercially inept as to make his heroes outdated cavemen or suave, shallow smoothies. As usual, brainless thugs who mistreated women were the object of his scorn, and Quinlan's rampant sexism was often pilloried in the scripts. Cannell and his writers never divided men and women into categories of rescuer and victim, or perpetrator and captive. When women were menaced (as people must be in an action/adventure show), men were often in trouble with them, and when the women alone were threatened, the man doing the menacing was always portrayed as weak and cowardly. The women were part of the adventure, rather than part of the props department, something many critics chose to ignore or were incapable of noticing.

---

*See the introduction to this book for more comments from the critics on Riptide.

The *Riptide* boys were ordinary guys who, as the publicity material for the series succinctly pointed out, "sometimes got the girl." As a result of this, *Riptide* was never offensive towards women in the manner of say, *Starsky and Hutch* or *Miami Vice*—it was better perceived as the male response to *Cagney and Lacey!* And, just as that series mellowed in its hostile attitude toward the male characters as the show matured and developed self-confidence, so did *Riptide* gradually dispense with Mama Jo and her boatload of bimbos. Gradually, the writers gave Nick, Cody and Boz real relationships with real women, although the view was always from a strictly male perspective. As *Riptide* had been created with the sole aim of holding on to the *A-Team* audience for an extra hour, the series catered for women only in the sense of providing likeable and recognizable male characters—and thus naturally became a huge fan favorite with female viewers.

But the most interesting aspect of *Riptide* was the nature of the bond between the men. Unlike Simon and Simon, who are brothers, and the male teams in *Starsky and Hutch, Black Sheep Squadron, Greatest American Hero, The A-Team, Hardcastle and McCormick, Miami Vice, Houston Knights* and others of the time, the *Riptide* men have not been thrown together by job or circumstance. They are together simply because they are friends. Friendship and the particularly strong loyalty of male camaraderie is an integral part of all Cannell's fantasies, but this is one of the few series from any producer in which it is the only reason for a team, rather than the inevitable *result* of that teaming.

Producing were Babs Greyhosky, formerly of *Magnum, Greatest American Hero,* and *Rousters,* and Cannell's old high-school buddy J. Rickley Dumm, who also performed similar chores on *Hardcastle and McCormick.* For the third season, Tom Blomquist took over from Greyhosky, who continued to contribute to the show extensively throughout its run. Jo Swerling, Jr., was ever-present as executive producer. Greyhosky had been put in charge of the whole shebang when Cannell commissioned scripts from his regular pool of contributors following the pilot, and considered her scripts to be the ones which had the best handle on what he was trying to do. For a male-orientated show like *Riptide,* this was perhaps both ironic and inevitable—who better to understand men than a woman?

The best episodes were undoubtedly those written by Cannell, Lupo and Greyhosky (although Mark Jones turned in quite a few zingers too), and it may well have been the presence of a female writer/producer that helped the series avoid any clumsy sexism of the sort rife in non–Cannell adventure series. "We put bikini-clad girls into it at first," Cannell told *Hollywood Reporter* (and indeed, episodes such as "Hatchet Job," "The Mean, Green Love Machine" and "The Hardcase" were festooned with bimbos), "but we dropped it. It wasn't what we were trying to accomplish."

What Cannell, Lupo, and Greyhosky *did* accomplish with *Riptide* was to successfully subvert the traditional Hollywood nerd stereotype (as portrayed superbly by Thom Bray as Murray Bozinsky) while skillfully and willfully exploiting the cliché. Cannell in particular took great delight in sending up Boz and subverting expectations at the same time. While Boz was busy making a fool of himself with his gawky naiveté and innocent enthusiasm ("Enthusiasm is my strongest suit!"), this was never played for sentiment, and he would often simultaneously show up the tough guys, bad guys, and authorities with his superior ability, knowledge and qualifications; in the opening episode, "Conflict of Interest," written by Cannell, and directed by Ron Satlof, the guys trip straight into an ambush after turning down Murray's suggestion. In one of the series' best episodes, the second season's "The Orange Grove," by Cannell and director Michael Lange, he defuses a bomb ("Oh, geeky Murray should be sitting shivering in the john, is that it?") and humbles two cocksure FBI men before the show is ten minutes in. In Greyhosky's "Someone Is Killing the Great Geeks of America"(!), directed by Bruce Kessler, the story centers around a meeting of the High-Q club for "mental giants," of which Boz is an honored member. It's Boz who is famous and smart, and recognized wherever they go, and even though Nick and Cody are constantly bailing him out of trouble with their muscle, Murray's unassuming modesty concerning his bookish brainpower is constantly reminding them how ordinary they are, and it is this that provides much of the show's humor at their expense. In the episode "A Matter of Policy," written by Steven Sears and Burt Pearl, Bray is clearly unavailable, and there is an amusing scene in which Nick and Cody struggle with an elementary computer, fail to access it, and have to raid the company offices after being unable to hack into their records. (There's also a hilarious running gag as the guys try to phone Boz at his hotel hideaway, only to be greeted by the tumultuous sounds of a wild party, and find themselves unable to get past the gorgeous party girl who keeps misunderstanding them and hanging up! It eventually transpires, in a brief insert filmed by Bray to cover his absence from that episode, that Murray changed rooms!).

Not that Boz isn't the butt of the show's humor as well, of course. In the hilarious "The Mean, Green Love Machine," by Cannell and director Guy Magar, James Luisi (*Rockford's* spiteful Lt. Chapman) guests as a bad guy in a story in which the highlight is a hilarious scene with Boz wired up as a rich, white-suited sucker for a scam in which the pigeons are being seduced by beautiful hookers. All plugged in, but ignoring his radio instructions from Nick and Cody (who are watching aghast from a nearby table), Boz suddenly falls hook, line and sinker for the scam he's supposed to be exposing; in Babs Greyhosky's "Diamonds Are for Never," Boz is packed off to the movies like an awkward younger brother to lose himself for the night, while Nick and Cody entertain women from the neighboring floating escort agency run by the formidable — but absent — Mama Jo. Weeping his way through *Bambi* (it's the tough guys' turn to bawl over a weepie in the later "Catch a Fallen Star," written by Tom Blomquist), Boz discovers that the woman sitting next to him in tears is actually hiding out after witnessing a murder. Boz manages to destroy half of King Harbor in pursuit of the culprits while trying to master the intricacies of Nick's treasured Corvette, and then, in a wildly over-the-top sequence, spends the night in jail with a flamboyant pimp who has managed to convince him that he's an encyclopedia salesman being persecuted for the way he's dressed!

It might be argued that the show patronized the Bozinsky character, and in some episodes they undoubtedly did,* but even though he was clearly there as a comic foil for Nick and Cody, Cannell and his writers effortlessly avoided the offensiveness of Murray's spiritual predecessor, Bart Braverman's Binzer character in *Vegas,* who was there purely for the audience to feel superior to and for the hunky heroic leading man to patronize. Unlike *Vegas* and its ilk, in which the hero was tough and smart and the nerd is just a nerd, *Riptide* went to great lengths to show that the three of them were a team, each weaker without the others. Their relationship is funny, but rarely tips over into the condescending. Where other producers might have turned Bozinsky into a stooge to boost the egos of those identifying with the hero (as was Binzer's function in *Vegas*†), Boz is one of the team, often indispensable, and because Can-

---

*Patrick Collins and Kim Darby find their characters similarly teetering on the borderline between acceptance and condescension in their respective episodes "Catch of the Day" and "A Matter of Policy," by Dectar and Lupo and Sears and Pearl, but the messages are well-intentioned and free of the ridicule and malice that such stereotypes attract on other shows.
†Ironically, Braverman guest stars in an episode of Riptide, Cannell's "Be True to Your School," directed by Michael Lange.

nell's heroes have the self-confidence and good nature not to intimidate Boz for cheap laughs or gratification, all three men look bigger for it.

Like Brockelman and Brownshoe before him, Boz is enthused with the idea and mythology of being a detective, and is very much an early prototype for *Revenge of the Nerds* star Curtis Armstrong's Burt Viola in *Moonlighting*. Ironically, it was the cult success of *Moonlighting* that finally edged *Riptide* off the air in 1986 ... but not before Blomquist and Greyhosky had exacted their revenge and taken an inspired and hilarious poke at their argumentative rivals in the very last episode "If You Can't Beat 'Em, Join 'Em" ... not to mention taking good-natured satirical jabs at *Miami Vice* (Murray adopts the "Don Johnson look" in "Does Not Compute") and *Simon and Simon* (in the third season opener "Wipe Out") on the way!

Inevitably, *Riptide* has many similarities with *The A-Team,* including a comic-strip attitude towards fire-power and stunts and that all-important score by Mike Post and Pete Carpenter. The players breeze through their lines with the same light touch as most of the Cannell series of the early '80s, and it's clear the cast take their various predicaments no more seriously than the viewers, although Cannell series can lay on the heavy stuff when they need to. In "Home for Christmas" for example, Nick escorts the body of a fellow soldier for burial in a sensitive and touching episode by Tom Blomquist in which James Whitmore, Jr., directs his father in a moving story about the effects of the Vietnam war on a military family, and in "Echoes," written by Babs Greyhosky, and directed by Perry King, Murray must deal with the possibility that he has shot and killed an innocent man. In "Prisoner of War," also by Babs Greyhosky, the death of a young soldier in a traffic accident triggers Post War Stress Syndrome in Nick's girlfriend, a nurse in the Vietnam war, while "The Twisted Cross," by Cannell bit-player James Andronica and Tom Blomquist, takes a grim look at the nature of racism in America and the behavior and *modus operandi* of the American Nazi Party. As with *Magnum* and *Simon and Simon,* both of which had their darker moments, Cannell and his writers were quite capable of delivering drama when they wanted to.

Other episodes gingerly explored the relationship between Nick, Cody and Murray when, in true buddy movie fashion, an outsider — usually a woman — intruded on their friendship. Tom Blomquist's "Double Your Pleasure" trotted out the old split personality schizo girlfriend routine so beloved of detective dramas, while Frank Lupo's hilarious "Something Fishy" dared to dust off the old drug-smuggling dolphin chestnut for a storyline, although it was mostly about Nick's dilemma when a woman Murray is sweet on misses Murray's signals, and takes a fancy to him instead.

Mostly though, the *Riptide* plots were happily original as well as being blissfully Rockfordian in content. In Cannell's series opener, the aforementioned "Conflict of Interest," Boz has accepted a case in the guys' absence involving protecting a young woman whose mobster husband is trying to kill her; in the meantime, Nick and Cody have been coerced into helping the mobster locate his fleeing wife! In "Four Eyes," by Babs Greyhosky, the guys take on a sleazy divorce case while desperate for work, only to discover that their client is a major creep and his supposedly wicked wife sweetly pristine perfect. Perhaps most Rockfordian of all is the third season gem "The Frankie Kahana Show," in which the guys are driven against their better instincts to protect a phony cabaret singer with a gruesome Hawaiian routine from his mob bosses.

Tuesday night on NBC was now guys' night, just as Monday nights on CBS were geared to grab the female audience fleeing the ABC football. *Riptide* had no aspirations to examine male angst as *Cagney and Lacey* so functioned for women; it was there simply to crack a beer open to. For three seasons, it crumpled a lot of cans.

Episode Guide

regular and recurring cast: Perry King (Cody Allen), Joe Penny (Nick Ryder), Thom Bray (Murray "Boz" Bozinsky), Jack Ging (Lt. Ted Quinlan), June Chadwick (Lt. Joanna Parisi), Ken Olandt (Kirk Dooley), Anne Francis (Mama Jo), Marsha Warfield (Mama Max), Gianni Russo (Straightaway)

First Season (1984)

RIPTIDE (pilot)

wr. Stephen Cannell, Frank Lupo, dir. Chris Nyby II

Nick and Cody, two beach bums scraping a living from running tours in their motor boat and broken-down helicopter, are reunited with a computer whiz they knew in the armed forces, and find his electronic genius invaluable when they form a detective agency to exploit his abilities. Their first task is to clear the survivor of a boat explosion of smuggling for the mob after a hijacking at sea.

with Karen Kopins, Robert Viharo, Patrick Dollaghan, Marla Heasley, Eugene Butler, Lee Patterson, Frank McCarthy, Ray Girardin, Robin Evans, Ingrid Anderson, Patrika Darlo, Greg Lewis, Dave Adams

CONFLICT OF INTEREST

wr. Stephen Cannell, dir. Ron Satlof

When a young woman overhears her mobster husband ordering a contract killing, she becomes a target herself before the hit can be safely carried out.

with Kristen Meadows, Robert Desiderio, Bill Overton, Eli Cummins, Charles Hyman

SOMEONE IS KILLING THE GREAT GEEKS OF AMERICA

wr. Babs Greyhosky, dir. Bruce Kessler

A contract killer is picking off members of an intellectual society Murray belongs to, but there is conflict when the next target turns out to be someone Nick had a bad relationship with in high school.

with Cindy Pickett, Joe Michael Terry, Rodney Kageyama, Jeffrey Lampert, Vahan Moosekian

HATCHET JOB

wr. Mark Jones, dir. Ron Satlof

Although they are supposed to be pursuing the elusive Pier 56 burglar for the residents, the guys get roped into investigating a long-closed murder case by a disorientated young woman Boz has befriended.

with Maylo McCaslin, Beau Starr, Randi Brooks, Deborah Shelton, Mike Genovese, Tom Pletts, Katherine Kelly Lang

THE MEAN, GREEN LOVE MACHINE

wr. Stephen Cannell, dir. Guy Magar

The guys are hired by a friend to find her father, last seen in Mexico, which results in Murray posing far too authentically as the pigeon for a seduction scam.

with Mary-Margaret Humes, Tamara Stafford, James Luisi, Robert Sampson, Sam Scarber, East Ismael Carlo, Bruce Tuthill

DIAMONDS ARE FOR NEVER

wr. Babs Greyhosky, dir. Gloryette Clark

Bought off with a movie ticket and the use of the Corvette so that he is absent from the *Riptide* while Nick and Cody make out, Boz befriends a stewardess who has been duped into carrying contraband through customs, and the guys work to clear her name while avoiding the murderous perpetrator of the scheme.

with Kathryn Witt, John Anderson, Pepper Martin, Peter Hobbs, Robin Evans, K.C. Winkler

THE HARDCASE (a.k.a. There Goes The Neighborhood)

wr. Mark Jones, dir. Victor Hsu

The boys adopt a variety of disguises to discover the identity of a thuggish drugs runner who has stolen a boat and menaced their neighbors on Pier 56.

with William Smith, Kelly Preston, Jeffrey Josephson, Joshua Bryant, Paul Gleason, Robin Evans, K.C. Winkler, Karl Johnson, Lew Saunders, Lewis Arquette, James Edgcomb, Ken Lerner, Xander Berkeley

FOUR-EYES

wr. Babs Greyhosky, dir. Bruce Kessler

Desperate for work, the guys take on a sleazy divorce case, only to find that their client is a scuzzo and the supposedly wicked wife one of the sweetest people on the Earth. Their dilemma is exacerbated by the arrival of two wisecracking rival investigators, their female counterparts (this was a backdoor pilot for the girls which went no further).

with Stepfanie Kramer, D.D. Howard, Michael Baseleon, Joan Freeman, Danny Wells, Craig Littler, Mary Beth Evans

NUMBER ONE WITH A BULLET

wr. Stephen Cannell, dir. Arnold Laven

A rock band's manager plots the murder of his two young obnoxious stars in order to capitalize on a memorial album.

with Ed Winter, Brant Van Hoffman, Kelbe Nugent, Murphy Cross, Reid Smith, Peter Leeds, Ted Sorel, Mary Betten, Brian Libby, Jack Shea, Gary Houston Phillips, Richard Kuhlman

LONG DISTANCE DADDY

wr. Babs Greyhosky, dir. Bruce Kessler

When Nick's Cambodian foster children stow away on an airplane to reach America, they witness the killing of a mobster's son by a gun runner.

with John Louie, Julia Kono, Joseph Sirola, Frank Annese, Doug France, David Graf, Marshall Teague, Dean Wein, Bobby Kelton, Tony Ciccone, James Emery

DOUBLE YOUR PLEASURE

wr. Tom Blomquist, dir. Michael O'Herlihy

When Nick and Cody are persuaded to attend a dismal singles night at the shabby Cupid Connection by the socially inept Bozinsky, Cody falls head over heels for a young woman he meets there, only to discover a dark secret involving the case of her missing sister.

with Marta Dubois, Dennis Franz, Ron Karabatsos, Eric Server, Debi Richter, Robert Rothwell, Ellen Crawford, Sandra De Bruin

RAIDERS OF THE LOST SUB

wr. Mark Jones, dir. Dennis Donnelly

Murray's loopy sister, Melba Bozinsky, enlists the aid of the guys to help her in her profession of historian to find the wreck of a German submarine laden with gold bullion.

with Geena Davis, Stefan Gierasch, Lance Henriksen, Steven Keats

SOMETHING FISHY

wr. Frank Lupo, dir. Michael O'Herlihy

Unintentional frustration between Nick and a lovestruck Murray over the attentions of a young dolphin trainer hinder an investigation into the mysterious death of her colleague.

with Elyssa Davalos, Anthony Charnota, Christopher McDonald, Victor Mohica, Morgan Hart, Judd Omen

Second Season (1984–'85)

WHERE THE GIRLS ARE

wr. Babs Greyhosky, dir. Ron Satlof

Charged with chaperoning three dim teenaged girls, the guys discover that the vacationing airheads are the targets of a kidnapping scheme to bleed their wealthy parents (this episode is the first seen to feature Ken Olandt as Dooley, although it probably wasn't the first to be filmed; for the record, Dooley gets what appears to be his proper introduction to the series in "It's a Vial Sort of Business").

with Daphne Ashbrook, Juliana Donald, Claudia Christian, George Clooney, Alex McArthur, Don Stark, J. Warren Davis, Charlie Dell

THE ORANGE GROVE

wr. Stephen Cannell, dir. Michael Lange

When the guys are hired to investigate their former commanding officer in Vietnam for drugs running, they furiously deny his involvement but take the case to try to prove his innocence.

with Gerald S. O'Loughlin, Stanley Kamel, Kurtwood Smith, Al White, Michael Swan, Allan Graf, Arnold Turner

CATCH OF THE DAY

wr. Edward Dectar, Frank Lupo, dir. Michael Lange

The Riptide detectives are accompanied by an unpleasant reporter from the gutter press when they investigate the claim of a local fisherman that he has seen a mermaid who begged him for help.

with Patrick Collins, Tricia O'Neil, Christopher Stone, Burr DeBenning, Lana Clarkson, Ken Foree, David Clover, Gene Ross, Randy Hamilton

MIRAGE

wr. Tom Blomquist, dir. Bruce Kessler

Infatuated by a student in a computer class he is teaching, Murray can't believe his luck when she slips him a note after school ... but things go sour when he attempts to rescue her from the overbearing clutches of her Middle East husband.

with Wendy Kilbourne, Randolph Powell, Kabir

Bedi, Jacqueline Scott, Adam Ageli, Eric Goldner, Tony Di Stefano, Brendon Blincoe

Beat the Box

wr. Stephen Cannell, dir. Arnold Laven

A device invented by Murray that signals loudly whenever someone tells a lie proves invaluable when the guys investigate the mysterious death of an author, high as a kite on hallucinogenics, and discover a grim Vietnam war crime.

with Ray Wise, Joan Sweeney, William Traylor, Jack Hogan, Sal Viscuso, Geoff Prysirr, Larry Gilman, Robert O'Reilly

Father's Day

wr. Tom Blomquist, dir. Tony Mordente

When a baby is left on the doorstep of a local priest, the search for the mother causes the guys to unravel a web of intrigue that leads to mob infiltration of the police force at the highest level.

with Paul Gleason, Sherry Hursey, Robert Logan, Charles Cooper, Dennis Haysbert, Elaine Wilkes, Liz Sheridan, Steve Allie Collura

Be True to Your School

wr. Stephen Cannell, dir. Michael Lange

Cody's envy at his former classmates' success while attending his high school reunion turns to dismay when hooded gunmen crash the party and dark secrets are exposed.

with Sam Jones, Arthur Rosenberg, Bart Braverman, Gerard Prendergast, Mark Harrison, Howard George, Barbara Whinnery, Charles Guardino, David Kagen

It's a Vial Sort of Business

wr. Babs Greyhosky, dir. Bruce Seth Green

It's a typical day at Pier 56 ... Dooley has stolen a vial of horse sperm that gangsters are extremely eager to have returned to them, and a missing youngster turns out to be a runaway hamburger.

with Alan Fudge, Joe Dorsey, Clarence Gilyard, Jr., Jason Bernard, Kim Hamilton, Vince McKewin, Fil Formicola, Ken Wright, James Andronica

Peter Pan Is Alive and Well

wr. Babs Greyhosky, dir. Tony Mordente

When the Riptide agency is hired to investigate thefts of jewelry on an exclusive private beach, Murray nails the thief while Cody encounters an old friend working as a lifeguard and uncovers a blackmail operation.

with Jonathan Perpich, Peter Brown, Fionulla Flanagan, Lynn Herring, Thomas McGreevy, Beth Miller, Robyn Peterson, Steve Tannen

Catch a Fallen Star

wr. Tom Blomquist, dir. Mike Vejar

An elderly movie star who used to own Pier 56 draws the boys into a confrontation with mobsters who have stolen from her while she was in care.

with Edith Fellows, David Ackroyd, Paul Stewart, Byron Morrow, Rachel Bard

Gams People Play

wr. Tom Blomquist, dir. Ron Satlof

Nick isn't too thrilled when Cody and Boz gleefully jump at the chance to investigate chicanery at a beauty pageant in his absence.

with Bill Macy, Kelly Ann Conn, Rod McCary, Bridget Hanley, Dennis Pratt, Gene Rayburn, Bob Eubanks, Mindy Iden, Lesa Lee

Prisoner of War

wr. Babs Greyhosky, dir. Michael O'Herlihy

Nick's girlfriend goes missing after being struck by post–Vietnam trauma after a road accident revives all her bad memories of the war from her subconscious.

with Nancy Stafford, Glynn Turman, Ji-Tu Cumbuka, Anthony James, Eve Roberts, Bill Quinn, Yung Sun

Baxter and Boz

wr. Bill Nuss, dir. Michael Lange

At the patent office, Murray befriends a down-and-out who turns out to be eccentric millionaire Baxter Bernard, who employs the Riptide agency to discover why his new helicopters are developing deadly flaws.

with John Astin, Ann Turkel, James Sloyan, Kenneth Gray, Clara Perryman, James Hornbeck, Lou Felder, Terri Ann Linn, Phil Hoover

Curse of the Mary Aberdeen

wr. Steven Sears, Burt Pearl, dir. Ron Satlof

Nick and Cody are rather skeptical about the client Murray has taken on for them — he's a ghost! But during the course of their investigations they discover some interesting facts about the *Riptide*.

with Richard Kiley, Bert Freed, Jack Riley, John Sanderford, Jeffrey Osterhage

Boz Busters

wr. Babs Greyhosky, Tom Blomquist, dir. Bob Bralver

Boz reluctantly leaves the Riptide detective agency to take up a promising position at a new electronics company, unaware that he's being lured into a trap by a former military man with a grudge against him.

with Mitchell Ryan, Rosalind Cash, Cathie Shirriff, Joseph Chapman, Robert Symonds, Will MacMillan, Clare Nono, Tom Williams, Sue Giosa

Oil Bets Are Off

wr. Paul Bernbaum, dir. Michael Lange

The guys pose as wealthy high-flying gamblers while investigating the mysterious death of Murray's friend, a geologist whose latest discovery is a threat to a ruthless oil cartel.

with Joanna Johnson, Seth Jaffe, Shawn Southwick, Castulo Guerra

Girls Night Out

wr. Steve Beers, Alan Cassidy, dir. Bob Bralver

The guys are forced to investigate a series of break-ins and apprehend the real culprits, after Lt. Quinlan gleefully jumps to the conclusion that they've been committing the crimes.

with Belinda J. Montgomery, Lenore Kasdorf, Jeanetta Arnette, James Cromwell, Michael Schneider, Milt Oberman

Polly Want an Explanation

wr. Jim Carlson, Terrence McDonnell, dir. Michael Switzer

The guys become involved with an enthusiastic fledgling spy when an old friend of Nick and Cody attempts to arrange his own disappearance in order to author a critical book about the CIA.

with Robin Riker, William Russ, John McLiam, Richard McGonagle, Gary Wood, Phil Rubenstein, Bob Larkin

The Twisted Cross

wr. James Andronica, Tom Blomquist, dir. Robert Sallin

A woman resorts to desperate measures to get her impressionable young teenage son away from his father, who is a crazed racist.

with Robert Gray, Randy Norton, Katherine Cannon, Jere Burns, Millie Slavin, Cameron Thor

Fuzzy Vision

wr. Paul Bernbaum, dir. Bruce Kessler

Stranded in a weird small town, the guys try to help out one of the saner citizens, who has been accused of murder.

with Jan Sterling, Kevyn Major Howard, Bill McKinney, Lynn Hamilton, Woody Eney, Arnold Johnson, Jon Van Ness, William Bronder, Scott Lincoln, William Boyett, Med Flory, Kay Freeman

Arriverderci Baby

wr. Babs Greyhosky, dir. Michael Lange

While Nick and Cody vie for the attentions of a colorful oceanographer's Italian daughter, they also attempt to discover who is trying to sabotage the adventurer's latest explorations.

with Cesar Romero, Ava Lazar, Dana Elcar, Russell Todd, Glenn Morrissey, Steve Lattanzi, Brad English, Nick Cavenaugh, James Andronica

Harmony and Grits

wr. Tom Blomquist, Babs Greyhosky, dir. Bob Bralver

Murray's attempts to get Nick and Cody involved in the activities of a Peace and Harmony seminar he is attending end with a western saloon-bar style punch-up, and the guys argue and bicker their way through an investigation into military espionage.

with Lee Bryant, Lyle Alzado, Dean Wein, Christopher Thomas, Kathryn Skatula, Francine York, Peter Jason

Third Season (1985–'86)

Wipe Out

wr. Tom Blomquist, dir. Bob Bralver

While the Riptide agency is plagued by the activities of new competitors for their clients, the guys investigate a surfing accident that leads them to a pop singer trying to make a comeback.

with Richard Hatch, Simone Griffeth, Suzanne Snyder, Ted Neeley, David Penhale, Mitchell Anderson, Michael Galardi, A.J. Freeman

Thirty Six Hours 'til Dawn

wr. Babs Greyhosky, dir. Bob Bralver

Nick falls in love with the ex-wife of a mobster, who the guys are trying to bring back safely from Mexico to testify against him, and who will then disappear forever into the Witness Relocation Program.

with Christina Raines, Michael MacRae, Stewart Moss, Castulo Guerra, George Clifton

Does Not Compute
wr. Tom Blomquist, dir. Michael Lange
A liberal politician is slowly having his life ruined and his career destroyed by a group of right-wing conspirators who are manipulating and altering computer data. When the Riptide agency investigates, they find their own records being falsified.
with Larry Linville, Nicholas Pryor, Tracy Reed, Sharon Barr, Johnny Lee, Howard Caine, Jack Wells, Toni Attell, Jerry Potter

The Bargain Department
wr. Stephen Cannell, dir. Kim Manners
When the guys, down on their luck, are offered positions with a new hi-tech investigating agency, Cody and Boz are quickly seduced, but Nick risks his friendship with the guys to dig deeper into the company's background.
with Robert Walker, Kate Charleson, Thom McFadden, Bill Cort, George Solomon, Jan Merlin, Sol Trager

Who Really Watches the Sunset?
wr. Steven Sears, Burt Pearl, dir. Michael Lange
The guys race against time to help out a terminally ill young journalist who has been fatally slow-poisoned by the callous conspirators she is investigating and has only a few months left to bring them down and break the biggest story of her career.
with Darleen Carr, Daryl Anderson, Harvey Vernon, Paul Willson

Still Goin' Steady
wr. Terry Nelson, dir. Michael Switzer
When Murray wins a small fortune on a TV game show, two former class-mates come out of the woodwork to dupe him into saving their skins with the cash.
with Kay Lenz, Michael Lombard, James Carroll Jordan, Johnny Mountain

Robin and Marian
wr. Paul Bernbaum, dir. Robert Sallin
A daydreaming fantasist with a Robin Hood complex steals from the rich to give to a poor young widow he is attracted to ... but his activities implicate him with mobsters searching for a counterfeit money plate he has inadvertently looted.
with Walter Olkewicz, Miriam Flynn, Frank Ramirez, Michael Champion, Olivia Burnett, Scott Nemes, Gino Silva

Requiem for Icarus
wr. Steven Sears, Burt Pearl, dir. Chuck Bowman
The daughter of a hell-raising friend of Nick's begs him to help her father, who has become involved with illegal aliens (this episode writes out the character of Lt. Quinlan).
with Clu Gulager, Lisa Denton, Carl Franklin, Carl Strano, Gus Corrado

Home for Christmas
wr. Tom Blomquist, dir. James Whitmore, Jr.
Escorting the casket of a former army buddy home to his father, Nick uncovers a military conspiracy.
with James Whitmore, Ken Swofford, James David Hinton, Fred Holliday, Hugh Gillin, Anne Bellamy, Stephen Liska

Lady Killer
wr. Babs Greyhosky, Tom Blomquist, dir. Michael Lange
The guys are pleasantly surprised when they meet Quinlan's replacement, a friendly, attractive and co-operative young woman who, they are disappointed to discover, is engaged to get married. Unfortunately, a serial killer with a grudge against blonde brides-to-be is on the loose, and has the new Lt. all picked out as his next victim (this episode introduces June Chadwick as Lt. Parisi).
with Robin Strand, Lina Pousette, Eli Marder, Brian Matthews

A Matter of Policy
wr. Steven Sears, Burt Pearl, dir. Michael Preece
Deprived of most of their resources by Murray's absence and Nick's carelessness, Nick and Cody must investigate an insurance swindle with the *Riptide* in the repair shop, the Corvette in the hands of a second-hand car dealer, and the *Ebbtide* blown to bits.
with Kim Darby, John S. Ragin, Richard Sanders, James F. Kelly, Jay Ingram, F. William Parker, Alice Nunn, Brad Harris

The Wedding Bell Blues
wr. Tom Blomquist, Babs Greyhosky, dir. Michael Switzer
A young millionaire hires the guys to find out the identity of, and locate for him a beautiful young model over whom he's been obsessing ... but the boys are unaware that she's the daughter of a mob kingpin...!

with Richard Lewis, Molly Fontaine, Al Ruscio, Paul Lambert, James Purcell, Arthur Taxier, Christian LeBlanc, James Staley

The Frankie Kahana Show

wr. Frank Lupo, dir. Bruce Kessler

An obnoxious idiot flees the mob with a valuable set of accounts, but then seeks fame and fortune as a night-club singer, leading the gangsters right to him...! Unfortunately, Murray has just hired this ridiculous specimen as the lead act for Straightaways, and the next gig is to be at a police benefit.

with Andy Bumatai, Cal Bellini, Jeri Gaile, Charles Tyner, Jineane Ford-Passolt, Harold Ayer, Nathan Jung

Smiles We Left Behind
(double-length episode)

wr. Babs Greyhosky, dir. Tony Mordente

Cody's passion for a former flame is re-ignited when he and the guys travel to San Francisco to search for a missing wedding guest who flew to the U.S. from China but never showed up.

with Jane Badler, George Kee Cheung, Scott DeVenney, Christopher Pennock, Joel Brooks, Rosalind Chao

The Pirate and the Princess

wr. Terry Nelson, dir. Kim Manners

The guys are reunited with Italian oceanographer Angelo Guirilini and his daughter (from the episode "Arrividerci Baby"), and join them on a treasure hunt.

with Cesar Romero, Ava Lazar, Christopher Neame, Christopher Cary, Paul Land, Warren Berlinger, Russell Todd, Stan Haze

Playing Hardball

wr. Paul Bernbaum, dir. Bob Bralver

Nick is enthused by the prospect of going undercover with a baseball team to investigate suspicions of drug dealing.

with Steve Allen, Nicholas Guest, Ray Abruzzo, Linda Thompson Jenner, Barbie Benton, Robert Hanley

The Play's the Thing

wr. Tom Blomquist, dir. Richard J. Forrest

The guys are reunited with would-be secret agent Gloria Burghoff (from "Polly Want an Explanation") when an English teacher who claims to have discovered an undiscovered work by Shakespeare is subsequently murdered.

with Robin Riker, Frances Bay, Gino Conforti, Bernard Fox, Terry Kiser, David Ruprecht, Joseph Ruskin, David White

Dead Men Don't Floss

wr. Steven Sears, Burt Pearl, Tom Blomquist, Babs Greyhosky, Frank Lupo, dir. Chuck Bowman

Weary of the guys' bickering about who is the best detective, Lt. Parisi challenges them each to take a case out of the small ads, and see who can solve the mystery solo first.

with Dennis Burkley, Danny Cooksey, Stephen James, Lu Leonard, Christopher McDonald, Lee Wilkof, Lisa Nelson, Peggy Walton Walker, Laurie Ambert, Kit Fredericks, Carmen Filipi, Jeff Silverman

Chapel of Glass

wr. Steven Sears, Burt Pearl, dir. Bob Bralver

The guys suspect Lt. Parisi's fiancée of fixing government contracts.

with Vincent Bagetta, Michael Lally, Cliff Emmich, R.J. Bonds, Lewis Dauber

Echoes

wr. Babs Greyhosky, dir. Perry King

In this pre-empted episode, shown some months after the series had ceased production, and a little darker than most, Murray undergoes severe trauma when he's forced to shoot and kill a man who has seriously wounded Cody, but may have been innocent of the crime they were pursuing him for, and was possibly acting in self-defense.

with Lonny Chapman, Elinore Donahue, Erik Stern, Linda Hoy, Chuck Lindsley, Hap Lawrence, Jon Locke, Walker Edmiston

If You Can't Beat 'Em, Join 'Em

wr. Tom Blomquist, Babs Greyhosky, dir. Tony Mordente

In this final episode, the guys reminisce about past adventures while working as advisors to the bickering stars of a show that bears an uncanny resemblance to *Moonlighting* ... the show that pushed *Riptide* off the air!

with Annette McCarthy, Richard Greene, Danny Wells, Thom Sharpe, Al Pugliese

series ends

Unsold Pilots (2)

Cannell could do no wrong in getting series on the air until 1984, when — at the height of his success with buddy-actioners — he conceived *Brothers-in-Law,* which starred singer-songwriter Mac Davis and Joe Cortese (later of Frank Lupo's *Something Is Out There*) but was mostly notable for the presence of a villainous Robert Culp as their father-in-law and worst enemy in the world. Davis and Cortese were highway patrolman T.K. Kenny and shady trucker Mickey Gubiacci, who naturally hated each other (especially after Gubiacci's testimony secured Kenny's wife's divorce), but had married bimbo twin sisters (Candi and Randi Brough), the daughters of a super-rich, super-powerful, and slightly maniacal tycoon Winston Goodhue (Culp). Now, as Gail Williams put it in her review for *Hollywood Reporter,* "the marriage has soured, and Culp is bent on revenge against these two common fellows who have defiled his progeny!" A number of Cannell regulars guest-starred, including Daphne Ashbrook, John Saxon, Dennis Burkley, Alan Fudge, and Frank McCarthy. In a sarcastic review in *Variety,* the reviewer criticized the show (along with Larson's *The Fall Guy,* Spelling's *T.J. Hooker* and *Matt Houston,* and previous Cannell productions) for its casual car chases and gunplay, its vigilantism ("the world's problems are solved through force"), and cynicism towards the suits ("the law is the plaything of evil power-mongers") — which is a bit like criticizing a burger for having beef in it. Culp's villainy was a resounding hit with the critics, but he may

Joe Cortese and Mac Davis would have been *Brothers-in-Law.*

have been just a little too successful; American audiences are notorious for rejecting losers, and by the end of the pilot the two brothers-in-law had reluctantly teamed up after losing their jobs and their most prized possessions. Cannell learned from his mistake — the *Riptide* pilot appeared that same year, with three guys who were the best of friends and who enjoyed all the boyish trappings that Kenny and Gubiacci had lost.

Destination: America, a busted pilot from the 1986 season, was not really series material, and seemed to be about to duplicate the same mistake Cannell ultimately made with *Stingray,* which did go to series that year; his strength was buddy shows, but Bruce Greenwood's Corey St. James is a loner, traveling across America in search of the murderer of

Bruce Greenwood sets off for *Destination: America.*

his father (Rip Torn), with whom he'd had a rocky relationship, but was about to patch things up. The script was more somber for Cannell than usual, and had *Destination: America* gone to series it would have been a show more in the spirit of his late-'80s shows than his early-'80s fun-tasies, even though all Cannell's standard trademarks are to hand; freedom, individualism, a blue-collar hero, a white-collar antagonist, the sensitive machismo, the white knight, the rednecks and the hoods are all in there. Directed by Corey Allen, the indoor shots, including some beautiful tracking shots, are better than the outdoor scenes, which fail to utilize the wide open spaces to best advantage. Co-starring were Corinne Bohrer, Alan Autry, Joe Pantoliano, Henry Kingi, Robert Newman, Norman Alden, Steve Kahan, and Kim Morgan Greene, with Luke Andreas, Judith Barsi, Booth Colman, Anthony Carbone, Dennis Robertson, Robert Rockwell, and Elsa Raven (Vinnie Terranova's mother in *Wiseguy*) in support. Patrick Hasburgh and Steve Beers, later of *21 Jump Street,* collaborated.

PART THREE:
FROM L.A. TO CANADA

Hunter
September 1984–April 1991

"Works for me!"

Given the direct influence that the films of Clint Eastwood have had on television since the early '70s, and in particular on the shaping and forming of Cannell's attitude to his material, it was perhaps almost inevitable that it would be Cannell who eventually — and perhaps somewhat belatedly — provided the long overdue TV version of Eastwood's *Dirty Harry* for the 1984 debut of *Hunter*. The only surprise was that it had taken so long.

The premise of the angry cop, hampered in doing his job to the best of his ability by the constraints of the wicked, corrupt, politically motivated bureaucratic system had appeared throughout the cop shows and films of the 1970s in numerous guises, sometimes in the form of liberal despair with the system's inadequacies and unfairness, sometimes as hawkish frontier justice fantasy. While the cliché of the surly, snapping, rule book-waving boss (sometimes loveable and respected, sometimes just plain nasty) had become a staple ingredient to the point of necessity in all 1970s and early '80s TV cop shows, only Glen Larson's *McCloud* had been inspired directly by an Eastwood cop movie, 1968's *Coogan's Bluff*.*

Hunter starred Fred Dryer, a six-foot-plus giant of a man, and a former football player for the New York Giants and the L.A. Rams. He was rebel cop Rick Hunter, the bad apple in a gangland family who had crossed over like a character in a Chinese gangster film to the side of law and order to dispense justice in his own unique way. This gave him quite an edge when it came to hunting down information, but didn't do much for his credibility when his unorthodox methods got him into hot water ... as they naturally frequently did. The critics did not take long in figuring out Cannell's — and creator Frank Lupo's — source material. Dryer was described immediately and variously as "a younger, more cadaverous version of Clint Eastwood," "a cross between Richard Widmark and Clint Eastwood," "like Richard Widmark grown a foot taller and right out of Clint Eastwood territory," looking "like Clint Eastwood and may even have been carved from the same piece of wood" and "bearing a striking facial resemblance to Eastwood, especially when he's talking to the punks that make his day." "He has the kind of easily defined presence that works especially well in television" wrote John J. O'Connor in the *New York Times*. But the best description of Dryer's Rick Hunter came from writer John Leonard, who wrote of "a furtiveness, the thumbprints of a sneaky

---

*In McCloud *though, the folksy amiable and pleasant presence of Dennis Weaver (later the lead in Cannell's failed paint-by-numbers cop show* Stone*) had ensured that the subsequent series, while following the standard requirements of the 1970s cop show formula, bore little resemblance to the feature film that clearly inspired the pilot.*

mind that suggests a long Richard Nixon and a tidy Jack Nicholson ... his blank uneasiness, his friendly menace ... marble-eyed, laconic to the point of catatonia...!" "I knew from the moment I read the script that he was going to be a Clint Eastwood sort of character," Dryer told interviewer John Kercher, "but I certainly didn't try to imitate him."

Co-starring with Dryer was 5'6" Stepfanie Kramer as his petite pal and equally tough partner, Dee Dee McCall. Despite having a name like a stripper, and in the early episodes make-up and clothing to match, McCall was as capable and as dedicated as Hunter. The premise of the series was essentially an extension of the situation Eastwood's Harry Callahan found himself in during the third, excellent *Dirty Harry* escapade *The Enforcer* (1976), in which Callahan had been reluctantly paired with determined lady cop Tyne Daly (later to virtually recreate her role for the 1981–'89 series *Cagney and Lacey*). The idea in both stories was that the presence of a female partner should act as both punishment and restraining leash to appease the maverick cop's seething superiors.

In *Hunter,* Cannell and series creator Frank Lupo hatched a thinly-disguised *Dirty Harry* figure to join their growing canon of macho vigilantes, but then threw in Kramer's Dee Dee McCall as a sort of "Dirty Harriet."* More like a tougher, smarter member of *Charlie's Angels,* but with a brain, than a Cagney or a Lacey, she had married a cop who had been shot down shortly after their marriage.† This loss not only enabled the producers to include a little will-they-won't-they sexual tension between Hunter and McCall, but gave Kramer's character her motivation for being as resolutely single-

Fred Dryer and Stepfanie Kramer as Rick Hunter and DeeDee McCall.

This nickname was later given to the lead character of David Gerber's Chicago-based 1985 magnum and mayhem cop show Lady Blue, *starring Jamie Rose and Danny Aiello.*

†*Foolishly and carelessly, there are two versions of how McCall lost her husband, one in the first season episode "The Shooter," written by Mark Jones and directed by Michael Lange, in which he is said to have been a motor-cycle cop shot by a maniac, and another in the third season, "Requiem for Sergeant McCall," written by Joe Gannon and Douglas Heyes, Jr., and directed by Charles Picerni, in which we are told that he was killed while investigating a supposed suicide/suspected murder. In the latter, the male McCall is portrayed by Franc Luz, a player in three short-lived series of the '80s,* Hometown, Kay O'Brien, *and* Free Spirit.

minded as Hunter. Consequently, far from having difficulty getting along, as their superiors had hoped, the dynamic duo give their bosses a hefty dose of double trouble each episode, while — of course — Cannell and Lupo deviously send up an already self-parodic genre with over-the-top humor and stunts (a quite spectacular and ludicrous stunt sequence in the opening scene of the second-season episode "Blow Up" occurs when a car is catapulted literally the entire length of a suburban street!). Hunter shares Dirty Harry's grim attitude to the bad guys, and adds an evil smile on top of it. When bad guy Brian Dennehy plummets to his death from a rooftop in the pilot film, Hunter stands grinning like a demon at the edge of the parapet and coins his own make-my-day catch-phrase "Works for me!"* In one priceless scene in the pilot which almost compensates for all the absurdities and inadequacies of the rest of the story, Hunter strides over to a totally wrecked ball of metal that used to be an automobile, points his gun at the delirious sub-human spillage crawling out of the mess, and says — no doubt in a rare attempt to "do it by the book"—"Stop ... or I'll shoot!"

Like many of the action/adventure shows of the 1980s in well-worn genres (*Magnum, Mike Hammer, Riptide, Simon and Simon, Remington Steele, Moonlighting,* and indeed almost all the Cannell p.i. shows of the previous decade), *Hunter* was very much tongue-in-cheek during the early '80s, a comic-strip cop show in the manner of *The A-Team, Riptide,* and *Hardcastle and McCormick* that frequently went wildly over-the-top.† Hunter has the same mental block where authority and rule-books are concerned as the rest of Cannell's catalog of Lone Rangers, but all attempts to dispose of him or discredit his methods end in disaster for a variety of harassed superiors (placed opposite *Dallas* in its first year, and one of the few 1980s series to survive such a fate, *Hunter* was plagued by lack-of-direction decisions while trying to find its feet, and went through constant minor format and co-star changes).

However, the primary difference between the development of *Hunter* in comparison with *The Enforcer* is also the one unflinching, unchallenged constant of the series, and the factor that makes *Hunter* unique in American male/female shows — the inviolable notion that Hunter and McCall are only partners and workmates, and not passionate or unrequited lovers. And whereas the one underlying theme in all Cannell's series has been the bonds and loyalties of male friendship, *Hunter* is one-of-a-kind for offering viewers a platonic and respectful male-female friendship.§

This deliberate policy decision not to turn the relationship into an inevitable love affair — and its acclaim from this writer — does not come from prudishness or misguided moralizing; indeed, many 1980s series benefited from a romantic frisson or sexual tension between the two leads, including *Remington Steele, Moonlighting,* and *Cheers.* It's the originality of the partnership that's so refreshing, the notion that it's not necessary to have a romance. By not making a big deal out of the partnership and just getting on with the action, the partnership becomes a big deal because of its understatement; there have only been two other shows to

---

*Lupo had coined this phrase himself some years ago as a running gag in "The Shock Will Kill You," an episode of Greatest American Hero.

†Hunter *also has the dubious honor of having helped to inspire — along with the* Dirty Harry *mentality generally — a spoof of the spoofs, Alan Spencer's amusing* Sledge Hammer, *starring David Rasche as a Reaganite Aryan psycho cop who sleeps with and talks to his gun and "blows away" or "wastes" jaywalkers and litterbugs. By sheer coincidence,* Sledge *also has a tough and attractive female partner assigned to him as a calming influence, Anne-Marie Martin as Dori Doreau, who becomes a best friend instead in a hilarious closing scene to the pilot in which she gleefully dons a pair of* Stingray-*like shades the same as Sledge to signify her going over to his side.*

§*In the sixth season episode "Unfinished Business," written by Morgan Gendel and directed by Corey Allen, one of the last to co-star Kramer, and towards the end of the series itself, we learn that Hunter and McCall did once tumble into bed some years earlier just the once, but had never spoken about it again until a traumatic incident brings it to the fore.*

take this route — *The Avengers* in the 1960s and *The X-Files* in the 1990s (and *The X-Files* was persuaded to succumb to pressure from internet fans). As discussed in the introductory chapter, Cannell was one of the first producers in dramatic TV to include strong, independent women and realistic male/female relationships in his series, despite the strong male bias of every one of his shows, and this is a factor that has not gone unnoticed by the audience; *Hunter* had a huge following with women aged sixteen to forty-five, says ratings research. A further giveaway, perhaps unintentional, shows up in the early publicity material for the show. "Hunter is tough ... he's ornery ... he's the best cop on the L.A. beat!" booms the copy. "There's no-one more dedicated or resourceful — except his partner!"

Careless writing possibly, but unintentionally or not, it does reflect the situation between the team accurately. McCall may not be "more" dedicated, but she certainly is the smarter of the two in those early seasons ... even if Hunter's numerous "gut-feelings" and "hunches" are, in the grand tradition of the TV cop, as righteous as his flagrant abuses of the rule-book as he wades through the L.A. vermin oblivious to the cautions of his more careful partner.

Dryer, a lifelong resident of L.A. with a fondness for Europe, spent three years with the New York Giants before returning home to spend the next ten with the L.A. Rams. During his last two years on the field, he wisely took acting classes, playing only bit-parts prior to being cast in *Hunter*, with minor roles in *Hart to Hart, Laverne and Shirley*, and a suitably furrowed-brow episode of *Lou Grant* titled "Violence," which dealt rather patronizingly with the hand-wringing subject of mindlessly violent TV shows! Incredibly in retrospect, he was short-listed for the role of Sam Malone in *Cheers*, going on to make two brief walk-on appearances as a sports-buddy pal,* and had come to the attention of Cannell Productions after playing a heavy in the pilot film for *Rousters*.† Dryer's film roles include *Cannonball Run II* with Burt Reynolds and the hawkish, stunt-filled murder and mayhem action film *Death Before Dishonor*, directed by *Hunter's* assistant director, stunts supervisor Terry Leonard, and co-starring Brian Keith of *Hardcastle and McCormick*. He's also done some TV movie work, including *Something So Right*, a melodrama directed by *Rockford* regular Lou Antonio.

Stepfanie Kramer had shone in the dire 1983–'84 bimbo sit-com *We Got It Made* (two young men employ a gorgeous live-in maid, much to the chagrin of their respective lady-friends), through which she sat patiently and wryly rising above her material as one of the suspicious girlfriends for a season before getting her well-deserved break as McCall. Kramer is no second fiddle in her role in *Hunter* despite the imposing size and presence of Dryer, and often can be seen stealing the scene with her lovely facial expressions (a ploy that saw her through that dismal year on the sit-com). Protesting to the directors that she could hardly convincingly pursue the criminal element in the series' numerous chase sequences in her high-heeled wardrobe, she made television history of a minor variety by boldly kicking them off before belting through the L.A. alleyways. McCall is very much an equal to Hunter, more so than the women in many other male/female adventure teams, and can give as good as she gets. In a typical Cannell flourish, her nickname — speedily discarded after the pilot — is not "the Iron Lady" but "the Brass Cupcake" (similarly hastily dropped was Hunter's nickname in the pilot, "the Head Hunter")!

One of these before Hunter *had started production, the other well after the show had become established — "Sam at Eleven" and "I on Sports."*

†*His partner in crime had been Robert Davi, later to appear as Albert Cerrico in the better third season episodes of* Wiseguy *and "Million Dollar Misunderstanding," a Lupo-penned second season* Hunter *involving the same crime he and Dryer had been attempting in the* Rousters *pilot — an armored car heist!*

Kramer's previous TV work includes guest-roles in *Starsky and Hutch, Vegas, Fantasy Island,* and *Dynasty* for Aaron Spelling, as well as *Cliffhangers* (in which she played a sword-and-sorcery princess), *Trapper John, Mike Hammer, Knot's Landing, The Devlin Connection,* and *The A-Team* and *Riptide* for Cannell. The *Riptide* episode was "Four Eyes," a back-door pilot by Babs Greyhosky, produced only months before *Hunter* commenced filming; interestingly, the real name of the actress playing her partner in the "Four Eyes" pilot was billed as D.D.

Appearing as the resident nerd during the early seasons with diminishing regularity was James Whitmore, Jr., as a bow-tied by-the-book Aunt Sally named Bernie Terwilliger, who was eventually promoted Frank Burns/*M*A*S*H*-style to Internal Affairs and gradually faded away. Whitmore, a regular director on *Hunter* and guest-star on numerous Cannell and Bellisario productions, co-starred in the first season of *Black Sheep Squadron* as the tough Lt. Jim Gutterman, but perfected his nerd persona as the bogus p.i. Fred Beamer in two episodes of *The Rockford Files* ("Beamer's Last Case" and "Nice Guys Finish Dead") and two episodes of *The Greatest American Hero,* first as a mean-minded tax inspector in "There's Just No Accounting," and then as the gormless creator of a role-playing game in the episode "Wizards and Warlocks."

As a Cannell show that survived several seasons until the beginning of the 1990s, *Hunter* managed to embrace various passing trends in Cannell's own productions and in American television generally during its run, rather than being solely representative of one. However, like many series that eventually become long-runners, *Hunter* got off to a dire start in the ratings, not helped by an absurd plot for the pilot film that — although graced with some excellent action scenes and brilliant one-liners from Frank Lupo — was otherwise dismally stupid. Written by Lupo and directed by Ron Satlof, the splendid character actor Brian Dennehy, a player with a superb string of performances in film and TV to his credit, was wasted in every sense of the word as a psychotic country and western fan with a murderous grudge against blonde-haired women. Hunter's superiors are trying to take him out of commission by sending him to a psychiatrist who has orders from upstairs to pronounce him unfit for duty. In a plot development that would have the most lenient critic banging his or her head repeatedly against the wall, the psychiatrist just happens to be the loony on the loose as well, thus allowing Hunter to effectively kill two birds with one stone. With a prurient mentality and artless contrivance more readily associated with a 1970s Aaron Spelling farrago, and a storyline that for all of Dryer and Kramer's obvious potential and compatibility, stretches credibility and circumstance way beyond the bounds of probability, this was not a particularly auspicious start for the series; things could only get better for the simple reason that they could not get any worse.

Of the first season of eleven episodes, the best was easily "The Hot Grounder," written by Cannell himself and directed by Bill Duke, in which Hunter goes after the police commissioner himself for murder! The title of the episode is derived from the nick-name Hunter's fellow officers have for an impossibly awkward case nobody else wants. When the news of murder at the commissioner's stately home first comes in, there is an amusing scene as the entire squadroom hides out in the men's washroom until the case has been assigned. Naturally it "works for Hunter" (and Cannell and Lupo) because it gives Hunter and McCall the perfect opportunity to upset the most superior of superiors ... a murderous police commissioner blaming the mob for his wife's car-bomb demise. Inevitably, even after the suit-and-tie guys have told Hunter and McCall that the case is closed, the duo persist with relish, creating a major scandal in the process. The fact that an above-average cast included *The Rockford Files'* Joe Santos very much at home in the squad room and the always excellent William Windom as the commissioner (Windom was severely under-used in the pilot for *The A-Team*, playing Amy Allen's abducted colleague) helped considerably, although Santos had already been a focal point of the same plot in a *Rockford Files* episode "Kill the Messenger." This was everything the pilot should have been. Lupo's own "A Long Way from L.A.," directed by Arnold Laven, also offered an unconventional episode away from the norm in what appeared to be a half-hearted attempt to recreate Eastwood's superb feature *The Gauntlet* as a small-town conspiracy yarn.

But while indulging in the familiar tried-and-true clichés of vigilante action/adventure, Cannell and Lupo and their colleagues cleverly managed to ring a few changes on some well-worn themes with their usual skilful and slyly subversive humor. In "Avenging Angel," written by Brian Lane and directed by James Whitmore, Jr., it is not an unfortunate female co-star or guest star being stalked by a deranged and murderous male admirer, but big Rick Hunter himself! The episode opens to a scene strongly reminiscent of Juanita Bartlett's *Rockford Files* episode "Crack Back," in which Rockford's lady lawyer friend had been pursued by an obsessive tormentor, and — in one particularly powerful and memorable scene — had stumbled into a room where the walls had been plastered with candid voyeuristic snap-shots of her, a veritable shrine which, in fact, had been devised as a psychological device to distract her from a case in progress (the creepy candid camera display has since become a cliché, parodied superbly in the *Seinfeld* episode "The Opera"). As this episode of *Hunter* opens, the camera lovingly pans over a display of similarly secretly-shot pictures of Hunter in action, which — in the red-hued tint of the photographer's darkroom — sweeps seductively over the picture gallery to the haunting strains of the pop song lyrics "every breath you take, I'll be watching you...!" In Cannell's "The Hot Grounder," William Windom's wicked police commissioner kills the tennis coach his wife has been having a secret affair with, not because of his wife's infidelity, but because the bi-sexual gigolo has jilted him for her!

Despite all this innovation and exploitation, ratings were disastrous. Quite simply, no-one was watching ... not the least because the Ewing clan of *Dallas* were then at the height of their popularity on the rival CBS network. *Hunter* was a doomed show whatever its failings or merits. Fortunately, the pairing of Dryer and Kramer was a winner that even a network executive could spot, and NBC had reaped great dividends at the time by giving eventual hit shows like *Hill Street Blues, Cheers* and *St. Elsewhere* a chance to find their footing. Even though *Dallas* clobbered *Hunter* spectacularly, the networks were at last beginning to perceive that not every series gathered lousy ratings because it just didn't work, and that the schedules of rival networks and the success of opposing shows just might play some significant part in determining the performance of the series against it. Obviously, any new series scheduled against an established hit at the height of its popularity was going to have a much lower chance of succeeding than a show placed opposite a tired, fading series or a brand new program, whatever its quality or potential.

Cannell's impressive track record and the obvious charm and charisma of Dryer and Kramer and their rapport together as partners clearly entitled *Hunter* to a more deserving fate than to be yet another virginal sacrifice to the great god *Dallas*. NBC, already running *The A-Team* and *Riptide* as the mainstays of their successful Tuesday night line-up, had nothing to lose by giving *Hunter* another chance, but everything to gain from another strong Cannell show to build around. After much table-thumping by Cannell, NBC were willing to concede that *Hunter* might have a chance in another slot.

Realizing that the show had come to the brink of cancellation, Cannell wasted no time in giving the show an overhaul. *Hunter* went briefly off the air in mid–January of 1985, and when it returned in March of that year a few weeks later it was with the dazzling and memorable two-parter "The Snow Queen," written by Frank Lupo and directed by Tony Mordente and Richard Colla. With the new lease of life for the show came glossier, sharper photography and a whole new slick look; "The Snow Queen" was a colorful, beautifully photographed, tightly edited foretaste of the weeks to come, presented with the same style and flair of the 1984–'85 season's surprise smash hit, Michael Mann's *Miami Vice,* also for NBC. Guesting was Dennis Franz, a regular Cannell villain here playing his usual sleazy cop role.

After a television debut in the 1982 series *Chicago Story* as a salt-of-the-earth good guy uniformed cop, Franz had appeared twice on *Hill Street Blues,* first in a storyline as the corrupt doomed thug Detective Benedetto. Although Benedetto was written out and killed off, he had been so charismatic a character that he was reincarnated as Benedetto-clone Sgt. Norman Buntz and later, when *Hill Street* finally closed, enjoyed a brief spell in his own spin-off show, the promising but thoroughly disappointing *Beverly Hills Buntz.* During and since his tenure in *Hill Street Blues,* he'd slimed his way through guest spots in just about every adventure show of the '80s, often in what appeared to be the same wardrobe, until securing the starring role in the superb *NYPD Blue* in the '90s. Also in the cast of this superior episode was former cop turned actor Dennis Farina, ironically cast as a hood named Vic Terranova; a couple of seasons later, two excellent mob shows would burst onto the air, one starring Farina as the tough cop Mike Torello in *Crime Story,* the other, Cannell's own production *Wiseguy,* starring a lead character named Vinnie Terranova.

With the arrival of the influential and successful "cop video" *Miami Vice,* the look of many new television series suddenly changed to accommodate the trend, taking on the rapid-cut, glossy presentation of that series. Apparently, the notion of "MTV cops" was NBC president Brandon Tartikoff's idea, and he'd originally offered it for development to Cannell, who had turned it down. "We haven't invented the Hula-Hoop or anything," Michael Mann told *Rolling Stone* reporter Emily Benedek with mock modesty. "If anything, we're only *contemporary.* And if we're different from the rest of TV, it's because the rest of TV isn't even contemporary." Of course today, like all hip shows of their time, *Miami Vice* looks hilariously dated, while shows like *Hunter* have retained their longevity by *not* immersing themselves in the fashions of the moment. Cannell, knowing that television is about longevity and long-term profit, was right to wave it away.

Hunter, searching for an identity since it began, very quickly latched onto this style of presentation, particularly since it was on the same network as *Miami Vice,* and in a similar slot. From a shabby-looking back-street shoot-'em-up, *Hunter* transformed from an inauspicious 1984 debut distinguished only by Cannell and Lupo's dialogue and Dryer and Kramer's screen presence to begin 1985 as a sharply-photographed, tightly-edited visual treat.

The other innovation of *Miami Vice* had been, of course, the use of contemporary pop music on the soundtrack. Cannell had been toying with this otherwise new development as early as *The Greatest American Hero* in 1981, which had often included musical segments composed by Joey Scarbury, whose theme for the show had made the U.S. pop charts (as indeed did Mike Post and Pete Carpenter's theme for *The Rockford Files,* and Sammy Davis, Jr.'s, title vocals for *Baretta*), although these interludes were more time-fillers than mood-setters. Many of the 1985 episodes of *Hunter,* particularly in the early half of the year, were distinguished by their liberal use of familiar rock tracks to punctuate the story, most noticeably in the opening scenes. As one program-buyer pointed out to me in reference to such a scene in Cannell's flashy 1986 pilot for his series *Stingray*, "it must have taken him twenty minutes to get out of his car!"

As with *Miami Vice*, *Hunter* was concentrating for a while on style rather than content, although *Hunter* had the advantage of two leads with more charisma, and a relationship already established in the preceding episodes. With the absence of a scenic Miami backdrop to the stories, this minimalist, uncomplicated, almost comic-book approach to the series produced some quite extraordinary results. In episodes such as Thomas Szollosi's and Richard Christian Matheson's "The Beach Boy" and "Fire Man," Mark Jones' "The Shooter" and "Guilty," and Sidney Ellis' "Sniper" (the latter clearly inspired by the theme of the pilot), Hunter and McCall pursued a succession of crazed, murderous loonies who had assumed the almost mystical status of a supernatural horror from the classier end of the monster market. The faceless killer cop of "The Shooter" resembled nothing less than the super-human horrors of films like *Hallowe'en* or *Friday the 13th;* "The Beach Boy," clad in Hawaiian shirt and toting an enormous machine-gun, shrugs off bullets like a Kryptonian super-villain, and "The Death Machine," by Tom Lazarus, offers former football player John Matuszak as a mob enforcer known only as Lincoln, a bone-breaking torturer for hire. "Fire Man," seen only in silvery fire-proof suit, and lugging a flame-thrower around with him, looks as though he just stepped out of the 1990s TV incarnation of *The Flash*, meeting his end in a shadowy graveyard where he has, in a manner of speaking, risen from the dead. (Ironically, actor Robert Englund—Freddy Krueger himself, from the *Nightmare on Elm Street* film series—has a minor bit-part in Frank Lupo's "Million Dollar Understanding" at around this time, but in a brief comic turn rather than as one of the villains). These encounters took place against a backdrop of near-continuous modern music and rapid-fire visual imagery as Hunter and McCall became vigilante executioners every bit as formidable as their demonic opponents, and were as fantastic as anything Lupo would later turn out for his solo supernatural series *Werewolf* and *Something Is Out There* a few years later, with Hunter and McCall up against adversaries as bizarre, insane, elusive and ethereal as any even the Batman ever had to confront! The murders in "Guilty" even resemble an early *Batman/Joker* story, with a killer systematically bumping off the citizens who put him away, and seem as relentless, inevitable and unstoppable as the bullets of "The Beach Boy." Stephen Katz' "Killer in a Hallowe'en Mask" takes us into *Phantom of the Opera* territory with a deformed Joker/Half-Face type, and Herbert Wright's "Blow Up" offers us the insane, cackling Otto Minsky (Anthony James), a demented mad bomber systematically knocking off grudges and—like the Riddler—daring Hunter to catch him! And all this, long before Tim Burton's *Batman* film or the *Flash* television series!

This short run ended in May 1985, and when *Hunter* returned for its official second season in September, there was another change of direction, with Cannell bringing in his old colleague from his Universal days, Roy Huggins, to take over from him as executive producer (some sources have implied that *Hunter* was "taken away" from Cannell, either before or after Huggins' tenure, but if so, there seems to have been no animosity or ill-feeling apparent). Huggins had years of experience behind him, and had worked with Cannell on *The Rockford Files* a decade earlier.

"Roy Huggins was my mentor, my godfather," Cannell told interviewer Duane Byrge in the late '80s. "He gave me my first producership when I was a writer under contract with Universal. The time I was with him was a very important time in my career, a time when I didn't know anything. Roy believed in me and taught me. When I was really in trouble on

Hunter, we were just spread real thin. I needed somebody to come in and absolutely run things. Roy didn't need the job or anything, but I said 'I'd sure appreciate it if you'd bail me out here,' and he did."

The network picked a typically lurid episode to lead off with, as Hunter and McCall investigated the murders of a number of porn stars in "Case X," written by Tom Lazarus and directed by David Soul, the former star of Aaron Spelling's 1970s cop show *Starsky and Hutch* and later the lead in Cannell's own short-lived 1989 cop series *Unsub*. Soul had edged his way into directing with an episode of *Starsky and Hutch* ("Survival") as part of the standard contract carrot that Dryer and Kramer themselves would later enjoy (both Dryer and Kramer negotiated directing assignments during the series' run), and had since directed episodes of *Miami Vice*. With *Hunter* and a number of other shows going for the glossy *Miami Vice* image, Soul was clearly perceived as a natural choice to bring such an approach to *Hunter*, but for whatever reason, this was to be his only episode (Michael Mann had written the *Starsky and Hutch* pilot, among other Spelling vehicles; later, Soul would guest star and direct on *Crime Story*).

Despite *Hunter's* brief flirtation with mid-'80s TV chic, critics remained unconvinced, with Fred Schruers, marking the show's 100th episode in 1989, commenting in the U.S. bible of cool *Rolling Stone*, "In contrast to *Miami Vice*, *Hunter* remains remarkably un-'80s, decidedly un-hip." Button-holing the ambience of the early Friday night episodes opposite *Dallas* perfectly, Schruers observed "a hard-to-define aura of shabbiness (that) clung to the show — from the stars' costuming (Hunter's jeans and Sears-rack shirts, the *haute*-tart suits of his partner, DeeDee McCall) through its locales (blank-walled homes, the dingy station-house) and its '50s-retro look (flat lighting, *Jetsons*-style furniture, artificially barren streets) to its losing bouts with street-cop reality and its over-worked tag-line 'Works for me....'"

The second season also featured scripts by Cannell regulars Stephen Katz, a frequent *A-Team* contributor, and Rudolph Borchert of *The Rockford Files, Kolchak—the Night Stalker*, and *Greatest American Hero*, while Cannell's later Canadian operation co-worker, Randall Wallace, made an inauspicious debut with the feeble "Fagin 1986," directed by Douglas Heyes and guest-starring Trinidad Silva (gang leader Jesus Martinez in *Hill Street Blues*) in his traditional clichéd role of street-smart gangster-in-charge. In the station-house, John Amos (as Captain Dolan) and Gary Crosby (as patrolman Dabney Smith), had departed, and Bruce Davison was introduced as Hunter's new fuming superior, Captain Wyler. Half-way through the third season he would be replaced by the more sympathetic Captain Devane (Charles Hallahan), who would stay with the series until its demise, and in the second season episode "Blow Up," John Shearin (formerly one of the cast of James Garner's *Bret Maverick* in 1981–'82) gave Hunter support against the short-tempered Wyler as Lt. Ambrose Finn. With Devane more supportive of Hunter in subsequent episodes, and Hunter and McCall not so easily lead astray from the rule-book now that they were away from Cannell and Lupo's influence, Finn was surplus to requirements as the series went on, and was written out at the close of the fourth season in the final episode of the year, Dallas and Joanne Barnes' "Silver Bullet." A disastrous addition to the series during Huggins' tenure (in "The Return of Typhoon Thompson," by Rogers Turrentine) was the appallingly dated cliché of jive-talkin' black hustler and pimp Arnold "Sporty" James (Garrett Morris), a tired and over-used caricature that had worn out its welcome way before the close of the '70s, and who became a regular but thankfully often brief fixture during the third season (interestingly, Hunter and McCall rarely ever seemed to *pay* for Sporty's information!).

Hunter made a point of featuring a number of minor regular recurring characters during its lengthy run, who drifted in and out of the show providing welcome continuity and familiarity, sometimes making an impact, sometimes not. Apart from the occasional appearances of Terwilliger, Finn and Sporty, there was Martin E. Brooks (a semi-regular on the 1970s bionic super-hero shows) as devious criminal lawyer Mike Snow, morgue attendants Carlos (Richard Beauchamp) and Reuben (Rudy Ramos, formerly of the '60s series *Garrison's Gorillas*), and coroner Barney (Perry Cook), and whenever a certain role came up in the script, all efforts would be made to bring back an appropriate familiar face, rather than just introduce another one-off role. It wouldn't have been a cop show without the occasional appearance of Bruce Kirby in some of the early episodes, who's been in virtually every police precinct on TV, while Paul Mantee, occasionally seen as a cop in *Cagney and Lacey*, made periodic appearances in the final season. Jack Bannon (Donovan in *Lou Grant* and a regular on the 1980s guest-star circuit) made a handful of appearances (with a ludicrous shaven head) as Drug Enforcement Agency operative Stevens, and a now silver-haired Robert Colbert (of *Maverick* and *The Time Tunnel*) showed up as Internal Affairs investigator Dryden.* Furthermore, Hunter's previous nemeses in the department, Captains Cain and Wyler, didn't just disappear, but were promoted upstairs; Arthur Rosenberg's Captain Cain (portrayed by Michael Cavenaugh of the *Starman* TV series in the pilot) even returned to be exposed as corrupt and caught in Dallas Barnes' fourth season three-parter "City of Passion."

With Huggins' arrival, and a move to Saturday nights (a placing destined to be *Hunter's* regular time-slot for the years to follow, excepting a couple of brief ill-judged aberrations), *Hunter* inherited a sort of non-identity and a mystery audience that helped it reach that 100th episode long after the brief star that was *Miami Vice* had burned out. By the third season, the show was plainly Huggins', but the second season was a curious hodgepodge of familiar themes with a twist. Interspersed with the mayhem, mobsters, terrorists, Russian agents and other Cannell trademarks of such second season episodes as Sidney Ellis' "Scrap Metal," Rudolph Borchert's "62 Hours of Terror," and Jo Montgomery's and Roy Huggins' "The Beautiful and the Dead" (a typical Huggins title if ever there was), the dazzling gunfights of Herbert Wright's and Patrick Barry's "Night of the Dragons," the small-town B-movie ambience of Stephen Katz' "The Biggest Man in Town" (which even offered up such inevitable casting as Don Stroud as the town sheriff and Stuart Whitman as the local big shot), the tired junior delinquents, intrusive hostile reporters and victimized vagrants of Randall Wallace's "Fagin 1986" and Marianne Clarkson's and Allison Hock's "Saturday Night Special," and the recognizable Cannell territory of Allison Hock's "War Zone" and Rogers Turrentine's "The Return of Typhoon Thompson" (Isaac Hayes as yet *another* vengeful ex-con), were traditional cop show/detective stories such as Stephen Cotler's "Rich Girl," Turrentine's "The Big Fall" and "Waiting for Mister Wrong," Jo Montgomery's "Burned" (guest starring 1950's movie queen Jane Russell) and Allison Hock's "The Set Up." Cannell — unusually — had not contributed an actual script to the series since providing the early episode "The Hot Grounder" and co-writing "Hard Contract" with Lupo, although his presence had always been strongly felt in the script, plots, and themes, and Lupo bowed out spectacularly with "Million Dollar Misunderstanding," which featured some brazenly self-parodic Lupo dialogue ("Hey, what *is* this?"—"It's a *boat* chase!").

Colbert's co-star in The Time Tunnel, *James Darren, frequently directed for Cannell and Lupo, working on episodes of* The A-Team, Stingray, Werewolf, Hardball, Something Is Out There, Renegade *and others, including several episodes of* Hunter—*but none with Colbert.*

Gradually, Huggins reintroduced stories to the proceedings, as some very typically Huggins-influenced plot-lines transfused themselves to the existing *Hunter* formula. Huggins was a member of the old school of script-writing, having begun his career writing pulp detective mysteries, and those traditions rapidly found their way into the series. The blaring pop music cautiously disappeared, although the show retained its new-found glossy sheen and crisp quality of photography, and episodes such as "Rich Girl," with its plush settings of wealth and easy living, contrasted sharply with the visual shabbiness of the opening episodes in 1984, an endless succession of back alleys and bars filled with trash, literal and living. By the beginning of the third season, Cannell's writers had also departed, but for Lupo, still keeping an eye on proceedings as the show's creator. The most conspicuous change in the series was brought about by Roy Huggins' old school attitude toward women; while Stepfanie Kramer's character didn't change, the women Hunter and McCall encountered were now beautiful creatures of mystery, devious, alluring, and manipulative in the grand tradition of pulp detective novels and 1960s television series. Nevertheless, the series and its two lead characters were well established enough by now for the changes in tone to be subtle and seamless. By 1986, in the most difficult time-slot of the week, *Hunter* was outrating not only *Miami Vice* and its more contemporary clones, but such stylish and successful competitors as *Magnum* and *The Equalizer* as well, to become the most successful cop/detective show of the '80s.

"All this hoopla for *Hunter* is extremely odd," mused a critic writing in the *St. Louis Dispatch* in 1989 as *Hunter* reached the magic 100 mark of a bona-fide, 24 carat hit series. "It is a fairly well-crafted show, but other than that it is overwhelmingly ordinary, essentially indistinguishable from scores of middling cop shows that have preceded it, and scores that will follow. We are not talking *Hill Street Blues* here."

Indeed we were not, which was probably why *Hunter* had cornered its own little niche in the marketplace. Despite some familiar plots and cop show traditions, *Hunter,* while being very much a typical cop show, was a cut above the rest more for what it *didn't* do rather than for what it did. The late-night weekend time-slot kept it free of teenage elements such as pretty-boy sidekicks and emotional sops for the thirtysomething demographics, while rarely descending to the idiocies of other out-of-time '80s shows like *T.J. Hooker* or *Spenser: for Hire.*

In the first two seasons, *Hunter* avoided sophistication in its dialogue, and ambiguities in the plots; we knew who did it — let's go get 'em! There were no sub-plots or moral debates standing in the way of Hunter and McCall, just technicalities and bureaucracies. Just under 50 minutes a week would be spent whittling these away with short-cuts and car chases; the problem was not so much figuring out who did it, but how to cut through the red tape to waste the suckers. By the third season, Huggins had reintroduced mystery to the stories, complete with twists, turns, surprises, and red herrings. As with his first season *Rockfords,* the stories were awash with romanticized mystery women who baffled men with their treacherous allure. Huggins slowly phased out the angry bosses, rotten assignments, broken-down cars (a running gag in the show had our dynamic duo being handed the worst rattle-trap in the police car pound to minimize the catastrophic costs when Hunter wrecked it), the "Works for me" catch-phrase, with Hunter freed to do his job unhindered by the complexities and subtleties of other 1980s cop shows that had moved on from the pulp detectives into gritty urban realism. Before long, *Hunter* was sitting squarely in the top thirty — sometimes top twenty — TV shows where it firmly stayed for the remainder of the decade.

The mystery audience that put it there was also more easily defined by what it wasn't. Aired on the lowest sets-in-use night of the week (Saturday), *Hunter* actually raised the HUT

(Homes Using Television) average, which — Huggins delighted in pointing out — was unheard of. Its competition consisted mostly of modestly successful mediocrities (*Hotel, Spenser*) or brave adventurous failures (*Murphy's Law* and *Men*), and it followed a string of four quaint family sit-coms, the latter two being the elderly-skewed duo of *Golden Girls/Amen* and later *Golden Girls/Empty Nest,* hardly perceived as compatible shows with similar audience profiles. Presumably, after two hours of sit-coms (and who wouldn't be ready for some violence after two hours of loveable irascible old folks?), NBC's audience was ready for a change of pace, while the rival networks' viewers changed channel to join *Hunter* in preference to the competition. Kids were out on the town, so it seemed as though *Hunter* in the 1980s, like *Hawaii Five-O* a decade earlier, had outlived its numerous fellow cop shows of the period simply by catering for the formidable number of over-thirties who wanted a regular weekly dose of polished, professional, no-nonsense conventional cop heroics. *Hunter* now dispensed with the trendy trimmings and contemporary affectations to be found in the likes of such classy productions as *Miami Vice, Moonlighting, Crime Story, L.A. Law, Hooperman, Private Eye, Stingray, Legwork, Sonny Spoon,* or *Wiseguy,* and also offered (mostly) far superior stories to the dated and illogical bilge being served up in other older-skewed crime shows like *Matlock, Murder She Wrote, The Father Dowling Mysteries, Jake and the Fat Man* and *The Law and Harry McGraw,* etc. *Hunter* certainly laid its share of eggs, but usually the plots were intelligent without being complex, and sensible without being sophisticated; a degree in sociology, criminology, law, modern politics or pop culture was not required. As the others came and went, *Hunter* retained its audience share. NBC moved it at its peril.

Huggins had come out of retirement as a favor to Cannell, and — having accomplished his assignment to save the show beyond anybody's wildest hopes or dreams — chose to depart at the end of the fourth season (1987–'88). Although Cannell's contribution in setting the show up should not be minimized, by now, Cannell and his early-'80s canon of writers had no connection with the series at all, which had long been entrusted to the capable hands of Huggins and the considerable and growing input into the series of Fred Dryer himself (although Frank Lupo was drafted in to supervise the scriptwriting chores that would allow Dryer his first shot at directing). Cannell's operation had now moved to Canada, in Vancouver, and only *Hunter* and the short-lived *Sonny Spoon* (1987–'88) were still being produced in L.A.*

A legacy that the pulp detective origins of Huggins had left the series during his fourth and final season was a series of often multi-part stories adapted from both novels and true-life cases. These included "Flashpoint," "City of Passion," "Naked Justice," and "Silver Bullet," all from novels by Dallas Barnes, Robert Hamner's "The Black Dahlia," and "Death Signs," from a novel by H. Edward Hunsberger. It was one of these stories that caused a falling-out between Stepfanie Kramer, who took a brave stand over something she believed in, and the producers and the network. Ironically, this dispute stemmed from one of the best episodes in the series, the two-parter "Rape and Revenge" from the second season, written by Tom Lazarus, and directed by Cannell exec. Gary Nelson and the highly regarded Richard Colla.

In this story, amid all the murder and mayhem that distinguished the second season, Hunter pursued a rapist pleading diplomatic immunity for his crimes all the way back to his home country, a tin-pot banana dictatorship, where he hunts him down like a dog and pro-

---

*See the chapter on *Stingray* for details on this development.

vokes him into a fatal gunplay. Despite the exploitative title and nature of the story, the actual treatment of a rape perpetrated on McCall by this man was intelligently and carefully handled, portrayed neither luridly, dishonestly, nor voyeuristically. The rapist was no slavering, psychopathic animal, as film usually chooses to portray such men (although such specimens undoubtedly exist), but a powerful, wealthy, and good-looking diplomat who had every option open to him to obtain the pleasures of women in other ways. His crime was a cool, calculating and completely careless act of brutality that could not make use of such feeble excuses as frustration or misunderstanding. Similarly, McCall was not shown as instantly recovering from the ordeal in the next scene; neither was she shown to be a victim for life, but portrayed working hard to recover from her ordeal. Kramer apparently played a large part in ensuring that the rape storyline was played horrifically and authentically, without encouraging the section of the audience likely to find such brutality exciting or entertaining. The storyline also avoided the glib clichés of both film and feminism, showing that McCall's initial attraction to the diplomat's attentions were not a welcome mat for his aggression, that his success in flattering and intriguing her did not entitle him to take things further than she was ready for, and that while this man had proven himself a vicious pig, there were plenty of other men, including Hunter himself, revolted by the rape and ready to offer support and sympathy.

As the story progresses, we learn several factors that allow the audience to appreciate the revenge motif of the second half (episode one deals with McCall's recovery and Hunter's helplessness, both in bringing the rapist to justice and helping his friend and colleague through her trauma). We discover that the American authorities are powerless to arrest the diplomat, that he has no qualms about repeatedly flouting the law (at one point, he brazenly puts a bullet in Hunter), that he drove his wife to suicide, and that he may have perpetrated similar crimes, including a rape/murder in the U.S. Finally, when McCall informs the diplomat's father of the son's crimes, it becomes clear that this callous disdain for women is a family trait. Consequently, while surrounded by all the usual trappings of a classic exploitation revenge shoot-'em-up, everyone concerned with the story went to great lengths to ensure that the sensitive sequences were handled in just that way, complete with genuine aftermath and long haul back to confidence and self-respect.

During the third season, an inevitable sequel, "*High Noon in L.A.*" appeared — inevitable, because after killing the rapist diplomat, Hunter and McCall are pursued across the country by the enraged father for a nerve-jangling hair-breadth escape. In this story, written by Erica Byrne and Howard Chesley, and directed by James Whitmore, Jr., the brother of the dead man arrives in America to return fire. The book was now closed.

However, in the three-parter "*City of Passion*" exactly a year later, adapted from his own novel by Dallas Barnes, the storyline called for McCall to become the latest victim of a serial rapist. Kramer rightly felt that the producers had returned to the well one too many times, and refused point blank to film such a scene, declaring it a point on which she was prepared to walk off the series completely. To her credit and courage, a compromise was reached, with the attack being rewritten as an attempted rape, and Kramer managing to incorporate a few more points about the after-effects of such a terrible attack into the script. Kramer finally announced her departure from the series some years later in early 1990, for completely unrelated reasons.

At one point, during 1987, NBC — noting the element of playful camaraderie between Dryer and Kramer — slid *Hunter* over to Tuesdays at 9:00 to compete with ABC's smash hit *Moonlighting.* In the weeks that the troubled *Moonlighting*— beset with various production problems — ran repeats, *Hunter* outrated it, but otherwise *Hunter* came in second. Despite this, the presence of *Hunter* caused the ratings for the whole night to marginally improve across the board. In the meantime, *Hunter's* Saturday night slot had been occupied by the short-lived Cannell series *J.J. Starbuck*. When Cannell's new baby failed to hold the Saturday night audience for NBC (*Starbuck's* second attempt to find a home on the schedule), NBC wisely returned *Hunter* to its old home. NBC tampered with success again briefly during *Hunter's* final year, during a mass program-shuffling panic on the part of all three networks during the 1990–'91 season. The series survived NBC's efforts to do it in, but a crisis was on the way....

For the fifth season, George Geiger, a veteran producer with credits including *Magnum, Miami Vice,* and *Scarecrow and Mrs. King,* took over from Huggins. The new story editor was to be Fred McKnight, a TV scriptwriter who had spent 25 years in the narcotics division of the police force. After his partner was killed in a drugs operation, McKnight turned to a desk job, entering television through an introduction from his friend, the cop-turned-novelist Joseph Wambaugh, whose career had formed a loose inspiration for Cannell's *Stone*. Wambaugh had fought the Hollywood establishment constantly over the film versions of his books, and his efforts to keep the TV series inspired by his works, *Police Story,* on the straight and narrow in terms of credibility had been well publicized. McKnight had been brought in by Wambaugh to work on *Police Story,* and eventually ended up scriptwriting for the spin-off series *Police Woman,* as well as other series including *Hollywood Beat* and *MacGyver*. Many of his real-life cases had been adapted for the *Dragnet* TV series.

Dryer was unhappy with the first season of *Hunter,* and while he approved of Huggins' work on the series, saying that Huggins had "turned the show around," he was less happy with the direction Geiger wanted to take. With Huggins gone, Lupo now off producing series of his own, and Cannell busy elsewhere, Dryer was left practically running the show, and that was just the way he liked it. With the series still a hit, and Kramer one of the most supportive and amiable of co-stars, the new people found themselves being constantly over-ruled and vetoed by the show's protective star.

Geiger had spoken to the press about "more depth and dimension" for the characters, with stories revolving around Hunter and McCall's personal lives. McCall's mother was to make an appearance, and Hunter was to be hassled by a landlord and a flirtatious neighbor, with flashbacks exploring the leads' histories. Dryer immediately trashed these plans, telling reporters that "getting involved in the private lives of the characters would be death to the show. This series is about what happens to Hunter and McCall in the line of police work. The show should come out of that, not what I think about my next-door neighbor." For her part, Kramer seemed diplomatically non-plussed about all this off-screen to-ing and fro-ing, having told journalist Kay Gardella earlier, "I'm hoping ... there'll be more expansion, more growth. TV is a restrictive environment. Once a structure is found that works, people adhere to it without deviation. It's important to change and expand on what you know that works," but adding that "The relationship we have on the screen is the core of the show. It's what distinguishes us from other cop shows. Fred and I do whatever we can to enhance it, including ad-libbing back and forth. The basis for the relationship is strong respect and friendship." But she did want, she said, "more depth in the storylines ... an effort to progress and develop the characters." Geiger, McKnight, and the others worked out their contract for a year and departed. The following year, Dryer and his manager Larry Kubik were officially in charge.

"Television is an executive producer's medium," Kubik told Richard Hack for *Hollywood Reporter*. "Movies are a director's medium. We're in television, so to become the executive producer of this show puts us right in the center of the action." "I want to write, produce, and direct," Dryer told reporter Pat Hilton for *USA Today* during the series' fourth season (Huggins' last). "There's more to life than hanging out in this trailer. I want to be in control of my life. I'm not sitting by the phone waiting. I'm active and extremely aggressive. I have a lot of things that are going to be popping in a year or two."

"Input is what I expect," Dryer told *Hollywood Reporter*. "Now that I have the final say, I want to share it. Every actor, every director, every first assistant director, every truck driver that shows up on that set will have a true working relationship. No longer will people be asked to perform miracles without any say in the direction of the show." But by the following year, Dryer was prominent in a list of people who were difficult to work with in an anonymous poll in *TV Guide* of directors and production staff. "Fred has been described to me by some of his very closest friends as one of the most charming, nicest, brightest men they have ever met," supervising producer Tom Chehak told Fred Schruers in *Rolling Stone*, "but I don't think there's anybody on this staff on a professional side who can say that. There's two Freds. I don't know the other socially, I know the one that I work with. When he's working, he knows what he wants. There is no time for any politeness. And that about sums it up for me. Because I am one who wants to collaborate and communicate. I mean, this is a job, it's not life. Perhaps for Fred it's his life, and not just a job."

"Let me just say this about the bank of writers and the executive producers," Dryer said to Schruer. "They're here, and doing the job of supplying us with storylines and ideas. I say what my character does, and when it comes down to what goes on television Saturday night, it's my face with the *Hunter* logo on it. They want to see myself and they want to see Stepfanie do what we do.... And I don't want anybody monkeying with it!" "Fred's reputation was all over the place before he joined *Hunter*," Frank Lupo had said after the first season. "But when you start a new series, you don't get the rehearsal time you need, the hours are long, the scripts are late, and the principal actors have to take the brunt of all that. I have to say that Fred's been a team player all the way."

"We started off at the beginning of the (fifth) year trying to make the shows a little bit different — richer, fuller, more tangled, interwoven stories — and it's been stripped right back by Mr. Dryer," said Chehak, who departed to work on the sci-fi cop series *Alien Nation*. "Mr. Dryer *knows* what he wants to do, and he says this is the kind of show we will do. This is hard for a writer to say, but it really is the character that people fall in love with."

"There's never been anyone like me on TV, and there never will be," Dryer told *TV Guide* in 1991. "The absence of my name on the Emmy nomination lists has become so conspicuous, it's ridiculous. Because the series is produced by Stephen Cannell, who produced *The A-Team*, and because *Hunter* stars an ex-football player running around with a gun in his hand, it's not supposed to be quality — which is ludicrous! It took them ten years to discover Ted Danson! They don't know nothing!" "I was replaceable in the NFL," Dryer told the *New York Times* in 1988. "But there's only one person who can play Hunter, and that's me."

Dryer was right — as Hunter, he made the show what it was, and given the show's audience of traditional Saturday night stay-at-homes, he was probably intuitively correct in keeping things simple and less ambitious. But at the start of the 1990–'91 season, Kramer left the series, as characteristically and diplomatically silent regarding her reasons as ever, but allegedly over Dryer's decision to cut down Kramer's screen-time and prominence in the credits. Kramer's silence over whatever ups and downs there had been behind the scenes on *Hunter* were almost certainly for the sake of how her professionalism was viewed, but the diminishing of her role in the credits was of equal relevance to her career prospects, and she had little choice but to call the producers on it. As a result, she departed the series and Dryer and Kubik were forced to shop around for a new female partner, which they found in the form of Darlanne Fluegel, who had portrayed Dennis Farina's wife on the *Crime Story* series, guested on a number of other shows including *Wiseguy*, and appeared in the films *The Eyes of Laura Mars, Once Upon a Time in America, To Live and Die in L.A., Running Scared, Tough Guys,* and *Freeway*. By the middle of the season, Fluegel had also departed over "creative differences" after her thirteen week contract was up, and another new actress, Lauren Lane, was drafted in to take her place. For the audience, the spark had gone, and *Hunter* was canceled after seven seasons, the most popular and commercially successful cop show of the 1980s.

Episode Guide

regular cast: Fred Dryer (Sgt. Rick Hunter), Stepfanie Kramer (Sgt. DeeDee McCall), Charles Hallahan (Captain Charlie Devane)

recurring cast: Garrett Morris (Sporty James), James Whitmore, Jr. (Bernie Terwilliger), Bruce Davison (Captain Wyler), John Shearin (Lt. Ambrose Finn), Darlanne Fluegel (Joanne Molenski), Lauren Lane (Chris Novak), Brion James (Thomas Duffy), Perry Cook (Barney), Rudy Ramos (Reuben), Richard Beauchamp (Carlos), Arthur Rosenberg (Captain Cain), John Amos (Captain Dolan), Gary Crosby (Officer Dabney Smith), Ronald William Lawrence (Officer Dorsey), Martin E. Brooks (Mike Snow), Jack Bannon (DEA Agent), Kate Zentall (Esther Wyman), Shelley Taylor Morgan (Kitty O'Hearn), Robert Colbert (Dryden), Beah Richards (Pockets), Dirk Blocker (Randall Fane), William Smith (Sgt. Sal Drasso), Robin Thomas (Al Novak), Courtney Barilla (Alison Novak), Paul Mantee (Commander Clayton)

First Season (1984–'85)

HUNTER (pilot)

wr. Frank Lupo, dir. Ron Satlof

Rick Hunter, a rebellious rule-breaking cop, is teamed up with DeeDee McCall, a female officer with a similar reputation, to pursue a homicidal maniac with a liking for country and western music. In the meantime, Hunter's harassed superiors pursue him with a psychiatrist with orders to discredit him and find them an excuse to get him off the force.

with Brian Dennehy, Joanna Kerns, Steven Williams, David Labiosa, Michael Cavenaugh (as Cain, pilot only), Richard Young, Lee Patterson, Luke Andreas, Marilyn Tokuda

HARD CONTRACT

wr. Sidney Ellis, dir. Arnold Laven

McCall discovers that her former partner is now a freelance hit-man.

with David Ackroyd, Joan Sweeny, Michael Delano, Ron Karabatsos, Arnold Turner

THE HOT GROUNDER

wr. Stephen Cannell, dir. Bill Duke

When the police commissioner is suspected of killing his wife, the cops in the squad room are delighted to discover that Hunter and McCall have drawn the short straw and been saddled with this career-killing investigation.

with William Windom, Thomas Carter, Sam Jones, Joe Santos, Ray Girardin, William Schilling, Jason Bernard

A LONG WAY FROM L.A.

wr. Frank Lupo, dir. Arnold Laven

Forced to stay overnight in a hick town when their car breaks down while transporting a prisoner back to L.A., Hunter and McCall find that their charge has been set up as a patsy for a crime he didn't commit by the local sheriff.

with Bo Svenson, Morgan Woodward, Paul Eiding, Maylo McCaslin, Bill Quinn, Ted Gehring, Joe Colligan, Jeffrey Josephson

LEGACY

wr. Chris Bunch, Allan Cole, dir. Ron Satlof

A young girl is picked up in a bar by a syndicate man so that he can frame her for the murder of his father.

with Vincent Bagetta, Mary Margaret Humes, Ken Gilman, Al Ruscio, Tony Giorgio, Tony Longo,

Fil Formicola, Jude Farese, Judi Boeke, Alfred Dennis, Chip Johnson, Bill Capizzi

FLIGHT ON A DEAD PIGEON

wr. E. Nick Alexander, dir. Michael Preece

A young girl goes to the police when her father, who has been using her homing pigeons for drugs-running activities, is killed by gangsters.

with Marissa Mendenhall, Robert Costanzo, Anthony Charnota, Eric Stern

PEN PALS

wr. Babs Greyhosky, dir. Larry Stewart

Hunter is framed for the murder of a drugs runner he's been roughing up after a boy dies from the merchandise. While McCall investigates, Hunter tries to survive prison....

with Tim Thomerson, Tracey Walter, Billy Drago, Jack O'Halloran, James Victor, Forbsey Russell, Deborah Wakeham, Paul Drake, Cynthia Eilbacher, Michael Fox, Phil Hoover, J. Jay Saunders, Michael Laskin, Karl Johnson

DEAD OR ALIVE

wr. Frank Lupo, dir. Guy Magar

Hunter pursues a ruthless and vicious cowboy bounty hunter.

with Wings Hauser, Sally Julian, Jimmie F. Skaggs, Ann Weldon, Diane Robin, Eddie Zammit, W.T. Zacha, Bob Goldstein, Charlie Stavola, Jesse Dizon

HIGH BLEACHER MAN

wr. Sidney Ellis, dir. Arnold Laven

Hunter must protect a particularly unpleasant informant from the mob.

with Michael Cornelison, Michael Baseleon, Richard Romanus, D.D. Howard, Alan Autry, Beau Starr, Silvana Gallardo, Suzanne Lederer, Joey Pento, Diane Turley Travis, Robert Denison

THE SHOOTER

wr. Mark Jones, dir. Michael Lange

Hunter poses as a motorcycle cop to investigate the death of a fellow officer whose death has intriguing parallels with that of McCall's husband some years earlier.

with Robert Dryer, Marc Alaimo, Shawn Weatherly, Steve Sandor

THE GARBAGE MAN

wr. Sidney Ellis, dir. Bruce Kessler

Hunter and McCall hunt down someone who has been killing parolees.

with Ed O'Neill, Christopher McDonald, Lynne Topping, Norman Alden, Abraham Alvarez, Will MacMillan, Fran McDormand, Dave Shelley, Nicholas Worth

THE AVENGING ANGEL

wr. Brian Lane, dir. James Whitmore, Jr.

Hunter gains an unlikely admirer in the form of a surveillance expert who turns vigilante to win Hunter's favor and then attempts to do away with Hunter's female co-workers.

with Robert Gray, Nancy Stafford, Angus Duncan, Lee Wilkof, Michael Cornelison, Charles Lampkin, Robert Pastorelli, Rod Haase

THE SNOW QUEEN (two parts)

wr. Frank Lupo, dir. Tony Mordente, Richard Colla

Hunter and McCall find themselves allied with a bad apple from the Big Apple when a brutish N.Y. cop arrives in town to track down a young girl acting as a drug courier.

with Dennis Franz, Dennis Farina, Lycia Naff, Ron Max, Brendan Hughes, Joseph Cali, Daniel Chodos, Bob Dubac, Lesa Lee, J.D. Hall, France Mayot, Marc Adams, Daniel Faraldo, Christie Claridge, Dennis Stewart, Pepper Martin, Vojo Soric, Janine Ford

THE BEACH BOY

wr. Thomas Szollosi, Richard Christian Matheson, dir. Richard Colla

Hunter and McCall pursue a machine-gun-toting hit-man from Hawaii.

with Brett Clark, Tony Plana, Jason Ronard, Castulo Guerra, Steven Williams, Jere Burns, Kimberly Beck, Cyndi James-Reece, Kellye Nakahara, John Roselius, Kathryn Lytton

GUILTY

wr. Mark Jones, dir. Michael Lange

Hunter and McCall track down a psychopath who is killing off all the members of the jury who put him away.

with Ken Foree, Devon Ericson, Phillip Coccioletti, Al White, Willard E. Pugh, Nina Wilcox, Will MacMillan, Elizabeth Hoffman, Hank Rolike, William E. Bassett, Tom Everett

THE LAST KILL

wr. Jeff Wilhelm, dir. Bruce Kessler

The unpleasant husband of an ex-girlfriend is Hunter's prime suspect as a hit-man, but his emotional stake in the girl's well-being gives McCall cause for doubt.

with Madison Mason, Stephanie Blackmore, Judd Omen, Tony Giorgio, Danny Wells, George Skaff, James Jeter

Fire Man

wr. Thomas Szollosi, Richard Christian Matheson, dir. Tony Mordente

A TV newsman hampers Hunter and McCall in their pursuit of an unhinged Vietnam veteran turned arsonist.

with Mark Schneider, Robert Desederio, William Russ, Julie Fulton, Belinda Balaski, Carol Culver, Bruce Tuthill, Vivian Bonnell

Sniper

wr. Sidney Ellis, dir. James Whitmore, Jr.

Hunter and McCall hunt down a sniper who only picks on blonde-haired women after a girlfriend snubs him.

with Joe Dorsey, Jack Starrett, Sandy Martin, James Cromwell, John Sanderford, John Walcutt, Daniel Chodos, Michael Galardi, Phil Brock, J. Bill Jones

Second Season (1985–'86)

Case X

wr. Tom Lazarus, dir. David Soul

McCall poses as a porn film actress to investigate the murders of two young teenagers who were making sex films for a photographer.

with Leo Rossi, Sam Anderson, Rita Taggart, Tracy Vaccaro, Cal Gibson, Lori McGinley, Davie Wiley

Night of the Dragons

wr. Herbert Wright, Patrick Barry, dir. James Whitmore, Jr.

Hunter and McCall become implicated in a gangland war between Chinese and Vietnamese factions in Chinatown.

with Clyde Kusatsu, James Hong, Arsenio Sonny Trinidad, Robert Kim, Nathan Jung

The Biggest Man in Town

wr. Stephen Katz, dir. Bob Bralver

An investigation into the murder of a blackmailer is hindered by a town sheriff in the employ of a local big shot.

with Stuart Whitman, Don Stroud, Nana Visitor, Gregory Itzin, Stephen Roberts

Rich Girl

wr. Stephen Cotler, dir. James Whitmore, Jr.

An elderly millionaire is shot, and his young bride, cleared of the crime, is then murdered herself.

with Dorian Lopinto, John Calvin, K. Callan, John McLiam, Robert Rockwell, Richard Vath, Lois Hamilton, Tonja Walker, David Sage, Karen Hughes

Killer in a Hallowe'en Mask

wr. Stephen Katz, dir. Sidney Hayers

Hunter and McCall are assigned as technical advisors to a trashy TV cop show to get them out of the spotlight for a while ... but the star of the series is murdered.

with Gary Graham, Jan Murray, Randee Heller, Stephen Shortridge, Jordan Charney, Tony Plana, Robin Evans, Jesse Ventura, Gerry Gibson, Rick Fitts, Dianne McCannon, Julie Hayek, William Utay, Tim Russ

Rape and Revenge (two parts)

wr. Tom Lazarus, dir. Gary Winter, Richard Colla

A diplomat who rapes McCall when she resists his romantic overtures is protected by diplomatic immunity ... but not as far as Hunter's concerned. In Part Two, Hunter pursues McCall's attacker to his home country for a grim resolution.

with Richard Yniguez, Michael Ansara, Jack Starrett, Danny Ponce, Nate Esformes, Lisa Wilkinson, Larry Hankin, Sam Vlahos

Million Dollar Misunderstanding

wr. Frank Lupo, dir. Michael Preece

A ruthless robber kills his partners after an armored car robbery, but then has his car, with the money inside, stolen by juveniles.

with Robert Davi, Phil Rubinstein, Robert Englund, Christie Claridge, Jack Andreozzi, Pamela Brull, James Crittenden, Maurice Sneed

The Big Fall

wr. Rogers Turrentine, dir. James Whitmore, Jr.

Hunter and McCall are part of a team guarding a valuable informant, but one of their fellow officers has been bought off, bribed to dispose of the witness himself.

with Jonathan Banks, Mills Watson, Vic Polizos, Richard Foronjy, Patti Tippo, Lou Felder, Michael Pasternak

WAITING FOR MR. WRONG

wr. Rogers Turrentine, dir. Ron Satlof
Hunter befriends the girlfriend of a jewel thief in the course of an investigation, but is seduced by her charms instead.

with Ada Maris, Fernando Allende, John Lansing, Steve Peterman

THINK BLUE

wr. Sidney Ellis, dir. Michael O'Herlihy
An informant gives Hunter a tip-off that a series of warehouse robberies have been committed by police officers ... and a fellow officer is accused of murdering his unfaithful wife.

with Ramon Bieri, William Smith, Justin Lord, Joey Green, Bill Cross, Paul Jenkins, Toni Attell

BLOW UP

wr. Herbert Wright, dir. Douglas Heyes
Hunter pursues a vindictive psychopath who is using bombs triggered by telephone calls to kill the people who put him away.

with Anthony James, Kate Zentall, Brad English, Henry Sanders, Steve Fifield

WAR ZONE

wr. Allison Hock, dir. Bob Bralver
Hunter pursues a group of mercenaries who intend to break a drug dealer out of jail.

with Billy Drago, Vernon Wells, Robert Hanley, Don Hood, Gela Jacobson, Mike Moroff, Diana Bellamy

BURNED

wr. Jo Montgomery, dir. Charles Picerni
While visiting New Orleans, McCall is convinced she has seen somebody declared dead years earlier, and Hunter reluctantly agrees to investigate with her.

with Anthony Caruso, Victoria Bass, George McDaniel, Jane Russell, Peter Hobbs, Branscombe Richmond

SCRAP METAL

wr. Sidney Ellis, dir. Michael Preece
A deathbed confession from a hit-man sends Hunter on the trail of the man who killed his father.

with Frank Campanella, Joe Cortese, Kay Lenz, Douglas Dirkson, Ji-Tu Cumbuka

FAGIN 1986

wr. Randall Wallace, dir. Douglas Heyes
While investigating the activities of a modern-day Fagin using juvenile delinquents to pull off robberies, Hunter shoots a youngster.

with Trinidad Silva, Ron Joseph, Richard Coca, Jeannie Linero, Jacob Vargas, Carlos Cervantes, Ruth Zakarian

62 HOURS OF TERROR

wr. Rudolph Borchert, Rogers Turrentine, Richard Breen, James Polster, dir. Michael Preece
A terrorist group tries to cash in on the murder of a diplomat that they were not responsible for.

with Persis Khambatta, Thom Christopher, Rod Arrants, Allen Williams, Freeman King, Ben Slack, J.P. Bumstead, Tom Henshel, Michael Zand, Dallas Cole

DEATH MACHINE

wr. Tom Lazarus, dir. Kim Manners
Hunter poses — ludicrously — as a "punker" to track down a giant thug who is leaving a trail of tortured bodies in his wake as he tracks down some stolen jewels he has been paid to locate.

with John Matuszak, Ron Karabatsos, Lou Richards, Whitney Kershaw, Allen Williams, Brett Porter, Charles Boswell, Don Edmonds, Danil Torppe, Joe Shea, John Chandler, S. Marc Jordan, Rhonda Dotson

THE SET-UP

wr. Allison Hock, dir. James Whitmore, Jr.
A young woman is murdered when her lover fears that her interest in a new romance may cause her to reveal that he committed a murder some years earlier.

with Jack Colvin, Reid Shelton, Sydney Walsh, Marshall Teague, Robert O'Reilly, Elsa Raven, Regina Richardson

THE BEAUTIFUL AND THE DEAD (two parts)

wr. Jo Montgomery, Roy Huggins, dir. Gary Winter
A straightforward investigation into a murder at a motel suddenly turns into a Russian spy melodrama, and when a dead body appears and then disappears in Hunter's apartment, Hunter and McCall travel to San Francisco to unravel the mystery.

with Kabir Bedi, Sandy McPeak, Katherine Justice, Dan Lauria, Rita Zohar, Andrew Masset, Marc McClure, Norman Alden, Kim Ulrich, Kasey Walker

THE RETURN OF TYPHOON THOMPSON

wr. Rogers Turrentine, dir. Peter Kiwitt

Here's Isaac Hayes doing his vengeful ex-con routine again, tracking down the guys who set him up ... (this episode introduces the character of Sporty James).

with Isaac Hayes, Sheryl Lee Ralph, Miguel Fernandes, Luke Andreas, Mel Carter

SATURDAY NIGHT SPECIAL

wr. Marianne Clarkson, Allison Hock, dir. Peter Kiwitt

McCall poses as a down-and-out and befriends an eccentric pickpocket to capture a murderer who has been killing vagrants for media notoriety.

with Anne Marie-Johnson, Beah Richards, William Frankfather, Richard Lineback, John DiSanti, Patrick Cranshaw, Virginia Peters

Third Season (1986–'87)

OVERNIGHT SENSATION

wr. Richard Okie, dir. Tony Mordente

Hunter becomes a suspect when a TV reporter who has been repeatedly criticizing him on air suddenly becomes the target of murder attempts.

with Michael Wren, Alex Courtney, Anne Curry, Jeff Doucette, Sal Lopez, Joseph Chapman, Heidi Banks, Liz Torres, Victor Brandt, Larry Carroll

CHANGE PARTNERS AND DANCE

wr. David Lightstone, dir. James Whitmore, Jr.

McCall is mystified when she and Hunter are suddenly assigned new partners, apparently at Hunter's request.

with Tim Thomerson, Norbert Weisser, Brynn Thayer, Stephen Apostle-Pec, Robert Firth, Wayne Grace, Martin Azarow

CRIME OF PASSION

wr. Jo Montgomery, Douglas Heyes, dir. Charles Picerni

McCall becomes romantically involved with a murder suspect.

with Kristoffer Tabori, Candy Clark, Ray Wise, Granville Ames

THE CASTRO CONNECTION

wr. Carlton Hollander, Dennis Rodriguez, Douglas Heyes, Jr., dir. James L. Conway

Hunter becomes involved in a top secret drug smuggling and gun running operation when he goes to the aid of a former partner.

with John Beck, Hector Mercado, Peter MacLean, Jack Bannon, Al Israel, Juanita Jennings, Nat Bernstein

HIGH NOON IN L.A.

wr. Erica Byrne, Howard Chesley, dir. James Whitmore, Jr.

The younger brother of the diplomat Hunter pursued and shot after McCall was sexually attacked by him travels to L.A. for revenge ... with the same diplomatic immunity his rapist brother enjoyed.

with George DeLoy, East Ismael Carlo, Ethan Phillips, Nate Esformes, Zitto Kazann

FROM SAN FRANCISCO WITH LOVE

wr. Ira Besserman, Chris Ruppenthal, Stephanie Garman, Hollace White, dir. Charles Picerni

Looking into an attempted murder in L.A., Hunter and McCall are joined by a San Francisco cop investigating the suicide of the victim's father, and a tangled romantic web unravels.

with Laura Johnson, Philece Sampler, Mark Withers, Dana Kimmell

TRUE CONFESSIONS

wr. Jo Montgomery, Rogers Turrentine, dir. Michael Preece

When three college kids rape and kill a young girl, and are then methodically killed off themselves, Hunter and McCall find that their chief suspect is the girl's vengeful sister.

with Lauren Tewes, Timothy Patrick Murphy, Will Curran, Kenneth Tigar, H. Richard Green, Melvin Belli, Moose Drier, John J. York, Grand Bush, Robert Gooden

LOVE, HATE, AND SPORTY JAMES

wr. Marianne Clarkson, dir. Don Chaffey

Informant Sporty James withholds valuable information from Hunter and McCall so that he can blackmail the mobster involved.

with Marco Rodriguez, Tyra Ferrell, Claudia Christian, John Lisbon Wood, Don Edmonds, Danil Torppe

The Contract
wr. Paul Ehrman, Roy Huggins, dir. Les Sheldon
A kidnap scam suddenly turns into a trail of clumsy murders.
with Peter Haskell, Katherine Moffat, Kenneth David Gilman, Katherine Cannon, Brent Spiner, Anne Navarro, Eda Reiss Martin

The Cradle Will Rock
wr. E. Nick Alexander, Roy Huggins, Rogers Turrentine, dir. Kim Manners
McCall poses as a singer chasing the big time to investigate the murder of a missing rock star.
with Chaka Khan, John Hancock, Kim Langford, Clebe Hartley, Lisa Peluso, Jack Kehler, Raymond O'Connor, Nick Savage

Bad Company
wr. Dick Nelson, dir. Charles Picerni
Hunter and McCall become the captives of a group of racist survivalists.
with Dean Stockwell, Lar Park Lincoln, Big John Studd, George Dickerson, Forry Smith, Jack Stryker

Down and Under
wr. Roy Huggins, Charlotte Clay, Howard Chesley, dir. James Darren
Hunter travels to Australia to investigate the mysterious circumstances surrounding the murder of an elderly lady on holiday.
with Shelley Smith, Marina Sirtis, Anthony La Paglia, Mike Preston, Richard Blade, Michael St. Clair, Brendan McKane

Straight to the Heart
wr. Eric Estrin, Michael Berlin, Roy Huggins, dir. James Whitmore, Jr.
Hunter is sent to a lakeside retreat when a mobster he is to testify against puts out a contract on him.
with Lydia Cornell, Wolf Muser, Robert Miano, Owen Bush, Ted Markland, DeeDee Rescher, Lori Birdsong

Requiem for Sergeant McCall
wr. Joe Gannon, Douglas Heyes, Jr., dir. Charles Picerni
Completely contradicting background revealed in the first season episode "The Shooter," this episode flashes back to the murder of McCall's police officer husband.
with Cesare Danova, Leslie Hope, Jeff Kaake, Paul Leiber, Franc Luz, Kathleen Freeman

Double Exposure
wr. Thomas Huggins, Charlotte Clay, dir. James Whitmore, Jr.
McCall poses as a hopeful model to infiltrate a ring of hookers who are drugging and robbing their clientele.
with George Clooney, Fern Fitzgerald, Art Hindle, Mimi Coutelier, Marie Cheatham, Jason Wingreen, Terri Hoyos, Antony Alda

The Girl Next Door
wr. Thomas Huggins, Charlotte Clay, dir. James Whitmore, Jr.
Hunter and McCall travel to small-town Texas to investigate the macabre death of an apparently ordinary young girl.
with Byrne Piven, Stanley Kamel, Caroline McWilliams, Charles Lane, Robert Firth, Gloria LeRoy, Kandace Keuhl, Curtis Taylor, Adam Gregor

Any Second Now
wr. Charlotte Clay, Roy Huggins, Stephanie Garman, Hollace White, Marianne Clarkson, dir. James Darren
Hunter and McCall lay a trap for a knife attacker who has threatened a concert pianist he attacked some years ago that he is going to finish the job.
with Theresa Saldana, Andy Wood, Richard Bakalyan, Barbara Townsend, Daniel Ziskie, Martin Speer, Conroy Gideon

Shades
wr. Frank Lupo, dir. Michael Preece
Investigating the disappearance of Hunter from a dockside rendezvous, McCall inadvertently causes a fellow officer to break her cover (Fred Dryer appears only in the opening and closing scenes of this episode, cautiously supervised by Frank Lupo, so that Dryer could prepare for his directorial debut the following episode; also, this episode introduces Shelley Taylor Morgan as Sgt. Kitty O'Hearn).
with Shelley Taylor Morgan, Joseph Mascolo, Jared Martin, Michael Gregory, Peter White, Frank Silvera, Chip Heller, Jon St. Elwood, Christie Claridge

A Child Is Born
wr. Erica Byrne, Marianne Clarkson, Janice Meyer, dir. Fred Dryer

When the wrong woman is murdered by a hitman, Hunter and McCall travel to Vegas to prevent the killing of the real target and apprehend the murderer.

with Tracy Vacarro, Carmen Argenziano, Rhoda Gemignani, Raymond St. Jacques, Leif Garrett, Carmen Zapata, Corrinne Michaels, Grand Bush, William Bronder, Jana Marie Hupp, Jennifer Anglin

CROSSFIRE

wr. Herman Groves, Terry Nelson, Roy Huggins, dir. Charles Picerni

When a former girlfriend returns to Hunter's life, he contemplates marriage ... but she's brought mob trouble from her current romantic involvement with her (this episode introduces Martin E. Brooks as occasional character Mike Snow, shady lawyer).

with Leigh Christian, Shawn Elliott, J.E. Freeman, Martin E. Brooks, Richard Cox, Mark Arnott

HOT PURSUIT (two parts)

wr. Thomas Huggins, Charlotte Clay, dir. James Darren, Stepfanie Kramer

When McCall is hospitalized by a gunman while investigating a traveling prostitution operation (thus enabling Kramer to make her directorial debut), Hunter sets out to complete the investigation in his own distinctive fashion. (This episode introduces Kate Zentall as occasional character Esther Wyman).

with Jeanna Michaels, Robert Ridgely, Gela Nash, Dana Lee, Ji-Tu Cumbuka, Nick Angotti, Susan Peretz, Michele Tobin, Maggie Sullivan, Arnold Turner, David Froman, Larry Drake, Kate Zentall, Eloy Casadas, Joe Sicari

Fourth Season (1987–'88)

PLAYING GOD

wr. Richard Okie, dir. James Whitmore, Jr.

Hunter and McCall investigate the murder of a community leader who turns out to have been less a pillar of the community than his image had implied.

with Castulo Guerra, Christopher Allport, Geno Silver, Ken Tobey, John Di Santi, Mike Moroff, Tasia Valenzia

THE JADE WOMAN

wr. Joe Menosky, dir. Fred Dryer

Hunter helps an old friend from Vietnam trace his missing mail-order bride, who has some interesting traveling luggage.

with Dirk Blocker, Richard Bakalyan, James Wainwright, Clare Nono, Brent Jennings, Stanley Brock, Victoria Carroll, Arnold Turner, Jim Boeke

FLASHPOINT

wr. Dallas Barnes, dir. Michael Preece

A supposed racial killing by police officers being exploited by a local community leader running for office turns out to be more complex than first assumed (Arthur Rosenberg returns as first season character Commander Cain in this episode).

with Gregory Sierra, Hector Mercado, Deborah Pratt, Beau Billingsley, Israel Juarbe, Leonard Salazar, Rudy Negrete, Billy Kane, Nora Gaye, Tony Montero

NIGHT ON BALD MOUNTAIN

wr. Roy Huggins, Marianne Clarkson, dir. Dennis Dugan

Comedic spooky episode, with Hunter and McCall stranded in an old house with members of an eccentric family who are gradually being bumped off one by one.

with Tricia O'Neil, Richard Kline, Dann Florek, Frank Ashmore, Mary Jackson, Parley Baer, John O'Connell, Carolyn Clarke, Frank Telfer

CITY OF PASSION (three parts)

wr. Dallas Barnes, Charlotte Clay, dir. James Whitmore, Jr.

Hunter and McCall hunt a serial rapist while McCall is being pressured by high office to drop charges made against a judge, who propositioned her while she was posing as a prostitute on vice (this episode features a second appearance of Shelly Taylor Morgan as Sgt. Kitty O'Hearn, and the first appearance of Robert Colbert as Dryden).

with Erik Estrada, Shelly Taylor Morgan, Frederick Coffin, Margaret Gibson, Gail Young, Lezlie Deane, Barbara Treutelaar, Raye Birk, Susan Cash, Rony Clanton, Rosemary Forsythe, Robert Colbert, Conrad Bachmann, Hank Woessner, Robert Reed, Howard George, Carel Struyken, J. Michael Flynn, Jon Menick, Danil Torppe, Don Edmonds

TURNING POINT

wr. Paul Schiffer, Robert Bielak, dir. Dennis Dugan

A car thief is killed detonating a car bomb intended for an unethical reporter who is blackmailing the head of a powerful construction company instead of writing up the story.

with Richard Gilliand, Valerie Wildman, Jon Cypher, Ernie Sabella

HOT PROWL

wr. Joseph Gunn, Joe Menosky, dir. Jeff Kibbee

A thief starts a deadly chain of events when he steals a necklace from a wealthy woman who has sold the valuable original and replaced it with a fake without telling her husband.

with Cindy Morgan, Alex Rocco, Henry Stolow, Cliff Emmich, Brett Clark, Ken Lerner, Joe Ross

ALLEGRA

wr. Roy Huggins, Joe Menosky, dir. James Whitmore, Jr.

A typical Huggins story, as Hunter investigates the mysterious death of a beautiful woman he once knew.

with Kim Morgan Greene, Michael Delano, Tony Jay, Marisa Redanty, Anne Bellamy

RENEGADE

wr. Frank Dandridge, Terry Nelson, dir. Jeff Kibbee

When the son of one of Hunter's former partners becomes involved with drug dealers and causes his mother to be seriously injured, Hunter must try to prevent his friend from exacting his own justice before the law can sort it out.

with James McEachin, Kevin Best, Pepe Serna, Brion James, Rene Assa, Paul Miceli-Sanchez, Conrad Bachmann

THE BLACK DAHLIA

wr. Robert Hamner, dir. Michael Preece

Hunter and McCall investigate a fifty year old unsolved murder and family cover-up in this story that speculates on a factual 1947 murder case.

with Lawrence Tierney, Jeanette Nolan, Macon McCalman, Billie Bird, Logan Ramsey, Ian Abercrombie, John Finnegan, Jessica Lee Nelson

NOT JUST ANOTHER JOHN DOE

wr. Douglas Heyes, Jr., dir. James Darren

An eccentric pickpocket (previously seen in the second season episode "Saturday Night Special") witnesses the murder of a fellow vagrant, but won't accept police protection.

with Beah Richards, Mark Blankfield, Robert Glaudini, Grand Bush, Don Dubbins, Anthony Pena, Ben Rawnsley, Richardson Morse

NAKED JUSTICE (two parts)

wr. Dallas Barnes, Joanna Barnes, dir. James Whitmore, Jr.

Hunter and McCall investigate the murder of a popular movie actress.

with Nestor Serrano, John Standing, Donna Mitchell, David Beecroft, Harris Laskawy, Randi Brooks, Kasey Walker, Gianni Russo, Tony Mockus, Barry Jenner, Tommy Highcastle, Lynn Hamilton, Meg Register, Tom Spackman, Tony Perez, Shaun Toub

GIRL ON THE BEACH

wr. Douglas Heyes, Jr., dir. Fred Dryer

Hunter and McCall investigate the murder of Captain Devane's ex-wife, who has witnessed a murder before the perpetrator can make it look like an accident.

with Frances Lee McCain, Vincent Bagetta, Alexa Hamilton, Mark Sivertsen, Virgil Frye

THE BOGOTA MILLION

wr. Jo Montgomery, dir. Michael Preece

Informer Sporty James' previous attempt to blackmail a mobster comes back to haunt him when gangsters believe he got his money.

with Richard Bakalyan, Victor Campos, Brent Jennings

DEATH SIGNS

wr. H. Edward Hunsberger, Thomas Huggins, Charlotte Clay, dir. James Whitmore, Jr.

Hunter and McCall investigate an art fraud after the murder of a prominent dealer.

with Brant Van Hoffman, Catherine Richardson, Howie Seago, Walter Addison, Tony Carrero, Mary Vreeland, Rob Neukirch

BOOMERANG

wr. Jo Montgomery, dir. Jeff Kibbee

Hunter tries to prove the guilt of a woman he believes arranged for her husband to die in a boating accident.

with Wendie Malick, Michael Durrell, Elizabeth Savage, Barbara Tarbuck, Roy Brocksmith, Dennis Bailey

THE FOURTH MAN

wr. Thomas Chapman, Joe Menosky, Rogers Turrentine, dir. John Peter Kousakis

Internal Affairs reopens an investigation into a five year old drug theft which was never resolved in which Hunter was under suspicion with his partner and two other officers.

with John Carter, Darnell Williams, Leon Rippy, Janet Hubert, Robert Colbert, Peter Crook, Kellie Overbey

Murder He Wrote

wr. Roy Huggins, dir. Jeff Kibbee

When the brakes of his car are tampered with, a millionaire asks the police to look to his family for possible suspects ... but his friend, an elderly mystery writer, hampers Hunter and McCall in their investigations. Yes, it's a send-up of *Murder She Wrote*.

with Marge Redmond, Efrem Zimbalist, Jr., Tony Goldwyn, Peter Fox, Dawn Arnemann, Michael Ryan, Patrick O'Connell, Bennett Guillory, Gary Lee Davis

Silver Bullet

wr. Dallas Barnes, Joanne Barnes, dir. Michael Preece

Hunter and McCall pursue a vigilante cop who leaves a silver bullet behind at each of his murders (this episode writes out John Shearin as Lt. Finn).

with Leslie Bevis, Edward Riley, Tony Abatemarco, Alan Toy

Fifth Season (1988–'89)

Heir of Neglect

wr. David Lightstone, dir. Alexander Singer

Hunter and McCall investigate an apparently motiveless shooting when the parents of a young boy are killed while he is in the house.

with Chad Allen, Lucy Butler, Rick Lieberman, Yuji Okumoto, David Spielberg, Michele Marsh, Bill McLaughlin, Jack Yates

The Baby Game

wr. Tom Chehak, dir. James Fargo

Hunter and McCall inadvertently become baby sitters when the only witness to the murder of a prostitute is a tiny child.

with Wayne Tippit, Margot Rose, Stan Ivar, Michael Keys Hall, Stephen Young, Yuji Okumoto, Sid Melton, Cynthia Szigeti, David Partington, Mark Drexler, Kit Paraventi, Aimee and Danielle Warren

Presumed Guilty

wr. Joe Menosky, dir. Alexander Singer

A young thief protests his innocence after a dead woman is found at the scene of his robbery.

with Dack Rambo, George Denesky, Debra Sandlund, James O'Sullivan, Terry Boseman, Nora Heflin, Corinne Carroll, Otto Felix, Michael Canavan, Warren Stanhope, Toni Naples

Dead on Target (two parts)

wr. George Geiger, dir. Corey Allen

Hunter investigates a complex cover-up over a military accident in Vietnam and some valuable stones after a friend from his unit dies in mysterious circumstances.

with Dirk Blocker, Gary Frank, John Bennett Perry, Mario Rocuzzo, Clare Nono, Patrick Bishop, Michael D. Roberts, Michael Bell, Jesse Welles, Tom Biener, Ann Duran, Evelyn Guerrero, Carol Swarbrick

No Good Deed Ever Goes Unpunished

wr. Whitney Wherett Robinson, dir. Tony Mordente

When McCall's art class is bombed, the target is revealed to be an elderly lady who has discovered some uncomfortable facts about toxic waste dumping.

with Louise Latham, John Anderson, J.A. Preston, Bradley White, Daphne Eckler, Carlos LaCamera, Daniel Chodos, Liz Reavey, Duke Stroud

Honorable Profession

wr. Fred McKnight, dir. Michael O'Herlihy

Hunter goes to the defense of an injured patrol cop set to get the blame for a shooting incident that ended in several deaths.

with Tim Thomerson, William Smith, Patrick Bishop, James Hong, Beulah Quo, Betty Carvalho, Diane Delano, Kimberley Delfin, Douglas Seale, Robert Colbert, Arsenio "Sonny" Trinidad, Aki Aleong, Oz Tortora, Patrick Matthew, Robert Benedict

Payback

wr. Lee Maddux, dir. Alexander Singer

Hunter goes to the aid of a small-time crook who once saved his life, and has now been set up to take the fall for a mob heist by his treacherous partners.

with David Wohl, Michael Constantine, Lisa Sutton, Stephen Liska, Gary Hudson, Tim Haldeman, Ivan G'Vera, Alfred Dennis

Partners

wr. Terry Nelson, dir. James Fargo

Hunter and McCall are teamed with another male/female duo when kids pulling apart a car discover the body of the female officer's husband.

with Julia Montgomery, Scott Jaeck, Peter Brown, Gerald Castillo, William Frankfather, Med Flory, Miguel Sandoval, Dale Swann

The Pit

wr. Joe Menosky, dir. Randy Roberts

A police despatcher is blackmailed into assisting a gang of gold bullion thieves after her young son is abducted by them.

with Dorothy Lyman, Christopher Stone, Darren Powell, Frank Papia, Tim DeZarn, Sheldon Feldner, Sam Hennings, Christopher Carroll, Joe Hart

City Under Seige (three parts)

wr. George Geiger, Tom Chehak, Joe Menosky, dir. James Fargo

McCall goes undercover in a troubled high school and runs into the local vigilante, while Hunter is being stalked by a psychotic killer he put away years ago, now freed by her boyfriend.

with Cec Verrell, Daniel Quinn, Robert Vaughn, Robin Strand, Craig Hurley, James Horan, Robert Clotworthy, Brynn Horrocks, James B. Sikking, Tom Taglang, Barbara Collentine, Lee Arnone, Saida Rodriguez Pagan, Gene Butler, Conor O'Farrell, Laurelle Brooks, S. Marc Jordan, Howard S. Miller

Me, Myself, and Die

wr. David Brown, dir. Jeff Kibbee

McCall investigates the case of a mentally ill girl who has apparently committed a murder after her medicine was tampered with by a chemist who is exploiting her condition for his own purposes.

with Rosemary Dunsmore, John Harkins, Angela Paton, Ron Kuhlman, Bill Morey, Terry Bozeman, Robert Clotworthy, Annie Gagen, Eric Tull

Informant

wr. Tom Chehak, dir. James Whitmore, Jr.

Hunter refuses to identify an informant, even though it will lead to the recovery of an armored truck heist.

with Henry Brown, Clare Wren, Rick J. Porter, Meg Wittner, Joshua Shelley, Danil Torppe, Howard Beckler

Blood Line

wr. Richard Raskind, dir. Michael Preece

Hunter and McCall investigate the fatal drugging of a horse which has resulted in the death of a stablehand.

with Charles Bateman, Jeff Allin, Maurice Roeves, Amy Bendict, Linda Henning, Hank Brandt, Catherine Parks, Lou Wagner, Prince Hughes, Alvin Ing, T.D. Smith, Allan Wasserman

Shoot to Kill

wr. Terry D. Nelson, dir. Tony Mordente

McCall is up on charges of shooting an unarmed burglar when the gun he was using is not present at the scene of the crime.

with Robert Miranda, Maggie Roswell, Todd Jeffries, Ron Mychal Hayes, John Mahoney, Rick Hill, Louis Tucker, Gregory Beecroft, Tom McGreevy, Danil Torppe, Don Edmonds

Code Three

wr. Van Gordon Sauter, David Percelay, dir. Michael Preece

After postponing a meeting with a doctor friend who needs her help and is subsequently murdered, a guilt-ridden McCall discovers a medical conspiracy.

with Mark LaMura, Jeanna Michaels, Michael Toland, Bebe Drake-Massey, Paul Collins, Mary Gregory, Kay Cole, Victoria Christian

Ring of Honor

wr. Asher Brauner, dir. Fred Dryer

Hunter and McCall investigate corruption in the boxing game.

with Sammy Davis, Jr., Nicholas Coster, Scott Colomby, Val Avery, Patrick St. Esprit, Frank Campanella, Nurit Koppel, Tracy Vacarro, Nicky Blair, Peter Noel Duhamel

Teen Dreams

wr. Tom Chehak, dir. David Phinney

Hunter and McCall pursue a serial killer who is murdering prostitutes while disguised as a cop.

with Brynn Horrocks, Peter Lapis, Sheila Wills, Lauren Woods, Caroline Barclay, Anne Elisabeth Ramsey, Robert Axelrod, LaRita Shelly

Last Run

wr. Fred McKnight, dir. James Whitmore, Jr.

An arson investigation ends in tragedy for a cop with a long-standing grudge.

with Bill Lucking, Terry Kiser, Margarita Franco, Marco Rodriguez, L. Scott Caldwell, Jason Edwards, Martyn St. David

RETURN OF WHITE CLOUD

wr. Stepfanie Kramer, Erin Conroy, Joe Menosky, dir. Stepfanie Kramer

Murders in the art world occur when ancient indian artifacts are stolen from sacred ground.

with Rion Hunter, Michael Fairman, Ruth Britt, David Hayward, John Quade, Robert Clotworthy, Leslie Woods, Patti Been, Petrea Burchard, Jeff Chayette, Kit Paraventi, Robert Lopez

Sixth Season (1989–'90)

ON AIR

wr. Lee Goldberg, William Rabkin, dir. Tony Mordente

The hostess of a sexy radio show that caters for lonely men becomes the target of a deranged obsessive who starts killing her lovers.

with Erin Gray, Don Swayze, Scott Marlowe, Michael McManus

SHILLELAGH

wr. Jerome Lew, dir. David Phinney

Captain Devane's new lady love is visited by her brother, a spokesman for peace in Ireland who has now decided to resort to violence.

with Fionulla Flanagan, Nicholas Guest, Jay Ingram, Alan Scarfe, Jonathan Emerson, Kenneth Kimmins

INVESTMENT IN DEATH

wr. Jerry Jacobuss, Nick Gore, dir. Corey Allen

Racial unrest brews when a reformed juvenile delinquent turned successful college student is senselessly murdered by his former fellow gang members (in this episode, Hunter's squad move into the William Parker Centre, although due to network running order choices, they were already there in the previous episode!).

with Bernie Casey, Joel Brooks, Steve Eckholdt, Russell Curry, Cylk Cozart, Brent Jennings

A GIRL NAMED HUNTER

wr. Catherine Bacos Clinch, dir. Dennis Donnelly

After Hunter helps a young runaway when she suddenly goes into labor in the street, he makes it his personal business to find out why she was killed shortly afterwards, and discovers she reneged on a baby-selling deal.

with Bobbi Jo Lathan, Elizabeth Ashley, Mary McDonough, Allison Smith, Dan Peterson, Amy Lynne, Stephen Johnson

THE LEGION (two parts)

wr. Marvin Kupfner, dir. Corey Allen

When a psychotic racist captured by Hunter breaks out of prison with the aid of his equally deranged brother, Hunter pursues him; in the meantime, McCall is reunited with her mentor, now retired and miserable that he's out of the force.

with Richard Lynch, Claude Akins, Jerry Douglas, Richard Lineback, Ken Foree, Jacqueline Schultz, Paul Koslo, Paul Mantee, Michael Strasser, Pat Skipper, David Froman, Karl Johnson

YESTERDAY'S CHILD

wr. Lee Maddux, dir. Winrich Kolbe

Hunter tries to clear a young teenager of murder after he's caught at the scene of a crime where two other youths have killed a late-working employer and fled.

with Joon Bi-Kim, Soon Teck-Oh, David Groh, Jeb Brown, Scott Kraft, Steven Anderson

SHIELD OF HONOR

wr. Leonard Mlodinow, Scott Rubenstein, dir. James Darren

The son of a retired and much decorated officer attempts unsuccessfully to follow in his father's footsteps, his recklessness and his father's stubbornness endangering his fellow officers.

with Harry Guardino, Sheree North, K. Callan, Eric Larson, Michael Shaner, Gregory Scott Cummins

THE FIFTH VICTIM

wr. Kevin Droney, dir. Michael Preece

While the authorities are eager to tie up a rash of serial killings of gay men after apprehending a bigoted thug, Hunter suspects that one of the deaths might not be his work.

with William Smith, Rick Giolito, Don Galloway, William Joyce, Michael Champion, Laurie Prange

BROTHERLY LOVE

wr. Terry Nelson, dir. James Fargo

After accidentally killing the drug dealer he's been working for, a juvenile steals his money and runs.

with Mark Pellegrino, Tim Griffin, Gretchen Corbett, Gary Grubbs, Tim Rossovich, G. Adam Gifford

The Nightmare

wr. Terry Nelson, dir. James Whitmore, Jr.

When McCall's housekeeper is found murdered after recognizing a killer from her homeland, Hunter and McCall find themselves on the trail of a barbarous torturer who has come to L.A. under an alias to start a new life.

with Carlos Carrasco, Joe Renteria, Ingrid Oliu, Kamala Lopez, Barbara Luna, David Combs

Broken Dreams

wr. Mark Lisson, David Balkan, Terry Nelson, Kevin Droney, dir. Michael Preece

When an old college friend of Hunter witnesses a murder, her shady husband sees an opportunity to cash in.

with Christina Raines Crowe, Granville Van Dusen, Michael Greene, Steve Rankin, Deborah Strong

Son and Heir

wr. Kevin Droney, dir. Winriche Kolbe

A mobster's son kills an undercover cop — and then discovers that the cop was his half-brother.

with Paul Regina, Jerry Orbach, Bette Ford, Brian Libby, Geoffrey Blake, E.J. Peaker, Gary Wood, Blake Bahner, Brooks Gardner, Tony Amendola

Unacceptable Loss

wr. Catherine Bacos Clinch, dir. Corey Allen

Hunter and McCall investigate toxic waste dumping after a young boy is killed by cyanide in an open sewer.

with Robert Gentry, Kathleen Noone, Tony Plana, Brooke Bundy, Ken Lerner, Steve Kahan, Tina Lifford

Unfinished Business

wr. Morgan Gendel, dir. Corey Allen

After McCall and Hunter nearly shoot each other while pursuing a hold-up man, they are ordered to see a police psychiatrist, and a surprising secret is revealed.

with Allan Arbus, Karen Austin, Don Gibb, Thomas Geas, Julie Ow

Lullabye

wr. Terry Nelson, Kevin Droney, Marvin Kupfer, David Balkan, dir. Corey Allen

A serial killer murdering prostitutes moves his base of operations from London to L.A., and Hunter is joined by a London detective to end the reign of terror.

with Gary Sinise, Rosalyn Landor, Clive Revill, Ross Kettle

Final Confession

wr. Terry D. Nelson, dir. Tony Mordente

An ex-con with a grudge inflicts a perverse revenge on a priest by confessing to murder in advance of the crime.

with John Pleshette, Jeff Pomerantz, Sally Spencer, Donna Lynn Leavy, James Sutorius, Roy Dotrice

Blind Ambition

wr. Marvin Kupfer, Mark Lisson, dir. Michael Preece

McCall and a federal prosecutor she's been dating are held hostage before leaving for a long weekend by the brother of an allegedly innocent youth found dead in his cell.

with John Beck, Harold Sylvester

Sudden Withdrawal

wr. Terry Nelson, Kevin Droney, dir. Tony Mordente

A ruthless woman seduces married bank officials and flatters them into revealing suitable times for her gang to strike.

with Leslie Bevis, Mark Pinter, Paul Drake, Mark Bringelson, Will Jeffries, Ann Gillespie, Mark L. Taylor

Second Sight

wr. Daniel Chodos, Michael Kerwin, dir. Winrich Kolbe

A psychic with a proven track record predicts that McCall will be the next victim of a killer.

with Tom Villard, Time Winters, Luana Anders, Michael Whaley

Street Wise (two parts)

wr. Mark Lisson, Kevin Droney, David Balkan, dir. James Whitmore, Jr., Winriche Kolbe

Hunter goes to the aid of a homeless man who has had his war medal stolen by a mugger, while McCall considers a proposal of marriage.

with Robert Connor Newman, Daniel Southern, Ryan Cutrona, Christopher Curry, Charles Walker, Sal Landi, Jeffrey Josephson, Dan Bell, Margaret Blye, M.C. Gainey, Lou Beatty, Jr., Robert Silver

Seventh Season (1990–'91)

DEADLY ENCOUNTERS (two parts)

wr. Mark Lisson, Terry D. Nelson, dir. Winriche Kolbe

Hunter and Charlie Devane move to a new division and investigate the murders of two immigrants with the assistance of Officer Joanne Molenski, who becomes Hunter's new partner.

with Andreas Katsulas, Bill McKinney, Ramsey Midwood, Brad Tatum, Beth Grant, Dennis Moynahan, Pamela Gien, Jan Triska, Cyril O'Reilly

WHERE ECHOES END

wr. Walter Brough, dir. James Darren

The murder of an undercover Treasury agent is witnessed by an undercover cop, who is surprisingly unhelpful in Hunter's investigations.

with Beau Starr, Lynne Thigpen, Asher Brauner, Kim Walker, Ismael East Carlo, Shawn Thompson

KILL ZONE

wr. Kevin Droney, dir. Corey Allen

Molenski is personally affected by an investigation into a series of brutal murders.

with David Ledingham, Mary Kohnert, Andi Chapman, Richard Grove, Al Pugliese, William Smithers

THE INCIDENT

wr. Kathy McCormick, dir. Fred Dryer

An innocent man becomes the victim of an overenthusiastic vigilante group, while the police are harassed by the press and a local community group.

with Barry Primus, Mitch Pileggi, Rugg Williams, Cort McCown, Devon Odessa, Anne Gee Byrd, David Heavener, Al Ruscio

A SNITCH'LL BREAK YOUR HEART

wr. Jeff Benjamin, dir. Tony Mordente

Hunter investigates a seventeen-year-old murder, while Molenski defends an informant who is failing to deliver.

with Seth Isler, Katherine Cannon, Jeff McCarthy, Steven Leigh, Christina Carlisi, Gloria Cromwell

WHEN THE SHARK BITES

wr. Simon Muntner, dir. Peter Crane

Captain Devane is investigated when his name is discovered on a mob's money list.

with Nehemiah Persoff, Carmine Caridi, Geoff Pryssir, John Capodice, Richard Yniguez, Marcia Rodd

THE USUAL SUSPECTS

wr. Deborah Baron, dir. Alan Myerson

A computer operator releases the night's catch and selects one of the prisoners from the police files to murder her husband.

with Rebecca Stanley, Jesse Ventura, Gregory Alan-Williams, Tuck Milligan, Cecile Callen

THIS IS MY GUN

wr. Robert Vincent O'Neill, dir. Winriche Kolbe

Molenski goes undercover as bait for burglars following lone women home to rob them, but loses her gun ... which is used in a murder.

with Lewis Van Bergen, Charles Boswell, John Michael Bolger, Breon Gorman, Scott Burkholder, Tony Capozzola, Monty Bane

LA FAMILIA

wr. Walter Brough, dir. Tony Mordente

A gang member trying to go straight is intimidated by his family into continuing warfare.

with Joe Santos, Luis Guzman, Raymond Cruz, Grand L. Bush, Teresa DiSpina

ACAPULCO HOLIDAY

wr. Jeff Benjamin, dir. Tony Mordente

Hunter is sued for wrongful arrest.

with Nina Foch, David Neidorf, Kasey Walker, Scott Getlin, Dick Christie, Paul Linke

FATAL OBSESSION (double length)

wr. David Balkan, Terry D. Nelson, dir. Corey Allen, Winriche Kolbe

Molenski is killed by a cop killer during an investigation into a number of serial killings, and Hunter gains a new partner when an old friend joins the squad after a drunk driver runs into one of the fleeing victims.

with Ellen Wheeler, Ken Marshall, Jeffrey Combs, Courtney Barilla, Marcus Giamatti, Kevin

Wixted, Frances Bay, Seth Jaffe, Alex Kubik, Jack Jozefson, Red West

Under Suspicion

wr. Daniel Chodos, dir. Gus Trikonis

Hunter races against time to locate a witness before a bounty hunter does.

with Gregory Alan Williams, Teresa Ganzel, Jeff Silverman, Danny Woodburn, Robert Schuch, Christopher Morley, Barry Doe, Brion James

The Reporter

wr. Simon Muntner, dir. Corey Allen

Novak discovers that a reporter friend accompanying her on her cases for a story is taking cocaine.

with Kelly Curtis, Arlen Dean Snyder, David Kimball, Joey Aresco, Don Fischer, Danny Wells, Joe E. Tata

Room Service

wr. Terry D. Nelson, dir. Peter Crane

Novak's ex-husband joins Hunter on a case to catch a pair of muggers picking on tourists whose last attack ended in murder (this episode introduces Robin Thomas as Al Novak).

with Kevin Page, Cindy Morgan, Jeremy Roberts, Brian George, Biff Manard, Stephen Rowe, Saxon Trainor

Shadows of the Past

wr. Mark Lisson, dir. Tony Mordente

A family dispute looms over Novak's assignment to protect a witness to a murder.

with Mitchell Ryan, Joe Marinelli, Alex Colon, Carl Strano, Jeff Austin, Annie Grindlay, Ron Max, Antony Ponzini

The Grab

wr. Morgan Gendel, dir. Corey Allen

Novak's ex-husband's cover is at risk when a counterfeit investigation goes sour.

with Robin Thomas, Vincent Guastaferro, Christopher Neame, Joris Stuyck, Courtney Barilla, Greg Collins, Casey Sander, Edith Diaz

All That Glitters

wr. Daniel Chodos, dir. Tony Mordente

Two prostitutes, one the daughter of a councilman, become the targets of a thief when they make off with a valuable coin he's stolen.

with Denise Crosby, Patrick St. Esprit, Alan Fudge, Kimberly Neville, Patricia Berry, Sal Viscuso, David De Luise, Cindy Brooks, Lee Kessler

Cries of Silence

wr. David Balkan, dir. Peter Crane

Hunter and Novak pursue a runaway girl who can help them in a murder inquiry.

with Michael Fernandes, Pierette Grace, Greg Mullavey, Melissa Hayden, Victor Rivers, Tony Vatsula, Jodi Benson, Marc Riffon, Phyllis French

Ex Marks the Spot

wr. Simon Muntner, dir. Gus Trikonis

A dry cleaner laundering more than clothes incurs the wrath of the mob when his bitter ex-flames conspire to raid his business.

with Don Rickles, Leslie Easterbrook, Bonnie Burroughs, Teri Copley, Ron Karabatsos, Tony Longo, Stacey Nelkin, Michael Tomlinson, Lou Beatty, Jr.

Little Man with a Big Reputation

wr. Tom Blomquist, dir. James Darren

Hunter and Novak are suspicious when Charlie Devane is asked to be the best man at the wedding of a minor villain.

with Jean Kasem, Ted Markland, Thom McFadden, Gary Wood, Art Metrano, Tony Mordente

series ends

Stingray
March 1986–May 1987

In many ways, *Stingray* was a typical Cannell show, featuring a one-man *A-Team* with a Lone Ranger complex in the Judge Hardcastle tradition. If you had melded both Hardcastle and McCormick into one, and swapped the noise, buddy banter and checked shirt machismo for silent, sleek, solo sophistication, the end result would have been Stingray. Like Hardcastle and McCormick, Ray — as he calls himself when absolutely forced to give a name — has a fast car, a Stingray Corvette. As the publicity material for the series declares, "You call him when you're in trouble, when the wheels of justice are moving too slowly, and the villains are too big. Stingray doesn't go through channels, doesn't fill out reports. And he never does anything for money." "What bull," as Cannell had said when explaining *Rockford*, the antithesis of *Stingray*. Ten years after *The Rockford Files*, Cannell was back doing formula TV.

Vigilante series starring futuristic and/or resourceful Lone Ranger types were in great abundance during the 1980s. While numerous series offering heroes who worked for recognized government agencies fell at first post (*Masquerade, Cover Up, Blue Thunder, Automan, Manimal, The Highwayman*, and others), series featuring heroes who worked outside the law enjoyed a healthy run — *Knight Rider, The Fall Guy, The A-Team, Hardcastle and McCormick, MacGyver, Mike Hammer, Airwolf, The Equalizer*, and so on. Consequently, Cannell was well within reason to expect that *Stingray* would also enjoy a worthwhile run on NBC, even though the network had commissioned it specifically to take on CBS' show-killer, *Dallas*.

However, there was one fatal difference between this show and the Cannell programs that had preceded it. The major drawback of the show was that *Stingray* had no regular supporting cast of characters for the hero to bounce Cannell's distinctive and unique trademark banter back and forth with in the manner of all his previous series, which had to date proven to be Cannell's greatest strength. With no other recurring characters to hand, and with Stingray himself a mobile drifter and mystery man, the series relied entirely on the appeal of its newface leading man, a traditionally good looking shop window mannequin with reflective shades. As Stingray had no roots and no background, there was little beyond this shallow surface smoothness for men to identify with or women to be attracted to. The result of this was that *Stingray* was heavily reliant on the short-term benefits of the briefly popular *Miami Vice*-inspired "cop video" approach so beloved of NBC in the mid-'80s; indeed, Stingray's first adversary in the pilot film is played by Gregory Sierra, the original boss of Crockett and Tubbs in the first few episodes of *Miami Vice*.

Cast as the enigmatic Stingray was the Italian-born Canadian actor Nick Mancuso, who had emigrated to Toronto with his family when he was six years old. Well-educated, with a degree in psychology and fluent in several languages, Mancuso worked extensively in the theater during the 1970s before breaking into films, TV movies, and mini-series such as the successful *Scruples* in the early '80s. He had previously worked for Cannell as the star of the unsold 1978 pilot *Doctor Scorpion,* and his feature film credits have been mostly minor low-budget endeavors. "I've got Latin looks," Mancuso told the press, "and if you're dark, you'll be cast as someone who's intense, moody, and flawed." Sadly, "intense, moody and flawed" was a description that was to fit *Stingray.*

An adult *Knight Rider* with flashy visuals, *Stingray's* closest neighbor was the 1985–'88 series *The Equalizer,* created by Michael Sloan, whose other claims to fame were the highly rated TV movies *Return of the Man from UNCLE* and *Return of the Six Million Dollar Man.* In *The Equalizer,* Edward Woodward was cast as a former government agent turned hero for hire, Michael Caine's Harry Palmer playing out Michael Winner's *Death Wish* to a television moral code. Woodward, who had played a weary, hard-edged spy already in the '60s British-made tape series *Callan,* had been remembered by Sloan after they had worked on a low-budget feature together in the early '70s. Now, Woodward was cast as the weary Robert McCall, a jaded secret agent who had turned wild card and somehow been allowed to quit. He had subsequently set himself up as a vigilante avenger with a brief but concise ad in the newspaper and an answer-phone to take the calls for help. After weeding out the time-wasters, he would get in touch with various victims, and turn up on the doorstep to take care of business for free. Unlike the A-Team, who worked from a similar premise, McCall was known to the police, who covertly supported him. The anonymous and mysterious Stingray also worked for free via a newspaper ad and answer-phone, but with Stingray, there was a catch. He wanted a favor in return. It could be anything, at any time, simple or complex, legal or otherwise, but the client would only be called on once, and they had to do it. He might call tomorrow, ten months, or ten years later, but they had to be there for him, and calling these favors from former customers in all trades and from all walks of life has enabled Stingray to build up a network of convenient contacts, colleagues and experts in every field. It was a novel idea that could have been fascinating, had the series run long enough for writers to exploit it. As it was, all but one of the people who aided Stingray were those he had supposedly met and helped before the series began. During the course of the first six episode run, Stingray — who also has a comprehensive computer system and a hazy undisclosed history with a government agency — was able to pose convincingly as a doctor, a diver, an illegal alien, student, and psychologist. In the second season, which ultimately took the

Nick Mancuso as Stingray sits in his Stingray to advertise ***Stingray.***

entire series to a total of 23 episodes, he masquerades as a chemist, hoodlum, longshoreman, and military man. Each time, his sources are able to provide him with credible credentials.

Although originally commissioned by NBC as an 8:00 show, the pilot film turned into something very different, and both Cannell and the network decided they had a 10:00 show on their hands. Indeed, if *Stingray* achieved anything at all, it was to open the door for Cannell to late night slots and a darker, grimmer terrain that later shows like *Unsub* and *Wiseguy* would continue to explore. In retrospect, the series was a major turning point for Cannell, taking him away from bright and breezy action/adventure. Cannell pitched the *Stingray* pilot to NBC as it was, but NBC passed on it, and ran it in the summer months as a TV movie. Reviewing the pilot, trade bible *Variety* had pointed out that NBC's decision to pass on the show was a bad idea, but that the series' "*Miami Vice* pretensions" had "hurt it more than it helped it." They had called it "a decision worth reappraising," and NBC was inclined to agree. When the pilot rated surprisingly high, NBC had second thoughts and revived the show, placing an order with Cannell for eight episodes. These aired on a Tuesday night that was then dominated entirely by Cannell product; the evening opened with *The A-Team,* moved on with *Riptide,* and closed with *Stingray.* However, so solid did this triumvirate look on the NBC line-up, that *Stingray* was a victim of a scheduling snafu — the shows running directly opposite *Stingray* on the rival networks were *The Equalizer* and *Spenser: for Hire,* both very similar (and more traditional) vigilante action shows aimed at much the same audience. This disastrous double-punch from two series already well established with the viewers effectively ensured *Stingray's* demise that season. On the other hand, NBC wasn't about to ignore a promising series from the man who had already given them *The A-Team, Riptide,* and *Hunter* (another slow-burner that patience paid off with), and with Mancuso's face starting to show up in assorted teen magazines, NBC still felt the show had potential. "It wasn't renewed based on ratings," NBC head Brandon Tartikoff told trade paper *Electronic Media* in October '86. "It was renewed on faith. They came on in March, they had to make the shows in a hurry, and they didn't really have the time on the scripts they would have liked. I think in Nick Mancuso they have a guy who has the same kind of break-out potential that Don Johnson had."

Tartikoff placed an order for another seven episodes, but this time it was the Cannell organization itself that started to have doubts. "With the syndication market being what it is, and with licence fees being what they are," explained Cannell's executive vice-president Mike Dubelko to journalist Lee Goldberg, "...it didn't make sense to even *make* the show. It would have been questionable if we could ever have recouped our money." It was Mancuso himself, a native Canadian, who gave both his series and Stephen J. Cannell Productions a new lease of life by suggesting that Cannell move the series out lock, stock and barrel to Vancouver, where the series could be made for literally half the cost. "We sent a location scout and crew to Toronto, Calgary, and Vancouver," Cannell told Ken Winikoff of *Hollywood Reporter* in 1988. "They came back with miles of videotape and said hey, this is great. So we pushed the button and shot the second year of *Stingray* in Canada and found a new and energetic industry there with people who were real excited about the influx of film."

The move to Canada was an easy one for *Stingray,* as the only regular cast member was Mancuso himself. However, while *Stingray* fought gamely for its existence, a number of significant events were occurring in Hollywood.

Early in 1987, *The A-Team* had ceased production. In fact, it had been *Stingray's* second season that initially replaced it, and when the early evening slot that had been intended for the concept right from the start didn't work, *Stingray* was moved back to late nights. It then darted back to early evenings for the summer, which further confused the audience. Was it a kids' show? An adult show? A family show? Nobody knew from one week to the next, further adding to the series' already quite schizophrenic quality.

Riptide had closed at the end of the 1985–'86 season, as had *Hardcastle and McCormick*. It was the end of an era, the end of the line for a certain style of Cannell show, the good-natured, humorous, rough and tumble, smash and crash, don't-take-us-too-seriously-we're-just-having-fun period of buddy show programming dominated by *The Greatest American Hero, The Quest, Rousters, The A-Team, Riptide, Hardcastle and McCormick,* and the early *Hunter* (which would survive, but change significantly as it entered the late–'80s, the sole survivor of Cannell's early–'80s mayhem). At the same time, Cannell's *The Last Precinct,* an ambitious but misfired comedy about misfit cops in the *Police Academy* tradition, had made its (expensive) debut one month after *Stingray* in April '86 and closed down just one month later. Two Cannell pilots, *Destination: America,* a *Fugitive*-style yarn starring Bruce Greenwood of *St. Elsewhere,* and *Return of the Greatest American Hero,* with Catherine Mary Stewart as a female in the super-suit under Bob Culp's supervision, had failed to sell. Another earlier Cannell pilot, *Brothers-in-Law* in 1984, with Culp, Mac Davis and Joe Cortese (later of Lupo's *Something is Out There* series), had also failed to fly. The feeling now was that this sort of programming, expensive to produce and less successful in the ratings, had seen its best days. Sit-coms, cheaper to produce, but not Cannell's *forte* (as a number of busted late–'80s pilots unhappily demonstrated) were beginning to prove more popular both on the networks in primetime and in the all-important syndication market where producers such as Cannell made their real money once the series had ceased production. It was only another temporary trend, but a financially crippling one for Cannell.

Hollywood production people, who had been gainfully employed by the prolific Cannell's output, had their worst fears confirmed when a stop-gap measure designed to enable the border-line *Stingray* to be financially viable turned into a whole new venture for Stephen J. Cannell Productions, which eventually built studios and set up permanent residence in Vancouver.

"We have to realize," Cannell told the trade press in 1987, "that if it's not a profitable business for studios and independent producers to make this kind of material here, then we'll leave."

"We don't believe that shooting series in Canada is going to be financially profitable," said freelance writers Chris Bunch and Allan Cole, contributors to a number of L.A.–based series including *The A-Team* and *Hunter,* in 1987. "The reason we shoot in Los Angeles is not because L.A. is pretty, 'cause it ain't, but because it's got mostly dependable weather. Now I know that a number of movies have been shot in Toronto, but on a series you're talking about 26 weeks straight through. Now, suppose this is the day you're going to shoot the chase ... and this is the day it happens to rain, or you get a couple of inches of snow — what are you going to do then? This is an example of false economy. We think that in about a year and a half they'll bring every show back from Canada down to L.A."

But Cannell had reinvented the wheel. Cannell has acknowledged in print that "the only reason that (the film) business was originally in L.A. was because of the weather," and that as a result of that, all the sound stages were built there too. But, he pointed out, advances in technology have made the film business portable now ("you've got fast film that can shoot in normal light, and there's no need for a sound stage any more") and as for the weather, "anyone who's seen an NFL game knows that as long as you don't shoot into the lights, you can barely tell it's raining." Indeed, as the unique closing device of showing pictures of the show being produced demonstrated on *Stingray*, wet weather gear was an essential new part of the film-maker's equipment. Bunch and Cole, and many others dubious of the move, were right in assuming that Cannell's traditional type of show would have been a tough shoot in Canada, but Cannell's shows were changing their look and m.o. Outdoor action scenes were thinner on the ground, and chases almost non-existent. Cannell was also now shooting more after dark; after the pilots of *Wiseguy* and *21 Jump Street*, which were heavy on stunts, the series themselves spent more time indoors, more time talking, and more time on the streets at night.

Initially attempting to film *Stingray* in Mancuso's home ground of Toronto, Cannell found that there were so many American producers already shooting in Canada that no crews were available in that town! Ultimately, Cannell and his crew would shoot the seven new episodes of *Stingray* in Calgary, moving down to Vancouver for the remainder of the series. At the same time *Stingray* was in production, the *21 Jump Street* series was commissioned by the then-new Fox network, and Cannell immediately entertained the notion of shooting that series in Vancouver too. "There's places that look like New York, others that look like downtown L.A.," enthused Cannell to the trade press at the time. "They've got the ocean, the mountains, the big city.... On *Starbuck*, we even doubled Hollywood!"

With seventy-five percent of Stephen J. Cannell Productions shot in Canada, the building of the North Shore studios, a twenty million dollar base of operations with production offices, facilities, and seven sound stages (this last to free Cannell from the endless search for warehouses and offices to rent for standing sets) was inevitable.

"We're in a world market," Cannell reiterated to journalist Martin Borycki in 1987. "The reason that the film business has been in Los Angeles all these years is climate. It's been here for fifty years, so the crews and technology exist here. But all those things exist in other countries as well. The idea of putting the Studio together happened over the last year or so. There were no facilities in Vancouver at the time, and we were one of a number of American companies shooting there that were looking for suitable warehouse space and just couldn't find any. Building a studio in Vancouver made economic sense, because we never know from year to year just how much production we'll be doing. The studio will operate independently from our production company and the facilities will be offered for use to other production companies."

Having experienced such shooting problems himself, Cannell had ingeniously turned the one drawback to filming in Canada that he had encountered into a commercial advantage. On thirteen acres with one hundred thousand square feet of office space, interior courtyards and plaza, Cannell was well-equipped for any eventuality. "We were fighting with everybody for locations and stage space," Cannell told *Hollywood Reporter* for its special British Columbia edition. "It occurred to us that the town was really in desperate need for some sort of a home plate for films, and that because we were up there, it seemed like it was maybe a good thing to get involved with."

The North Shore Studios subsequently provided thousands of jobs from acting to administration in Canada, and took a Canadian company as partner for the enterprise. While *Hunter*, by necessity, stayed in L.A., with only minimal involvement from Cannell at this point in its history, subsequent series — such as *Wiseguy, JJ Starbuck, 21 Jump Street, Booker, Unsub, Top of the Hill,* and others — were all produced in Vancouver. And while *Wiseguy* and *21*

Jump Street flourished, an L.A.–based co-production with NBC, *Sonny Spoon,* collapsed after only a few episodes. There seemed no reason why Cannell shouldn't stay in Canada.*

As for *Stingray,* it may have been the anonymity and ambiguity of the lead character that ultimately caused its downfall. The similar vigilante series *The Equalizer* offered an equally enigmatic hero to the audience, but with more vulnerability, character and humanity. Furthermore, Edward Woodward's Robert McCall was a somewhat more reassuring father figure to see arrive on the doorstep to take on impossible odds, and unlike Stingray, he required no favor in return for his services. In *The Equalizer* (filmed not in Hollywood or Canada, but on location in New York) the only icy chills of apprehension were caused by the bad guys. Perhaps the series' greatest problem was that not only did the viewers not know who Stingray was, but the format of the show clearly indicated that we were never going to find out. Ironically, what *Stingray* really needed was one of the oldest clichés in the book — someone to pursue him. Had *Stingray* applied the corny old standby of including an adversary dedicated to following him around and exposing his true identity, there might have been some friction in the series, but what drove Stingray to do what he did was never explored or explained. Without even the illusion that all might be revealed, the audiences' only hope of involvement was to be drawn into the plight of the person needing Stingray's help. Here too though, the viewer was thwarted, by the shows's glossy, visuals-dominated approach. Not only did Stingray remain an enigma, but often, so did the person he was assisting. In the best episodes, Stingray has some sort of relationship with the person he has decided to aid. But mostly, even they are left out in the cold. Even the Lone Ranger had Tonto!

In many ways, with its lone undercover hero, *Stingray* was a precursor of the exemplary *Wiseguy,* one year later — but where *Wiseguy* had plot and substance and characters with charisma, *Stingray* offered only flashy edits and tricksy camera shots. More significantly, *Wiseguy* was about undercover cop Vinnie Terranova's relationship with the people he was investigating. Frequently, Vinnie would get too close to the people he was deceiving or working alongside, particularly mobster Salvatore "Sonny" Steelgrave in the opening episodes. Just as the relationship between Vinnie and Sonny made *Wiseguy* the gripping and involving saga it was, so the lack of any camaraderie or contact in *Stingray* made the series sterile and uninvolving. In comparison with the compelling *Wiseguy,* in which the warmth of friendship and wealth could be instantly subverted by sudden blasts of violence, horror and deceit, *Stingray* came over as bland and devoid of any humanity at all.

Another problem with the show's chance for success was, ironically, the diversity of the plots, which — while they all offered familiar TV scenarios — dropped our hero into a different atmosphere and ambience each week with a completely fresh locale. *Stingray* perversely suffered from a *lack* of formula, the very factor which often drives some series into a rut. Yet, a series can be familiar without being predictable, as shows such as *Magnum* and *The Rockford Files* have demonstrated, to name but two. Shows like those, and *Hill Street Blues, M*A*S*H, Cheers, Taxi, L.A. Law, St. Elsewhere* and many other quality productions have all offered audiences a recognizable set of ground rules and expectations without being predictable. With *Magnum,* for example, the audience would never know if they were going to get a light comedy, moody drama, murder mystery, war story, parody, or something else

---

Although the doubters could not have foreseen the change in program style that would facilitate shooting in Canada in the late '80s, or indeed the preponderance of dark and gloomy shows in the wake of the Canadian-shot X-Files *and its imitators, it is worth noting that when Cannell returned to action/adventure in the early '80s style with the superb return to form series* Renegade *in the 1990s, he shot in San Diego.*

entirely, but they *did* know that they were going to see Hawaii, Robin's Nest, Rick, T.C., and Higgins. Similarly, *The Rockford Files* varied its premise each week while relying on the same set of recurring characters and even recurring incidents. Every *Rockford* story was different, but followed a set premise; the viewer knew that Angel would be up to no good, that Dennis Becker would be harassed, and Chapman obnoxious. If Rockford was locked up, we knew that Beth would be there in the following scene; if he got into his car, we knew that there would be a couple of gun-toting hoods in the car behind. In *Stingray,* there were no constants, and every episode took the audience to a new unfamiliar destination with new, unfamiliar people, in the company of a cool, unemotional mystery man they knew nothing about. One week, a grim story about a Vietnam veteran would be offered, the next, a sinister research establishment ... another week, a conceited movie star ... another, a grim investigative thriller of corruption, the next, a spoofy scam. From producing *The A-Team,* a series with the same premise of people in need of outside-the-law assistance, which rapidly got trapped in a mire of predictability and had to be pulled out mid-series, Cannell had moved across to the other extreme.

This did not mean that there weren't individual episodes worth watching. Among the more unusual episodes were Carol Mendelsohn's and Larry Hertzog's "Payback," guest starring Jack Blessing (*Moonlighting's* McGillycuddy) and the reliable character actor Eugene Roche (*Magnum's* Luther Gillis) in a story about murder at a scientific establishment experimenting with living conditions in space, and Hertzog's "Autumn," in which Mary Jackson (housekeeper Sarah Wickes in the first season of *Hardcastle and McCormick*) plays a mystery writer who leads Ray on a wild goose chase to provide her with good book material. More familiar ground was covered in Mendelsohn's "The Neniwa," the old "noble savage" cliché already covered by Mancuso in his film *Nightwing* and TV movie *Legend of the Walks Far Woman,* and Mendelsohn's "Echoes," a beautifully executed piece of direction by second season producer David Hemmings, but with a hopelessly telegraphed ending.

"The First Time Is Forever," written by *The A-Team's* Steven Sears, "Second Finest Man Who Ever Lived," by another *A-Team* regular Burt Pearl, and "One Way Ticket to the End of the Line," written by Judy Burns, were all competent and comprehensible standard TV thrillers, while only "Gemini," written by Harold Apter, and the aforementioned "The First Time Is Forever" offered the slightest hint of Stingray's background and motivation. The latter, which had Stingray turn down a reporter who won't reveal the nature of his story to him, only to be consumed with guilt when that refused client is murdered, was a novel idea; "Gemini," with its impostor darkside Stingray, was an old chestnut.

Perhaps the best episodes were Mendelsohn's "Night Manoeuvres," set in a military academy, and "Blood Money," written by Tom Blomquist. Here, John Amos, a regular in early *Hunter* episodes, plays a high school principal trying to keep three of his students out of the seductive thrall of a charismatic and psychotic gang leader, which offered TV cop show regular and *Hooperman* co-star Felton Perry a much meatier role than his usual suit-and-tie parts. Cannell's own episodes found the man on familiar form, with yarns about drugs smuggling, mobsters, and Russian spies. "Sometimes You Gotta Sing the Blues" is typical *Rockford* stuff, with Stingray saddled with a lovestruck lady cop trying to clear her boss, while "Cry Wolf," also strongly in the *Rockford* tradition, is full of gangsters, real estate frauds and federal agents, and revolves around a phoney, self-obsessed and strung-out minor league actor on a TV medical show. A colleague supposedly minding his affairs has implicated him in a drugs scam, and his life is under threat from the vengeful mob victims of two warring factions, one Vegas, one Yakuza, but because the vain, career-obsessed actor (Jeff Conaway, still typecast after his stint on *Taxi*) has pulled a death threat publicity stunt the year before, the cops don't want to know. As well as the typical trademark confrontations between hero and client, all the richness and humor of Cannell's dialogue is present, but Mancuso is no James Garner, and so *Stingray*, even at its erratic best, never comes across as anything more than an interesting diversion on a bad TV night.

Lawrence Hertzog was executive producer on *Stingray*, having crossed over to the series (with a number of the writers) following the cancellation of *Hardcastle and McCormick*, and would later perform the same duties on *J.J. Starbuck*. Hertzog also contributed five episodes, one with Carol Mendelsohn, who herself wrote three episodes. J. Rickley Dumm, Cannell's old college buddy hired to assist on *Hardcastle and McCormick* and *Riptide*, had produced the pilot. As usual, Cannell wrote the pilot and the first episode (from a first draft from producer and sometime *Hunter* writer Herbert Wright), and then another five. Wright and Edward Vaughn, two newcomers to the Cannell contingent, produced the first season, but when the series went to Canada, director David Hemmings was producing, later to be assisted by Tom Blomquist from *Riptide* and Judy Burns (who each contributed an episode); Cannell's second season opener, "The Greeter," is directed by Hemmings, who also features in a small cameo role. Hemmings directed several of the better episodes of *The A-Team*, as well as episodes of Glen Larson's *Masquerade* and Donald Bellisario's *Airwolf* (guesting in both series). He also directed two episodes of the first season of *Stingray*, three of the second, and an episode of *The Last Precinct* (also providing narration). Towards the end of the series, Frank Lupo and Chuck Bowman were pitching in to keep things running.

Episode Guide

regular cast: Nick Mancuso (Stingray)

First Season (1986)

STINGRAY (pilot)
wr. Stephen Cannell, dir. Richard Colla
While searching for a city official who has been abducted to prevent him prosecuting an underworld leader, Ray discovers the existence of a clinic performing mind-altering operations.
with Robyn Douglass, Gregory Sierra, Susan Blakely, Joe Renteria, Lee Richardson

ANCIENT EYES
wr. Stephen Cannell, Herbert Wright, dir. Charles Picerni
Ray poses as an illegal alien to infiltrate a marijuana plantation where drug traffickers are exploiting Mexican immigrants.
with Rachel Ticotin, J.E. Freeman, Marco Rodriguez, Georgeann Johnson, Isela Vega, Richard Roat, Robert Curtin, Joe Flores, Linda Salcedo, Frank Doubleday, Carlos Cervantes

ETHER
wr. Lawrence Hertzog, dir. David Hemmings
Stingray investigates a hospital where routine operations are regularly resulting in patients' deaths, and unearths a macabre scheme to keep a wealthy man supplied with donors.
with James Laurensen, Ray Wise, Walter Barnes, Carolyn Ann Clark, Joel Colodner

BELOW THE LINE
wr. Tom Lazarus, dir. Larry Shaw
Stingray poses as a Naval diver to investigate the disappearance of a diver at a research center, and uncovers a massive million dollar oil fraud.
with James Wainwright, Steve Vinovich, Kelbe Nugent, Lee Garlington, Patricia Wettig, Randy Holland, John Macchia

SOMETIMES YOU GOTTA SING THE BLUES
wr. Stephen Cannell, dir. Kim Manners
A police captain enlists Ray's help to clear him of the charge of murdering his wife, and Ray is

teamed with the officer's love-struck secretary to clear his name and reveal the true murderer.

with Kathleen Lloyd, Tom Atkins, James Handy, Kurtwood Smith, James Carroll

ABNORMAL PSYCHE

wr. Lawrence Hertzog, dir. Michael Preece

Stingray joins the class of a psychologist who is programming his students to become assassins ... and collects his favor from the police captain in the previous episode (broadcasters, watch out!).

with Robert Vaughn, Scott Paulin, James Handy, Lori Lethin, Patricia Ayame Johnson

ORANGE BLOSSOM

wr. Stephen Cannell, dir. Rob Bowman

Stingray investigates the bizarre claim that patients from a psychiatric hospital are being abducted by Russian agents.

with Robyn Douglass, Kate Charleson, Erica Yohn, Stewart Moss, J. Patrick Macnamara, Mark Lowenthal, Donegan Smith, Tony Longo, Granville Ames

LESS THAN THE EYE CAN SEE

wr. Lawrence Hertzog, dir. Gary Winter

Stingray investigates a government health cover-up over a deadly stolen virus.

with Raymond Singer, Larry Keith, Kenneth Tigar, Frank Dent, James Newell, John Welsh, Thom Rachford, Gary Bowen, William Hayes, Eugenia Bostwick

THAT TERRIBLE SWIFT SWORD

wr. Tom Lazarus, dir. David Hemmings

Stingray investigates the murders of a number of prostitutes, all of which occur when a traveling religious group are in the vicinity.

with Barbara Williams, James McKrell, David Froman, Dick Anthony Williams, Stuart Pankin, John Lawlor, James Hornbeck, Bill Gratton

Second Season (1987)

THE GREETER

wr. Stephen Cannell, dir. David Hemmings

Stingray poses as a chemist to close down an illegal drug manufacturing fraud exploiting the Third World.

with Ann Wilkinson, Daniel Trent, Vernon Weddle, Steven Williams, Howard Siegel, J.C. Quinn, John Bluethener, Gordon Signor, David Hemmings

GEMINI

wr. Harold Apter, dir. Kim Manners

Stingray is framed for a series of murders of young women answering Stingray's newspaper ads and committed by a man last seen entering a black Corvette.

with William Hayes, Marcia Strassman, Lisa Rafel, Frank McCarthy

PLAYBACK

wr. Carol Mendelsohn, Lawrence Hertzog, dir. David Hemmings

Stingray investigates the deaths of a number of scientists experimenting with duplicating conditions in outer space.

with Eugene Roche, Jack Blessing, Charles Lucia, Evan Kim, Lisa Hart Carroll, Charles Boswell, Richard Kuss, James Louis Watkins, Maureen Malone

BRING ME THE HAND THAT HIT ME

wr. Stephen Cannell, Frank Lupo, dir. Don Chaffey

Stingray poses as a punk mobster to help a young girl stop her brother from being involved with the mob.

with Lori Petty, Tom O'Brien, Gregg Henry, Roberts Blossom

ECHOES

wr. Carol Mendelsohn, dir. David Hemmings

Stingray must return to a case he thought solved three years ago when a ghost from the past comes back to haunt an artist with fragile mental health.

with Samantha Eggar, Joseph Maher, Robert Harper, Joseph Hacker, Cliff Potts, Mark Taylor, Julianne McCarthy, Walker Edmiston

THE FIRST TIME IS FOREVER

wr. Steven Sears, dir. Rob Bowman

Stingray is consumed with guilt when he turns down a plea for help from an investigative reporter who won't divulge the nature of his investigation and is then murdered.

with Margaret Michaels, Stanley Grover, Raleigh Bond, John Carter, Jeff Altman, Dennis Madalone, Lucinda Neilsen

Autumn

wr. Lawrence Hertzog, dir. Charles Picerni

An elderly mystery writer creates a fictional puzzle for Stingray to solve, to trick him into providing a perfect plot for what will be her last novel.

with Mary Jackson, Shannon Tweed, Bibi Osterwald, Louise Claire Clark, Kit Fredericks

Neniwa

wr. Carol Mendelsohn, dir. Les Sheldon

Stingray becomes involved in an escalating confrontation between American Indians and a construction company that wants to build on the site of an Indian burial ground.

with Nick Ramus, Jenny Gago, Frank Sotanoma Salsedo, Craig Richard Nelson, Robby Romero, John Wesley

The Second Finest Man That Ever Lived

wr. Burt Pearl, dir. Larry Shaw

Stingray investigates the death of a former client who has uncovered smuggling on the waterfront where he works.

with Dennis Christopher, Lee Taylor, Mike Genovese, Kabir Bedi, David Peterson, Stephen E. Miller, Carmine Caridi

Night Manoeuvres

wr. Carol Mendelsohn, dir. James Darren

A cadet at a military academy witnesses a cold-blooded execution, and Stingray poses as a drill instructor to investigate his story.

with Doug Savant, James A. Watson, Jr., Bill Calvert, George McDaniel, Joe Higgins, Anthony Darren, Steve Walker, Roman Padhora

Cry Wolf

wr. Stephen Cannell, dir. Don Chaffey

Stingray investigates attempts on the life of a vain, self-obsessed actor with little credibility, who is starring in a minor medical soap.

with Jeff Conaway, Renny Temple, Thalmus Rasulala, Joseph Ruskin, Tony Abatemarco, Lindsay Bourne, Tom Kuwahara, Howard Story

Blood Money

wr. Tom Blomquist, dir. Lyndon Chubbuk

Stingray goes to the assistance of a high school principal who is trying to prevent three of his students becoming involved with a homicidal gangster.

with John Amos, Felton Perry, David Raynr, Miguel Nunez, Dee White, James Handy, Kareem Abdul-Jabarr

Anytime, Anywhere

wr. Randall Wallace, dir. Chuck Bowman

Temporarily blinded by a terrorist explosion, Stingray is stranded in Ho Chi Minh City with only an embittered Vietnam veteran, also blinded, to help him complete his mission.

with Leo Rossi, John Fujioka, Rosalind Chao, James Hong, James Pax, Clyde Kusatsu, Stephen Chang

Caper

wr. Evan Lawrence, dir. Rob Bowman

Stingray collects favors from a somewhat reluctant bunch of frauds to rescue the father of a Russian defector.

with Judith Chapman, Robert Mandan, Todd Sussman, Robert Swan

One Way Ticket to the End of the Line

wr. Judy Burns, dir. Larry Shaw

And it is indeed the end of the line for the mysterious man in the Corvette, in an above average episode involving a war between drug barons and a missing crop-duster pilot.

with Barbara Williams, Robert Gray, Cec Verrell, Douglas Dirkson, Lonny Chapman

series ends

The Last Precinct
April 1986–May 1986

> *"People say what they're going to say.*
> Police Academy *was only ripping off* Animal House.
> *What you try to do is make a fresh application to things"*

"*Adam 12* was never like this," remarked Tim Brooks and Earle Marsh in their *Complete Directory to Prime-Time Network TV Shows,* and this was indeed a show that would have reduced Jack Webb (that series' producer and one of Cannell's earliest employers) to tears. With that saving grace as one of the few virtues of the show, the pilot film for *The Last Precinct* made its debut after the Super Bowl on ABC in January 1986. The series followed belatedly in April.

With *The Last Precinct,* Cannell and Lupo took the manic comic energy of *The A-Team* to its extreme, lost the subtle element of parody deep within that series, and fell flat on their faces to the tune of many million dollars. Presenting outright chaotic comedy in the spirit of drive-in/video rental humor, *The Last Precinct* was based quite shamelessly on a cynical mix of the 1978 feature *Animal House* with the 1980s series of *Police Academy* films. Cannell had come full circle now, from the straight, humorless stodgy police melodramas of Jack Webb to this, his first fatal stab at pure cop comedy. But of course with Cannell and Lupo — the team behind *Riptide, Hunter* and *The A-Team*— at the helm, this was no three-set, three-camera sit-com. Instead, Cannell presented ABC with an hour-long multi-cast-member concoction of mayhem that had at least offered him the therapeutic opportunity to finally clear his system of those early days submitting story ideas to *Mission: Impossible, Ironside* and *Chase.* This tasteless farrago of stupidity and lunacy set out to shoot the square-jawed, clean-cut heroes of the past straight between the eyes ... if only they'd offer the courtesy of bending over....

The Last Precinct is a dumping ground on the outskirts of L.A., where the authorities have decided to create a Siberian limbo-land to be occupied by every misfit and nitwit on the police force. Headed by the upright and uptight Captain Rob Wright (Adam West, formerly of the strait-laced *The Detectives*), the precinct resembles nothing less than a ramshackle frat house, where the oddball outfit is locked in eternal competition with the neighboring sheriff's office, headed by Lt. Ron Hobbs (a splendid portrayal of slack-jawed redneck fascism from B-video action star Wings Hauser) and his gormless kiss-up assistant Dial (Geoffrey Elliott).

Manning the precinct is Steve Guttenberg lookalike Jonathan Perpich (who had then recently guested on *Riptide,* in the episode "Peter Pan Is Alive and Well") and his colleague Tremaine "Night Train" Lane, played by busy film and TV player Ernie Hudson of *Ghostbusters* fame. The assortment of crackpots and looney tunes who work with them consisted of Keenan Wynn and Hank Rolike as the elderly "Butch and Sundance," the vampish sex-changed Mel Brubaker (portrayed by Randi Brooks, who specialized in bimbo roles for Cannell shows and other series), Vijay Amritraj as the Indian exchange officer with an unpronounceable name (so they call him Alphabet), Elvis fan and Elvis impersonator King (Pete Willcox, who had taken several sit-com assignments as an — or the — Elvis), prissy Rina Starland (Lucy Lee Flippin), hulking motorcycle cop Raid (Rick Ducommun), and the steel-gripped, stone-faced Martha "Ziplock" Haggerty, played by Yana Nirvana. Had each of these characters been allowed to develop individually, and been given witty, comical lines to speak, they would still never have transcended their stereotypical origins.... As it was, Cannell and Lupo chose to have them running around for a long 48 minutes each week all in one huge blue mass like modern-day Keystone Cops. The result was a shambolic mess.

Cast as the unflappable but incompetent Rob Wright was Adam West, star of the 1960s cult TV series *Batman,* and easily the project's greatest asset. Initially groomed as a heroic lead by Warner Brothers, and guest-starring in such Warners training ground vehicles as *Maverick, 77 Sunset Strip, Sugarfoot,* and *Colt .45* while under contract, West was spotted by *Batman* producer William Dozier after sending up the James Bond spy genre in a number of TV commercials. West, never the straight actor his male model looks condemned him to, resented his success in the *Batman* series for many years, claiming that its three season, two year run from 1966 to 1968 ruined his career prospects, and as a victim of his own success as the legendary Caped Crusader of the comics, West spent the next few years of his career trying to exorcise the ghost of *Batman* before later treasuring and protecting his claim to fame. In fact, as the pilot film for *The Last Precinct* more than adequately demonstrates, his true forte remains comedy. "Great comedy timing and droll delivery made him the front runner from the minute his name was mentioned," Cannell told *People* magazine. Shrugging off the *Batman* label, Cannell laughed, "We'll create a *new* stereotype for him!"

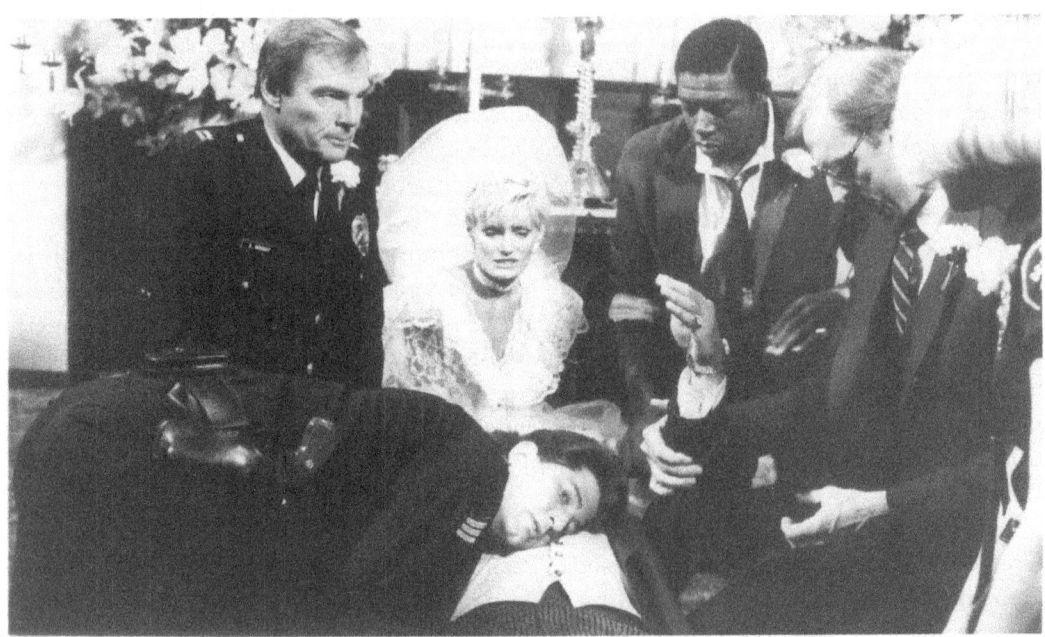

Adam West (top left) received a brief opportunity to demonstrate his flair for comedy and superb comic timing in *The Last Precinct.* Clockwise from West are Randi Brooks, Ernie Hudson, James Cromwell, Yana Nirvana, and Jonathan Perpich.

The pilot for *The Last Precinct* was directed by Hy Averback, who had worked with Cannell on *The Rockford Files* and directed the *Richie Brockelman* pilot. As with the pilot films for *21 Jump Street, Wiseguy,* and *J.J. Starbuck,* the higher budget for the movie-length opener allowed Cannell to go all out on the action stunts he was best known for, a luxury the budgets for the series themselves could not afford. In the case of *Jump Street, Wiseguy,* and *Starbuck,* such window dressing was not essential, but it was quite a different situation with *The Last Precinct,* and the action stunts and mechanical mayhem in the pilot, orchestrated by veteran stunt man and sometime director Bob Bralver, elevated the pilot for *The Last Precinct* to the status of a standard drive-in comedy or video release, a compliment that could not be paid to the lame content of the series itself. In one of the stunt sequences that raises the pilot film head and shoulders above the subsequent series, a squad of cop cars take off after a monstrous garbage truck carrying drugs and attempt to force it violently off the road. As the truck sails invincibly off into the sunset unscathed, the cops manage to completely destroy a fleet of vehicles in every manner imaginable. To add insult to injury, the cars are equipped with a calm computerized voice that, as the bemused officers climb out of an unrecognizable ball of twisted metal, informs them that "You have a cracked tail-light!"

The network's faith in Cannell and Lupo allowed them to go much further than any TV show had gone before in content, and the whole production was remarkably similar to the sort of tasteless teenage fare that television will not or cannot produce, with lines like "Let's do the chainsaw bit" and "I like him — I can always use a homicidal nut!" chasing easy knee-jerk laughs. Besides chainsaw gags, Cannell and Lupo were also able to throw in a blind gangster, Tex Avery–style signpost captions, a doped-up dog and an inflatable doll — although this last one was in the form of a male.*

Weekly episodes of *The Last Precinct,* far better suited to a half-hour slot than the hour-length format the show was given, offered such corny plotlines as disappearing corpses, gorilla suits, haunted houses, vampires, wrestling, and a missing mummy — storylines that went back to the Poverty Row time-fillers of the 1940s. Notable guest stars included Anthony Charnota, a frequent player of gangster roles in previous Cannell productions, Michael Delano (forever typecast as Vegas lounge-lizard Johnny Venture in MTM's *Rhoda*), Kenneth Mars (a regular in Mel Brooks comedies) and familiar TV and B-film heavy Richard Lynch, all of whom had worked for Cannell before.

The 1980s offered two other cop show spoofs of merit, which — while being equally as short-lived — were far superior to *The Last Precinct.* In 1982, Jim Abrahams and David and Jerry Zucker, makers of the highly successful *Airplane!* send-ups for the big screen, devised *Police Squad!,* a six episode series that parodied the Quinn Martin school of cop shows with wicked center-target accuracy, but allegedly failed to take off because, said network execs explaining the cancellation, inattentive viewers missed the proliferation of sight gags — the audience just wasn't paying attention. This reasoning seems highly dubious, and *Police Squad!* became something of a cult show, while Abrahams and the Zucker brothers got their revenge on the TV industry with a *Police Squad!* feature film, *The Naked Gun,* which raked in millions at the box office and ultimately spawned sequels and a whole new direction for former TV movie and cop show face Leslie Nielsen. This was followed by the insane *Sledge Hammer,* ironically a wicked lampoon of the *Dirty Harry/Hunter* school of cop show, with a won-

---

Perhaps the network censors had forgotten Don Adams' altercation with an inflatable girlfriend in "Satan Place," an episode of the 1960s spy spoof Get Smart, *another cult show of the* Batman *era.*

derful central performance from David Rasche, maniacally gleeful as the hawkish, misogynist gun-toting loony of the title. *Sledge Hammer,* devised by industry journalist Alan Spencer and produced by Leonard Stern of *Get Smart* fame, stumbled through an amazing 39 episodes despite being suicidally scheduled against not just *The Cosby Show,* but also *Dallas* (on CBS) and *Miami Vice* (on NBC) at the same time!* Proving the lie to ABC's *Police Squad!* theory (and *Sledge Hammer* was also aired by ABC), *Sledge Hammer* was rife with sight gags as well as great one-liners, titles and themes satirizing films of the day, and a plethora of sideswipes at other, less novel TV series. So convinced was creator Spencer that *Sledge* wouldn't see a second season, that he blew up Sledge, his co-stars, and the entire city in the final first season episode ... only to have ABC pick it up for a second year!†

Tellingly, both *Police Squad!* and *Sledge Hammer* were only half an hour long, which was quite enough for heavy-handed comedy. *The Last Precinct,* being nowhere near as funny, not only lasted an hour, but seemed much, much longer.... More telling though, in the search for a reason for the show's failure (sheer awfulness has never been a ratings factor) were the claims by Cannell and his advocates that *The A-Team* was "one of the best comedies" on television. With *The Last Precinct,* Cannell and Lupo, the best comedic writers at Stephen J. Cannell Productions, were simply trying too hard to be funny. When Cannell and his writers put comedy into their adventure shows, the series worked superbly; Cannell and Lupo's scripts for *The A-Team, Riptide,* and *Greatest American Hero* were often the best in those series, because the humor came from the characters and the situations, not from stereotypical ciphers taking obvious prat-falls in contrived set-ups. But the infuriating thing about *The Last Precinct* was that it could have worked. In the lead roles, Cannell had a great cast; West, Perpich, and Hauser in particular would have excelled in a standard Cannell and Lupo adventure show. If Cannell had ditched the idiotic supporting characters and the *Animal House/Police Academy* aspirations, and built one of his regular action/adventure shows around West, Perpich, Hudson, and Hauser, he might very well have had a hit show. Instead, the cynical, transparent approach that was taken shrunk the potential audience and buried the stronger elements under a torrent of juvenilia.

More than one commentator has described Cannell as "stretching himself a little thin," and most of Cannell's late-'80s endeavors exhibited all the hallmarks of having not been thought out properly before the cameras rolled. From *Stingray,* where—by his own admission—Cannell had delivered a completely different type of show to the one discussed, to the obvious omissions and errors evident in that series and *The Last Precinct,* to the lack of direction and brazen stealing in *J.J. Starbuck,* the recycling of old hits in *Sonny Spoon* and *Unsub,* and the misguided and ill-advised digressions into sit-com and—disastrously—tabloid TV with the horrible *Scandals,* it seemed that in the late '80s, Cannell had lost his way. However, if his mantle as flawless hit-maker was to be tarnished by a string of unsold pilots, misfires, and short runs in the late '80s, his reputation during that period would be partially redeemed by two smash hit series—the worthy and innovative *21 Jump Street,* and the passionately and deservedly exalted cult mob show *Wiseguy.* The critical and commercial acclaim for these two shows, and no doubt the continued income from his piece of *Hunter,* kept his financial and creative head above the water. Stephen J. Cannell Productions was still a force to be reckoned with.

---

*One of the show's numerous TV-related gags has Sledge, on hearing the whereabouts of a fleeing fugitive, turn to the camera and say "Gee—between Dallas and Miami! What a terrible place to be!."

†The series duly returned, and for the first few weeks was sub-titled The Early Years! ... until ABC finally realized that nobody cared too much!

Episode Guide

regular and recurring cast: Adam West (Captain Rob Wright), Jonathan Perpich (Sgt. Price Pascall), Ernie Hudson (Tremaine "Night Train" Lane), Randi Brooks (Mel Brubaker), Keenan Wynn (Butch), Hank Rolike (Sundance), Vijay Amritraj (Alphabet), Rick Ducommun (William "Raid" Raider), Pete Willcox (King), Wings Hauser (Lt. Ronald Hobbs), Lucy Lee Flippin (Rina Starland), Yana Nirvana (Sgt. Martha Hagerty)

(1987)

THE LAST PRECINCT (pilot)

wr. Stephen Cannell, Frank Lupo, dir. Hy Averback

The members of the "last precinct" compete with the equally bumbling sheriff's office to apprehend gangsters who are transporting drugs in garbage trucks.

with Carl Strano, James Cromwell, Robert Miranda, Misty Rowe, Jere Burns, George Pentecost, Derek McGrath, Katherine Kelly Lang, Jack Andreozzi, Geoffrey Elliott

GORILLA-GRAM

wr. Frank Lupo, dir. Michael Lange

After a sick gorilla in the zoo is found to have a valuable diamond in his stomach, Raid dons a gorilla suit to act as a decoy to capture the diamond smugglers who put it there.

with Anthony Charnota, John Di Santi, Robert Pastorelli, Rick Hurst

MR. COOL

wr. Robert Goethals, dir. Michael Lange

A mobster's bodyguard, turning state's evidence against his boss to protect himself after being caught seducing the mobster's girlfriend, is put in the protective custody of the sex-changed Mel.

with Art Metrano, Michael Delano, James Cromwell, Beau Starr, Antony Ponzini

I WANT MY MUMMY

wr. Paul Bernbaum, dir. Bob Sweeney

The 56th Precinct steal a sarcophagus from a museum themselves after being unable to convince Dial that terrorists plan to grab it.

with Kenneth Mars, Don Calfa, Nicholas Kadi, Vahan Moosehian

NEVER CROSS A VAMPIRE

wr. Paul Bernbaum, dir. Michael Lange

Hampered by the attentions of a sensationalizing journalist, the 56th Precinct pursue the thief of several pints of blood from a hospital.

with Richard Lynch, Ernie Sabella, Gary Frank, Barbara Whinnery, Joey Travolta, Samantha Harper

A GHOST OF A CHANCE

wr. Frank Lupo, dir. Bruce Kessler

Members of the 56th Precinct gradually disappear at a party in a haunted house.

with Joseph Ruskin, Leslie Bevis, Tony Giorgio, Miguel Fernandez

TOEHOLD

wr. Jim Mulligan, dir. David Hemmings

An unaccredited David Hemmings narrates this tale of mob infiltration into American wrestling when the 56th Precinct investigates the murder of the "Mad Apache."

with Carl Strano, Robert Miranda, Richard Brose, Audra Johnson

THREE RING CIRCUS

wr. Paul Bernbaum, Robert Goethals, Jim Mulligan, dir. Michael Lange

Night Train and Price discover that the company they have invested in is a cover for a call-girl operation.

with Henry Jones, Frances Bay, Jonathan Goldsmith, Charles Lane, John Fujioka, Alex Henteloff, Mark Taylor, Leeza Vinniechenko

series ends

21 Jump Street
April 1987–May 1991

Traditionally, the teenage audience has always been the toughest to reach for the television industry. Children bounce excitedly before what the author and TV critic Harlan Ellison termed "the glass teat," while jaded adults slump in front of it after they've started a family, but teenagers have better things to do. They don't sit still, they're out and about — sometimes at the cinema, keeping the widescreen medium alive. Furthermore, television doesn't reflect their values or their social milieu — television often doesn't work as entertainment for teens because it's not tough enough, clever enough, relevant enough, or honest enough; television's questions and answers are shallow and simplistic at a time when the young are asking bigger questions and open to more complex answers. And at the same time television doesn't work as an educator — the young are media-literate, its dishonesty is too obvious, and it invariably adopts an authoritarian stance riddled with misinformation, disinformation, nostalgia, tradition, phony morality, propaganda, liberal presumptions and conservative values. Even in a television environment of themed channels, demographic targeting, and households with more than one TV set, MTV is heavily censorious, and the big three networks still chase the family audience above all others ... and teenagers are notorious for their inclination to break free of the family environment, perhaps even (temporarily) reject it.

Perhaps the most bizarre attempts by the television industry to pander to the teenage audience were made in the late '60s and early '70s, at the height of student unrest over events in Vietnam, and — according to the aforementioned TV critic Ellison, a writer of SF novels and short stories who was also regularly contributing to TV series at the time — it was a move instigated at the express wishes of then–President Nixon, who apparently hoped that television might fulfill the same propaganda function as Hollywood had during World War II. According to Ellison, writing in the early '70s, the networks — notably ABC, but all to a degree — duly caved in and complied. The medium had become a little more sophisticated by then (although not much, as the subsequent series concerned demonstrated), but so had media awareness. Furthermore, while World War II was a tragedy that was virtually unavoidable once specific relevant events were in motion, Vietnam was a far more questionable conflict and hardly had the full support of the public. This was particularly true of the American youth of the day, who were being drafted into service as cannon-fodder (and television series in the 1970s, unlike '80s shows which made the Vietnam vet a hero, were not particularly kind to those who returned, due to the numerous horror stories that littered the nightly news).

Whatever the truth in Ellison's remarks (made in the radical *L.A. Free Press,* and repeated in a collection of his columns titled *The Other Glass Teat*), the schedules of the period speak for themselves. While many established series of the time had token "hippie" episodes featuring the "generation gap" and "the youth of today" (including *Batman, Get Smart, F Troop,*

The Lucy Show, The Man from UNCLE, Amos Burke — Secret Agent, Lost in Space, Bewitched, Star Trek, I Dream of Jeannie, Ironside, The Name of the Game, and *The Bold Ones*) — many of them as hilariously off the mark as the average '50s j.d. movie — a slew of series specifically aimed at exploiting the youth culture of the day started springing up on America's TV screens.

At the start of the 1969–'70 season, there was the awkwardly titled *Then Came Bronson* (NBC), which related the spiritually enhancing travels of a wealthy lawyer who had begun to question his values after the suicide of a colleague, and decided to ride the highways of America in search of the meaning of life — on a motorbike of course, as *Easy Rider* (1969) had just hit cinema screens. *The New People,* on ABC (from Rod Serling, would you believe), were a group of 40 teenagers stranded on an abandoned desert island earmarked — but never used — for atomic target practice, and fully equipped with all the basic necessities with which the youngsters could start — and shape — a new society. *The Young Lawyers,* idealistic attorneys working for free against corrupt cops, police brutality, slumlords, and drugs busts, and *The Young Rebels* (these rebellious kids were fighting authority in the American War of Independence!) started within a day of each other on ABC as the 1970–'71 season commenced, closely followed by *The Storefront Lawyers* (more refugees from the legal system working without pay for the underprivileged), and — most bogus of all — *The Headmaster* (Andy Griffith and Jerry Van Dyke!), both on CBS. *Matt Lincoln* (bearing a remarkable resemblance to super-doctor *Ben Casey,* on account of also being played by Vince Edwards) ran an inner-city hot-line for troubled teens and a free clinic for the poor on ABC ... but just in case things got too depressing for him (or indeed, the audience), he somehow found the money to maintain such materialistic accessories as a beach-house, sailboat, and sports car.

None of these hip, trendy young things lasted beyond a season; *The Young Lawyers* quickly took on a WASP member (Ellison gleefully relates how the writer Stephen Kandel named the new boy forced on them Christian White, until the censors caught it at the last minute), and were out of business by the end of the TV year, while *The Storefront Lawyers* actually returned to the prestigious firm their leading light had fled, and the safety of a more conventional courtroom show (now titled *Men At Law,* which also failed to take). The Americans managed to defeat the British without the aid of the eighteenth century teeny boppers, and Andy Griffith retreated to the safe confines of his more traditional and successful rural hick persona for all further post–*Mayberry* endeavors. The American networks' flirtation with the values and ideals of the counter-culture were brief and unproductive — although they may have helped Nixon in a way he hadn't envisaged, by destroying whatever appeal the values of the '60s might have had to successive generations by misrepresenting, trivializing and corrupting them, and reducing them to naive sloganeering and fashionable posturing. How dangerous and anti-establishment could this lifestyle be, if TV was all for it?

Two shows *were* a success. *Room 222* — initially conceived as a comedy — was a rather more credible campus-based college show created by James Brooks and Allan Burns, later of MTM, and which — like *Jump Street* — won many awards and commendations for tackling drugs, racism, and other civil rights issues, running for five years until 1974. The other was Aaron Spelling's *The Mod Squad,* which actually began in 1968, a year earlier than all the other cash-ins, and outlived the entire "relevance" phenomenon, closing its own five year run in 1973.*

---

*By the 1990s, two of the leads, Peggy Lipton and Clarence Williams III, were considered sufficiently hip for nostalgic thirtysomethings' sensibilities to secure roles in the trendy Twin Peaks *series.*

The Mod Squad was presumed by many to be the inspiration for *21 Jump Street,* although the formula was slightly different. In *Jump Street,* the kids were actually cops who looked younger than their years, and so work undercover in schools and colleges cleaning up the mess that society leaves behind; in the pilot, Tom Hanson (series star Johnny Depp) is assigned to the secret undercover group when his youthful appearance fails to command the respect or credibility of the citizens he comes into contact with, to the detriment of his work and the danger of his partner. In *The Mod Squad,* the three leads were not cops to start with, but former anti-establishment troublemakers who had seen the light—a wealthy rebel, an Afrohaired black with a history of rioting in the ghettoes, and the vagrant daughter of a hooker. Assigned to a special hip squad under the guidance of a suit-and-tie guy, their work consisted of weeding out the bogus hippies and wicked over-thirty types who were exploiting the naive counter-culture kids, thus cunningly incorporating the authorities into the youth culture, and the youth culture into the mainstream.* Spelling was a master at covering all the bases, as he proved with the likes of *Starsky and Hutch, Charlie's Angels,* and *Vegas* later that decade, and *The Mod Squad* was no exception. As farcical as the series was, *The Mod Squad* offered prurient or concerned adults a window on the teenage world they were struggling to comprehend (and perhaps were even vaguely excited by), while simultaneously imposing traditional authoritarian values onto the younger audience with a nod to their concerns. A series of straw men were lined up throughout the series' run to show that, hey, the other side's not so bad after all, the kids are okay, the cops are okay, the system's okay, it's just a few people in each category who are spoiling it for everybody. Peace and harmony, man. In the meantime, in the real world, the kids were as high as kites, the cops were breaking heads, and the campuses, the ghettoes, and the jungles and villages of Vietnam were in flames.

In less than two years, the trend was over; the networks turned away from youth unrest and back to the business they knew best—reassurance. The early '70s cop show explosion was about to begin, and TV's more liberal writers drifted into these series, solving social issues through official channels rather than change-the-world protest. But television had been changed. One other new series made its debut in the 1970–'71 season, and was far more radical and long-lasting than any of the hip shows—*The Mary Tyler Moore Show. All in the Family* followed in 1971, and *M*A*S*H* in 1972. The times, they really were a-changin'.

Flash forward to the late '80s. When media mogul and newspaper magnate Rupert Murdoch launched Fox TV in 1987, the television industry laughed at him, and his ambitious plans to make Fox "the fourth network." There hadn't been a fourth network in the U.S. since Dumont closed in the late '50s, leaving the cake to be divided between NBC, CBS, and ABC. Furthermore, the market had been invaded by cable, satellite, and the VCR by then, not to mention home entertainments provided by personal computers (many of which used the TV screen). The cake was smaller—there was less to go around, not more.

They were still laughing when several big name producers, including James Brooks (*The Mary Tyler Moore Show, Taxi, Cheers*), Gary David Goldberg (*Family Ties*), and Cannell and Lupo were invited to pitch ideas for shows with the promise that Fox would be more liberal, daring, and adventurous in what they allowed on the screen. The laughter died down when, amid the expected flurry of early cancellations and failures not too dissimilar to the networks' own annual performance, shows such as the cheap reality-based tabloid TV show *America's*

---

*Oddly enough, not only was this ludicrous concept allegedly based on fact (creator and former cop Bud Ruskin had headed an undercover drugs squad made up of kid-cops in the 1950s), but the pilot script had been floating around the nets looking for a home since 1960. The Mod Squad weren't so mod after all—they'd taken eight years to get on the air!

Most Wanted and the outrageously vulgar and subversive (for TV) sit-com *Married—with Children* became smash-hits. The smiles faded when the teen-oriented, issue-based cop drama *21 Jump Street* hit the air bang in the middle of cutesy-pie family hour Sunday evening TV and kept the teenage audience transfixed for a whole sixty minutes while the other broadcasters aired news, semi-educational pap and Disney ... and their faces positively paled when *The Simpsons,* a superbly funny and witty primetime cartoon from Brooks and cartoonist Matt Groening became the first major cult show of the 1990s.

Very soon, the networks were not only taking Murdoch's endeavors seriously, but brazenly copying his companies' innovations, looking at Fox programming, and wondering how far they dare go in emulating their content without completely abandoning their own self-imposed constraints. *America's Most Wanted* begat *Unsolved Mysteries* (NBC) and *Rescue 911* (CBS), *Married—with Children* paved the way for *Roseanne* (ABC) and less successful shows such as *Lenny* and *Uncle Buck* (both CBS), while *21 Jump Street* clones included the flops *Knightwatch* (ABC) and *Nasty Boys* (NBC). Frank Lupo's *Werewolf* ("Of all the shows that have been pitched to me, I hate this one the most ... but this is the one I'm going to go with!" said Fox head Barry Diller, according to the series' story editors) caused NBC to green-light Lupo's hit sci-fi/horror mini-series and less successful weekly show *Something Is Out There,* and *21 Jump Street's* guiding light, Patrick Hasburgh, left the show mid-run to try in vain to recreate the *Jump Street* ambience with a procession of similar but shortlived teen-oriented pilots and short-runs including *Glory Days, Sunset Beat,* and *HELP.**

Fox had won the attention of the big-name producers like Brooks, Goldberg, Cannell and Lupo by promising the only thing they were in a position to offer that the big three couldn't or wouldn't—creative freedom. The Fox network, they promised, would offer less censorship, and tougher programs.†

Inviting creators to pitch ideas that they felt the other broadcasters wouldn't go for, most took them at their word. For *Happy Days* scriptwriters Michael Moye and Ron Leavitt, veterans of the likes of *Diff'rent Strokes* and *Silver Spoons,* it was the chance to finally let rip and produce a totally immoral family sit-com ... and *Married—with Children* became the *All in the Family* of the late-'80s/early '90s, as Archie Bunker moved aside for Al Bundy. For Frank Lupo, it was the opportunity to let loose his dark side with *Werewolf* ("No, the *hero* is the werewolf!" he told stunned Fox execs) ... which was something of a loss to Cannell Productions, given his ability to match Cannell's superb ear for funny, witty dialogue. For his own part, Cannell kept true to form by producing a series out of what was, on paper—like *Rockford* and the *A-Team*—a highly unsuitable candidate for a heroic show. On the credibility scale, kids who were really courageous cops and cops who were really likeable kids were probably somewhere in between corporate executives who were really communists and big game hunters who were really animal rights campaigners, but if there was one TV producer who could make *The Mod Squad* work in the '80s, it was Cannell. After all, this was the guy who turned a cowardly, bad tempered ex-con p.i. into a six-year smash, and a band of Vietnam vet fugitive mercenaries into the cult heroes of the '80s. He'd given ABC a vigilante judge,

---

**A spin-off series from* Jump Street, *provisionally titled* City Court *and then later* Return of the Prince, *was to follow the cases into the courtroom, but never happened; the pilot was to guest-star Johnny Depp in a story in which Tom Hanson is accused of murder.*

†*It is interesting to note that as both Fox in the U.S. and Sky in the U.K. have grown more successful and become part of the television mainstream, they have simultaneously become more traditional and conservative now that they're part of the club.*

and NBC a rebel cop with mob connections—why not a team of juvey finks aimed at the teen market for Fox?

The show *People* magazine called "Hill Street Babes" was originally titled *Jump Street Chapel*, after the abandoned church the undercover cops use as a headquarters. Assigned to making *21 Jump Street* a reality was Patrick Hasburgh, a former Colorado ski-instructor and truck driver who had last written kid characters while working on *The Greatest American Hero*, the series on which he'd made his first sale at thirty years of age. From there, he'd dallied briefly with *The A-Team* before taking the helm of *Hardcastle and McCormick*. Even at Fox, there was some debate about how far to go, and whether the market even wanted another socially conscious cop show — particularly the teen market. Nevertheless, Hasburgh belonged to that generation that Nixon's people had allegedly tried to dupe — a generation that at least had a social conscience, if not a credible gameplan, and with the gift of hindsight through adult eyes he brought commitment and credibility to the contemporary themes that *21 Jump Street* would tackle during its three year run. "The switch," as critic Michael Hill pointed out in the *Baltimore Sun*, "is that the captain in charge is a Mod-Squadder grown up unrepentant,

So how cool are we? The cast of *21 Jump Street* model what all the hip undercover cops are wearing in the late '80s. Left to right, Holly Robinson, Dustin Nguyen, Peter De Luise, Steven Williams, Johnny Depp.

while the main kid represents the by-the-book cop." *Jump Street* "puts young-looking officers undercover in high schools investigating the kids. In *The Mod Squad,* they went after adults."

Cast as baby-faced cop Tom Hanson, the cop "who looks so young he ought to have training wheels on his police car" was cute and surly Johnny Depp. Described by *Rolling Stone* magazine as having "everything that makes little girls wriggle," he reluctantly succumbed to the inevitability of becoming America's latest in a long line of teen dreams. Coaxed into an acting career by his actor friend Nicolas Cage, Depp was pursuing a rock and roll lifestyle until he was persuaded to go along for an audition for Wes Craven's *Nightmare on Elm Street* (1984), the first of the Freddy Krueger films. He got the part, and a good experience in Oliver Stone's Vietnam war film *Platoon* hooked him. Filming of the *Jump Street* pilot was already underway with Jeff Yaegher of *V* in the lead when the producers realized the actor looked too old for the role, and began recasting, securing the reluctant and unsure Depp at the last minute. It was Cage who pointed out that a spell on *Jump Street* would give him the money and the clout to call his own shots in the years to come.

At 25 years of age, Depp—like his character—was older than he looked, but whereas baby-faced Tom Hanson had the relatively square upbringing that might be expected for a cop, Depp's own youth, according to the plethora of magazine articles he featured in, was more typically close to the edge. According to published material, he'd discovered sex at thirteen and drugs at fourteen, left school at sixteen, and survived a brief marriage shortly after. His resume then consisted of the teen-sex movie *Private Resort,* the cable TV movie *Slow Burn,* and a guest-shot in the short-lived cop series *Lady Blue.* "I had the flu so bad that day I tested for *21 Jump Street,* I didn't care, and that was the attitude they wanted!" he told journalist Jim Bawden. "I was told to hop the next plane and get to Vancouver." Required to be little more than a male bimbo, he deeply resented the teen idol image he was saddled with, and wisely used his new-found fame to segue into more substantial roles and innovative films. Following *21 Jump Street,* Depp quickly shed his teen-mag status with a role in professional sleaze merchant John Waters' off-the-wall *Cry Baby* (1990) and won critical acclaim for his portrayal of the title character in the bizarre fantasy *Edward Scissorhands* (1991). He has pursued other weirdo roles enthusiastically ever since. Enthused with youthful integrity, he refused to release one of his beloved rock and roll records while in the glare of the *Jump Street* spotlight, and the string of letters resulting from his work on the show that made him agony aunt to America's more weak and impressionable teens distressed him.

Another cast change following Depp's arrival occurred five episodes into the show, when the Jump Street cops' hippie boss Captain Jenko (Fredric Forrest) was written out. Jenko, wrote reviewer Michael Hill, "wears a leather jacket with Jim Morrison on the back, his office is plastered with Jimi Hendrix posters, and when he says 'Child is father to the man' you figure he's the only one in the office who knows that's the name of Blood, Sweat and Tears' first album."

The problem with Jenko was that he was the only one among the viewers who knew it too, and his inclusion—a sop to older demographics—was quickly deemed irrelevant when the show become a smash-hit with more difficult to reach teens, who saw not a hipster hanging on to his values, but an old hippie. Jenko was laid to rest courtesy of a drunk driver and replaced by cool, steely-eyed Captain Adam Fuller, played by Steven Williams ("a real solid, terrific actor" said Hasburgh). There was some irony to this, as Williams had himself been dropped from *his* role as Lt. Jefferson Burnett in *The Equalizer* after the first few episodes, and, while there seemed to be no antagonism about the change, Depp had previously stated that one of the reasons he was enticed to the show was the opportunity of working with Forrest.

A former salesman and model from Chicago, Williams worked in film and theater before moving to L.A. in the early '80s. His TV work before *Jump Street* included a number of TV movies and roles in *Hill Street Blues, Chicago Story, MacGyver, Dallas,* and *The Dukes of Hazzard,* as well as the Cannell series *The A-Team, Hunter* and *Stingray*. During *Jump Street's* run he also made an unmissable cameo appearance in *Wiseguy,* in a jail cell scene in "The One That Got Away" during the rock industry storyline. Later, he would take on one of his most unusual roles for the short-lived failed Cannell show *The 100 Lives of Black Jack Savage*. "I played a lot of stereotyped bad guys — pimps and cons" he told journalist Anna Marie Kukec. "Then one day I shaved off my beard and moustache and started getting roles as doctors and lawyers!" Since *Jump Street,* Williams has also kept busy, starring in the single season of cop show *L.A. Heat* and playing the enigmatic Mr. X in *The X-Files* series.

Much the same stereotyping confronted Holly Robinson, cast as Officer Judy Huffland. "At the audition, I asked if I had the right script," she told *TV Guide;* recent offers had included a hooker, a pimp's girlfriend, and a pregnant teenager. "I really thought it was a white actress' part." It was — but when Hasburgh saw Robinson, he was bowled over, and rewrote the part, and Judy Huffland became Judy Hoffs. "In walks this black kid with enormous brown eyes and a sleek body, and so intelligent she made me feel outmatched," said Hasburgh. "My old Judy began to look like a naive sap!"

"My role is colorless," said Robinson. "You could put a young white actress in every situation I've been in. People come up to me in the street to say how we've helped with their problems and I get letters all the time from girls asking for advice. If you think back to Martin Luther King's time, I'm sure you can't name one black woman that any teenage white girl would be running up to and saying 'I want to be like you when I grow up.' That's a sign that times have changed for the better."

Johnny Depp as Tom Hanson and Holly Robinson as Judy Hoffs in the teen hit *21 Jump Street*.

A budding pop singer from a show-biz family (her father was a story editor and producer on *The Cosby Show* and her mother an agent and manager), it's Robinson singing the show's theme. Her earliest show-biz memory was begging and pleading her father, then working on *Sesame Street,* to get her on the show. She blew her one line! From Big Bird as an infant, she moved on to *Howard the Duck* (1986) as a teen, working for three months and ending up with three minutes on the screen. The duck was a turkey, and it was three minutes too many. Like Depp, she had aspirations to be more famous as a singer than a TV cop, and maintained that she only auditioned for TV work to pay for her demo tapes! "It's hard for people to take you seriously in one medium when you're already well known in another," she told *TV Guide*. "I had four great years on *Jump Street,* and I felt lucky to have the role of Judy Hoffs because it wasn't stereotyped, but I'm making a conscious choice not to do more television work. I'm committed to being a singer."

Another actor to defy the script's initial stereotyping was cast as Officer Doug Penhall. "Hanson is assigned to a small squad of young cops who infiltrate youth gangs," wrote Martin Burden in the *Washington Post*. "The rest of the squad is the usual mix so dear to army movies — a black, an Oriental, and the big loud guy." The big loud guy was Peter DeLuise, son of oversized comedian Dom DeLuise, and originally hired to play the big *fat* guy until he turned up for shooting several pounds lighter.

Just as Cannell and Hasburgh's Judy Huffland had transformed from early publicity releases' idiotic "lady cop whose beauty causes criminals to look at least twice" into "a compassionate, well-educated black woman who rejects her roots to be a cop"(?), so DeLuise's typical smart-mouthed slob of a thousand and one dud teen-films transformed from someone who "seems to be just another pudgy teenager but is an experienced cop who knows the score" into "a wisecracking rookie cop." A fellow biker and friend of the moody Depp, DeLuise had already chalked up roles in the films *Solar Warriors, Free Ride,* and *Hot Stuff,* with TV guest shots in *Diff'rent Strokes* and *Facts of Life*. Like Robinson, he had an early TV role with his father, portraying a junior version of DeLuise Sr., at the end of a comedy skit; later, Hasburgh would cast him on *seaQuest*. His real-life girlfriend — and later wife — Gina Nemo was cast in the series later as Penhall's girlfriend.

Completing the cast was Dustin Nguyen, who had previously guested on *The A-Team, Shell Game,* and *Magnum,* and had featured in a recurring role on the daytime soap *General Hospital*. Nguyen was to play Japanese-American cop H.T. Ioki (the H.T. stood for Harry Truman!), who — following DeLuise's post-casting transformation — lost the wisecracking label and underwent a minor transformation to a shyer, quieter soul. Another offspring of a showbiz family, Nguyen is a black belt in the martial arts, and his film work includes *Good Morning, Vietnam*. "I was lucky to get started quick and with good parts," he told Ivy Miller of *Modern Screen*. "My first part was a two-hour *Magnum*. After that, it was hard to do gang leaders and other stereotypical roles. When I was offered the role of Ioki, I was being offered a lot of movies at the time, but everyone told me I'd be making a big career mistake if I turned it down. They were right, I've never regretted it." Although Nguyen was Vietnamese by birth, the character of H.T. Ioki was Japanese until a memorable Christmas episode, "Christmas in Saigon," revealed him to be an illegal Vietnamese immigrant, with some scenes based on Nguyen's own harrowing experiences when his family fled their homeland after the war due to his father's work on a U.S. radio station. "Basically it was a propaganda station to discourage the Viet Cong to defect to the South ... so, politically, my father was not very popular with the new establishment!" Nguyen told journalist Monika Guttman. Unlike Ioki's parents in the episode, his family survived the escape, and are all American citizens. With the flashback scenes involving explosives and action, Nguyen was obliged to play Ioki at fourteen years of age himself. "Being able to do that two-part special about escaping Saigon was great for me," he told *Modern Screen.* "It was a real release, a real catharsis. I keep my real feelings bottled up a lot, so it really helped me to do that show."

Careful not to point the finger either at kids, parents or teachers, but also not to weasel out of apportioning blame or taking a stand either, *Jump Street* quickly caught the attention of its youthful audience as much for its honesty as its pretty cast. The series consequently managed to keep the cake and eat it, winning numerous awards and accolades from various concerned organizations for its constructive and credible portrayals of the blotches on the teenage skin of society. Speaking to interviewer Frank Spotnitz for *US* magazine, Holly Robinson said, "Sometimes there are happy endings, and we hate 'em! We cringe when we read those happy endings!"

The series pulled no punches in tackling racism, runaways, sexual promiscuity, drugs, substance abuse, illiteracy, child molestation, date rape, child porn, steroids, teenage pregnancies, incest, interracial dating, parental kidnapping, child prostitution and gang violence. Many shows dealing with a contentious topic closed by giving a hot-line number for kids to call relating to that problem. While '80s kids were more conservative than their '60s and '70s counterparts, the cast regretfully admitted that society had reached the point where undercover cops in high schools were genuinely necessary, an unpleasant reality of contemporary America. The kids may be squarer, but they grow up faster, and in more dangerous times.

"We know it's difficult to grow up now," said DeLuise. "I just got out of high school three years ago. Our show, in its music, clothing, and style gives an accurate picture of what it's like in high school today. When kids see the clothes and they know they're right, and they hear the music and know it's right, then maybe they'll think the message is right too." *Jump Street,* Hasburgh told the *New York Post,* "won't be as controversial as I originally would have liked. We both bent a little." Citing "huge fights at Fox," Hasburgh announced, "They want to be responsible and not offend the Moral Majority, but when kids react to a friend's suicide, they don't say 'Golly Gee.' I don't want some conservative station owner in Iowa telling the audience what to watch. If people are offended, they can turn me off, but don't censor me."

"We had to fight the network to let us be as ballsy and as gutsy as we wanted to be," confirmed Robinson in an interview for *TV Guide,* whose budding romance and bedroom scene with Peter DeLuise was disallowed by the network; "Our original script would probably be acceptable to them now," Hasburgh lamented some months later to *US* magazine.

"Graphically showing, rather than artfully implying has been the way Fox's *21 Jump Street* has taken to the screen," wrote reviewer Miles Beller in *Hollywood Reporter.* "The series has tried to be 'relevant' while fostering a *cadre* of adolescent heart-throbs whom young viewers can lust after. An irresistible jittery energy surges through the weekly show — a factor that is beyond traditional elements such as story or plot — catapulting the viewer into the show's milieu with undeniable force."

"Fox picked an experienced team," wrote Don Merrill in *TV Guide,* praising the presence of Cannell and Hasburgh, "who worked together on *Hardcastle and McCormick* and *The A-Team,* and their expertise is evident in what appears on the screen." "Like *Miami Vice,* the series uses popular rock music to enhance the story," wrote journalist Sandra Knipe, "but *Jump Street* doesn't have to rely on videos to substitute for a literate script."

"We're the number one show in the country for teenagers," enthused Hasburgh to the *Washington Post* at the start of the second season. "I'm real proud of that. We're doing real drama for kids, without wrapping them up neatly at the end. Kids like to be talked to like adults. My concern is that I don't want to come off sounding pretentious. We're not trying to preach."

Williams, Depp, and Robinson all accompanied real cops in the back seat of a patrol car during their preparation for the series, and it proved to be a sobering experience for all concerned. But everybody on the show was insistent that the moment they tried to deliver lectures, they'd be washed up. "I thought the show would be about busting a friend for smoking a joint in the bathroom," Robinson told the *New York Post*. "In one hour, I saw four gang murders, a drug-related suicide, and a car chase. All the perpetrators were under sixteen. Besides," she laughed, "the way we portray the bad guys, you can't help but like us!"

"Getting through adolescence has never been easy," Williams told the *Denver Weekly News,* "but it's never been as hard as it is today. Kids are bombarded by problems — drugs, child abuse, absent parents, peer pressure.... Sure, they make a lot of problems for themselves, but even worse are the adults who go into the high schools to prey upon and exploit our children."

"The typical thing is for a parent to point his finger and say 'don't'," DeLuise told a Sacramento paper. "We don't do that. We show what happens if you *do*. When I was in high school, you weren't popular unless you did cocaine. I was captain of the football team, but I was a social outcast because I didn't do dope." "The way we were back then," Williams told journalist K.J. Scotta, "we thought we could use drugs to make the world better. We may have been stupid, but that's what we thought. Our hearts were in the right place, even if our heads weren't!"

But not all the *Jump Street* plots were standard dope-related themes. As well as the usual cop show scenarios (the team hunt a pyromaniac, bust an auto ring, get taken hostage, guard star athletes and even aid a defector during the first season), more adventurous episodes include Paul Bernbaum's "Bad Influence," which has Ioki joining the macho locker-room element of a gym class to track down a teenage hooker working her way through the school, and Clifton Campbell's "16 Blown to 35," in which the team break up an underage pornography ring. At least two episodes deal with drunk driving and the tragic consequences, while "Higher Education," by E. Paul Edwards, focuses on teenage pregnancies. Racists and homophobes received a well-deserved dressing down throughout the series, and the highly praised "Little Disease with a Big Name," by Hasburgh, has been hailed as one of the most perceptive and constructive U.S. TV episodes to deal sensitively and non-exploitatively with the subject of AIDS, when a schoolkid who has the disease is ostracized by the locals who don't want him to continue attending the school. "I struggled with the blood transfusion angle," Hasburgh told *Emmy* magazine, "but halfway through I decided to turn it around, to say that he was homosexual, that he was a guy we like and we know, and he got the disease the way most people get it. I felt I had to deal with the subject honestly. The whole point is that the only way we're going to beat AIDS is out of love."

Another prominently praised episode was "The Best Years of Your Life," written by Jonathan Lemkin and directed by Bill Cocoran, dealing with the cause, effects, and emotional fallout of a teenage suicide. Each character in the story represents a different reaction as observed by researchers into the phenomenon of teen suicide, the highest cause of adolescent death in the U.S., even above drugs. There are those who see the act as heroic, or are romantically inclined to copy it for attention, while others blame themselves for their colleague's death, or become depressed themselves because of it. Hanson is tormented by the notion that he might have been able to prevent it (he and Penhall were undercover in the school at the time), while Penhall suffers from having memories of his mother's suicide vividly recalled. If the episode has any failings, it is probably also the show's virtue — it panders to teenage self-absorption and self-pity.

Inevitably, the show was liberally decorated with contemporary chart sounds from the popular bands of the day, and equally inevitably the series was rich in self-obsessed, self-pitying teen angst, with the pilot film offering a sharply observed portrait of a spoilt suburban kid indulging in drugs-related teen rebellion. Before long, he's out of his element, and being menaced by big time drug dealers, for whom drugs mean serious money rather than teen protest. The series often employed the A-plot, B-plot structure of other "message shows" such as *M*A*S*H* and *Lou Grant* in most episodes, with the heavy themes of the main storyline interspersed with a comic or romantic plotline to lighten and contrast. During the course of the series, most of the team have romantic entanglements, and in one unusual episode, "Chapel of Love," written by Jonathan Lemkin and Bill Nuss, the guys sit around in the station house playing cards and relating worst-case scenario bad date stories. Other storylines included a sexually abused teenager whose policeman father is the target of her bitter plan for revenge; a community where born-again wackos (lead by Dann Florek of *L.A. Law* and *Law and Order*) are burning school science books; false accusations of rape; and a neighborhood watch group that goes over the top.

Novelty shows included "Wooly Bullies," written by Bruce Kirschbaum, Eric Blakeney, and Bill Nuss, and directed by Bill Cocoran, in which each Jump Streeter narrates a flashback story relating to how they dealt with bullying incidents in their childhood, "High High" written by Eric Blakeney and Bill Nuss, and directed by Mario Van Peebles, in which the team have to demonstrate various skills while working undercover at a performing arts school (Booker becomes a performance artist, Ioki a video film-maker, Penhall and Hoffs join acting class, and Hanson plays guitar), "Back from the Future," written by David Stenn and directed by Peter DeLuise, in which a youngster fifty years into the future interviews the now elderly Jump Street cops about their careers, and "How I Saved the Senator," written by Gary Rosen and directed by James Whitmore, Jr., in which each Jump Street cop tells a different and wildly exaggerated story about the same arrest.

"I liked the pilot," said Depp. "We were all getting to know one another, and it was a great time. But my very favorite episode was one called "Orpheus Three Point Three," where my girlfriend gets shot and killed, and I have to make a decision in my own mind whether I had time enough to save her or not. I have to make a decision whether I'm going to track this killer down on my own, or let the law take its course."

At the start of the third season in 1988, a new team member was introduced as Richard Grieco made his debut as Officer Dennis Booker. Opinions differed as to exactly why Grieco had been brought in to join the existing cast. Mostly, the character was supposed to introduce a new element to the show, a spark that would shake up the regular cast. "He's an intense egomaniac whose unorthodox style and interpretation of the justice system leave a lot to be desired," said Grieco of his role. "Booker will be the kind of guy who knows how to push people's buttons," said producer Steve Beers. "He is a good cop, but he enjoys turmoil. His guest role will be explosive."

This Booker achieved, but not necessarily in the way intended. Having recently been vocal about the quality of some of the scripts and the lack of material for Nguyen and Robinson, adding fresh competition for screentime just didn't add up for the existing cast. Furthermore, Johnny Depp, reluctant teen idol and budding movie star, had been making noises about moving on — he wasn't even too keen about being the focal point of the show. "Look at shows like *L.A. Law* or *St. Elsewhere,*" he objected, "They use everybody!"

"I've been doing mainstream television for three and a half years now," Depp told *TV Guide*. "I don't think I have more to offer that type of thing any more. I can't hold the revolver any differently ... I've had six nervous breakdowns on the show, I've lost a father on the show, I've lost girls on the show.... Oh, and I've also murdered someone and went to prison for it. I think Hanson should be put in a mental institution, or someone should put him to death!"

"Johnny Depp really altered the mood of the cast," said Holly Robinson. "He wasn't into it. He wanted to go and be a big movie star. It was like pulling teeth just to get him to be happy on the set." "It's obvious, isn't it?" Peter DeLuise told *USA Today*. "This guy has been brought in as insurance in case Johnny leaves."

"I can only go to high school for so long," Depp had told *Modern Screen* some years earlier. "I have to age at some point. If the show ever got fluffy or started to lie or mislead people, and not remain true to its original intention, that's when I wouldn't want to be a part of it. As long as we stick to our guns and send out the right messages, I'm there." "We're not thinking of Grieco as a replacement," retorted Fox exec Kevin Wendle. "We brought him in to creatively stir up the ensemble and add some new dramatic tension."

In one episode ("Nemesis," written by John Truby and directed by Ken Wiederhorn), Booker is involved in an undercover operation when the gang he has infiltrated become aware that a spy is in their midst, but finger — and murder — the wrong gang member, giving Booker a severe case of self-doubt. In a thoughtful character piece, he also discovers that he can tell a girl he is romancing for information that he loves her, but can't say the words to his real girlfriend.

21 Jump Street was canceled in 1990 due to a sudden outbreak of corporate bravado, and while the decision was ultimately regretted (Fox flirted with the idea of reviving the show, and Robinson, DeLuise and Williams were all ready to return), the series was never restored to the schedule. A move to Monday nights to accommodate the Richard Grieco spin-off *Booker* was a mistake, and resulted in the demise of both shows, but by the time the error was assessed, a worthy replacement had been found for both Depp and *Jump Street* in the form of the series *Beverly Hills 90210* and series star Jason Priestley; both Priestley and his co-star Shannen Doherty had guested on *Jump Street,* as had other up-and-coming new faces including Josh Brolin (*Private Eye, The Young Riders*), Sherilyn Fenn (*Twin Peaks*), Christina Applegate (*Married — with Children*), Blair Underwood (*L.A. Law*), Billy Warlock (*Baywatch*), John J. York (*Werewolf*), Bridget Fonda, Brad Pitt, Vince Vaughn, and Mario Van Peebles. *Beverly Hills 90210* owed much of its attitude and content to the ground broken by Hasburgh and *Jump Street,* and ironically, it came to Fox from Aaron "*Mod Squad*" Spelling's new company.

"They encouraged me to do some controversial issues," stressed Hasburgh, "but they asked me to make the show more fun, entertaining, and less socially conscious. In fairness, I'm not sure my original show would have worked. I didn't fully appreciate the kind of impact real controversial programming would have at 7:00." "*The Mod Squad* was too serious," Holly Robinson told Jill Brooke for the *New York Post*. "They never smiled. We have lots of laughs on this show!"

However, Hasburgh's no-preaching, social issues approach paid off. The supposedly risky and contentious AIDS episode gained the series its highest ever ratings, and the series regularly trounced softer fare on the big three networks, gleefully exploiting Fox's exclusion from the family hour obligations of its rivals.

But there were other less mercenary rewards, too. "Last year we ran a show on sexual abuse, and that night the hot line got 6,000 calls," Hasburgh told journalists proudly. "The average number is 900. With the one we ran involving under-age porn, two porn rings in the mid–West got busted. Films of that episode are being used as training films across the country for police officers. We're getting letters from teachers who use our show as a classroom exercise." "The best thing about the series," Depp told *TV Guide,* "is getting positive fan letters. We've gotten tons of response on shows we've done on sexual abuse and cocaine — calls to the cocaine hot line went way up after we did a show on it. Maybe we can make a difference." "*Jump Street* never takes the easy way out," said Robinson to *TV Guide.* "That's one of the things I like about the show."

"We're not preaching," said Depp, echoing the rest of the cast. "In high school, everyone is impressionable and susceptible. We're saying, we are going to show you something here, take a look and tell us what you think. What looks right to you? What looks wrong to you?" "We lose kids to the first person who tells them they're special," said Steven Williams, ruefully quoting a line of his dialogue from Clifton Campbell's first season story "16 Blown to 35." "Why can't it be the parent who delivers that message?"

Episode Guide

regular and recurring cast: Johnny Depp (Tom Hanson), Peter DeLuise (Doug Penhall), Dustin Nguyen (H.T. Ioki), Holly Robinson (Judy Hoffs), Steven Williams (Captain Adam Fuller), Richard Grieco (Dennis Booker), Michael Bendetti ("Mac" McCann), Michael DeLuise (Joey Penhall), Sal Jenco (Sal "Blowfish" Banducci), Gina Nemo (Dorothy Pezzino), Dorothy Parke (Amy Pearson), Yvette Nipar (Jackie Garrett), Marcia Rodd (Mrs. Hanson), Linda Darlow (Mrs. Booker), Mindy Cohn (Rosa Banducci), Frederic Forrest (Captain Richard Jenko), Frank McCarthy (Captain Brody), Kurtwood Smith (Spencer Phillips), David Barry Gray (Dean Garrett), Alexandra Powers (Katie Rocky), Tony Dakota (Clavo)

First Season (1987)

Pilot

wr. Patrick Hasburgh, dir. Kim Manners

Cop Tommy Hanson looks five years younger than he really is, and the bad guys are laughing so hard they can't shoot straight — it's putting his fellow cops at risk. Turning a disadvantage into a plus, Hanson is assigned to a squad of youthful undercover cops based in a church who pose as high-school students to cope with juvenile crime. Hanson has to learn how to be a kid all over again ... or blow his cover.

with Frank McCarthy, Barney Martin, Claude Earl Jones, Charles Payne, Reginald T. Dorsey, Brandon Douglas, Cheryl Anderson, Scott Kraft, Niles Brewster, Noelle Harling

America, What a Town

wr. Bill Nuss, dir. Larry Shaw

Hanson and Penhall are assigned to break up an auto-theft ring, while Hoffs is given the supposedly easier task of looking after a foreign visitor to the U.S. ... but it doesn't work out that way.

with Tracy Lin, Billy Jacoby, Steve Antin, Ray Abruzzo, Merek Czuma, Dale Wilson, Paula Brooke, Robert Miranda

Don't Pet the Teacher

wr. Clifton Campbell, dir. Les Sheldon

Hanson, posing as a student, finds himself falling for his teacher — an "older woman" as far as she's concerned — while at the same time she's being plagued by the unwanted attentions of a mysterious admirer.

with Leah Ayres, Tony Mockus, Mark Lowenthal, Geoffrey Blake, Lillian Lehman

My Future's So Bright, I Gotta Wear Shades

wr. Bill Nuss, dir. Gary Winter

Hanson and Penhall go undercover in an expensive private school to investigate the murder of a local girl.

with Josh Brolin, David Oliver, Jamie Bozian, John DiAquino, Robyn Stevan, Norman Alden, Mitchell Anderson, Linda Darlow, William Samples, Anthony Holland (later in the series, Linda Darlow appears as Booker's mother)

The Worst Night of Your Life

wr. Patrick Hasburgh, dir. Rob Bowman

The Jump Street cops are assigned to find a high-school firebug before the night of the school prom.

with Troy Beyer, Lezlie Dean, Winifred Freedman, Mary Gregory, Jackson Davis, Jane McDougall, Kerry Remsen

Gotta Finish the Riff

wr. Patrick Hasburgh, Bill Nuss, dir. Kim Manners

Recovering from the death of Captain Jenko, killed by a drunk driver, the Jump Street cops are ill-prepared for the tougher Captain Fuller ... then Hanson and Hoffs are taken hostage while undercover in a school riot.

with Blair Underwood, Robert Picardo, Panchito Gomez, Lance Slaughter, Richard McKenzie

Bad Influence

wr. Paul Bernbaum, dir. Kim Manners

Holly and Ioki investigate reports that a young girl has become a classroom hooker, while Hanson and Penhall pursue two youngsters who are on a joyride with twelve thousand dollars...!

with Liane Curtis, Scott Schwartz, Byron Thames, Anne Wyndham, David Kagen, Tom Schell, Hagan Beggs

Blindsided

wr. Jonathan Lemkin, dir. David Jackson

While posing as an aggressive lout, Hanson is offered a huge sum of money from one of the pupils to kill her father, who has been sexually abusing her.

with Sherilyn Fenn, Harold P. Pruett, Courtney Gains, Robert Hallack, Tom O'Rourke, Jim McKrell

Next Generation

wr. Paul Bernbaum, dir. David Nutter

The Jump Street cops investigate a young man following in the footsteps of his father — as an extortionist operating a protection racket — and Penhall gets a taste of fatherhood when he babysits for a stranded stewardess.

with Stephen Gregory, Andy Romano, Jane Windsor, Michael Ensign, Jason Lively, Ned Bellamy, Dale Robins

Low and Away

wr. Bill Nuss, Paul Bernbaum, dir. Bill Cocoran

The Jump Street cops are assigned to protect a student who's a whiz at both his studies and baseball ... but they haven't been told why he's at risk.

with Patrick Breen, Michael Fairman, Tom O'Brien, Kurtwood Smith, Al White, Dorothy Fielding

16 Blown to 35

wr. Clifton Campbell, dir. James Whitmore, Jr.

Holly infiltrates an underage school pornography operation (director and Cannell regular James Whitmore, Jr. puts in an unaccredited cameo appearance in the teaser as one of the cops).

with Lisa Fuller, David Paymer, Sarah G. Buxton, David Raynr, Tasia Valenza, Gayle Harbor

Mean Streets and Pastel Houses

wr. Jonathan Lemkin, dir. James Whitmore, Jr.

Hanson puts himself at risk when he joins a vicious punk gang.

with Steve Marshall, David Sherrill, Bradley Gregg, Jason Oliver, Jason Priestley, Greg James, William Taylor, Jeff Schultz

Second Season (1987–'88)

In Custody of a Clown

wr. Clifton Campbell, dir. Kim Manners

A frightening kidnapping outside a junior school turns out to be a grandfather taking his son away from two bickering parents in the throes of a messy divorce and custody battle.

with Barney Martin, Joshua Miller, Robert Hooks, Ray Walston, Lillian Lehman, Kurtwood Smith, Caren Kaye, Robert Lipton, Jerry Wasserman

Beseiged (two parts)

wr. Jonathan Lemkin, dir. Bill Corcoran

The Jump Street cops investigate the death of a teenage drug dealer who got his girlfriend addicted to crack, while Penhall is partnered with a cop he's afraid may be a vigilante killer.

with Bruce Young, Renee Jones, Josh Richman, Carlos Cervantes

Two for the Road

wr. Paul Bernbaum, dir. Steve Beers

When a young teenager severely injures his best friend after crashing a car while drunk driving, he commits a mercy killing to honor a pact they made.

with Rob Stone, Pauly Shore, Alan Miller, Susan Ursitti, Lynne Moody, Bill Dow

After School Special

wr. and dir. David Jackson

Fuller and Hoffs go undercover as teacher and student to investigate the shooting of a teacher, only to have to prevent the teacher and his colleagues from taking revenge.

with Keith Amos, Patrick Cronin, Kenneth Edwards, Thomas Ryan, Sheryl Piland, Marcia Rodd, James Staley, Michele Goodger

Higher Education

wr. E. Paul Edwards, dir. Larry Shaw

To cover up a rape, a teenage girl accuses Ioki of having made her pregnant.

with Christianne Hirt, Deborah Wakeham, Michael Horton, Michael MacRae, Gretchen Corbett, Joel Colodner, Ross Schafer

Don't Stretch the Rainbow

wr. Patrick Hasburgh, dir. Kim Manners

The Jump Street cops try to ease tensions at a high school where a race riot is brewing.

with Gretchen Palmer, Ned Vaughn, Alvin Alexis, J.A. Preston, Hal Havins, Barry Sobel

Honor Bound

wr. Stephen J. Abert, Scott Smith, E. Paul Edwards, dir. Bill Corcoran

The Jump Street cops go undercover to put a stop to a series of assaults on homosexuals by a gang of louts from a nearby military academy.

with Bo Foxworth, Manfred Melcher, Dean Hamilton, Charles Boswell

You Oughtta Be In Prison

wr. Bill Nuss, dir. Kim Manners

Hanson is assigned to protect a Hollywood film star, but they are both kidnapped by a fugitive.

with Tom Brenahan, Reginald Dorsey, Annie Oringer, Shannon Tweed, Bart Braverman, Tony Todd

How Much Is That Body in the Window?

wr. Clifton Campbell, dir. Neal Fearnley

The Jump Street cops investigate the supply of steroids to a high school athletics team.

with John Doolittle, Forry Smith, Dorothy Parke, Geri Betzler, Dan Gauthier, Carolyn Mignini

Christmas in Saigon

wr. Bill Nuss, dir. Kim Manners

Ioki is exposed as a Vietnam refugee, rather than the Japanese officer everybody thought he was.

with Arthur Taxier, Haunani Minn, Keone Young, Mindy Cohn, Marcia Rodd, Dorothy Parke, C.K. Tan, Joseph Hieu, Paul Jarrett

Fear and Loathing with Russell Buckins

wr. Gary Skeen Hall, dir. Kevin Hooks

The usually straight-as-an-arrow Hanson starts behaving uncharacteristically, while under the influence of a freewheeling high-school chum from his past.

with Angelo Tiffe, Marc Alaimo, Anthony Starke, Liz Keifer, Ivan Kane

A Big Disease with a Little Name

wr. Patrick Hasburgh, dir. Neill Fearnley

Hanson is assigned to protect an embittered AIDS sufferer who has been ostracized from his community and his school.

with Philip Tanzini, Gary Beyer, Janet Carroll, Deborah Sandlund

Chapel of Love

wr. Jonathan Lemkin, Bill Nuss, dir. Mike Robinson

A dateless Jump Street team gather for a Valentine's Day poker game and relate the stories of their worst ever dates.

with Deborah Lacey, Kent McCord, Carmine Caridi, Liz Sagal, Jean Sagal, Mindy Cohn, Tom Wright, Robert Costanzo, Bradford English, Ken Olfson

I'm Okay, You Need Work

wr. Clifton Campbell, dir. Neill Fearnley

Hanson investigates stories of abuse at a psychiatric center for disturbed adolescents after discovering that one youngster has been placed there by his parents after a bad episode with drugs.

with Brandon Douglas, James Stephens, Richard McGonagle, Christina Applegate, Allen Williams, Todd Eric Andrews

ORPHEUS 3.3 (a.k.a. The Convenience Killer)

wr. Bill Nuss, dir. James Contner

Hanson cracks up following the murder of his girlfriend Amy during a hold-up (this episode writes out the character of Amy played by Dorothy Parke).

with Brent Jennings, Frank Annese, Dorothy Parke, Art Hindle, Scott Kraft

CHAMPAGNE HIGH

wr. Paul Bernbaum, dir. Larry Shaw

The Jump Street cops encounter a shoplifting rich kid and an impoverished yuppie while trying to solve the theft of a Porsche that threatens to disrupt a bussing scheme from a poor neighborhood.

with Charles Stratton, Andrew Ross, Peter Berg, Andrew Koenig, Gabe Jarret, Philip Richard Allen

BROTHER HANSON AND THE MIRACLE OF RENNERS POND

wr. Eric Paul Jones, dir. Bill Corcoran

Hanson investigates book-burning after the discovery that a schoolteacher is preaching Genesis rather than teaching the theory of evolution.

with Dann Florek, David Greenlee, Gregory Itzin, Patti Johns, Cami Cooper, Bruce French

PRIVATEERS AND PUBLIC SCHOOLS

wr. Jonathan Lemkin, dir. Bill Corcoran

Judy Hoffs comes close to getting too personally involved with a drug smuggler she has been romancing while undercover.

with Christian Clemenson, Mark Arnott, Noah Blake, Dennis Moynahan, Sam McMurray

BEST YEARS OF YOUR LIFE

wr. Jonathan Lemkin, dir. Bill Corcoran

Memories of his mother's suicide return to haunt Penhall when a teenage burglar the team have apprehended kills himself.

with H. Richard Greene, Brad Pitt, Cheryl Pollak, Tiffany Helm, Carey Scott, Laura Austin, Trevor Weaver, Gina Nemo

CORY AND DEAN GOT MARRIED

wr. Clifton Campbell, dir. Kim Manners

When a young girl is taken into custody after her teenage husband-to-be escapes an attempt to arrest him for murder, he takes Hoffs hostage for an exchange.

with Rainbow Harvest, Kevin Wixted, Joseph Whipp, Frances E. Williams, Gina Nemo

SCHOOL'S OUT

wr. Eric Blakeney, dir. Kim Manners

It looks like the end of the team when the authorities debate the closure of the Jump Street operation.

with Kris Kamm, Elaine Wilkes, Sam Anderson, Michael Laskin, Max Perlich, Gina Nemo

Third Season (1988–'89)

FUN WITH ANIMALS

wr. Eric Blakeney, dir. James Whitmore, Jr.

Hanson suspects a new officer on the team of being involved in the racially-motivated crime they are trying to solve.

with Ken Abraham, Todd Bryant, Lossen Chambers, Janet Hubert, Antony Holland

SLIPPIN' INTO DARKNESS
(a.k.a. Date with an Angel)

wr. Clifton Campbell, dir. James Contner

A vigilante gang attempting to avenge the death of their leader are unaware of the presence of Jump Street undercover cops in the drug operation they are attempting to close down, and ruin the arrest.

with Richard Coca, Leo Rossi, Tim Russ, Tony Colitti, Jaime Gomez, Mark Aaron Eliot, William Taylor, Gerry Bean, Deryl Hayes, Jerry Wasserman, Bill Ontiveros, Steffania Ciccone, Matt Hill, Roman Podhora, Gloria Reuben, Mike Andaluz

THE CURRENCY WE TRADE IN

wr. Eric Blakeney, dir. Neill Fearnley

Penhall pursues a sports writer accused of sexually abusing his daughter relentlessly, only to discover that the man is innocent.

with Richard Holden, Peri Gilpin, Michelle Joyner, David Froman, Art Frankel, Jay Brazeau, Garwin Sanford, Stephen E. Miller

COACH OF THE YEAR

wr. Bill Nuss, dir. James Whitmore, Jr.

When a footballer is permanently crippled, Penhall and Booker investigate charges of criminal negligence against the Coach.

with Scott Allan Campbell, Gary Lahti, Charles Cyphers, Michael Laskin, Cliff Bemis, Linda Darlow

WHOSE CHOICE IS IT, ANYWAY?

wr. David Abramowitz, Michelle Ashford, dir. Bill Corcoran

Hoffs poses as a pregnant teenager to investigate the vandalizing of pregnancy clinics.

with Stacy Edwards, James Sutorius, Jill Andres, Dana Ashbrook, Sarah Essex

Hell Week

wr. Bill Nuss, dir. Jonathan Wacks

The Jump Street cops join a number of college fraternity houses and endure the absurd initiation pledges to tease out the identity of a rapist.

with Doug McKeon, Gary Hershberger, Greg Kean Williams, Deborah Goodrich, Peter Fox, Mark Sussman, Allan David Fox

The Dragon and the Angel

wr. E. Paul Edwards, dir. Jefferson Kibbee

Ioki infiltrates a gang running a protection racket, and in a staged robbery to assist Ioki in establishing a cover, Hanson is accidentally shot by Penhall.

with Russell Wong, Danny Kamekona, Andrew-Huy Nguyen, Kelly Hu

The Blue Flu

wr. Clifton Campbell, dir. Bill Cocoran

The Jump Street team have some spare time on their hands when the police force must go on strike.

with Robert Romanus, Art Metrano, Kevin Dunn, John Lindstrom, Brian Walton

Swallowed Alive

wr. Eric Blakeney, dir. James Contner

The Jump Street cops go undercover in a juvenile penitentiary to discover how drugs are getting in to the inmates, and Penhall has serious doubts about the system he works within.

with Ian Tracey, Duane Davis, Michael Champion, Joshua Cox, Jeremy Roberts, Tim Henry, Randi Brooks

What About Love?

wr. Michelle Ashford, dir. David Jackson

Penhall moves in with Ioki after his wife throws him out, while Judy inadvertently falls for a married man and ends up making accusations of sexual harassment.

with Michael Laskin, Bobby Hosea

Woolly Bullies

wr. Bruce Kirschbaum, Eric Blakeney, Bill Nuss, dir. Bill Corcoran

When Penhall confronts a bully in the course of his undercover investigations, it provokes other members of the team to recall incidents of bullying in their youth.

with Larenz Tate, Casey Ellison, Maia Brewton, R.J. Williams, Michael DeLuise, Dom DeLuise, Luke Edwards, John Lavachielli, Marcie Warren, Christopher Titus

The Return of Russell Buckins

Marc Abraham, Paul Bernbaum, dir. Rob Iscove

Hanson is distraught to find that his old friend, tearaway, journalist, and bad influence Russell Buckins has written an exposé about the Jump Street operation, which results in his suspension. Hanson finds Buckins at the home of a wealthy politician, where he is about to marry into money.

with Angelo Tiffe, Jane Sibbett, Joseph Campanella, Joseph Kell, Arthur Malet

AWOL

wr. Peter L. Dixon, Glen Morgan, James Wong, dir. Mike Robinson

Captain Fuller's old army buddy turns up absent without leave, and Penhall and Hanson are assigned to get him back before being officially declared a deserter.

with Patrick Labyorteaux, Harrison Page

Nemesis

wr. John Truby, dir. Ken Wiederhorn

Booker infiltrates a drugs gang, but when the kids suspect the presence of a police officer within their number, Booker suffers the guilt when they kill one of their group under the impression that he was the informer.

with Doug Greenall, Krista Errickson, Craig Hurley, Daniel Beer, Olivia Barash, Diana Barton, Cal Evans, Savannah Smith Boucher, Linda Darlow, Gilbert Desautels, John Novak, Franklin Johnson

Fathers and Sons

wr. John Truby, dir. Jefferson Kibbee

The leader of a group of kids doing cocaine turns out to be the son of the Mayor, who steps in to stop the Jump Street operation.

with Ricky Paull Goldin, Michael Laskin, Timothy Owen, Bobbie Eakes, Steve Prutting, Warren Selko

High High

wr. Eric Blakeney, Bill Nuss, dir. Mario Van Peebles

A performing arts school is threatened with closure when it is discovered that drug-taking is rife, and the Jump Street team must discover their hidden talents to pose as students; Booker becomes a performance artist, Ioki a video film-maker, Penhall and Hoffs join acting class, and Hanson plays guitar.

with Michael Des Barres, David Coburn, Philip Linton, Michael Harris, Michael Bowen, Tom Fridley, Jackson Davies

BLINDED BY THE THOUSAND POINTS OF LIGHT

wr. Glen Morgan, James Wong, dir. Jorge Montesi

The Jump Street cops encounter homeless runaways while trying to catch a vicious man offering money for abusive sex.

with Damon Martin, Bridget Fonda, Neil Barry, Heather Fairfield, Darin Morgan, Robert Sampson, M. Scott Wilkinson

NEXT VICTIM

wr. Bruce Kirschbaum, dir. James Contner

Booker and Hoffs go undercover to take opposing sides in a vicious battle between racist agitators and their militant opponents.

with Calvin Levels, Brian Bloom, Paul Abbott, John Zarchen

LOC'D OUT (two parts)

wr. John Truby, Glen Morgan, James Wong, Eric Blakeney, Michelle Ashford, Bill Nuss, dir. James Whitmore, Jr.

Ioki is in critical condition after being shot following a drive-by shooting. Hanson goes undercover to break the gangs, but ends up on the run after shooting a corrupt cop.

with Gerardo Mejia, Andrew Lauer, James Whitmore, Jr., Claude Brooks, Conor O'Farrell, J.W. Fails, T. Rogers, Frank Sanchez, Jr., Margot Rose, Robert Krantz, Marcia Rodd, Barry Primus

Fourth Season (1989–'90)

DRAW THE LINE

wr. Glen Morgan, James Wong, dir. Kim Manners

Having been found guilty of murder following the close of last season's two-part story "Loc'd Out," Hanson finds himself in prison, exposed as a cop; in the meantime, Booker stumbles on to the identity of the true murderer, ends up unjustly persecuted for breaking department regulations to clear Hanson, and resigns from the force rather than take an unfair punishment (note: at this point, the Booker character gets his own series, which lasted one season).

with Conor O'Farrell, Greg Callahan, Robert Romanus, Rich Hebert, Stu Nahan

SAY IT AIN'T SO, PETE

wr. Bill Nuss, dir. Jefferson Kibbee

Penhall goes undercover as a doorman at a local college bar where customers have been beaten up.

with Robert Estes, Jill Carroll, Rick Aiello, Stu Nahan

ETERNAL FLAME

wr. David Stenn, dir. Mario Van Peebles

Hanson is made the manager of a night-spot he is working in undercover, and becomes involved with an ex-flame, now married to the owner of the club.

with Tracy Griffith, Thomas Haden Church, Kim Valentine, Michael Des Barres, Mario Van Peebles

COME FROM THE SHADOWS

wr. Sharon Elizabeth Doyle, Larry Barber, Paul Barber, dir. David Nutter

While investigating a black market in babies, Penhall gets involved with a young woman from El Salvador and marries her so that she can stay in the U.S.

with Kristoffer Tabori, Billy Warlock, Tony Plana, Kamala Lopez, Julie Warner, Barbara Tarbuck

GOD IS A BULLET

wr. John Truby, dir. Jefferson Kibbee

Penhall and Hoffs argue over the tactics of a new get-tough principal when they go undercover in the crisis-hit school he has inherited to clean up.

with Richard Cummings, Jr., Tim Thomerson, Christopher M. Brown, Anthony Thompkins, Dayna Winston

OLD HAUNTS IN A NEW AGE

wr. Glen Morgan, James Hong, dir. Jefferson Kibbee

When a girl claiming to have psychic powers predicts the moves of an arsonist, Penhall believes her while Hanson suspects her of the crimes.

with Pamela Segall, Ian Abercrombie

Out of Control

wr. Thania St. John, dir. Mario Van Peebles

When a rash of burglaries break out in wealthy households protected by the same security firm, the team go undercover to investigate claims and counter-claims from the victims and the company.

with Todd Allen, Christine Elise, Jim Calvert, Adam Biesk, John Putch

Stand By Your Man

wr. Michelle Ashford, dir. Daniel Attias

While undercover at a medical school, Hoffs is raped by a classmate, but finds herself unable to report the crime.

with Ken Olandt, Philip Reeves, Seth Isler, John Short, Darcy Marta

Mike's P.O.V.

wr. John Truby, Glen Morgan, James Wong, dir. Jorge Montesi

A teacher bribes a disenfranchised youth to commit a murder for him, but the boy finds that the pay-off can't buy him respect.

with Donovan Leitch, Paul Linke, Robin Lively, Vince Vaughn, Robert Metcalfe, Wendy Van Riesen

Wheels and Deals

wr. Thania St. John, dir. Jefferson Kibbee

Penhall, Booker, Ioki and Captain Fuller pose as bikers when they get the opportunity for revenge on the gangster who put Hanson in prison and cost Booker his police career; this episode is the second part of a crossover with the *Booker* series.

with Ray Baker, Mickey Jones, Cynthia Mace

Parental Guidance Suggested

wr. Sam Bushwick, Glen Morgan, James Wong, dir. Jeffrey Auerbach

Hoffs falls out with Fuller when she neglects a burglary case to interfere with a series of domestic disturbances near her stake-out.

with Jay Underwood, Lenore Kasdorf, Paul Gleason, Charles Siegel

Things We Said Today

wr. Glen Morgan, James Wong, dir. Tucker Gates

Ioki becomes personally involved in the case of a young boy who turned in his own family for doing drugs.

with Keith Coogan, Shannen Doherty, Stephen Godwin, Dirk Blocker, Lise Cutter

Research and Destroy

wr. Gary Rosen, dir. Jefferson Kibbee

While attempting to track down the chemist who is flooding the streets with synthetic heroin, Hanson and Ioki find themselves involved with the CIA and the Chinese government.

with Scott Fults, Ping Wu, Sari Chang, Don Keith Opper, Grant Heslov, Wallace Langham

Change of Heart

wr. Michelle Ashford, dir. Jan Eliasberg

Fuller and Hoffs pose as teacher and student again to solve the murder of a teacher, and uncover a tangled web of secret love affairs between women.

with Katy Boyer, Kathryn Leigh Scott, Lela Rochon, David Kriegel, Olivia Negron, Larry Cedar, Eileen Conn, Steven Garr, Shawn MacDonald, Kelly Duncan, Doug Millar

Back from the Future

wr. David Stenn, dir. Peter DeLuise

In the 21st century, a young police officer attempts to restart the Jump Street operation, and speaks to the now elderly original team members about their recollections of the period.

with Michael Bays

2245

wr. Michelle Ashford, Glen Morgan, James Wong, dir. Kim Manners

Hanson witnesses an execution, and recalls the events leading up to the young man's crimes and eventual capture.

with Josh Richman, Rosie Perez, Myles Thoroughgood, LaRita Shelby, George Buck

Hi, Mom

wr. Bill Nuss, dir. James Whitmore, Jr.

Hanson, Penhall and Fuller go undercover at a high school to uncover a drugs problem in a basketball team and discover the games are being fixed.

with David Raynr, Jacques Apollo Bolton, Chick Hearn, Kareem Abdul-Jabbar, Joseph Hacker, Wesley Jonathan, Nigel Miguel, Spencer Garrett, Don Barnes

Spring Break

wr. Glen Morgan, James Wong, dir. Jorge Montesi

A radical militant student is distraught to see a picture of his girlfriend in a men's magazine, and heads for Florida to find her, but the Jump Street team — unaware his little group only faked a bombing campaign out of a fortuitous lab accident — follow him under the impression he's gone to plant a second bomb.

with Shawn Levy, Jensen Daggett, John Waters, Denney Pierce

La Bizca

wr. Larry Barber, Paul Barber, dir. David Nutter

Hanson and Penhall head for El Salvador when the girl Penhall married (in "Come from the Shadows") in a vain attempt to keep her in the U.S. is reported missing.

with Richard Roundtree, Elpidia Carillo, Don Barnes, Wesley Jonathan, Mike Gomez

Last Chance High

wr. Michelle Ashford, dir. Kim Manners

Investigating robberies, Hanson and Penhall discover a young girl who has kidnapped her baby sister.

with Dietrich Bader, Sarah Trigger, Mark Ballou, Andrew Bloch, Drew Snyder, Christine Jansen, Terrence Kelly

Unfinished Business

wr. Geri Jewell, Mark Powell, Julie Friedgen, dir. Daniel Attias

Hoffs goes undercover to catch a rapist whose cowardly attacks have been made against handicapped women, but a handicapped officer demands Fuller put her on the case rather than sending Hoffs to pose as a disabled person.

with Geri Jewell, Maria Serrao, John J. York

Shirts and Skins

wr. Larry Barber, Paul Barber, dir. Jorge Montesi

The Jump Street team reluctantly investigate the murder of the leader of a neo–Nazi group, with a local community leader as the prime suspect.

with Steven Eckholdt, Morgan Woodward, Castulo Guerra, George Kiek, Brent Hinckley, Karl Weidergott

Business as Usual

wr. Alan McElroy, Larry Barber, Paul Barber

Investigating a rape, Hanson, Hoffs, and Penhall are trapped in a riot situation which gets wildly out of hand.

with Robert Munic, Jon Maynard Pennell, Patrick Malone, Jeremy Applegate, Kristen Datillo, Peter Zapp, Robert Metcalfe, Stephen E. Miller, John Destrey

How I Saved the Senator

wr. Gary Rosen, dir. James Whitmore, Jr.

Each of the Jump Streeters has their own wildly fantastic variation on how a politician's life was saved — each favoring their own heroism! This is the last episode to feature Johnny Depp.

with Christian Hoff, Elena Stiteler, Jim Ishida, Ray Parker, Jr.

Rounding Third

wr. Gary Rosen, dir. Jefferson Kibbee

A missing youngster turns up as a member of Penhall's junior baseball team.

with Sam Bottoms, Chris Wilding, Lindy Nisbet, Mitchell Roche

Every Day Is Christmas

wr. David Gascon, Glen Morgan, James Wong, dir. Ken Wiederhorn

Penhall's life starts to fall to pieces as he loses his job and fails a rookie partner (this is the last episode to feature Dustin Nguyen, and introduces David Barry Gray as Dean Garrett).

with David Barry Gray, Stephen Shellen, Michael Pniewski, Ronald William Lawrence, Tim Streeter, Ivory Ocean

Tunnel of Love

wr. Michelle Ashford, dir. Jorge Montesi

While attempting to put a massage parlor owner suspected of drugs dealing and prostitution out of business, the team stumble onto a DEA operation.

with David Barry Gray, Alexandra Powers, Joe Maruzzo, Meredith Scott Lynn, Dolores Drake, Stephen E. Miller, Beverley Hendry, Stephen Bland, Jennifer Copping

Back to School

wr. Glen Morgan, James Wong, dir. Steve Beers

Dean Garrett, introduced in "Every Day is Christmas," and Kati Rocky, introduced in "Tunnel of Love," have briefly joined the team, and pose as a brother and sister starting a new school (although these two new characters were intended to be new regulars, this is their final appearance; the fifth season was produced as an off-network, straight-to-syndication series and featured a different cast, with only DeLuise, Robinson, and Williams remaining).

with David Barry Gray, Alexandra Powers, Justin Louis, Lisa Dean Ryan, Austin Pendleton, Judy Prescott, Michael Cerveris, Ken Douglas, Morris Panych, Scott Bremner, John Kirk Connell, Peter Yunker, Frances Flanagan, Rochelle Greenwood, Peter Hanlon, Janet Hodgkinson, Pat Bermel, Mark Lundie

Fifth Season (1990–'91)

THE BUDDY SYSTEM

wr. Jonathan Glassner, David Levinson, dir. Jorge Montesi

Hoffs and Penhall take an instant dislike to their new team member, and attempt to find out the cause of his bad attitude during their investigation into the murder of a mentally disabled student by a security guard.

with Scott Grimes, Fred Henderson, Sheelah Megill, Nigel Leach, Matt Hill, Maggie Donaghy, Brigitta Dau, Peter Gaitens, Whitney Stuart

POISON

wr. Ann Donahue, dir. Don McBrearty

Doug is attracted to an undercover drugs cop who joins the team on temporary assignment, but other members of the team suspect she may be hooked on heroin herself.

with Perrey Reeves, Richard Leacock, Johannah Newmarch, Paul Jarrett, Byron Lucas

JUST SAY NO HIGH

wr. Sharon Doyle, dir. Randy Bradshaw

Penhall and Hoffs go undercover in a school where the students are being tested for drugs, but Hoffs is discovered to test positive herself.

with Peter Outerbridge, Peter Stebbings, Garry Chalk, Pat Bermel, Maurice Verkaar, Delia Brett, Deanna Milligan, Jordan Pratt, Michael Puttonen

BROTHERS

wr. Jonathan Glassner, dir. Don McBrearty

Doug's brother Joey, also a cop, joins Jump Street, but on an investigation into a religious cult, appears to be getting sucked in (this episode introduces Michael DeLuise as Joey Penhall to the cast).

with John Pyper-Ferguson, Alison Quinn

THIS AIN'T NO SUMMER CAMP

wr. Morgan Gendel, dir. Peter Marshall

Doug and Joey investigate a death at a teenage camp where offenders are treated by hard work and severe punishment in an attempt to set them straight.

with Zachary Ansley, Leon Russom, Donna Peerless, Jano Frandsen, Merrilyn Gann, Terence Kelly, Janne Mortil, Andrew Markley, D. Neil Mark, Katherine Banwell

THE GIRL NEXT DOOR

wr. Jonathan Glassner, dir. Brenton Spencer

A number of false trails hinder an investigation into the murder of a high-school football player.

with Ocean Hellman, Michael Davies, Ken Camroux, Chris Boyd, Lochlyn Munro, Wes Tritter

DIPLOMA FOR SALE

wr. Tom Perry, Jo Perry, dir. Randy Bradshaw

A blackmailer who sells term papers to students causes a youngster to turn to robbery to buy his silence, but when the youth is killed, Jump Street cops investigate the crime and uncover the true depth of his operations.

with Jayeson Boyd, Anna Hagen, Noah Beggs, Venus Terzo, Leslie Carlson, Channing Mitchell, Alex Bruhanski

NUMBER ONE WITH A BULLET

wr. Ann Donahue, dir. Peter DeLuise

Critically wounded and in a coma, Doug faces a strange near-death experience while his teammates complete his undercover mission.

with David DeLuise, Kamala Lopez, Andrea Mann, Ken Tremblett, French Tucker, Alec Burden, Margo Pinvidic

EQUAL PROTECTION

wr. Jeff Myrow, dir. Brad Turner

Hoffs witnesses and investigates racism in a police gang patrol.

with Richard McGregor, Peter Williams, Charles Payne, Timothy Webber, Todd Waite, Deryl Caitlyn, Patricia Forte, Lenno Britos, Charlene Fernetz

THE EDUCATION OF TERRY CARVER

wr. Tom Perry, Jo Perry, dir. Randy Bradshaw

When a young woman is raped at the university, Hoffs and McCann investigate and discover there has been a cover-up over the fact that the rape even happened.

with Christianne Hirt, Jonathan Crombie, Doug Abrahams, Jan D'Arcy, Dolores Drake, Roark Critchlow, Rebecca Toolan, James Kidnie, Suzanne Andersen

BABY BLUES

wr. Deborah Seibel, dir. Zale Dalen
Joey becomes involved with a woman addicted to drugs who has her baby taken into care.

with Heather Hess, James Purcell, Alfonso Quijada, Troy James, Candus Churchill, Jane Mortifee, Gerry Nairn

FILM AT ELEVEN

wr. David Levinson, dir. Peter DeLuise
After the hunt for a newswoman's missing daughter, the Jump Street cops discover some curious loose ends that lead to an unsolved murder.

with Renda Rae Norman, Jennifer Milmore, Don S. Davis, Jim Lacamell, Tim Henry, Michael Rogers, Paula Bellamy, Noah Beggs, Walter Marsh

IN THE NAME OF LOVE

wr. Jonathan Glassner, James Novak, dir. Zale Dalen
McCann's personal life threatens to endanger his uncomfortable mission to get close to the daughter of a dangerous drug dealer.

with Kelli Fox, Beth Toussaint, Duncan Fraser, Andrew Johnston, Ron Chartier

COPPIN' OUT

wr. Simon Ayer, dir. Brad Turner
The Jump Street cops investigate the intimidation of the elderly residents of a rest home.

with Fay Hauser, Markus Redmond, Joy Coghill, Doug Williamson, Rik Kiviaho, Scott Swanson

UNDER THE INFLUENCE

wr. Sharon Doyle, dir. Jorge Montesi
Investigations reveal that attacks on homeless vagrants are being perpetrated by a Satanic cult.

with J.J. Makaro, David Longworth, Leslie Bega, Jennifer Copping, Todd Schaeffer, Stacy Grant, Charles Siegel, Tasha Sims, Jed Reese, Bruce Corkum

CROSSFIRE

wr. Ann Donahue, dir. Jorge Montesi
Fuller is concerned over Hoffs' new boyfriend, who is continuously borrowing money from her.

with Geoffrey Thorne, Renee Jones, Janisha Culp, Vincent Gale, Jennifer Haley, Barry K. Mickelson, Kevin McNulty, William B. Davis

WASTED

wr. Sharon Doyle, dir. Brenton Spencer
McCann poses as a football player to investigate the possible use of steroids after a student dies.

with Byron Lucas, Robert Sidley, Michael A. Jackson, Steve Bacic, Dale Wilson, Marie Stuillin, Keith Bearwood, Sam Malkin, Mitchell Kosterman

BAD DAY AT EAGLE ROCK

wr. Thomas Perry, Jo Perry, dir. Brenton Spencer
Fuller goes undercover in a school where three students running an extortion ring have beaten a teacher to death.

with Michael Cudlitz, Thomas Mitchell, Phil Mitchell, Dale Walters, Howard Storey, Lalania Lindbjerg, Marc Baur

HOMEGIRLS

wr. Jeff Myrow, dir. Brad Turner
Hoffs infiltrates an all-girl gang after a drive-by shooting.

with Brenda Critchlow, Carol-Ann Feffers, Jada Pinkett, Gemma Lovett, Chuck Perry, Don Fullilove, Dafina Beasle, Freda Perry, Sandra P. Grant

SECOND CHANCES

wr. Jim Brown, dir. Steven Williams
Hoffs is upset that McCann is investigating a teenager she had put into a rehabilitation program.

with Martin Cummins, Peter La Croix, Brock Johnson, Raimund Stamm, Jennifer Griffin, Bill Dow, Deanna Milligan

series ends

Wiseguy
September 1987–December 1990

*"You're a great player in a dangerous game.
But the game takes its toll — you lose your edge
and the consequences can be fatal."*

Two Cannell series made their debut in September 1987 for the '87–'88 season, *JJ Starbuck* and *Wiseguy*, and while both were good shows, there could not have been a greater difference between the two.

With *Stingray, The Last Precinct,* and now Patrick Hasburgh's *21 Jump Street* safely tucked under his belt, Cannell's output was beginning to look positively schizophrenic. Whereas all his series until then had seemed to occupy the same television universe, Cannell was suddenly throwing out shows with a diversity of styles at a variety of potential audiences.

What was really happening of course was inevitable — Cannell's colleagues and co-workers of the 1980s were starting to develop their own themes and directions, just as DeGuere, Bellisario, Chase and Bartlett had before them. Hasburgh was fully committed to *Jump Street*, which bore few recognizable Cannell trademarks after the first season, while Frank Lupo, although pitching in on the early development of *Wiseguy*, had left Cannell after *The Last Precinct* to develop his own projects, the dark horror shows *Werewolf* and *Something Is Out There* and the disappointing cop show *Hardball*. But if *Wiseguy* was another digression for Cannell, the underlying themes were all too familiar, an obvious extension of everything he'd ever written about before. If any of Cannell's late '80s shows belonged to his main body of work it was this one ... and yet, it was also a major departure for him.

While remaining true to the Cannell ethos, *Wiseguy* dismissed his standard flying car crashes and guns that didn't hurt for a dark, grim and brooding atmosphere that, unlike *Rockford, Tenspeed* and *The A-Team et al.,* took his usual familiar territory deadly seriously. The hero was New Jersey toughie Vinnie Terranova (Ken Wahl), an undercover agent whose mission is to infiltrate the mob and destroy it from the inside by gaining the trust of the bad guys and feeding information to the cops. When the series opens, Terranova has just spent eighteen months in the slammer for the sole purpose of establishing a credible identity for himself as a hood — or a "wiseguy" — a cheap slab of mob muscle who in fact is working under deep cover for the OCB, a division of the FBI. In order to avenge the murder of his mentor ("These guys ain't all that smart. They're just mean"), Vinnie's first target as a mob mole is the Steelgrave family, led by brothers Mike and Sonny Steelgrave. Terranova's new contact is the surly, cynical, slow-burning Frank McPike (portrayed superbly by Jonathan Banks), and his first tense and traumatic assignment is complicated by the fact that while he has an affinity with his mobster target, who comes from the same side of town as him, trusts him, and treats him like a brother, his police liaison is a cold, unfriendly, and uncompromising man who can't manage as much as a smile, and is constantly suspicious and critical of Terranova's actions.

The growing expense of smashing up cars and overturning jeeps had combined with the television market's move toward the cheaper half-hour sit-com form to make the sort of action/adventure mayhem of Cannell's early '80s period financially unviable and unattractive. Furthermore, big screen bullies like Schwarzenegger, Stallone, and their copyists, and later the *Die Hard, Lethal Weapon* and *Under Siege* franchises had stolen their thunder. When Cannell's only competition had been Roger Corman and other low budget drive-in kings, his shows could match them bullet for bullet, car for car; now he was competing with blockbuster budgets. In the search for ways to cut costs, Cannell had moved his operations to Canada, where he had sought out new approaches to the hour format he specialized in — the murder mystery format of *Starbuck,* to be discussed next, or the flashy, visual graphics of *Stingray,* a series that was all mood and no substance. The last smash-and-crash show Cannell had produced was the pilot for *The Last Precinct,* and the budget for that ill-fated action/comedy had been severely and noticeably trimmed in series format. While the pilots for Cannell's new hour dramas still had their fair share of squealing tires and gunplay, the series that resulted from them were forced to rely more on mood, suspense and dialogue. The pilot for *Wiseguy* continued this trend, with some spectacular action sequences emerging from a terrorist sub-plot (there's a wonderful scene where a female terrorist fires a huge concealed gun from between her legs, thus effectively blowing every cod–Freudian slice of film imagery from macho movies into the middle of next week with one well-aimed blast!), but the main body of the film concerned itself with setting up the powerful nine episode drama to follow, with the death of mobster Dave Steelgrave (Cannell regular Gianni Russo) and the hiring of undercover cop Vinnie as chauffeur and then lieutenant by his manic feisty younger brother Salvatore "Sonny" Steelgrave (Ray Sharkey). Best of all, Cannell didn't make the mistake of keeping the plot stagnant in order to hang on to the premise or the characters. There are no neverending storylines here, and no instant solutions — each weekly episode is a separate story but forming part of a whole, with a new adversary every few weeks.

Careful, Vinnie, someone's always watching ... Ken Wahl in *Wiseguy*.

"Conceived by producer-writer Stephen J. Cannell, who gave us such idiosyncratic classics as *The Rockford Files* and *Baretta*, *Wiseguy* shows no respect for the genre's storytelling conventions," wrote Harry Waters and Janet Huck for *Newsweek*. "Instead of confining its bad guys to one night stands, it fleshes out their characters by keeping them around through a string of episodes (known in the scriptwriting trade as "arcs"). The result? Nothing less than the most mesmerising, vividly-drawn villains in the annals of prime-time crime."

"My idea was that we would reinvent the show every half year," Cannell told *Rolling Stone* magazine, as he explained to journalist Elvis Mitchell how he had pitched the show to CBS after ABC had passed on the series. But beyond that, Cannell couldn't crack it ("The story was told okay, but there was no real relationship with anyone..."). When he and co-writer Frank Lupo, a reluctant collaborator pitching in for old times sake, came up with the idea of making the (heterosexual) relationship between undercover cop and hood the main theme, rather than the gangster's niece, it all fell into place. But it was still just a very good TV movie setting up a premise.

The cop masquerading as crook is, of course, is one of the oldest plot formulas in the history of cinema, best and most famously represented by the classic 1949 feature *White Heat*, with Edmond O'Brien and James Cagney in the confrontational roles of betrayer and betrayed.* *Wiseguy*, with its long-form format, could take the time to set the scene properly and explore characters and relationships at a comfortable pace, but it was still essentially *White Heat* for television — and in actor Ray Sharkey's mesmerizing portrayal of gangster Sonny Steelgrave, Cannell had stumbled onto a celluloid mobster to rival Cagney's finest hour ... and who would be equally adored by the audience.

With the death of Dave Steelgrave in the pilot, the Steelgrave storyline focuses on Sonny, his brotherly love relationship with Vinnie, and his attempts to hold together his Atlantic City empire in the face of covert attacks by Pat "the Cat" Patrice (Joe Dallesandro) and the slimy accountant Sid Royce (Dennis Lipscombe), whom Patrice insists on installing in the Steelgrave building (in Dave's office, no less), but who is really there not to oversee Sonny's operation, but to undermine it.

Joe Dallesandro, formerly associated with the sleazy avante-garde art films of Andy Warhol in the '60s, had turned to television in the early '80s via a guest appearance on the fashionable *Miami Vice*, and was a revelation as Pat the Cat. As social-climbing snake Sid Royce, Dennis Lipscombe, a career TV bad guy with a number of Cannell show appearances to his credit, created a worthy adversary for both Sonny and Vinnie. By his own admission, Lipscombe was mostly occupied with playing "scumbag of the week" on a variety of '80s shows, one of his favorite roles being a psychotic killer in *Moonlighting*. He had briefly had a semi-regular role as the mayor in *In the Heat of the Night*, but didn't want to be tied down to a series. With the exception of Sid, the only other recurring role he had been unable to resist was that of the actor Harlan Keyvo in the sit-com *The Famous Teddy Z*.

Wiseguy took the moody, aggressive darkness that Lupo had originally intended for *Hunter* and married it to a more sober study of Cannell's usual obsessions — the mob, confidence scams,

---

**Wiseguy wasn't one of those corny old cop shows where it takes the hero all of five minutes to con his way into the confidence of the dumber-than-dumb bad guys though; *Wiseguy* opens with Vinnie having spent eighteen months in jail just to establish a cover—a pleasant change from those episodes of* The Untouchables *and* Hawaii Five-0, *to recall just two offenders in otherwise fine series, where the instantly recognizable media hound heroes would turn up in a jail cell to befriend a future stool pigeon that same afternoon!*

deceit and self-deceit, bluff and double-bluff, buddy movie camaraderie, moral rightness against the letter of the law, and male bonding. All Cannell's series have been about the nature of friendship, but none more so than this one. In many ways, *Wiseguy* consolidated the themes of Cannell's earlier, lighter shows into a new, darker, more serious framework.

"Not since David Janssen's Richard Kimble character on *The Fugitive* has a television hero been as angst-ridden as Vinnie Terranova," wrote Daniel Ruth in the *Chicago Sun-Times*, "struggling week to week with the pressures of his dual life and the moral ambiguity of his actions." "*Wiseguy* infuses the most predictable of genres with the intoxicating sense that anything can happen," announced *New York Woman*; "*Wiseguy* is full of suspense," wrote Don Merrill in *TV Guide*. "Each episode has Vinnie's life at stake if his real identity is revealed, and since he becomes friendly with the head honchos, there are always some underlings who are jealous (and) suspect him.... Around this dramatic core, Cannell and his writers offer all-too-believable background on the powerful outlaws who control large-scale crime in this country."

"*Wiseguy* is people-rich," noted Michael Dougan in the *San Francisco Examiner*. "Cops and crooks are drawn in three full dimensions — including Sonny, one of the most personable ruffians ever seen on television." "Sonny Steelgrave, dynamically portrayed by Ray Sharkey, proved to be the most personable villain ever to enter our living room," agreed Mark Esslinger in *Hollywood Gazette*. "For more than a moment Sonny's genuine charisma made us forget Vinnie's altruistic mission to bring this mob boss to his knees."

Sonny Steelgrave, a tour-de-force performance from Sharkey, was the best TV gangster since Bruce Gordon's barbaric brute-in-a-suit Frank Nitti in *The Untouchables* (1959–'63) — and probably would still have been, even if the competition had been less scarce. Wrote James Wolcott in *Vanity Fair*, "(Sharkey's) Sonny entered the great gangster tradition of aggrieved goombahs — Edward G. Robinson's Little Caesar, Robert De Niro's Capone, Marlon Brando's and Al Pacino's Corleones — but it was a continuation, not a major break." Sonny, says Elvis Mitchell in his *Rolling Stone* piece, "is a New Jersey outlaw who has bought into the glass-and-marble facade of the new wave of corporate crime. He probably picks up his clothes at the casual shop of the same men's store that Gordon Gekko of *Wall Street* frequents — Thugs 'R' Us!"

The matter-of-fact violence of *Wiseguy* is real and absolute, and vitally important to the integrity of the theme. It's also horrifically sudden and shocking for both Vinnie and the audience. Vinnie's major problem, and the focal point of the series' first storyline (and subtext of many later stories to follow), is that like a lot of villainous characters, on the surface Sonny is a very likeable, charismatic guy, and because Vinnie must live the life of a mobster, with all its ill-gotten trappings, Sonny quickly becomes Vinnie's best friend. This was never a problem for Edmond O'Brien in *White Heat*, because he and Cagney's mad dog Cody were either in jail or on the run! The term "the villain you love to hate" was never truer than when Ray Sharkey portrayed mobster Sonny Steelgrave; while O'Brien felt a twinge of sympathy for Cagney's miserable thug, Steelgrave's brutish insanity is unleashed in short, sharp, sickening bursts, and the rest of the time he's a likeable rogue with whom Terranova feels a growing affinity — they *socialize*. "We did episodes to prove that Ray was the bad guy, simply because everyone was terrified that once Ray went down, we'd lose the series," said first season story editor Eric Blakeney to interviewer and writer Ed Gross for his intriguing fan publication "*The Unofficial Story of the Making of a Wiseguy*" (Pioneer Books Inc.). "'A Deal's a Deal' was supposed to show Ray kicking the dog," said Sharkey to Gross, "and I have the knack of kicking the dog and making you feel sorry for me! That's what acting is all about. They really wanted this episode to make Sonny look bad, and it didn't work. I warned them. I said, don't you get it by now? Nobody is ever going to dislike me. They said 'but Sonny is a murderer, he's about to kill Patrice!' I said, I'm doing it because he deserves it. They're going to love me killing him. 'No, no, no' ... Well, sure as shit...!" But every time Vinnie starts to get in so deep that he begins to be seduced by Sonny's lifestyle and friendship, something so horrific occurs that it snaps the tormented "wiseguy" back to reality; the title of the episode "The Birthday Surprise," written by Eric Blakeney and directed by Robert Iscove, refers to a particularly horrific shock ending instigated by Sonny, while the strangulation scene in Blakeney's "The Marriage of Heaven and Hell" (directed by Zale Dalen)—with added attraction of a shooting and a vomiting on the sidelines—is memorable shock television that ultimately snaps Vinnie out of his dilemma and seals Sonny's fate.

But not all the horrific violence in the Steelgrave storyline is dished out by Sonny. A powerful scene in Cannell's "Loose Cannon," directed by Larry Shaw, has David Marciano's psychotic and bogus Lorenzo Steelgrave, an opportunistic impostor, following Terranova into the car park of a night club after a loutish altercation over which man went home with which woman; Lorenzo has his eye on Vinnie's girl, even though Sonny has laid on whores for everybody, and a brutish spectacle has culminated in a foolish power game from which Lorenzo must save face. As he swaggers toward Vinnie and Sonny with mad eyes and a leering idiot grin on his face, he snaps car aerials off the vehicles he passes in an act of seemingly mindless vandalism ... but once he's finished, he has a handful of potentially lethal metal rods in his hand, which he savagely and unexpectedly swipes across Vinnie's face. After callously and randomly raping and murdering throughout the episode, he discovers Vinnie's identity as a federal agent and joyously taunts Terranova secure in the knowledge that Vinnie must respect the procedures of the law. But Vinnie is a wiseguy now — and blows the demented bandit into oblivion.

The conclusion of the second season's anti-racist storyline provoked Cannell to comment, "I've been in this business twenty years, and that's the single most violent episode I've ever been associated with!," but nothing tops the Steelgrave stories for brutality. The pilot is ruthless, and "New Blood," written by David Burke and directed by Lyndon Chubbuck, has a gloriously clever and gruesome twist ending with splattered pizza suggestively standing in for an assassin's innards. "One on One," written by Stephen Kronish and directed by Ray Villalobos, has a grim torture scene for Frank McPike when the cavalry arrives a little bit later than is the norm for series regulars, while "The Squeeze," written by Gina Wendkos and directed by Bill Cocoran, sees Vinnie inflicting a cathartic beating on two suave deceivers who have attempted to harm his mother. "A Deal's a Deal," by Burke, Kronish, and Correll, offers up some spectacularly grim and offhand police brutality.

Despite all this, Cannell's strong sense of morality triumphs. Every single character who commits these acts of violence ultimately pays for his sins, and Sonny himself is ultimately undone by his tendency toward solving every situation with actual or threatened physical violence. As Vinnie states in the climactic "No-One Gets Out of Here Alive" from Burke and Iscove, Sonny would have served time rather than met his maker if he hadn't resorted to murder. Vinnie *was* looking after him in his own way.

"You stupid bastard," he rages. "I had my men rocking in there at seven o'clock this morning, plenty of time to keep Patrice from killing you. You were going to be the victim, Sonny. I dealt you the best hand I could. I was giving you a position from which you could negotiate. But you screwed it up, man. You had to indulge your bloodlust!" "It's because of Ray, I thought he was wonderful" Dennis Lipscombe told Gross. "I think the scene that sticks out in my mind the most is when I'm under the table throwing up as he's killing my boss, thinking I'm next. I was praying they would leave that in, and I'm glad they did."

Said Blakeney to Gross, "I was really turned on by the whole concept of the good things that bad people do and the bad things that good people do. For me, there's no drama in a guy who does the right thing all the time. Vinnie went in there to arrest the bad guy, but he was betraying a friend. And Sonny Steelgrave was completely open and honest and gave himself over to this relationship, and he was the bad guy. In the relationship between them, Sharkey was pure and Kenny was the deceiver, and that, for me, was the series."

"We play moral dilemmas," stated Les Sheldon to Martha Hindes in *The Cincinatti Enquirer*. "Basically, there are three guys — the undercover guy who works for the government, the guy he has to become to *go* undercover, and the guy that's really him in his personal life." "We don't follow the formula where it's white hats and black hats, and that's the thing I'm proudest of," Wahl told journalist Hugh Boulware. And to Daniel Ruth of the *Chicago Sun-Times,* he said, "That's the whole point of the series — to show that everybody's not all good, not all bad. Vinnie could have gone either way. Sonny could have gone either way. It wasn't just Gene Autry riding into town with his white hat on. He blew that guy away and got away with it ("The Loose Cannon"). He got away with murder. He's not always just a goody-two-shoes guy. He's a guy who can't talk to his mother. He has nowhere to go. The only time he has any kind of good time at all is with Sonny."

While *The Rockford Files* and *The A-Team* are the series with the fame and longevity, Cannell fans and critics alike regard the Sonny Steelgrave series of stories in *Wiseguy* to be the apotheosis of the prolific producer's output, and it's not difficult to see why. For all the false hopes and false starts, missteps and misjudgments that Cannell may have made in the late 1980s, most Cannell fans and critics will excuse him anything for *Wiseguy*— particularly that first, fabulous season — the most thrilling and exciting television drama since the heyday of *Hill Street Blues*. "The last fifteen minutes of 'The Marriage of Heaven and Hell' was the bachelor party," Sharkey told Ed Gross in an extensive and detailed interview for his book. "Even Cannell came up, sat at the top of a ladder so that he could see the whole thing. Everybody was there, and I remember doing that speech in one take, and we moved on. Everybody was in overtime, but nobody cared. Stephen Cannell gave this great speech from on top of the ladder — 'There's magic happening here tonight' — and everybody was into it. We had a young Canadian crew and they really got spoiled. Even I got spoiled. Rarely in my life do those things happen. Rarely are you on the set and looking into the eyes of the crew, and you're aware of what's happening."

"*Wiseguy* is a keg of video dynamite," wrote Ron Miller in the *San Jose Mercury News;* "The most exciting, the most credible, and above all, the most literate crime drama to surface on television in quite some time," wrote David Friedman in *Newsday;* "Vintage Stephen J. Cannell," announced Kay Gardella in the *New York Daily News*. "Intelligent, hard-boiled crime drama," said *Time* magazine; "The best crime series in years," said *TV Guide;* "The best, toughest, and most tension-filled..." wrote Matt Roush in *USA Today,* "and it just keeps getting better." And on and on they went — "this season's surprise quality crime show," "the best new drama," "one of the best new shows," "the best new show," best, best, better.

Unfortunately, this blitz of positive reviews was not reflected in the initial ratings for the show, which had the misfortune to go out against NBC's double-bill of the ever-popular

Cheers and its back half-hour *Night Court*. "*Wiseguy* must have set some kind of record this season for being the best show on prime-time network television to be completely overlooked," complained one journalist. However, when the football season ended, CBS moved *Cagney and Lacey* and put the re-runs of *Wiseguy* out in that slot and at last, slowly but surely, *Wiseguy* built a steady loyal audience. Those figures (a two-hour re-showing of the Steelgrave storyline's climax did particularly well), numerous supportive articles in the press ("Get Wise," "Smarten Up to *Wiseguy*," "*Wiseguy* much too good to be rubbed out," and so on) and a write-in campaign that produced 20,000 letters of support, secured a second season. Ultimately, it settled into a Wednesday night slot following *The Equalizer* and opposing the disastrous *Tattingers* on NBC and the classy but difficult *China Beach* on ABC. "We feel it has evolved into a most extraordinary drama—beyond even the high expectations we had for it," said CBS president Kim LeMasters.

Like Johnny Depp in *Jump Street*, and Tony Musante of *Toma* before him, Cannell had cast another lead actor who wasn't interested in attaining heart-throb status. Ken Wahl rarely consented to give promotional interviews for the series, and was a private man with much the same blue-collar New Jersey background as his character. Exactly how he made the move from mechanic to movies is shrouded in myth, with Wahl giving Vinnie Terranova–like speeches about grabbing for the brass ring, etc., but his only other TV work had been in another undercover cop show with Billy Dee Williams, the 1985 series *Double Dare*, which made its debut at the end of the 1984–'85 season and was instantly canceled. His film work had been slightly more prolific, but anonymous and insignificant. Wahl had never modeled, never done commercials, and never performed on the stage, and he greeted his sudden stardom with a mix of beginner's naiveté ("If we make a terrific show and I take my shirt off in one scene with a woman, I guarantee you that is the only clip they will use to promote the show") and arrogance ("If you ever see me on another series after *Wiseguy*, you know I am going to be hurting for money").*

According to legend, Wahl just jumped in his car in Chicago and headed west. It was 1977, and the hot new movie stars were Italian-Americans Sylvester Stallone and John Travolta. "I said 'Sure, let me grab my suitcase and I'll go with you!'" said Wahl's brother Chuck—"Look who's laughing now!" Fortunately, Wahl's lack of professional training didn't matter, as his role in *Wiseguy* was mostly reactive, or as Cannell put it, "he's a counter-puncher"; his role was to respond to the actions and insanity around him, rather than provoke or provide them. Wahl's job was mostly just to stand there looking convincingly tough, a task he mastered effortlessly.

"Ken Wahl is what some might call a hunk," wrote Don Merrill in *TV Guide*, "a good-looking, intelligent, articulate version of Sylvester Stallone." "Physically, Wahl fits the part of a Mafia mannequin," wrote James Wolcott, reviewing *Wiseguy* in *Vanity Fair*. "His eyebrows join together, his jawline is long and equine, and he seems to have a big 'Duh?' drawn above his head. Even Wahl's dense responses as an actor help make Vinnie a believable soldier in the mob." "Wahl is a convincing sufferer," wrote Mitchell in *Rolling Stone*. "His eyes cloud up at a moment's notice, and he gets plenty of moments to be noticed, one of *Wiseguy*'s few flaws." "If Wahl had more technique at his disposal," he added cruelly, "he might muck up the show with reflective migraines of the soul. But he simply doesn't have the skill to bring

---

*In fact, following Wiseguy, *Wahl completely disappeared from film and TV just a couple of years later. An older, heavier Wahl resurfaced in a bizarre "return of..." TV movie trying to resurrect the series with a reincarnated Vinnie Terranova in the early 1990s.*

the proceedings to a crawl." But it was Cannell himself who summed up Ken Wahl's Vinnie Terranova persona the most succinctly. "If Ken Wahl walked across a room toward me, I'd be worried!" he joked to journalist Jane Lane on a promo tour for the show's second season.

"Just because I'm pragmatic about this occupation doesn't mean I don't take it seriously," Wahl told journalist Kathryn Baker. "I do to the extent that I try to do the best job that I can. I just keep it on an occupational level. I don't take it to another level of being all artistic and everything. If somebody else wants to think it's artistic, that's fine. But to me, it's my job. I'm supposed to do it well. If I don't do it well then I won't be able to continue to work. And then you get hungry. And that's my point."

But Wahl wasn't as dumb as he sounded. "The acting challenge," Wahl told the *Chicago Sun-Times,* "is that you have to give to the other characters in the storyline enough to believe Vinnie playing that part. He's acting as well. But on the other hand, Vinnie can't give too much away — the underlying fear and all that — because the bad guys will catch on. But you *do* have to give some of that to the audience, so *they* know what's going on. All of that is the toughest thing."

However, it was Jonathan Banks' Frank McPike who was the true savior of the show after Steelgrave's demise, the one constant in every single story in the series and the glue that held all four seasons together (the last without Wahl). While star-names and super-villains came and went, McPike was there, solid as a precariously balanced rock about to follow Wile E. Coyote off the cliff edge. Banks, a powerful character actor and a familiar face on series TV, including Cannell's, had generally specialized in playing deranged, sleepy-eyed psycho roles. He appeared in a memorable episode of *Hunter* as a sleazy corrupt cop in "The Big Fall," was a chillingly convincing rapist/intruder in *Lou Grant,* played a powerful role in *Hill Street Blues* as a murderer with multiple frightening personalities, and came to *Wiseguy* having just portrayed a "space-Nazi" as he put it, in the science fiction series *Otherworld.*

"Even when I was a little kid I wanted to be the bad guy," says Banks. "I wanted to wear black. I *have* played a good guy, but it's hard for me to be a straight arrow." In more ways than one it seems; for a while, poor Banks was getting cast as a scuzzo in pastels and floral prints, dragging up for appearances in *Mike Hammer, Crazy Like a Fox, and* one of his episodes of *Otherworld!* Over fifty other TV roles have included more traditional sleazoids in *Hardcastle and McCormick, Falcon Crest,* and many more; he even got to slime all over *The Waltons!* His character of McPike has been described variously as a "caustic, bespectacled misanthrope" (*USA Today*) and "the nastiest nice guy on television, a sheep in wolf's clothing!" When cast in the role, Banks' first thought was to make him "a good guy you don't like." But, says Banks, "I like Frank. I like Frank when Frank's up against it. I think I like his quarrelsomeness the most. That he is irritable. That he is a guy who wakes up and hates going to the cleaners, and hates the noise of the kids and the color of the carpet, and he still goes out and does his job. And at the same time, I think if Frank saw a lost dog in the neighborhood, he'd try and ignore it, and couldn't."

"Originally, the McPike character was written as a big, red-headed guy, strong and a lot more straightforward and burly," explained Banks to a journalist. "I think I brought the acerbic quality to it and they started playing on it. It's evolved into McPike doesn't know how to be friendly. McPike is the kind of guy who could go watch people having a good time and really enjoy it. But he could never take part in it. He just doesn't know how."

In fact, Banks couldn't be more removed from the likes of Frank McPike — an active football and baseball player coaching Little League in his spare time, he worked as a stage director in Australia before moving to Hollywood, directing productions of the musicals *Hair, Grease,* and *Jesus Christ, Superstar.* Having worked his way up from assistant stage manager to artistic director, Banks stepped before the cameras to essay a succession of sleazoids in films such as *Beverly Hills Cop, Stir Crazy, 48 Hours, Freejack,* and *Cold Steel.* But, said Banks, not entirely in jest, "I've sure liked some of the bad guys I've played. You bet. My bad guys usually have a pretty good time being bad. I'm starting to play nice people. Not that I like it very much!"

McPike has a very simple philosophy where the mob is concerned, and when McPike mocks a gangster's abuse in an early episode with the line "My mother thinks I'm adorable," he's not entirely convincing! "I've been jealous of every villain that's been on this show!" Banks told Tom Green of *USA Today,* but, he says, "I knew what I was signing on for! Everybody was honest about McPike from the beginning. I like Frank, although I've never played a character for so long, and he does go home with me at times!"

But if mother does love little Frank McPike, then gangsters certainly love their mothers. In *White Heat,* James Cagney's Cody Jarrett is as electrically volatile and swiftly violent as Sonny Steelgrave, and as psychotically crazy as Mel Profitt, Vinnie's target for the second half of the first season; like Cody, Sonny loves mother, but its Vinnie's mother who enjoys his attentions in a key turning point in Carol Mendelsohn's "The Prodigal Son," while mother (Elsa Raven) is equally sly at hiding her contempt for him. Unlike Cagney's mother (Margaret Wycherly, excellent), Vinnie's mother is smart enough to ask the question "What good is a man who loves his children but kills somebody else's?"*

As Frank McPike, Banks was also supposed to be dislikeable, but with the culmination of the Steelgrave story, McPike rapidly became a loveable, sympathetic cuss, and any conflict between the two rapidly dissolved into a die-for-each-other best-friends buddy relationship that later embraced Terranova's initially faceless intermediary with McPike, the mysterious paraplegic Lifeguard, Uncle Mike.† Actor Jim Byrnes, cast as Terranova's phone-link with the OCB, really is a double amputee, having been injured in a car accident, and while the series' opening credits carefully skirted the fact with some tricky camerawork, the series itself had few qualms about putting the actor in the limelight. "I told the network that if we couldn't cast the part with a disabled actor then we would have to change the character," Cannell told an awards ceremony at the 1989 Media Access Awards. "I wouldn't put a guy who can walk in a wheelchair," said Cannell, adding that every time an actor with disabilities was cast, "it makes it easier for the next person to do it." Also acknowledged that night was deaf actress Marlee Matlin's role in the *Hunter* episode "Death Signs."

Byrnes' casting failed to raise any eyebrows other than over at the network, and enabled further castings for disabled performers, including players in the sit-com *Sister Kate* and the drama *TVIOI,* the legless Bob Wieland as "Skates" in the short lived *Sonny Spoon* series and former *Lancer* co-star James Stacy, injured in a motorcycle accident, in a later *Wiseguy* storyline in the third season. The outcome of this sudden burst of humanitarianism in the previ-

---

*Poor Mel Profitt, who makes his debut shortly after Sonny's electric Cody-like demise, doesn't have a mother, only an incestuous and equally conspiratorial relationship with his sister to provide parental protection, and it is his upbringing in an orphanage without motherly love and fatherly guidance that has created both the monster he has become and the demon within him.

†Although Banks has claimed that he didn't want to see McPike in a "buddy-buddy relationship," he has said that his favorite episode is the male-bonding camping trip filler, "Call It Casaba."

ously disadvantaged-less environment of network television was a flurry of series episodes endeavoring to include the disabled (Byrnes himself guest-starred in an episode of the syndicated series *Out of This World*) that culminated in the modestly successful Sunday night schmaltz show *Life Goes On,* starring Chris Burke, an actor with Down Syndrome, and Matlin's co-starring role with Mark Harmon (formerly of *St. Elsewhere*) in the 1991–'92 sea-

This bizarre cast shot features a bunch of characters many of whom shouldn't know each other! Sonny, look behind you! Posing in character are (left to right) Gerald Anthony, Ken Wahl, Jonathan Banks, Ray Sharkey, and seated, Jim Byrnes.

son's debut of the detective series *Reasonable Doubts*. Ultimately though, despite it opening doors by creating precedent, it was just another TV trend.

"The role is the best thing that's ever happened to me," said Byrnes, who heard he got the part on the anniversary of his accident. A player in a blues band, Byrnes was born in St. Louis, Missouri, and attended Boston University, moving to Toronto in 1969. Following *Wiseguy*, he took a substantial supporting role in the TV series *Highlander*. "Somebody came up to me in a restaurant once, and asked me 'How do they film it so you look like you don't have any legs?'" Byrne told a journalist. "I told him it was done with mirrors.... My attitude towards being handicapped is that it's a non-issue, and I'm playing a role that demonstrates that. We don't make a big deal about the fact that I'm in a wheelchair. He is good because he's good, not because he's handicapped." Says Cannell, "I hope we would get to the point where it isn't important whether the character is disabled, or black, or a woman. It's all a part of life. All I'm really looking for is a good performer."

Cannell certainly had a good performer in Brooklyn-born Italian Ray Sharkey; many critics regarded it outrageous that he was not awarded an Emmy for his performance as Sonny Steelgrave. "'The Marriage Between Heaven and Hell' dealt with love between these two guys without homosexual overtones," enthused Sharkey. "It was the first time you got to see that. It was the first time that two guys got to look at each other with 'Nights in White Satin' in the background, no dialogue, just them looking at each other, and no homosexual bullshit. That's a testament to David Burke, Eric Blakeney, Stephen Cannell, Steven Kronish, because they wrote the material. Really, all I had to do was act it. I would love to able to say that I deserve all the credit, but that's not true. It was all on paper for me."

There had been talk of lengthening the Steelgrave storyline, but Sharkey was committed to a film in Greece, an obligation that kept the production honest. However, with hindsight, a full season would have been workable. "We'd love to keep him," Cannell told *TV Guide*, "but that would have violated the credibility of the show." "There was definitely a shared feeling that maybe we jumped too soon on his death," Sharkey told journalist Roberta Plutzig, "but once the wheels are in motion and commitments were made to the format of the show, there was no turning back. When I accepted the assignment, I thought it was going to be good for me as an actor to do this pilot, but I didn't know it would go any further and I liked the idea that it was a part with closure. In the second or third week of the run, I knew it was going to take off. Then I realized I would have loved to play it for at least a year! To have altered the character to make him live on would have been a bad decision, though it would have appeased my ego!" By the time he returned, the series had aired and was into re-runs, and he was mobbed at the airport and from there on. "I was turning around to see who they were goggling over. Boxes of mail arrived.... People were giving us these Sonny-isms! It was insane, it was crazy time. Half the people who are fans caught it on the re-runs. CBS put me on this promo tour, which was unprecedented. Nobody ever went on a promo tour for re-runs!"

The response of the networks to Sharkey's success was embarrassingly typical and depressingly predictable; they first tried to cast him as a *detective* in his own series, then tried to place him in a sit-com that changed its title over half-a-dozen times before being canned, and finally had him playing a cartoon of Steelgrave as real-life gangster Al Capone — whom he resembled not in the slightest — in the TV film *The Revenge of Al Capone*. Coincidentally, Sharkey had also appeared in a poor Danny De Vito comedy called *Wiseguys*, which had primarily proven that horror director and Hitchcock admirer Brian De Palma couldn't do comedy, and equally coincidentally, De Palma had directed the superbly gory and successful gangster movie *Scarface,* a film which was to have a strong influence on the series' final season. One of Sharkey's more controversial roles was in the poorly-received anti-drug feature *Wired,* an adaptation of Watergate reporter Bob Woodward's notorious book on the life and death of comedian John Belushi (Sharkey had guest-starred with Belushi on *Saturday Night Live,* and had endured a much-publicized run-in with the drug culture himself, delivering fervent anti-drug messages during numerous PR pieces for *Wiseguy*).* Tragically, he failed to listen to his own lectures, returning to heroin in the 1990s, and dying amid a flurry of grim and highly unfavorable publicity in 1993 from an AIDS–infected needle.

From Little Caesar and Cody Jarrett, Cannell and new aide David Burke moved on to Emperor Nero. The first two episodes of the Profitt storyline were written by Cannell himself, and in many ways resembled the emphasis of the pilot on action, *femmes fatales,* cool killers, and hardware. Faced with the challenge of topping Ray Sharkey's villainy, Cannell conceived Mel Profitt, a Napoleonic loon who has based his massive drug and arms empire on Malthusian philosophy, which he expounds to Wahl's Terranova in a superbly deranged and passionate drawn-out rant in Burke's "Smokey Mountain Requiem." Cannell introduces Mel (Kevin Spacey) and his faithful and devoted sister Susan (Joan Severance) in the second of his two opening salvos, using the first to return to his recurring theme of the hero figure's darkside persona, here represented by Vietnam vet and CIA recruit Roger Loccoco (William Russ), a Terranova gone bad.

Terranova joins the Profitt organization after befriending Loccoco, a weapons-crazy nihilist who is one of the Profitts' leading lights in their global set-up. "Everywhere he goes, the coroner is working overtime," says McPike. Although their initial meeting smacks of contrivance (two arms enthusiasts just happen to be sitting next to each other at a poolside table?), the remainder of the season is beautifully constructed and performed. The Profitts (a.k.a. Martin, after the foster family who took them in, and whose son they subsequently murdered) are orphaned and abandoned by society and live in their own paranoid playground, where their sky-high intellects are matched only by their detached and deranged killer tendencies. Mel is having an incestuous relationship with his sinister sister, and when Susan is abducted in Cannell's "Fascination for the Flame," explodes into a childish tantrum (the sequence in which Profitt reacts to the information of his sister's abduction is a fabulous performance). To further complicate things, the sultry and seductive Susan has her doe-eyes on Vinnie. Loccoco, who obviously has an agenda of his own, has not been corrupted by the flashy wealth and strutting machismo of a Steelgrave empire, which — as he disdainfully points out — is a drop in the ocean to someone like Mel Profitt, but by the corruption and distortion of the notion of democracy that had been exposed and popularized during the Vietnam/Nixon period. In a storyline that reeks of "Irangate," Loccoco, a child of the McCarthy era, truly believes — or has forced himself to believe — that his covert operations against the law and the Constitution have been done in the name of preserving and safeguarding American ideals of freedom and security against a hazily-defined Enemy. However, just as McCarthy did more damage to the national spirit and American pride with his witch-hunts than any cabal of Russian spies could have achieved, so Loccoco has corrupted the American ideals in his efforts to maintain them. To Loccoco, genuinely concerned about ecology and underdeveloped nations,

---

Playing Belushi was the versatile Michael Chiklis, who played a minor thug in the third season of Wiseguy *and went on to star in Cannell's 1991 series* The Commish.

the national interest is all, and when his mentor, the darkside McPike Herb Ketcher (David Spielberg, in one of the finest of his many character parts), is revealed as a deceitful and cynical phony as greedy and deranged as Profitt, Loccoco's perception of the world falls apart before his eyes. In a twist from the standard scenario in which the CIA warns the hero not to get involved with CIA business (a scenario which makes an appearance in more traditional form in the series' final year), the agency beg Vinnie to stay inside the Profitt organization as he's already closer to Mel and Susan than any other agent is likely to get. Vinnie still feels he's out of his depth, but Loccoco coolly points out that if Vinnie quits on Mel, even with a legitimate story, Mel will assume he's a cop and order him killed ... by Loccoco. And he'll have no choice but to do it.

Kevin Spacey, cast as Mel Profitt, was a Juilliard-trained theater actor and usually invisible supporting player in features who was then unknown, and, like Sharkey, seized the moment. "He's fun to play because there are no boundaries," Spacey told Alan Carter for the *New York Daily News*. "You never know which way he's going to go. [*Wiseguy*] is a great arrangement for an actor like myself who doesn't want to do a weekly series as a steady diet. [Ray Sharkey] was very popular with the audience and the cast and crew, and here I was, dropped from the sky, this New York stage actor...!"

Wrote James Wolcott in his colorful and perceptive *Vanity Fair* piece, "The Profitt empire was a floating politburo of illicit fantasies, a woozy casino unconcerned with national borders and normal hours. The show became a dusk-to-dawn study in disorientation as everyone lost sleep hunting down Mel's whims. The starkest toll was taken on Mel himself. As this amoral schizo with a genius IQ, Kevin Spacey had a field day splicing his moods in a mercurial flash from giddy joy to killer hate... As Susan, Joan Severance showed less range but was a fabulous camera subject, with a model's full armory of shotgun nostrils, thrust lips, inch-long lashes, heaping handfuls of hair, and firm, frank, mobile hips." Said Severance's manager Erwin More to *Hollywood Reporter*, "Here's a person who could get 20,000 dollars to walk down a fashion runway. She came to us (the Larry Thompson Organization) and said 'I'm willing to give you a year. I'll do no modeling, just work on an acting career.' She was thirty-one, and knew it was time. Her work on *Wiseguy* was complicated and sexy. She refuses to play bimbo roles." Features included a reteaming with Kevin Spacey to play the villains in the Gene Wilder/Richard Pryor comedy *See No Evil, Hear No Evil*, and *No Holds Barred*, with "Hulk" Hogan, while Spacey, perhaps ill-advisedly, seemed to be recreating the Mel Proffitt role as a crazy eccentric businessman in a later episode of *L.A. Law*, before moving into the big time on stage and screen.

Cast as Roger Loccoco was William Russ, an actor with features that were too much man to be a teenager, but suggested too much of the boy in his face to look adult. As the duped but wily assassin Loccoco, emotional enough to be propelled by a passionate love for the flag, emotion*less* enough to kill anyone, anything, or any number in its name, Russ was perfect casting, the man conveying enough authority and experience to represent his tough experiences in Vietnam and his capabilities as an ice-cool, shit-hot hit-man, the boy looking immature enough to have been sucked in by the middle-aged evil of David Spielberg's dumpy devil Herb Ketcher, an unassuming, insignificant-looking man so drably normal in his appearance that he had no choice but to be completely mad.

Russ started out on TV in the soap *Another World,* guested as a wacky CIA agent in an episode of *Riptide* some years earlier (the light and loony "Polly Want an Explanation," by Babs Greyhosky), appeared in *Hunter,* and inevitably chalked up roles in Michael Mann's

Miami Vice and the pilot for *Crime Story;* he went on to play a nondescript role in the disappointing MTM flop *Capital News* and the thankless role of the father in the dire but popular Disney sit-com *Boy Meets World*. "Basically, I'm a very shy, boring guy," Russ told journalist Frank Lovece. "Roger Loccoco is totally unlike me. I'm an ex-altar boy! I don't really care much for guns!" Russ later secured another juicy one-off showpiece in an early episode of *Stargate—SG-1* in an *Apocalypse Now*–style madman role. David Spielberg, occasionally a faceless precinct cop in the likes of *The Rockford Files* and *Hardcastle and McCormick*,* has since made a far more interesting career out of playing evil slit-eyed non-entities as he became balding and portly, and just keeps getting better and better. Imagine a dark, cold, confident, joke-free and unspeakably evil George Costanza.

On the surface, the Proffitt storyline was Ian Fleming's James Bond on the screen, even down to Roger Loccoco's souped-up supercar with built-in Gatling gun and the punnish names of the decadent duo (who trade under the '60s spy movie-ish company name of S & M Profitt). But the difference was that the Profitts, Ketcher, and Loccoco were fascinating, well-performed, complex and contradictory characters, far more finely-drawn and intriguing than the cartoon cut-outs of *James Bond* movies, and a much-needed change of direction to avoid emulating the mob milieu of the Steelgrave saga. This was a captivating mix of political adventure and undercover agent action, espionage as it should be played, and built on the premise that fact-based fiction is far more incredible and alluring than death-ray fantasies. As the series spun it, "When he's in the mood, nobody lives like Mel Proffit. And once you've lived with him, the rest of the world seems very dark and very cold."

"The Profitts were tough to write," Burke told Ed Gross, "but actually when you threw all your preconceived notions away and just started to write, they were fun. Cannell defined them pretty well. They were a psychotic critical mass, and they needed each other to be functional... Anyone outside that relationship was a potential threat, because Mel was crazy."

But in many ways, like Roy Thinnes' David Vincent character in the '60s sci-fi series *The Invaders*, or Patrick McGoohan's Number Six in *The Prisoner*, Mel's madness was justified—because everybody *was* out to get him. His friends were phonies, his enemies were high-rolling killers, both Terranova and Loccoco had their own motivations for their supposed loyalty, and Washington's hierarchy conspired to prove that what they giveth, they could also take away. Ultimately, Mel is destroyed by Machiavellian machinations in the corridors of power that he could never have begun to comprehend, and in a superb twist in Cannell's "Fascination for the Flame," which introduces and establishes the character of Mel Profitt, Mel's paranoiac and unreasonable suspicion that drug-lord Paco's new beautiful blonde wife might be a CIA spook simply because she comes from Virginia turns out to be right on the button...!

The third episode, "Smokey Mountain Requiem," written by David Burke from a story by Hans Tobeason, was an entertaining actioner with some nice character play between Lococco and Terranova out in rural farmland and some wonderful dialogue; "We were seeded by the cocoa leaf, but it's not where our power comes from now!" announces Susan dreamily. "Like most boys of nineteen, he knew he'd never die" says a tired mother, bitterly. "Lead us not into temptation!" whines a religious zealot shooting vermin in his farmyard barn, "if that rat was a Christian, he'd be alive today!" "You know, it's going to be a major disappoint-

---

*He was also Richie Brockelman's *older brother in that series' episode "The Framing of Perfect Sidney."*

ment in my life if I don't get a chance to kill that guy!" mutters Lococco as a bloated drug kingpin jeers at him — and later, from a Fed cleaning up: "Hey, there's a guy in here with his head on backwards!"

While "Smokey Mountain Requiem" is a nice, taut mini-feature with some strong moments, enjoyable action sequences and the feel of a small drugs'n'guns feature film, "Player to Be Named Now," although neatly illustrating the way rich men can buy and sell human lives on a whim and interfere on impulse in the lives of hundreds of people in both a large and small way, can only offer some superb performances from Spacey and Russ, a scary scene as Loccoco terrorizes a washed-up party girl, and a nice bit of business between McPike and Clyde Kusatsu's cop Sashousa. For most shows, this is more than can be hoped for — from first season *Wiseguy*, it's short change.

"The Merchant of Death," written by Carol Mendelsohn, has a wonderfully cynical plot development in which Profitt buys a small country, Isle Pavot; that way, they reason, they won't have to buy and sell weapons any more because the U.S. will just throw them at them! When McPike tries to prevent the subsequent arms deal going through, it does anyway, and the episode has established that Mel's influence reaches inside the labyrinth of Washington. Inevitably — in Gina Wendkos' "The Squeeze" — it is these connections which betray Vinnie's deep cover to Loccoco and Herb Ketcher, who are also working to destroy the Profitts for their own ulterior motives.

"Not for Nothin'" takes Vinnie safely away from the farm and back to the big city, resurrecting the ghost of Sonny Steelgrave in the form of jerky hood Aldo Baglia (Robert Mangiardi), the two-bit son of the Baglia family who was cheated out of his piece of Atlantic City by Terranova's termite job on the house of Steelgrave. When the whole shaky edifice finally tumbled down, Baglia lost his franchise, and when he hears that his father "Joey Bags" (Nathan Davis) has died of a heart attack, he makes a clumsy and brutal hit on Vinnie after following him to the Profitt organization. The shooting sequence is a typical *Wiseguy* moment, with Vinnie downed during the split second McPike has left his telescope to grab his burger from room service.

Returning almost immediately to the window, McPike is mortified to be greeted by the scene of chaotic pandemonium below. Mel's vanity and Loccoco's logic both cause them to assume that Vinnie simply got in the way of a bullet for Mel, but Loccoco begins to have his doubts, and in a wonderfully creative scene ingeniously rigs up a pair of sticky-tape shoes and plays dumb to tramp around the scene of the crime picking up an assortment of clues as he traipses around the sealed apartment to the uncomprehending irritation of the police!

Ultimately, Mel slips completely over the edge, and become obsessed with the voodoo background of Louis Cabra, the political rival of Isle Pavot's despot-in-residence, who the Washington cabal want taken out of the picture. Loccoco and Ketcher fall out when the pompous buffoon Henri Lalonde (Ben Halley, Jr.), a puppet politician to be installed on Isle Pavot turns out to be a greater liability than first thought with his delusions of grandeur. Although he's antagonized Loccoco, Ketcher insists that this absurd figure must be installed in the newly-created banana republic regime Mel's money is to finance. Eric Blakeney's "Blood Dance" is followed by Stephen Kronish's "Phantom Pain," which wraps up the Susan Profitt storyline, and Burke's "Dirty Little Wars," in which the theme of betrayal comes up yet again, when Loccoco learns of the deceit of his darkside McPike, Herb Ketcher. While Loccoco's deeds have all been done in the name of democracy as he perceives it, Ketcher's motivation has been nothing more complex than money. The follow-up, "Date with an Angel," has a wonderful double-meaning as Ketcher, deserted by his Washington spooks, blows his brains out after being duped during a liaison with a superbly played hooker (Traci Lords, notorious former porn actress).*

"*Wiseguy* has the craziest charge of endangerment since the hallelujah days of *Hill Street Blues*," raved James Wolcott in *Vanity Fair*—"Kevin Spacey did stuff I've never seen anyone do on TV before." "*Wiseguy* featured the best action drama writing of the year," wrote Bob Knight in *Variety*, "and probably the best acting job by Ray Sharkey of any series on the air this season." "Briskly paced, deftly plotted, consistently interesting," wrote Steve Sonsky in the *Miami Herald*. "When a show is this well produced, this well-stocked with sensational bad guys, this taut, action-packed, and pulse-racing, you have to give it its due," insisted Bill Carter in the *Baltimore Sun*—"It is better than every other crime or cop drama on TV, a genuine thrill ride." *Wiseguy* found itself renewed for another year.

Wiseguy came back for a second season with two imposed concessions—shorter stories and the new feature of a weekly update scene opening each episode with McPike briefing his superiors—and thus the audience—on the situation so far. These made *Wiseguy* a little more conventional, but could be lived with. Replacing Eric Blakeney as story editor was John Schulian, later to spend a number of years on the series *Midnight Caller* and *Reasonable Doubts*. Also departing (to Vietnam war series *Tour of Duty*) was story editor Carol Mendelsohn. Remaining with the series was Stephen Kronish, formerly a story editor on the revived early-'80s *Alfred Hitchcock Presents* and a co-producer on *MacGyver*† and Alfonse Ruggerio, Jr., who had cut his teeth on *Baretta* and *Airwolf*.

The second season began with a classy, well-observed study of the cancer of racism, which notably avoided the clichés of redneck Southerners to remind the audience that racism is everywhere, not just the domain of purely evil people, but a disease that can warp the minds of otherwise good but simple souls. Knox Pooley, as portrayed by real-life Watergate lawyer Fred Dalton Thompson, is a silver-tongued immoral salesman, as happy to sell hate as encyclopedias ... or indeed, condos, which is where he ends up at the close of this adventure after destroying lives and communities during the course of a powerful, intense and thoroughly downbeat and depressing four-parter. Pooley's activities in turning a profit out of hate and misery as he breeds racial resentment in Vinnie's neighborhood are the business of Vinnie's next assignment, a mission made personal by the murder of his brother....

Ray Sharkey had suggested in the press that the *Wiseguy* writers had plundered his 1981 TV feature *The Idolmaker* for ideas, and this certainly also seems to be the case with Ken Wahl's two early films *The Omega Syndrome* (elements of which turn up in the racist storyline) and *The Gladiator*, which features an encounter group scene very similar to that found in the first season bridging episode "Last Rites for Lucci." As with Nick Mancuso and *Stingray*, the writers had apparently been rifling through the actor's personal background and previous work for ideas. In "Goin' Home," which bears a passing resemblance to the themes explored

---

Lords' previous performances were swept off video rental shelves across the U.S. when she blithely announced she was underage when she made almost all of them! She then neatly segued into a more conventional acting career on the strength of all the publicity, including a remake of '50s SF cheapie Not of This Earth, *and the film* Cry Baby *alongside Jump Street's Johnny Depp. TV appearances include a role on the sit-com* Married—with Children, *which delighted in occasionally—but not exclusively—employing other genuine porn actresses as fantasy females!*
†*Following his stint on* Wiseguy, *Kronish worked his way up the ladder within the Cannell operation, co-creating and co-executive producing* Unsub, *executive producing* The Commish, *and creating pilots.*

in *The Omega Syndrome,* a washed out Vinnie returns to his roots in New Jersey to reassess his life, and the second season opener begins some weeks after the end of the previous season, with a weary and bearded Vinnie (he looks ridiculous with a beard), exhausted from the horrors of the high life with Mel Profitt, now working as a mechanic—Wahl's own real-life profession before leaving New Jersey for the bright lights. Before long, he's drawn into a battle with a new adversary when he finds his neighborhood slowly but surely being infiltrated by the poison of a vicious but charismatic fascist who is fermenting hatred and resentment in Vinnie's depression-hit community. As a mobster in the eyes of the locals, Terranova is hardly in a position to preach, and before long McPike sees a way to lure Terranova back into the fold.

One character who was in a position to preach was Vinnie's brother Pete Terranova, played by Gerald Anthony—he was a Catholic priest who had been Vinnie's Jiminy Cricket since the pilot. One of the more interesting aspects of the character of Father Pete was that he was as big a phony as Terranova, and the series had some interesting observations to make about the role of the church in Vinnie's Italian-American neighborhood. In the first season episode "Last Rites for Lucci," the knowing next target of a hit-man comes to him for the last rites (Pete can't give them because he's not dead, and besides, suicide is a mortal sin and he's accepting his fate instead of trying to prevent it), and Pete himself admits to Vinnie that he feels "forbidden" urges when he sees an attractive woman. In a later scene he is shown patronizing a member of his parish on the phone he regards as a nuisance, and sacking the woman who answered the phone and ignored his instructions to say he wasn't available! But the ways of the Lord are indeed mysterious—this unwanted delay gives Vinnie valuable minutes to get to the church and save Father Pete from becoming the next victim of the hit-man.* Also returning from a single first-season appearance (in "The Birthday Surprise") was Kerry Sandomirsky as Vinnie's neighborhood girl Angela Tessio; Sandomirsky had first worked for Cannell in the *JJ Starbuck* episode, "The Full Circle."

The storyline featuring Fred Dalton Thompson as race-hate preacher Knox Pooley may also have inadvertently made some comments about the performances lawyers give in court. Thompson began his acting career in only-in-America style, after replaying his role in a real-life court case that was dramatized on film (*Marie,* starring Sissy Spacek, in 1985). "I'd never even been in a high-school play," said Thompson to the press, but the director asked to use him again, in the feature *No Way Out.* Until then, his major claim to fame had been the Watergate trial ("I was just thirty years old at the time. It was quite an education for a young man. It proved to me that the process works. There were some miscarriages of justice, but the way the country faced up to it and dealt with it was peaceful and according to Constitutional process"). He's since had a prolific film and television career and entered politics, representing Tennessee in the U.S. Senate from 1994 to 2003 and running unsuccessfully for the 2008 Republican presidential nomination. "I get a certain amount of ribbing from my lawyer buddies," Thompson told reporter Gary Mullinax, "but I get them back by telling them about the great hours and the excitement and all those other lies that make them eat their hearts out!"

Playing Pooley's expendable racist stooge, the sad and pathetic Calvin Hollis, was Paul

---

*Steve Kronish and director Bill Corcoran pull the most outrageous cheat on the audience in this episode, by playing sinister music as a man enters the confessional, only to then reveal him as an ordinary parishioner—the real hit-man has yet to take his turn!

Guilfoyle, a talented stage performer in Boston and New York whose film appearances include *Wall Street, Three Men and a Baby, Beverly Hills Cop II, Howard the Duck, Cadillac Man,* and *The Local Stigmatic,* a two character movie with Al Pacino. His television credits include the inevitable *Miami Vice* and *Crime Story,* along with *Kojak, The Equalizer, Kate and Allie, Spenser: for Hire, A Man Called Hawk, Law and Order,* and Cannell's *Unsub.* A Method actor, Guilfoyle spent much of his time on set in character! "There was that wonderful Calvin Hollis scene," recalled David Burke to Ed Gross, "where he's given his first opportunity to speak, but he can't because he's a stutterer. But when he gets out there, he suddenly becomes Hitler, and Paul Guilfoyle was spectacular. No-one said 'Do Hitler,' but when we got the dailies back, his mannerisms were subtle enough to not be an imitation, but you could see this is where he drew his spirit." Hollis, agreed Guilfoyle, "was locked into the whole Nazi sensibility right down to the way he dressed. I wore clothes that were too small for me because everything I did was designed to make me feel tighter, more restricted, repressed."

Perhaps more sinister than either Pooley or Hollis is the way the impressionable and mentor-hungry local boy Richie Stamm is drawn into their corrupting influence. By the third of the four episodes, Richie has begun to realize what a horrible bunch he's fallen in with, but now — as with a religious cult — he feels he's in too deep to get out. Portraying Stamm was Tim Guinee, a stage actor who had also chalked up appearances in *Crime Story, Spenser,* and *The Equalizer.* Guinee was cast in *Wiseguy* after working with Les Sheldon on Cannell's failed sit-com pilot *Livin' Large.*

Once again, the theme is betrayal. In Cannell's superb "Revenge of the Mud People," directed by Bill Corcoran, Vinnie is betrayed by the system when the man who killed Father Pete is beaten to death in the cells by the police after Vinnie has resisted the urge to execute vigilante justice (in order to prove to the gullible locals under Pooley's influence that the system works). Stamm has been betrayed by Pooley's words, and Vinnie (in a weakly considered plot development) reveals his FBI identity to Stamm to persuade him to betray Pooley's thugs. At the same time, Vinnie is posing as an arms dealer to infiltrate the increasingly militarist 'Pilgrims of Progress' under Hollis' command. Finally, in Schulian's concluding episode, "Last of the True Believers," directed by Rob Iscove, Pooley and Hollis actually betray *each other;* Pooley is let down by Hollis' murderous excesses, and in a wonderful climatic scene that sends Hollis completely over the edge as he regresses to childhood (and is thus betrayed in turn by Pooley, who abandons him with an angry "I ain't your daddy!!!"), Pooley admonishes Hollis' pitiable militarism, berating him for destroying perfectly good business. Earlier in that same episode, Burke and Schulian have brilliantly demonstrated the way the media naively and inadvertently colludes with the racist manipulators during a pious talk-show, on which Pooley is perfectly happy to be shouted down in the knowledge that the segment of the audience he wants to reach and exploit will perceive him as a persecuted underdog. The producers have agreed to the condition that he will only appear if they will flash his phone number on the screen during the interview! This publicity ultimately escalates into the murders of the talk-show host and a civil rights activist, neither of which would have occurred if the media-hungry Pooley hadn't been accorded a platform in the first place. With uncanny finger-of-fate precision, the fascist storyline first aired just after the headline-making confrontation between racists and a civil rights activist on the tabloid TV show *Geraldo.* All who worked on *Wiseguy,* already concerned that they might inadvertently be publicizing racist viewpoints through their characters, were at pains to point out that it was an ugly but fortuitous coincidence that the Knox Pooley story included a talk show debacle with a somewhat grimmer, but similar outcome.*

In many ways, the superior quality of the first season served to obscure just how good this four-parter was. Thompson and Guilfoyle made excellent villains, with Thompson superb as the shrewd but ethically bankrupt manipulator Knox Pooley, who no more believes his racist diatribes than he does a used car spiel, but understands human weaknesses perfectly, and Guilfoyle in particular offering an instantly recognizable and thoroughly embarrassing portrait of the breed of self-loathing bitter simpletons who embrace racism's allure to bolster their own inferiority complex by bullying and persecuting others. Unlike the sadly all-too-real but nevertheless tired stereotype of the racist redneck slob, Guilfoyle's Calvin Hollis offers no appealing good ol' boy characteristics or justifiable anger whatsoever for real racists to latch on to. So instantly recognizable is Guilfoyle's sniveling dupe, that he is the worst advertisement for fascism ever presented on television.

Pooley, confirms Thompson, is equally pathetic underneath his salesman's confident veneer. "He's using white supremacism as his latest venture to make a buck," he told Mullinax. "He uses fear and prejudice to go out and raise money through the sale of books and cassettes for instance. But in his more private moments he's insecure. He doesn't get any respect from his wife and kids. He's kind of pitiful."

Indeed he was, but the racist storyline was the first in the series where the viewer couldn't really feel any empathy for the villains. Steelgrave and the Profitts were victims of their environment and their upbringing and had a certain enviable charisma about them; Pooley and Hollis were undeniably nasty pieces of work, genuinely hateful specimens with no redeeming qualities at all. In fact, if the story has a flaw, it is that whereas the villainous excesses of Steelgrave and Profitt were fun, the racism episodes are so powerfully put together that they are by necessity profoundly difficult to watch. There's not even the satisfaction of seeing the villains ultimately come to grief— though Pooley is routed and Hollis is returned to his maker stamped "reject," nothing is ultimately resolved; the racists have not learned their lesson but simply end up leaderless, gullible and malleable pawns for the next easy-answer huckster. The circumstances which bred their fearful hate have not gone away (it would have been shamefully bogus to suggest otherwise), and Pooley ends up in the Florida sunshine, happily selling retirement homes to clientele of all religious and ethnic groups. By creating real racists, rather than obvious straw men to be knocked down, writers Cannell, Burke, Kronish, and Schulian manage, during the course of the four parts, to offer numerous insights into the nature of racism through a variety of interesting character portraits of weak men. Particularly valuable is the picture painted of Vinnie's friend and boss at the garage; beset by the influx of Japanese industry in the U.S., his business suffers, and in his distress and fear it is a small step to the empty but uplifting evangelical simplicity of Pooley's Bible of hate. Before long, he has accompanied the cowardly and anonymous sheet-clad pack-rats to desecrate a synagogue, only to recoil in tearful remorse when he realizes what his bitterness has taken him to. For others though — the natural bullies and the impressionable — the horror of what they are doing escapes them until Pooley disappears into the night and Hollis comes to his end in a fiery conflagration that sends him to hell most definitely not rare but certainly prematurely well-done.

---

*The Geraldo debacle might have possibly inspired "It's How You Play the Game," a superb episode of the sit-com Murphy Brown written by Russ Woody and directed by Barnet Kellman. The final bringdown closing scene packs a punch unseen since the classic "Guess Who's Coming to Brefnish?" by Barry Kemp and James Burrows that introduced Carol Kane's character of Simka to the immortal Taxi.

"Ray Sharkey as vicious mob boss Sonny Steelgrave generated enough histrionic juice to blow all the fuses at San Quentin," wrote Harry Waters and Janet Huck for *Newsweek*. "Then came the sinuously creepy Profitt siblings (Joan Severance and Kevin Spacey), a pair of incestuous drug merchants. Intrigued by offbeat casting, Cannell next enlisted Watergate lawyer turned part-time actor Fred Thompson to portray a rabble-rousing bigot. And last week, he launched a Jerry Lewis arc, in which the comedian plays a garment industry mogul...."

Jerry Lewis, as they say, needs no introduction! Best known for his series of buddy movies with Dean Martin in the 1950s, he attracted Cannell's attention following his memorable dramatic performance in Martin Scorsese's *The King of Comedy* (1982). Born Joseph Levitch, he is a native of Newark, New Jersey who was firmly ensconced in show business by the early 1940s, and making films by 1949. Ten years later, he had signed the biggest movie contract for a single star in the history of Hollywood, and was writing, producing and directing. While his comedy career went into decline during the '70s following a string of incredibly popular physical slapstick fantasies in the '60s, much mirth of a different kind has always been drawn in the U.S. from the fact that while in his home country his style of humor is now considered absurdly broad and dated, he is revered in France where the critics and academics rave with as much passion and conviction as American audiences blanch. With his extraordinary performance in *The King of Comedy*, a portrayal far removed from the jerky adolescent nerd of his '50s and '60s features, he once again attracted favorable reviews. His role as garment industry boss Eli Sternberg in *Wiseguy* bore no relation to his portrayal of Scorsese's talk show host and added another string to his bow.

Wrote Matt Roush in *USA Today*, "The setting is New York's garment district, where self-made success Eli Sternberg (Lewis) finds his clothing business near tatters — probably thanks to the mob, which he must turn to for financial help. Lewis plays Eli with forceful 'love-ya-babe' show-biz savvy, brow-beating his workers, gladhanding the right people, and sustaining a love-hate relationship with his son David."

Portraying David was Ron Silver, an award-winning Broadway actor whose film credits include *Silkwood, Garbo Talks, Blue Steel, Semi-Tough* and *Timecop*. His TV work includes *The Rockford Files, Hill Street Blues,* and a recurring role in *Rhoda,* and he won further acclaim for the mini-series *The Billionaire Boy's Club,* which earned him an Emmy.

Due to the writers' strike of '88, the new season started late, in October, and Jerry Lewis started filming on the rag trade storyline in November '88 straight from a two week engagement in Vegas with Sammy Davis, Jr. "We thought Jerry wouldn't do it," Burke told Moira Farrow of the *New York Times*, "but he was a good mental picture to have in mind as we were writing"— but it turned out that Lewis was impressed by the show and its concept of multi-episode storylines, enabling the series to achieve the depth of characterization Burke enjoyed writing. Both Lewis and Silver referred to their work, and their motives for doing *Wiseguy,* as being like doing "a five-hour movie."

Terranova is drawn into the story posing as a euphemistically titled security consultant after Sternberg's son — more hip to the ways of modern day mobsters than his father, who believes that a man's word is his bond — calls in the Feds after Sternberg Sr., does his deal with slimy mobster Ricky Pinzolo. As Eli Sternberg, the Lewis character sees nothing wrong with doing business with shady characters — it's part and parcel of everyday business — but only his son realizes the nest of vipers his father is getting into. Absurdly, David is forced to go to the extreme of approaching the authorities because he is completely unable to communicate with his overbearing and domineering father, and it is this inability that is the catalyst for both the story and their ultimate destruction. Burke, Kronish, and director Rob Iscove draw comparisons with the mobs of the old days and the new breed of yuppie gangsters by having Pinzolo show off his snazzy new juicer and talk health with Lewis' proud businessman. In the old days, if a gangster talked of health as he held court, it meant bullets for somebody; Pinzolo is talking diet, and in a brutally wicked twist Pinzolo gets popped viciously and painfully in the mouth twice when the tables are turned, condemning him to a painful few months with a wired jaw drinking nothing *but* liquids! Pinzolo was superbly played by Stanley Tucci, a familiar provider of smug, weasely gangsters during the '80s, who — it hardly needs to be said by now — did a wonderful mob turn in *Miami Vice* as the strutting Frank Mosca, who in one memorable scene in the fourth season opener "Conflict of Interest," sits in court eating and offering chocolates!

With the exception of Tucci's splendidly ugly Steelgrave-wannabe, there are no real clearcut villains in this storyline, which instead is more of a character piece that ends in tragedy. Unlike most cop show scenarios, Sternberg doesn't really deserve the misery that he is left to live with at the series' end. For this reason, the story is not terribly satisfying and the rag trade series ambles along a little longer than it might have done, the five episodes seeming more like ten, with a few nice scenes mixed in with some dumb ones. The casting and performances, which are uniformly excellent, hold the piece together, but the storyline was further hampered by an accident on the set that wrote out Ken Wahl's Vinnie Terranova from the plot.

Although it was Wahl who had first suggested casting Jerry Lewis as Sternberg, he hardly got the chance to appear with him. Shortly into shooting, a heavy camera trolley ran over Wahl's foot not once, but twice, hospitalizing the star and throwing the entire storyline into disarray. *Wiseguy* was not a movie, despite the quality and integrity of its scripts, and the show had to go on ... or come off. There was no way the series could be put on hold for a few weeks until Wahl could return to work — weekly episodes had to appear. The scripts were hastily rewritten to put Vinnie in the hospital, and McPike was faced with abandoning the operation or bringing in someone else — a dilemma the writers were now certainly well-equipped to write about! Into the storyline came John Henry Raglin, an equally troubled fellow undercover operative played by Anthony Denison, another *Crime Story* alumnus (Denison's actress wife, Jennifer Evans, also secured a part in the deal). Conversely, just as the *Wiseguy* villains had appeared in minor and unnoticeable roles in *Crime Story*, Denison — who played *Crime Story's* charismatic continuing antagonist Ray Luca with such power and presence — appeared to little effect as Wahl's replacement in *Wiseguy*. As Raglin, Denison was totally uninteresting and lacking in charisma; as Ray Luca, *Crime Story's* answer to Sonny Steelgrave, he was fabulous. However, Burke's frantic eleventh hour call to his friend saved the show from closing down completely.

The storyline was further restricted by Silver's insistence on returning home for the holidays, and he was written out of episodes two and three, a demand he claimed he later regretted, before being killed off in part four at his own suggestion (one wonders what his conditions would have been if he had disliked the role!). As a result of all this, the writers had to rebuild their story around Wahl's accident, Denison's arrival, and Silvers' absence and strict contractual demands. The rag trade story staggered toward the end of its storyline buoyed by the presence of the excellent Stanley Tucci, Lewis, Silver, and two other *Crime Story emigrees*, Patricia Charbonneau and John Santucci.* Santucci has some marvelous, insanely violent scenes

---

*Denison later went on to take the lead in a short-lived CIA series from the makers of China Beach, *titled* The Company, *while Tucci was efficient but wasted as a good guy in the syndicated cop show* The Street. *Later he played a key role in the first season of Steven Bochco's* Murder One *in the mid–'90s.*

as he attacks Vinnie with a baseball bat in Burke and Kronish's "Seventh Avenue Freeze-Out" (directed by Iscove), and is later repaid in full in a back alley, finally calmly stepping out of a window to his doom while in police custody rather than wait for an inevitable assassin's bullet! Not for him the hysteria of the suicidal mob stoolie in Bogart's 1952 classic *The Enforcer!* Wahl's accident, which resulted in the second and third episodes being completely restructured (the hospital scenes in "Next of Kin" consist of plot exposition that has plainly been written to fill in newly created holes in the plot and other bits of business transposed from a party scene), effectively cut down Charbonneau's planned romance with Vinnie and making her a peripheral character.

"Eli is a mix of ego, drive, and pride, qualities Lewis portrays cannily," wrote Roush in his *USA Today* review. "But beneath the bluster is a man on the edge of deflation, as he reluctantly borrows two million from a cold-eyed crook who specializes in rag trade takeovers. As David, who approaches the Feds because he's worried for his dad and for the business he'll inherit, Silver is a quivering bundle of nervy energy."

And of Jerry Lewis' closing scene, Kronish summed up the feelings of everyone concerning Lewis' extraordinary performance when he told Ed Gross, "That final speech I had written just came out right, and it was enhanced by Jerry's playing it the way he did.... There aren't many times when you can watch your own stuff and get emotionally moved by it, because you know it so well and you know what it took to put it down on paper, but that was a moment where I got a little choked up when I heard him saying those things. If I had to pick one of the big moments that had affected me, that would be number one."

While good, solid drama, the Steelgrave and Profitt sagas of the fabulous first season were a tough act to follow, and the rag trade storyline had no chance, even with Wahl. Without the star, the audience forgivingly coasted along.

Wiseguy was, unfortunately, a variable series in its second and third seasons. Part of the problem was that if a regular weekly series had a bad episode it was over in an hour — but if *Wiseguy* went off on a wayward tangent, the damage lasted for the duration of the storyline — which might be weeks. It was a long time for the audience to stick around waiting for things to get better. This was never truer than when *Wiseguy* segued into a name-bloated rock industry storyline that was too long at seven weeks, and was then extended to nine to stroke Wahl.

It had been decided, perhaps rightly, that the racist and rag trade storylines had been heavy going for audience and staff alike, and so the writers contrived to allow Vinnie to probe corruption in the record industry to lighten things up. As a four-parter, this star-studded diversion — Glenn Frey (acting debut: *Miami Vice*), Deborah Harry, Tim Curry, Paul Winfield, Patti D'Arbanville, Mick Fleetwood — would have been fun and different, a healthy breather for both Vinnie and the audience from the save-the-world storylines with rabid mad-dog mobsters and super-monsters. The bloated egos of the rock industry sharks hurt nothing but the rock industry itself, which frankly, could stand the pressure. Its denizens were not the most sympathetic people in the world, and neither its victims nor its tortured villains solicited much sympathy. Like the glossy cartoon characters of the prime-time soaps, even when suffering, they were living better than most ordinary folk.

Things improved marginally with a return to the mob environment for a six-parter starring the charismatic Robert Davi, and a brief slither in the labyrinthine corridors of power in Washington with Norman Lloyd as another monster in a suit, this time a fanatical politician. While these stories kept the flagging show's head above the water, they were essentially second trips to the well that had been dug in the first season, and highlighted all too clearly the limited lifespan of the series and its concept. They were two perfectly adequate stories, had we not seen what the series was truly capable of. *Wiseguy* still had yet to return to the heights scaled during that first glorious season.

Sadly, this was something the series would never do. The show rapidly lapsed into a macho soap opera, a blue-collar *thirtysomething* made up of single episode sob stories more concerned with the personal lives of Vinnie, McPike, and the Lifeguard. Once in a while, these stories were welcome and desirable; "Last Rites for Lucci" had been all right, with just enough novel touches to keep it from resembling an average *Streets of San Francisco, Kojak,* or *Baretta* episode — but instead of scattering such diversions amid powerful storylines, they became the body of the series itself, with Vinnie's increasingly disappointing assignments being the rarity.

"Call It Casaba" (the title is a sly macho tit joke) was a fun episode primarily for the fans and the actors in which Terranova, McPike, and the Lifeguard all head for a mountain retreat and some R & R. Unfortunately, in the process it completely destroyed the relationships built up between the three characters; Terranova and McPike were better when they were at odds with each other, and the valued anonymity between the agent and his "lifeguard" was lost forever. "Casaba" was also a bridging episode between the rock industry storyline and the new mob saga, which was laboriously introduced in "Le Lacrime D'Amore" (the title taken from an opera by Donizetti, parts performed by the very competent Robert Davi) during an interminable and indulgent romance between Wahl's Vinnie and the rock industry character Amber Twine, played by Patti D'Arbanville. D'Arbanville was the wife of *Miami Vice* lead Don Johnson, and had appeared in both that series and Mann's *Crime Story*.

The mob story, in which Terranova palled it up with Davi's family man mobster Albert Cerrico, was well-cast (Anne DeSalvo was fun as a shrewish wife, with John Snyder playing the henpecked Joey Grosset as a cross between David Marciano's ersatz Lorenzo Steelgrave and Ed O'Neill's Al Bundy of *Married — with Children*) and had its share of moments (Davi, an opera-trained singer in real life, creates a nice *la familia* ambience with his moving party-piece arias contrasting curiously with the blithely sanctioned business-like violence of the mob, and the scenes of the Cerrico family heading for the hills in the dead of night in a convoy of bullet-proof limos as war breaks out is marvelously fearful and exciting as the wives pack bags and the babies are pulled from their beds). There was plenty of murder, treachery and gunplay to be had in the yarn, and while it never once gave the illusion of returning the series to the Steelgrave era, it was a welcome and reassuringly tight, if overly familiar, return to the show's favored gangland territory after the crashing boredom of the rock industry story.

This energy was immediately dispelled by a series of no less than four single episodes which plunged the show into weepy, self-absorbed pathos of the *thirtysomething* variety. "Sleepwalk," by David Burke and Clifton Campbell, was an aptly titled angst-ridden interval in which Vinnie and Amber were advised by a therapist (!) to explore their relationship with each other while refraining from each other's bodies. As absurd as it sounds (how many New Joisey toughies have analysts? How many would agree to such a treatment?), it made a mockery of Vinnie that must have had Mel and Sonny rolling in their graves with laughter (this was the wimp they partied with?) and D'Arbanville, although a beautiful woman, was not really compatible with Vinnie. Although likeable, her character couldn't help but give the impression she had Terranova under her thumb and was running rings around him.

"How Will They Remember Me?," by Stephen Kronish and Alfonse Ruggerio, attempted to explain what drove Vinnie to the OCB, an interesting gap in the show's premise filled by an entirely predictable series of flashbacks — yes, in black and white — relating a clichéd yarn which creatively, if illogically, was played out by actors more familiar for different, previous roles in the series. By now, the series seemed hopelessly lost and self-indulgent, giving the unavoidable impression that the writers were treading water while trying to come up with a new multi-part plot-line.

"People Do It All the Time," by David Braden, David Curran, and Suzanne Oshry, was a Lifeguard episode which gave the formerly mysterious Uncle Mike his turn in the spotlight (this weepie alone would have been more than enough as a bridge between multi-episode stories), and "The Reunion," by Don Kurt, Burke, and Ruggerio, was Cannell's standard high school reunion plot.

The Washington arc which followed was a bungled conspiracy yarn with an improbable plot so ridiculous — high-powered politicos conspire to destroy the Japanese economy and avenge themselves on Terranova at the same time — that it was of course quite plausible compared with the known machinations of certain real world political figures. The unbelievable elements in the storyline came from the flaws in the telling of it — Vinnie's blinkered, starry-eyed naiveté and lack of cynicism in Washington after everything that he'd witnessed during the Steelgrave and Profitt investigations (which had now apparently been magically wiped from his brain), the incompetence of the assassin who was ordered to make his hit look like a random hold-up shooting, but then used a poison instead of a plain ol' bullet (a story development that would have embarrassed the audience for *Diagnosis: Murder*), and an outrageous revelations and confessions climax — complete with shut-up-you-fool gunfire — that would have been rejected by the writers of *Matlock* or *Perry Mason*. A series that was once known for its originality, subtlety, inventiveness and subversion now wallowed in dramatic clichés and formula developments of the worst kind.

Three more fillers straggled behind this four-parter, the best of which was "To Die in Bettendorf," written by Morgan Gendel and directed by Jorge Montesi, which enlightened the audience on the fate of Patrice pawn Sid Royce. Another vain attempt — like "White Noise" — to recapture the glory days of the first season, it didn't quite achieve its aim, but didn't disgrace the show or spoil old memories either. There was some entertainment to be had over witnessing Syd's fate as determined by a spiteful McPike, who had sent this social snob and culture vulture to the mid-West to live the FBI-manufactured life of a shoe salesman called Elvis Prim, but the story was a standard hostage scenario seen a hundred times before in regular cop shows and Dennis Lipscombe, saddled with the unenviable task of portraying smooth and slimy Sid as a guy who had slipped over the edge, had been away from the character for too long, reducing the subtle characteristics he displayed so effectively in the first season to the sort of cardboard recreation another actor might have pulled trying to recreate a role defined by another performer. Bookending this curiosity was the corny "Meet Mike McPike" by Frank Megna, in which we did indeed meet Frank's wayward cantankerous Dad for the usual paint-by-numbers wily-old-coot story, and the dreadful "The Romp," written by Ruggerio and directed by Wahl, which was the dumbest of the lot, with Wahl actually waking up at the end of the story to find out that gee, it wuz all a dream.... Anybody walking into the *Wiseguy* offices with a yarn like that during the first season would have been taken out to the back alley for a touch of the Johnny Coke-Bottles treatment...!

The third season closed with an adventurous and bizarre story mixing elements of *Dark Shadows* with *Twin Peaks,* and which Wahl appears to have abandoned midway to pursue a second storyline involving a waste disposal firm poisoning school playgrounds with the cooperation of corrupt local government. The first section of this confused rambling oddity takes place in a chilly logging town nudgingly named Lynchboro (this once original show was now paying homage to other, less original shows), and stars Steve Ryan (one of Torello's goons in *Crime Story*) as Barnabas Collins lookalike Volchek, a crazed local big shot who runs the local industry, sheriff's office, and whorehouse, and is vampirically draining the will of the inhabitants and the resources of the town by making them dependent on him. Into this strange broth, writers David Burke and Frank Engel (with an assist from Stephen Kronish and Clifton Campbell) throw a serial killer and a standard horror-film crypt given over to cryogenics. Burke was clearly trying to do a horror film for the present day while incorporating as many of the traditional trappings of a vintage example of the genre (Volchek is obsessed with the 1961 minor-league feature *Mr. Sardonicus*), but unfortunately, despite finally bringing back the originality and inspiration the show had once reveled in, he doesn't pull it off. As Wahl segues into the waste disposal storyline by way of having Vinnie crack up during the Lynchboro serial killer revelations and become a rogue agent, Burke brings back William Russ as Roger Loccoco to replace his errant star. For all his craziness, Ryan's Volchek is not a charismatic villain, and other notable guest stars, including Darlanne Fluegel (of *Crime Story* and the last season of *Hunter*) and Bonnie Bartlett (Dr. Craig's wife in *St. Elsewhere*) have little opportunity to strike sparks. Having started out as a meticulously crafted television masterpiece that broke the rules skillfully and purposefully, *Wiseguy* staggered to the end of Terranova's OCB career in a shambolic disarray of scissors and paste scripting, off the wall misfires, tired clichés, and clumsy misjudgments. Compare the complexity and integrity of "Last Rites for Lucci" with the soppy religious romanticism of the final Wahl storyline with the waste disposal firm, which climaxes with church bells ringing symbolically as McPike revives from that ol' TV writer's standby the coma, and it readily becomes apparent just how lost the series had become.

With the close of the third season and the Volchek/Lynchboro debacle, Wahl had a falling out with Cannell Productions and abruptly left the series. He had often complained of "the grind" of doing a weekly series, admitting that he had been "spoiled" by starting out in movies. The show was called *Wiseguy* and not Terranova, and the events at the close of the third season would have made it very difficult to continue with Wahl's cover anyway, so the production immediately started casting around for a third undercover agent (Wahl had, after all, been temporarily replaced by Anthony Denison as John Henry Raglin during his hospitalization in the second season). At the same time, David Burke also left the series, only to resurface as one of three writers on Wahl's next — and disastrous — movie project, the Sidney Furie–directed *The Taking of Beverly Hills*. The film was announced with some fanfare in the trade press, and then it, and Wahl, disappeared from view.

The seeds for Wahl's departure had been sown at the close of the first season, during a promotional tour in which he remarked to at least two journalists that he thought three years of the show would be enough; in fact, the reality of a hit show is that while three years is enough to secure some sort of afterlife in syndication, a five year run is essential to turn a serious profit — indeed, to set everybody up for life. *Wiseguy's* ratings had always been precarious; after a first half-season against *Cheers* and a second half-season against mini-series conclusions (which did no good at all for a series with a continuing storyline; you don't just dip in to *Wiseguy*, you're either hooked or you're not), it had some quality competition during its second and third seasons from the amusing and appealing George Segal flop *Murphy's Law*, the frothy time travel adventure *Quantum Leap,* and the intense, beautifully performed, but sometimes inaccessible *China Beach.*

CBS execs were a little unsure about the series' future without Wahl, but Cannell was no quitter, and his past efforts with *Toma, Black Sheep Squadron, Hunter,* and *The A-Team* had proven he didn't let a series die easily. Cannell squeezed an extra thirteen episodes out of the series by recasting and revamping the show, and produced a stylish and intriguing production that instantly erased memories of Vinnie Terranova as efficiently and permanently as the Salvadoran death squad that disposed of his character. In a double-length series premiere ("The Fruits of the Poisonous Tree," by Cannell and new executive producer Peter Lance), McPike discovers that Vinnie has been snatched from his New Jersey house, and a white paint palm print left on the wall. Backtracking Vinnie's whereabouts, McPike learns that Vinnie had been investigating the disappearance of the missionary son of a friend of his mother in El Salvador, and that the symbol is the sign of a notorious death squad.

Cannell had always demonstrated an admiration for Michael Mann's *Miami Vice,* and had perhaps regretted turning down then–NBC chief Brandon Tartikoff's offer to take the concept under his wing. Just as he had hired staff from Mann's follow-up show *Crime Story* to initially helm *Wiseguy,* his new man in the hot seat was another former *Miami Vice* staffer, Peter Lance. This was more than just a happy coincidence, as *Wiseguy*'s latest setting was to be Miami, the new wiseguy a Cuban-American immigrant, and the target a hypocritical Cuban crime-lord.

Like Burke, Lance had a background in television news and was well-equipped to tackle a series with the depth of *Wiseguy.* A Bachelor of Philosophy, he had a master's in journalism, numerous awards for investigative reporting, Emmys for broadcast journalism, and a degree from Fordham University School of Law. The numerous topics he covered for ABC News would have provided a fascinating selection of potential storylines far beyond the mob war constraints of the Terranova series. Determined to move from news to drama, Lance had turned up in Michael Mann's office in the early '80s without an appointment and was given "five minutes to blow Mann against the wall with a story idea." He was given a job on the spot, rapidly rising to the position of story editor on *Miami Vice* and *Crime Story.* He was an obvious and exciting choice to succeed Burke and the other Mann operation emigrees.

The new *Wiseguy* was different enough to be new, but familiar enough to still possess traces of the show it had been. McPike had grown a beard, and much humor was derived from his prowling around a sultry, sun-drenched Miami in his double-knit dark suit; there was another pop-world guest star in the form of the equally sultry Martika (whose previous television work prior to chart fame had included *Hardcastle and McCormick,* as well as the likes of *Silver Spoons* and *Diff'rent Strokes*); and the new OCB operative, Michael Santana, was a public disgrace and a private hero just as Vinnie had been (the episode ends with a moving funeral service for Vinnie with neither body nor congregation, as McPike keeps a promise made to Mrs. Terranova that, if Vinnie should ever be killed in action, he would reveal his status as an FBI agent and clear his reputation). There was also a devoted father (Manolo Villaverde) to substitute for Vinnie's mother; and whereas the Vinnie Terranova series had opened with a bogus buddy-buddy friendship that culminated in betrayal, the new Michael Santana series began with a phony father-son relationship between Santana and the crime-lord Guzman, who in a superb scene scripted by Cannell for the episode "The Gift," laughs disdainfully at Santana's father's life and beliefs and so further strengthens Santana's resolve to destroy him, demonstrating compellingly that he stood no better chance of understanding the nature of such a relationship than if Santana really had been blood. Just as Vinnie knew he had to take down Sonny Steelgrave the moment he witnessed him throttling the last drop of life from Patrice, so we realize that it is at this point that Santana has decided to bring down Guzman.

Amusingly, the "gift" of the title is a beautiful phallic jeweled rifle which has been passed down through Guzman's family from father to son for generations (echoing the gift Sonny receives posthumously from his brother Dave in "A Deal's a Deal" way back in the beginning of the series)— amusingly because Santana is the recipient and because Guzman is impotently shooting blanks in the bedroom (hence his fatherly adoption of Santana). Like Sonny Steelgrave, who was on the verge of perpetuating the family name with Theresa Baglia before being fried on the morning of the wedding that would have kept his name alive, Guzman is unable to continue the family line.* And where Steelgrave controlled the docks, Guzman, a fabulously oily portrayal by Maximilian Schell, owns a freight operation for which Santana's father works, and which is also a cover for numerous illegal business transactions.

Cast as McPike's newfound ally (Cannell had previously used the name Michael Santana for the drug-smuggling villain of the *Riptide* pilot) was Steven Bauer; Bauer was a Cuban-American expatriate raised in Miami himself, and became interested in acting while at college. His first prime-time acting job was on Cannell's *The Rockford Files,* and he met and befriended later *Miami Vice* lead Don Johnson while they were working on the 1979–'80 series *From Here to Eternity.*† A succession of daytime soaps and busted pilots followed, and Bauer returned to the theater until attracting critical attention in Oliver Stone and Brian De Palma's 1983 gangster classic *Scarface,* which — like this second *Wiseguy* pilot — had a strong subtext involving the constant flood of Cuban refugees to Miami. During the 1970s, Bauer had starred in a multi-part drama series for public television — *Que Pasa USA*— which educated Cuban immigrants in the American way, and Manolo Villaverde, who played Santana's father on *Wiseguy,* had also played his character's father on that series. Prior to taking the role of Michael Santana on the revamped *Wiseguy,* Bauer had attracted further critical praise for his role as the ill-fated DEA agent Kiki Camarena in Michael Mann's 1990 *Drug Wars* mini series, and with amazing gall, one *Wiseguy* episode actually refers to the Camarena case!

As the corrupt businessman Guzman, Maximillian Schell made the most of a superbly-scripted multi-faceted and contradictory role, building an aura around him that suggested both strength and weakness, and guile and gullibility at the same time, and also succeeded in simultaneously provoking a mixed reaction of contempt and respect, ridicule and fear. Equally impressive was the character of the intelligent and obstinate patsy Hillary Stein, evoking memories of the Washington storyline's Kay Gallagher (Kim Griest), but played by Cecil Hoffman in an entirely different way, clear-minded and coolly ambitious where Gallagher had been impulsive and flamboyantly efficient. While Greist's Gallagher had reveled in her sexuality, Hoffman's Stein subdued it beneath stiff suits and a sharp veneer of don't-mess-with-me business, defiantly attractive in spite of herself, but unable to fully suppress giving the impression of being stupidly vulnerable. Ironically, it was the upright Stein who had been professionally embarrassed by Santana and sexually compromised by the deceitful Guzman, a victim of her career's failures, while Gallagher, far more comfortable in a woman's body,

---

*In an extraordinary conversation in Eric Blakeney's "The Marriage of Heaven and Hell" as Steelgrave asks for his daughter's hand in marriage, Nathan Davis' Don Baglia, in a bizarre amalgam of respect and derision, remarks regretfully that he "always knew" Sonny's brother Dave was a "girl-maker!"
†Robert Davi and David Spielberg were also among the cast.

had been a helpless patsy through no fault of her own other than her success, and came across as much more competent and efficient. Hoffman, who had come to prime-time via the *thirtysomething* team's short-lived follow-up series *Dream Street,* stayed with the series to its close, segueing neatly into a near-identical role in the fifth season of Steven Bochco's ailing but still enjoyable *L.A. Law.*

"Fruits of the Poisonous Tree" (also a title for a *Hill Street Blues* episode) was a reference to Santana's attempt to introduce tainted evidence into the trial of leering *Miami Vice*–style drugs kingpin Martinez-Gacha, which results in the disbarring of both himself and the innocent Hillary. His career ruined, he is found by McPike living in a sleazy houseboat with sexy local songbird Dahlia Mendez (pop vocalist Martika) and reluctantly recruited to the cause. "Fruits of the Poisonous Tree" was a classy and enjoyable two hours, much better than anyone had a right to expect, that dealt with Vinnie's demise credibly and creatively within the context of the series, but which was bookended by two absurd flaws. In the scene that introduces the audience to Santana, he is attending the drugs bust that will take the evil Martinez-Gacha (Alex Panas) to trial and culminate with the tainted evidence scandal that will destroy his career as a Federal prosecutor, and strides into the drug lord's den in nothing but a cotton shirt after refusing a bullet-proof vest; this idiotic display of machismo, supposed to show us what a tough cookie Santana is, simply makes him look like the biggest fool on the block, surrounded as he is by both a hail of bullets and SWAT team officers protected like football players. It was hardly the best introduction to the series' new hero, making him look like a suicidal buffoon. And, at the other end of the episode, McPike locates the man who gave the order for Vinnie's execution lolling around luxuriously in a hot-tub. With the promise of a marvelously cathartic denouement, McPike picks up an electric fan and threatens to throw it into the tub ... only to be talked out of the audience's retribution by that ghastly old cliché, the "it'll make you as bad as he is" speech! (To add insult to injury, this dreary cop-out had already been blown away along with David Marciano's bogus Lorenzo in the first season classic "The Loose Cannon"). In a cowardly and pointless tag that lets McPike off the hook and belatedly tries to compensate, we are offered a contrived scene showing the culprit come to a grisly and unexplained end in the slammer. But the damage has been done — McPike has been cheated out of his revenge, and both Vinnie and the audience have been let down by one of the oldest and corniest routines in crime shows.

Nevertheless, the new *Wiseguy* was a breath of fresh air for a series which had never quite recaptured the thrill and energy of that first fabulous season, and despite a few classy moments and small victories along the way, the Ken Wahl version had undeniably been on its last legs at the close of the third season due to the exhaustion of the writing staff and what seemed to be to the outsider constant efforts to sweeten Wahl, every one of which had been to the detriment of the series. The *Variety* review for the new pilot, which aired as a mid-season replacement in November 1990, was unreasonably harsh, announcing that "Only the stabilizing presence of Jonathan Banks salvages the premiere of what was once the smartest, classiest crime drama on television ... efforts to write around the departure of Ken Wahl will leave fans of the original show feeling jerked around.... Any successes in this season debut can be credited entirely to Banks' tremendous intensity, although his character worked better as a stoic and cynical counterpoint to Wahl's passionate Terranova. Perhaps the episode's biggest drawback is Peter Lance's penchant for long, preachy speeches about Central American atrocities and U.S. complicity."

Variety's reviewer went on to complain about the vocal interludes with Martika and the montages of Miami life, but these undoubtedly served to create an ambience that would distance it from the dreary realism of the series' previous Vancouver locations. Cannell — as ever, going flat out to save his show — had bravely coughed up the cash for a Miami shoot to launch the Santana series and best exploit the expertise of Lance, whose predilection for intriguing political complexities was no great change from the David Burke worldview that had so enhanced the Wahl storylines and raised even the most clichéd storylines above the plots of standard police actioners. The continued political savvy of the show was one of its saving graces, and even if the Miami locale had been played out somewhat during the 1980s by Mann's *Miami Vice*, it was a much-needed change of venue for *Wiseguy*, and Lance's script clearly indicated that there was still much to say about this extraordinary stretch of coastline.

Jeff Salamon, reviewing the new series in *The Village Voice*, was a little fairer, stating that "except for some Latin beats slipped beneath the theme music, and the leap from Italian Brooklyn to Cuban Miami, this is still *Wiseguy*," even though he was justly inclined to point out that "swathed in a canary yellow cardigan, archvillain Amado Guzman leers from behind his wraparound shades like a refugee from *Miami Vice*— which he is." Although critical of some elements, Saloman noted that "Raised in an anti–Castro milieu by his Bay of Pigs veteran dad, Santana is appalled at the compromises his people have made to wage their struggle. These compromises, we're told, include assisting Salvadoran death squads and Colombian drug cartels, as well as orchestrating — with CIA assistance — unrest against Allende in Chile. As far as prime-time goes, these are stunningly lefty premises. (To establish Guzman's wickedness, we're shown photos of him shaking hands with Nixon and Reagan). Yet Santana, who scoffs at the obsessiveness of his father's generation, never denies the legitimacy of their hatred.... These intra-ethnic strains extend beyond the generation gap; at one point Guzman, played with appropriate slime by Maximilian Schell, disparages his bodyguard as 'Marialito trash.' Yesterday's immigrant, we're reminded, is today's true blue American...."

However, *Wiseguy* had no intention of becoming the next *Miami Vice* or remaining in the Miami milieu following the close of the Guzman storyline. In the final few episodes, the OCB is disbanded by government cutbacks, and McPike and the newly-recruited Santana and Stein (Jim Byrnes still appeared as the Lifeguard, but now his OCB call-code was Uncle Bill) move to New York, where they will work for U.S. Attorney Winston Chambers (Fredric Lehne recreating his similar politician's puppet role from the seriously underrated 1989–'90 series *Mancuso FBI*). The show was just launching into a potentially fascinating arc (concerning the growing sophistication of the high-school drug market and the despair of the people trying to work within the school system in an environment where dealers carry guns and phone-beepers) when the introductory episode, wisely complete in itself, became a single and final installment.

The rapid cancellation of the new *Wiseguy* was not unexpected, but it was much too soon, and the true potential of the Bauer/Hoffman/Banks version was never explored, and there was a distinct nagging feeling that a potential slow-burner had been nipped in the bud. It was entirely possible that given two years, the Santana version could have exorcised the ghost of Vinnie Terranova forever. *Wiseguy* could — and should — have gone onto better things. Perhaps some consolation can be taken from the comments of Les Sheldon, who saw the writing on the wall for *Wiseguy* at the close of the second season. "We really do believe there's an audience out there that would love the show if they would just give us a shot," he told Ed Gross. "But let's face it, we're never going to be a number one show. We're not *Cosby*. Even if we were to get canceled, it wouldn't be a bad moment, because every moment we were fortunate to work on this show was worth it."

Episode Guide

regular and recurring characters: Ken Wahl (Vinnie Terranova), Jonathan Banks (Frank McPike), Steven Bauer (Michael Santana), Jim Byrne (Lifeguard — Uncle Mike/Bill), Elsa Raven (Mrs. Terranova), Gerald Anthony (Father Pete Terranova), Patti D'Arbanville (Amber Twine), John Jackson (Daryl Elias), Ken Jenkins (Paul Beckstead), Cecil Hoffman (Hilary Stein)

First Season (1987–'88)

WISEGUY (pilot)

wr. Stephen Cannell, Frank Lupo, dir. Rod Holcomb

Vinnie Terranova, an OCB agent so deep undercover that only his brother, a Catholic priest, knows that he's not really a mob wiseguy, attempts to infiltrate the Steelgrave gang of Atlantic City and avenge the death of his mentor.

with Ray Sharkey, Gianni Russo, Robert Miranda, Jessica Steen, John Wesley, Adriana Baron, Leon Pownall, John Jackson, Jack Ging, Mark Rolston

NEW BLOOD

wr. David Burke, dir. Lyndon Chubbuck

Sonny's mob bosses, unsure that he can run the Atlantic City operation alone now that Dave Steelgrave is gone, send in a sly accountant to oversee his operations ... who promptly sets up Sonny to take a fall.

with Ray Sharkey, Dennis Lipscomb, Joe Dallesandro, Vic Polizos, Eric Christmas, Joe Shea, Kevin McNulty, Frank Ferrucci, Morris Panych, Fred Pleasure

THE LOOSE CANNON

wr. Stephen Cannell, dir. Larry Shaw

While waiting for the arrival of his nephew from Sicily, Sonny finds a gang war breaking out with local Jamaicans, and Vinnie becomes romantically involved with a cop's widow.

with Ray Sharkey, Dennis Lipscomb, Joe Dallesandro, David Marciano, Yvette Heyden, Raymond Forchion, Gerald Anthony, Blu Mankuma, Beverly Hendry, Venus Terzo

THE BIRTHDAY SURPRISE

wr. Eric Blakeney, Gene Miller, dir. Robert Iscove

Sonny arranges a unique birthday gift for Vinnie and McPike takes a junkie for a ride when Vinnie endangers his cover with a personal vendetta.

with Ray Sharkey, Dennis Lipscomb, Aharon Ipale, Nestor Serrano, Sal Lopez, Eric Christmas, Gerald Anthony, Richard Lion, Eddie Ross Pagliaro, Kerry Sandomirski, Jerry Wasserman, William Nunn, Michael Naxos, Daryl Hayes, Mike Winlaw

ONE ON ONE

wr. Stephen Kronish, dir. Reynaldo Villalobos

An undercover operation initiated by a status-seeking minor official endangers Vinnie's cover when police turn a string of Sonny's deals sour, and the hunt is on for the informant.

with Ray Sharkey, Dennis Lipscomb, Annette Bening, James Handy, Eric Christmas, William Bronder, Elaine Church, Dan Muldoon, Pat Bermel, Tom McBeath, Jon Pallone, Edward Greenhalch

THE PRODIGAL SON

wr. Carol Mendelsohn, dir. Charles Correll

When Vinnie's mother is mugged, Sonny lays on the royal treatment at the hospital while Vinnie is forced to re-examine his priorities when he sees how his mother and the rest of the neighborhood react to him.

with Ray Sharkey, Gerald Anthony, Elsa Raven, John Jackson, Eddie Zammit, Michael Benyaer, Rhonda Bukowski, Babs Chula, Stefania Ciccone, Bernie Coulson, Bruno Gerussi, Umberto Menghi, Sean Morgan

A DEAL'S A DEAL

wr. David Burke, Stephen Kronish, dir. Charles Correll

Two crooked cops on Steelgrave's payroll inadvertently come close to exposing Vinnie's true identity when intimidating a vocalist from one of Sonny's casinos who wants out.

with Ray Sharkey, Joe Dallesandro, Billy Vera, Dan Lauria, Steve Vinovich, Nathan Davis, Joe Shea, Martina Finch, Ken Camroux, Ernie Prentice, Todd Shaffer

THE MARRIAGE OF HEAVEN AND HELL

wr. Eric Blakeney, dir. Zale Dalen

As Sonny plans to wed the daughter of a former power in the Bronx, Sid Royce decides that Vinnie might be ripe for taking into the Patrice organization.

with Ray Sharkey, Dennis Lipscomb, Joe Dallesandro, Nathan Davis, Robert Mangiardi, Martina Finch, Eric Christmas, Joe Shea, Elsa Raven, Alex Bruhanski, George Catalano, Peter Yunker

No-One Gets Out of Here Alive

wr. David Burke, dir. Robert Iscove

As the Federal agents swoop down on the Steelgrave party, Vinnie pursues a devastated Sonny to a deserted theater of Sonny's childhood for a final emotional showdown.

with Ray Sharkey, Dennis Lipscomb, Nathan Davis, Robert Mangiardi, Martina Finch, Eric Christmas, Joe Shea, John Jackson, Richard Donat, Ric Reid, Allan Lysell, Keith Martin Gordey

Last Rites for Lucci

wr. Stephen Kronish, dir. Bill Corcoran

With a contract out on him, a neighborhood failure goes to Father Terranova for the last rites, but Vinnie — attending therapy with other cops after the Steelgrave incident — intercedes to protect him.

with James Andronica, Gerald Anthony, Matt Landers, Ricardo Gutierrez, Jon Slade, Michele Goodger, Jackson Davies, Lee Taylor, Dwight McFee

Independent Operator

wr. Stephen Cannell, dir. Aaron Lipstadt

A minor investigation into the activities of a busy hit-man and Vietnam veteran unearths a multi-million-dollar-a-year drugs and arms operation being run by a jet-set psychopath.

with William Russ, Joan Severance, Clyde Kusatsu, Will Zahrn, Terry Bozeman, Bernadette Leonard, Antony Holland, Garwin Sanford, Frank Ferrucci, Sean O'Byrne

Fascination for the Flame

wr. Stephen Cannell, dir. William Fraker

When Mel embarrasses a drugs baron at his wedding, a war breaks out that results in the kidnap of Susan Profitt.

with William Russ, Kevin Spacey, Joan Severance, Clyde Kusatsu, Franklyn Seales, Will Zahrn, Rene LeVant, Frank Ferrucci, Leroy Schulz, Alvin Lee Saunders, Herbert Lewis

Smokey Mountain Requiem

wr. Hans Tobeason, David Burke, dir. Neill Fearnley

Terranova and Loccoco find themselves out in the boonies of the American midwest, where a godfearing family has been coerced into housing an out-of-control drugs operation on the pretext of helping their son out of a jail sentence.

with William Russ, Kevin Spacey, Joan Severance, Fred Asparagus, Lou Hancock, Rance Howard, Mark Pillow, Will Zarhn

Player to Be Named Now

wr. Stephen Kronish, dir. Ron Rapiel

Profitt throws a party on his yacht to entrap a treacherous mobster, and exploits his friends in high places and a washed-up party girl to bully the gangster out of ownership of his baseball team.

with William Russ, Kevin Spacey, Joan Severance, Jon Polito, Jane Brucker, Clyde Kusatsu, Helena Yea, Marc Bourrel, Marilyn Chin

The Merchant of Death

wr. Carol Mendelsohn, dir. William Fraker

An attempt to bribe a corrupt French official to secure an important weapons deal goes wrong, and it becomes apparent that hit-man Roger Loccoco is not what he seems. In the meantime, Vinne and McPike learn just how powerful Mel already is.

with William Russ, Kevin Spacey, Joan Severance, Michael Ensign, Paul Verdier, Bill Ontiveros, William B. Davis, Andrew Rhodes, Nathen Vanering

Not for Nothin'

wr. David Burke, Don Kurt, dir. Bill Corcoran

His career ruined by the death of Sonny Steelgrave, an embittered Aldo Baglia — brother of Sonny's intended bride and set to play a key role on Sonny's Atlantic City operation when his sister married — learns of his father's death and makes an attempt on Vinnie's life.

with William Russ, Kevin Spacey, Joan Severance, Melanie Chartoff, Robert Mangiardi, Joe Shea, David Spielberg

Squeeze

wr. Gina Wendkos, dir. Bill Corcoran

As the Profitts' munitions empire crumbles around them from the sabotage being inflicted both outside and within his organization by Roger Loccoco and his masters, Mel throws a spanner in their plans by ordering Vinnie to use his mob contacts to get him back into the drugs business.

with William Russ, Kevin Spacey, Joan Severance, Melanie Chartoff, George O. Petrie, David Spielberg, Vito D'Ambrosio, Clayton Corzatte, Peter Yunker, Terry Arrowsmith, Elsa Raven

BLOOD DANCE

wr. Eric Blakeney, dir. Kim Manners

Mel goes ahead with Roger's plan to purchase a banana republic, selecting the heroin-rich Isle Pavot (Island of Poppies) in the Caribbean as planned, but rejects Ketcher's intended puppet dictator out of an irrational fear of voodoo.

with William Russ, Kevin Spacey, Joan Severance, Richard Portnow, Charlaine Woodard, David Spielberg, Mabel King

PHANTOM PAIN

wr. Stephen Kronish, dir. Dennis Dugan

With Mel out of the picture, Ketcher orders his plans to secure Isle Pavot stepped up, and Loccoco begins an elaborate deception to drive Susan off the deep end by playing on her insecurities.

with William Russ, Joan Severance, David Spielberg, Melanie Chartoff, Ben Halley, Jr., Ron Dean, Terry Moore, Rob Roy, Sean O'Byrne

DIRTY LITTLE WARS

wr. David Burke, dir. Robert Iscove

Loccoco and his mercenaries assemble for the coup, but Ketcher's plan falls to pieces when Loccoco realizes his true motivation is dollars.

with William Russ, David Spielberg, Ben Halley, Jr., Denis Arndt, Frank Megna, Christopher Thomas, Richard Sargent, Andy Rhodes, Garry Chalk, Helena Yea

DATE WITH AN ANGEL

wr. David Burke, Stephen Kronish, dir. Les Sheldon

Ketcher and Loccoco face bleak futures as the Senate Hearing into the attempted coup of Isle Pavot commences in a media circus.

with William Russ, David Spielberg, Stephen Joyce, Robin Gammell, Ben Halley, Jr., Georgann Johnson, Ray Stricklyn, Jerry Wasserman, Traci Lords, Tom Hammond, Cecilia Warren, Dana Still, Ty Haller, Max Reimer

Second Season (1988–'89)

GOING HOME

wr. David Burke, dir. Les Sheldon

A weary and disillusioned Vinnie returns to his old neighborhood to find a number of locals in thrall to a two-bit racist organization called the Pilgrims of Progress that is beginning to penetrate his community on the back of economic distress.

with Marshall Bell, Tim Guinee, Gerald Anthony, Elsa Raven, Kerry Sandomirsky, Jesse Doran, Jack Orend, John M. Jackson

SCHOOL OF HARD KNOX

wr. Stephen Kronish, dir. Robert Iscove

Local boy Richie Stamm begins to realize just how dangerous the racist group Pilgrims of Progress are when they reveal their true madness in a robbery and murder, and Vinnie enlists his aid to bring them down.

with Fred Dalton Thompson, Paul Guilfoyle, Tim Guinee, Marshall Bell, Kerry Sandomirsky, Elsa Raven, Jack Orend, Meredith Woodward, Connie Marie Brazelton, John M. Jackson, Walter Marsh, Dwight Koss, Ric Reid

REVENGE OF THE MUD PEOPLE

wr. Stephen Cannell, dir. Bill Corcoran

Vigilante cops beat up Vinnie and kill a suspect in their custody, cheating Vinnie out of justice for his brother's death.

with Fred Dalton Thompson, Paul Guilfoyle, Tim Guinee, Kerry Sandomirsky, James DiStefano, William Taylor, J.J. Johnston, Jack Orend, John M. Jackson, Janet Wright, Terry Barclay, Lindsay Bourne, Raimund Stamm, Alexander Boynton

LAST OF THE TRUE BELIEVERS

wr. John Schulian, dir. Robert Iscove

The racist agitator's entrepreneurial plans are spoiled when his stooge kills a talk show host who pilloried the Pilgrims on the air, but had given them valuable publicity he intended to exploit.

with Fred Dalton Thompson, Paul Guilfoyle, Tim Guinee, Alan Burke, Richard Lawson, Charles Siegel, Dwight McFee, Mark Acheson, Meredith Woodward, Catherine Pope, Ken Jenkins

ARIA FOR DON AIUPPO

wr. Alfonse Ruggiero, Jr., dir. Jan Eliasberg

Vinnie is alarmed to discover that a retired Mafioso is courting his elderly mother.

with Elsa Raven, George O. Petrie, Kerry Sandomirsky, Karen Kandazian, Paula Shaw, Tony Romano, James Costy, Ken Jenkins, Dwight Koss, John Destrey

SEVENTH AVENUE FREEZE OUT

wr. David Burke, Stephen Kronish, dir. Robert Iscove

When David Sternberg, the son of a New York garment businessman fears his father Eli is getting too deeply involved with the local mobsters, he seeks the intervention of the OCB, and Vinnie poses as a security consultant for the firm.

with Ron Silver, Jerry Lewis, Stanley Tucci, Patricia Charbonneau, John Santucci, Harry Goz, Jack Wohl, Blu Mankuma, Dwight Koss, Lovena Fox, Pedro Salvin, Jennifer Griffin, Pamela Hart, Paul Beckett

NEXT OF KIN

wr. Alfonse Ruggiero, Jr., John Schulian, dir. Bill Corcoran

When Vinnie is injured protecting Eli Sternberg from thieves, McPike calls in a second agent, the retired John Henry Raglin, who infiltrates the organization of Sternberg's mob benefactor, the gangster Pinzolo.

with Anthony Denison, Ron Silver, Jerry Lewis, Stanley Tucci, Patricia Charbonneau, Harry Goz, Alex Bruhanski, John Nesci, Matthew Walker, Deryl Hayes, David Petersen, Alex Kliner, Jennifer Griffin, Pamela Hart

ALL OR NOTHING

wr. Suzanne Oshry, dir. Gus Trikonis

While watching one of Sternberg's shipments, Raglin discovers a dangerous sweat-shop, and finds a young girl being intimidated to prevent her campaigning for better conditions.

with Anthony Denison, Jerry Lewis, Stanley Tucci, Patricia Charbonneau, Harry Goz, Joan Chen, Salem Ludwig, Frederick Neumann, Gillian Barber, Janet Wright, Dwight Koss, Jennifer Griffin

WHERE'S THE MONEY?

wr. David Burke, Alfonse Ruggiero, Jr., dir. Robert Iscove

Seeing his father's business crumble, and taking the law into his own hands, David Sternberg abducts the gangster Pinzolo to force him to reverse his father's fortunes.

with Anthony Denison, Ron Silver, Jerry Lewis, Stanley Tucci, Patricia Charbonneau, Harry Goz, Tony Ganios, Ken Jenkins, Dwight Koss, M. Jennifer Evans

POSTCARD FROM MOROCCO

wr. Stephen Kronish, John Schulian, dir. Roy Campanella II

Raglin and McPike make a last-ditch attempt to bring down Pinzolo before he can leave the country with blood on his hands.

with Anthony Denison, Jerry Lewis, Stanley Tucci, Patricia Charbonneau, Harry Goz, Tony Ganios, Dwight Koss, Sheila Paterson, Pamela Hart, Dale Robins, Sid Filkow

STAIRWAY TO HEAVEN

wr. Alfonse Ruggiero, Jr., dir. James Contner

A distraught McPike faces a crisis of conscience when the only way to save his wife's life is with tainted mob money.

with Jessica Harper, David Wilson, Ken Jenkins, Dwight Koss, Don S. Davis, Marc Reid, Dolores Drake

WHITE NOISE

wr. Ken Wahl, David Burke, Alfonse Ruggiero, Jr., dir. James Whitmore Jnr

While Vinnie is in hospital for a psychiatric evaluation to enable him to continue working undercover, a former disaffected agent who is now a patient alters the hospital's computer records and has Vinnie classified dangerous. While subdued by drugs, Vinnie hallucinates encounters with Sonny Steelgrave and his deceased brother Pete.

with John Jackson, Ken Jenkins, David Schramm, Ray Sharkey, Gerald Anthony, Garwin Sanford, John Novak

DEAD DOG LIVES

wr. David Burke, Stephen Kronish, dir. Gus Trikonis

Vinnie sets up a record company with confiscated mob money to probe corruption in the record business, and is soon living out his fantasies as a benevolent talent scout.

with Glenn Frey, Deborah Harry, Paul McCrane, Pamela Segall

AND IT COMES OUT HERE

wr. David Burke, Stephen Kronish, dir. Bill Corcoran

Vinnie antagonizes an industry mogul by signing his new comeback star Diana Price to his biggest rival.

with Glenn Frey, Deborah Harry, Paul Winfield, Tim Curry, Patti D'Arbanville, Deidre Hall, Mick Fleetwood, Ken Jenkins

THE RIP-OFF STICK

wr. Alfonse Ruggiero, Jr., John Schulian, dir. Mario Azzapardi

Following a successful launch party for Diana's new album, devious industry mogul Winston Newquay attempts to woo her away from Vinnie's protective embrace.

with Glenn Frey, Deborah Harry, Paul Winfield, Tim Curry, Patti D'Arbanville, Pamela Segall, Deidre Hall, Paul McCrane, Peter Williams, Ron Taylor, Billy Wirth, Paul Jarrett, Peter Yunker, Ken Jenkins

HIGH DOLLAR BOP

wr. Alfonse Ruggiero, Jr., John Schulian, dir. Douglas Jackson

Vinnie's plans are nearly ruined when a high stakes poker game ends up with his company absorbed by Newquay's operation.

with Glenn Frey, Paul Winfield, Tim Curry, Patti D'Arbanville, Pamela Segall, Deidre Hall, Paul McCrane, Ron Taylor, Billy Wirth

HIP HOP ON THE GRAVY TRAIN

wr. Suzanne Oshry, dir. Helaine Head

As protagonists fall like ninepins, Vinnie tries to hold his increasingly shaky operation together long enough to bring down Newquay.

with Glenn Frey, Paul Winfield, Tim Curry, Patti D'Arbanville, Deidre Hall, Billy Wirth, William Calhoun, Ken Jenkins

THE ONE THAT GOT AWAY

wr. David Burke, Alfonse Ruggiero, Jr., dir. Jorge Montesi

Through a bizarre twist of fate, Vinnie's partner in his record company discovers that he is an OCB agent.

with Glenn Frey, Paul Winfield, Tim Curry, Patti D'Arbanville, Mitchell Kosterman, Jeff Irvine, Ken Budd, Steven Williams

LIVING AND DYING IN 4/4 TIME

wr. Stephen Kronish, John Schulian, dir. James Contner

Newquay is freed on a technicality, and Vinnie's mission draws to a close.

with Glenn Frey, Paul Winfield, Tim Curry, Patti D'Arbanville, Anthony J. Schembri, Stephen E. Miller, Lee Taylor, Rod Menzies, Christine Zastrzembska, Ken Jenkins

CALL IT CASABA

wr. David Burke, Clifton Campbell, Alfonse Ruggiero, Jr., dir. Gus Trikonis

Heading for the hills for a well-deserved break, Vinnie, McPike and the Lifeguard all confront their feelings for the women in their lives.

with Patti D'Arbanville, Lisa Waltz

Third Season (1989–'90)

LE LACRIME D'AMORE (two parts)

wr. Suzanne Oshry, John Schulian, dir. Frank Johnson (part one)

wr. Alfonse Ruggerio, Jr., Clifton Campbell, dir. Bill Corcoran (part two)

Vinnie contemplates a marriage to rock widow Amber Twine that neither Vinnie's mother, Amber's lawyer, or McPike want to happen for their own ulterior motives ... but a mob war is brewing.

with Patti D'Arbanville, Elsa Raven, George O. Petrie, Robert Davi, Patricia Harty, Mike Starr, Thomas Ian Griffith, Mimi Lieber, John Snyder, Richard Sarafian, Tony Romano

A RIGHTFUL PLACE

wr. David Burke, dir. Robert Iscove

When an attempt is made on the life of his stepfather Don Aiuppo, Vinnie allies himself with mobster Albert Cerrico to infiltrate the highest echelons of the mob and find the man who ordered the hit.

with Robert Davi, Tony Mike Romano, Patti D'Arbanville, George O. Petrie, Elsa Raven, Mariangela Pino, John Snyder, Michael Chiklis, Alex Bruhanski, Sean Christien Davi

BATTLE OF THE BARGE

wr. Clifton Campbell, dir. Robert Iscove

Vinnie and Cerrico suspect henpecked hood Joey Grosset of ordering the hit on Don Aiuppo, but in the course of their investigations stumble onto a terrorist bomb factory.

with Robert Davi, Tony Mike Romano, Patti D'Arbanville, John Snyder, Anne DeSalvo, George

O. Petrie, Elsa Raven, Michael Chiklis, George Kee Cheung, Francois Chau

Sins of the Father

wr. Stephen Kronish, dir. David Burke

When a desperate politician plans to make capital out of the impending mob war, McPike tries to defuse the situation.

with Robert Davi, Tony Romano, John Snyder, Anne DeSalvo, George O. Petrie, Elsa Raven, Michael Chiklis, Chazz Palminteri, Mariangela Pino, Walter Olkewicz, Sean Christien Davi

Heir to the Throne

wr. Alfonse Ruggiero, Jr., dir. Bill Corcoran

To the anger and frustration of Cerrico and Grosset, Don Aiuppo puts Vinnie in charge of operations until he is well again.

with Robert Davi, Tony Mike Romano, John Snyder, Anne DeSalvo, George O. Petrie, Michael Chiklis, Chazz Palminteri, Alex Bruhanski, Tom McBeath, Norman Browning, Kevin McNulty

Sleepwalk

wr. David Burke, Clifton Campbell, dir. Matthew Meshekoff

Afraid that Vinnie's luck is running out, McPike and Lifeguard consider taking him out of the field while he's still winning, and Vinnie himself is tempted to resign and begin a life with Amber.

with Patti D'Arbanville, Scott Harlan, Ebbe Roe Smith, Pamela Dunlap, Kim Wilson

How Will They Remember Me?

wr. Stephen Kronish, Alfonse Ruggiero, Jr., Ken Wahl, David Burke, dir. William Fraker

When a box of belongings left at the church by the late Father Terranova is discovered, Vinnie discovers some background on his father, and gains an insight into his father's past. As Vinnie plays the story out in his head, characters from previous stories play the roles as he sees them in his mind.

with Patti D'Arbanville, Chazz Palminteri, Robert Miranda, Jesse Doran, Mimi Lieber, Joe Shea, Rhoda Gemignani, Walter Marsh

People Do It All the Time

wr. David Braden, David Curran, Suzanne Oshry, dir. Jonathan Sanger

When Lifeguard's son-in-law is ordered to overlook safety conditions at a local building site or lose the job he is desperate to keep, McPike moves in to close the operation down, creating conflict between Lifeguard's daughter and her husband. In the meantime, Lifeguard has trouble coming to terms with his daughter's new life as wife and expectant mother.

with Lisa Waltz, John Philbin, Dion Anderson, Geoffrey Rivas, Pamela Dunlap, Martin Garner, Stephen E. Miller, Walter B. Davis

The Reunion

wr. Don Kurt, David Burke, Alfonse Ruggiero, Jr., dir. William Fraker

A high school reunion reunites supposed mobster Terranova with mob lawyer Mike and police officer Denise, and a bizarre triangle of deception and self-deception is formed.

with Tony Ganios, Cathy Moriarty, Lenny Termo, Beverley Elliott

Day One

wr. David Burke, Stephen Kronish, Alfonse Ruggiero, Clifton Campbell, dir. Mario Van Peebles

Admiral Strichen, whose corrupt and self-serving political agenda was thrown into disarray by Vinnie's operations during the Profitt saga, plots an elaborate revenge.

with Kim Greist, Norman Lloyd, Stephen Joyce, Georgann Johnson, Robin Gammell, Robert Harper, Stan Shaw

Day Four

wr. David Burke, Stephen Kronish, Alfonse Ruggiero, Clifton Campbell, dir. Ray Villalobos

An absurd bungle on the part of Strichen's hired assassin puts collaborator Leland Masters' plan to destabilize the Japanese economy at risk.

with Kim Greist, Norman Lloyd, Stephen Joyce, Georgann Johnson, Robert Harper, Ray Stricklyn, Stan Shaw

Day Seven

wr. David Burke, Stephen Kronish, Alfonse Ruggiero, Clifton Campbell, dir. William Fraker

While Masters guides the OCB investigation in the direction he wants it to go, Vinnie works at persuading the skeptical Kay Gallagher that she is a pawn in Strichen and Masters' game.

with Kim Greist, Norman Lloyd, Stephen Joyce, Georgann Johnson, Robin Gammell, Robert Harper, Ray Stricklyn, Ford Rainey, Stan Shaw, Jason Bernard, Eric Menyuk, Joe Verroca

Day Nine
wr. David Burke, Stephen Kronish, Alfonse Ruggiero, Clifton Campbell, dir. Les Sheldon

As the noose tightens, McPike is sent to arrest Vinnie and Kay attempts suicide.

with Kim Greist, Norman Lloyd, Stephen Joyce, Georgann Johnson, Robert Harper, Ray Stricklyn, Ford Rainey, Stan Shaw, Jason Bernard, Eric Menyuk, Joe Verroca

Meet Mike McPike
wr. Frank Megna, dir. Robert Woodruff

McPike's recalcitrant father moves in with him after being ejected from yet another retirement home, and proceeds to attempt to bring Frank and his wife together again.

with John Kellogg, Elizabeth Ruscio, Matthew Faison

To Die in Bettendorf
wr. Morgan Gendel, dir. Jorge Montesi

McPike and his wife are held hostage by a demented Sid Royce, formerly of the Patrice organization, who has been living in misery courtesy of McPike, and has now fled the witness protection program after his wife abandons him for a new life.

with Dennis Lipscomb, Elizabeth Ruscio, Holland Taylor, David Myers

The Romp
wr. Alfonse Ruggiero, Jr., dir. Ken Wahl

Vinnie dreams that he goes on a stag night with some old buddies.

with Tony Ganios, Xander Berkeley, Mariska Hargitay, Jim Youngs

A One Horse Town
wr. David Burke, dir. Peter Marshall

Vinnie poses as a truck-driver to investigate corruption in Lynchboro, a small Washington logging town, and meets the bizarre and quite crazed town benefactor, who is running a private kingdom out in the sticks.

with Steve Ryan, David Strathairn, Darlanne Fluegel, James Stacy, Neil Gray Giuntoli, John Nesci, Lochlyn Munro

His Master's Voice
wr. Robert Engels, dir. James Contner

Vinnie is made a local deputy in Volchek's Lynchboro community after two of the deputies are found dead by the river, and a bizarre series of killings are exposed.

with Steve Ryan, David Strathairn, Darlanne Fluegel, James Stacy, Frank C. Turner, Neil Gray Giuntoli, Cavan Cunningham, Roman Podhora

Hello Buckwheat
wr. David Burke, Stephen Kronish, dir. Jonathan Sanger

Vinnie cracks up with a nervous breakdown, and McPike finds himself allied with Roger Loccoco, who assumes Vinnie's role in the continuing investigations into local crackpot Volchek.

with Steve Ryan, William Russ, Darlanne Fluegel, James Stacy, Frank C. Turner, Neil Gray Giuntoli, Michele Goodger, Peter Yunker, Dwight Koss, Ken Jenkins, Jeffrey Lyons, Lora Zane, Karen Campbell, Cavan Cunningham, Roman Podhora

Let Them Eat Cake
wr. Clifton Campbell, Robert Engels, dir. James Contner

Loccoco betrays McPike's carefully laid plan in order to keep Volchek in charge of Lynchboro.

with Steve Ryan, William Russ, Darlanne Fluegel, James Stacy, Neil Gray Giuntoli, Lora Zane, Vinnie Guastaferro, French Tickner, Jim Smith, Jerry Wasserman, Karen Campbell, Cavan Cunningham, Roman Podhora, Natasha Morley, Peter Hanlon

Melt Down
wr. Stephen Kronish, Clifton Campbell, dir. Frank Johnson

Vinnie works to expose the activities of a waste disposal company illegally dumping near a school playground.

with Steve Ryan, William Russ, Darlanne Fluegel, James Stacy, Neil Gray Giuntoli, Lora Zane, Vinnie Guastaferro, Arnie Walters, Lochlyn Munro, Cavan Cunningham, Roman Podhora, Frank C. Turner, Gerry Rousseau

Sanctuary
wr. David Burke, Robert Engels, dir. William Fraker

Near to breaking point, Vinnie finds that the waste disposal company has corrupt friends in high places with mob connections.

with Vinnie Guastaferro, Bonnie Bartlett, Leo V. Gordon, Eddie Bracken, Lora Zane, Lochlyn Munro, Cavan Cunningham, Roman Podhora, Frank C. Turner

BRUMMP-BUMP
wr. Robert Engels, dir. Peter Marshall
A political cover-up goes awry when the guilty parties fail to take into account the growing madness of their henchman.
with Vinnie Guastaferro, Bonnie Bartlett, Leo V. Gordon, Eddie Bracken, Lora Zane, Arnie Walters, John G. MacLaren, John Bear Curtis, James R. Zachery, Peter La Croix, Matthew Walker

Fourth Season (1990–'91)

THE FRUITS OF THE POISONOUS TREE
(double-length)
wr. Stephen Cannell, Peter Lance, Rafael Lima, dir. Jan Eliasberg
Fearing the worst, McPike follows the trail of a kidnapped Vinnie, snatched by a Salvadorean death squad after looking into the disappearance of the missionary son of a friend of his mother.
with Maximilian Schell, Manolo Villaverde, Martika, James Rebhorn, Stephen Markle, Elsa Raven, George O. Petrie, Jody Wilson, James Baldwin, Alex Panas, Ken Jenkins, Mario Ernesto Sanchez, Iris Acker, Ellen Beck, John Archie, Chaz Mena

BLACK GOLD
wr. Stephen Cannell, Peter Lance, Rafael Lima, Bill Bludworth, dir. Jorge Montesi
McPike finds a new ally in disbarred lawyer Michael Santana, and together they work to bring down corrupt businessman and murderer Armado Guzman, starting with a cocaine operation.
with Maximilian Schell, Manolo Villaverde, Martika, Carlos Gomez, Badja Djola, Colson F. Gilkes, Joshua Sussman, Charles Matheny

THE GIFT
wr. Stephen Cannell, Peter Lance, dir. Jorge Montesi
The lives of Santana's father and girlfriend are endangered by Guzman and his treacherous bodyguards.
with Maximilian Schell, Manolo Villaverde, Martika, Carlos Gomez, Tony Bolano, Kevin Quigley, Lynn Ladner

LA MINA
wr. Stephen Cannell, Peter Lance, dir. Colin Bucksey
Santana's operations inside Guzman's criminal empire take him full circle to drug lord Martinez-Gacha, who escaped justice after Santana's enthusiasm to put him away got him disbarred and ended his legal career.
with Maximilian Schell, Manolo Villaverde, Martika, James Rebhorn, Raul Santidrian, Chaz Mena, Rene Rokk, Marc Macaulay, Felecia Rafield

WITNESS PROTECTION FOR
THE ARCHANGEL LUCIFER
wr. Peter Lance, Rafael Lima, Stephen J. Cannell, dir. Jorge Montesi
Santana discovers that Guzman is being offered immunity for testifying against drug lord Martinez-Gacha.
with Maximilian Schell, Manolo Villaverde, Martika, Alex Panas, Fredric Lehne, Rene Rokk, Marc Macaulay

POINT OF NO RETURN
wr. Brock Choy, dir. Colin Bucksey
As Santana's sister gives birth to a baby boy, her cop husband disappears from a blood-stained patrol car, found abandoned and full of money.
with Michael Learned, Jim Youngs, Ada Maris, Art La Fleur, Vanessa Marquez, Tony Rosato

DEAD RIGHT
wr. James Kearns, dir. Tucker Gates
Hilary Stein investigates the claims of three army widows that their husbands died because of cost-cutting defective helicopter parts.
with Michael Learned, Fredric Lehne, John Cothran, Jr., Stephen Root, Michele Goodger, Ken Jenkins

CHANGING HOUSES
wr. Stephen Cannell, dir. Gus Trikonis
Santana tries to break a high school drugs operation after his niece is critically injured, but his new reputation as a wiseguy offends a crusading high school principal who is in the process of humiliating a bandwagon-jumping politician.
with Billy Dee Williams, Wayne Tippit, Oliver Platt, Vanessa Marquez, Ada Maris, Beverly Todd, Fredric Lehne
series ends

J.J. Starbuck
September 1987–February 1988*

*"Now don't get me wrong, but every day I'm rubbing shoulders
with these young lions, you know. Believe me, they don't go around drivin'
20 year old Lincolns. They get a new car every other year, they own a house,
they own a boat, a lot of them ain't one bit brighter 'n you.
The problem is, bein' all those things, you got yourself spread too thin."*

Silver-haired good-ol'-boy J.J. Starbuck, as played with great amusement and professionalism by silver-haired good-ol'-boy Dale Robertson (formerly the lead in '50s western *Tales of the Wells Fargo* and '60s western *Iron Horse*) is a colorful, sanctimonious, walking, talking larger-than-life cliché who travels around in a mile-long motor vehicle with steer horns on the front and a car horn that plays "Yellow Rose of Texas." Starbuck's a millionaire who uses his fortune to travel round the country doing good deeds for nice people and driving nasty people nuts with his down-home charm and country-boy platitudes.

"Starbuck lost his wife and son in a plane crash, and he just never really went back to the office" explained Robertson about his character in a TV interview. "He kind of rolls around in an automobile just like I do now. I've flown for so many years, I'm tired of flying. I love to drive, and so does ol' Starbuck! He drives around in his ol' Lincoln, he's read every *Perry Mason* book, *Charlie Chan*, *Sherlock Holmes* ever written. He's always been a student of criminology, and once in a while he runs into a mystery. And he goes pokin' his nose in where he's not wanted, usually! It's a nice character. I like the show very much."

Some critics labeled the show "Matt Houston's Dad," after Lee Horsley's younger but very similar mustachioed Texan millionaire do-gooder, which on the surface is fair comment, but deep down *J.J. Starbuck* is a Cannell show through and through, far removed from the shallow, gratuitous unpleasantness of Spelling's crime shows. A demographic dud, *J.J. Starbuck* struggled its way through a sixteen episode run searching for a formula, but despite the *Dallas* hats and the critical allusions to Spelling product, Cannell's black hat/white hat morality and sly self-parody are well in evidence. *Starbuck* is a show that wants its audience to feel good rather than emotionally mugged.

J.J. runs around in his massive Lincoln "setting things straight" as one character puts it in the pilot, after the loss of his family gave the millionaire businessman a new sense of priorities. His philosophical gems are almost religiously simplistic—"Happiness isn't getting what you want, it's wanting what you get"/"We can easily forgive a child who's afraid of the dark—the real tragedy is when men are afraid of the light!"—and this is appropriate as J.J. has been very much "born again" following the loss of his wife and son. There hasn't been

---

*Two final new episodes eventually aired in April and June respectively, with some re-runs.

cornpone cracker-barrel philosophy like this since Walter Brennan rode into the sunset on Spelling's delightful 1967 western *The Guns of Will Sonnett,* but where *Starbuck* excels, and rises above the moronic stroking of the feel-good, second chance absolution of the religious preacher is with the withering streak of sarcasm he reserves for some wonderfully cast bad guys, and it's here that *Starbuck* betrays both its true origins as a dyed-in-the-wool Cannell show and its very real debt to Richard Levinson's and William Link's 1971–'78 series *Columbo.*

Early in his career at Universal, Cannell had in fact written a *Columbo* episode,* and, as the publicity material for the *Columbo* series indicates, the premise had always warmed to several themes that Cannell sympathized with. Columbo, as the press release emphasizes, "is a modest man, stumbling through the world of the very rich and famous, who regard him as a slow-witted nuisance. The killers in Columbo's world are the high-priced executives and members of the jet-set who live in showplaces with pools, servants, and private 'planes. Into the lives of the privileged bumbles Columbo, who is tolerated by his adversaries." Given the late–'80s success of the murder mystery format and the decline of smash-and-crash action/adventure, it was perhaps inevitable that Cannell would eventually try his hand at a *Columbo*-style show himself; he had, after all, specialized in cops and detectives at Universal, the busiest breeding ground for the genre.

One significant difference in the case of Starbuck, however, is that he too is wealthy, and often uses that factor to hook a bad guy, as in "The Circle Broken," written by Randall Wallace, in which his wealth becomes a lure for a dangerous cult organization. Starbuck's targets often indulge him because he *has* money; unlike Columbo, Starbuck is not a cop, and has no legal authority to investigate anything. In Cannell's own superb "A Killing in the Market," it is the killer's lust for even greater wealth that causes his confrontation with the wily Starbuck, when he attempts to buy out J.J.'s company. His insistence that Starbuck travel to meet him, even though Starbuck has repeatedly insisted that his company is not on the market, is his ultimate undoing.

Columbo was the creation of New York playwrights Richard Levinson and William Link, who had written '60s TV to finance their stage plays until discovering the power of television and the allure of the audience size. One of these plays was "Prescription: Murder," which was turned into a TV movie in 1968 and became the *Columbo* series in 1971. "We can all identify with Columbo," says Everett Chambers, one of the producers on *Columbo,* and later on Cannell's *Baretta* and Donald Bellisario's *Airwolf.* "He's the little man, who proves that those who dwell in marble halls and dress in satin often don't deserve it. And in the end, they are done in by a man of street wit who is afraid to fly, can't stand the sight of blood, and never uses force."

Running until 1977 as one of the *Mystery Movie* series (it accumulated 44 episodes and was revived in 1988 for a horribly disappointing second run), *Columbo* began a minor cottage industry during the '70s and '80s, as murder mystery series flourished, some successful, some not; none used *Columbo's* device of showing the identity of the murderer and challenging the audience to guess how he or she would be caught, but all rode on the back of Columbo's grubby macintosh, and many came from former *Columbo* staffers. Levinson and Link tried their hand with a new *Ellery Queen* series (1975–'76), and *Blacke's Magic* (1986), a rehash of the *Banacek Mystery Movie* formula, while Peter Fischer, Levinson and Link's story editor on

---

*"Double Negative," directed by Richard Quine and starring future Cannell regular Robert Culp as a documentary maker who uses subliminal techniques to commit a murder.

Columbo, Ellery Queen, and *Blacke's Magic,* branched out on his own with *The Eddie Capra Mysteries,* which starred Cannell villain Vincent Bagetta as a heroic sleuth. Levinson, Link and Fischer eventually hit the big time again together with the cynical confection *Murder She Wrote,* a contrived mix inspired by Agatha Christie's *Miss Marple* character and their own *Columbo* episode "Murder by the Book." Former *Columbo* producer Dean Hargrove and ex-network chief Fred Silverman brought Raymond Burr out of retirement to return as *Perry Mason* for a series of new TV movies beginning in 1985 (a move which almost certainly provoked Peter Falk's return as *Columbo* in '88), following it up with *Matlock* in 1986 (Andy Griffith as a legal Columbo in *Perry Mason*–like courtroom *denouements*), the silly *Jake and the Fat Man* in 1987 (whose first season was at least graced with a superb credits sequence and theme), and the equally idiotic *Father Dowling Mysteries* in '89. With *J.J. Starbuck,* Cannell was belatedly climbing on the bandwagon.

Dale Robertson as *J.J. Starbuck*

The guest players signed on to confront Starbuck were, in the tradition of the TV murder mystery begun by Spelling's campy *Burke's Law* and perpetuated by Levinson and Link's *Columbo* and *Murder She Wrote* and the Silverman/Hargrove series, often one of the highlights of the genre, and — following a weak pilot film with the ratings-reliable Bill Bixby as a bland bad guy — the *J.J. Starbuck* series opened with an episode starring Cannell's old buddy and big TV draw Robert Conrad, whose appearance helped launch the show in style as the first of a string of inspired guest villains. If Columbo's targets were the arrogant rich, reveling in their status, then Starbuck's investigations invariably steered themselves toward the cold and the heartless. All Starbuck's adversaries in the series are insensitive, murderous philistines, a point Cannell hammers home in the Conrad opener, "A Killing in the Market," directed by Larry Shaw. We know that Robert Conrad's murderous Wall Street wizard Corbett Cook III is a bad guy, because he not only commits an appallingly cold-blooded killing, but ducks out on the ballet to do it, and his evil deeds are expertly intercut with the performance he is missing.* Conrad's ballet-dodging insider-trader is followed by the soulless and callous Pierce Morgan (Kelsey Grammer — Frasier Crane himself — marvelous as a cold, cruel-eyed pianist), in Babs Greyhosky's "Murder in E Minor" (directed by Kim Manners), who, upon realizing that he can never win an all-important competition while a judge (Eric Christmas of the Steelgrave *Wiseguy*) considers his work precise but lacking in passion, cooly and methodically arranges an infallible alibi, strangles him, and fakes his suicide. Once again,

---

Conrad, the lead in a number of television series over the years, including Cannell's Black Sheep Squadron *and* The Duke, *had also appeared in an excellent* Columbo, *"An Exercise in Fatality," written by Larry Cohen and Peter Fischer, and directed by Bernard Kowalski.*

Starbuck's dogged perseverance, unerring eye for the murderer's identity, and gee-schucks mock-gullibility reeks of the Levinson and Link *Columbo*.* So much so, in fact, that writer Burt Pearl revisits no less than two *Columbo* plots (Steven Bochco's "Murder by the Book" for the idea and Peter Fischer's "Negative Reaction" for the solution) of "The Blimpy Who Yelled Blue," directed by Bill Cocoran and featuring a superb central performance by Richard Mulligan (Burt Campbell of *Soap*) as a publicity hound and plagiarist ghost writer. *Stingray* and *Wiseguy* writer Carol Mendelsohn goes even closer to home for her inspiration, reworking the premise of *Rockford Files* episode "Three Day Affair with a Thirty Day Escrow" for her story "The Ten Percent Solution," guest starring Patrick O'Neal as an unscrupulous property dealer. Other guest villains included John Schuck of *McMillan and Wife* as the ghoulish administrator of a mortuary (later Schuck essayed Herman Munster in the ghastly *The Munsters Today*), Alan Rachins (Douglas Brackman in *L.A. Law*) as a swindling swami guru, Ed Nelson (of *Peyton Place* fame) as a murderously competitive talk-show host on a tabloid TV show, Jill St. John and Jessica Walter as femme fatale executives, and Barry Nelson as a corrupt businessman and political manipulator.

As in *Columbo,* the bad guys are all arrogant, rude, sophisticated smoothies, but Starbuck's self-deprecating posturing lays them low every time. It's also an unusually soppy and sentimental series at times for Cannell, and but for a typical and thoroughly enjoyable car chase in the pilot, on the surface it doesn't even seem like a Cannell show at all. There's even a confused orphaned juvenile delinquent and an adopted stray dog in the pilot, which is the weakest contribution to the entire series, and a couple of scenes of overwhelming generosity in the earliest episodes that come across like *Fantasy Island/Love Boat* fantasy rewards. The charismatic David Huddleston, cast as Starbuck's wonderfully named business partner Charlie Bullets in the pilot, is all but wasted; in the series, his role is reduced to deskbound inserts essayed by country and western singer Jimmy Dean, a performance which Dean literally phones in.

At first, Robertson's Starbuck does come over like a character who's fallen head-first out of an Aaron Spelling show onto the hard concrete. As *TV Guide* wryly observed, "J.J.'s barrage of bromides—'Nobody ever lost his eyesight lookin' on the bright side of things'/'The way I look at life, only about ten percent's what you make it—ninety percent's how you take it!'—would overpower anyone!" But Starbuck's sugar-coated homilies are often wittier than those moral platitudes served up in other sentimental feel-good shows, and it's the Cannell team's usual keen sense of funny dialogue contrasting against the uptight angry targets of Starbuck that saves the show as an entertainment. "They couldn't get the smile off his face with a crowbar," J.J. jovially informs someone in one episode; in another, he's "harder to get rid of than a barbecue stain on a Sunday suit."

But for all the obvious similarities to the *Columbo/Murder She Wrote* school of television, the real clue to the inspiration for *J.J. Starbuck* lies hidden in the knowledge that he is exactly the sort of character Cannell would have been cynically sending up in his *Rockford/Riptide* days. Recalling the origins of *Matt Houston,* which came to TV as a cynical attempt to marry TV mega-hits *Dallas* and *Magnum* in a shotgun wedding, we can trace *Magnum* star

---

*Just as Peter Falk's irascible and rumpled raincoat-clad detective continuously bamboozled his wealthy suspects with feigned stupidity, and continuously referred to his unseen wife and various assorted family members, so does Starbuck play dumb with his targets and possess a string of quotable relatives, all spouting the same virtuous platitudes as himself. In one superb moment of intense aggravation in Babs Greyhosky's "Murder in E Minor," Grammer's cold, cruel-eyed pianist is compelled to snap "Your family just never shut up, do they, Mr. Starbuck?!" in a splendid Frasier-like outburst.

Tom Selleck's TV persona back to his two guest appearances on *The Rockford Files* as Lance White ("White on White and Nearly Perfect" and "Nice Guys Finish Dead," both by Cannell). And there, in all his youthful glory is J.J. Starbuck, Jr. Robertson's Starbuck *is* Lance White, right down to the white suit, cheerful optimism, and buffoonish grin — a little older, a little wiser, and not quite so heavy handedly parodic ... but that's him, with the wealth of funds, wealth of friends, and "parade float" vehicle.

Although *Starbuck,* perhaps fatally, strayed adventurously but confusingly from the formula to turn out non-murder storylines as Cannell and writer Babs Greyhosky played with the format, it easily measured up to the poorly thought-out plots of the Hargrove/Silverman-produced efforts, where humorless scripts were matched by their witless plotting. Cannell tinkered with *J.J. Starbuck* all through the series' brief one-season run, but it's difficult to believe from the finished product that his heart was really in it. The series was too much an obvious contrivance for that. Throughout the pilot and fifteen episodes produced, *Starbuck* was a good idea searching for a format.

Cannell wrote the pilot, and six of the fifteen hours, including the series opener featuring Conrad and two of the three episodes that sought to break from the rigid *Columbo* format. In the first, "Incident at Sam September," directed by *Wiseguy* director Lyndon Chubbuk and guest-starring Kent McCord (formerly of Jack Webb's *Adam 12* and Glen Larson's *Galactica '80,* later of Cannell's *Unsub*), Starbuck confronts terrorists occupying one of his oil rigs. In the second, "Gold from the Rainbow," directed by John Peter Kousakis, J.J. enjoys the hospitality of a Greek family headed by patriarch Telly Savalas (of *Kojak*), and stays on to resolve a family quarrel with the son (Peter Riegert). After this two week interlude, it was back to the murder mysteries, and, as entertaining as these diversions were, the crime stories were certainly the best episodes.

Story editors were Randall Wallace, who wrote five of the episodes (one with Cannell), most of them with a light touch, and former *A-Team* stalwarts Burt Pearl and Steven Sears (although only Pearl contributed an episode, the aforementioned and derivative "Blimpy Who Yelled Blue"). Of all the writers on the show, it was the ever reliable Babs Greyhosky, former *Magnum, Greatest American Hero* and *Riptide* scripter, who provided the only episodes to come up to the standard of Cannell's own. Like Cannell, she understood and accentuated the notion that the villains must be shown to be callous and soulless brilliantly in the clever but unlikely "Murder in E Minor," when Kelsey Grammer's icy-eyed and vindictive pianist disposes of his gentle, educated and impassioned elderly music teacher, and taking the taming-of-the-delinquent sub-plot of the pilot and turning it into the splendid "First You Got to Go to the Picnic," directed by Cannell regular Bruce Kessler. In this, the third and final of Cannell's departures, Starbuck takes custody of an old friend's troublesome son, a street smart black youth (Mykel T. Williamson), and drops him in the middle of a whitebread Idaho college football team as coach to a bunch of losers who couldn't so much as manage a draw with Charlie Brown's All-Stars.

Williamson, whose numerous TV appearances include regular roles in *Cover Up* and *The Bronx Zoo,* makes the most of some great lines as the delinquent son of elderly janitor Hank Rolike (of *The Last Precinct*), particularly in the scenes where he's being spirited away, screaming for help as J.J. carts him off in "a car with horns on it" to Idaho, where he feels like "we just drove through a bowl of Corn Flakes." Williamson's street smart screaming ("For those of you who have never been outside of Sparta," he bellows at the bemused citizens, "I am a Negro" ... and is greeted with a sea of stony faces) makes an amusing contrast with Robertson's hick complacency, but naturally Starbuck's Hollywood fantasy of a winning team and reformed youth inevitably wins out. It's very professional slop.

As was often the case with Cannell series, Cannell's tendency to throw in extra trimmings and trappings to either develop or discard is well in evidence in *J.J. Starbuck,* which — unlike the meticulously conceived *Columbo*— gave every indication of having been put into production half-cocked. Just as *The A-Team* had ultimately found no use for its female cast members, and just as Anne Francis and Mary Jackson had been found surplus to requirements in *Riptide* and *Hardcastle and McCormick* respectively, so Cannell and his writers found they had no use for Shawn Weatherly as Jill, the surviving Starbuck family member (Weatherly went on to co-star in the first season of *Baywatch*), and Jimmy Dean as Charlie Bullets. Indeed, Weatherly's most prominent role in the series came as a guest-star (still cast as Starbuck's daughter) after she had left the series, in the episode "Rag Doll," written by Randall Wallace and directed by William Fraker, in which she investigates a fearful phone call from a desperate friend.* Cannell would always overload his series with gimmicks and characters for the writers to play with and the networks to choose from, and then use the ones the writers felt most comfortable with. It was tough for the players, but Cannell was loyal to those performers who were loyal to him, and often performers dropped from a show were given guest roles elsewhere. Once you were on Cannell's roster of players, there was a good chance you'd be offered further work, and in both L.A. and Canada, Cannell built up a stable of stock players who, if a series runs long enough, will show up in almost everything at one time or another.

Perhaps the saddest loss to the series was the character of Lt. Casperson, an L.A. cop ultimately ushered out of the plots by Starbuck's habit of traveling round the country, and portrayed in the pilot by Glynn Turman (later to co-star in the Cosby series *A Different World*). Casperson demonstrates a wonderful streak of Cannell cynicism that suggests that he too has seen the entire 44 episode run of *Columbo.* His muted aggression in the pilot, aimed at both Starbuck's sly buffoonery and guest bad guy Bill Bixby's bogus act of concerned stifled *angst* at his wife's demise, is a joy to behold. Sadly, Casperson appeared only once in the series proper, and played by another, more subdued performer (Robert Hooks), but Turman's slow-burning fuse might have been a major asset to the series, creating a McCloud/Clifford–style relationship between the two. Turman's 3-d performances have been the saving grace of many a TV turkey, including the pilot for Glen Larson's infantile *Manimal* (Michael D. Roberts of *Baretta* took over his role for the series), and the surprisingly poor "Paladin of the Lost Hour," written by the usually excellent Harlan Ellison for the 1980s incarnation of *The Twilight Zone,* in which he offered a sublime antidote but discordant contrast to the saccharine performance of co-star Danny Kaye's Hollywood-humble lead.

Clearly Cannell realized that Starbuck needed somebody to spar with, and when former *Tenspeed and Brownshoe* star Ben Vereen became available, Cannell contrived the audacious idea of bringing his beloved E.L. "Tenspeed" Turner character back to life in *Starbuck.* It seemed like a foolproof idea — *Tenspeed and Brownshoe* had been a critical success if not a ratings hit, and Vereen was considered a good draw with audiences. Those who remembered Tenspeed would be pleased to see him back, and those who didn't would simply regard him as a new character (only a fleeting reference was made to Vereen's former partner Lionel Whitney, played in the 1980 series by Jeff Goldblum, then very much in demand for features).

---

*Indeed, the pilot and four episodes with Weatherley in the credits had passed before Jill Starbuck made her first appearance.

Cannell, as we have discussed already, was big on returning characters, and frequently used the same names for gangsters, buddies, and corporations alike, partly because it appealed to the sense of humor of his close-knit team of writers (his series are littered with private jokes utilizing the names of friends and co-workers), and partly because it performed the practical function of saving lawyers clearing new fictional names for use.

Tenspeed makes his reappearance in a Cannell-scripted episode titled "Cactus Jack's Last Call," directed by Zale Dalen, and with guest player Pat Corley, a rotund, gravel-voiced character actor with numerous guest roles on quality shows such as *Hill Street Blues* and *Moonlighting* to his credit, and a recurring role on the sit-com *Murphy Brown*. Here, he's cast as the title character of Cactus Jack, a name well familiar to that handful of people who watched *Rousters*. Cannell even has Tenspeed pulling his old phony reverend routine from the *Tenspeed* pilot again. Vereen co-starred with Robertson (replacing Weatherly and Dean in the opening credits*) for four episodes, with what appears to be a telephone call insert in the fifth remaining episode presumably for continuity purposes. The show still didn't rise in the ratings, and NBC pulled the plug.

Starbuck had made its debut on Tuesday nights in a difficult slot. It followed the remarkably similar but dumber *Matlock,* a sort of cornpone mix of *Columbo* and *Perry Mason* itself, which may have meant that the audience had already had their fill of wily old silver-haired investigators for the evening and served only to signpost how derivative *J.J. Starbuck* was. It also opposed *Jake and the Fat Man* on CBS, which was another murder mystery courtroom show from the same producers as *Matlock* and which co-starred Joe Penny of *Riptide,* thus siphoning off Cannell aficionados as well as murder mystery fans. Also, Levinson and Link's *The Law and Harry McGraw,* yet another show in the same post–*Columbo* vein as *Matlock* and *Jake and the Fat Man* actually followed the latter, further saturating the Tuesday night line-up with detective shows. To further compound matters (although it was aimed at an entirely different audience), *Starbuck* was also directly opposite *Moonlighting,* a hit show that had not yet hit the production problems that would later sink it (to add insult to injury, the debut of *Moonlighting* had driven *Riptide* off the air). Perhaps sensing that the evening was overloaded with five shows of the same genre (hey, nothing gets past these network scheduling wizards), NBC switched the show to Saturday nights, swapping it with Cannell's hit *Hunter*. In the Saturday slot, *Starbuck* won its time period, but was still rating lower than *Hunter* had in that slot; *Hunter* was actually beating the now production-troubled *Moonlighting* on the evenings when ABC was forced to run repeats, but on the nights when a new episode of *Moonlighting* was ready, the audience went back to it and *Hunter* lost out. Consequently, NBC chose to return *Hunter* to Saturdays to protect it and *Starbuck* was put on hold, finally being canceled after re-runs in a Wednesday night slot rated poorly.

But while *Starbuck* must ultimately share some of the blame for being aimless and unsure of itself, most of the blame — given the show's improvement on Saturday — can be apportioned out to NBC's schedulers, who placed *Starbuck after* a similar show, *opposite* a similar show, and as a highly unlikely and unhelpful lead-in to Michael Mann's *Crime Story*. And although it might also be argued that *Starbuck's* chances were killed by the popularity of *Hunter,* NBC were not faced with an either/or situation; they could have had both shows if they'd had the inclination. The real problems had begun with the Tuesday night line-up; *The Law and Harry McGraw* also bit the dust, while *Jake and the Fat Man,* which initially fared badly and flirted

---

*Dean had departed the series a little earlier than Weatherley.

with the axe, flourished later in a different slot. There, but for the grace of network stupidity, went *Starbuck*.

The one constant that *J.J. Starbuck* had going for it throughout its entire short history was the sparkle of former school teacher and former TV western star Dale Robertson, who was marvelous in the lead.* The night before *Starbuck* made its debut, Robertson turned up to promote the new series on *The Tonight Show*, explaining that he had returned to television from retirement to his ranch in Oklahoma after losing a lot of money in the oil business. Guest spots had followed — typically — on *Dallas, Dynasty,* and *Matt Houston*.

"There are actors and there are personalities," explained Robertson, now an elected member of the Cowboy Hall of Fame, and "motion pictures and television have usually been a business for personalities. And the difference, in my opinion, is the way an actor can change himself to fit a role, a personality, out of necessity, must change the part to fit himself. You know, I don't have the ability...." He paused to consider. "Well, nobody ever asked me to play Shakespeare! And I wouldn't have done it anyway! They wouldn't let me ad-lib, y'know...!" Amusingly, there was a lot of J.J. in Robertson himself as he discussed the bad press Hollywood gets in the media ("33,000 people in this industry, and the only ones you read about in a negative way are a handful") and launched into a J.J.–style wry observation about charity events ("I told all them husbands that if we got together and counted up what we spend on shoes, dresses, jewelry for the ladies, and to rent the hall, buy the food, pay the orchestra and everything else — if we forgot all that and took the money and sent it straight to the charity — I believe they'd come out a whole lot better off!").

Throughout it all, Robertson's Starbuck waddled through the show oozing charm and decency like Santa Claus in a ten-gallon hat, and Cannell and his writers almost have you believing this horse manure ... but J.J. Starbuck only works his magic for an hour at a time, and ultimately, perhaps even inevitably, common sense and cynicism must win out over posturing and platitudes. And deep down, not in the heart of Texas, and certainly not in the heart of Cannell the TV producer, you get the feeling that Cannell the writer probably wouldn't really have it any other way.

Episode Guide

regular and recurring cast: Dale Robertson (J.J. Starbuck), Ben Vereen (E.L. "Tenspeed" Turner), Shawn Weatherly (Jill Starbuck), Jimmy Dean (Charlie Bullets)

with Bill Bixby, Patty Duke, Jay Underwood, Glynn Turman, Donna Mitchell, David Huddleston, Katherine Moffat, H. Richard Greene, Doug Shanklin, Amy Yasbeck, Eric Server, Patrick Cronin, Luke Andreas, Michael Laskin, Lora Staley

(1987)

J.J. STARBUCK (pilot)

wr. Stephen Cannell, dir. Corey Allen
Visiting Beverly Hills, Starbuck noses around the murder of a troublesome young boy's mother by his stepfather and business associates.

A KILLING IN THE MARKET

wr. Stephen Cannell, dir. Larry Shaw
Traveling to New York to placate a Wall Street businessman who wants to buy out J.J.'s company, Starbuck uncovers an insider dealer trading scam

---

*One of Cannell's earliest story idea sales had been to Robertson's 1966–'68 western series Iron Horse, in which Robertson's character loses — and wins back — his railroad in a poker game, in much the same way he acquired it in the first place.

and exposes the faked suicide of a young businesswoman who had her own suspicions.

with Robert Conrad, Christine Hirt, Kim Ulrich, Trent Dolan, Christine Haber, Tracey Olson, Don Mackay

Murder in E Minor

wr. Babs Greyhosky, dir. Kim Manners
A technically brilliant but passionless pianist masterminds the murder of his piano teacher with a foolproof alibi.

with Kelsey Grammer, Eric Christmas, Peggy McCay, Don Hood

The Blimpy Who Yelled Blue

wr. Burt Pearl, dir. Bill Corcoran
When a publicity hound learns that the true author of a successful series of children's books he is co-credited with intends to retire, he arranges murder to keep the secret.

with Richard Mulligan, Sherry Hursey, William Frankfather, Lisa Nelson

First You've Gotta Go to the Picnic

wr. Babs Greyhosky, dir. Bruce Kessler
J.J. hauls the troublesome son of an old friend to a hick farming community to help sort out the fortunes of an ailing football team.

with Mykel T. Williamson, Joshua Bryant, Roy Brocksmith, Hank Rolike, Don Michael Paul

Incident at San September

wr. Stephen Cannell, dir. Lyndon Chubbuk
An oil-rig occupied by employees of Marklee, Starbuck's company, is invaded by terrorists intent on capturing a shipping freighter transporting missiles.

with Kent McCord, Wolf Muser, James Louis Watkins, J. Patrick McNamara, Nehemiah Persoff, Duncan Fraser

Gold from the Rainbow

wr. Stephen Cannell, dir. John Peter Kousakis
Starbuck stumbles into a family feud between a Greek restaurateur and his property developer son.

with Telly Savalas, Paul Regina, Raye Birk, Candace Savalas, Christine Anton, Vanessa Santos.

Graveyard Shift

wr. Randall Wallace, dir. Bob Bralver

On the word of a gravedigger, Starbuck investigates mysterious goings-on at a local mortuary.

with John Schuck, Geoffrey Lewis, Karole Selman

The Six-Percent Solution

wr. Carol Mendolsohn, dir. Zale Dalen
Starbuck poses as a simple-minded speculator to expose an estate agent deliberately breaking up marriages to obtain valuable sales on desirable properties.

with Patrick O'Neal, Bibi Besch, Lena Pousette, Robert Hooks, Larry Parrish, Andrew Cavadas

The Circle Broken

wr. Randall Wallace, dir. Kim Manners
Starbuck sets out to expose a phony religious cult that is milking the fortunes of the gullible by joining their ranks.

with Alan Rachins, Marta Dubois, Jill Carroll

Murder by Design

wr. Randall Wallace, dir. Charles Picerni
When a talentless designer attempts to blackmail the editor of an influential fashion magazine into running a spread on his work, he becomes the target for murder ... and the object of an investigation by J.J. Starbuck, who knew his father.

with Jessica Walter, John Kapelos, Jack Elam, Michelle Goodger

Cactus Jack's Last Call

wr. Stephen Cannell, dir. Zale Dalen
Tenspeed Turner from *Tenspeed and Brownshoe* returns in this story of gambling debts gone sour.

with Pat Corley, Stuart Whitman, Dakin Matthews

A Song from the Sequel

wr. Stephen Cannell, dir. James Whitmore, Jr.
Starbuck helps a ruined and despondent young man regain his self-respect by solving a ten year old murder committed by a film executive who killed the man's father.

with Jill St. John, Joe Regalbuto, John Ireland, Silvano Gallardo

Permanent Hiatus

wr. Stephen Cannell, Randall Wallace, dir. Neill Fearnley
Starbuck becomes suspicious that an old war

buddy, now hosting a tabloid TV talk show, has murdered a rival producer.

    with Ed Nelson, Melody Rogers, Jackson Davies

RAG DOLL

    wr. Randall Wallace, dir. William Fraker

Starbuck's daughter receives a frantic phone call and investigates the death of a friend who was prostituting herself for a hedonistic video producer.

    with Michael Des Barres, Xander Berkeley, Raymond O'Connor, Beverley Hendry, Caryn West

THE RISE AND FALL OF JOE PIERMONT

    wr. Carol Mendelsohn, dir. Bob Bralver

An old business colleague wants Starbuck to hit the campaign trail for his politician son, but although the son appears to be on the level, J.J. has reservations about the integrity of his old pal.

    with Barry Nelson, Joseph Hacker

    series ends

Sonny Spoon
February 1988–December 1988

*"They wanted a guy who could go anywhere, from the
White House to the outhouse — use his wits and not his mitts"*

With *Sonny Spoon*, Cannell returned to his roots, and the ground he had covered in the '70s with *The Rockford Files, Baretta, The Duke* and *Tenspeed and Brownshoe,* elements of all of which were to be found in this lively detective show. Salvatore "Sonny" Spoon was a streetwise p.i. who managed to be black without being a cliché — he could have been any nationality — and who had a phone box next to his best pal's newsstand which doubled as his office.

Unfortunately, the supporting characters — an army of street people on tap as contacts — did not avoid stereotyping quite so easily, and *Sonny Spoon* offered a collection of '70s throwbacks so bogus that they would have made even *Baretta* think he'd entered a comic-book; these included loveable news vendor Lucius DeLuce, played by Joe Shea, a former trumpet player from Brooklyn turned actor and guest star on such other Cannell series as *Hunter* and *Wiseguy*,* physically handicapped actor Bob Wieland as the legless, skateboard-riding "Skates," and Jordana Capra as tart-with-a-heart Monique, three of many who lived only for the moment when they could justify their existence on this mortal coil by throwing a curve-ball for Sonny.

In the early 1970s, when street life was being romanticized in both cop shows and black super-hero flicks, *Sonny Spoon* might have been the hit show that Cannell's *Baretta* or Spelling's *Starsky and Hutch* was; in the late 1980s, when every film from Martin Scorsese's 1976 nightmare *Taxi Driver* to the most Z-grade straight-to-video exploiter had acknowledged and deconstructed the myth of neon-bathed glamour-sleaze nightlife, the spruced-up shabbiness of *Sonny Spoon*'s close-to-the-edge urban environment was as phony as a three dollar bill, a point not lost on the more perceptive reviewers. "As might be expected from producer Stephen J. Cannell, who also gave us *The Rockford Files, Hunter,* and *The A-Team* among others, *Sonny Spoon* has a salable premise, interesting characters and snappy dialogue," said *TV Guide*. "The plots are vintage Cannell, fast-paced and convoluted. What it doesn't have is a feeling of reality, a sense that these are real people, rather than fugitives from comic strips." "Secondary characters," noted *Variety*, "offer some texture but suggest they may have been acquainted with Baretta when he was jumping fences a decade ago...." But in the affluent '80s, nobody fantasized about slumming it with the street-life any more, as Aaron Spelling had found out a few years earlier with his rapidly canceled 1984 show *Hollywood Beat*.

Sonny Spoon was a fresh contribution to that stale myth, a dozen years too late and unable to revitalize the lie; it had taken a while for television to catch up with the movies, but the

---

*Shea was "No Money" Mahoney in the Steelgrave story, but his finest moments came in the middle of the Proffit saga in the episode "Not for Nothin'."

days when *Charlie's Angels* or *Police Woman* could glam up as hookers to spice up the lives of the American mid-west for two-faced exposes that gave double-meaning to the word bust were over. If some of that mentality has since been revived in the 1990s and 2000s by rap and "gangsta" videos, it is for a far more insular and less all-pervasive market since.

What *Sonny Spoon* did have going for it was the multi-talented Mario Van Peebles in the lead role, who was highly tipped as a hot new talent by NBC boss Brandon Tartikoff, and was the son of film-maker Melvin Van Peebles, who later briefly co-starred with him in the show as Spoon's dad. Although an otherwise complimentary review in *TV Guide* suggested Van Peebles should "tone it down" a few notches (and the author agrees that a little of Sonny Spoon goes a long way — a Sonny teaspoon rather than a Sonny tablespoon perhaps), the critics were almost unanimous in agreeing that it was Van Peebles (alongside the Cannell m.o.) who made the show special. "*Sonny's* big plus is Van Peebles," said *Variety*; "Van Peebles ... adds dash to a TV creation that reads better on paper than he would normally play on TV as conveyed by most other video actors," agreed *Hollywood Reporter*.

One element of *Sonny Spoon* that was original was that it was a drama series with a black lead; previous attempts on TV — *Shaft, Tenafly, Paris, Fortune Dane* — had been few and far between. "I'm aware that none have been successful in the past," Van Peebles told Eirik Knutzen of the *Toronto Star*, "but NBC is taking a chance, hoping that the mass audience will look beyond color. I'm at a loss to explain why parts for black leading men only come along every five years while Americans completely accept black comedic performers." Ironically, Sonny Spoon as a character is so manic and scene-stealing that he might have worked better as a supporting player rather than the star ... but too charismatic to play sidekick or co-star without completely stealing the show, Van Peebles' ultimate aim, even then, was to become a director and producer, and he accomplished his aim remarkably quickly during the production of *Sonny Spoon*.

"I was told that I looked like a young Harry Belafonte when I first came to Hollywood, and I knew it meant unemployment because of the black leading man thing," said Van Peebles to Knutzen (and others), "So I concentrated on getting character parts." As an actor, Van Peebles' film work includes films of such variable quality as *The Cotton Club, Jaws: the Revenge, Heartbreak Ridge*, and *Exterminator II*. Born in Mexico City to a black father and a blonde German mother ("the original hippie — she even got me drum lessons with The Grateful Dead"), the young Van Peebles traveled Europe as a child with his family, before they settled in San Francisco, and later New York. He appeared in numerous stage productions as an actor and dancer, speaks four languages, worked as a model, and even directed a pop video.

At a meeting with the NBC suits, Van Peebles outlined his hopes for the show. "I said I'd like to have a character who doesn't carry a gun, who uses his mind, who does all these different characters — because I don't want to be pigeonholed — and I'd like to have my dad on the show!" Van Peebles told Pat Hilton for *USA Today*. "I insisted the cops and villains be mixed, so we break away from this silly color stuff. I want a human show. If we have a black show, then I've lost." In a few months, wrote Hilton, "he got a call from someone named Steve, who said that NBC wanted him to work with Van Peebles. The actor was polite, but asked, 'What do you do, Steve?' Stephen J. Cannell explained that he'd produced *The Rockford Files, The A-Team*, and *Hunter*."

Cannell had viewed a short film Van Peebles had written, directed, and performed called *Juliet*, in which he played all the boyfriends the title character had worked her way through. As for the name Sonny Spoon, Van Peebles told interviewer Joe D'Agnese for *Right On* magazine "Later on (NBC chief Brandon Tartikoff) said 'How do you like the name Sonny Spoon?' Now that I knew who he was, I said 'Do *you* like that idea, Brandon?' He said yes. I said 'I love that idea! Great name, great name!'"

Another asset was co-star Terry Donahoe, a former player in daytime soaps, as ambitious assistant D.A. Carolyn Gilder (a similar character materialized a couple of seasons later on the series *Gabriel's Fire*), who was introduced in the pilot while Sonny is investigating the murder of his friend and mentor, newly retired p.i. Sam Abramowitz. At first, Donahoe played a role not unlike that of Gretchen Corbett's Beth Davenport in *The Rockford Files,* but, said

Joe Shea, Mario Van Peebles, and Terry Donahoe ham it up for the camera at this publicity shoot to promote *Sonny Spoon's* first season.

producer Randall Wallace to *TV Guide*, "We want to see more of them together. Initially, we found her convenient as someone for Sonny to call for help when he's in jail. We won't actually change the format of the show, but we'd be idiots not to use her more."

Donahoe's best moments are in "The Story of Daring Dick Darling..." and Cannell and Wallace's enjoyable and obvious-with-hindsight "Too Good to Be True...," two episodes which successfully define a three-dimensional friendship in the Hunter and McCall tradition between the two of them. Ultimately, the street life element was quietly phased out, and Shea's Lucius the news-vendor dispatched to the limbo-land occupied by such other disappearing Cannell characters as Jill Starbuck, Mama Jo and Sara Wickes, and Donahoe and Van Peebles Sr., were built up.

Also working in the show's favor were a variety of 1970s Cannell trademarks and plots, most often found in the likes of *Baretta*, *The Rockford Files* and *The Duke,* and perhaps last used in *Riptide* and *Hardcastle and McCormick.** Like Rockford, Baretta and Tenspeed (not to mention Hannibal, Face and the *Riptide* boys), Sonny has a variety of disguises, false identities and scams to hand, and some worked better than others. In the otherwise excellent "Too Good to Be True...," Sonny's masquerade as a Japanese chef right under Carolyn Gilder's nose would require the myopia of Superman's girlfriend Lois Lane not to see through; other gags are much funnier. Van Peebles' other masquerades in the series include a Rastafarian, a blonde, blue-eyed Frenchman, an old fat man, a priest, a snobbish attorney, and a Motown-like nightclub singer. "I'll also be doing a Chinese houseboy, a one-armed Jamaican hit-man, a pregnant woman ... and Elvis!" he enthusiastically informed Laurie Werner of *USA Weekend*. "I just love watching people and copying them. We traveled so much when I was a kid that I was always hearing new voices to copy. I still do it. It drives my friends nuts because I'm always throwing new voices at them." To Stephannia Cleaton of the *Boston Herald,* he said "I speak a little French, I speak a little Spanish, a little uptown, a little downtown...."

"I didn't want him to be a black James Bond," Van Peebles told Werner. "He has a Bugs Bunny philosophy. He doesn't carry a gun. When you're confronted by the Tasmanian Devil, you don't shoot him, you dress up as a girl Tasmanian Devil and walk him off a cliff!" "Sonny is kind of like Artemus Gordon from *The Wild Wild West* meets *The Rockford Files* with a Bugs Bunny philosophy," he told Leslie Van Buskirk for *US* magazine.

The writers took Van Peebles' Bugs Bunny reference to heart, even incorporating familiar gags and touches from the legendary Warner Bros. cartoons, such as the scene used in the opening credits in which a maniacally grinning Sonny waves goodbye to some pursuing hoods from the back window of his getaway car. "It's easy to write that a character gets out of a car and pulls a gun," Van Peebles told journalists during his promotional campaign for the show. "It's much harder to have him suddenly become a Hispanic taxi driver!" Fortunately, if anyone was adept at writing both kinds of scenes, it was Cannell!

The tone of the series is best exemplified by Cannell's "The Story of Daring Dick Darling..." which guest-stars David Marciano, then recently seen as the crazed psychotic Lorenzo in Cannell's *Wiseguy* script "The Loose Cannon," but later to co-star in *Due South*. Here, under the appellation Insane Wayne (which Cannell aficionados will quickly recognize from the *A-Team* extravaganza "Waiting for Insane Wayne" by Cannell and Frank Lupo), Marciano mugs furiously in a virtual parody of his Lorenzo role and, whereas in *Wiseguy* we could believe him of any act of violence, in *Sonny Spoon*—even when he is repeatedly dangling Spoon out

---

**Cannell even resurrected the "tough nun" cliché from the* Black Sheep Squadron *episode "Poor Little Lambs" for the episode "The Tough Habit."*

of a window *A Fish Called Wanda*–style — we are never remotely unsure that Spoon will be hauled back in to crack wise another day. Similarly, Leigh McCloskey's Angel Martin clone Dick Darling brings back memories of Ken Olandt's Kirk Dooley in "It's a Vial Sort of Business" for *Riptide* and numerous other pretty-boy wastrels.

Cannell's episodes of *Sonny Spoon* are easily the best, despite their almost overpowering familiarity, the last gasp of his late–'70s, early '80s freewheeling primetime persona, but if *Sonny Spoon* achieves anything it is the overwhelming sense of the end of that particular era. As good as Randall Wallace's "Semper Fi" is — and it is good — the viewer can't help but recall the similar scenarios from *The Rockford Files*' "Two into 2:56 Won't Go" or *Riptide*'s "The Orange Grove"; all three are excellent entertainments, but the idea has been round the block one too many times. Cannell's "The Tough Habit" is fun, but as with the sucker punches laid on Spoon by McCloskey's pathetic Dick Darling in "The Story of Daring Dick Darling…" and David Ackroyd's masterful portrait of the uptight and repressed military man Colonel McClanahan in "Semper Fi," it's difficult to respect a hero who lets himself be trampled over by so many people, especially one who — unlike Rockford or Nick and Cody — is so cocksure of himself. Even Thom Bray's Murray Bozinsky of *Riptide* wouldn't put up with the treatment Spoon receives from McClanahan or super-nun Sister Elizabeth Mary, and the viewer is left with the overwhelming impression that if Spoon can't handle a tight-ass reactionary, or abrasive old woman, or whitebread leech, then he's not as smart as he thinks he is. Spoon is just a little too smug — when kidnapped by thugs in "Crimes Below the Waist," he responds with assorted put-downs and *Rockford*-isms but this viewer at least suffered a guilty and shameful desire to see the despondent thugs wipe the grin from his face!

There was also a sense that rather than let the stories develop from Spoon and his co-stars, these classic Cannell storylines were being shoe-horned into the format and the character organized to fit the rehashed plot of the week. Spoon comes across more like the sort of character who would have successfully ducked military service rather than the noble preacher who lectures McClanahan in "Semper Fi" on the camaraderie of the Marines as if they were Mouseketeers. Cannell and/or writer Wallace attempt to circumvent this by creating a sort of *M*A*S*H*–like Bilko/Hawkeye Pierce military identity for Spoon as rebellious clown and finagler, but this not only undermines Spoon's speech about loyalty to fellow officers but is totally at odds with Chip McAllister's portrayal of the ill-fated Titus, Spoon's partner-in-mischief according to the script, but who comes across as virtually mentally retarded in the finished program.

"Crimes Below the Waist" — written by everyone-and-Cannell — gives every indication of being cobbled together out of scenes and ideas crowded out of the pilot, but does seem more deliberately styled to the *Sonny Spoon* format, even if it does resurrect the famous elaborate sting storyline best represented by Juanita Bartlett's "The Farnsworth Stratagem" and "The Great Blue Lake Land and Development Company" for *The Rockford Files* and — again — Cannell's "The Orange Grove" for *Riptide*. Once again, it's fun to see it all coming together, but also once again, it's the last gasp of something we've seen far too often and far too recently; whereas Cannell's vigilante shows of the early '80s resurrected pseudo Republic serial stories that hadn't seen the light of day in the mass market for thirty or forty years, and film-makers like Lucas, Spielberg and De Palma have carved movie careers out of forgotten themes and formulae from the outer edges of ancient pop culture, these gags won't really be good for reviving until the 2020s … and that's assuming the *Rockford/A-Team/Riptide* re-runs haven't been too prolific!

So familiar were the storylines and situations of the first season, that when the second season opened with a blatant rewrite of *Riptide's* "Be True to Your School," a Cannell script pulled from the drawer due to the writers' strike of '88, it made little noticeable difference to the established tone of the series. "Never Go to Your High School Reunion," revised for *Sonny Spoon* by producer Jo Swerling, Jr., was the only script Cannell and NBC were forced to re-use before the dispute was settled and — even without the rehash — was already a well-worn Cannell theme that had already been employed in episodes of *The Rockford Files* ("Rattler's Class of '63"), *Greatest American Hero* ("The Price is Right"), and *The A-Team* ("Beneath the Surface").

Robert Bielak's painfully punnish "Papa Rotzi" and Randall Wallace's "Ratman Can" are typically entertaining Cannell forays into mob-land, while Cannell's own "Deuce's Wild," with Cannell regular Ken Swofford playing Deputy Chief "Bricktop" Jones, bears a strong resemblance to *Rockford's* "Kill the Messenger" and *Hunter's* "The Hot Grounder," while Jonathan Glassner's "Diamonds Aren't Forever" echoes themes explored in *Hunter's* "Burned." The last episode, "The Final Exam," written by Jack Bernstein, resurrects Cannell's old standbys the medical conspiracy and the Nazi war criminal.

Corey Allen (director on *Hill Street Blues, L.A. Law, Murder She Wrote, Star Trek: The Next Generation,* and anything else with a large cast to manipulate) helmed the pilot, with the usual Cannell team behind the scenes, including Stuart Segall (*Hunter, Thunderboat Row, Renegade*), Alan Cassidy (*Hunter*), and Jo Swerling, Jr. Creation of the character was credited to Cannell and Wallace, Michael Daly and Dinah Prince. The series was co-financed by NBC themselves, and consequently was the only other Cannell production of the period besides *Hunter* (also on NBC) to be shot on the streets of L.A. (for the first season, the series was set in an unspecified East Coast city, but for the second season facelift, logic prevailed and Sonny moved to Los Angeles). This accounted for the number of *Hunter* personnel also working on *Sonny Spoon,* and when the show was written off so early, it also effectively spelled the end of Cannell's operations in Hollywood.

Mario Van Peebles had co-starred in *L.A. Law* for a couple of episodes (a similar character to his was later reintroduced, played by Blair Underwood) and guest-starred in *The Cosby Show,* and both Cannell and Tartikoff were convinced they had a major new star on their hands. It turned out that they did — but not in the way they expected. *Sonny Spoon* did reasonably well in its first short series of episodes (although not as well as some other higher-rated shows that NBC canceled), but bombed when it returned for the new season, with even lower ratings; stung by accusations of favoritism because it was an NBC show as opposed to an outside commission, this drop sealed its fate. For a show which had been hailed as the Second Coming only a few months earlier, it was axed with undignified haste, without earning even a second chance in a different time-slot, a stay of execution both *Hunter* and *J.J. Starbuck* had been granted. However, Van Peebles had not been idle — he'd been using his time with the Cannell organization to hone his skills as a director on *Sonny Spoon* (he helmed Cannell's "Cheap 'n Chili," which — although it had the feel of a back-door pilot — was actually supposed to introduce the two cops owning the nicknames of the title as continuing characters; this idea never went any further) and other Cannell shows like *Hunter, 21 Jump Street, Top of the Hill,* and *Wiseguy.* During the break between seasons of *Sonny Spoon,* he and his father made the film *Identity Crisis* together, and which he had written during the making of *Jaws: the Revenge* "while we were sitting around waiting for the shark to work." Jr. and Sr. co-directed and co-produced, and Cannell himself took a role; "But when you're directing your boss and your dad in a scene together, what do you say—Do it over?" lamented Van Peebles, Jr. jokingly to journalist Marilyn Beck.

It was quite unusual for a producer of Cannell's clout to have a show canned so rapidly, but Van Peebles barely had time to mourn the Wile E. Coyote–style dive his promising television career had taken—he was too busy being hailed as one of the exciting new directors of the '90s for his critically-acclaimed feature *New Jack City*.

Episode Guide

regular and recurring cast: Mario Van Peebles (Salvatore "Sonny" Spoon), Terry Donahoe (D.A. Carolyn Gilder), Melvin Van Peebles (Melvin Spoon), Joe Shea (Lucius Luce), Bob Wieland ("Skates"), Jordana Capra (Monique)

First Season (1988)

SAM'S PRIVATE EYE (pilot)

wr. Randall Wallace, Michael Daly, Dinah Prince, Stephen Cannell, dir. Corey Allen

Sonny Spoon, a novice p.i. working from a phone booth near a newsstand, becomes the target of mobsters after his friend and mentor is gunned down while working on his last case before retirement.

with Nathan Davis, John Snyder, Matthew Faison, Greg Collins, Anthony DeFonte, Kathleen Freeman, Charles Fleischer, Henry Kingi, J. Bill Jones, Ben Rawnsley, Eric Server, Jimmie F. Skaggs

THE STORY OF DARING DICK DARLING, WIZARD OF ODDS

wr. Stephen Cannell, dir. Rob Bowman

Reformed burglar and professional leech Dick Darling has returned to crime in the worst way, ripping off gangster "Insane Wayne" Bataglia, and—in turning to Sonny for protection—implicates him in the mess.

with Leigh McCloskey, David Marciano, Gregory Wagrowski, Lorry Goldman, Harvey Jason, Clare Carey, Robert Schuch, Jon Slade, John Tuell

CRIMES BELOW THE WAIST

wr. Randall Wallace, Michael Daly, Dinah Prince, Stephen Cannell, dir. Rob Iscove

Sonny is busy helping out two old friends, one accused of murder, the other being blackmailed by compromising photographs.

with Robin Givens, Phill Lewis, Thomas Ryan, Bernie Hern, Gary Werntz, David Partington, Jack McGee, J.P. Bumstead

WHO'S GOT TONSILLITIS?

wr. Randall Wallace, dir. Roy Campanella II

Sonny searches for a missing blues singer involved with an unscrupulous and dangerous record promoter.

with Leon Isaac Kennedy, Jeff Silverman, Roderick Cook, Dan Lauria, Steve Vinovich, Ricardo Guitterez, Raymond O'Connor, Denise Gordy, Charles Walker

SEMPER FI

wr. Randall Wallace, dir. Alan Cooke

Sonny is "drafted" back into the Marines by an unpleasant and cold military man to hunt down an old friend of his who has gone absent without leave while on a secret assignment.

with David Ackroyd, Ron Mychal Hayes, Chip McAllister, Melinda Mallari, Rex Ryon, Troy Beyer, Irving Mosley, Jr., Lance Reed

THE TOUGH HABIT

wr. Stephen Cannell, dir. Dick Miller

Sonny is coerced by a tough local nun into hunting down a runaway orphan girl, a young trickster who turns out to have a number of different aliases! (This episode introduces Melvin Van Peebles as Melvin Spoon).

with Conchata Ferrell, Blanca DeGarr, Seth Jaffe, Kim Milford, Michael Delano, Benji Schulman, Pierre Epstein, David Coburn

TOO GOOD TO BE TRUE, TOO GOOD TO GET CAUGHT

wr. Stephen Cannell, Randall Wallace, dir. Roy Campanella II

Sonny sets up Carolyn with a hot date ... only to discover that he may be a wanted killer...!

with Antony Hamilton, Brenda Strong, Joe

Highcastle, Robert Silver, Frantz Turner, Guy Christopher

Second Season (also 1988)

NEVER GO TO YOUR HIGH SCHOOL REUNION

wr. Stephen Cannell, Jo Swerling, Jr., dir. Roy Campanella II

Sonny's high school memories are sullied by the discovery that a number of his friends have fallen into a drug smuggling operation with their former chemistry teacher (this episode is a remake of a *Riptide* episode, dusted off during a writers' strike).

with Forry Smith, Jack Bannon, Jeff Lester, Julius Carry III, Ray Brocksmith, Annabelle Gurwitch, Stuart Mabray, Ron Regasner, Nicholas Schaeffer, Reid Smith, Carl Strano

CHEAP 'N CHILI

wr. Randall Wallace, dir. Mario Van Peebles

Spoon gets involved with a couple of seedy maverick cops who have lost valuable evidence in a double-or-nothing scam that's gone horribly wrong.

with Nestor Serrano, Mark Thomas Miller, Richard Brooks, Larenz Tate, Ron Taylor, James Avery, Mark Lonow, Julie Inouye, Irwin Keyes, Andre Nunez

BLIND JUSTICE

wr. Jack Bernstein, dir. Dennis Dugan

Sonny befriends an accident-prone blind girl visiting the city, unaware that she is an undercover assassin setting him up for a frame.

with Claudia Christian, Rita Wilson, Dwier Brown, Kenneth Tigar, Dan Bell, Johnny Haymer, David McKnight, Ralph Monaco, Jeremy Roberts

PAPA ROTZI

wr. Robert Bielak, dir. Randy Roberts

Sonny becomes the target of a vengeful movie stuntman after a news photographer takes a picture of the tough guy with a starlet and sets up Sonny to take the fall.

with Kevin Dunn, Gregory Wagrowski, Matt Landers, Gerald Prendergast, Floyd Levine, Charles Boswell, Sam Scarber, Anthony Charnota, Elizabeth Hoffman, David McKnight, John Tuell

RATMAN CAN

wr. Randall Wallace, dir. Dick Miller

Sonny is coerced into exposing a mob plot by impersonating a deranged hit-man ... who then escapes from police custody.

with Kario Salem, David Hunt, Joseph Cali, Jill Carroll, Al Ruscio, Mitch Pileggi, Robert Tessier, Perry Anzilotti, Paul Joynt, Scott Lincoln, Ralph Manza, Robert Miano, Charlie Murphy

DEUCE'S WILD

wr. Stephen Cannell, dir. Bruce Kessler

Sonny is reluctantly teamed up with a useless and deceitful on-staff detective at a law firm to assist in clearing the name of a client accused of murder.

with Shadoe Stevens, Ron Glass, Ken Swofford, M.K. Harris, David Labiosa, Tim Neil, Jennifer Rhodes

DIAMONDS AREN'T FOREVER

wr. Jonathan Glassner, dir. Bruce Kessler

A successful author is convinced that she has collided in the street with one of the men who killed her mother many years ago — but with a new book just released based on her relationship with her parents, the police suspect a publicity stunt.

with Kristen Meadows, Andy Romano, Andrew Masset, Michael Gates, Mike Genovese, David Froman, Marilyn McCoo, Anne Bellamy, Chris Crone, Ben Hartigan

THE FINAL EXAM

wr. Jack Bernstein, dir. Winriche Kolbe

Sonny poses as a cantankerous old man to investigate a nursing home where the patients are dying mysteriously, and discovers that he's not the only person there who isn't what he seems to be.

with Nicholas Pryor, Ray Walston, Joyce Hyser, Mark L. Taylor, John O'Leary, Phil Leeds, Mabel King, Arnold Johnson, Laurel Lockhart, Johnny Silver, Tatiana, Hank Woessner

series ends

Unsub
February 1989–April 1989

Like *Sonny Spoon*, *Unsub* was a series which took Cannell full-circle back to his origins, this time to the territory of hard, grim, factual crimebusting shows like *Chase* and *Adam 12*; *Unsub* even starred Kent McCord of *Adam 12*, alongside David Soul of *Starsky and Hutch* fame. Soul, whose TV career began with embarrassing bit parts on *Gilligan's Island* and *Star Trek*, but progressed to lead roles in pilots like Spelling's *Hong Kong Harry* and such later short-run series as *Casablanca* and *The Yellow Rose* (and directing assignments on such classy '80s productions as *Miami Vice, Crime Story, Hunter, Heart of the City,* and *China Beach*), was John "Westy" Grayson, head of an elite force of crime-busters based in Washington, who are called in when the authorities are up against a particularly slippery serial killer. A Universal Studios contract player for a decade and a half, Kent McCord starred in Glen Larson's revamped *Galactica '80* and had known Cannell since his days on *Adam 12*, guesting on *Black Sheep Squadron, J.J. Starbuck,* and *21 Jump Street.* McCord played Grayson's colleague Alan McWhirter, with the other members of the team consisting of Joe Maruzzo as psychic Tony D'Agostino, Jennifer Hetrick as Amy Madison, M. Emmet Walsh as hardened old timer Ned Platt, and Richard Kind (later of *Mad About You* and *Spin City*) as young inexperienced eager beaver Jimmy Bello.

Using state of the art equipment, forensic evidence, and psychological profile to get inside the mind of the deranged souls they attempt to neutralize, *Unsub* (short for unknown subject) was primarily about the mechanics of catching criminals and killers, but ultimately, the very nature of the television medium caused the series to play on people's fears of senseless, random murder and the seemingly increasing number of insanely complicated madmen, psychopaths, bombers, fanatics, and mental cases that might be loose across America.

Although both Cannell and the show's publicists claimed that *Unsub* would show the team arriving on the scene *after* the crime was committed, rather than show the deed being done, the pilot at least showed just enough of the ugly build-up to a murder for the rest to be squeamishly filled in by the imagination, and for all its cleverness, *Unsub* quickly degenerated into just another sicko psycho crime show. The name of Cannell however, and the presence of David Burke and Stephen Kronish hot from *Wiseguy* in the credits bought the show a credibility from the critics earned from their work on that acclaimed series, and gave them the benefit of the doubt.* *Variety* called the show "surprisingly substantial," but considered that NBC had nevertheless put themselves in for 'Bad Taste of the Year Award, Non-Tabloid TV Division!' However, *Variety's* reviewer also wrote that "in a surprising and welcome touch, the tough-edged drama didn't paint its killer as a depraved sicko, but rather a victim

---

Many of the performers who guested in Unsub *had previously appeared in* Wiseguy, *including Paul Guilfoyle, Kevin Spacey, Patricia Charbonneau, John Snyder, and Kerry Sandomirsky.*

himself whose story is as tragic as the crimes he commits. But in one of several U-turns into silliness for an otherwise sterling Cannell script, Soul inexplicably starts referring to the villain as a 'murderous bastard.'" Inexplicably? It's true that the perpetrator of these horrendous crimes (Paul Guilfoyle, of the *Wiseguy* racism story) is a victim of tragic circumstances, but it's also difficult to deny that he *is* a murderous bastard ... and even more difficult to forget that perfectly innocent individuals who had done nothing to deserve such an early and barbaric end to their lives died horrible, vile deaths at his hands, making them far more deserving of sympathy than Guilfoyle's mad killer.

Writing in *USA Today,* Matt Roush commented, "*Unsub* should rivet those who devour police procedurals and look for grisly authenticity in their crime fiction. Meticulously and intensely, they construct profiles of their prey with high-tech hardware and a battery of unfathomable terminology. Beneath all the printouts and techspeak, however, these pros are walking wounded, psychologically battered by their proximity to the heinous acts they're investigating ... *Unsub* is unpleasant, nearly humorless, and leaves you with a sour taste. But it also grabs you and rarely insults you...." Wrote Kay Gardella in the *New York Daily News,* "The information forthcoming is fascinating (but) one weakness in this police drama is that it's too talkative, and information flies by too fast. A more deliberate approach is needed ... *Unsub* needs work, but otherwise it's different enough to be intriguing to viewers."

Whereas *Sonny Spoon* had arrived on TV ten years too late, and explored what everybody at the time felt was over-familiar territory (ten years later it would be parody, ten years after that, nostalgia), *Unsub* saw Cannell ahead of the game by ten years. What he was aiming to produce, said Cannell, was "something that wasn't on the air, something that you haven't seen before, and something you would go home and watch."

M. Emmet Walsh, Kent McCord and David Soul lead the *Unsub* team.

Given the gory, voyeuristic tabloid fascination with disgusting murders, the failure of *Unsub* was quite surprising, and only a few years later the television industry's insistence in persevering with the concept produced a modest hit with *Millennium* and later still an ongoing franchise with the *CSI* series of horrific crime dramas, the modern day equivalent of lurid pulp paperbacks and detective magazines. *Unsub* was such a damp squib that Cannell can hardly be blamed for opening the door to this material on television, as the public voted to keep it firmly wedged shut on this occasion. Sadly, such a commendable display of good taste would not be evident from audiences just ten years later, and television in the

Promotional leaflet for *Unsub*, showing Jennifer Hetrick and David Soul.

early 21st century is awash with voyeuristic unpleasantness that makes one long for the anodyne innocence of *Rockford, The A-Team,* and *Riptide* ... or even *Burke's Law* and *Charlie's Angels!*

Episode Guide

regular and recurring cast: David Soul (John "Westy" Grayson), Kent McCord (Alan McWhirter), Joe Maruzzo (Tony D'Agostino), Jennifer Hetrick (Ann Madison), M. Emmet Walsh (Ned Platt), Richard Kind (Jimmy Bello)

(1989)

WHITE BONE DEMON

wr. Stephen Cannell, dir. Corey Allen
The Unsub team race against time to put together a profile of a bizarre serial killer before he strikes again.
with Paul Guilfoyle, Andrea Mann, Grace Zabriskie, Terrence Kelly, Tom Heaton

SILENT STALKER

wr. David Burke, dir. William Fraker
The Unsub team make the mistake of letting a young student join an active investigation to catch a child molester, and her emotional involvement in the horror of the case disrupts the operation to catch him.
with Patricia Charbonneau, John Snyder, Jackson Davies, Florence Patterson

CLEAN SLATE

wr. Joe Menosky, dir. Jim Johnston
When the activities of a serial bomber cause distress and injury to members of his family, Tony calls in the rest of the team to help the police put an end to the bombings.
with Kevin Spacey, Blu Mankuma, Kerry Sandomirsky

DADDY DEAREST

wr. Stephen Kronish, dir. Reynaldo Villalobos
The Unsub team pursue a serial killer whose victims are left castrated.
with Lora Zane, Alex Bruhanski, Jo DeWinter

AND THEY SWAM RIGHT OVER THE DAM

wr. Michael Berlin, Eric Estrin, dir. Jorge Montesi
A young boy could be the only link to discovering vital information about the serial killer who murdered his parents and other couples.
with Sherman Howard, Matt Landers, Codie Lucas Wilbee

BURN OUT

wr. Gene Miller, dir. James Contner
Ann and Ned lead an investigation to locate a pyromaniac.
with Anthony Lucero, Don S. Davis, Jerry Wasserman, Vicki Maxwell, Meredith Bain Woodward

AND THE DEAD SHALL RISE
TO CONDEMN THEE (two parts)

wr. Anthony J. Schembri, Randall Wallace, dir. Bill Corcoran
Wes takes a personal interest in the hunt for two young girls who may have become the victims of a religious zealot.
with Jason Bernard, Virginia Capers, Andi Chapman, Alec Burden
series ends

Unsold Pilots (3)

In 1990, Bruce Greenwood (who was in the deserved 1983 flop *Legmen* and featured in the later seasons of the superior off-the-wall soap *St. Elsewhere*) appeared in a second busted pilot for Cannell, *Dead End Brattigan* (a.k.a. *The Great Pretender*). In this, he was an award-winning writer who'd got a little too big for his boots and been fired after he'd done a number on his publisher (Donald Moffat) in his column. Then he went to court to get reinstated and won his case for unfair dismissal — but rather obviously, did not win any guarantee to get plum assignments, and so is handed all the bottom of the barrel jobs and a crummy basement office in revenge. In true TV fashion, Brattigan finds jewels in the trash, and with the aid of a gradually defrosting icy colleague (Jessica Steen) and a number of impersonations, breaks a big story anyway. It was an okay film, with Greenwood doing the standard Cannell Rockford/Faceman scam-a-minute routine, but nothing special. Written by Cannell with *Top of the Hill* collaborator Art Montarastelli, the pilot film co-starred Gregg Henry, Aharon Ipale, Paul Guilfoyle, Harris Laskawy, H. Richard Greene, Robert Ito, Don Keith Opper, and Elizabeth Hoffman.

Prior to this, Cannell had attempted a second series starring *Rousters'* Chad Everett, but the pilot for *Thunderboat Row* (a.k.a. *Walk on Water*), a proposed series about a group of drug squad ocean patrol cops in Florida, was an incomprehensible shambles. The cast also included Nick Coree, Rob Estes (later of Cannell's absurdly-titled off-peak crime show *Silk Stalkings*), Peter Murnick, Freddie Simpson, Anthony Rene Jones, and Todd Schaffer, with John J. York of Frank Lupo's *Werewolf* as a guest star.

Bruce Greenwood, Jessica Steen, and dog in *Dead End Brattigan*.

The Wrap-Up

Time and television stand still for no mortal, and this book had to close somewhere. With *Sonny Spoon, Starbuck* and *Unsub,* which took Cannell full circle back to his origins with *Chase, Baretta,* and *Columbo,* it seemed that the 1988–'89 season was the best option. Few people will want to read a chapter on *Top of the Hill.* For completists though, let's sum up.

The 1989–1990 season began with Cannell Productions' ill-advised forays into sit-coms, game-shows, TV movies, and other offshoots in a spectacularly unsuccessful attempt to break into more financially healthy parts of the television industry and away from the reputation for being solely suppliers of the action/adventure genre. The reasoning behind this is difficult to fault, backed up by Cannell's recent lack of a hit show in primetime and the cost and failure rate of the action/adventure genre in general — but with hindsight, Cannell, economics permitting, may well have been better off biding his time while waiting for his next hour-long primetime hit to appear than throwing bad money after good on a succession of costly misfires.

Pilot projects such as *Sirens,* a half-hour sit-com about female cops, and *Not Quite Beverly Hills,* a vehicle for his good friend Ben Vereen of *Tenspeed and Brownshoe* and *J.J. Starbuck,* were the most prominent of a number of non-starter sit-com projects, many others of which apparently died in pre-production. The horrendous *Scandals,* an embarrassing attempt to enter the tabloid TV reality market pioneered by such series as *America's Most Wanted, Unsolved Mysteries,* and *Rescue 911,* provoked a follow-up attempt, *Scandals II,* which was notable solely for the embarrassing spectacle of host Robert Culp trying to defend it on media magazine *Entertainment Tonight,* and was swiftly passed over by the network. Neither Cannell nor Culp, two of the greatest talents in television, perhaps *the* two greatest talents in their respective fields, should have come to this. A game-show format and animation projects met similar Bermuda Triangle–like fates.

Top of the Hill *and* Booker

Cannell's two entries into the hour-long drama arena he knew best for that 1989–'90 season were *Lame Duck,* later retitled *Top of the Hill* (September 1989 — December 1989), with William Katt (formerly of *The Greatest American Hero*) in the lead, and *Booker* (September 1989 — May 1990), a spin-off from *21 Jump Street* originally intended to be a lawyer show titled first *Return of the Prince,* and then *City Court. Top of the Hill* turned out to be a dreary affair, in which Katt played a *Riptide*-style beach-bum turned crusading junior politician coerced into substituting for his ailing Democrat dad (TV veteran Dick O'Neill, Cagney's father in *Cagney and Lacey*). Co-starring were Jordan Rowe Baker and Tony Edwards as his aides Susan Pengilly and Link Winslow, alongside Robby Weaver, who had previously appeared in a recurring role with Katt in *The Greatest American Hero.* "If somebody can figure out what this show's about, tell the producers" wrote Jay Martel, reviewing the new season's shows for *Rolling Stone*. "Thomas Bell, Jr. is a twenty-nine year old surfer who has been elected to fill the congressional office that his father, Thomas Bell, Sr.,* was forced to leave for medical reasons. Happens all the time! But Tom Senior hangs around trying to get Tom Junior to compromise his values in the name of Washington deal-making. All the ingredients are in place

Bill Katt, formerly the *Greatest American Hero,* is flanked by his associates (Jordan Baker, Tony Edwards) in *Top of the Hill.*

*In fact, Tom Bell's father is named Pat Bell in the series.

for some father-son fisticuffs mixed with a little populist-politico bashing, but in the pilot, Junior suddenly flies to some tiny Latin American nation to rescue an imprisoned drug agent, and the result is a shoot-'em-up 'Mr. Smith Goes to Central America.'"

After a standard fish-out-of-water introduction as he meets his assistants in the process of giving one of his constituents the bum's rush, Bell defies his new colleagues to help the citizen, who is trying to trace a DEA agent son who has disappeared while on assignment. "The adventures in the fictional *Mission: Impossible* style country of Costa Verde drag on incessantly as Bell bumbles through his rescue efforts. An obvious villain fools him to the last," wrote *Variety*. In return for assistance in getting the DEA agent out alive, Bell must agree to vote for a motion by the party whip that he doesn't believe in. "He'll learn that political life is a compromise" said Cannell. (Or that he's been swiftly corrupted).

Nevertheless, as improbable as the pilot may have been (it has escaped the author at time of writing), it sounds vastly more entertaining than the series episodes (many of which have been viewed by the author), a collection of hackneyed plots with few new wrinkles, no action, and numerous humorless clichés. And in its favor, the pilot has a fabulous cast, including veteran character actor Kenneth McMillan as the intimidating party whip, the delightful and sexy Corinne Bohrer (whose series include *Free Spirit* and James Garner's *Man of the People*, and who appeared in the earlier Cannell pilot *Brothers in Law*) as his daughter, and — in a straight role — *Frasier's* Kelsey Grammer. Scripted by Cannell (who surprisingly claimed he had conceived the series' concept back in his *A-Team* days), the pilot boasts such superbly Cannell-esque names as Steele Cooley, Dutch Vanderhill, and Enrique Falcone, with Katt's Tom Bell playing Lone Ranger and Rebel with Several Causes in a familiar Cannell scenario. Tellingly, given the difference between pilot and series, a desperately dull affair, the pilot was shot a year and a half before the series went into production, which had been slowed down by the Writers' Strike.

Booker starred future teen idol Richard Grieco — who went on to fifteen minutes of fame with modest movie success — as a hip, unconventional teenage investigator working for a large, staid, and very conservative corporation. Grieco had started out in television, serving daytime soap apprenticeship on *One Life to Live* before guesting on series like *Who's the Boss?*, *Rags to Riches*, and as a gay student in *The Bronx Zoo*. His Booker character had originally been introduced into *21 Jump Street* as a safety net in case Johnny Depp departed the show, with the reassurance that he was only intended to be in "two or three" episodes before being writ-

Richard Grieco as *Booker*.

ten out. In the event, he stayed the season. "The casting director had probably looked at fifty guys for the role of Booker," Bill Nuss told *US* magazine, "but by the time it got down to me, there were two people we really liked. We weren't quite sure which way to go, so we put them both on tape. He really came across. The camera loved him. You could see the devil in his eye." "Eric Blakeney called and said 'We're going to do this spin-off,'" Grieco told *US* magazine. "I said 'What is it?' He said 'It's you, man!'"

Now off the force as of the close of *Jump Street's* third season, Booker is hired by the Teshima Corporation of America to run a new Investigative Operations Department, where he reports to the imposing Alicia Rudd (Marcia Strassman), known to her colleagues as "the Dragon Lady." Co-starring with Grieco and Strassman were Carmen Argenziano (later of *Equal Justice* and *Stargate SG-1*) as their boss, Charles "Chick" Sterling, and Katie Rich as Booker's secretary Elaine. Mid-way through the series, newcomer Lori Petty appeared in an episode (Carleton Eastlake's "Flat Out") as Suzanne Dunn and was on the fast track to break-out status as a new co-star (replacing Rich) just as the series got canned. She also later caught her fifteen minutes of fame as cinema's *Tank Girl*. In fact, many of the episodes of *Booker* were better than they had any right to be, offering up some good ideas and a number of clever twists and turns. Most of the scripts were written by *Jump Street* staffers (Holly Robinson and Steven Williams put in a number of guest appearances to link the show), but, said Cannell, who wrote the pilot and two episodes of the 21 hours, "I chose to write for *Booker* because I feel so strongly about the guy. This isn't to denigrate *Jump Street*, but it has a fairly narrow story target. With *Booker*, we can send Richard in any direction because he's an ex-police officer who gets himself involved with a company, dealing with all the stuff that corporations throw at you. And Booker is not a guy who belongs in a corporation, so we can get some humor out of that."

Variety's reviewer was not optimistic. "The novelty of a hero who wears an earring is bound to wear off by, say, ten minutes into the second episode.... Unless *Booker* improves substantially, or the yahoos who watch *America's Most Wanted* are willing to tune in early, Greico may soon find himself back on the road to *Jump Street*."

In fact, there was no *Jump Street* to go back to at the end of the season. The network had moved *Jump Street* to Monday nights to accommodate *Booker* in the old *Jump Street* slot, and at the close of the season, both series were canceled. As Grieco and Depp segued effortlessly into wide-screen features, former *Jump Street* stars Steven Williams, Holly Robinson, and Peter DeLuise joined newcomers Michael DeLuise (Peter's younger brother) and Michael Bendetti for a fifth and final season of the show for the syndication market, financed solely by Cannell Productions to build up the numbers for the future full syndication package (an odd decision, as *Jump Street*, by its very nature, rapidly dated and became redundant).

Broken Badges

For the 1990–'91 season, Cannell created *Broken Badges* (November 1990–December 1990, June 1991), an intriguing amalgam of one of his greatest hits—*The A-Team*—and one of his biggest disasters—*The Last Precinct*. The show had a great title, and was about a group of misfit cops who each had some sort of stress-related psychological disorder that made them difficult to work with (evoking memories of the *Hunter* pilot, in which the brass tried to get rid of Hunter by declaring him psychologically unfit for duty). Miguel Ferrer, who met memorable fates as a big screen bad guy in the likes of *Robocop* and *Deepstar Six* and was one of the highlights of the 1990–'91 supernatural series *Twin Peaks* as disdainful city cop Albert Rosenfield, played Beau Jack Beauman, an unconventional Cajun cop. Co-starring was Ernie Hudson of the ill-fated *The Last Precinct* as kleptomaniac Toby Baker, who has the added handicap of occasionally transforming Murdock-like into fictional Texas Ranger Cactus Cole Watson, and ventriloquist Jay Johnson (fondly remembered as both Chuck and Bob in the spoof series *Soap* of the late-'70s and who had recently guested on Frank Lupo's *Something is Out There*) as Officer Stanley Jones, who has the unnerving habit of working with Officer Danny — a ventriloquist's dummy. Rounding out the cast was the striking newcomer Eileen Davidson as Judy J.J. "Bullet" Tingreedies (initials *and* a nickname!), a wildcat Harley-straddling leather-clad tearaway who looks positively normal next to the others but whose appearance recalled such striking and lethal ladies as *Wiseguy's* female terrorist from the pilot and Susan Profitt (Joan Severance). The *Broken Badges* pilot had the added advantage of including the attractive Terry Donahoe of *Sonny Spoon* in the cast as the criminologist who assembles the team, now billed as Teresa Donahoe, but who was replaced in the six episodes of the series by Charlotte Lewis as a psychiatrist in charge of the group. It was an adventurous and unusual concept and had a fascinating collection of characters, but was handed the lowest audience night of the week — Saturday — and bombed instantly.

The cast of *Broken Badges;* **left to right, Terry Donahoe, Miguel Ferrer, Jay Johnson, Ernie Hudson, and Eileen Davidson.**

The 100 Lives of Black Jack Savage

As the 1990–'91 season came to a close, Cannell allied himself with Walt Disney Productions, of all people,* to produce the schizophrenic fantasy adventure *The 100 Lives of Black Jack Savage* (March 1991— May 1991), a mid-season try-out in the luckless Friday night graveyard of over a dozen other short-run sci-fi and fantasy productions that failed to buck the trend. The series took elements of *Riptide, Hardcastle and McCormick,* and Cannell's failed pilot *Thunderboat Row* and put them in Cannell's first fantasy setting since *The Greatest American Hero.* Cleverly contrasting seventeenth century callousness with the modern-day piracy of Wall Street (the traditional pirate figure of Black Jack against wealthy corporate-raiding, asset-stripping yuppie Barry Tarberry, the modern-day equivalent), the series starred Daniel Hugh-Kelly as the disreputable Tarberry and Steven Williams as the ghostly Black Jack Savage.

Both Hugh-Kelly and Williams were former leads in Cannell series, Hugh-Kelly having been Mark McCormick in *Hardcastle and McCormick,* and Williams having played Captain Fuller in *21 Jump Street* (in the pilot, Stoney Jackson of the absurd 1985 series *The Insiders* had played Black Jack, but had declined the series; Williams, said *Variety,* had brought "a swashbuckling style to what had been more of a jive portrayal!"). When Tarberry buys the ancient Blackbird Castle as a status symbol and hideaway on the Caribbean island of San Pietro, he discovers that it's haunted by the restless spirit of Black Jack (shades of *The Ghost and Mrs. Muir*), who has been denied his final rest and warns Tarberry that he's headed for the same dire fate. Just as *Hardcastle and McCormick* featured 100 cases that Judge Hardcastle wanted tidied up after his retirement, so pirate Black Jack Savage found that he was obliged to meet a target of 100 lives saved to atone for his sins before he could be allowed to rest in peace ... and Tarberry's headed the same way unless he joins up with Black Jack and starts making amends for his unethical modern-day piracy.

While writer Paul Lomartire's location report for the Cox News Service supposed that "the Disney-Cannell marriage would seem perfect — Disney's deep pockets plus Cannell's vast imagination," *Variety* reviewed the finished product less enthusiastically, noting that "the script mixes grown-up nastiness with juvenile fantasy to disquieting and unentertaining effect. Cannell's script is generally witty and nicely crafted, but the poorly structured, schmaltzy story and an overall mean-spiritedness do it in." However, as kids are generally a gore-loving bloodthirsty bunch anyway, particularly where pirate stories are concerned, it's difficult to view this as a failing. In fact, *The 100 Lives of Black Jack Savage* had so many appealing elements thrown into the mix — a haunted castle, a special effects wizard (Steve Hytner as a sort of Murray Bozinsky/Frankie Santana hybrid), modern-day pirates and bandits — that it's difficult to work out exactly why the show didn't catch on, other than the fatal weekend time-slot that networks persist in giving to SF and fantasy.

Off Prime-Time

Eventually, Cannell began looking at the straight-to-syndication or off-peak late-show slots that have proved comfortable homes for re-runs of *Wiseguy* and *Unsub,* and at this point

---

*Cannell Productions regularly did technical work for Disney on sound.

Carl Weathers gets tough in *Street Justice*.

things started looking up again. The most innovative of these was the intriguing *Scene of the Crime* (April 1991–'92), an anthology mystery show with a stock ensemble cast playing different roles each week, and hosted by Cannell himself for CBS latenights. These tolerable potboilers were bookended by Cannell's delightful and sparkling cameo introductions and conclusions, which were the highlight of the entire show — a forerunner of things to come. Less inspired — but watchable — was *Street Justice,* with a number of former *Jump Street* personnel behind the cameras and former boxer and *Rocky* co-star Carl Weathers as tough cop Adam Beaudreaux, allied with long-lost adopted son Grady Jamieson (Bryan Gennesse), a martial arts expert, and the appallingly titled *Silk Stalkings,* which has two cops investigating crimes in high society in a Palm Beach locale and, despite a number of cast changes, chalked up five seasons on cable.

Weathers' previous series attempt was the short-lived 1986 cop show *Fortune Dane,* and co-starred Joe Dallesandro, *Wiseguy's* "Pat the Cat"; here, his co-stars were Liam Blackwood, Charlene Fernetz, and Timothy Webber. Reviewing *Street Justice, People* magazine wrote, "Because of the star's athleticism, the action sequences are unusually good, and there's greater ethnic diversity than on most shows. Still, the series is only so-so when it comes to production values and storytelling. But for those who miss the big bang of *Hunter,* here's your fix."

Bryan Genesse and Carl Weathers enforce *Street Justice* ... "for those who miss the big bang of *Hunter*...."

Starring in *Silk Stalkings,* the later time-slot (and later cable venue) of which allows the material to be marginally more daring than primetime sometimes allows, was the strikingly attractive Mitzi Kapture as Detective Rita Lee Lance (whose best known previous credit was taking over from B-queen Betsy Russell as hooker-turned-cop Angel in the low-budget feature film series as of *Angel 3*), and Rob Estes (of the failed *Thunderboat Row* pilot) as her partner Chris Lorenzo. Playing their boss for a while was Cannell's old buddy Ben Vereen.

The Commish *and* Palace Guard

However, Cannell's track record of 1970s and early-'80s successes had not left him without interest from the networks for primetime, and the 1991–'92 season gained him two fresh commitments, from ABC for the clumsily titled *The Commish,* relating the work life and home life of a loveable Italian police commissioner who hits the streets with the boys, and from CBS for *Palace Guard,* a clumsy opposites-attract detective fantasy in the *Remington Steele/Moonlighting* tradition easily overpowered by *Reasonable Doubts,* a similar, slightly darker but also short-lived show in the same vein from *Midnight Caller* creator/producer Robert Singer and former *Wiseguy* story editor John Schulian.

Starring in *The Commish* was the chameleonlike Michael Chiklis, who previously played John Belushi in the anti-drugs pseudo-biopic *Wired* alongside Ray Sharkey, and made a memorable guest appearance on the quality sitcom *Murphy Brown* as unsavory stand-up comic and hate-merchant Tony Rocket. He had also guested in *B.L. Stryker, L.A. Law, Miami Vice,* and the unsold pilot *Maverick Square,* and appeared in the role of Italian mobster Carlo in the Albert Cerrico storyline that opened the third season of *Wiseguy*. Most series exploit an actor's known image, whereas Chiklis was clearly a superbly capable all-rounder, which made his already unlikely and larger-than-life smiling "Commish" an even more dubious TV creation, a curious combination of Hannibal Smith's

Michael Chiklis and Theresa Saldana cuddle up for the cozy *The Commish.*

humor and daring, Kojak's world weary savvy and authority, and Baretta's preachy commitment. Or, as the critic for the *Boston Sunday Globe* put it, *The Commish* has "uncompromising honesty, outright decency and vigilante heart."

As Commissioner Tony Scali, Chiklis commands a panting respect and admiration from his men that makes *Hill Street's* saintly Frank Furillo and revered Phil Esterhaus look like a couple of Cannell's suit and tie time-servers in comparison. It was difficult to imagine *The Commish* succeeding where *Eischeid, Paris, The Oldest Rookie* and *Mancuso FBI* had failed, but someone had to be the next Kojak, and stranger shows have survived to buck the odds. Despite being almost completely forgotten already (Chiklis went on to star in the diametrically opposed but equally populist pandering *The Shield* and portray Marvel Comics icon the Thing in the *Fantastic Four* movie franchise), *The Commish* plodded along for an astonishing four seasons. Noted Ken Tucker of *Entertainment Weekly*, "It's clear that ... Cannell and (Stephen) Kronish — who also worked on *Wiseguy*— want to tap into the frustration we all feel about so many of the rude, overworked bureaucrats and public officials we encounter in our lives ... but Chiklis is such a happy saint that he verges on the insufferable — no-one can be this generous, this clever, this jolly!" "There's more than a tad of schmaltz and stage business afoot here" agreed *Hollywood Reporter*, "yet *The Commish* outperforms the usual cop operas this year." "Chiklis turns in such a magnetic performance that he pushes himself and this series onto a higher plane," wrote the *New York Post*. "Chiklis is a marvel of believability, vividly creating a character who is disarming, droll, clever, and compassionate," announced *People* magazine's reviewer. "*The Commish* works because star Michael Chiklis is genuinely appealing and auteur Stephen Cannell is so playful," said *New York Magazine*. And, conceded *Entertainment Weekly*, "Scali is the role of a lifetime, which Chiklis performs with wild-eyed abandon, leaving everyone else in the cast in the proverbial dust." Coughing and sneezing in that recurring cast on *The Commish* were David Paymer as a freeloading brother-in-law, Kaj-Erik Eriksen as Scali's son David and Theresa Saldana (of Scorsese's *Raging Bull*) as his wife Rachel. Saldana's other TV work includes guest appearances on *MacGyver, Hunter, Cagney and Lacey, Matlock,* and *Simon and Simon*. Curiously, the show's two-hour pilot actually aired as the fifth episode. Writers on the series have included Cannell and Stephen Kronish, who wrote the pilot, co-producer Robert Cochran, executive script consultant Tammy Adler, and *Jump Street* writers Glen Morgan and James Wong, the supervising producers. All of the people with important positions on the series worked as writers on the show. "This is the only studio in town that I know of that's run by a writer for writers," says Cannell. "If I ever stopped producing or running a studio, I'd still be writing. I spend too much time at a typewriter to be called anything but a writer."

The possibility of the undistinguished *Palace Guard*, one of a number of fire-ice/chalk-cheese boy-girl pairings of the 1991–'92 season following in the footsteps of such successful male/female investigating teams as those of *Remington Steele* and *Moonlighting*— or even *Scarecrow and Mrs. King*— was even less hopeful. *Palace Guard* starred D.W. Moffett (formerly of the short-lived 1987 series *The Oldest Rookie*, one of the Disney Touchstone series for which Cannell Productions did some technical work) and daytime soap star Marcy Walker, best known for long-running roles on *All My Children* and *Santa Barbera*. Moffett's guest-starring roles have included *Miami Vice, Midnight Caller,* and *The Equalizer*. Co-star Tony Lo Bianco, an actor and director (he directed episodes of *Police Story* and *The Duke*) plays hotel magnate Arturo Taft, who — much against the wishes of image-conscious Palace Hotel PR manager Christy Cooper (Walker) — hires former fresh-out-of-prison jewel thief Tommy Logan (Moffett) to protect his resorts as security chief on the assumption that it takes one to know one. As one of Cannell's earliest script sales was to the series *It Takes a Thief*, we can again see Cannell plundering the past. What we know — but nobody else does — is that Logan is actually Taft's long-lost son (shades of the short-lived *The Devlin Connection*). Jacob Epstein and Ken Solarz executive produced with Cannell, with the reliable names of Alan Cassidy and Alex Beaton as producers.

Praising Cannell's familiar trademarks of "characters with history"

Marcy Walker and D.W. Moffett are the *Palace Guard*.

and "vivid villains each week," *People* magazine's reviewer wrote that "Moffett is energetic, bordering on vainglorious as the fast-talking sharpie. Walker, as his watchdog, hits just the right two-tone note of dignified disapproval and grudging attraction. Leave it to Cannell to reforge *Remington Steele*." Other reviewers were less thrilled. "CBS has said it wants to give viewers light entertainment over the weekend, and it doesn't get much lighter than this," announced Brian Lowry in *Variety*. Referring to a "half-baked plot," "predictable twist," and "*Moonlighting* wannabe banter that couldn't power a 60 watt bulb," Lowry wrote that "Cannell spared no cliché in putting the pilot together. The near-saving grace is the casting of Moffett as the improbable lead ... Walker fares less well as the flak, who waffles between brave and helpful on one hand and shrewish and petty on the other, but tends to come off as more of the latter, thanks in large part to the script." Referring to the show as "*Moonlighting* on steroids," *Hollywood Reporter* critic Miles Beller pronounced *Palace Guard* "a ridiculous creature operating on clunky wisecracks and leaden quips" and added that "the alleged 'chemistry' between Logan and Cooper is microscopic, and isn't much bolstered by the contrived storyline." *Palace Guard*, much less well-received than *The Commish*, quickly joined Cannell's growing collection of instant flops.

Missing Persons *and Missing Inspiration*

The Hat Squad had to be Cannell's most desperate idea yet (and this CBS picked up, while passing over *Renegade*— about which, more later). Nestor Serrano, who very nearly became a supporting character in *Sonny Spoon* when he was introduced in the episode "Cheap 'n Chili," starred with Billy Warlock of *Baywatch* fame and James Tolkan, the bald-headed guy from the *Back to the Future* films. Don Michael Paul completed the team. Yes, it was four cops in silly fedoras, the poor man's *Mulholland Falls*. When *Hat Squad* failed to "do an *A-Team*" on Wednesday nights at 8:00, CBS moved it to Saturday at 10:00 in the hope it would "do a *Hunter*." But poor Cannell — ABC already had the same idea with *The Commish,* so two Cannell series ended up going head-to-head.

Failing to get on the air as a series was a promising pilot titled *Greyhounds,* which starred four veteran old coots (Dennis Weaver, James Coburn, Pat Morita, and the slightly younger-looking Robert Guillaume) as a bunch of male Angela Lansburys who shore could show them young 'uns a thing or two, if'n only they'd lissen up (a typical scene from the opening has Weaver nosing in unwanted at a crime scene and picking up a clue all the sniffy young suits have been trampling over). This would have been a sure thing for Saturday nights, but sadly, they never got the chance.

Another show that had promise, but only lasted thirteen episodes (the author viewed the pilot but has not been able to catch the series) was the following seasons (1993–'94) *Missing Persons.* Apart from the innumerable man-on-the-run chase shows, most track-'em-down series have been glossy romances, like *Lottery,* in which lucky individuals were sought to hand them a fortune, or the horrendous *Finder of Lost Loves,* in which Tony Franciosca endeavored to reunite the separated. *Missing Persons* was such an obvious idea it's surprising no-one had thought of it before (the concept has since enjoyed modest success — it's all about timing — as another producer's *Without a Trace*). A now greyer Daniel J. Travanti (formerly of *Hill Street Blues*) was Ray McAuliffe, the leader of a team of police investigators whose job it is to locate the lost and missing. The team were the typical late '80s/early '90s assortment of non-entities, including a rule-bending cop studying law on the side, a young female first-timer trying to prove herself, a naive chump with a lot to learn, an elderly guy who's seen it all before (rather like the audience), and a young/middle-aged new dad. The strength of the series was not in this nondescript bunch, none of whom you would recognize in the street half an hour after watching the show, but in Travanti and the strength and originality of the concept, which is the irresistible stuff of drama.

Travanti's Ray McAuliffe was another Cannell hero in the style of *The Commish.* Tough but likeable, he's the sort of guy you'd feel comfortable working for but who keeps you on your toes. All memories of *Hill Street* were instantly expunged — the tight-assed saintly Furillo (a persona Travanti always said he was quite unlike in real life) had been replaced by a more emotional, but still cool cop. The hand-held camera was used sparingly, but the series had a busy, everyday look, and some of the dialogue suffered from being deliberately garbled and messy. The setting was Chicago, and the mood grey and tense. This was not a stylish, glossy show — it strived to look ordinary.

As a pilot, the feature-length opener tried to show the diversity of the concept — a task it achieved admirably — with a variety of ongoing investigations. The story opens with every mother's nightmare — a young Polish woman loses her little girl in the crush of a tube train and is separated from her at the station. At the next stop — no little girl. A young rich kid pressured by exams and a looming arranged marriage between powerful families ("more of a merger" sniffs her best friend disdainfully) vanishes, a young soldier goes AWOL for an illicit encounter (a then-fashionable touch of feminist spite had the young female investigator delighting in exposing him), and an elderly lady vanishes from a nursing home. The linking theme is that all of the investigators are getting personally involved. The twist was that the missing person the viewer expects to turn up dead doesn't, but another one does. As with

Cannell's other late-'80s/early '90s shows, this one abandons the gags, guns and car chases for straightforward storytelling bereft of jokes and gimmicks; it was written and directed by TV-to-film-to-TV grasshopper Gary Sherman, and it was his first decent piece of work. Cannell, however, was now producing the "ordinary" cookie-cutter shows he had been accused of doing ten years earlier. Less intriguing was the corny *Cobra*, for syndication (initially marketed as *Viper*, Cannell was obliged to concede the title to Paramount, who had their own show with that less-than-inspired title in the works), which starred former straight-to-video star Michael Dudikoff alongside the luckless Hat Squadder James Tolkan, cast in another stiff.

Cannell attempted to climb upmarket again with *Traps*, a well-intentioned, sober and dull-as-dishwater cop show that got an end-of-season try-out starring George C. Scott as Joe Trapchek, a tough old ex-cop who comes out of retirement to work on unsolved cases from the past. His much-loved cop son died in the line of duty, but he doesn't get on with grandson Chris (Dan Cortese), who's followed in the family footsteps, and therein lies the show's conflict ... Cannell wrote three of the six; perhaps somewhat inevitably for the time (we were now in 1994), the first case was tracking a serial killer ... *Traps* went out against two news shows and came third! Two more turkeys followed — the brave but dreary *Hawkeye*, starring rent-a-hero Lee Horsley and former *Wonder Woman* Lynda Carter in a revival of the legendary folk hero, and another vehicle for Richard Grieco, a rehash of *Stingray* titled *Marker* for UPN and co-starring Gates McFadden, fresh from her lengthy run on *Star Trek: The Next Generation*. Despite upping the Grieco earring quotient to two (the short-lived gimmick mocked in the *Booker* review was now being referred to as his "familiar sideburns and earrings"), the show and its fleet of Hawaiian-based helicopters were soon grounded.

Cannell's straight-to-syndication series have been mostly a disappointment when compared with his earlier work. While syndicated series have lower budgets, and so enjoy fewer sets and less competent acting performances, the real flaw lies in the content. The unfair accusation, ten years earlier, that Cannell has his "finger on the pulse of the yahoo market" by now seemed painfully accurate — it was hard to believe that Cannell was laughing while he devised these series, as he once claimed with *Rockford Files* and *The A-Team*, or that he was writing what he himself would enjoy watching. His pleasures during this period clearly came from his periodic onscreen turns as corrupt cop "Dutch" Dixon on the *Renegade* series (which we shall discuss next), and beginning in earnest his long-desired career as a novelist — always his long-term ambition. A series like *Silk Stalkings* was the sort of show he would have been parodying, not producing, even as recently as 1988, *The Commish* and the others smacked of cynical contrivance, and as a string of uninspired syndicated series sprung forth from the Cannell castle, it began to seem as though the man's heart wasn't in it. The rather more upmarket *Profit*, praised by the critics but an instant cancellation for the Fox network, was a nasty, cynical and irredeemable exercise about a ruthless young yuppie and ten years out of date to boot. There have even been the inevitable TV movie "Return of's...," with a short series of *Rockford Files* and *Hunter* TV movies beginning in 1994 and 1995 respectively, and, in 1996, a bizarre attempt to revive the original *Wiseguy* with an older and — it has to be said — somewhat overweight Ken Wahl back from the dead as Vinnie Terranova. Unlike the awful second series revivals of such diverse shows as *The Jetsons* and *Columbo* in the 1980s, or the ghastly feature films of classic TV shows, none of these efforts have spoiled or embarrassed the memory of the originals, they just seemed terribly pointless and redundant (the *Wiseguy* script even featured some of the old magic in terms of inspiration and plot twists), perhaps because in the case of *Rockford* and *Hunter,* the originals have never really gone away, and in the case of *Wiseguy,* it's too little, too late. All the performers are, naturally, older and look tired and weary. It's not how we want to remember them; better for Cannell's heroes to be frozen in time as fond memories of the '70s and '80s than for us to meet the middle-aged *Riptide* detectives in the 21st century.

However, Cannell seemed to have been stricken by a touch of Peter Pan syndrome himself, having progressed from simply hosting *Scene of the Crime* and the unintentionally hilarious *U.S. Customs Classified* on-camera to role-playing himself, taking the plum part of rogue cop Dutch Dixon in his successful syndicated show *Renegade*.

Renegade

Cannell's way-over-the-top feel-good actioner *Renegade* in 1992, starring hunky girl-bait Lorenzo Lamas, likeable Native American everyman Branscombe Richmond, and the gorgeous Katherine Kinmont, despite a slow and uncertain start, turned out to be the master in top form again as it progressed. Sold straight to syndication and then picked up by U.S. cable, *Renegade* was corny, clichéd, self-parodic and extremely familiar stuff—but better to be old hat than *Hat Squad.* And, in a swath of uninspired ensemble cast clones of '80s cop, lawyer and doctor shows, poker-faced SF, and dark, grim serial killer and conspiracy series, it was a delight. Come home to Cannell, as an ad might say. Or, as pro-wrestler Jesse Ventura, playing a psychotic thug, points out in one episode with a leer and a sneer, *"There's gonna be some major badness going down...!"* How true in so many ways, but the cast and show were irresistible. It perhaps helped that they were already friends, rather than thrown together. Lamas (the son of actor Fernando Lamas and actress Arlene Dahl) met both Richmond and Kinmont (who he was later briefly married to) on the set of his previous series, *Falcon Crest,* Richmond when he came to choreograph a fight scene, Kinmont when she came to visit her actress mother Abby Dalton, also in the large *Falcon Crest* cast. When Lamas was offered the lead in *Renegade,* he knew immediately who to call for his co-stars.

Both *Walker, Texas Ranger,* the Cannell-ish but dull TV vehicle for video star Chuck Norris, and Frank Lupo's *Raven* were made for network TV, but *Renegade* looked better than both. Incredibly—perhaps ominously—despite Cannell's 1980s track record, and the cautious familiarity of the concept (Huggins' tried-and-tested man-on-the-run formula) all four networks had declined it. "The networks didn't believe that anybody wanted to see a guy on a motorcycle chasing bad guys," said Lamas to *Variety.* "Well, we're in our fourth year and once again Stephen proved that he has a quick mind in discerning public tastes. I was glad he remembered me for the part. He remembered me from tests I did for *21 Jump Street* and other shows. I hung in there and he gave me the opportunity to show the industry that I was capable of doing more than just wear a fancy suit for nine years on *Falcon Crest.*" Renegade cop Reno Raines is an ex-cop turned flowing-maned biker-on-the-run accused of the usual crime he didn't commit and pursued *Fugitive*-style by Cannell himself as Lt. Dutch Dixon, the cop who really done it.... In the meantime, Reno travels around the country doing *A-Team*–style acts of helpfulness as a sort of long-haired Lone Ranger ... and trying to look soulfully sad about his predicament, which any fool can see is the most fun he's ever had in his life.... He's aided by former bit-player and stunt-man Richmond in his break-out role as thrifty bounty hunter Bobby Six Killer and his sister Cheyenne Phillips (Kinmont), who's sweet

Lorenzo Lamas as Reno Raines with his co-stars Kathleen Kinmont and Branscombe Richmond in *Renegade*.

on Reno—but as Reno hides his pain for murdered fiancée Val (Deprise Brescia, gunned down in the pilot), so Cheyenne hides her love for Reno. At least Cannell made no attempt at hiding *his* glee at playing a bad guy after twenty years behind the typewriter.... He is so wonderful in the role, one can only marvel at how he held back from turning up to terrorize *The A-Team* or *Hardcastle and McCormick*. Such indulgence would ruin a *Wiseguy*, or be laughable in *Jump Street* or *The Commish*, but *Renegade* is plainly such a huge romp for all concerned. "I had always wanted to create a contemporary western," said Cannell. "I liked the idea of a show with some moral dilemma and simple storytelling. Reno Raines is a guy on the run who will stop in between to fix something and then silently move on."

Renegade began life as exactly the kind of series the less perceptive critics thought he was making ten years earlier. Early episodes were plagued by bad performances, bad ideas and bad scripts (even Cannell's own scripts show a marked decline in quality of plotting and dialogue), but while the latter two problems faded as the cast grew into their roles, the bad performances eventually became part of the fun. In one first season episode, Reno beats the stuffing out of a local bully and forces him to undo all the harm he's done over recent months, but is somehow unable to do the same again to discover the location of a kidnapped girl — instead taking a staged public beating from the bully to keep the girl safe. As the thug in question has already gotten away with murder in the past, there seems little to gain from this capitulation other than the melodramatic sound thrashing he endures. As silly as *The A-Team* was, it was always credible and logical within the parameters of the fantastic it had set for itself. And in the same episode, co-stars Richmond and Kinmont pull a scam that is cruel and unjustified, albeit for a worthy outcome; in Cannell's earlier series scams were pulled only on the guilty — or they were harmless.

However, as the series progressed it turned into the one bright light of the 1990s from the Cannell company, proving that the story of Stephen J. Cannell Productions — by then Cannell Entertainment — or at least the legacy of the Cannell contribution to television may not yet be over after all (the only other great action adventure show of the '90s outside of the *Hercules/Xena* genre turned out to be the Cannell-esque Pamela Anderson vehicle *V.I.P.*, a flashy, frothy confection which cleverly made a virtue out of Anderson's failings by casting this would-be actress out of her depth as a would-be heroine out of her depth; it was overseen by sometime Cannell writer Morgan Gendel). "*Renegade* was a work in progress the first season," Cannell claimed, perhaps sensing its failings. "I wrote five or six episodes because I had certain concepts in mind that I was trying to keep going throughout. This year, I brought in another executive producer (Bill Nuss of *The A-Team*) and we're extremely pleased at how the show looks. We have added more humor in the scripts and there already seems to be a certain buzz on the show. I'm really excited, as I think we're off to a great second season!" Stu Segall oversaw the series as it went on. *Renegade* also benefited from one of the

Lorenzo Lamas enjoying himself far too much as the tortured *Renegade*.

most superb opening credits scenes in years (by Ralph Hemecker — watch for the Z-for-Zorro desert road) graced of course by one of Mike Post's best themes in years.

By the end of the 1980s, audiences and critics were getting tired of the once radical, innovative and inspirational Cannell approach. "*Sonny Spoon* certainly doesn't lead us to any new entertainment frontiers," mused a *TV Guide* critic in 1987, as yet another Cannell show premiered. Reviewing the same show's second season premiere the following year, *Variety* began "Sometimes it seems like every Stephen J. Cannell show depicts the world as one giant Beach Boys song, except that everyone's got guns, half the people are dealing drugs, and something always gets blown up." Reviewing Cannell's 1995 series *Marker,* another in a long list of swift cancellations, *Variety's* reviewer wrote "If it sounds familiarly far-fetched, one only has to look at show's creator, Stephen Cannell, for an explanation ... (Andy) Bumatai is often too clownish, but the Cannell m.o. requires a buddy for the lead and he ably fulfills that responsibility." It was more observation than insult, but the writing was on the wall. What had once been fresh and surprising was now predictable and expected.

They say that you don't know the value of what you've got until you've lost it. When I first started researching this book between magazine assignments in 1987, Cannell was already on his way to Canada, and his writers from his days in L.A. had already started scattering to the four winds, diversifying into their own areas of interests. With all due respect, none of Cannell's co-workers have equaled or bettered their work on the Cannell series since their departure from the fold,* although there certainly have been items of interest (David Chase's short-run *Almost Grown* springs to mind, but his later *The Sopranos* feels like *Rockford* without Rockford, or indeed any moral center). Creatively, the Cannell years may have been the best times for all of them. As I put the finishing touches to this latest and last draft of my text twenty years later in 2007, there are no shows so delightfully mindless yet gloriously amusing on the air. But in television, the pendulum swings....

In recent years, the television industry has declared the action/adventure format if not terminal then critical, depending on who you speak to and what mood they're in. But then, when Cannell was reigning supreme, the sit-com form was supposed to be dead until Robert Culp's former partner from the '60s hit the ratings with a simple and sugary confection called *The Cosby Show,* and science-fiction has been pronounced stone cold dead on U.S. TV twice, and on both occasions it was just before NBC spent a bomb launching *Buck Rogers in the 25th Century* and then later *V,* two of the most expensive SF series ever made for television. Since then, it has found a new lease of life, not on the faithless networks, but on cable and in syndication, where it flourishes. The best of the few action adventure series around in recent years have also been in non-network marketplaces (*Renegade, Raven, Hercules, Xena, V.I.P.*). On TV, what goes around, comes around again, and again, and then again, not only in eternal re-runs, but in trends and concepts (Roy Huggins' once totally unacceptable and unthinkable man-on-the-run format turns up regularly every two or three years). As this book makes clear, there are few new ideas, only fresh ways to present them, just as Cannell and his writers themselves so ingeniously and skillfully tapped into the public consciousness and restructured the trends of the past into programming for the '70s and '80s.

The action/adventure series *will* be back with a vengeance, somewhere, somehow, and you don't have to be Nostradamus to see it; the genre thrives even now in feature films and

---

*Splitting Cannell and Lupo as a team has been the television equivalent of the break-up of the comic industry's Lee and Kirby; how great might Werewolf or Hardball have been as Cannell and Lupo shows?

computer games, and these mediums — with their growing budgets and special effects technology — are most likely part of the reason for the decline of their like in the television arena. But just as the generation before me mourns the end of the era of Cagney and Bogart, Astaire and Rogers, Karloff and Lugosi, Rogers and Hammerstein, Ford, Hawks, and John Wayne, so my generation will miss the television icons of the '60s, '70s and '80s.

Action/adventure will be back — but it probably won't be Cannell and Lupo, it probably won't have Mike Post's familiar musical trademark, it won't be the same familiar good guy and bad guy faces on the screen (time marches on), and no matter what the quality, be it better *or* worse, my generation will say it's not as good!*

In the course of chasing cuttings, quotes, tapes, and program information on Stephen J. Cannell Productions, there have been two recurring constants. I record them here for what they are worth. The first is that nobody — not in person or in print, in public or in private — has a single bad thing to say about Stephen J. Cannell as a person, program provider, or employer. I have been told this emphatically and authoritatively more than once. This man, as they say in the opening scenes of a murder mystery, has no enemies. And secondly — and it's quite extraordinary how this phrase just kept cropping up verbatim — that, in producing his series, he "spreads himself a little thin."

This is a fair criticism — *The Greatest American Hero, Riptide,* and the first few episodes of *Hunter* were visually very threadbare compared with other emptier but glossier shows, and the stand-out episodes of the later seasons of *Wiseguy* were always those written by Cannell. While it's thrilling that a producer and businessman of Cannell's stature could still find the time and the inclination to sit at the typewriter and write his own scripts (even as late in the day as the middle of a Steven Bauer *Wiseguy* storyline — the middle, mind you), one can only speculate as to what might be achieved if he could have spent some time on every episode. Perhaps if Cannell threw himself into fewer series at one time after he lost Chase, Bartlett, Lupo, and Greyhosky *et al.,* he could have avoided the careless, obvious errors that flawed *Stingray* and *The Last Precinct,* or the confusion that marred *Sonny Spoon* and *J.J. Starbuck.* Perhaps *Renegade* flourished because it had his attention.

In recent years, Cannell has forsaken TV to busy himself with writing his novels, just as his alter-ego Mark Savage did in *Tenspeed and Brownshoe* all those years earlier. In an amusing twist for a writer who has given himself unswervingly to the small screen over the years, they are often being optioned as potential film treatments. American TV is poorer without him, and even poorer when he misses the mark, as he did so often following the golden era of *Rockford* and *The A-Team.* Still, as barren as the U.S. TV drama scene may be without a Stephen J. Cannell, trends in American television are like the weather in Britain as once described by the visiting Frank Sinatra — if you don't like it … wait a minute. Somewhere out there is another populist, satirist and storyteller waiting to pick up the gauntlet dropped so provocatively by the reluctant heroes of the Cannell universe. They would do well to study the Cannell m.o. before they scoop it up.

---

*No doubt the fathers of those youngsters sitting enthralled in front of The A-Team *were tut-tutting as they reminisced fondly about the days of* The Cisco Kid *and* The Lone Ranger…. *When* are *you comin' back,* Range Rider?

Sources of Quotations

This book has been a work in progress since the very late 1980s. During that time, as a result of the rise of the internet and a handful of high profile frauds, credibility, provenance, and fact-checking have become a far greater issue than they were two decades ago when mistakes were often obvious and honest (as the ones in this book will be). Some of the cuttings and quotes referred to in this book date back twenty years and came from second-hand or sometimes even third-hand sources (such as newspaper articles reprinted in fanzines or press releases).

Every effort has been made to trace the original source and provide authors and dates, but when not possible the secondary source has been credited. Any contentious or controversial quote that could not be sourced was removed from the text. In a few cases of non-contentious quotes, no source could be confirmed. However, every major or extensive quote in my text has been credited below and following this appendix is a bibliography to provide readers with additional reading.

Introduction

page 4: "I said to myself..." Cannell quoted by Ellen Torgerson, in "James Garner believes in good coffee — and a mean punch," *TV Guide,* June 2, 1979.

page 4: "What I try and do..." TV interview with Louis Rukeyser, *Wall Street Week,* 1986.

page 4: "I don't really think too much about demographics," TV interview with Louis Rukeyser, *Wall Street Week,* 1986.

page 6: "Chances are that any action show of the last few years..." Tom Carson, "*The A-Team* — Macho Goes to Camp," *The Village Voice,* February 22, 1983.

page 6: "He has to write," colleague Frank Lupo to Jerry Roberts, "Working Formulas," *Variety,* August 17, 1995.

page 6 "One of the things about Stephen is he loves to write," Charles Johnson to Jerry Roberts, "Working Formulas," *Variety,* August 17, 1995.

page 6: "We asked him once about writing," William Katt to Jerry Roberts, "Working Formulas," *Variety,* August 17, 1995.

page 8: Helicopter story related on camera by Cannell on U.K. television program *Bring Back The A-Team,* Channel Four, 2005.

page 9: "Ordinary" and "typical" quoted from *Adventures on Prime-Time,* Robert Thompson, 1990, Praeger.

page 13: "There isn't much space left to discuss *Riptide...*" unidentified review of *Riptide* and *Blue Thunder,* credited to *New York,* 1984 by British Film Institute Information Department.

page 13: TV review of the *Rockford Files* episode "The Empty Frame," Keith Howes, *Gay Times,* (U.K.), September 20, 1979, British Film Institute Information Dept.

page 13: "I'll tell you how off the money I was..." TV interview with Wil Shriner, *Wil Shriner Show,* October 2, 1988.

page 13: "*Riptide's* lead couple have laid-back appeal..." "Bok," TV review of *Riptide, Variety,* 4 January, 1984.

page 16: "It is the one truly non-sexist TV series on the air," letter from viewer/reader Salli B. Madden to *TV Guide;* no date available, but published following June 2, 1979 article in *TV Guide* on Cannell and *The Rockford Files.*

page 16: Many critics suggest that Cannell "can't write women"; Thompson cites *Black Sheep Squadron* and *The A-Team* in *Adventures on Prime-Time,* Robert Thompson, 1990, Praeger.

page 16: Heasley, it transpires, was summoned to Peppard's trailer (related on camera by Heasley on U.K. television program *Bring Back The A-Team,* Channel Four, 2005), but Peppard's attitude was frequently commented on elsewhere, sometimes by himself!

page 17: "What I've basically been trying to do..." Cannell to Alan Ginsberg, "Stephen J. Cannell: Writing His Own Ticket," 54th anniversary edition of *Hollywood Reporter,* 1984.

page 18: "Cannell focusses not on the woebegone wealthy, smothered in mink..." Alan Ginsberg, "Stephen J. Cannell: Writing His Own Ticket," 54th anniversary edition of *Hollywood Reporter,* 1984.

page 18: "It was purely a matter of convenience..." Frank Lupo to Robert Greenberger, "The Secret Force Behind *The Greatest American Hero,*" *Starlog,* November 1982.

page 19: "*Hunter* is really unique I think..." fan Sue-Anne Hartwick, quoted in fanzine *The Cannell Files.*

page 19: "...It was refreshing to see a woman as such an equal..." fan Jean Thrower, quoted in fanzine *The Cannell Files.*

page 19: "Bill Maxwell reminds me a little of my dad," Patrick Hasburgh to Robert Greenberger, "The Secret Force Behind *The Greatest American Hero,*" *Starlog,* November 1982.

page 20: "Unlike every other glossy TV crime-buster, Hunter seems to treat women as friends," Hilary Kingsley, TV review of *Hunter,* London *Daily Mail,* mid-'80s.

page 20: "Heavies aren't always guys with bent noses and 42 inch necks," Patrick Hasburgh to Robert Greenberger, "The Secret Force Behind *The Greatest American Hero,*" *Starlog,* November 1982.

page 20: "A guy who knows he's a villain is a bad character. The best villains at worst think they're misunderstood!" Cannell to Jane Lane, "Talking Television with Stephen Cannell," *Women's Wear Daily,* October 20, 1988.

page 20: "Steve loves to make fun of high rollers," David Chase quoted by Chris Wicking, "From the Files of James Scott Rockford," *Time Out* magazine (London), December 7, 1979.

page 21: "The B-hero is a noble drifter who comes into town, sometimes with a comical sidekick..." Kim Newman, in his book *Wild West Movies,* 1990, Bloomsbury.

page 21: "He's able to write about what is for the most part youthful in all of us..." Rod Holcomb to Jerry Roberts, "Working Formulas," *Variety,* August 17, 1995.

page 22: "He brings a good-heartedness to all his work," Rod Holcomb to Jerry Roberts, "Working Formulas," *Variety,* August 17, 1995.

page 22: "Cannell certainly has his finger on the pulse of the yahoo element..." anonymous rival producer cited in U.S. trade paper.

page 23: "This is the kind of show in which anyone in a suit and tie..." Robert MacKenzie, TV review of *Hardcastle and McCormick, TV Guide,* date n/a.

page 23: Steve McQueen suit and tie anecdote sourced several times by the author, most recently in Penina Spiegel's biography *Steve McQueen,* Fontana/Collins 1986.

page 23: "Cannell specialises in despising institutionalised authority..." John Leonard, reviewing *Riptide* for the *New York Herald Tribune,* circa 1984, date n/a.

page 25: "He always came at shows with a very odd, quirky perspective..." Frank Lupo to Richard Setlowe, "First and Foremost a Writer," *Variety,* August 17, 1995.

page 25: "Steve brought humor and sass to television drama..." David Burke to Richard Setlowe, "First and Foremost a Writer," *Variety,* August 17, 1995.

page 25: "He has a wonderful way of writing dialogue..." Rod Holcomb to Richard Setlowe, "First and Foremost a Writer," *Variety,* August 17, 1995.

page 28: "I always try to be as pragmatic as I possibly can about the business we're in, and not tilt at windmills just because they're there," roundtable discussion: "Independent Producers and their Uncertainty about the Future," *Emmy* magazine, March/April 1983.

page 28: "We've had no real problems with ABC," Juanita Bartlett to James Burns, "Juanita Bartlett: The View From the Top, Part Two," *Starlog* January 1982.

page 29: "Some bad guys try to stop us..." Robert Culp to Don McGregor, "Starlog Interview: Robert Culp, Part Two," *Starlog,* February 1982.

page 29: "On American TV, at 8.00, you can't kill people," freelance writers Chris Bunch and Allan Cole to the author at Sci-Fi WorldCon, 1987 for unpublished feature on *Werewolf.*

page 33: "Well, I just love to write," TV interview with Wil Shriner, *Wil Shriner Show,* October 2, 1988.

page 33: "They didn't call it dyslexia in those days," Cannell to Peter Rigby, "Top TV Writer Has a Problem — He'll Never Read or Spell Properly," *Star,* October 1, 1985.

page 33: "Because of it, I've become an over-achiever," Cannell to Dusty Saunders, "Dyslexia Didn't Block Cannell's Path to Success," *TV Ledger,* September 26, 1987.

page 33: "...Because I was so taken with his energy and enthusiasm..." Grace Curcio to Sylvia Souza for *Cannell Channel* in-house magazine, Feb./March 1985.

page 33: "In six years, I never had to send back a script..." James Garner to Jeff Silverman, "Mr. Write," *U.S.* magazine, February 24, 1986.

page 33: "I see what I'm writing..." Cannell to Jeff Silverman, "Mr. Write," *U.S.* magazine, February 24, 1986.

page 33: "And I also like television," Cannell to Kathryn Baker, "Prolific Producer Thought He Was a Loser," Associated Press, January 1987.

page 34: "A series is ongoing maintenance in a strange way," Cannell to Jane Lane, "Talking Television with Stephen Cannell," *Women's Wear Daily,* October 20, 1988.

page 36: "Cannell is not especially fond of freelancers, and we are one of the few freelancers that have done a significant number of shows for Cannell series," freelance writers Chris Bunch and Allan Cole, to the author at Sci-Fi WorldCon, 1987 for unpublished feature on *Werewolf.*

page 36: "We work in total collaboration," Juanita Bartlett to James Burns, "Juanita Bartlett: The View From the Top, Part Two," *Starlog,* January 1982.

page 37: "I was a little suspicious..." David Chase quoted by Chris Wicking, "From the Files of James Scott Rockford," *Time Out* magazine (London), December 7, 1979.

page 37: "It's one thing writing a scene, but it's another out in the field," William Katt to Brian Lowry, "Starlog Interview: William Katt, I Knew Flying Was Part of the Job," *Starlog,* May 1985.

page 37: "Most of the guys directing episodic TV are not very imaginative," Robert Culp to Don McGregor, "Starlog Interview: Robert Culp, Part Two," *Starlog,* February 1982.

page 37: "The thing that sticks out in my mind was that the actors were treated like adults," Ron Silver to Edward Gross, *The Unofficial Story of the Making of a Wiseguy,* 1990, Pioneer Press.

page 39: "They're good writers, the whole staff," Anthony Denison to Edward Gross, *The Unofficial Story of the Making of a Wiseguy,* 1990, Pioneer Press.

page 39: "We never had a relationship after that," Roy Huggins, quoted by Vance Durgin, "Running Man Roy Huggins," *Emmy* magazine, September 1988.

page 40: "He's my godfather in television," Cannell quoted by Vance Durgin, "Running Man Roy Huggins," *Emmy* magazine, September 1988.

page 40: "He was someone who couldn't write a dull scene..." Roy Huggins to Richard Setlowe, "The Epitome of Success," *Variety,* August 17, 1995.

The Rockford Files

page 43: "We used to tell him what to say," James Garner to Robert Ward, "Never Play Poker with James Garner," *Gentleman's Quarterly,* March 1984.

page 43: "Jim's kind of a 1930s actor," Meta Rosenberg quoted by Chris Wicking, "From the Files of James Scott Rockford," *Time Out* magazine (London), December 7, 1979.

page 43: "It's the best work I've ever done," James Garner to Robert Ward, "Never Play Poker with James Garner," *Gentleman's Quarterly,* March 1984.

page 44: "It was literate, moving, and funny," Meta Rosenberg quoted by Chris Wicking, "From the Files of James Scott Rockford," *Time Out* magazine (London), December 7, 1979.

page 46: "I said to myself..." Cannell quoted by Ellen Torgerson, in "James Garner believes in good coffee — and a mean punch," *TV Guide,* June 2, 1979.

page 47: "...So when I wrote *The Rockford Files* I had Joe Rockford really embarrassed..." Cannell to Richard Setlowe, "The Epitome of Success," *Variety,* August 17, 1995.

page 49: "Garner is one of the best actors around," Robert Altman quoted in *Video Today,* "The James Garner Files," May 1985.

page 49: "Garner looks comfortable on screen, and it's relaxing to watch him," Kate Stevens, "The James Garner Files," *Video Today,* May 1985.

page 49: "No-one could do exasperation like Garner could," Richard Meyers, *TV Detectives*, 1981, A.S. Barnes and Co.

page 50: "I won't do movies that glorify killers and bank robbers," James Garner to Robert Ward, "Never Play Poker with James Garner," *Gentleman's Quarterly*, March 1984.

page 50: This from James Coburn (who would later direct the *Rockford* episode "Irving the Explainer" and complain bitterly about the editing) in *Time Out* magazine (London), circa 1979.

page 50: "I was always picking up someone else's fight when they couldn't defend themselves," James Garner to Jo Weedon, *Weekend* magazine (U.K.), date n/a, 1981.

page 50: "They want *Mannix* in a shroud," he fumed, "chases through graveyards!" Rod Serling, quoted and requoted, ad infinitum; notably in *Night Gallery* section of *Fantastic Television*, LSP/Harmony.

page 50: "We were just punched to death," Cannell to Jean Vallely, feature on *The Rockford Files, Esquire*, July 3, 1979.

page 51: "We're free now to do what we want to do," Meta Rosenberg quoted by Chris Wicking, "From the Files of James Scott Rockford," *Time Out* magazine (London), December 7, 1979.

page 51: "What are the heavies doing?" David Chase, interviewed by Mark Lawson for the BBC in 2006.

page 57: "I'll never retire as such," James Garner to Jo Weedon, *Weekend* magazine (U.K.), date n/a, 1981.

page 57: "He's getting better and better..." Stuart Margolin to Robert Ward, "Never Play Poker with James Garner," *Gentleman's Quarterly*, March 1984.

Baretta

page 73: "Twelve producers..." Cannell quoted by Ellen Torgerson, in "James Garner believes in good coffee — and a mean punch," *TV Guide*, June 2, 1979.

City of Angels

page 82: "Rogers was deeply critical of the series in the trade press..." Richard Meyers, *TV Detectives*, 1981, A.S. Barnes and Co.

page 83: "Rogers had plenty of chances to be the charming, cynical, raffish gumshoe beloved of popular fiction," "Mick," TV review *City of Angels, Variety*, February 11, 1976.

page 83: "The casting is ideal throughout," Morna Murphy, *Hollywood Reporter*, February 1976.

page 83: "1934 model Rockford, an investigator who uses wide-eyed guile when he can," Blaik Kirby, the *Toronto Globe and Mail*, February 1976.

Black Sheep Squadron

page 87: Former Black Sheep member Fred Avey was interviewed at length by John Wukovits for *Aviation Heritage*, 1970s.

page 87: "When we did *Black Sheep*, and I started to write shows with more and more emotional content..." Cannell in unidentified TV interview.

page 88: Robert Conrad's Golden Girls remarks during CBS press conference for *High Mountain Rangers* related in *Variety*, late '80s.

page 88: "Robert Conrad's home movies," Jeff Jarvis, TV review of *High Mountain Rangers, People* magazine, April 1987.

page 88: "I knew it was going to be a hit, it had all the right ingredients," Robert Conrad in unidentified TV interview.

Stone

page 102: [*Police Woman* would] "...fly in the face of everything Wambaugh had attempted to achieve with *Police Story*," Richard Meyers, *TV Detectives*, 1981, A.S. Barnes and Co.

Unsold Pilots (1)

page 106: "...Such a remarkably consistent portrayal of an unsympathetic character..." "Mor," TV review of *Scott Free, Variety*, October 20, 1976.

Tenspeed and Brownshoe

page 110: "It was like sailing a ship with no rudder. It was much worse than I ever thought it would be..." Cannell quoted by Lee Goldberg, "Cannell Runs Studio Like a One Man Show," *Electronic Media*, April 14, 1986.

page 110: "Elements of the *Tenspeed* pilot resembled sequences to be found in the feature films *What's Up, Doc?* and *The In-Laws*..." "Demp," TV review of *Tenspeed and Brownshoe, Variety*, January 1980.

page 110: "Like Cannell's earlier detective series *Richie Brockelman*, the fun comes from watching two basically nice but inept guys bungle their way to success," writer n/a, TV review of *Tenspeed and Brownshoe, Hollywood Reporter*, January 1980.

The Greatest American Hero

page 119: "Bob and I relied on our own sense of truth," William Katt to Brian Lowry, "Starlog Interview: William Katt, I Knew Flying Was Part of the Job," *Starlog*, May 1985.

page 121: "This is like *I Spy* in a lot of ways. You take two really human, ordinary people and you drop them into remarkable situations," Robert Culp to Don McGregor, "Starlog Interview: Robert Culp, Part Two," *Starlog*, February 1982.

The A-Team

page 133: "I'm the only woman (on the set) besides the wardrobe lady, the lady in hair, and the lady in make-up!" Judith Ledford, talking to *Modern Screen*, 1986.

page 136: "A sort of raunchy *Mission: Impossible*," "Bok," TV review of *The A-Team, Variety*, date n/a, January 1983.

page 136: "A revved-up version of *Mission: Impossible*," writer n/a, *New York*, 28 February, 1983.

page 136: "*The Dirty Dozen, The Magnificent Seven, The Road Warrior*, and *Mission: Impossible*," admitted NBC president Brandon Tartikoff, quoted in several sources, in-

Sources of Quotations

cluding Sally Bedell, "How TV Hit *The A-Team* Was Born," *New York Times*, 28 April, 1985.

page 136: "A hybrid of *The Dirty Dozen, Garrison's Gorillas,* and *The Four Just Men,*" Leslie Halliwell, quoted in *Television Weekly* (U.K.), January 26, 1983.

page 136: "The first episode was a 90 minute special which combined (with that lurid enthusiasm only the Americans can muster)..." Mary Harron, TV review of *The A-Team,* "All Our Fantasies," *New Statesman,* (U.K.), July 1983.

page 136: "I can think of ten ways in which this nonsense was depressing or offensive," Patrick Stoddart, TV review of *The A-Team,* "Sunset Boulevard Blues," *Broadcast,* (U.K.), 8 August, 1983.

page 138: "It wasn't tough enough for an appropriate A-Team response," *Adventures on Prime-Time,* Robert Thompson, 1990, Praeger.

page 138: "Often a writer would get this part of the equation wrong, and Cannell, like a maths teacher, would have to correct it," *Adventures on Prime-Time,* Robert Thompson, 1990, Praeger.

page 138: "It's the best comedy show on the air," Cannell in numerous interviews.

page 138: "The fun comes in the action scenes," Walter Goodman, TV review of *The A-Team, New York Times,* 21 January, 1983.

page 138: "The exploits of *The A-Team* (are) so outrageous that it is impossible to take them seriously," John J. O'Connor, "The Rise of *The A-Team* Guarantees More Violence," *New York Times,* 8 May, 1983 (this headline does not accurately reflect what O'Connor was trying to say).

page 139: "The stars of *The A-Team* keep throwing us a wink to let us know that they're in on the mischief," writer n/a, *New York,* 28 February, 1983.

page 139: "...Climaxed with a car chase that was the funniest thing I've seen on TV in a while," Tom Carson, "*The A-Team*— Macho Goes to Camp," *The Village Voice,* February 22, 1983.

page 139: "When the Hulk throws a man through a plate-glass window..." freelance writers Chris Bunch and Allan Cole, to the author at Sci-Fi WorldCon, 1987 for unpublished feature on *Werewolf.*

page 139: "*The A-Team* doesn't seem to me to be nearly as 'mindless' as many critics find it," John Leonard, TV review of *The A-Team, New York,* 8 October, 1984.

page 139: "As showcased in the pilot, *The A-Team* looms as escapist action adventure, to be played all stops out for the action trade..." "Bok," TV review of *The A-Team, Variety,* date n/a, January 1983.

page 140: National Coalition on Television Violence, quoted in several sources, including Sally Bedell, "How TV Hit *The A-Team* Was Born," *New York Times,* 28 April, 1985.

page 140: "The show isn't working because we're flipping jeeps over," Cannell, quoted by Sally Bedell, "How TV Hit *The A-Team* Was Born," *New York Times,* 28 April, 1985.

page 140: "It has a much broader appeal than we thought it would," NBC researcher Jerry Jaffe, quoted by Sally Bedell, "How TV Hit *The A-Team* Was Born," *New York Times,* 28 April, 1985.

page 141: "These are crazy times," Brandon Tartikoff quoted by Sally Bedell, "How TV Hit *The A-Team* Was Born," *New York Times,* 28 April, 1985.

page 141: "We are not looking for Emmy award nominations," Brandon Tartikoff quoted by Sally Bedell, "How TV Hit *The A-Team* Was Born," *New York Times,* 28 April, 1985.

page 141: "As long as 42 million people keep watching, I don't see any reason to change," Brandon Tartikoff quoted by Douglas Thompson, "Girl No. 2 gets the A-Team Bullet," *London Daily Mail,* date n/a, circa 1984.

page 141: "There is always going to be a section of the audience which has natural concern over particular programmes," John Whitney (regulator), interviewed by Martin Jackson and Steve Clarke in *Broadcast,* March 7, 1986.

page 141: "I think the A-Team are either the *worst* shots in the world...!" George Peppard interviewed by Terry Wogan on *Wogan,* BBC U.K. talk show, March 13, 1987.

Hardcastle and McCormick

page 155: "I never wanted to do a car chase show..." Patrick Hasburgh quoted by Jefferson Graham, "Fans Rally to Save *Hardcastle and McCormick,*" *USA Today,* date n/a, early '80s.

page 162: "There's nothing logical about the cases that come their way. Trouble just sort of tracks them down..." Gail Williams, TV review third season premiere *Hardcastle and McCormick, Hollywood Reporter,* September 26, 1985.

Rousters

page 170: "...The pack of lies Earp told writer Stuart Lake," Kim Newman, *Wild West Movies,* 1990, Bloomsbury.

Riptide

page 175: "Lately I have been reading about the Peter Pan syndrome..." Robert McKenzie, TV review of *Riptide, TV Guide,* March 17, 1984.

page 179: "If you are male, well-built, and a good guy..." Cynthia Broadwater, writing about *Riptide, Daredevils* no. 10, August 1984.

page 181: "We put bikini-clad girls into it at first," Cannell to Alan Ginsberg, 54th anniversary edition of *Hollywood Reporter,* 1984.

Unsold Pilots (2)

page 190: "The world's problems are solved through force" ... "the law is the plaything of evil power-mongers," writer n/a, TV review for *Brothers in Law, Variety,* April 1985.

Hunter

page 192: Descriptions of Fred Dryer as Hunter: "a younger, more cadaverous version of Clint Eastwood"; "a cross between Richard Widmark and Clint Eastwood"; "like Richard Widmark grown a foot taller and right out of Clint Eastwood territory"; "like Clint Eastwood and may even have been carved from the same piece of wood," from various early 1980s reviews.

page 192: "...Bearing a striking facial resemblance to Eastwood, especially when he's talking to the punks that make his day," Bridget Freer, *TV Guide* (U.K.), September, 1989.

page 192: "He has the kind of easily defined presence that works especially well in television," John J. O'Connor, reviewing *Hunter* in the *New York Times,* date n/a.

page 192: "A furtiveness, the thumbprints of a sneaky

Sources of Quotations

mind that suggests a long Richard Nixon and a tidy Jack Nicholson..." John Leonard reviewing *Hunter,* source n/a.

page 193: "I knew from the moment I read the script that he was going to be a Clint Eastwood sort of character," Fred Dryer to John Kercher, "Move Over Clint, Hunter's Here," *Woman's Weekly* (U.K.), 1984.

page 198: "We haven't invented the Hula-Hoop or anything," Michael Mann quoted by Emily Benedek, *Rolling Stone,* date n/a, early '80s.

page 199: "Roy Huggins was my mentor, my godfather," Cannell in an interview with Duane Byrge in the late '80s. Original source cannot be found.

page 200: "In contrast to *Miami Vice, Hunter* remains remarkably un-'80s, decidedly un-hip" Fred Schruers, "Can 800 million Chinese Be Wrong?" *Rolling Stone,* May 4, 1989.

page 202: "All this hoopla for *Hunter* is extremely odd," writer n/a, "As *Hunter* hits 100," *St. Louis Dispatch,* 11 January, 1989.

page 205: "Getting involved in the private lives of the characters would be death to the show. This series is about what happens to Hunter and McCall in the line of police work. The show should come out of that, not what I think about my next-door neighbor," Fred Dryer, circa 1988.

page 205: "I'm hoping ... there'll be more expansion, more growth..." Stepfanie Kramer to Kay Gardella, *New York Daily News,* circa 1988.

page 205: "Television is an executive producer's medium," Larry Kubik to Richard Hack, *TeleVisions* column, *Hollywood Reporter,* July 18, 1989.

page 206: "I want to write, produce, and direct," Fred Dryer to Pat Hilton, "Fred Dryer, the Restless Hunter," *USA Today,* December 1987.

page 206: "Input is what I expect," Fred Dryer to Richard Hack, *TeleVisions* column, *Hollywood Reporter,* July 18, 1989.

page 206: "But by the following year, Dryer was prominent in a list of people who were difficult to work with..." Bridget Freer, "Head Hunter," *TV Guide* (U.K.), June 1990.

page 206: "Let me just say this about the bank of writers and the executive producers," Fred Dryer to Fred Schruers, "Can 800 million Chinese Be Wrong?" *Rolling Stone,* May 4, 1989.

page 206: "Fred's reputation was all over the place before he joined *Hunter,*" Frank Lupo quoted by Bridget Freer, *TV Guide* (U.K.), September, 1989.

page 206: "We started off at the beginning of the (fifth) year trying to make the shows a little bit different..." Tom Chehak to Fred Schruers, "Can 800 million Chinese Be Wrong?" *Rolling Stone,* May 4, 1989.

page 206: "There's never been anyone like me on TV, and there never will be," Fred Dryer to Marilyn Beck, *Insider Grapevine* column, *TV Guide,* 1991.

page 206: "I was replaceable in the NFL," Fred Dryer to Dave Anderson, "*Hunter* on the Hunted," *New York Times,* 2 October, 1988.

Stingray

page 221: "You call him when you're in trouble..." Columbia publicity material for *Stingray,* 1987.

page 222: "I've got Latin looks, and if you're dark, you'll be cast as someone who's intense, moody, and flawed," Nick Mancuso, unidentified press cutting, 1987–88.

page 223: "*Miami Vice* pretensions ... hurt it more than it helped it," TV review of *Stingray* pilot, writer n/a, *Variety,* March 1986.

page 223: "It wasn't renewed based on ratings," Brandon Tartikoff to Lee Goldberg, "*Stingray* still breathing after two executions," *Electronic Media,* October 1986.

page 223: "With the syndication market being what it is..." Mike Dubelko to Lee Goldberg, "*Stingray* still breathing after two executions," *Electronic Media,* October 1986.

page 223: "We sent a location scout and crew to Toronto, Calgary, and Vancouver," Cannell to Ken Winikoff, "Stephen J. Cannell: The Producer Who Came to Dinner," British Columbia Special Report, *Hollywood Reporter,* October 4, 1988.

page 224: "We have to realise that if it's not a profitable business..." Cannell to Morrie Gelman, "Canell Copes with Deficit Financing," *Hollywood Reporter,* date n/a, 1987.

page 224: "We don't believe that shooting series in Canada is going to be financially profitable," freelance writers Chris Bunch and Allan Cole, to the author at Sci-Fi WorldCon, 1987 for unpublished feature on *Werewolf.*

page 224: "The only reason that (the film) business was originally in L.A. was because of the weather," Cannell to Ken Winikoff, "Stephen J. Cannell: The Producer Who Came to Dinner," British Columbia Special Report, *Hollywood Reporter,* October 4, 1988.

page 224: "You've got fast film that can shoot in normal light, and there's no need for a sound stage any more," Cannell to Ken Winikoff, "Stephen J. Cannell: The Producer Who Came to Dinner," British Columbia Special Report, *Hollywood Reporter,* October 4, 1988.

page 225: "Anyone who's seen an NFL game knows that as long as you don't shoot into the lights, you can barely tell it's raining," Cannell to Ken Winikoff, "Stephen J. Cannell: The Producer Who Came to Dinner," British Columbia Special Report, *Hollywood Reporter,* October 4, 1988.

page 225: "There's places that look like New York, others that look like downtown L.A.," Cannell to Martin Borycki, "On the Canadian Experience," *Reel West,* May/June 1987.

page 225: "They've got the ocean, the mountains, the big city.... On *Starbuck,* we even doubled Hollywood!" Cannell to Ken Winikoff, "Stephen J. Cannell: The Producer Who Came to Dinner," British Columbia Special Report, *Hollywood Reporter,* October 4, 1988.

page 225: "We're in a world market," Cannell to Martin Borycki, "On the Canadian Experience," *Reel West,* May/June 1987.

page 225: "We were fighting with everybody for locations and stage space," Cannell to Ken Winikoff, "Stephen J. Cannell: The Producer Who Came to Dinner," British Columbia Special Report, *Hollywood Reporter,* October 4, 1988.

The Last Precinct

page 231: "People say what they're going to say," Cannell quoted in news piece, "NBC's *Last Precinct* cops a large audience," *Hollywood Reporter,* January 1986.

page 231: "*Adam 12* was never like this," Brooks, Tim, Marsh, Earle, *The Complete Directory to Primetime Network and Cable TV Shows, 1946—present,* 1999, Ballantine.

page 232: "Great comedy timing and droll delivery made him the front runner from the minute his name was mentioned," Cannell to Jeff Yarbrough, "Adam West trades his cape for a cop's badge," *People* magazine, 12 May 1986.

21 Jump Street

page 236: According to Ellison, writing in the early '70s, the networks duly caved in. All of this is discussed in detail in Ellison's two books *The Glass Teat* and *The Other*

Glass Teat (Pyramid), collections of his TV review columns from the *L.A. Free Press,* 1969–1972, specifically 27 November, 1970, 4 December 1970.

page 239: "Of all the shows that have been pitched to me, I hate this one the most..." freelance writers Chris Bunch and Allan Cole, to the author at Sci-Fi WorldCon, 1987 for unpublished feature on *Werewolf.*

page 240: "Hill Street Babes," Jeff Jarvis, TV review of *21 Jump Street, People* magazine, April 1987.

page 240: "The switch is that the captain in charge is a Mod-Squadder grown up unrepentant..." Michael Hill, "*21 Jump Street* could be seductive," *Baltimore Evening Sun,* April 11, 1987.

page 241: "...Who looks so young he ought to have training wheels on his police car," Jeff Jarvis, TV review of *21 Jump Street, People* magazine, April 1987.

page 241: "...Everything that makes little girls wriggle," Johanna Schneller, "Johnny Depp: Girl's Best Friend," *Rolling Stone,* December 1, 1988.

page 241: "I had the 'flu so bad that day..." Johnny Depp to Jim Bawden, "Young actors take quick jump to fame," *Toronto Star,* November 1, 1987.

page 241: "...Wears a leather jacket with Jim Morrison on the back..." Michael Hill, "21 Jump Street could be seductive," *Baltimore Evening Sun,* April 11, 1987.

page 242: "I played a lot of stereotyped bad guys — pimps and cons," Steven Williams to Anna Marie Kukec, unidentified cutting from Burrell's via fan source.

page 242: "At the audition, I asked if I had the right script," Holly Robinson quoted by Bridget Freer, "Jump Street Kid," *TV Guide* (U.K.), 1989.

page 242: "In walks this black kid with enormous brown eyes and a sleek body, and so intelligent she made me feel outmatched," Patrick Hasburgh quoted by Bridget Freer, "Jump Street Kid," *TV Guide* (U.K.), 1989.

page 242: "My role is colorless," Holly Robinson quoted by Bridget Freer, "Jump Street Kid," *TV Guide* (U.K.), 1989.

page 243: "Hanson is assigned to a small squad of young cops who infiltrate youth gangs," Martin Burden, TV review of *21 Jump Street, Washington Post,* April 1987.

page 243: "I was lucky to get started quick and with good parts," Dustin Nguyen to Ivy Miller, "Surviving One Jump at a Time," *Modern Screen,* 1989.

page 243: "Basically it was a propaganda station to discourage the Viet Cong to defect to the South..." Dustin Nguyen to Monika Guttman, "The refugee's story has a happy ending in Hollywood," Tribune Media Services, 1987.

page 244: "Sometimes there are happy endings, and we hate 'em! We cringe when we read those happy endings!" Holly Robinson to Frank Spotnitz, "Bows for Holly," *US* magazine, October 3, 1988.

page 244: "We know it's difficult to grow up now," Peter DeLuise, quoted in Cannell Studios press release.

page 244: "...Won't be as controversial as I originally would have liked. We both bent a little," Patrick Hasburgh to Fred Rothenberg, "Toned-down *Jump Street* still tackles tough issues," *New York Post,* April 9, 1987.

page 244: "We had to fight the network..." Holly Robinson quoted by Jessica Brighty, "Holly Goes Pop," *TV Guide* (U.K.), 1991.

page 244: "Our original script would probably be acceptable to them now," Patrick Hasburgh to Frank Spotnitz, "Bows for Holly," *US* magazine, October 3, 1988.

page 244: "Graphically showing, rather than artfully implying..." Miles Beller, TV review of *21 Jump Street* episode "Fun With Animals," *Hollywood Reporter,* November 4, 1988.

page 244: "Fox picked an experienced team" Don Merrill, TV review of *21 Jump Street, TV Guide,* November 7, 1987.

page 244: "Like *Miami Vice,* the series uses popular rock music to enhance the story," Sandra Knipe, "Fox's new police show is arresting," *Evansville Courier,* April 11, 1987.

page 244: "We're the number one show in the country for teenagers," Patrick Hasburgh to Patricia Brennan, "Getting a Jump on the competition," *Washington Post/New York Post,* December 10, 1987.

page 245: "I thought the show would be about busting a friend for smoking a joint in the bathroom," Holly Robinson to Jill Brooke, "Teen crime tackled by Jump Street crew," *New York Post,* April 11, 1987.

page 245: "Getting through adolescence has never been easy," Steven Williams, quoted in *Denver Weekly News,* 1987.

page 245: "The typical thing is for a parent to point his finger and say 'don't,'" Peter DeLuise, quoted in *Sacramento Vision,* June 28, 1987.

page 245: "The way we were back then..." Steven Williams to K.J. Scotta, unidentified cutting from Burrell's via fan source.

page 245: "I struggled with the blood transfusion angle," Patrick Hasburgh quoted by Kerry Sullivan, "Out of the Shadows," *Emmy* magazine, September 1988.

page 246: "I liked the pilot," Johnny Depp to Ivy Miller, "Modern Screen interviews Johnny Depp," *Modern Screen,* 1990.

page 246: "He's an intense egomaniac..." Richard Grieco, quoted in *Elizabethtown News Enterprise* (Kentucky), October 30, 1988.

page 246: "Booker will be the kind of guy who knows how to push people's buttons," Steve Beers, quoted in *Elizabethtown News Enterprise* (Kentucky), October 30, 1988.

page 247: "I've been doing mainstream television for three and a half years now..." Johnny Depp quoted in *TV Guide,* date n/a.

page 247: "Johnny Depp really altered the mood of the cast," Holly Robinson quoted in news pages, *TV Guide* (U.K.), July 28, 1990.

page 247: "This guy has been brought in as insurance in case Johnny leaves," Peter DeLuise to Tom Green, "Young Cast finds itself at crossroads," *USA Today,* November 1988.

page 247: "I can only go to high school for so long," Johnny Depp to Ivy Miller, "Modern Screen interviews Johnny Depp," *Modern Screen,* 1990.

page 247: "We're not thinking of Greico as a replacement," Fox exec Kevin Wendle to Tom Green, "Young Cast finds itself at crossroads," *USA Today,* November 1988.

page 247: "They encouraged me to do some controversial issues," Patrick Hasburgh to Fred Rothenberg, "Toned-down *Jump Street* still tackles tough issues," *New York Post,* April 9, 1987.

page 247: "*The Mod Squad* was too serious," Holly Robinson to Jill Brooke, "Teen crime tackled by Jump Street crew," *New York Post,* April 11, 1987.

page 248: "Last year we ran a show on sexual abuse, and that night the hot line got 6,000 calls," Patrick Hasburgh at press call, 1988.

page 248: "The best thing about the series..." Johnny Depp quoted in *TV Guide,* date n/a.

page 248: "*Jump Street* never takes the easy way out," Holly Robinson, quoted in *TV Guide,* date n/a.

page 248: "We're not preaching," Johnny Depp to Bill Cosford, "Johnny Depp turns street smart," *US* magazine, June 13, 1988.

page 248: "We lose kids to the first person who tells them they're special," Steven Williams, quoted in *Sacramento Vision,* June 28, 1987.

Wiseguy

page 260: "Conceived by producer-writer Stephen J. Cannell... *Wiseguy* shows no respect for the genre's storytelling conventions," Harry Waters and Janet Huck, "The Fine Arc of a Crime Hit," *Newsweek*, December 26, 1988.

page 260: "My idea was that we would reinvent the show every half year," Cannell to Elvis Mitchell, "Thugs 'R' Us," *Rolling Stone*, March 24, 1988.

page 260: "The story was told okay, but there was no real relationship with anyone..." Cannell quoted by Edward Gross, *The Unofficial Story of the Making of a Wiseguy*, 1990, Pioneer Press.

page 261: "Not since David Janssen's Richard Kimble character on *The Fugitive* has a television hero been as angst-ridden as Vinnie Terranova," Daniel Ruth, "Ken Wahl follows a dream, winds up a Wiseguy," *Chicago Sun-Times*, July 17, 1988.

page 261: "*Wiseguy* infuses the most predictable of genres with the intoxicating sense that anything can happen," Cannell Studios press release quoting *New York Woman*, April 1988.

page 261: "*Wiseguy* is full of suspense..." Don Merrill, "TV review of *Wiseguy*," *TV Guide*, March 5, 1988.

page 261: "*Wiseguy* is people-rich," Cannell Studios press release quoting Michael Dougan, *San Francisco Examiner*, 1988.

page 261: "Sonny Steelgrave, dynamically portrayed by Ray Sharkey, proved to be the most personable villain ever to enter our living room," Mark Esslinger, "Wise Up to *Wiseguy*," *Hollywood Gazette*, May 25, 1988.

page 261: "Sonny entered the great gangster tradition of aggrieved goombahs..." "Mixed Media, James Wolcott," *Vanity Fair*, May 1988.

page 261: "...A New Jersey outlaw who has bought into the glass-and-marble facade of the new wave of corporate crime" Elvis Mitchell, "Thugs 'R' Us," *Rolling Stone*, March 24, 1988.

page 261: "We did episodes to prove that Ray was the bad guy," Eric Blakeney to Edward Gross, *The Unofficial Story of the Making of a Wiseguy*, 1990, Pioneer Press.

page 261: "'A Deal's a Deal' was supposed to show Ray kicking the dog," Ray Sharkey to Edward Gross, *The Unofficial Story of the Making of a Wiseguy*, 1990, Pioneer Press.

page 262: "I've been in this business twenty years, and that's the single most violent episode I've ever been associated with!" Cannell quoted on "Last of the True Believers," to Edward Gross, *The Unofficial Story of the Making of a Wiseguy*, 1990, Pioneer Press.

page 263: "It's because of Ray, I thought he was wonderful," Dennis Lipscombe to Edward Gross, *The Unofficial Story of the Making of a Wiseguy*, 1990, Pioneer Press.

page 263: "I was really turned on by the whole concept of the good things that bad people do and the bad things that good people do..." Eric Blakeney to Edward Gross, *The Unofficial Story of the Making of a Wiseguy*, 1990, Pioneer Press.

page 263: "We play moral dilemmas," Les Sheldon to Martha Hindes, "The Wiseguy's star rises," Gannett News Services, *The Detroit News*, September 4, 1988 and "Double Life means Double Trouble," *The Cincinnati Enquirer*, September 25, 1988.

page 263: "We don't follow the formula where it's white hats and black hats, and that's the thing I'm proudest of," Ken Wahl to Hugh Boulware, title n/a, 1988/89.

page 263: "That's the whole point of the series..." Ken Wahl to Daniel Ruth, "Ken Wahl follows a dream, winds up a Wiseguy," *Chicago Sun-Times*, July 17, 1988.

page 263: "The last fifteen minutes of 'The Marriage of Heaven and Hell' was the bachelor party," Ray Sharkey to Edward Gross, *The Unofficial Story of the Making of a Wiseguy*, 1990, Pioneer Press.

page 263: "*Wiseguy* is a keg of video dynamite," Cannell Studios press release quoting Ron Miller, *San Jose Mercury News*, 1988.

page 263: "The most exciting, the most credible, and above all, the most literate crime drama to surface on television in quite some time," Cannell Studios press release quoting David Friedman, *Newsday*, 1988.

page 263: "Vintage Stephen J. Cannell," Cannell Studios press release quoting Kay Gardella, *New York Daily News*, 1988.

page 263: "Intelligent, hard-boiled crime drama," Cannell Studios press release quoting *Time* magazine, 1988.

page 263: "The best crime series in years," Cannell Studios press release quoting *TV Guide*, 1988.

page 263: "The best, toughest, and most tension-filled..." Matt Roush, "Give CBS' *Wiseguy* a try on its new night," *USA Today*, January 4, 1988.

page 264: "*Wiseguy* must have set some kind of record this season for being the best show on prime-time network television to be completely overlooked," and "*Wiseguy* may be season's sleeper," publication n/a, Associated Press, January 1988.

page 264: "We feel it has evolved into a most extraordinary drama — beyond even the high expectations we had for it," Kim LeMasters (CBS president) quoted by Mark Schwed, *New York Daily News*, December 1988.

page 264: "If we make a terrific show and I take my shirt off..." Ken Wahl quoted by Bridget Freer, "Introducing Ken Wahl, Wiseguy," *TV Guide* (U.K.), 1989.

page 264: "If you ever see me on another series after *Wiseguy*, you know I am going to be hurting for money," Ken Wahl quoted by Bridget Freer, "Introducing Ken Wahl, Wiseguy," *TV Guide* (U.K.), 1989.

page 264: "I said 'Sure, let me grab my suitcase and I'll go with you'!" Chuck Wahl to Daniel Ruth, "Ken Wahl follows a dream, winds up a Wiseguy," *Chicago Sun-Times*, July 17, 1988.

page 264: "He's a counter-puncher," Cannell to Elvis Mitchell, "Thugs 'R' Us," *Rolling Stone*, March 24, 1988.

page 264: "Ken Wahl is what some might call a hunk," Don Merrill, TV review of *Wiseguy*, *TV Guide*, March 5, 1988.

page 264: "Physically, Wahl fits the part of a Mafia mannequin," "Mixed Media, James Wolcott," *Vanity Fair*, May 1988.

page 264: "Wahl is a convincing sufferer," Elvis Mitchell, "Thugs 'R' Us," *Rolling Stone*, March 24, 1988.

page 265: "If Ken Wahl walked across a room toward me, I'd be worried!" Cannell to Jane Lane, "Talking Television with Stephen Cannell," *Women's Wear Daily*, October 20, 1988.

page 265: "Just because I'm pragmatic about this occupation doesn't mean I don't take it seriously," Ken Wahl to Kathryn Baker, Associated Press, 1987.

page 265: "The acting challenge..." Ken Wahl to Daniel Ruth, "Ken Wahl follows a dream, winds up a Wiseguy," *Chicago Sun-Times*, July 17, 1988.

page 265: "Even when I was a little kid I wanted to be the bad guy," Jonathan Banks, quoted in Cannell Studios press release and subsequently *TV Guide* (U.K.), October 1990.

page 265: "Caustic, bespectacled misanthrope," "He's the chief good guy on CBS' *Wiseguy*," Tom Green in *USA Today*, date n/a.

page 265: "The nastiest nice guy on television, a sheep in wolf's clothing," "Nicest villain on TV," Richard Mann and Jonathan Banks in *The Washington Times*, mid-1988.

page 265: "A good guy you don't like," Jonathan Banks,

quoted in *TV Guide* (U.K.), October 1990 and Richard Mann, "Nicest Villain on TV," *The Washington Post*, mid–1988.

page 265: "I like Frank when Frank's up against it," Jonathan Banks to Richard Mann, "Nicest Villain on TV," *The Washington Post*, mid–1988.

page 265: "Originally, the McPike character was written as a big, red-headed guy," Jonathan Banks to AP journalist, "*Wiseguy* may be season's sleeper," publication n/a, Associated Press, January 1988.

page 266: "I've been jealous of every villain that's been on this show!" Jonathan Banks to Tom Green, "He's the chief good guy on CBS' *Wiseguy*," *USA Today*, date n/a.

page 266: "I told the network that if we couldn't cast the part with a disabled actor then we would have to change the character," Cannell quoted by Jane Lieberman at 1989 Media Access Awards, "For Disabled Entertainers, a Champion in Hollywood," *Variety*, February 15, 1989.

page 268: "The role is the best/greatest thing that's ever happened to me," Jim Byrnes, all press interviews, circa 1988.

page 268: "Somebody came up to me in a restaurant once..." Jim Byrnes, quoted in *TV Guide* (U.K.), circa 1990, possibly from earlier source.

page 268: "I hope we would get to the point where it isn't important whether the character is disabled, or black, or a woman," Cannell quoted by Jane Lieberman at 1989 Media Access Awards, "For Disabled Entertainers, a Champion in Hollywood," *Variety*, February 15, 1989.

page 268: "'The Marriage Between Heaven and Hell' dealt with love between these two guys without homosexual overtones," Ray Sharkey to Ed Gross, *The Unofficial Story of the Making of a Wiseguy*, 1990, Pioneer Press.

page 268: "We'd have loved to keep him," Cannell quoted in *TV Guide*, "So Long Sonny," November 1987.

page 268: "There was definitely a shared feeling that maybe we jumped too soon on his death," Ray Sharkey to Roberta Plutzig, "Playing Sonny Was the Ultimate High," TV Record, *New York Daily News*, June 15, 1988.

page 268: "I was turning around to see who they were goggling over..." Ray Sharkey to Edward Gross, *The Unofficial Story of the Making of a Wiseguy*, 1990, Pioneer Press.

page 270: "He's fun to play because there are no boundaries" Kevin Spacey to Alan Carter, *New York Daily News*, 1988.

page 270: "The Profitt empire was a floating politburo of illicit fantasies..." "Mixed Media, James Wolcott," *Vanity Fair*, May 1988.

page 270: "Here's a person who could get 20,000 dollars to walk down a fashion runway..." Erwin More (Joan Severance's manager) to *Hollywood Reporter*, "Talent Special Report," May 1990.

page 271: "Basically, I'm a very shy, boring guy..." William Russ to Frank Lovece, "Behind the Scenes," publication n/a, 1988.

page 271: "The Profitts were tough to write," David Burke to Edward Gross, *The Unofficial Story of the Making of a Wiseguy*, 1990, Pioneer Press.

page 273: "*Wiseguy* has the craziest charge of endangerment since the hallelujah days of *Hill Street Blues*," "Mixed Media, James Wolcott," *Vanity Fair*, May 1988.

page 273: "*Wiseguy* featured the best action drama writing of the year," Cannell Studios press release quoting Bob Knight in *Variety*, 1988.

page 273: "Briskly paced, deftly plotted..." Cannell Studios press release quoting Steve Sonsky, *Miami Herald*, 1988.

page 273: "When a show is this well produced, this well-stocked..." Cannell Studios press release quoting Bill Carter, *Baltimore Sun*, 1988.

page 274: "I'd never even been in a high-school play," Fred Dalton Thompson quoted in press release from The Cannell Studios, 1988.

page 274: "I was just thirty years old at the time," Fred Dalton Thompson quoted in press release from The Cannell Studios, 1988.

page 274: "I get a certain amount of ribbing from my lawyer buddies," Fred Dalton Thompson to Gary Mullinax, "Fred Thompson does about-face," Gannett News Services, *Des Moines Sunday Register*, October 30, 1988.

page 275: "There was that wonderful Calvin Hollis scene," David Burke to Edward Gross, *The Unofficial Story of the Making of a Wiseguy*, 1990, Pioneer Press.

page 275: "...Was locked into the whole Nazi sensibility ... I wore clothes that were too small for me..." Paul Guilfoyle to Edward Gross, *The Unofficial Story of the Making of a Wiseguy*, 1990, Pioneer Press.

page 276: "He's using white supremacism as his latest venture to make a buck," Fred Dalton Thompson to Gary Mullinax, "Fred Thompson does about-face," Gannett News Services, *Des Moines Sunday Register*, October 30, 1988.

page 277: "Ray Sharkey as vicious mob boss Sonny Steelgrave generated enough histrionic juice to blow all the fuses at San Quentin," Harry Waters and Janet Huck, "The Fine Arc of a Crime Hit," *Newsweek*, December 26, 1988.

page 277: "The setting is New York's garment district..." Matt Roush, TV review of *Wiseguy*, *USA Today*, December 14, 1988.

page 277: "We thought Jerry wouldn't do it," David Burke to Moira Farrow, "*Wiseguy* mini-series format appeals to Jerry Lewis," *New York Times*, late 1988.

page 277: "A five-hour movie," Edward Gross, *The Unofficial Story of the Making of a Wiseguy*, 1990, Pioneer Press.

page 279: "Eli is a mix of ego, drive, and pride..." Matt Roush, TV review of *Wiseguy*, *USA Today*, December 14, 1988.

page 279: "That final speech I had written just came out right, and it was enhanced by Jerry's playing it the way he did..." Stephen Kronish to Edward Gross, *The Unofficial Story of the Making of a Wiseguy*, 1990, Pioneer Press.

page 283: "Five minutes to blow Mann against the wall with a story idea," Columbia press release for Peter Lance, fourth season of *Wiseguy*.

page 285: "Only the stabilizing presence of Jonathan Banks salvages the premiere..." "Bril," TV review of *Wiseguy*, fourth season premiere, *Variety*, November 19, 1990.

page 286: "Except for some Latin beats slipped beneath the theme music, and the leap from Italian Brooklyn to Cuban Miami, this is still *Wiseguy*," Jeff Salamon, "Miami Wise, TV review of *Wiseguy* fourth season premiere," *The Village Voice*, November 12, 1990.

page 286: "We really do believe there's an audience out there that would love the show if they would just give us a shot," Les Sheldon to Edward Gross, *The Unofficial Story of the Making of a Wiseguy*, 1990, Pioneer Press.

J.J. Starbuck

page 295: "Starbuck lost his wife and son in a plane crash, and he just never really went back to the office," TV interview; Dale Robertson to Johnny Carson on *The Tonight Show*, 25 September, 1987.

page 295: "Matt Houston's dad" Elvis Mitchell, "Thugs 'R' Us," *Rolling Stone*, March 24, 1988.

page 296: "...[Columbo] is a modest man, stumbling through the world of the very rich and famous, who regard him as a slow-witted nuisance..." MCA press release for *Columbo*.

page 296: "We can all identify with Columbo," Everett Chambers, one of the producers on *Columbo*, quoted in MCA press release for *Columbo*.

page 298: "J.J.'s barrage of bromides would overpower anyone!" staff writer, New Season Review, *TV Guide*, 12 September, 1987.

page 302: "There are actors and there are personalities," TV interview; Dale Robertson to Johnny Carson on *The Tonight Show*, 25 September, 1987.

Sonny Spoon

page 305: "They wanted a guy who could go anywhere, from the White House to the outhouse — use his wits and not his mitts," Mario Van Peebles to Joe D'Agnese, "Make Room for Sonny Spoon," *Right On*, 1988.

page 305: "As might be expected from producer Stephen J. Cannell...," Merrill Panitt, "TV review of *Sonny Spoon*," *TV Guide*, 29 October, 1988.

page 305: "Secondary characters offer some texture," "Tone," TV review of *Sonny Spoon*, *Variety*, 24 February, 1988.

page 306: "I'm aware that none have been successful in the past," Mario Van Peebles to Eirik Knutzen, "Sonny Outlook," *Toronto Star*, June 11, 1988.

page 306: "I was told that I looked like a young Harry Belafonte when I first came to Hollywood, and I knew it meant unemployment..." Mario Van Peebles quoted by Stephannia Cleaton, "Fighting for Better Roles for Blacks," *Boston Herald*, May 15, 1988, and Eirik Knutzen, Sonny Outlook, *Toronto Star*, June 11, 1988.

page 306: "The original hippie — she even got me drum lessons with The Grateful Dead," Steve Malins, *TV Guide* (U.K.), September 8, 1990.

page 306: Van Peebles has an economics degree, and also once worked as a budget analyst for a mayor's office, Eirik Knutzen, "Sonny Outlook," *Toronto Star*, June 11, 1988.

page 306: "I said I'd like to have a character who doesn't carry a gun, who uses his mind...," Mario Van Peebles to Pat Hilton, "A Spoonful of Fame for Mario," *USA Today*, 17 March, 1988.

page 306: "I insisted the cops and villains be mixed.... If we have a black show, then I've lost," Mario Van Peebles quoted by Pat Hilton, "A Spoonful of Fame for Mario," *USA Today*, 17 March, 1988, and Stephannia Cleaton, "Fighting for Better Roles for Blacks," *Boston Herald*, May 15, 1988.

page 307: "Later on (NBC chief Brandon Tartikoff) said 'How do you like the name Sonny Spoon?'" Mario Van Peebles to Joe D'Agnese, "Make Room for Sonny Spoon," *Right On*, 1988.

page 308: "We want to see more of them together," Randall Wallace to *TV Guide*, July 16, 1988.

page 308: "I'll also be doing a Chinese houseboy, a one-armed Jamaican hit-man, a pregnant woman ... and Elvis!" Mario Van Peebles to Laurie Werner, "A Detective who's Totally Disarming," This Weekend's TV, *USA Weekend*, November 11, 1988.

page 308: "I speak a little French, I speak a little Spanish, a little uptown, a little downtown..." Mario Van Peebles to Stephannia Cleaton, "Fighting for Better Roles for Blacks," *Boston Herald*, May 15, 1988.

page 308: "I didn't want him to be a black James Bond," Mario Van Peebles to Laurie Werner, "A Detective who's Totally Disarming," This Weekend's TV, *USA Weekend*, November 11, 1988.

page 308: "Sonny is kind of like Artemus Gordon from *The Wild Wild West* meets *The Rockford Files* with a Bugs Bunny philosophy," Mario Van Peebles to Leslie Van Buskirk, "Mario Van Peebles' Sonny Skies," *US* magazine, March 21, 1988.

page 310: "But when you're directing your boss and your dad in a scene together, what do you say — Do it over?" Mario Van Peebles to Marilyn Beck, *Washington Times*, September 16, 1988.

Unsub

page 313: "Surprisingly substantial," "Bier," TV review of *Unsub*, *Variety*, February 15, 1989.

page 314: "*Unsub* should rivet those who devour police procedurals..." Matt Roush, TV review of *Unsub*, *USA Today*, February 3, 1989.

page 314: "The information forthcoming is fascinating..." Kay Gardella, "Intelligent crime-busting," *New York Daily News*, 3 February, 1989.

page 314: "...Something that wasn't on the air, something that you haven't seen before, and something you would go home and watch," Cannell to Kay Gardella, "Intelligent crime-busting," *New York Daily News*, 3 February, 1989.

The Wrap-Up

page 318: "If somebody can figure out what this show's about, tell the producers," Jay Martel, "Heading for a Fall," *Rolling Stone*, September 21, 1989.

page 320: "The adventures in the fictional *Mission: Impossible* style country of Costa Verde drag on incessantly..." "Tone," TV review of *Top of the Hill*, *Variety*, October 4, 1989.

page 321: "The casting director had probably looked at fifty guys for the role of Booker," Bill Nuss to *US* magazine, writer n/a, May 28, 1990.

page 321: "Eric Blakeney called and said, 'We're going to do this spin-off,'" Richard Greico to *US* magazine, writer n/a, May 28, 1990.

page 321: "I chose to write for *Booker* because I feel so strongly about the guy," Cannell quoted by Glenn Esterly, TV Guide (U.K.), June 1990.

page 321: "The novelty of a hero who wears an earring is bound to wear off by, say, ten minutes into the second episode..." "Bril," TV review of *Booker*, *Variety*, September 1989.

page 323: "A swashbuckling style to what had been more of a jive portrayal," "Bier," TV review of *100 Lives of Black Jack Savage*, *Variety*, April 15, 1991.

page 323: "The Disney-Cannell marriage would seem perfect — Disney's deep pockets plus Cannell's vast imagination," Paul Lomartire, location report, *100 Lives of Black Jack Savage*, for the Cox News Service.

page 323: "The script mixes grown-up nastiness with juvenile fantasy..." "Bier," TV review of *100 Lives of Black Jack Savage*, *Variety*, April 15, 1991.

page 324: "Because of the star's athleticism, the action sequences are unusually good, and there's greater ethnic diversity than on most shows," TV review of *Street Justice*, *People*, 4 November, 1991.

page 326: "Uncompromising honesty, outright decency and vigilante heart," *Boston Sunday Globe*, quoted in press ad for *The Commish*.

page 326: "It's clear that ... Cannell and Kronish — who also worked on *Wiseguy*..." TV review of *The Commish*, Ken Tucker, *Entertainment Weekly*, October 11, 1991.

page 326: "There's more than a tad of schmaltz and stage business afoot here," Miles Beller, TV review of *The Commish, Hollywood Reporter,* September 27, 1991.

page 326: "Chiklis turns in such a magnetic performance..." *New York Post,* quoted in press ad for *The Commish.*

page 326: "Chiklis is a marvel of believability..." *People* magazine, quoted in press ad for *The Commish.*

page 326: "*The Commish* works because star Michael Chiklis is genuinely appealing and auteur Stephen Cannell is so playful," *New York Magazine,* quoted in press ad for *The Commish.*

page 326: "Scali is the role of a lifetime..." Ken Tucker, TV review of *The Commish, Entertainment Weekly,* October 11, 1991.

page 326: "This is the only studio in town that I know of that's run by a writer for writers," Q and A with Stephen J. Cannell, Warner Bros. press release for *Renegade.*

page 327: "Moffett is energetic, bordering on vainglorious..." TV review of *Palace Guard, People* magazine, quoted in Columbia Television press release.

page 327: "CBS has said it wants to give viewers light entertainment over the weekend, and it doesn't get much lighter than this," Brian Lowry, TV review of *Palace Guard, Variety,* October 18, 1991.

page 327: "A ridiculous creature operating on clunky wisecracks and leaden quips," Miles Beller, TV review of *Palace Guard, Hollywood Reporter,* October 18, 1991.

page 331: "I had always wanted to create a contemporary western," Q and A with Stephen J. Cannell, Warner Bros. press release for *Renegade.*

page 332: "*Renegade* was a work in progress the first season," Q and A with Stephen J. Cannell, Warner Bros. press release for *Renegade.*

page 333: "Sonny Spoon certainly doesn't lead us..." Merrill Panitt, TV review of *Sonny Spoon, TV Guide,* 29 October, 1988.

page 333: "Sometimes it seems like..." "Bier," TV review of *Sonny Spoon, Variety,* October 11, 1988.

Bibliography

Books

Brooks, Tim, and Earle Marsh. *The Complete Directory to Prime Time Network and Cable TV Shows, 1946–Present.* New York: Ballantine Books, 2003.

Gross, Edward. *The Unofficial Story of the Making of a Wiseguy.* Las Vegas, Nev: Pioneer Books, 1990.

Meyers, Richard. *TV Detectives.* San Diego: A.S. Barnes, 1981.

Newman, Kim. *Wild West Movies, or, How the West Was Found, Won, Lost, Lied About, Filmed, and Forgotten.* London: Bloomsbury, 1990.

Thompson, Robert J. *Adventures on Prime Time: The Television Programs of Stephen J. Cannell.* Media and society series. New York: Praeger, 1990.

Major Features on Cannell Shows

Abbott, Jon. "*The Greatest American Hero.*" *Starburst* no. 95, late 1980s, revised, rewritten, and extended for this book.

Bedell, Sally. "How TV Hit *The A-Team* Was Born." *New York Times,* 28th April, 1985.

Burns, James, and Juanita Bartlett. "The View From the Top, Part One." *Starlog,* December 1981.

———. "The View From the Top, Part Two."*Starlog,* January 1982.

Cannell, Stephen J. "Roundtable Discussion: Independent Producers and their Uncertainty about the Future." *Emmy* Magazine, March/April 1983.

Carson, Tom. "*The A Team*—Macho Goes to Camp." *The Village Voice,* February 22nd, 1983.

Durgin, Vance. "Running Man Roy Huggins." *Emmy* Magazine, September 1988.

Gansberg, Alan L. "Stephen J. Cannell: Writing His Own Ticket." *Hollywood Reporter,* 54th Anniversary issue, 1984.

Goldberg, Lee. "Cannell Runs Studio Like a One Man Show." *Electronic Media,* April 14th, 1986.

Greenberger, Robert. "The Secret Force Behind *The Greatest American Hero.*" *Starlog,* November 1982.

———. "Starlog Interview: Connie Sellecca." *Starlog,* January 1982.

Hochman, Steve. "The Flip Side of *Wiseguy.*" *L.A. Times,* March 22nd, 1989.

McGregor, Don. "Starlog Interview: Robert Culp, Part One." *Starlog,* January 1982.

———. "Starlog Interview: Robert Culp, Part Two." *Starlog,* February 1982.

Mitchell, Elvis. "Thugs 'R' Us (*Wiseguy*)." *Rolling Stone,* March 24th, 1988.

O'Connor, John J. "The Rise of *The A-Team* Guarantees More Violence." *New York Times,* 8th May, 1983.

Peck, Stacey. "Marcia and Stephen Cannell." *L.A. Times* Home magazine, October 2nd, 1980.

Rensin, David. "Hooks and Crooks." *Rolling Stone,* April 20th, 1989.

Roberts, Jerry. "Working Formulas: Thousand Episode Producer Stephen J. Cannell." *Daily Variety,* August 17th, 1995.

Rousch, Matt. "Sharkey, a *Wiseguy* no more." *USA Today,* June 14th, 1988.

Ruth, Daniel. "Ken Wahl follows a dream, winds up a Wiseguy." *Chicago Sun-Times,* July 17th, 1988.

Saunders, Dusty. "Dyslexia Didn't Block Cannell's Path to Success." Scripps Howard Service, *TV Ledger,* September 26th, 1987.

Schruers, Fred. "Can 800 million Chinese Be Wrong?" *Rolling Stone,* May 4th, 1989.

Setlowe, Richard. "Thousand Episode Producer Stephen J. Cannell." *Daily Variety,* August 17th, 1995.

Silverman, Jeff. "Mr. Write." *US,* February 24th, 1986.

Stanley, John. "Stephen Cannell on His Own." *San Francisco Sunday Examiner and Chronicle,* 27th January, 1980.

Torgerson, Ellen. "James Garner believes in good coffee—and a mean punch." *TV Guide,* June 2nd, 1979.

Vallely, Jean. "*The Rockford Files.*" *Esquire,* July 3rd, 1979.

Van Buskirk, Leslie. "Working Class Hero." *US* magazine, April 17th, 1989.

Ward, Robert. "Never Play Poker with James Garner." *Gentleman's Quarterly,* March 1984.

Waters, Harry, and Janet Huck. "The Fine Arc of a Crime Hit." *Newsweek,* December 26th, 1988.

Wicking, Chris. "From the Files of James Scott Rockford." *Time Out* (London, U.K.), December 7th, 1979.

Wolcott, James. "Mixed Media." *Vanity Fair*, May 1988.

Zukowski, Helena. "Hanging On to Creative Control." *MediaScene*, 1989.

Brief Articles, Interviews, Cuttings and News Pieces

Adamo, Susan. "Log Entries: Ratings and Court Favor Hero." *Starlog*, June 1981.

_____. "Log Entries: Say Hi to Ralph Hinckley." *Starlog*, July 1981.

_____. "Log Entries: Final Word on *G.A.H.* Lawsuit." *Starlog*, May 1982.

Anderson, Dave. "*Hunter* on the Hunted." *New York Times*, 2nd October, 1988.

Baker, Kathryn. "Prolific Producer Thought He Was a Loser." Associated Press, January 1987.

Bauer, Patricia E. "Go North, Young Man. *Channels*, July/August 1987.

Bawden, Jim. "Young actors take quick jump to fame." *Toronto Star*, November 1st, 1987.

Beck, Marilyn. "Dryer Blasts TV Academy." *Insider Grapevine* column, *TV Guide*, 1991.

Beller, Miles. "TV review of *21 Jump Street*: 'Fun With Animals.'" *Hollywood Reporter*, November 4th, 1988.

_____. "TV review of *The Commish*." *Hollywood Reporter*, September 27th, 1991.

_____. "TV review of *Palace Guard*." *Hollywood Reporter*, October 18th, 1991.

"Bier." "TV review of *100 Lives of Black Jack Savage*." *Variety*, April 15th, 1991.

_____. "TV review of *Sonny Spoon*." *Variety*, October 11th, 1988.

_____. "TV review of *Unsub*." *Variety*, February 15th, 1989.

"Bok." "TV review of *The A-Team*." *Variety*, date n/a, January 1983.

_____. "TV review of *The Quest*," *Variety*, October, 1982.

_____. "TV review of *Riptide*." *Variety*, 4th January, 1984.

_____. "TV review of *Stone*." *Variety*, 16th January, 1980.

Borycki, Martin. "On the Canadian Experience." *Reel West*, May/June 1987.

Brennan, Patricia. "Getting a Jump on the competition." *Washington Post/New York Post*, December 10th, 1987.

Brighty, Jessica. "Holly Goes Pop." *TV Guide* (U.K.), 1991.

"Bril." "TV review of *Booker*." *Variety*, September 1989.

_____. "TV review of *Wiseguy* fourth season premiere." *Variety*, November 19th, 1990.

Broadwater, Cynthia. "*Riptide*." *Daredevils* no. 10, August 1984.

Brooke, Jill. "Teen crime tackled by *Jump Street* crew." *New York Post*, April 11th, 1987.

Buck, Jerry. "Father of *Jump Street*." Associated Press, *The Cincinatti Enquirer*, October 30th, 1988.

Burden, Martin. "TV review of *21, Jump Street*." *Washington Post*, April 1987.

Burns, Howard. "Silver pulls *Wiseguy* stint." *Hollywood Reporter*, November 7th, 1988.

Cosford, Bill. "Johnny Depp turns street smart." *US* magazine, June 13th, 1988.

Court, Clive. "Maple Leaf Treatment." *Broadcast*, May 22nd, 1987.

"Demp." "TV review of *Tenspeed and Brownshoe*." *Variety*, January 1980.

Donlon, Brian. "Stephen Cannell, Prime Time Adventurer." *USA Today*, Feb. 1988.

Esslinger, Mark. "Wise Up to *Wiseguy*." *Hollywood Gazette*, May 25th, 1988.

Freer, Bridget. "*Hunter!*" *TV Guide* (U.K.), September, 1989.

_____. "Head *Hunter*." *TV Guide* (U.K.), June, 1990.

_____. "Introducing Ken Wahl, *Wiseguy*." *TV Guide* (U.K.), 1989.

_____. "*Jump Street* Kid." *TV Guide* (U.K.), 1989.

Gardella, Kay. "Intelligent crime-busting." *New York Daily News*, 3rd February, 1989.

_____. "*Wiseguy's* Lifeguard." *New York Daily News*, October 14th, 1988.

Gelman, Morrie. "Cannell Copes with Deficit Financing." *Hollywood Reporter*, date n/a, 1987.

_____. "Pitching Ideas for Programs (is a) Skill." *Variety*, Wednesday, January 21st, 1987.

Goldberg, Lee. "*Stingray* still breathing after two executions." *Electronic Media*, October 1986.

Goodman, Walter. "TV review of *The A-Team*." *New York Times*, 21st January, 1983.

Green, Tom. "He's the chief good guy on CBS' *Wiseguy*." *USA Today*, date n/a.

_____. "Young Cast finds itself at crossroads." *USA Today*, November 1988.

Guttman, Monika. "The refugee's story has a happy ending in Hollywood." Tribune Media Services, 1987.

Hack, Richard. "TeleVisions." *Hollywood Reporter*, July 18th, 1989.

Harron, Mary. "TV review of *The A-Team*, All Our Fantasies." *New Statesman*, (U.K.), July 1983.

Hedges, Joyce. "From *Rockford* to *A-Team*, a series of Success for Pasadena's Stephen Cannell." *Business Monday*, Star-News, December 1st, 1986.

Hill, Michael. "*21, Jump Street* could be seductive." *Baltimore Evening Sun*, April 11th, 1987.

Hilton, Pat. "Fred Dryer, the Restless *Hunter*." *USA Today*, December 1987.

Hindes, Martha. "The *Wiseguy's* star rises." Gannett News Services, *The Detroit News*, September 4th, 1988.

_____. "Double Life means Double Trouble." *The Cincinatti Enquirer*, September 25th, 1988.

Hoggart, Simon. "The Tale of Mr. T." *New Society* (U.K.), 19th January, 1984.

Howes, Keith. "TV review of *The Rockford Files* episode "The Empty Frame." *Gay Times* (U.K.), September 20th, 1979.

Jarvis, Jeff. "TV review of *21, Jump Street."* *People* magazine, April 1987.

Kercher, John. "Move Over Clint, *Hunter's* Here." *Woman's Weekly* (U.K.), 1984.

Kirby, Blaik. "*City of Angels* best of new crime shows." *Toronto Globe and Mail,* February 1976.

Knight, Bob. "Webs' Midseason Shifts Hardly Cause for Alarm." *Variety,* January 27th, 1988.

Knipe, Sandra. "Fox's new police show is arresting." *Evansville Courier,* April 11th, 1987.

Lane, Jane. "Talking Television with Stephen Cannell." *Women's Wear Daily,* October 20th, 1988.

Leonard, John. "TV review of *The A-Team."* *New York Times,* 8th October, 1984.

Lieberman, Jane. "For Disabled Entertainers, a Champion in Hollywood." *Variety,* February 15th, 1989.

Lowry, Brian. "Starlog Interview: William Katt, I Knew Flying Was Part of the Job."*Starlog,* May 1985.

_____. "TV review of *Palace Guard."* *Variety,* October 18th, 1991.

Malins, Steve. "Master of Disguise." *TV Guide* (U.K.), September 8th, 1990.

Mann, Richard. "Jonathan Banks, Nicest villain on TV." *The Washington Times,* mid–1988.

Martel, Jay. "Heading for a Fall." *Rolling Stone,* September 21st, 1989.

McKenzie, Robert. "TV review of *Riptide."* *TV Guide,* March 17th, 1984.

"Mick." "TV review *City of Angels."* *Variety,* February 11th, 1976.

Merrill, Don. "TV review of *21, Jump Street."* *TV Guide,* November 7th, 1987.

_____. "TV review of *Wiseguy."* *TV Guide,* March 5th, 1988.

Miller, Ivy. "Modern Screen interviews Johnny Depp." *Modern Screen,* 1990.

_____. "Surviving One Jump at a Time." *Modern Screen,* 1989.

"Mor." "TV review of *Scott Free."* *Variety,* October 20th, 1976.

Mullinax, Gary. "Fred Thompson does about-face." Gannett News Services, *Des Moines Sunday Register,* October 30th, 1988.

Murphy, Morna. "TV review *City of Angels: The November Plan."* *Hollywood Reporter,* February 1976.

O'Connor, John J. "TV review of *Hardcastle and McCormick."* *New York Times,* September 16th, 1983.

_____. "TV review of *The Quest."* *New York Times,* October 22nd, 1982.

Panitt, Merrill. "TV review of *Sonny Spoon."* *TV Guide,* 29th October, 1988.

Plutzig, Roberta. "Playing Sonny Was the Ultimate High." TV Record, *New York Daily News,* June 15th, 1988.

Rigby, Peter. "Top TV Writer Has a Problem — He'll Never Read or Spell Properly." *Star,* October 1st, 1985.

Ross, Chuck. "Mr. *Wiseguy*—the Man who has Hollywood's ear." *San Francisco Chronicle,* October 26th, 1988.

Rothenberg, Fred. "Toned-down *Jump Street* still tackles tough issues." *New York Post,* April 9th, 1987.

Roush, Matt. "Give CBS' *Wiseguy* a try on its new night." *USA Today,* January 4th, 1988.

_____. "TV review of *Unsub."* *USA Today,* February 3rd, 1989.

_____. "TV review of *Wiseguy." USA Today,* December 14th, 1988.

Salamon, Jeff. "Miami Wise, TV review of *Wiseguy* fourth season premiere." *The Village Voice,* November 12th, 1990.

"Sax." "TV review of *21, Jump Street* ("Draw the Line"), *Variety,* September 20th, 1989.

Schindler, Harold, Jerry Lewis to play *Wiseguy* heavy, *Salt Lake Tribune,* October 27th, 1988.

Shister, Gail. Checking Out (news piece re: dropping characters from *Sonny Spoon*), *The Philadelphia Enquirer,* 5th November, 1988.

Souza, Sylvia. The C-Team: Cannell and Curcio, *Cannell Channel* in-house magazine, Feb./March 1985.

Spotnitz, Frank. Bows for Holly, *US* magazine, October 3rd, 1988.

Staff Writer. "Cannell Building Canadian Studio and Moves TV Production There," *Variety,* April 8th, 1987.

Staff Writer. "*Hunter* honored," *Hollywood Reporter,* October 25th, 1988.

Staff Writer. "TV review of *Hardcastle and McCormick,* New Season Review," *TV Guide,* 10th September, 1983.

Staff Writer. "TV review of *J.J. Starbuck,* New Season Review," *TV Guide,* 12th September, 1987.

Staff Writer. "So Long Sonny," *TV Guide,* November 1987.

Staff Writer. "Sonny's No Longer Solo," *TV Guide,* July 16th, 1988.

Staff Writer. "*Wiseguy, General Hospital* are among winners of Media Access Awards." *Variety,* February 1st, 1989.

Stoddart, Patrick. "TV review of *The A-Team,* Sunset Boulevard Blues," *Broadcast* (U.K.), 8th August, 1983.

Sullivan, Kerry. "Out of the Shadows," *Emmy* magazine, September 1988.

Teahen, Jack. "Focus on Canada: Building up Big Business," *Screen International,* August 20th, 1988.

Thompson, Douglas. "Girl No. 2 gets the *A-Team* Bullet," *London Daily Mail,* date n/a, circa 1984.

"Tone." "TV review of *Sonny Spoon,*" *Variety,* February 24th, 1988.

_____. "TV review of *Top of the Hill*," *Variety*, October 4th, 1989.
"Vors." "TV review of *Hunter*," *Variety*, October 25th, 1989.
Tucker, Ken. "TV review of *The Commish*," *Entertainment Weekly*, October 11th, 1991.
Warner Bros. press release for *Renegade*.
Weedon, Jo. "Interview with James Garner," *Weekend* magazine (U.K.), date n/a, 1981.
Wicking, Chris. "TV review of *Stone*," *Time Out* (London, U.K.), 12th September, 1980.
Wilkinson, Bud. "*Jump Street* grasps issue of teen suicide," *Arizona Republic*, April 28th, 1988.
Williams, Gail. "TV review: third season premiere *Hardcastle and McCormick*," *Hollywood Reporter*, September 26th, 1985.
Winikoff, Ken. "Stephen J. Cannell: The Producer Who Came to Dinner," British Columbia Special Report, *Hollywood Reporter*, October 4th, 1988.
Writer n/a. "TV review of *Palace Guard*," *People* magazine, quoted in Columbia Television press release.
Writer n/a. "TV review of *Sonny Spoon* second season premiere," *Los Angeles Sentinel*, September 15th, 1988.
Writer n/a. "TV review of *Stingray* pilot," *Variety*, March 1986.
Writer n/a. "TV review of *Tenspeed and Brownshoe*," *Hollywood Reporter*, January 1980.
Yarbrough, Jeff. "Adam West trades his cape for a cop's badge," *People*, 12th May 1986.

Index

References to main chapters on series are in **bold**; photographs are in *italics*.

The A-Team 1, 3, 4, 6, 7, 8, 9, 11, 12, 13, 16, 17, 18, 22, 23, 25, 27, 28, 29, 30, 32, 34, 35, 36, 48, 51, 56, 87, 91, 103, 106, 110, 119, 120, 127, *133*, **131–155**, *142*, 156, 157, 158, 160, 162, 170, 171, 172, 173, 175, 177, 178, 179, 180, 183, 194, 196, 197, 200, 201, 206, 221, 222, 223, 224, 227, 228, 231, 234, 239, 240, 242, 243, 258, 263, 283, 299, 300, 305, 306, 308, 309, 310, 316, 320, 321, 328, 329, 330, 331, 332, 334
"The A-Team" (pilot) 147
"The A-Team Is Coming, the A-Team Is Coming" 153
"The Aaron Ironwood School for Success" 60
Abatemarco, Frank 94, 100
Abatemarco, Tony 215, 230
Abbott, Paul 253
ABC 28, 53, 103, 109, 110, 111, 129, 156, 158, 173, 183, 204, 231, 234, 236, 237, 238, 239, 260, 264, 283, 301, 328
Abercrombie, Ian 214, 253
Abert, Stephen J. 250
Abraham, Ken 251
Abraham, Mark 252
Abrahams, Doug 257
Abrahams, Jim 233
Abramowitz, David 251
Abruzzo, Ray 189, 248
"Acapulco Holiday" 219
Acheson, Mark 289
Acker, Iris 294
Acker, Sharon 67, 68, 104
Ackroyd, David 154, 167, 186, 207, 309, 311
Adam 12 37, 45, 231, 299, 313
Adams, Dave 184
Adams, Don 233
Adams, Jeb 89, 91
Adams, Marc 165, 208
Adams, Nick 89
Adams, Richard C. 81
Addison, Walter 214
Addy, Wesley 64
Ades, Danny 66
Adler, Kay 78
Adler, Tammy 326
Adventures of Ellery Queen 96
Adventures on Prime-Time 9, 138

"The After Hours" 178
"After School Special" 250
*AfterM*A*S*H* 173
Ageli, Adam 152, 186
"Aggie" 77
Agolia Carey, Timothy 76, 81, 112
Aherne, Jean-Celeste 129
Ahsana, Rochelle 155
Aidman, Charles 65
Aiello, Danny 193
Aiello, Rick 253
Airplane 233
Airwolf 1, 11, 22, 27, 32, 33, 51, 88, 103, 113, 127, 131, 137, 138, 140, 142, 179, 180, 221, 228, 273, 296
Akins, Claude 217
Alaimo, Marc 75, 77, 125, 155, 166, 208, 250
Alan-Williams, Gregory 219, 220
Albert, Suzanne 150
Alda, Alan 82, 90
Alda, Antony 212
Alda, Robert 67, 112
Alden, Norman 67, 78, 126, 147, 149, 166, 191, 208, 211, 249
Aldrich, Robert 101
Aleong, Aki 155, 215
Alexander, E. Nick 79, 80, 81, 208, 212
Alexander, Grant 168
Alexander, Larry 73, 77, 78
Alexis, Alvin 250
Alfred Hitchcock Presents 45, 273
Alias Smith and Jones 3, 40, 44, 48, 52
Alice 16
Alien Nation 120, 206
"Alive at Five" 35, 145, 155
All in the Family 16, 39, 238, 239
All My Children 326
"All or Nothing" 290
"All That Glitters" 220
"All That Shatters" 80
Allan, Jed 166
Alldredge, Michael 32, 68, 123, 147, 148, 151
"Allegra" 214
Allen, Chad 215
Allen, Corey 13, 67, 68, 69, 104, 191, 194, 215, 217, 218, 219, 220, 302, 310, 311, 316
Allen, John 167
Allen, MacKenzie 154

Allen, Nancy 114
Allen, Phillip R. 81, 94, 251
Allen, Rae 124
Allen, Sian Barbara 59, 81
Allen, Steve 104, 189
Allen, Tod 254
Allende, Fernando 210
Allin, Jeff 216
Allport, Christopher 213
Allyn, Alice 75
Almost Grown 32, 51, 333
Altman, Jeff 229
Altman, Robert 3, 45, 46, 49, 82
Alvarez, Abraham 208
Alzado, Lyle 187
The Amazing Spider-Man (television series) 118, 121
Ambert, Laurie 189
Ambriz, Domingo 80
Ameche, Don 107
Amen 203
Amendola, Tony 218
"America, Whatta Town" 248
The American Girls 26
The American Vein 40
The Americanisation of Emily 50
America's Most Wanted 238, 239, 318, 321
Ames, Granville 211, 229
Amos, John 149, 165, 200, 207, 227, 230
Amos, Keith 250
Amos and Andy 84
Amos Burke—Secret Agent 237
Amritraj, Vijay 232, 235
"And Down Will Come Baby" 77
"And It Comes Out Here" 290
"And the Dead Shall Rise to Condemn Thee" 316
"And They Swam Right Over the Dam" 316
Andaluz, Mike 251
Anders, Luana 218
Andersen, Suzanne 257
Anderson, Cheryl 248
Anderson, Daryl 145, 153, 188
Anderson, Dion 292
Anderson, Gerry 146
Anderson, Ingrid 184
Anderson, John 63, 112, 123, 184, 215
Anderson, Ken 66
Anderson, Mitchell 187, 249

Anderson, Pamela 332
Anderson, Richard 144, 145, 153, 168
Anderson, Sam 169, 209, 251
Anderson, Steven 217
Anderson, Warner 60
Andre the Giant 126
Andreas, Luke 32, 53, 58, 64, 65, 67, 68, 104, 111, 112, 123, 147, 191, 207, 211, 302
Andreozzi, Jack 125, 209, 230
Andres, Jill 252
Andrews, Ben 69
Andrews, Brian 79
Andrews, Julie 50
Andrews, Todd Eric 250
Andronica, James 183, 186, 187, 288
Andy Warhol's Bad 177
Angel 3 325
"Angie's Choice" 167
Anglin, Jennifer 213
Angotti, Nick 155, 213
Annese, Frank 150, 152, 164, 185, 251
Another World 270
Ansara, Edward 149
Ansara, Michael 62, 168, 209
Ansley, Zachary 256
Anthony, Gerald 267, 274, 287
Anthony, Shirley 129
Antille, Lisa 151
Antin, Steve 248
Anton, Christine 303
Antonacci, Greg 67, 70
Antonio, Jim 148
Antonio, Lou 58, 60, 62
"Any Second Now" 212
"Anyone for Suicide?" 92
Anzilotti, Perry 312
Apocalypse Now 271
Apostle-Pec, Stephen 211
Applegate, Christina 247, 250
Applegate, Jeremy 255
"The Appointment" 81
Aprea, John 153, 166
Apter, Harold 227, 229
Aragon, Art 76
Arbus, Allan 67, 167, 218
Arcesi, Mike 100
Archer 162
Archie, John 294
Archie Bunker's Place 177
Ardito, Gino 78
Arena Productions 83
Aresco, Joey 60, 68, 89, *89*, 91, 148, 172, 174, 220
Argenziano, Carmen 69, 102, 104, 123, 125, 149, 213, 321
Argo, Victor 64
"Aria for Don Aiuppo" 289
Arkin, Adam 118
Armstrong, Curtis 183
Armstrong, Herb 67
Armstrong, R.G. 80
Armstrong, Todd 124
Armus, Burton 31
Arndt, Dennis 289
Arnemann, Dawn 215

Arness, James 170
Arnett, Jeanetta 153, 168, 187
Arnold, Madison 65, 81
Arnold, Victor 164
Arnone, Lee 216
Arnott, Mark 213, 251
Arquette, Lewis 112, 184
Arrants, Rod 210
"Arriverderci, Baby" 91, 187, 189
Arrowsmith, Terry 289
Ashbrook, Dana 252
Ashbrook, Daphne 151, 185, 190
Ashford, Michelle 251, 252, 253, 254, 255
Ashland, Camilla 169
Ashley, Elizabeth 217
Ashley, John 127
Ashton, John 35, 151, 169
Ashmore, Frank 213
Askew, Luke 63, 64, 126
Asparagus, Fred 288
Assa, Rene 66, 214
Ast, Pat 77
Astaire, Fred (and Ginger Rogers) 334
Astin, John 186
Atkins, Tom 48, 49, 58, 80, 229
Atkinson, Beverly Hope 81
Attell, Toni 153, 155, 188, 210
Attias, Daniel 254, 255
"The Attractive Nuisance" 66, 159
Atwater, Barry 65
Atwater, Edith 60, 78
Auberjonois, Rene 26, 68, 92, 98, 112
Auerbach, Jeffrey 254
"Aura Lee, Farewell" 53, 59
Austin, Jeff 168, 220
Austin, Karen 55, 67, 128, 129, 218
Austin, Laura 251
Automan 3, 137, 142, 160, 221
Autry, Alan 148, 155, 191, 208
Autry, Gene 263
"Autumn" 227
The Avengers 195
"The Avenging Angel" 197, 208
Averback, Hy 57, 66, 85, 96, 97, 98, 233, 235
Avery, James 153, 312
Avery, Tex 233
Avery, Val 80, 166, 216
Aviation Heritage 87
Avey, Fred 87
Avila, Christine 69
Avila, Cynthia 80
Avonne, Michael 147
"AWOL" 252
Axelrod, Robert 216
Axton, Hoyt 35, *171*, 172, 173
Ayer, Harold 189
Ayer, Simon 257
Ayres, Jerry 68
Ayres, Leah 150, 248
Ayres, Lew 155
Azarow, Martin 149, 211
Azzapardi, Mario 291
Azzarra, Candice 80, 112

Baa Baa, Black Sheep 27, 90, 91
Babcock, Barbara 65
Babes 12
Babson, Thomas 123
Baby 114
"Baby Blues" 257
"The Baby Game" 215
Baby Talk 115
Bacall, Lauren 69
Bacalla, Donna 64
Bachmann, Conrad 213, 214
Bacic, Steve 257
"Back from the Future" 246, 254
Back to the Future 328
"Back to School" 255
Backes, Alice 126
"Backlash of the Hunter" 52, 58
Bacos Clinch, Catherine 217, 218
"Bad Company" 212
"Bad Day at Eagle Rock" 257
"A Bad Deal in the Valley" 62
"Bad Influence" 245, 249
"Bad Time at the Border" 134, 144, 148
Bader, Dietrich 255
Badiyi, Reza 26, 48, 64, 65, 66, 67, 68, 73, 78, 79, 80, 81, 111, 112
Badler, Jane 189
Baer, Parley 149, 213
Bagetta, Vincent 32, 63, 65, 80, 150, 163, 168, 189, 207, 214, 297
Bahner, Blake 218
Bailey, Dennis 214
Bailey, Stephen 59
Bain, Sean 79
Bain Woodward, Meredith 316
Bakalyan, Richard 168, 212, 213, 214
Baker, Joby 104
Baker, Joe Don 158
Baker, Kathryn 265
Baker, Lenny 69
Baker, Ray 254
Baker, Rod 93, 94
Balaski, Belinda 75, 209
Baldavin, Barbara 76
Balding, Rebecca 66
Balducci, Dick 66, 151
Baldwin, James 294
Baldwin, Janit 77, 78
Baldwin, Katy 151
Balkan, David 218, 219, 220
Ball, Nora 154
Ballou, Mark 255
Balluck, Don 75
Baltimore Sun 240, 273
Bambi 182
Banacek 132, 296
Bane, Monty 219
Banks, Emily 167
Banks, Heidi 211
Banks, Jonathan 9, 32, 165, 167, 177, 210, 258, 265, *267*, 285, 286, 287
Bannon, Jack 201, 207, 211, 312
Banwell, Katherine 256
Banyon 83
Bar-Yotem, Reuven 174
Barak, Ari 124, 168

Barash, Olivia 252
Barbato, Rosa 75, 77
Barber, Gillian 290
Barber, Larry 253, 255
Barber, Paul 253, 255
Barclay, Caroline 216
Barclay, Terry 289
Bard, Rachel 186
Baretta 3, 4, 8, 9, 25, 31, 32, 33, 35, 37, 40, 49, 51, 52, **71–81**, 83, 88, 90, 103, 106, 107, 132, 145, 176, 198, 260, 273, 280, 296, 300, 305, 308, 318, 326
"The Bargain Department" 18, 188
Barilla, Courtney 207, 219, 220
Barker, Rick 126
Barnes, Dallas 11, 73, 79, 200, 201, 203, 204, 213, 214, 215
Barnes, Don 254, 255
Barnes, Joanna 11, 200, 214, 215
Barnes, Priscilla 65
Barnes, Suzanne 152
Barnes, Walter 228
Barnett, Eileen 153
"Barney" 74, 81
Barney Miller 88
Baron, Adriana 287
Baron, Deborah 219
Barr, Sharon 168, 188
Barry, Don "Red" 67
Barry, Gene 38
Barry, Ivor 62
Barry, Neil 253
Barry, Patricia 166
Barry, Patrick 201, 209
Barsi, Judith 191
Barth, Eddie 102, 104
Bartlett, Bonnie 282, 293, 294
Bartlett, Juanita 15, 18, 24, 25, 28, 29, 32, 36, 41, 51, 52, 54, 57, 58, 59, 60, 61, 62, 63, 64, 65, 66, 67, 68, 69, 102, 104, 112, 118, 119, 122, 123, 124, 127, 128, 129, 159, 197, 258, 309, 334
Bartold, Norman 59, 61, 62
Barton, Diana 252
Bartz, James 153
Basch, Harry 112
Baseleon, Michael 32, 78, 100, 125, 144, 145, 149, 150, 185, 208
Bass, Victoria 151, 210
Bassett, William E. 208
Basso, Bob 125, 148
Bateman, Charles 124, 216
Batman (character) 120, 199
Batman (movie franchise) 199
Batman (television series) 12, 19, 117, 118, 135, 138, 232, 233, 236
"The Battle Axe and the Exploding Cigar" 68
"The Battle of Bel-Air" 144, 149
"The Battle of Canoga Park" 64, 160
"Battle of the Barge" 291
Battlestar Galactica 3, 32, 89, 132, 139
Bauer, Jamie Lyn 77, 107
Bauer, Steven 146, 284, 286, 287, 334

Baur, Marc 257
Bawden, Jim 241
Baxley, Craig 32, 145, 150, 151, 152, 153, 154, 155
"Baxter and Boz" 186
Baxter Birney, Meredith 84
Bay, Frances 189, 220, 235
Bay City Blues 179
Bayer, Gary 168
Bays, Michael 254
Baywatch 247, 300, 327
BBC 51, 142
"Be True to Your School" 36, 160, 182, 186, 310
"The Beach Boy" 199, 208
The Beach Boys 333
Beach, James 126
Beale, Richard 129
"Beamer's Last Case" 55, 64, 196
Bean, Gerry 251
Bear Curtis, John 294
Bearwood, Keith 257
Beasle, Dafina 257
"The Beast from the Belly of the Boeing" 35, 148
"The Beast in the Black" 119, 124
"Beat the Box" 186
Beaton, Alex 88, 104, 106, 131, 327
Beatty, Lou, Jr. 219
Beatty, Ned 59, 63
Beauchamp, Richard 124, 201, 207
Beaumont, Gabrielle 123
"The Beautiful and the Dead" 201, 210
Beck, Ellen 294
Beck, John 211, 218
Beck, Kimberley 208
"The Becker Connection" 64
Beckett, Paul 290
Beckler, Howard 216
Beckley, William 69, 85
Beckman, Henry 70
Bedi, Kabir 186, 211, 230
Beecroft, David 214
Beecroft, Geoffrey 216
Been, Patti 217
Beer, Daniel 252
Beers, Steve 153, 168, 187, 191, 246, 250, 255
Beery, Bucklind 61, 64
Beery, Noah 48, 53, 58, 128, 129
Bega, Leslie 257
Beggs, Hagan 249
Beggs, Noah 256, 257
Behrens, Bernard 81, 123
Beir, Fred 59
Belafonte, Harry 306
Belford, Christine 124, 126
Bell, Dan 219, 312
Bell, Edward 111, 122, 125, 126, 155, 168
Bell, Jeannie 79
Bell, Marshall 289
Bell, Michael 62, 65, 215
Bellamy, Anne 69, 188, 214, 312
Bellamy, Diana 210
Bellamy, Ned 249
Bellamy, Paula 257
Beller, Miles 244, 327

Beller Airlines 35
"The Belles of St Mary's" 151
Belli, Melvin 211
Bellini, Cal 64, 106, 189
Bellisario, Donald 8, 11, 32, 33, 45, 51, 88, 89, 90, 91, 94, 95, 103, 104, 106, 113, 119, 127, 131, 144, 178, 179, 196, 228, 258, 296
Bellwood, Pamela 76
Belushi, John 269, 325
Bemis, Cliff 251
Ben Casey 43, 237
"The Bend in the River" 144, 150
Bender, Bob 125
Bendetti, Michael 248, 321
Benedict, Lawrence 123
"Beneath the Surface" 17, 154, 310
Benedek, Emily 198
Benedict, Amy 216
Benedict, Dirk 132, *133*, 135, 139, *142*, 145, 146
Benedict, Richard 215
Bening, Annette 287
Benjamin, Jeff 219
Benjamin, Julia Ann 67
Bennett, David 77
Benson 129
Benson, Jodi 220
Benson, Lucille 129
Bentley, Marc 68
Benton, Barbi 189
Benyaer, Michael 287
Berg, Peter 251
Berk, Howard 60
Berke, Lester 62, 70, 94
Berkeley, Xander 148, 151, 184, 293, 304
Berlin, Michael 212, 316
Berlinger, Warren 145, 153, 189
Bermel, Pat 256, 287
Bernard, Ed 160, 163, 166, 167
Bernard, Jason 125, 168, 186, 207, 292, 293, 316
Bernard, Joe 69
Bernbaum, Paul 145, 152, 155, 160, 177, 187, 188, 189, 235, 245, 249, 250, 251
Bernstein, Jack 23, 310, 312
Bernstein, Jay 8, 180
Bernstein, Nat 211
Berry, Al 69
Berry, Patricia 220
Berti, Dehl 106, 126
Besch, Bibi 64, 303
"Beseiged" 249
Besserman, Ira 211
Best, Kevin 214
"The Best Desk Scenario" 118, 123
"Best Three Out of Five" 92
"The Best Years of Your Life" 245, 251
Beswicke, Martine 80, 84
Betten, Mary 185
The Betty White Show 102
Betzler, Geri 250
The Beverly Hillbillies 173
"Beverly Hills Assault" 145, 152
Beverly Hills Buntz 198
Beverly Hills Cop 266

Beverly Hills Cop II 275
Beverly Hills, 90210 247
Bevis, Leslie 168, 215, 218, 235
Bewitched 17, 237
Bey, Markie 79
Beyer, Gary 250
Beyer, Troy 249, 311
Beyond Westworld 114
Bickel, Ray 150
Bickell, Ross 84
Bielak, Robert 213, 310, 312
Biener, Tom 215
Bieri, Ramon 57, 59, 210
Biesk, Adam 254
"Big Bad Charlie" 79
"The Big Cheese" 69
"A Big Disease with a Little Name" 250
"The Big Fall" 201, 209, 265
"The Big Hand's on Trouble" 72, 77
Big Hawaii 74
"The Big Rip-Off" 59
"The Big Squeeze" 151
"The Biggest Man in Town" 201, 209
Bilko 309
Billet, Don 61
Billingsley, Beau 155, 213
Billington, Michael 125, 128, 129
The Billionaire Boys' Club 277
Binns, Edward 50, 65
The Bionic Woman 52, 74, 118, 144
Bird, Billie 169, 214
Birdsong, Laurie 212
Birk, Raye 167, 213, 303
"The Birthday Present" 160, 167
"The Birthday Surprise" 262, 274, 287
Bishop, Donald 68
Bishop, Joey 166
Bishop, Patrick 215
Bisoglio, Val 59, 63, 75
Bissell, Whit 107
"A Bite of the Apple" 76
Bixby, Bill 297, 300, 302
"La Bizca" 255
B.J. and the Bear 3, 32
B.L. Stryker 325
"The Black Dahlia" 203, 214
"Black Day at Bad Rock" 144, 147
"Black Gold" 294
"Black Mirror" 67
Black Sheep Squadron 1, 3, 7, 8, 9, 16, 27, 33, 48, 71, **86–95,** *89,* 97, 99, 103, 106, 107, 111, 127, 132, 134, 145, 176, 181, 196, 283, 297, 313
"The Black Widow" 164
Blacke's Magic 296, 297
Blackman, Don 76
Blackmore, Stephanie 129, 209
Blackwood, Liam 324
Blade, Richard 212
Blair, Nicky 216
Blake, Geoffrey 218, 248
Blake, Noah 251
Blake, Robert 32, 35, 37, 40, 71, 72, 73, 75

Blake, Sondra 64, 75, 77, 112
Blakely, Susan 228
Blakeney, Eric 246, 251, 252, 253, 261, 262, 263, 268, 272, 273, 284, 287, 289, 321
Blanchard, Susan 57
Bland, Stephen 255
Blankenship, Norman 63
Blankfield, Mark 214
Blendick, James 105
Blessing, Jack 227, 229
"The Blimpy Who Yelled Blue" 297, 299, 303
Blincoe, Brendan 186
"Blind Ambition" 218
"Blind Justice" 312
"Blinded By the Thousand Points of Light" 253
"Blindsided" 249
Blissett, Julie 69
Bloch, Andrew 255
Block, Larry 76
Blocker, Dan 89
Blocker, Dirk 89, *89,* 91, 207, 213, 215, 254
Blomquist, Tom 18, 24, 25, 152, 154, 155, 158, 159, 161, 164, 165, 169, 177, 181, 182, 183, 185, 186, 187, 188, 189, 220, 227, 228, 230
"The Blood Bond" 77
"Blood Dance" 272, 289
Blood Feud 74
"Blood Line" 216
"Blood Money" 227
"Blood, Sweat and Cheers" 145, 152
Blood, Sweat and Tears 241
"The Bloodshot Eye" 85
Bloom, Anne 124
Bloom, Brian 253
Bloom, Lindsay 8
Blossom, Roberts 229
"Blow Up" 194, 199, 200, 210
Bludworth, Bill 294
"The Blue Flu" 252
Blue Steel 277
Blue Thunder 13, 40, 137, 140, 142, 179, 180, 221
Bluel, Richard 74, 79, 80, 81
"Blues for the Duke" 100
Bluethener, John 229
Blye, Margaret 68, 219
Blythe, Janus 79
Bob and Carol and Ted and Alice 116
Bochco, Steven 1, 3, 10, 54, 96, 97, 98, 101, 285, 298
Bochner, Lloyd 96, 98, 145, 152
"Body Slam" 153
Boeke, Jim 151, 154, 213
Boeke, Judy 208
Bogart, Humphrey 71, 96, 279, 334
Bogart, Paul 44
Bogert, William 23, 117, 122
"The Bogota Million" 214
Bohrer, Corinne 164, 191, 320
Bokar, Hal 93
Bolano, Tony 294
The Bold Ones 40, 52, 163, 237
Boles, Cliff 78

Bolger, John Michael 219
Bolger, Ray 81
Bolton, Jacques Apollo 254
Bonanza 45, 52, 89, 97, 127
Bond, James, III 112
Bond, Raleigh 229
Bond, Rudy 66, 81
Bonds, R.J. 189
Bongiorno, Frank 79
Boniface, Isabel 77
Bonnell, Vivian 209
Bonney, Gail 81
Bonnie and Clyde 50
Booke, Sorrell 67, 93
Booker 96, 102, 225, 247, **318, 319–320,** *320,* 329
"Boomerang" 214
Booth, James 80
Booth, Richard 85
Borchert, Rudolph 23, 26, 51, 60, 67, 68, 70, 112, 118, 121, 124, 125, 126, 159, 200, 201, 210
Borges, Jimmy 69
Borpujari, Shunil 126
Borycki, Martin 225
Bosson, Barbara 97, 98
Boston and Kilbride 35, 107, 179
Boston Herald 308
Boston Sunday Globe 326
Bostwick, Eugenia 229
Boswell, Charles 210, 219, 229, 250, 312
Bottoms, Sam 255
Boulware, Hugh 263
"Bounty" 145, 151
Bourne, Lindsay 230, 289
Bourrel, Marc 288
Bowen, Gary 229
Bowen, Michael 154, 253
Bower, Tom 63, 78, 168
Bowman, Chuck 32, 62, 112, 124, 125, 147, 172, 177, 188, 189, 228, 230
Bowman, Pamela 126
Bowman, Rob 229, 249, 311
"The Boxer" 164
Boxleitner, Bruce 77
Boy George 142, 154
Boy Meets World 271
Boyar, Sully 68
Boyd, Chris 256
Boyd, Jayeson 256
Boyer, Katy 254
Boyett, William (Bill) 61, 187
Boyington, Greg "Pappy" 27, 86, 87, 88
Boyle, Jim 167
Boyle, Michael 95
Boynton, Alexander 289
"Boz Busters" 187
Bozeman, Terry 215, 216, 288
Bozian, Jamie 249
Bracken, Eddie 293, 294
Brackett, Leigh 60
Bradbury, Lane 62, 107
Braden, David 281, 292
Bradford, William 50
Bradley, Wilbert 100
Bradshaw, Booker 64

Bradshaw, Randy 256
Bradshaw, Terry 167
Brady, Patrick 149, 167
Brady, Scott 53, 61, 64, 68
Bralver, Bob 32, 155, 168, 187, 189, 209, 210, 233, 303, 304
Brand, Neville 79
Brando, Marlon 261
Brandon, John 123, 165
Brandon, Michael 106
Brandt, Hank 67, 69, 216
Brandt, Victor 211
Brauner, Asher 216, 219
Braunstein, Alan 112
Braverman, Bart 182, 186, 250
Bray, Thom 14, *14,* 175, *176,* 177, 181, 182, 184
Brazeau, Jay 251
Brazelton, Connie Marie 289
Breaking Away 177
"Breakout" 145, 151
Breen, Patrick 249
Breen, Richard 210
Bremner, Scott 256
Brenahan, Tom 250
Brennan, Walter 296
Brescia, Deprise 331
Bret Maverick 46, 51, 57, 200
Brett, Delia 256
Brewster, Niles 248
Brewton, Maia 252
Brezany, Eugene 125
The Brian Keith Show 162
Brickell, Beth 104
Brinckerhoff, Burt 77, 79, 80
Bring 'Em Back Alive 127
Bringelson, Mark 218
Britos, Lenno 256
Britt, Melendy 64
Britt, Ruth 216
Broadcast 136, 141
Broadwater, Cynthia 179
Brocco, Peter 61, 67, 69, 111
Brock, Phil 209
Brock, Stanley 68, 69, 80, 98, 112, 123, 154, 167, 213
Brocksmith, Roy 214, 303, 312
Broken Badges 107, **321–322**, *322*
"Broken Dreams" 218
Brolin, Josh 247, 249
Bronder, William 78, 84, 104, 187, 213, 287
Bronson, Charles 10
The Bronx Zoo 299, 320
Brooke, Jill 247
Brooke, Paula 248
Brooke, Walter 58, 64, 65, 69, 169
Brooks, Cindy 220
Brooks, Claude 253
Brooks, Elizabeth 68
Brooks, Geraldine 78
Brooks, James 237, 238, 239
Brooks, Joel 189, 217
Brooks, Laurelle 216
Brooks, Martin E. 201, 207, 213
Brooks, Mel 233
Brooks, Randi 5, 126, 165, 172, 174, 184, 214, 232, *232,* 235, 252
Brooks, Richard (actor) 312

Brooks, Richard (director) 71
Brooks Swope, Tracy 81, 150, 166
Brose, Richard 235
"Brother, Can You Spare a Crime" 161, 168
"Brother Hanson and the Miracle of Renner's Pond" 251
"Brotherly Love" 217
"Brothers" 256
Brothers in Law 190, *190,* 224, 320
Brough, Candi and Randi 190
Brough, Walter, 219
Brown, Blair 61
Brown, Christopher T. 253
Brown, David 216
Brown, Dwier 312
Brown, Georg Stanford 112, 123, 164, 172, 174
Brown, Henry 216
Brown, Jeb 217
Brown, Jim 155, 257
Brown, Kathie 61
Brown, Kendall Carly 112
Brown, Lew 105
Brown, Peter 155, 186, 216
Brown, Reb 61
Browne, Robert Alan 124, 129
Browne, Roscoe Lee 106
Browning, Norman 292
Browning, Rod 68, 78
Brubaker, Tony 148
Bruce, Ed 57
Brucker, Jane 288
Bruhanski, Alex 256, 288, 290, 291, 292, 316
Brull, Pamela 112, 209
"Brummp-Bump" 294
Brundin, Bo 125, 155
Brunetti, Argentina 111
Bryant, Joshua 64, 84, 149, 184, 303
Bryant, Lee 84, 187
Bryant, Todd 251
Bryant, William 61
Buck, George 254
Buck James 103
Buck Rogers (comic strip) 127
Buck Rogers in the 25th Century 115, 333
Buckman, Tara 104
Bucksey, Colin 294
Budd, Ken 291
"Buddy" 80
"The Buddy System" 256
Buffalo Bill 170
Buffalo Bill and the Indians 45
Bugs Bunny 308
Bukowski, Rhonda 287
Buktenika, Ray 166
"Bullets and Bikinis" 144, 150
Bullitt 49, 71, 101, 146
Bullock, Earl 168
Bumatai, Andy 189, 333
Bumstead, J.P. 95, 124, 210, 311
Bunch, Chris 29, 36, 37, 56, 139, 149, 207, 224, 225
Bunch, Marianne 67
"The Bundle" 81
Bundy, Brooke 218

Burchard, Petrea 217
Burden, Alec 256, 316
Burden, Martin 243
Burghardt, Arthur 164
Burke, Alan 289
Burke, Chris 267
Burke, David 24, 25, 262, 268, 269, 271, 272, 275, 276, 277, 278, 279, 280, 281, 282, 283, 286, 287, 288, 289, 290, 291, 292, 293, 313, 316
Burke, Joseph 154
Burke, Mark 167
Burke, Ron 84
Burkely, Dennis 32, 63, 68, 81, 112, 123, 174, 189, 190
Burke's Law 3, 38, 297, 316
Burkholder, Scott 219
"Burn Out" 316
"Burned" 159, 201, 210, 310
Burnett, Mary Nancy 66, 68
Burnett, Olivia 188
Burns, Allan 237
Burns, Bart 76, 112
Burns, James 28
Burns, Jere 187, 235
Burns, Judy 227, 228, 230
Burr, Fritzi 62, 69, 76, 129
Burr, Raymond 106, 114, 297
Burroughs, Bonnie 220
Burrows, James 276
Burton, LeVar 132
Burton, Norman 59, 92, 104
Burton, Tim 199
Burton, Tony 65, 77, 111, 123, 149
Busey, Gary 74, 76
Bush, Grand L. 211, 213, 214, 219
Bush, Owen 212
Bushwick, Sam 254
"Business as Usual" 255
Bustin' 71
"But Can She Type?" 103, 104
Butch and Sundance: The Early Years 114
Butch Cassidy and the Sundance Kid 40
Butkus, Dick 62, 125
Butler, Eugene 184, 216
Butler, Lucy 215
Butler, Michael 74, 75, 76, 77
Buxton, Sarah G. 249
Byrge, Duane 199
Byrne, Erica 166, 204, 211
Byrnes, Jim 266, *267,* 268, 286, 287

"Cactus Jack's Last Call" 301, 303
Caddyshack 143
Cadiente, David 69
Cadillac Man 275
Caesar, Harry 76
Cage, Nicolas 241
Cagney, James 260, 261, 266, 334
Cagney and Lacey 9, 17, 53, 96, 102, 137, 158, 180, 181, 183, 193, 201, 264, 318, 326
Cahill, Barry 85, 94
Caine, Howard 188
Caine, Michael 222

Cain's Hundred 156
Caitlyn, Deryl 256
Calcote, Carolyn 67
Calderone, Sergio 147, 150
Caldwell, L. Scott 217
"Caledonia, It's Worth a Fortune" 59
Calfa, Don 77, 235
Calhoun, William 291
Cali, Joseph 208, 312
"Call It Casaba" 9, 266, 280, 291
Callahan 128
Callahan, Greg 253
Callahan, James 64, 95, 151
Callan 222
Callan, K. 209, 217
Callan, Michael 164, 169
Callen, Cecile 219
Calomee, Gloria 69
Calvert, Bill 230
Calvert, Jim 254
Calvin, John 64, 145, 151, 167, 209
Camacho Michaels, Corinne 59
Cameron, Patrick 129
Cameron, Rod 62
Campanella, Frank 60, 61, 62, 210, 216
Campanella, Joseph 40, 62, 252
Campanella, Roy, II 290, 311, 312
Campbell, Catherine 124
Campbell, Clifton 245, 248, 249, 250, 251, 252, 280, 282, 291, 292, 293
Campbell, J. Kenneth 94
Campbell, Karen 293
Campbell, Scott Allan 251
Campos, Victor 153, 214
Camroux, Ken 256
Canavan, Michael 215
Cannell, Stephen J.: acting 112, 310–311, 324, 330, 331; actors 31–32, 37, 300; call sheet 21; Canada (move to) 223–226; catch-phrases 34–35, 72, 179, 194; censorship 28–31, 139, 141, 244, 247; content 3–31, 48, 49, 72–74, 82, 86, 97, 101–103, 109, 120–121, 131–132, 134–146, 156, 161–162, 170–172, 175–176, 178–179, 180–183, 191, 221, 227, 259, 332, 333; critics 6, 7, 12–16, 18, 23, 83, 106, 110, 136, 138, 139, 162, 175, 179–180, 190, 192–193, 200, 202, 223, 231, 240–241, 244, 260, 261, 263, 264, 265, 273, 277, 279, 285–286, 298, 305, 306, 313–314, 318–320, 323, 326, 327, 329, 333; demographics 4, 14; directors 31–32; dress/clothing 9, 22, 23; dyslexia 33; early career 37–38, 39–41; episodes directed by 22, 55–56, 64, 67, 69, 104, 112; episodes written by (discussed) 9, 11, 13, 20, 22, 23, 24, 25, 27, 27–28, 30, 35, 52, 55–56, 72, 73, 86–87, 91, 96, 97, 101–102, 103, 106–108, 109, 110, 113–114, 118, 119, 120, 121, 122, 134, 142, 143, 144, 157–158, 158, 159–160, 161–162, 170–172, 181–182, 182, 183, 190–191, 196–197, 227–228, 233, 258–259, 262, 263, 269, 275, 283–286, 295, 296, 297, 298–299, 301, 305, 308, 308–309, 310, 313–314, 317, 318–320, 320–321, 321–322, 323, 324, 325–326, 326–327, 329, 332, 334; episodes written by (titles of) 58, 59, 60, 61, 62, 63, 64, 66, 67, 68, 69, 75, 84, 85, 91, 92, 93, 94, 98, 100, 104, 105, 106–108, 111, 112, 122, 123, 124, 125, 126, 130, 147, 148, 150, 151, 152, 153, 154, 163, 164, 166, 167, 173, 184, 185, 186, 188, 207, 228, 229, 230, 235, 287, 288, 289, 294, 302, 303, 311, 312, 316; finance 4, 37, 110, 121, 224, 318; friendship 14, 19, 181, 191, 194–195, 261, 262–263; in-jokes 35, 102, 145, 183, 301, 308; method 3–10, 10–31, 32–37, 48, 49, 51, 101–103, 118, 120–121, 131–133, 134–135, 162, 170–172, 179, 180–183, 194, 300, 301, 333; politics 6, 7–9, 10–16, 22–31, 38, 48, 49, 72–74, 90, 101–103, 131–132, 134–135, 156–159; quotes 4–6, 13, 17, 20, 28, 33, 34, 35, 46, 50, 51, 87, 109, 110, 138, 140, 181, 199–200, 221, 223, 224–225, 232, 260, 262, 263, 264, 265, 266, 268, 314, 320, 321, 326, 331, 332; repetition 35–37, 159–160, 301, 310, 333; satirical targets 16, 20–21, 22–31, 48, 72–73, 103, 159; sexual politics 13–19, 21–22, 30–31, 103, 132–133, 138, 180, 181, 194–195, 203–204; starting own company 110, 131; vigilantism 1, 10–13, 22, 23, 29–31, 73–74, 101, 103, 131–132, 137, 141, 156–159, 190, 192, 194, 203–204; villains 17, 20–21, 22, 23, 27, 29–31, 51, 72–73, 159, 190, 297–298; violence on TV 1, 97, 137–141, 190, 194, 195, 203–204, 261–263, 308–309, 313–316; women (presentation of) 14–17, 18, 18–19, 21–22, 31, 91, 103, 132–133, 180, 181, 203–204; writers 31–32
Cannon 74
Cannon, J.D. 49, 102
Cannon, Katherine 91, 187, 212, 219
Cannon, Vince 93
Cannonball Run II 195
"Can't Win for Losin'" 78
Cantero, George 80
"The Capelli Oath" 74, 75
Capers, Virginia 316
Capital News 26, 271
Capizzi, Bill 111, 112, 208
Capodice, John 219
Capone, Al 20
Capozzla, Tony 219
Capra, Frank 10
Capra, Jordana 305, 311
Capri, Anna 77
Captain America (pilot) 114
"Captain Bellybuster and the Speed Factory" 35, 125
Captain Nice 118
Captain Power 133
Carafotes, Paul 126
Carbone, Anthony 63, 105, 191
Cardea, Frank 127
"The Career Breaker" 159, 167
Carey, Clare 311
Carey, George 84
Carey, Timothy 75, 79, 123, 126
Caridi, Carmine 69, 219, 230, 250
Carillo, Elpidia, 255
"Carla" 79
Carlin, Lynn 84, 112
Carlisi, Christina 219
Carlo, East Ismael 80, 148, 151, 152, 184, 211, 219
Carlson, Jim 172, 174, 187
Carlson, Leslie 256
Carnell, Cliff 66
Carney, Art 46
Carney, Fred 65, 69
"The Carnival That Ate Sladetown" 173
Carpenter, Pete 106, 145, 172, 183, 198
Carr, Darleen 57, 85, 188
Carr, Paul 60, 67, 168
Carrarra, Don 76
Carrasco, Carlos 218
Carrere, Tia 154
Carrero, Tony 214
Carrie 114
Carrier, Albert 68
Carroll, Christopher 216
Carroll, Corinne 215
Carroll, David James 69
Carroll, James 229
Carroll, Janet 250
Carroll, Janice 63, 92
Carroll, Jill 253, 303, 312
Carroll, Larry 211
Carroll, Victoria 213
Carrott, Ric 66
Carry, Julius, III 153, 312
Carson, Tom 6, 7, 12, 139
Carter, Alan 270
Carter, Bill 273
Carter, Conlan 126
Carter, Dixie 125
Carter, Jack 64
Carter, John 59, 147, 151, 155, 166, 215, 229
Carter, Les 80, 81
Carter, Lynda 329
Carter, Mel 211
Carter, Thomas 207
Caruso, Anthony 81, 210
Caruso, Mickey 62
Carvalho, Betty 215
Carver, Mary 64
Cary, Christopher 65, 69, 189
Casablanca (television series) 313
Casadas, Eloy 213
"Case X" 23, 144, 200, 209
Casey, Bernie 217

Casey, Lawrence 66
Casey, Paul 77
Cash, Rosalind 187
Cash, Susan 213
Casper, Robert 111
Cass, Dave 69, 85, 125
Cassidy, Alan 168, 172, 187, 310, 327
Castillo, Gerald 216
"The Castle of Dreams" 85
"The Castro Connection" 211
CAT Squad 141
Catalano, George 288
"Catch a Fallen Star" 182, 185
"Catch of the Day" 26, 160, 182, 186
Cates, Leah 129
"The Cat's Whiskers" 92
Cattrall, Kim 107
Caulfield, Joan 79
Cavadas, Andrew 303
Cavenaugh, Michael 70, 105, 144, 150, 174, 201, 207
Cavenaugh, Nick 187
Cavonis, Paul 65, 123
CBS 37, 50, 53, 88, 102, 114, 121, 137, 163, 173, 178, 183, 197, 221, 237, 238, 239, 260, 264, 268, 301, 324, 325, 327, 328
Cedar, Jon 125, 166
Cedar, Larry 254
Celebrity Cop 101
Celozzi, Nik 150
Centano, Jose 79
Centennial 99, 103, 145, 162
Cervantes, Carlos 155, 210, 228, 249
Cervantes, Don 117, 122
Cervera, Jorge, Jr. 105
Cerveris, Michael 256
Cervi, Bruce 149
Chacon, Bobby 80
Chadwick, June 34, 152, 177, 178, 184
Chaffey, Don 211, 229
Chalk, Garry 289
Challenger, Rudy 59
Chambers, Everett 296
Chambers, Lossen 251
Chambers, Steve 148
"Champ" 151
"Champagne High" 251
Champion, Michael 188, 217, 252
Chan, Mike 79
Chandler, Alan 155
Chandler, Dave Ray 92
Chandler, John 210
Chandler, Raymond 44, 55, 96, 118
Chang, Stephen 230
"Change of Heart" 254
"Change Partners and Dance" 211
"Changing Houses" 294
Chao, Rosalind 155, 189, 230
Chapel, Loyita 125
"Chapel of Glass" 189
"Chapel of Love" 9, 246, 250
Chaplin, Sydney 79
Chapman, Andi 219, 316
Chapman, Joseph 123, 187, 211

Chapman, Judith 230
Chapman, Lonny 98, 155, 189, 230
Chapman, Thomas 214
Chappell, John 64
Charbonneau, Patricia 278, 279, 290, 313, 316
Charles, Gloria 153
Charles, Katherine 63
Charles, Keith 167
Charleson, Kate 188, 229
Charleson, Leslie 64, 93
Charlie Chan 295
"Charlie Harris at Large" 15, 60
Charlie's Angels 16, 26, 74, 91, 193, 238, 306, 316
Charney, Jordan 209
Charney, Suzanne 62
Charnota, Anthony 32, 64, 92, 122, 125, 126, 144, 149, 185, 208, 233, 235, 312
Chartoff, Melanie 288, 289
Chase 37, 231, 313, 318
Chase, Anzanette 61
Chase, David 20, 24, 26, 32, 35, 36, **51**, 53, 54, 62, 63, 64, 65, 66, 67, 68, 69, 160, 258, 333, 334
Chase, Lauren 149
Chastain, Don 66
Chau, Francois 292
Chauvin, Lilyan 93
Chayette, Jeff 217
Chayevsky, Paddy 50
"Cheap n' Chili" 310, 312, 327
Cheatham, Marie 212
Cheek, Molly 165, 168
Cheers 71, 119, 137, 194, 195, 197, 226, 238, 264, 282
Chehak, Tom 206, 215, 216
Chen, Joan 290
Cherokee Productions 43, 56, 57, 106
Chesire, Elizabeth 77
Chesley, Howard 204, 211, 212
Chester, Colby 104
Cheung, George Kee 67, 93, 154, 189, 292
Cheyenne 39, 43
Chicago Story 163, 198, 242
Chicago Sun-Times 261, 263, 265
"A Chicken in Every Plot" 124
"Chicken Little Is a Little Chicken" 54, 61
Chico and the Man 53
Chiklis, Michael 269, 291, 292, 325, *325*, 326
"A Child Is Born" 212
"Children of Jamestown" 138, 142, 147
Chiles, Linden 58, 155
Chin, Marilyn 288
China Beach 9, 90, 264, 278, 283, 313
Chinatown 46, 82
"The Chinese Typewriter" 107
Chinn, Ann 61
"A Chip Off the Old Milt" 169
CHiPs 32

Chodos, Daniel 125, 208, 209, 215, 218, 220
The Choirboys 101, 108, 177
Chopper One 132
"Chopping Spree" 149
Chow, David 112
Choy, Brock 294
Christi, Frank R. 81
Christian, Claudia 152, 185, 211, 312
Christian, Leigh 69, 213
Christian, Victoria 216
Christie, Agatha 297
Christie, Dick 219
Christie, Frank 75
Christie, Shannon 78
Christmas, Eric 287, 288, 297, 303
"Christmas in Saigon" 243, 250
Christopher, Dennis 230
Christopher, Guy 312
Christopher, Thom 210
Chromchak, Rudy 148
Chubbuk, Lyndon 230, 262, 287, 299, 303
Chula, Babs 287
Chung, Byron 67, 91, 93, 94
Chung, Esmond 69
Church, Elaine 287
Churchill, Candus 257
Ciccone, Steffania 251, 287
Ciccone, Tony 185
Cimmaron City 52
Cinardo, Nick 124
Cincinnati Enquirer 263
Cintron, Sharon 75, 81
Cioffi, Charles 144, 147
Ciral, Karen 78
"The Circle Broken" 24, 296, 303
The Cisco Kid (character) 12
The Cisco Kid (television series) 334
City Court 239, 318
City of Angels 9, 27, 46, 54, **82–85**, 88, 96, 97, 103, 106, 132, 158, 176
"City of Passion" 201, 203, 204, 213
"City Under Siege" 30, 145, 216
Civil Wars 35
"Claire" 60
Clanton, Rony 213
Claridge, Christie 152, 208, 209, 212
Clark, Blake 124
Clark, Brett 208, 214
Clark, Candy 211
Clark, Carolyn Ann 228
Clark, Damon 155
Clark, Gloryette 59, 76, 84, 85, 184
Clark, Joe 125
Clark, Louise Clair 168, 230
Clark, Matt 167
Clark, Michael 80
Clark, Robert 92
Clarke, Angela 79, 81
Clarke, Carolyn 213
Clarke, Gary 154
Clarkson, Lana 151, 185
Clarkson, Marianne 25, 158, 159,

162, 166, 167, 168, 169, 201, 211, 212, 213
"Classical Gas" 25, 118, 119, 123, 175
Clay, Charlotte 212, 213
Clayburgh, Jill 59
"Clean Slate" 316
Cleatton, Stephannia 308
Clemenson, Christian 251
Clements, Calvin 27
Clements, Stanley 77
Cliffhangers 196
Clifton, George 66, 187
Clooney, George 185, 212
Clooney, Rosemary 168
Close Encounters of the Third Kind 113
Clotworthy, Robert 66, 92, 104, 216, 217
Clover, David 185
"Coach of the Year" 251
Cobb, Randall "Tex" 167
Cobb, Vincent 62
Cobra 329
Coburn, David 253, 311
Coburn, James 50, 65, 328
Coca, Richard 210, 251
Coccioletti, Phillip 208
Cochran, Robert 326
Cochran, Wayne 100
"Code Three" 216
Codename: Foxfire 17, 137, 180
Cody, Kathleen 174
Coffin, Frederick 213
Coghill, Joy 257
Cohen, Larry 297
Cohn, Mindy 248, 250
Coit, Stephen 78
Colasanto, Nicolas 71, 76
Colbert, Robert 201, 207, 213, 215
Colbin, Rod 123, 124, 129, 149
Cold Steel 266
"Cold Streak" 174
Cole, Allan 29, 36, 37, 56, 139, 207, 224, 225
Cole, Dallas 210
Cole, Danny Lee 124, 126, 142, 149, 150, 153, 154
Cole, Dennis 152
Cole, Gary 273
Cole, Kay 216
Cole, Norman 76, 80
Coleman, Ann 75
Colitti, Tony 251
Colla, Richard 30, 166, 198, 203, 208, 209, 228
Collentine, Barbara 216
Colley, Don Pedro 112, 150
Collier, Richard 78
Colligan, Joe 150, 207
Collins, Burton 100
Collins, Greg 151, 220, 311
Collins, Jack 64, 66, 68
Collins, Joan 77
Collins, Patrick 125, 165, 166, 182, 185
Collins, Paul 216
Collins, Roberta 59
Collura, Steve Allen 81, 186

Colman, Booth 85, 93, 191
Colodner, Joel 228, 250
Colomby, Scott 78, 94, 153, 216
Colon, Alex 154, 220
Colt .45 39, 99, 232
Columbia 40
Columbo 7, 35, 39, 44, 53, 72, 96, 101, 104, 116, 133, 296, 297, 298, 299, 300, 301, 318, 329
Colvin, Jack 62, 76, 85, 210
Combs, David 218
Combs, Jeffrey 219
"Come from the Shadows" 253
Comer, Anjanette 78
Command Five 141
The Commish 269, 273, **325–326**, 325, 327, 328, 329, 331
The Company 278
"The Competitive Edge" 23, 66
Complete Directory to Prime-Time Network TV Shows 231
Compton, Richard 164
Compton, Sharon 63
Conaway, Jeff 228, 230
Conde, Eddie 80
Conde, Rita 80
"Conflict of Interest" (*Miami Vice* ep.) 278
"Conflict of Interest" (*Riptide* ep.) 35, 181, 183, 184
Conforti, Gino 189
Conlon, Noel 92
Conn, Eileen 254
Conn, Kelly Ann 186
Connell, John Kirk 256
Connors, Chuck 103, 104
Conrad, Michael 31, 61
Conrad, Nancy 89, 91
Conrad, Robert 28, 86, 87, 88, 89, 89, 90, 91, 94, 99, 100, 104, 297, 299, 303
Conroy, Erin 217
Considine, John 69, 153, 168
Constantine, Michael 215
Contner, James 251, 252, 253, 290, 291, 293, 316
"The Contract" 212
"Conventional Warfare" 161, 162, 168
The Conversation 46
Converse, Frank 94
Conway, Bert 112
Conway, Blake 155
Conway, James L. 168, 211
Conwell, Patricia 99, 100, 104
Coogan, Keith 254
Coogan's Bluff 49, 101, 192
Cook, Carole 75, 153
Cook, Doria 61
Cook, Elisha 78, 79, 153
Cook, Larry 61, 65
Cook, Perry 201, 207
Cook, Roderick 311
Cook, T.S. 77
Cooke, Alan 311
Cooksey, Danny 189
Cool Million 40, 52
Cooper, Cami 251
Cooper, Charles 61, 165, 186

Cooper, Jackie 59, 60, 62, 66, 92, 93, 97
Cooper, Jeff 124
"Cop" 177
Cop Rock 97
Copland, Rhonda 63
Copley, Teri 220
"Coppin' Out" 257
Copping, Jennifer 255, 257
Corbett, Glenn 68
Corbett, Gretchen 15, 48, 58, 308, 218, 250
Corbin, Barry 154
Corcoran, Bill 245, 246, 249, 250, 251, 252, 262, 274, 275, 288, 290, 291, 292, 298, 303, 316
Cordic, Regis 60
Coree, Nick 317
Corey, Jeff 71, 155
Corkum, Bruce 257
Corley, Pat 35, 167, 301, 303
Corman, Roger 259
Cornelison, Michael 108, 124, 167, 208
Cornell, Lydia 153, 212
Corrado, Gus 188
Correll, Charles 262, 287
Corso, John 83
Cort, Bill 188
Cortese, Dan 329
Cortese, Joe 190, *190,* 210, 224
"Cory and Dean Got Married" 255
Corzatte, Clayton 289
Cosby, Bill 37, 46, 116, 300
The Cosby Show 137, 234, 242, 286, 310, 333
Costanzo, Robert 81, 208, 250
Costello, Anthony 63
Costello, Ward 98
Coster, Nicolas 67, 81, 112, 164, 216
Cothran, John, Jr. 294
Cotler, Stephen 30, 201, 209
Cotten, Joseph 59
The Cotton Club 306
Coulson, Bernie 287
"Coulter City Wildcat" 63
"Count the Days I'm Gone" 77
"Counter Gambit" 60
"The Countess" 58
Courtney, Alexander 77, 211
Coutelier, Mimi 212
Covan, De Forest 78
Cover Up 17, 137, 140, 160, 221, 299
"Cowboy George" 153
The Cowboys 52, 127
Cox, Joshua 252
Cox, Richard 69, 76, 104, 213
Cox News Service 323
Cozart, Cylk 217
Crabtree, Michael 148
"Crack Back" 64, 197
"The Cradle Will Rock" 212
Crais, Robert 74, 80, 81
Crane, Barry 172, 174
Crane, Peter 219, 220
Cranshaw, Patrick 211
Crawford, Broderick 12, 84
Crawford, Ellen 185
Crawford, John 60, 168

"Crazy Annie" 78
Crazy Like a Fox 48, 127, 265
Crazy Tommy Todesco 35
Credel, Curtis 92
Crenna, Richard 66
"Cries of Silence" 220
"Crime of Passion" 211
"Crime School" 164
Crime Story 120, 137, 198, 200, 203, 207, 271, 275, 278, 280, 282, 283, 301, 313
"Crimes Below the Waist" 309, 311
Critchlow, Brenda 257
Critchlow, Roark 257
Crittenden, James 94, 167, 209
Crocker, James 65, 66, 93, 94
Crockett, Karlene 167
Crombie, Jonathan 257
Cromwell, Gloria 219
Cromwell, James 167, 187, 209, *232*, 235
Crone, Chris 312
Cronin, Patrick 249, 302
Crook, Peter 215
Crosby, Cathy Lee 165
Crosby, Denise 219
Crosby, Gary 65, 68, 200, 207
Cross, Bill 210
Cross, Murphy 185
"Crossfire" (*Hunter* ep.) 213
"Crossfire" (*21, Jump Street* ep.) 257
Crowe, Christopher 79
Crowley, Patricia 68
Crudup, Carl 78
Cruikshanks, Reid 150
The Crusader 162
Cruz, Raymond 219
Cry Baby 241, 273
"Cry Wolf" 227
"The Crystal Duck" 158, 159, 164
"The Crystal Skull" 155
CSI (franchise) 315
Cudlitz, Michael 257
Culea, Melinda 16, 132, *133, 142,* 146
Cullison, Barry 100
Culliton, Patrick 69
Culp, Janisha 257
Culp, Jason 126
Culp, Joseph 126
Culp, Robert 2, 7, 16, 23, 29, 34, 37, 46, 48, 113, *115,* 115–116, 117, 119, 121, 122, 125, 126, 162, 165, 190, 224, 296, 318, 333
Culver, Carol 209
Cumbuka, Ji-Tu 129, 152, 153, 186, 210, 213
Cummings, Quinn 81
Cummings, Richard, Jr. 253
Cummins, Eli 184
Cummins, Gregory Scott 217
Cummins, Martin 257
Cunningham, Cavan 293
Cunningham, Sarah 75
"A Cup of Joe" 35, 151
Curcio, Grace 33, 104
Curran, David 281, 292
Curran, Will 211
"The Currency We Trade In" 251

Curry, Anne 211
Curry, Christopher 219
Curry, Russell 217
Curry, Tim 25, 279, 291
"Curse of the Mary Aberdeen" 186
"Curtain Call" 150
Curtin, Robert 228
Curtin, Valerie 24, 65
Curtis, Howard 60
Curtis, Keene 76
Curtis, Kelly 220
Curtis, Liane 249
Cutler, Barry 123
Cutler, Brian 67
Cutrona, Ryan 219
Cutter, Lise 254
Cutter to Houston 173
Cypher, Charles 130, 251
Cypher, Jon 64, 124, 214
Czuma, Merek 248

The D.A. 88, 99
The D.A.: Murder One 90
"Daddy Dearest" 316
Daggett, Jensen 255
D'Agnese, Joe 306
Daheim, John 61
Dahl, Arlene 330
Daily Mail 20
Dakota, Tony 248
Dale, Tony 148
Dalen, Zale 257, 262, 287, 301, 303
Daley, Kathryn 167
Dallas 88, 121, 129, 156, 173, 194, 197, 221, 234, 242, 295, 298, 302
Dallenbach, Walter 62, 63
Dallesandro, Joe 260, 287, 288, 324
Dalton, Abby 168, 330
Dalton, Tyne 193
Daly, Michael 310, 311
Daly, Tyne 193
Damante, Susan 59
D'Ambrosio, Vito 289
Dandridge, Frank 214
Dandridge, Roy 76
Danese, Shera 79
Daniels, William 53, 62, 63, 107
Danilov, Raisa 153
Dannes, Nanette 78
Dano, Linda 63
Danova, Cesare 212
Danson, Ted 206
Danton, Ray 61
D'Arbanville, Patti 279, 280, 287, 291, 292
Darby, Kim 76, 182, 188
D'Arcy, Jan 257
Darden, Severn 84
Daredevils 179
"The Dark and Bloody Ground" 54, 58
Dark Shadows 107, 281
Darlo, Patrika 184
Darlow, Linda 248, 249, 251, 252
Darnell, Robert 154
Darren, Anthony 230
Darren, James 93, 155, 201, 212, 213, 214, 217, 219, 220, 230

Darrow, Henry 77
"Daryl Ross and the Supremes" 177
"Date with an Angel" 273, 289
Datillo, Kristen 255
Dau, Brigitta 256
Dauber, Lewis 189
Davalos, Dick 62
Davalos, Elyssa 185
Davey, John 68, 69
Davi, Robert 145, 151, 172, 173, 177, 195, 209, 279, 280, 284, 291, 292
Davi, Sean Christien 291, 292
David, Jeff 63
David, Thayer 60
Davidson, Eileen 322, *322*
Davidson, Jean 100
Davidson, Lewis 73, 78
Davies, Jackson 253, 288, 304, 316
Davies, Michael 256
Davies, Stephen 78
Davis, Anthony 125
Davis, Brad 79
Davis, Carole 151
Davis, Daniel 153, 169
Davis, Dawn 100
Davis, Don S. 257, 290, 316
Davis, Duane 252
Davis, Eugene 67
Davis, Gary Lee 151, 166, 167, 215
Davis, Geena 15, 19, 185
Davis, Gene 70
Davis, J. Warren 185
Davis, Jackson 249
Davis, Mac 190, *190,* 224
Davis, Nathan 272, 284, 287, 288, 311
Davis, Roger 58
Davis, Sammy, Sr. 72, 198, 216, 277
Davis, Susan 65
Davis, William B. 257, 288, 292
Davison, Bruce 48, 200, 207
Davy Crockett 133
Dawson, Gordon 23, 30, 51, 54, 57, 61, 62, 64, 65, 66, 67, 68, 93, 103, 104, 112, 160
Dawson, Ted 125
Day, Doris 39
"Day Four" 10, 292
Day George, Linda 166
"Day Nine" 10, 293
"Day One" 10, 292
"Day Seven" 10, 292
"The Day the Music Died" 161, 169
Dayton, Danny 98
"Dead Dog Lives" 290
Dead End Brattigan 317, *317*
"Dead Man Out" 77
"Dead Men Don't Floss" 189
"Dead on Target" 215
"Dead or Alive" 30, 208
"Dead Right" 294
"The Deadliest Enemy of All" 93
"Deadlock" 70
"Deadly Encounters" 219
"Deadly Manoeuvres" 30, 144, 150
"The Deadly Maze" 24, 66

"A Deal's a Deal" 261, 262, 284, 287
Dean, Jimmy 298, 300, 301, 302
Dean, Ron 100, 289
Dean Ryan, Lisa 256
Deane, Lezlie 213, 249
Dear Detective 178
"Dear Tony" 78
"Death and Taxes" 31
Death Before Dishonor 195
"Death Lends a Hand" 116
"The Death Machine" 199, 210
"Death on the Run" 77
"Death Run" 103, 104
"Death Signs" 203, 214, 266
Death Wish 10, 222
De Benning, Burr 60, 185
De Broux, Lee 75, 167
De Bruin, Sandra 185
De Camp, Rosemary 61
Dectar, Edward 160, 182, 185
Deen, Nedra 59
"The Deep Blue Sleep" 15, 20, 61
"Deep Sleeper" 104
Deepstar Six 322
The Deer Hunter 136
Dees, Rick 126
De Fonte, Anthony 311
De Garr, Blanca 311
De Guere, Phil 8, 12, 27, 32, 33, 48, 51, 73, 75, 76, 82, 84, 85, 88, 92, 93, 102, 104, 178, 258
Dehner, John 63, 167
Dein, Edward 94
De Kova, Frank 65, 81
De Lancie, John 108
Delano, Diane 215
Delano, Lee 67, 81
Delano, Michael 151, 152, 165, 172, 174, 207, 214, 233, 235, 311
Delany, Pat 60
Delegall, Bob 167
Delfin, Kimberly 215
Delgado, Luis 53, 57, 58
De Lisle, Christine 150
Deliverance 36
Dell, Charlie 166, 185
Dellasorte, Joe 59, 66
De Loy, George 211
De Luise, David 220, 256
De Luise, Dom 243, 252
De Luise, Michael 248, 252, 321
De Luise, Peter *240*, 243, 244, 245, 246, 247, 248, 254, 256, 257, 321
Denesky, George 215
De Niro, Robert 261
Denison, Anthony 37, 278, 282, 290
Denison, Robert 208
Dennehy, Brian 194, 196, 207
Dennis, Alfred 155, 208, 215
Dennis, Ron 81
Dent, Frank 229
Denton, Lisa 151, 188
Denver Weekly News 245
De Palma, Brian 114, 268, 284, 309
Depp, Johnny 238, 239, *240*, 241,
242, 243, 245, 246, 247, 248, 264, 273, 320, 321
De Sales, Francis 84
De Salvo, Anne 280, 291, 292
Desautels, Gilbert 252
Des Barres, Michael 69, 253, 304
Desiderio, Robert 145, 151, 164, 167, 184, 209
Desilu 37
"Desperado" 121, 126
Destination: America 191, 224
Destrey, John 255
The Detectives 231
"The Deuce" 68
"Deuces Wild" 310, 312
De Venney, Scott 189
"The Devil and the Deep Blue Sea" 124, 175
"Devil in the Slot" 93
De Vito, Danny 268
Devlin, Dean 168
The Devlin Connection 196, 327
De Windt, Sheila 81, 154
De Winter, Joanna 98, 312
"The Dexter Crisis" 59
Dey, Susan 114
De Zarn, Tim 216
Diagnosis: Murder 281
Diamond, Don 66
"Diamonds and Dust" 148
"Diamonds Are for Never" (*Riptide* ep.) 182, 184
"Diamonds Aren't Forever" (*Sonny Spoon* ep.) 21, 310, 312
"Diamonds Aren't Forever" (*Tenspeed and Brownshoe* ep.) 112
Di Angelo, Richard 79
Di Aquino, John 249
Diaz, Edith 79, 220
Di Cenzo, George 59, 75
Di Cicco, Bobby 155
The Dick Van Dyke Show 116
Dickerson, Beach 126
Dickerson, George 126, 212
Dickinson, Angie 102
"Did You See the One That Got Away?" 159, 165
Die Hard 259
Die Hard II 274
Dien, Edward 93
"A Different Drummer" 23, 68, 159
A Different World 300
Diff'rent Strokes 172, 173, 239, 243, 283
Di Fusco, John 123
Diller, Barry 239
Dimitri, Nick 63, 148
Dimitri, Richard 112
"Diploma for Sale" 256
"The Dippers" 77
Di Reda, Joseph 151
Dirkson, Douglas 93, 210, 230
The Dirty Dozen 136
Dirty Harry 21, 29, 31, 49, 101, 157, 192, 193, 194, 233
"Dirty Little Wars" 272, 289
"Dirty Money, Black Light" 64
Di Santi, John 211, 213, 230
"Dishpan Man" 154
Disney 114, 128, 239, 271, 323, 326
Di Spina, Teresa 219
Di Stefano, James 289
Di Stefano, Joe 75, 81
Di Stefano, Tony 186
"Divine Wind" 94
Divoff, Andrew 154, 155
"Divorce, Venusian Style" 120, 125
Dix, Richard 112
Dixon, Ivan 61, 64, 65, 66, 67, 68, 69, 92, 96, 98, 112, 123, 125, 126, 150
Dixon, Peter 252
Dizon, Jesse 69, 77, 93, 208
Djola, Badja 294
"Do Not Go Gentle..." 160, 167
Doc Holliday 39
"The Doctor Is Out" 143, 153
Doctor Kildare 120
Dr. No 120
Doctor Scorpion 106, 222
Doe, Barry 220
"Does Not Compute" 183, 188
"The Dog and Pony Show" 26, 35, 65, 120
Doheny, Lawrence 59, 60, 61, 62, 63, 92, 93, 94, 100, 124
Doherty, Shannen 247, 254
Dolan, Dee Dee 100
Dolan, Trent 303
Dollaghan, Patrick 184
Donaghy, Maggie 256
Donahoe, Terry 307, *307,* 308, 311, 322, *322*
Donahue, Ann 256, 257
Donahue, Elinor 189
Donahue, Patricia 66
Donald, Juliana 185
Donaldson, Lisa 70
Donat, Peter 92
Donat, Richard 288
Donfield, London 154
Doniger, Walter 92
Donizetti, 280
Donley, Robert 53
Donnell, Jeff 168
Donnelly, Dennis 32, 149, 150, 151, 152, 153, 166, 172, 173, 185, 217
Donner, Richard 117
Donner, Robert 85, 151
Donny and Marie 53
"Don't Kill the Sparrows" 74, 78
"Don't Mess Around with Jim" 30, 34, 120, 123
"Don't Pet the Teacher" 248
"Don't Stretch the Rainbow" 250
Doogie Howser M.D. 9, 97
Doolittle, John 250
Doran, Ann 154
Doran, Jesse 289, 292
Dorin, Jan-Ivan 126
Dorsey, Joe 166, 186, 209
Dorsey, Reginald T. 151, 164, 248, 250
Dotrice, Roy 155, 218
Dotson, Rhonda 210
Double Dare 264
"Double Exposure" 212

"Double Heat" 145, 150
"Double Image" 74, 76
"Double Negative" 116, 296
"Double Your Pleasure" 18, 183, 184
Doubleday, Frank, 125, 228
Doucette, Jeff 151, 211
Dougan, Michael 261
Doughty, Richard 92
Douglas, Brandon 248, 250
Douglas, Burt 78
Douglas, Diana 168
Douglas, Giles 85
Douglas, Jerry 67, 69, 98, 125, 217
Douglas, Ken 256
Douglas, Melvyn 50
Douglas, Robert 76, 77, 78, 80, 84, 85
Douglass, Robyn 111, 228, 229
Dow, Bill 250, 257
"Down and Under" 212
Downing, David 77
Downing, Steve 79
Downs, Fred 124
Doyle, Robert 100
Doyle, Sharon Elizabeth 253, 256, 257
Dozier, William 43, 117, 135, 138, 232
Dragnet 37, 38, 120, 205
Drago, Billy 167, 208, 210
"The Dragon and the Angel" 252
Drake, Dolores 255, 257, 290
Drake, Larry 213
Drake, Paul 151, 169, 208, 218
Drake Massey, Bebe 216
"Draw the Line" 253
"The Dream" 81
Dream Street 285
"Dreams" 121, 125
Dressler, Lieux 63
Drexler, Mark 215
Drier, Moosie 154, 211
Droney, Kevin 217, 218, 219
"Drought at Indian Head River" 63
Drug Wars 284
Dryer, Fred 7, 16, 23, *24*, 34, 172, 173, 192, 193, *193*, 195, 196, 197, 198, 200, 203, 204, 205, 206, 207, 212, 213, 214, 216, 219
Dryer, Robert 126, 149, 152, 166, 174, 208
Dubak, Bob 208
Du Barry, Denise 91
Dubbins, Don 66, 214
Dubelko, Mike 223
Dubin, Charles 59, 75
Dubois, Marta 150, 164, 185, 303
Duck Tales 140
Ducommun, Rick 5, 232, 236
Dudikoff, Michael 329
Due South 35, 308
"Duet for Two Wind Instruments" 159, 168
Duff, Howard 63
Dugan, Dennis 47, 58, 66, 68, 96, 97, 98, 213, 289, 312
Dugan, John 116
Duggan, Andrew 165
Duhamel, Peter Noel 216

The Duke 4, 35, 46, 87, **99–100**, 106, 111, 127, 297, 305, 308, 326
"The Duke" (pilot) 100
Duke, Bill 196, 207
Duke, Patty 302
The Dukes of Hazzard 54, 242
"The Dukes of Whispering Pines" 23, 154
Dullaghan, John 77
Dumm, J. Rickley 181, 228
Dumont 238
Dunard, David 154
Dunaway, Don Carlos 51, 60, 62, 63, 75, 100, 104
Duncan, Angus 62, 208
Duncan, Kelly 254
Dunigan, Tim 133, 147
Dunlap, Pamela 292
Dunn, Kevin 252, 312
Dunn, Larry 69
Dunn, Suzanne 154
Dunne, Dominic 129
Dunphy, Jerry 123
Dunsmore, Rosemary 216
Duran, Ann 215
Duran, Richard 153
Durbin, John 155
Durning, Charles 76
Durock, Dick 61
Durrell, Michael 94, 214
Durren, John 63, 75, 85, 92, 94
Dusenberry, Ann 164
Duvall, Shelley 74, 77
"The Dwarf in the Helium Hat" 25, 52, 66
Dynarski, Gene 85, 165
Dynasty 3, 53, 196, 302
Dysart, Richard 75

Eakes, Bobbie 252
Earl, Wallace 89
Earp, Wyatt 170
Easterbrook, Leslie 220
Eastin, Steve 153
Eastlake, Carleton 321
Easton, Joyce 66
Eastwood, Clint 3, 4, 12, 16, 29, 49, 101, 102, 144, 157, 192, 193, 197
Easy Rider 237
Ebbtide 179
Ebert, Michael 63, 85
Ebsen, Buddy 164
"Echoes" 183, 189, 227
Eckholdt, Steve 217, 255
Eckler, Daphne 215
Eddie Capra Mysteries 53, 96, 297
Edelman, Herb 168
Edgcomb, James 184
Edmiston, Walker 189, 229
Edmonds, Don 210, 211, 216
"The Education of Terry Carver" 256
Edward Scissorhands 241
Edwards, E. Paul 245, 250, 251
Edwards, Jason 217
Edwards, Kenneth 250
Edwards, Luke 252
Edwards, Stacy 252

Edwards, Tony 318, *319*
Edwards, Vince 237
Egan, Eddie 78
Eggar, Samantha 78, 229
Ehrman, Paul 212
Eiding, Paul 167, 207
87th Precinct 52
Eilbacher, Cynthia 208
Eilbacher, Lisa 98
Eischeid 53, 326
Eitner, Don 59
Elam, Jack 303
Elcar, Dana 32, 48, 61, 66, 72, 75, 90, 91, 93, 94, 100, 145, 150, 152, 165, 187
Electra Glide in Blue 71
Electronic Media 110, 223
The Eleventh Hour 178
Elias, Hector 76, 123
Elias, Lou 76, 81
Eliasberg, Jan 254, 289, 294
Elise, Christine 254
Elizondo, Hector 53, 60, 67, 76
Ellenstein, Robert 59
Ellery Queen 296
Elliot, Geoffrey 231, 235
Elliot, Mark Aaron 251
Elliott, Beverly 292
Elliott, Shawn 213
Elliott, Stephen 66, 84
Ellis, Sidney 30, 79, 80, 81, 149, 158, 199, 201, 207, 208, 209, 210
Ellison, Casey 252
Ellison, Harlan 236, 300
Emerald Point 103, 146
Emerson, Jonathan 217
Emery, James 185
Emmich, Cliff 189, 214
Emmy magazine 28, 39, 40, 109, 245
Empire 97
"The Empty Frame" 13, 67
Empty Nest 203
Eney, Woody 112, 123, 126, 187
The Enforcer (Bogart film) 279
The Enforcer (Eastwood film) 16, 49, 101, 193, 194
Engel, Frank 282
Engels, Robert 293, 294
English, Brad 150, 187, 210, 250
Englund, Robert 199, 209
Enriquez, Rene 81
Ensign, Michael 112, 123, 166, 249, 288
Entertainment Weekly 326
Epper, Tony 63, 148
Epstein, Jacob 327
Epstein, Pierre 311
Equal Justice 9, 321
"Equal Protection" 256
The Equalizer 1, 11, 131, 137, 138, 202, 221, 222, 223, 226, 241, 264, 275, 326
Ericksen, Leif 69
Ericson, Devon 147, 208
Ericson, John 148
Ericson, Karen 84
Eriksen, Kaj-Erik 326
Erlichh, Jayne 23, 154

Ernest (franchise) 172
Errickson, Krista 252
Escandon, Fernando 154
"Escape from a Velvet Box" 7, 130
"Escape from Caine Abel" 98, 159
Esformes, Nate 209, 211
Esquire 50
Essex, Sarah 252
Esslinger, Mark 261
Estes, Robert 253, 317, 325
Estrada, Erik 77, 213
Estrin, Eric 212, 316
"Eternal Flames" 253
"Ether" 23
Etienne, Roger 123
Eubanks, Bob 186
Evans, Cal 252
Evans, Gene 152
Evans, John Morgan 66
Evans, Linda 53, 60
Evans, Richard 153
Evans, M. Jennifer 278, 290
Evans, Mary Beth 185
Evans, Robin 173, 184, 209
Evans, Terrence 124, 150
Everett, Chad *171*, 172, 173, 317
Everett, Tom 208
Everhard, Nancy 154
Evers, Jason 65, 67, 145, 151
"Every Day Is Christmas" 255
"Everybody Loves a Clown" 174
"Everybody Pays the Fare" 79
Ewell, Tom 72, 75
Ewing, Diane 64
Ewing, Loren 94
"Ex Marks the Spot" 220
"An Exercise in Fatality" 297
"Exit Prentiss Carr" 59
The Exterminator 89
Exterminator II 306
The Eyes of Laura Mars 207
"Eyewitness Blues" 174

F Troop 236
Fabares, Shelley 59
Fabiani, Joel 61, 85, 93
Facts of Life 102, 243
"Fagin 1986" 200, 201, 210
Fails, J.W. 253
Fairfield, Heather 253
Fairman, Michael 111, 144, 149, 216, 249
Faison, Matthew 124, 293, 311
Falcon Crest 57, 107, 129, 265, 330
Falk, Harry 66
Falk, Peter 39, 82, 116, 297, 298
Falk, Tom 98
The Fall Guy 3, 119, 131, 137, 140, 190, 221
Faltas, Nick 155
"Fame Is the Name of the Game" 38
"La Familia" 219
Family Affair 162
"The Family Hour" 54, 62
"Family Reunion" 155
Family Ties 238
The Famous Teddy Z 260
Fann, La Velda 100

The Fantastic Four (feature film) 326
Fantastic Journey 134
Fantasy Island 3, 53, 196, 298
Faraldo, Daniel 151, 208
Farber, Arlene 75
Farentino, James 13, 40
Farese, Jude 208
Fargas, Antonio 164
Fargo, James 101, 151, 215, 216, 217
Farina, Dennis 198, 207, 208
Farmer, Frank 111
The Farmer's Daughter 17
"The Farnsworth Stratagem" 15, 60, 309
Farrell, Brioni 100
Farrow, Moira 277
"Fascination for the Flame" 269, 271, 288
"A Fast Count" 67
"Faster Heart" 161, 167
"The Fastest Gun" 28, 93
"Fatal Obsession" 219
The Father Dowling Mysteries 203, 297
"Fathers and Sons" 252
"Father's Day" 186
The FBI 82
"Fear and Loathing with Russell Buckins" 250
Fearnley, Neil 250, 251, 288, 303
Feather, Jon 149
Feds 274
"Feeding Frenzy" 63
Feffers, Carol-Ann 257
Feinstein, Alan 76, 164
Felder, Lou 155, 166, 186, 210
Feldner, Sheldon 112, 216
Felipi, Carmine 189
Felix, Otto 215
Fell, Norman 98
Fellows, Edith 186
Fenn, Sherilyn 247, 249
Ferdyn, Pamela 79
Ferguson, Jesse Lawrence 151
Fernandes, Michael 220
Fernandez, Miguel 126, 149, 211, 235
Fernetz, Charlene 256, 324
Ferrara, Al 76
Ferrell, Conchata 311
Ferrell, Tyra 211
Ferrer, Mel 79
Ferrer, Miguel 322, *322*
Ferrero, Martin 12
Ferring, Lynn 112
Ferris, Nick 61
Ferrone, Dan 92
Ferrucci, Frank 287, 288
Fiedler, John 66
Field, Gustav 77
Fielder, Pat 74, 79, 80, 81
Fielding, Dorothy 249
Fields, Edith 125
Fifield, Steve 210
"The Fifth Victim" 217
"Fighting Angels" 94
Figus, Lisa 105
Filkow, Sid 290

"Film at Eleven" 257
Fimple, Dennis 66, 93, 123, 155
"Final Confession" 218
"The Final Exam" 23, 143, 310, 312
Finch, Martina 287, 288
"Find Me If You Can" 54, 59
Finder of Lost Loves 328
"Finders Keepers" 173
Fink, Harry and Rita 101
Finley, Pat 58, 60, 64, 66, 67, 69
Finnegan, John 214
"Fire" 134, 145, 150
"The Fire Man" (*Baretta* ep.) 76
"Fire Man" (*Greatest American Hero* ep.) 123
"Fire Man" (*Hunter* ep.) 199, 209
Firestone, Eddie 60, 61, 63
"Firestorm" 27
"Firing Line" 155
First Love 114
"The First Time Is Forever" 227
"First You Got to Go to the Picnic" 299, 303
Firth, Robert 211, 212
Fischer, Bruce 111, 151
Fischer, Don 220
Fischer, Peter 53, 74, 75, 96, 98, 159, 296, 297, 298
A Fish Called Wanda 309
Fisher, George 98
Fisher, Shug 84
Fitts, Rick 154, 209
Fitzgerald, Fern 212
FitzSimmons, Jeannie 66
"The Five and a Half Pound Junkie" 75
"Five the Hard Way" 93
Fix, Paul 66
Flamingo Road 177
Flanagan, Fionulla 186, 217
Flanagan, Frances 256
The Flash 199
"Flashpoint" 203, 213
"Flat Out" 321
Fleer, Harry 92
Fleetwood, Mick 279, 291
Fleischer, Charles 311
Fleming, Ian 271
Fletcher, Bill 59, 66, 81, 92
Flicker, Ted 125
"Flight on a Dead Pigeon" 208
Flippin, Lucy Lee 5, 232, 235
Florek, Dann 213, 246, 251
Flores, Joe 228
Flory, Med 187, 216
Fluegel, Darlanne 207, 282, 293
"Flying Down to Rio" 161, 164
Flying High 53, 114
Flynn, Errol 136
Flynn, J. Michael 213
Flynn, Miriam 188
Foch, Nina 219
Foley Square 180
Fonda, Bridget 247, 253
Fonda, Henry 39
Fontaine, Eddie 59, 60, 62, 67, 75, 104
Fontaine, Molly 189
"Forbidden Fruit" 90, 91, 94

Forbidden Planet 178
Forbidden World 178
"Forced Retirement" 65
Forchion, Raymond 287
Ford, Anita 75
Ford, Bette 218
Ford, Faith 167
Ford, Glenn 39
Ford, Janine 208
Ford, John 334
Ford-Passolt, Jineane 189
Foree, Ken 185, 208, 217
Forman, Joey 104
Formicola, Fil 92, 147, 166, 186, 207
Foronjy, Richard 210
Forrest, Fredric 241, 242, 248
Forrest, Richard J. 189
Forrest, William 84
Forrester, Larry 168
Forster, Robert 83
Forsythe, Rosemary 213
Forte, Patricia 256
Fortune Dane 306, 324
48 Hours 266
Foster, Meg 75, 77
"Foul on the First Play" 62
"Four Eyes" 179, 183, 184, 196
The Four Just Men 136
"The Four Pound Brick" 54, 60
Fournier, Rift 80
"The Fourth Man" 62, 159, 214
Fowles, Jib 140
Fox, Allan David 252
Fox, Bernard 189
Fox, Kelli 257
Fox, Lavina 290
Fox, Michael 208
Fox, Peter 215, 252
Fox TV 238, 239, 240, 244, 247, 329
Foxworth, Bo 250
Fraker, William 288, 292, 293, 300, 304, 316
"The Framing of Perfect Sidney" 98, 271
Frampton, Peter 95
France, Doug 125, 185
Franciosca, Tony 38
Francis, Anne 34, 92, 166, 178, 184, 300
Francis, Carol 154
Franco, Abel 80
Franco, Margarita 217
Frandsen, Jano 256
Frank, Ben 62, 63, 104
Frank, Charles 57
Frank, Gary 215, 235
Frankel, Art 251
Frankenheimer, John 57
Frankfather, William 123, 211, 216, 303
"The Frankie Kahana Show" 183, 189
Franklin, Carl 67, 134, 147, 188
Frann, Mary 53, 60, 103, 104
Franz, Dennis 32, 144, 145, 150, 152, 163, 165, 166, 185, 198, 208
Fraser, Duncan 257, 303

Frasier 298, 320
Frazier, Sheila 126
Fredericks, Kit 168, 189, 230
Free Ride 243
Free Spirit 193, 320
Freed, Bert 186
Freed, Sam 167
Freedman, Winifred 249
Freejack 266
Freeman, A.J. 187
Freeman, J.E. 213, 228
Freeman, Joan 185
Freeman, Kathleen 212, 311
Freeman, Kay 187
Freeway 207
Freidrich, John 78, 79
Freilich, Jeffrey 78
French, Bruce 149, 164, 168, 251
French, Phyllis 220
Frey, Glenn 279, 290, 291
Friday the 13th 199
Fridley, Tom 253
Friedgen, Julie 255
Friedman, David 263
Friedrich, John 75
Frizzell, Lou 64
From Here to Eternity 284
"From San Francisco with Love" 211
Froman, David 213, 217, 229, 251, 312
Frost, Alice 79
"The Fruits of the Poisonous Tree" 283, 285, 294
Frye, Virgil 214
Fudge, Alan 32, 126, 144, 145, 147, 149, 150, 165, 186, 190, 220
The Fugitive 39, 40, 52, 131, 224, 261, 330
Fujioka, John 77, 94, 120, 124, 144, 148, 174, 230, 235
"The Full Circle" 274
Fuller, Lisa 249
Fullilove, Don 257
Fulton, Julie 209
Fulton, Wendy 145, 152
Fults, Scott 254
"Fun with Animals" 251
Funai, Helen 77
Furie, Sidney 282
Furlong, John 60, 62
Futureworld 114
"Fuzzy Vision" 160, 187

Gabriel's Fire 307
"Gadgo" 81
Gagen, Anie 216
Gagnier, Holly 151
Gago, Jenny 230
Gaile, Jeri 189
Gaines, Sonny Jim 81
Gainey, M.C. 148, 219
Gains, Courtney 249
Gaitens, Peter 256
Galactica '80 299, 313
Galardi, Michael 187, 209
Gale, Vincent 257
Galik, Denise 147
Gallanti, Jim 93
Gallardo, Edward 78

Gallardo, Silvana 208, 303
Galloway, Don 217
Gallup, Denise 154
Gallup, Dian 154
Gam, Rita 68
"Games People Play" (*Hardcastle and McCormick* ep.) 160, 168
"Games People Play" (*Riptide* ep.) 186
"The Games You Learn from Your Father" 159, 167
Gammell, Robin 67, 289, 292
"The Gang at Don's Drive-In" 66
The Gangster Chronicles 83, 177
Ganios, Tony 290, 292, 293
Gann, Merrilyn 256
Gannon, Joe 193, 212
Ganzel, Teresa 168, 220
Garas, Kaz 151
"The Garbage Man" 30, 158, 208
Garbo Talks 277
Garcia, Rick 153
Gardella, Kay 205, 263, 314
Gardner, Brooks 218
Garion, Buddy 150
Garlington, Lee 228
Garman, Stephanie 211, 212
Garner, Jack 53, 57, 62, 129
Garner, James 2, 6, 18, 20, 32, 33, 39, 40, 41, 43, 44, 46, 47, *47*, 48, 49, 50, 51, 52, 53, 56, 57, 58, 61, 97, 99, 101, 106, 162, 170, 180, 200, 228, 320
Garner, Martin 292
Garr, Steven 254
Garray, Alejandra 151
Garrett, Andi 93
Garrett, Dean 255
Garrett, Leif 213
Garrett, Spencer 254
Garrison, Sean 94
Garrison's Gorillas 133, 136, 201
Gascon, David 255
Gateaux, David 166
Gates, Michael 312
Gates, Tucker 254, 294
Gatlin, Larry 166
Gattys, Bennye 78
Gaul, Patricia 112
The Gauntlet 16, 102, 197
Gauthier, Dan 250
Gautier, Dick 58
Gay Times 13
Gaye, Nora 213
Gaynes, George 84, 92
Gazarra, Ben 52
Gazzo, Michael 79, 129
"Gearjammers" 60
Geas, Thomas 218
Gee Byrd, Anne 219
Geer, Ellen 80
Geeson, Judy 155
Gehring, Ted 61, 65, 84, 125, 126, 147, 207
Geiger, George 205, 215, 216
Gemignani, Rhoda 129, 213, 292
"Gemini" 227
Gendel, Morgan 194, 218, 220, 256, 281, 293, 332

General Hospital 243
Genesse, Bryan 324, *324*
Genovese, Mike 184, 230, 312
Gentle Ben 103
Gentleman's Quarterly (GQ) 43, 50, 52, 57
Gentry, Robert 218
George, Brian 220
George, Howard 64, 186, 213
"The Georgia Street Motors" 30, 158, 165
Geraldo 275, 276
Gerard, Gil 78, 114
Gerard, Merwin 84
Gerber, David 53, 101, 140, 193
Gerber, Jay 126
Gerussi, Bruno 287
Get Smart 233, 234, 236
Getlin, Scott 219
The Ghost and Mrs. Muir 323
"A Ghost of a Chance" 235
Ghostbusters 231
Giambalvo, Louis 32, 145, 152, 169, 177
Giamatti, Marcus 219
Giardino, Mark 111
Gibb, Don 218
Gibbs, Timothy *171*, 172, 173
Gibson, Cal 152, 209
Gibson, Gerry 168, 209
Gibson, Margaret 213
Gideon, Conroy 212
Gidget (television series) 17
Gien, Pamela 219
Gierasch, Stefan 79, 84, 125, 185
Gifford, G. Adam 218
"The Gift" 20, 283, 294
Gilbert, Edmund 92, 151, 166
Gilbert, Ron 67
Gilkes, Colson F. 294
Gill, Will, Jr. 66, 69, 79
Gillespie, Ann 218
Gilliam, Burton 148
Gilliand, Richard 214
Gilligan's Island 313
Gillin, Hugh 125, 166, 188
Gilman, Kenneth David 65, 207, 212
Gilman, Larry 186
Gilman, Sam 94
Gilpin, Peri 251
Gilyard, Clarence 186
Ging, Jack 27, 32, 48, 123, 134, 144, 147, 148, 164, 176, 177, 184, 287
Ginsberg, Alan 17, 18
Ginty, Robert 59, 89, *89,* 91
Giolito, Rick 217
Giorgio, Tony 207, 209, 235
Giosa, Sue 187
Girardin, Ray 104, 124, 129, 149, 165, 167, 184, 207
Giritlian, James 168
"The Girl in the Bay City Boys' Club" 61
"A Girl Named Hunter" 217
"The Girl Next Door" (Hunter ep.) 212
"The Girl Next Door" (*21, Jump Street* ep.) 256

"Girl on the Beach" 214
"Girls' Night Out" 187
Gjonola, Richard 123
The Gladiator 273
Gladstone, Dana 95
Glasier, Paul Michael 59
Glass, Ned 79
Glass, Ron 312
Glassner, Jonathan 256, 257, 310, 312
Glaudini, Robert 214
Gleason, Paul 150, 154, 165, 184, 186, 254
Gless, Sharon 53, 59, 62, 92, 96, 98
The Glitter Dome 57, 101
Glory Days 239
"The Glory Game" 76
Glover, Bruce 152
Glover, Danny 123
Glow Carr, Karen 78
Gnazzo, Angelo 61
"God Is a Bullet" 253
The Godfather 72
Godfrey, Alan 78, 80
Godshall, Liberty 150, 164
Godwin, Stephen 254
Goethals, Robert 235
"Goin' Home" 273, 274, 289
"Going Nowhere Fast" 164
Goins, Jesse D. 117, 122, 148
Gold, Donald 62, 70, 94
Gold, Harvey 85, 112
"Gold from the Rainbow" 299, 303
Goldberg, Gary David 238, 239
Goldberg, Lee 217, 223
Goldblum, Jeff 18, 109, 111, 300
Golden Girls 4, 88, 203
Goldin, Ricky Paull 252
Goldman, Danny 75
Goldman, Lorry 311
Goldner, Eric 154, 186
Goldsmith, Jonathan 67, 104, 153, 165, 168, 235
Goldstein, Bob 208
Goldwyn, Tony 215
Golonka, Arlene 66
Gomer Pyle 116
Gomez, Carlos 294
Gomez, Jaime 251
Gomez, Mike 255
Gomez, Panchito 80, 81, 249
Gonzales, Felix 147
Gonzalez, Diego 78
"A Good Clean Bust with Sequel Rights" 25, 54, 67
Good Morning, Vietnam 243
"The Good Samaritan" 121, 125
"The Goodbye Orphan Annie Blues" 76
Gooden, Robert 92, 123, 211
Goodger, Michele 250, 288, 293, 294, 303
Goodman, Walter 138
Goodrich, Deborah 152, 252
Goodrow, Gerry 168
Gordey, Keith Martin 288
Gordon, Bruce 261
Gordon, Leo 67, 69, 111, 293, 294

Gordon, Philip 148
Gordy, Denise 311
Gore, Nick 217
"Gorilla-Gram" 235
Gorman, Breon 219
Gortner, Marjoe 144, 148
Gosa, James 112
Gossett, Lou 47, 58, 62, 64
Gotell, Walter 143, 152
"Gotta Finish the Riff" 249
Gould, Elliot 45
Gould, Harold 68
Gower, Jon Andre 150
Goz, Harry 290
"The Grab" 220
Grace, Pierette 220
Grace, Wayne 61, 81, 211
Graf, Allan 185
Graf, David 148, 185
Graham, Gary 209
Graham, Gerrit 26, 75, 147
Grais, Michael 77
Grammer, Kelsey 297, 298, 299, 303, 320
Grand Prix 57
Grant, Beth 219
Grant, Faye 116, 117, 122, 163
Grant, Gillian 154
Grant, Harry 125
Grant, Sandra P. 257
Grant, Stacy 257
Grassoff, Alex 58
Grateful Dead 306
Gratton, Bill 167, 229
"Graveyard Shift" 303
Gray, David Barry 248, 255, 256
Gray, Erin 68, 217
Gray, Kenneth 186
Gray, Robert 125, 152, 187, 208, 230
Gray Giuntoli, Neil 293
Grayson, Katherine 81
Grayson, Kurt 112, 123, 124, 125
Grease 266
"The Great Blue Lake and Land Development Company" 61, 309
The Great Pretender 317
The Greatest American Hero 3, 4, 6, 7, 9, 11, 13, 15, 18, 19, 21, 23, 25, 27, 28, 29, 30, 32, 34, 35, 36, 37, 46, 48, 51, 52, 54, 97, 98, 102, 103, 106, 107, 110, **113–126**, *115,* 127, 128, 129, 131, 132, 135, 143, 156, 159, 161, 163, 172, 173, 175, 179, 180, 181, 194, 196, 198, 200, 224, 234, 240, 299, 310, 318, 323, 334
"The Greatest American Hero" (pilot) 122
The Greatest American Heroine aka *Return of the Greatest American Hero* 121
Green, Bruce Seth 186
Green, Daniel 150
Green, Gilbert 65, 70, 78
Green, Joey 100, 210
Green, Tom 266
The Green Berets 90
Green Bush, Billy 77, 84

The Green Hornet 107
Greenall, Doug 252
Greene, H. Richard 189, 211, 251, 302, 317
Greene, Kim Morgan 191, 214
Greene, Melissa 59
Greene, Michael 218
Greene, Sheckey 142, 153
Greenhalch, Edward 287
Greenleaf, Jim 125
Greenlee, David 251
Greenwood, Bruce 191, 317, *317*
Greenwood, Rochelle 256
Greer, Dabbs 62, 124
"The Greeter" 228
Gregg, Bradley 249
Gregg, Virginia 60, 78, 98
Gregor, Adam 125, 154, 212
Gregorio, Rose 68
Gregory, Mary 216, 249
Gregory, Michael 153, 166, 212
Gregory, Stephen 249
"The Grey Team" 155
Greyhosky, Babs 15, 18, 24, 25, 32, 119, 125, 126, 147, 148, 149, 172, 173, 174, 175, 177, 178, 179, 181, 182, 183, 184, 185, 186, 187, 189, 196, 208, 270, 297, 298, 299, 303, 334
Greyhounds 328
Grieco, Richard 246, 247, 248, 320, *320*, 321, 329
Griest, Kim 284, 292, 293
Griffeths, Simone 18, 111, 112, 117, 122, 187
Griffin, Jennifer 257, 290
Griffin, Tim 218
Griffith, Thomas Ian 291
Griffith, Tracy 253
Griffiths, Andy 237, 297
Grimes, Chester 165
Grimes, Scott 256
Grimm, Maria 67
Grindlay, Annie 220
Grizzard, George 107
Groening, Matt 239
Groh, David 217
Gross, Ed 37, 261, 263, 271, 275, 279, 286
Grove, Richard 219
Grover, Ed 72, 75, 124, 147
Grover, Stanley 125, 168, 229
Groves, Herman 213
Grubbs, Gary 124, 154, 218
Guardino, Charles 186
Guardino, Harry 217
Guardino, Jerome 60, 66
Guastaferro, Vincent 167, 220, 293, 294
Guerra, Castulo 155, 187, 208, 213, 255
Guerro, Evelyn 80, 215
"Guess Who's Coming to Brefnish?" 276
Guest, Nicholas 189, 217
Guilfoyle, Paul 274, 275, 276, 289, 313, 314, 316, 317
Guillaume, Robert 328
Guillory, Bennett 215

"Guilt" 68
"Guilty" 199, 208
Guinee, Tim 275, 289
Gulager, Clu 188
Gunn, Joseph 214
"Guns and Brothers" 79
The Guns of Will Sonnett 296
Gunsmoke 82, 102, 103, 170
Gurwitch, Annabelle 312
Guss, Louis 77
Gutierrez, Ricardo 288, 311
Guttenberg, Steve 231
Guttman, Monika 243
Guzman, Luis 219
G'Vera, Ivan 215
Gwynne, Michael C. 80, 112
The Gypsy Warriors 106, 179

Haase, Rod 85, 208
Haber, Christine 303
Hack, Richard 205
Hacker, Joseph 77, 152, 167, 229, 254, 304
Hackman, Gene 46
Hackney, Gerald 63
Haden Church, Thomas 253
Haddon, Laurence 85, 112, 123, 124
Hagen, Anna 256
Hagen, Erica 69, 77
Hagen, Stephanie 166
Hagman, Larry 65
Haig, Sid 59, 147
Hair 266
Haldeman, Tim 93, 215
Hale, Barbara 114, 116, 125
Hale, Doug 124
Haley, Jennifer 257
"The Half Million Dollar Baby" 75
Hall, Deirdre 291
Hall, J.D. 208
Hallack, Robert 249
Hallahan, Charles 65, 200, 207
Haller, Ty 289
Halley, Ben, Jr. 272, 289
Hallick, Tom 125
Halliwell, Leslie 136
Hallowe'en 199
Halma, Denise 123
Halsey, Brett 85
Halsey, Michael 124, 129, 144, 148
Halsted, Dana 100
Hambleton, Duffy 77, 79
Hamel, Veronica 15, 62, 63, 83, 85
Hamilton, Alexa 123, 130, 214
Hamilton, Antony 311
Hamilton, Colin 125
Hamilton, Dean 250
Hamilton, Frank 169
Hamilton, Kim 104, 186
Hamilton, Lois 209
Hamilton, Lynn 61, 187, 214
Hamilton, Randy 185
Hamilton, Richard 57
"The Hammer of C Block" 61
Hammond, Tom 289
Hamner, Ben 112, 151
Hamner, Don 84
Hamner, Robert 78, 203, 214
Hampton, James 60, 126

Hancock, John 124, 129, 145, 154, 160, 163, 212
Hancock, Lou 288
"The Hand-Painted Thai" 120, 124
Handy, Bill 165
Handy, James 229, 230, 287
Hang 'Em High 102
Hankin, Larry 209
Hankinson, Stephanie 68
Hanley, Bridget 186
Hanley, Robert 189, 210
Hanlon, Peter 256, 293
Hannie Caulder 116
Hansen, Al 60
Hanson, Judith 77
Hanson, Preston 153
Happy Days 91, 239
Harbor, Gayle 249
"The Hard Case" 24, 160, 181, 184
"Hard Contract" 158, 201, 207
Hardball 102, 119, 127, 201, 258, 333
Hardcastle and McCormick 3, 6, 7, 11, 12, 13, 19, 23, 30, 32, 34, 35, 54, 110, 116, 118, 119, 120, 131, 132, 133, 135, 137, 141, 143, **156–169**, *157*, *161*, 172, 175, 180, 181, 194, 195, 221, 224, 227, 228, 240, 244, 265, 271, 283, 300, 308, 323, 331
"Hardcastle for Mayor" 168
"Hardcastle, Hardcastle, Hardcastle and McCormick" 159, 160, 166
"Harder Than It Looks" 150
Hardin, Jerry 65, 70, 81, 84, 92
Hare, Will 124
Hargitay, Mariska 293
Hargrove, Dean 297, 299
Harker, Wiley 126, 150, 152
Harkins, John 80, 111, 216
Harlan, Scott 292
Harley, Amanda 98
Harling, Noelle 248
Harmon, Mark 267
Harmon, Tom 125
"Harmony and Grits" 24, 187
Harper, Diane 62
Harper, Jessica 290
Harper, Robert 229, 292, 293
Harper, Samantha 168, 235
Harrington, Curtis 73, 76, 77
Harris, Brad 188
Harris, Ed 67
Harris, M.K. 312
Harris, Michael 253
Harris, Ted 64
Harrison, Mark 186
Harrold, Kathryn 58, 67, 69
Harron, Mary 136
Harry 177
Harry, Deborah 279, 290, 291
Harry O 24, 46
Hart, Joe 216
Hart, John 11, 123
Hart, La Gena 152
Hart, Michele 68
Hart, Morgan 185
Hart, Pamela 290
Hart Carroll, Lisa 229

Hart to Hart 138, 195
Hartigan, Ben 312
Hartley, Clebe 212
Hartley, Marriette 69, 104
Hartwick, Sue-Ann 19
Harty, Patricia 169, 291
Harvest, Rainbow 251
Hasburgh, Patrick 13, 19, 20, 32, 36, 119, 120, 124, 125, 126, 144, 147, 148, 156, 158, 159, 160, 161, 163, 164, 165, 166, 167, 191, 239, 240, 241, 242, 243, 244, 245, 247, 248, 249, 250, 258
Haskell, Peter 100, 153, 212
Hasso, Signe 84
Hastings, Bob 61, 64, 95, 123, 125
The Hat Squad **327–328**, 329, 330
Hatch, Richard 187
"Hatchet Job" 181, 184
"Hate the Picture, Love the Frame" 166
Hauser, Fay 257
Hauser, Wings 5, 30, 78, 145, 151, 152, 167, 208, 231, 234, 235
Havins, Hal 250
Hawaii Five-O 48, 50, 51, 54, 73, 88, 203, 260
Hawaiian Eye 87, 99
"The Hawaiian Headache" 35, 69
Hawaiian Heat 89, 137
"The Hawk Flies on Sunday" 94
Hawkeye 329
Hawkins, Michael 163
Hawks, Howard 334
Haworth, Jill 78
Hayden, Melissa 220
Hayden, Sterling 45
Hayek, Julie 209
Hayers, Sidney 102, 124, 152, 154, 155, 168, 209
Hayes, Deryl 251, 287, 290
Hayes, Isaac 47, 58, 61, 64, 65, 142, 153, 158, 201, 211
Hayes, Ron 78, 147
Hayes, Ron Mychal 216, 311
Hayes, William 229
Haymer, John 92, 312
Hays, Robert 61
Hays Commission 28
Haysbert, Dennis 186
Hayward, David 217
Haze, Stan 189
Hazel 17
"He Stole'a My Art" 129
Head, Helene 291
The Headmaster 237
Health 45
Hearn, Chick 254
"The Heart of Rock and Roll" 153, 158
Heart of the City 313
"Heartaches of a Fool" 67
Heartbreak Ridge 306
Heartland 162
Heasley, Marla 16, 132, 144, 146, 148, 184
Heaton, Tom 316
"Heaven Is in Your Genes" 126, 143
Heavener, David 219

Hebert, Rich 253
Hedison, David 144, 145, 153
Heffley, Wayne 154
Heffron, Richard 52, 58
Heflin, Nora 215
Heiden, Janis 85, 111, 148
Heilveil, Elayne 61, 63, 111
"Heir of Neglect" 215
"Heir to the Throne" 292
Heldfond, Susan 79, 81
"He'll Never See Daylight" 72, 73, 75
Hell Town 72, 74
"Hell Week" 252
Heller, Chip 168, 212
Heller, Jack 152
Heller, Randee 209
Hellman, Ocean 256
"Hello, Buckwheat" 293
Helm, Tiffany 251
HELP 239
Hemecker, Ralph 333
Hemingway, Ernest 45
Hemmings, David 103, 143, 144, 150, 152, 153, 154, 227, 228, 229, 235
Henderson, Fred 256
Hendrix, Jimi 241
Hendry, Beverly 255, 287, 304
Henning, Linda 216
Hennings, Sam 216
Henriksen, Lance 149, 163, 185
Henry, Gregg 169, 229, 317
Henry, Tim 252, 257
Henshel, Tom 210
Hensley, Pamela 60
Henteloff, Alex 77, 93, 104, 235
Henzel, Richard 100
Hercules—The Legendary Journeys 88, 332, 333
Herd, Richard 61, 106, 122, 164, 167
"Here's Adventure, Here's Romance" 12
"Here's Looking at You, Kid" 122
Hern, Bernie 311
Hero at Large 118
Herrera, Anthony 69, 107
Herrick, Frederick 69, 93, 100
Herring, Lynn 186
Hershberger, Gary 252
Hertzog, Lawrence 23, 159, 160, 161, 165, 166, 167, 168, 227, 228, 229, 230
Heslov, Grant 254
Hess, David 154
Hess, Heather 257
Hesseman, Howard 78
Hetrick, Jennifer 313, *315*
Hewitt, Peter 168
Heyden, Yvette 287
Heyes, Douglas 77, 84, 85, 193, 200, 210, 211, 212, 214
"Hi Mom" 254
Hiatt, Michael 166
Hice, Fred 77
Hickey and Boggs 46
Hicks, Chuck 60, 79
Hieu, Joseph 250
Higgins, Joe 230

"High Bleacher Man" 208
The High Chaparral 133
"High Dollar Bop" 291
"High High" 246, 252
"High Jinx" 92
High Mountain Rangers 88, 99
"High Noon in L.A." 204, 211
Highcastle, Joe 312
Highcastle, Tommy 214
"Higher Education" 245, 250
Highlander 268
The Highwayman 137, 178, 221
Hill, Dean 100
Hill, Frankie 100
Hill, Matt 251, 256
Hill, Michael 240, 241
Hill, Rick 216
Hill, Walter 46
Hill Street Blues 4, 12, 15, 30, 31, 72, 96, 97, 98, 101, 102, 120, 128, 137, 145, 160, 179, 180, 197, 198, 200, 202, 226, 242, 263, 265, 273, 277, 285, 301, 310, 326, 328
Hiller, Arthur 50
Hillerman, John 8, 112
Hilton, Lawrence 78
Hilton, Pat 206, 306
Hinckes, C.J. 80
Hinckley, Brett 255
Hindes, Martha 263
Hindle, Art 78, 212, 251
Hindy, Joseph 68, 76
Hindy, Patricia 68
Hine, Roy 100
Hines, Grainger 149
Hingle, Pat 102, 104
Hinton, James David 188
Hiona, Sam 155
"Hip Hop on the Gravy Train" 291
Hippe, Laura 78
Hirsch, Steven 123
Hirschfield, Robert 112
Hirt, Christianne 250, 257, 303
"His Majesty, I Presume" 129
"His Master's Voice" 293
"The Hit Car" 122
Hoag, Mitzi 68
Hobart, Fenton 78
Hobbs, Peter 69, 184, 210
Hock, Allison 25, 201, 210, 211
Hodgkinson, Janet 256
Hoff, Christian 255
Hoffman, Cecil 284, 285, 286, 287
Hoffman, Elizabeth 125, 148, 208, 312, 317
Hoffman, Wendy 147
"Hog Wild" 123
Hogan, Hulk 142, 153, 155, 270
Hogan, Jack 152, 186
Hogan, Robert 66, 98, 104
Holbrook, Hal 29, 30
Holcomb, Rod 21, 22, 25, 105, 112, 113, 118, 122, 123, 124, 128, 129, 147, 287
Holden, Richard 251
"Holiday in the Hills" 147
Holland, Anthony 249, 251, 288
Holland, Erik 150, 167
Holland, John 98

Holland, Randy 167, 228
Hollander, Carlton 211
Holliday, Fred 188
Holliday, Kene 122, 126
Hollywood Beat 137, 205, 305
Hollywood Gazette 261
Hollywood Reporter 17, 83, 110, 162, 181, 190, 205, 206, 223, 225, 244, 270, 306, 326, 327
Holms, Lynn 77
Holt, Robert 75, 77, 78
Holt, Tim 22
"Home for Christmas" 183, 188
"Home to Judgement" 121
"The Homecoming" 161, 165
"Homegirls" 257
Hometown 193
"Homicide" 103, 104
Honey West 82, 178
Hong, James 77, 92, 149, 153, 209, 215, 230
Hong Kong Harry 313
Honig, Howard 65
"Honor Bound" 250
"Honorable Profession" 215
Hood, Don 154, 210, 303
Hooks, David 68
Hooks, Kevin 250
Hooks, Robert 160, 249, 300, 303
Hoopai, Jake 69
Hooperman 98, 118, 203, 227
Hoover, Phil 64, 186, 208
Hope, Leslie 212
Hopkins, Bo 58, 67, 68, 144, 149
Horan, Barbara 147, 167, 173
Horan, James 216
Hormann, Nicholas 105
Hornbeck, James 186, 229
Horrocks, Brynn 216
Horsley, Lee 295, 329
Horton, Michael 250
Horvath, Joe 164
Horwitt, Arnold 80
Hosea, Bobby 252
"The Hot Grounder" 159, 160, 196, 197, 201, 207, 310
"Hot Horse" 80
"Hot Pursuit" 213
"Hot Shoes" 161, 164
Hot Stuff 243
"Hot Styles" 151
Hotel 3, 115, 173, 203
"Hotel of Fear" 54, 65
"Hotshot" 94
House 114
"The House on Orange Grove Avenue" 84
"The House on Willis Avenue" 66, 97
Houseman, John 177
Houston Knights 181
"How I Saved the Senator" 246, 255
"How Much Is That Body in the Window?" 250
"How Will They Remember Me?" 280, 292
Howard, D.D. 151, 179, 185, 208
Howard, Dennis 104

Howard, Frank 100
Howard, Rance 167, 288
Howard, Sherman 312
Howard, Susan 63, 84
Howard, Vince 59
Howard the Duck 243, 275
Howell, Hoke 123
Howerton, Candace 62
Howerton, Charles 155
Hoy, Linda 126, 167, 189
Hoy, Robert (Bobby) 61, 84
Hoyos, Rodolfo 62
Hoyos, Terri 212
Hsu, Victor 184
Hu, Kelly 252
Hubert, Janet 215, 251
Huck, Janet 260, 277
Huckleberry Hound 140
Huddleston, David 61, 298, 302
Huddleston, Michael 126
Hudis, Norman 78
Hudson, Ernie 5, 95, 148, 231, *232*, 234, 235, 322, *322*
Hudson, Gary 215
Hudson, Rock 39
Hudson, Toni 126, 145, 152
Huffman, David 77
Huffman, Rosanna 98
Huge, Thom 100
Huggins, Roy 33, 39, 40, 41, 44, 48, 50, 51, 52, 54, 58, 59, 60, 71, 72, 73, 75, 76, 82, 83, 84, 106, 179, 199, 200, 201, 202, 203, 205, 206, 210, 212, 213, 215, 330, 333
Huggins, Thomas 212, 213, 214
Hugh-Kelly, Daniel *157,* 160, *161,* 162, 163, 169, 323
Hughes, Brendan 208
Hughes, Karen 209
Hughes, Prince 216
Hugo, Lawrence 84
Huguely, Jay 103
Humble, Gwen 122
Humes, Mary Margaret 149, 166, 174, 184, 207
Hunsberger, H. Edward 203, 214
Hunt, David 312
"Hunt for the White Tiger" 130
Hunter 3, 4, 7, 8, 9, 11, 13, 15, 16, 17, 19, 20, 21, 23, *24,* 25, 29, 30, 32, 34, 35, 36, 45, 48, 56, 57, 102, 107, 118, 119, 120, 132, 135, 137, 139, 140, 141, 144, 145, 146, 156, 157, 158, 159, 160, 172, 180, **192–220,** *193,* 223, 224, 225, 227, 228, 231, 233, 242, 260, 265, 266, 270, 282, 283, 301, 305, 306, 308, 310, 313, 321, 324, 326, 328, 329, 330, 334
"Hunter" (pilot) 207
Hunter, Kim 68, 78
Hunter, Rion 216
Hupp, Jana Marie 213
Hurley, Craig 216, 252
Hursey, Sherry 186, 303
Hurst, Gordon 63
Hurst, Rick 235
Hutcherson, Ray 79, 81

Hutton, Betty 79
Hyland, Patricia 81
Hylands, Scott 77, 94
Hyman, Charles 155, 184
Hyser, Joyce 31
Hytner, Steve 323

I Dream of Jeannie 17, 237
"I love it when a plan comes together" 35
I Love Lucy 17
I Married Joan 17
"I on Sports" 195
I Spy 37, 46, 116, 117, 121
"I Want My Mummy" 235
Iacangelo, Peter 155
IBA 141
"The Iceman" 90, 91, 94
Iden, Mindy 186
Identity Crisis 310
The Idolmaker 273
"If You Can't Beat 'Em, Join 'Em" 183, 189
"If You Can't Pay the Price" 72, 75
"If You Could See What I See" 160, 168
"I'll Take You to Lunch" 80
"I'm Okay, You Need Work" 250
"Immigrants" 134
Impert, Margaret 65
In Cold Blood 71
"In Custody of a Clown" 249
"In Hazard" 62
The In-Laws 110
"In Plane Sight" 149
"In Pursuit of Carol Thorne" 59, 159
"In the Eye of the Beholder" 160, 162, 169
In the Heat of the Night 260
"In the Name of Love" 257
"The Incident" 219
"Incident at Crystal Lake" 152
"Incident at San September" 299, 303
The Incredible Hulk 26, 29, 54, 118, 121, 139
"Independent Operator" 288
Indiana Jones (movie franchise) 127, 129
"Informant" 216
Ing, Alvin 104, 214
Ingersoll, James 62, 92
Ingham, Barrie 129, 153
Ingram, Jay 188, 217
Inouye, Julie 312
The Insiders 323
International Coalition Against Violent Entertainment 140
The Invaders 53, 82, 114, 271
"Investment in Death" 217
Ipale, Aharon 287, 317
Ireland, John 165, 303
Iron Eyes Cody 154
Iron Horse 295, 302
Ironside 37, 45, 106, 231, 237
Ironside, Michael 144, 148
Irvine, Jeff 291
"Irving the Explainer" 65, 143

Iscove, Rob 251, 262, 275, 278, 279, 287, 288, 289, 290, 291, 311
Ishida, Jim 64, 92, 93, 255
Ishimoto, Dale 92, 155
"The Island" 151
Isler, Seth 219, 254
Israel, Al 211
"It Could'a Been Worse, She Could'a Been a Welder" 161, 166
"It Goes with the Job" 74, 80
It Takes a Thief 37, 327
"The Italian Bird Fiasco" 54, 62
Ito, Robert 317
"It's a Boy" 81
"It's a Desert Out There" 149
"It's a Vial Sort of Business" 186, 308
"It's All Downhill from Here" 119, 120, 124, 175
"It's Easier to Pass an Elephant Through the Eye of a Needle..." 112
"It's Hard But It's Fair" 80
"It's How You Play the Game" 276
"It's Only Rock and Roll" 25, 121, 126
ITV 136, 141, 142
Itzin, Gregory 153, 209, 251
Ivar, Stan 215
Ives, Burl 39, 40

Jackson, David 249, 250, 251
Jackson, Douglas 291
Jackson, John M. 287, 288, 289
Jackson, Kate 163
Jackson, Mary 161, 163, 213, 227, 230, 300
Jackson, Michael 132
Jackson, Michael A. 257
Jackson, Sherry 61
Jackson, Stoney 164, 323
Jacobson, Gela 210
Jacobuss, Jerry 217
Jacoby, Billy 154, 248
Jacoby, Bobby 154, 167
"The Jade Woman" 213
Jaeck, Scott 216
Jaeckel, Richard 77, 94
Jaffe, Seth 187, 220, 311
JAG 32, 88
Jake and the Fat Man 203, 297, 301
James, Anthony 149, 152, 154, 186, 199, 210
James, Brion 65, 152, 207, 214, 220
James, Clifton 82, 83, 84, 144, 147, 149
James, Greg 249
James, John Thomas 51, 72
James, Rick 142, 153, 158
James, Stephen 189
James, Troy 257
James Bond (character/franchise) 232, 271, 308
James-Reece, Cyndi 208
Jameson, Joyce 59, 78
Janes, Robert 76
Janis, Conrad 12
Jansen, Christine 255
Janssen, David 38, 46, 52, 261

Jarrell, Andy 68
Jarress Brennan, Jill 93
Jarret, Gabe 251
Jarrett, Paul 250, 256, 291
Jarrett, Renee 85
Jason, Harvey 311
Jason, Peter 187
Jaws: The Revenge 306, 310
Jay, Tony 214
"the jazz" 35
Jefferson, Laurie 68
Jeffory, Dawn 174
Jeffries, Todd 216
Jeffries, Will 218
Jenco, Sal 247
Jenkins, Ken 287, 289, 290, 291, 293, 294
Jenkins, Paul 59, 63, 84, 210
Jenner, Barry 214
Jennings, Brent 213, 214, 217, 251
Jennings, Juanita 211
Jenson, Roy 64, 75, 108
"The Jersey Bounce" 67
Jesse Hawkes 99
Jesus Christ, Superstar 266
Jeter, James 66, 209
The Jetsons 200, 329
Jewell, Geri 255
J.J. Starbuck 7, 8, 24, 34, 35, 205, 225, 228, 233, 234, 258, 274, **295–304**, 297, 310, 313, 318, 334
"J.J. Starbuck" (pilot) 302
Joe Dancer 74
"Joey Blue Eyes" 53, 62
Johnny Ringo 82, 116
Johns, Patti 251
Johnson, Anne-Marie 25
Johnson, Arch 70
Johnson, Arnold 100, 187, 312
Johnson, Arte 142, 143, 153
Johnson, Audra 235
Johnson, Brock 257
Johnson, Charles "Chas" Floyd 6, 51, 61, 64
Johnson, Chip 125, 151, 208
Johnson, Don 183, 223, 280, 284
Johnson, Ed 150
Johnson, Frank 291, 293
Johnson, Franklin 252
Johnson, Georgeann 169, 228, 289, 292, 293
Johnson, James Burr 123
Johnson, Jay 322, 322
Johnson, Joanna 187
Johnson, Karl 151, 184, 208, 217
Johnson, Kenneth 26
Johnson, Laura 211
Johnson, Patricia Ayame 229
Johnson, Stephen 217
Johnson, Wyatt 60
Johnston, Andrew 257
Johnston, Jim 316
Johnston, J.J. 289
Johnston, John Dennis 64, 147, 152, 167, 172, 174
Jonathan, Wesley 254, 255
Jones, Anthony Rene 317
Jones, Carol 147
Jones, Christine 84

Jones, Claude 76, 125
Jones, Claude Earl 112, 151, 174, 248
Jones, Eric Paul 251
Jones, Henry 235
Jones, J. Bill 209, 311
Jones, Lindsay 68
Jones, L.Q. 154
Jones, Lynwood 100
Jones, Marilyn 165, 166
Jones, Mark 19, 24, 145, 150, 151, 152, 172, 173, 174, 181, 184, 185, 193, 199, 208
Jones, Mickey 152, 165, 254
Jones, Peter 118
Jones, Renee 165, 249, 257
Jones, Sam 150, 166, 174, 186, 207
Jones, Tommy Lee 77
Joon Be-Kim 217
Jordan, James Carroll 76, 188
Jordan, S. Marc 153, 168, 210, 216
Jordan, William 59, 62, 64
The Jordan Chance 106
Jory, Victor 66
Joseph, Allen 81
Joseph, Ron 210
Josephson, Jeffrey 148, 174, 184, 207, 219
Joyce, Elaine 82, 83, 84
Joyce, Stephen 289, 292, 293
Joyce, William 67, 217
Joyner, Michelle 251
Joynt, Paul 312
Jozefson, Jack 220
Juarbe, Isreal 213
"Judgement Day" 91, 145, 152
Julian, Sally 208
Juliet 306
Jump, Gordon 62, 93
Jung, Nathan 155, 189, 209
"Junk It to Me, Baby" 98
Jurado, Katy 79
"Just a Coupl'a Guys" 69
"Just a Little Blow Between Friends" 104
"Just Another Polish Wedding" 64
"Just Another Round of That Old Song" 159, 164
"Just Another Three Ring Circus" 9, 124
"Just By Accident" 60
"Just for Laughs" 81
"Just Good Friends" 119
"Just Say No High" 256
Justice, Katherine 211

Kaake, Jeff 212
Kadi, Nicholas 235
Kagan, David 153, 186, 249
Kagan, Jeremy 116
Kahan, Steve 123, 191, 218
Kaldor, Eric 60
Kalem, Toni 80
Kamekona, Daniel 69, 252
Kamel, Stanley 167, 185, 212
Kamm, Kris 251
Kanaly, Steve 84
Kandel, Stephen 237
Kane, Billy 213

Kane, Carol 276
Kane, Ivan 250
Kane, Michael 166, 169
Kanner, Jeff 77
Kapelos, John 303
Kapture, Mitzi 325
Karabatsos, Ron 185, 207, 210, 220
Kareem Abdul-Jabarr 230, 254
Karen, James 164
Karlen, John 67
Karloff and Lugosi 334
Karpf, Stephen and Elinor 84
Karron, Richard 77
Kasdorf, Lenore 151, 187, 254
Kasem, Jean 220
Kate and Allie 17, 180, 275
Katsulas, Andreas 219
Katt, William 6, 18, 34, 37, 113, 114, *115,* 117, 119, 122, 318, *319,* 320
Katz, Stephen 30, 102, 145, 149, 150, 151, 152, 158, 159, 161, 164, 168, 199, 200, 201, 209
Kavenaugh, Dorrie 66
Kawai, Leslie 151
Kay O'Brien 193
Kaye, Caren 164, 249
Kaye, Danny 300
Kazan, Laine 77
Kazann, Zitto 123, 211
Keach, James 93
Keach, Stacy 8
Keach, Stacy, Sr. 61, 78, 168
Kearns, James 294
Kearns, Sandra 70, 92, 106, 120, 125
Keats, Steven 60, 144, 150, 166, 185
Keefer, Don 76
"Keep Your Eye on the Sparrow" 72, 75
Kegeyama, Rodney 184
Kehler, Jack 212
Keifer, Liz 250
Keith, Brian 7, *157, 161,* 162, 163, 195
Keith, Larry 229
Kelbaugh, Rick 80, 81
Kell, Joseph 252
Keller, Susan 60
Kellogg, John 293
Kelly, Calvin 64
Kelly, Jack 56, 64
Kelly, James 152, 188
Kelly, Roz 81
Kelly, Terrence 255, 256, 316
Kelman, Barnet 276
Kelsey, Linda 59
Kelton, Bobby 185
Kelton, Richard 68
Kemmerling, Warren 59, 61, 147
Kemp, Barry 276
Kemp, Jeremy 124, 125
Kenneally, Phillip 58
Kennedy, Betty 69
Kennedy, Leon Isaac 25, 311
Kennedy, Tom 168
Kentucky Jones 103
Kenyon, Sandy 62

Kercher, John 193
Kerns, Joanna 148, 207
Kerns, Roger 80
Kerry, John 61, 76, 92
Kershaw, Whitney 210
Kerwin, Michael 218
Kessler, Bruce 32, 63, 77, 79, 123, 124, 125, 126, 129, 139, 147, 148, 165, 166, 167, 172, 174, 182, 184, 185, 187, 189, 208, 235, 299, 303, 312
Kessler, Lee 220
Kettle, Ross 218
Keuhl, Kandace 212
Keyes, Irwin 312
Keys Hall, Michael 215
Keystone Kops 232
Khambatta, Persis 210
Khan, Chaka 212
Kibbee, Jefferson 214, 215, 216, 252, 253, 254, 255
Kidder, Margot 44, 57, 76, 101
Kidnie, James 257
Kiek, George 255
Kiel, Sue 152
Kiger, Robby 150
Kilbourne, Wendy 151, 185
Kiley, Richard 186
"Kill the Messenger" 67, 159, 197, 310
"Kill Zone" 219
"Killer B's" 164
"Killer in a Hallowe'en Mask" 30, 102, 199, 209
"A Killing in the Market" 296, 297, 302
Kilpatrick, Lincoln 76, 106, 124
Kim, Evan 229
Kim, Robert 209
Kimball, David 220
Kimmel, Dana 148, 211
Kimmins, Kenneth 166, 217
Kincaid, Jason 108
Kind, Richard 313
King, Freeman 210
King, Mabel 289, 312
King, Martin Luther 242
King, Perry *14,* 22, 128, 129, 175, *176,* 177, 180, 183, 184, 189
The King of Comedy 277
Kingi, Henry 191, 311
Kingsley, Hilary 20
Kinmont, Kathleen 330, *331,* 332
Kino, Lloyd 92, 94, 126
Kinsey, Lance 100
Kirby, Blaik 83
Kirby, Bruce 61, 66, 119, 123, 201
Kirby, Jack 333
Kirkconnell, Clare 155
Kirkland, Sally 77
"The Kirkoff Case" 54, 58, 133
Kirschbaum, Bruce 246, 252, 253
Kiser, Terry 77, 84, 164, 173, 189, 217
Kiviaho, Rik 257
Kiwitt, Peter 211
Kleiner, Harry 101
Kline, Richard 213
Kliner, Alex 290

Knaub, Jim 149
Knell, David 57
Knight, Bob 273
Knight, Don 144, 148
Knight, Dudley 62, 84, 92, 123
Knight, Jack 60
Knight, Ted 114
Knight Rider 1, 11, 22, 32, 107, 121, 129, 131, 136, 137, 163, 221, 222
"Knights of the Road" 152
Knightwatch 239
Knipe, Sandra 244
Knots Landing 53
Knutzen, Eiric 306
Kodiak 53
Koenig, Andrew 251
Kogan, Milt 58, 62, 67, 84, 124, 125
Kohnert, Mary 219
Kojak 33, 72, 73, 120, 275, 280, 299, 326
Kolbe, Winriche 70, 104, 217, 218, 219, 312
Kolchak: The Night Stalker 51, 53, 71, 90, 200
Kono, Julia 185
Kopins, Karen 155, 184
Koppel, Nurit 216
Kordick, Moya 155
Koslo, Paul 32, 63, 68, 106, 123, 144, 145, 147, 152, 217
Koss, Al 125
Koss, Dwight 289, 290, 293
Kosslyn, Jack 81
Kosterman, Mitchell 257, 291
Kotto, Yaphet 144, 147
Kousakis, John Peter 155, 214, 299, 303
Kove, Martin 64, 111
Kowalski, Bernard 59, 72, 75, 76, 79, 81, 116, 297
Kozoll, Michael 96, 98, 101
Kraft, Scott 217, 248, 251
Kramer, Stepfanie 15, 16, 17, 31, 145, 150, 179, 185, 193, *193,* 194, 195, 196, 197, 198, 200, 202, 203, 204, 205, 206, 207, 213, 217
Krantz, Robert 253
Kriegel, David 254
Kronish, Stephen 262, 268, 272, 273, 274, 276, 278, 279, 280, 282, 287, 288, 289, 290, 292, 293, 313, 316, 326
Krugman, Lou 66
Kruschen, Jack 61, 85
Kubik, Alex 220
Kubik, Larry 205, 207
Kubota, Tak 95
Kucek, Anna Marie 242
Kuhlman, Richard 149, 185
Kuhlman, Ron 93, 216
Kumagai, Denise 104
Kupfner, Marvin 217, 218
Kurt, Don 281, 288, 292
Kusatsu, Clyde 32, 92, 209, 230, 288
Kuss, Richard 150, 164, 168, 229
Kutcher, Jack 104
Kuwahara, Tom 230

Kwan, Nancy 155
Kwong, Peter 149

L.A. Free Press 236
L.A. Heat 242
L.A. Law 12, 24, 30, 31, 54, 97, 114, 137, 142, 203, 226, 246, 247, 270, 285, 298, 310, 325
Labiosa, David 207, 312
"Labor Pains" 134, 148
Labow, Hilary 124
Labyorteaux, Patrick 252
La Camara, Carlos 148, 215
Lacamell, Jim 257
Lacey, Deborah 151, 250
Lacher, Taylor 67, 85, 104, 154
Lachow, Stan 123
"Le Lacrime D'Amore" 280, 291
La Croix, Peter 257, 294
Ladd, Diane 84
Ladner, Lynn 294
La Due, Joe 151, 164
Lady Blue 140, 193, 241
"Lady Killer" 177, 188
La Fleur, Art 150, 294
La Grue, Tom 79
Lahti, Christine 106
Lahti, Gary 251
Laird, Jack 33
Lake, Stuart 170
Lakso, Edward J. 51, 59, 60, 62, 77
Lally, Michael 154, 155, 169, 189
Lamas, Fernando 330
Lamas, Lorenzo 330, *331, 332*
Lambert, Paul 104, 189
Lambie, Joe 150
Lame Duck 318
Lampert, Jeffrey 184
Lampkin, Charles 208
La Mura, Mark 216
Lance, Peter 20, 283, 285, 286, 294
Lancer 266
Land, Geoffrey 59
Land, Paul 189
Landers, Judy 152
Landers, Matt 288, 312, 316
Landesberg, Steve 63
Landham, Sonny 151, 167
Landi, Sal 150, 219
Landon, Dana 85
Landor, Rosalyn 218
Lane, Brian 197, 208
Lane, Charles 212, 235
Lane, Jane 33, 265
Lane, Lauren 207
Lane, Michael 64, 107
Lane, Scott Edmund 81
Lang, Archie 154
Lang, Katherine Kelly 184, 230
Lange, Kelly 59
Lange, Michael 177, 181, 182, 185, 186, 187, 188, 193, 208, 235
Langford, Kim 212
Langham, Wallace 254
Langlois, Dar 168
Lannom, Les 93
Lansing, John 210
Lanyer, Charles 124

La Paglia, Anthony 212
Lapis, Peter 216
Laramie 133
Laredo 133
Larkin, Bob 187
Larkin, Kristine 85
Larkin, Sheila 81
Larroquette, John 89, *89,* 91
Larry Thompson Organization 270
Larson, Darrell 94
Larson, Eric 217
Larson, Glen 3, 11, 28, 32, 39, 40, 44, 48, 49, 51, 53, 55, 89, 101, 102, 106, 107, 108, 115, 119, 129, 131, 140, 144, 160, 175, 178, 190, 192, 228, 299, 300, 313
La Russa, Adrienne 79
Laskawy, Harris 214, 317
Laskin, Michael 208, 251, 252, 302
Lassick, Sidney 80, 166
Lassie 116
"Last Chance High" 255
"The Last Kill" 208
"Last Mission Over Sengai" 93
"Last of the True Believers" 275, 289
"Last One for Hutch" 93
"Last One There Is a Rotten Heir" 129
The Last Precinct 5, 5, 19, 107, 119, 224, 228, **231-235,** 258, 259, 299, 321, 322, 334
"The Last Precinct" (pilot) 235
"Last Rites for Lucci" 273, 274, 280, 282, 288
"Last Run" 216
The Late Show 46
Latham, Louise 215
Lathan, Bobbi Jo 217
Lattanzi, Steve 187
Lauer, Andrew 253
Laurensen, James 228
Lauria, Dan 168, 211, 287, 311
Lauter, Ed 65, 75, 144, 147, 150, 163
Lavachielli, John 252
Laven, Arnold 32, 67, 77, 96, 98, 111, 112, 118, 123, 124, 125, 126, 147, 148, 149, 151, 164, 172, 173, 174, 185, 186, 197, 207, 208
Laverne and Shirley 91, 195
The Law and Harry McGraw 203, 301
Law and Order 9, 30, 31, 246, 275
Lawlor, John 61, 92, 229
Lawrence, Evan 159, 164, 230
Lawrence, Hap 189
Lawrence, Marc 78, 154
Lawrence, Ronald William 207, 255
Lawrence, Steve 165, 169
Lawson, Eric 153
Lawson, Richard 164, 289
Lazar, Ava 152, 187, 189
Lazarus, Tom 21, 30, 199, 200, 203, 209, 210, 228, 229
Leach, Nigel 256
Leacock, Richard 256
"Leapin' Lizards" 12

Lear, Norman 3, 10
Learned, Michael 294
Leary, Brianne 91
"Lease with an Option to Die" 143, 152
Leavitt, Ron 239
Leavitt, Steve 166
Leavy, Donna Lynn 218
Le Blanc, Christian 189
Le Clerc, Jean 124
Lederer, Suzanne 208
Ledford, Judith 133, 146, 147
Ledingham, David 219
Lee, Anna 80
Lee, Dana 79, 154, 167, 213
Lee, Johnny 154, 188
Lee, Jonna 168
Lee, Lesa 186, 208
Lee, Ruta 174
Lee, Stan 120, 121, 333
Leeds, Adrian 81
Leeds, Peter 185
Leeds, Phil 312
Leek, Tiiu 154, 155
Lefcourt, Peter 94
"The Left Hand of the Devil" 77
"Legacy" 207
Le Gault, Lance 27, 32, 48, 60, 66, 92, 134, 146
Legend of the Walks Far Woman 227
"The Legion" 217
Legmen 179, 203, 317
Lehman, Lillian 248, 249
Lehmann, Ted 112
Lehne, Fredric 286, 294
Lehne, John 77
Lei, Lydia 149
Leiber, Paul 212
Leibman, Norm 75
Leigh, Steven 219
Leigh-Scott, Kathryn 129, 154, 164, 254
Leighton, Roberta 79
Leith, Virginia 79
Leitch, Donovan 254
Le Masters, Kim 264
Lemkin, Jonathan 245, 246, 249, 250, 251
Lennon, Jimmy 151
Lenny 239
Lenz, Kay 188, 210
Lenz, Rick 126
Leonard, Bernadette 288
Leonard, John 23, 139, 192
Leonard, Lu 189
Leonard, Sheldon 116
Leonard, Terry 61, 63, 195
Leong, Albert 167
Lerner, Fred 60, 63, 69, 123, 147
Lerner, Ken 126, 184, 214, 218
Lerner, Michael 58, 59, 63, 152
Le Roy, Gloria 76, 98, 212
Lessing, Norman 78
Lester, Jeff 312
"Let Me Hear the Music" 103
"Let Them Eat Cake" 293
Lethal Weapon 259
Lethin, Lori 150, 229

Le Vant, Renee 288
Levels, Calvin 253
Levine, Floyd 81, 112, 312
Levinson, David 256, 257
Levinson and Link, Richard and William, 101, 104, 116, 296, 297, 298, 301
Levitt, Alan J. 80
Levitt, Steve 169
Levy, Shawn 255
Lew, Jerome 217
Lewin, Robert 73, 77
Lewis, Arthur B. 80
Lewis, Charlotte 322
Lewis, David 66
Lewis, Diane 94
Lewis, Geoffrey 85, 144, 145, 150, 153, 303
Lewis, Greg 184
Lewis, Herbert 288
Lewis, Jerry 277, 278, 279, 290
Lewis, Marcia 77
Lewis, Richard 189
Libby, Brian 148, 185, 217
Libertini, Richard 79
Lichtman, Paul 78, 93
Lieber, Mimi 291, 292
Lieberman, Rick 215
The Life and Legend of Wyatt Earp 170
Life Goes On 267
Lifford, Tina 218
Lightfoot, Leonard 124
Lightstone, David 211, 215
Ligon, Tom 94
"Lilacs, Mr. Maxwell" 121, 125
Lillo, Marie 75
Lima, Rafael 294
Lin, Tracy 248
Lincoln, La Park 212
Lincoln, Scott 148, 187, 312
Lindbjerg, Lalania 257
Lindeman, Mitch 60
Lindsley, Chuck 189
Lindstrom, John 252
Lineback, Richard 167, 211, 217
Linero, Jeannie 77, 210
Linke, Paul 219, 254
Linn, Terri Ann 186
Linton, Philip 253
Linville, Larry 24, 66, 188
Lion, Richard 287
"Lions, Tigers, Monkeys and Dogs" 69
Lipari, Joanna 67
Lippe, Jonathan 60
Lipscombe, Dennis 32, 125, 126, 144, 148, 260, 263, 281, 287, 288, 293
Lipstadt, Aaron 288
Lipstick 177
Lipton, Peggy 237
Lipton, Robert 79, 249
Lisbon Wood, John 211
Liska, Stephen 151, 188, 215
Lisson, Mark 218, 219, 220
Little, Cleavon 63
Little, Tawny 126
"A Little Bit of England" 95

"Little Disease with a Big Name" 245
Little House on the Prairie 52, 127
"Little Man with a Big Reputation" 220
The Little Sister 44
"A Little Town with an Accent" 154
Littler, Craig 185
Liu, Frank Michael 60, 79
"Live at Eleven" 126
Lively, Jason 249
Lively, Robin 254
Livin' Large 275
"Living and Dying in 4/4 Time" 291
Lloyd, Kathleen 229
Lloyd, Norman 279, 292, 293
Lo Bianco, Tony 100, 326
"Local Man Eaten by Newspaper" 54, 68
The Local Stigmatic 275
"Loc'd Out" 253
Locke, Jon 189
Lockhart, June 116, 123, 126
Lockhart, Laurel 312
Lockwood, Vera 79
Lofton, Christopher 124
Logan, Robert 186
Logan's Run (television series) 54
Loggia, Robert 63, 64, 106
Lomartire, Paul 323
Lombard, Michael 69, 188
Lombardo, Joel 79
London, Jerry 60, 61, 62, 63, 64, 76, 85
London, Michael J. 123
The Lone Ranger (character) 10, *11*, 12, 141, 194, 221, 226, 320, 330
The Lone Ranger (comic books) 11, 156, 157
The Lone Ranger (feature film) 12
The Lone Ranger (television series) *11*, 12, 334
"A Lonely Way to Die" 84
"The Long Ago Girl" 161, 166
"Long and Thin, Lorna Lynn" 100
"Long Distance Daddy" 185
The Long Goodbye 45
"A Long Way from L.A." 159, 197, 207
Longo, Tony 166, 207, 220, 229
Longos, Lynn 155
Longworth, David 257
Lonow, Mark 69, 312
"Look Back in Terror" 78
"The Loose Cannon" 45, 262, 263, 285, 287, 308
"Loose Larry's List of Losers" 112, 159
Lopez, Kamala 218, 253, 256
Lopez, Ricardo 152
Lopez, Robert 216
Lopez, Sal 211, 287
Lopinto, Dorian 209
Lopresti, Jo 78
Lord, Jack 51
Lord, Justin 210
Lords, Traci 273, 289
The Lords of Flatbush 177

Loros, George 26, 32, 52, 57, 58, 64, 65, 68, 69, 75, 77, 79, 81, 124
"The Losers" 84
"The Lost Diablo" 29, 124
Lost in Space 116, 237
Lottery 328
Lou Grant 4, 24, 26, 51, 102, 134, 135, 145, 177, 195, 201, 246, 265
Lough, James 68, 151
Louie, John 185
Louis, Justin 256
"Love and War" 93
The Love Boat 3, 173, 298
"Love, Hate, and Sporty James" 211
"Love Is the Word" 69
Lovece, Frank 271
Lovett, Gemma 257
"Low and Away" 249
Lowe, Heather 84, 125
Lowens, Curt 153
Lowenthal, Mark 229, 248
Lowndes, Peter 174
Lowry, Brian 327
Lucas, Byron 256, 257
Lucas, George 309
Lucero, Anthony 316
Lucero, Enrico 147
Lucia, Charles 229
Lucking, Bill 27, 61, 92, 106, 125, 129, 134, 146, 217
Luckingbill, Lawrence 84
Lucky, Chris 80
The Lucy Show 17, 237
Ludwig, Salem 290
Luisi, James 32, 48, 49, 53, 58, 85, 92, 145, 151, 182, 184
Luke, Keye 149
Lukes, Jack 80
"Lullabye" 218
Luna, Barbara 218
Lund, Art 58, 84
Lundie, Mark 256
Lupo, Frank 6, 7, 12, 18, 25, 27, 30, 32, 34, 35, 36, 37, 102, 103, 118–119, 120, 123, 124, 125, 126, 127, 129, 132, 134, 135, 139, 142, 143, 144, 145, 147, 148, 149, 150, 152, 153, 154, 155, 158, 159, 160, 172, 174, 176, 178, 181, 182, 183, 184, 185, 189, 190, 192, 193, 194, 195, 196, 197, 198, 199, 200, 201, 202, 203, 205, 206, 207, 208, 209, 212, 228, 229, 231, 232, 233, 234, 235, 238, 239, 258, 260, 287, 308, 317, 330, 333, 334
Lupton, John 62, 63, 66, 85
Luz, Franc 193, 212
Lydon, James 62, 95, 124
Lyman, Dorothy 216
"Lyman P. Dokker, Fed" 80
Lynch, Ed 148
Lynch, Ken 66
Lynch, Richard 78, 145, 151, 217, 233, 235
Lynde, Janice 108
Lynley, Carol 98
Lynne, Amy 217
Lyons, Jeffrey 293
Lyons, Robert F. 148

Lysell, Allan 288
Lytton, Kathryn 208

M Squad 52
Mabray, Stuart 312
Macaulay, Marc 294
Macchia, John 228
Mace, Cynthia 254
Mace, Paul 68
Machon, Karen 64
MacDonald, Shawn 254
MacGyver 72, 90, 205, 221, 242, 273, 326
Mackay, Don 303
MacKay, Jeff 32, 88, *89*, 91, 100, 112, 122, 124, 167, 172, 173
MacKenzie, Philip Charles 93
MacKenzie, Robert 12, 23, 175
MacKenzie, Will 78
MacLachlan, Janet 61, 78
MacLaren, John G. 294
MacLean, Peter 111, 154, 164, 211
MacLeod, Murray 62
MacMahon, Karen 104
MacMillan, Will 123, 125, 126, 151, 187, 208
MacNamara, J. Patrick 229
MacRae, Meredith 65
MacRae, Michael 165, 187, 250
MacReady, George 38
Macy, Bill 168, 186
Mad About You 313
Madalone, Dennis 229
Madden, Salli B. 16
Maddux, Lee 215, 217
Magar, Guy 105, 147, 163, 164, 172, 174, 182, 184, 208
Magee, Jack 126
"The Magic Mirror" 121
The Magician 127
Magistretti, Paul 73, 75, 76, 77
The Magnificent Seven 136
Magnum Force 24, 29, 30, 55, 101, 158
Magnum P.I. 4, 7, 8, *8*, 32, 45, 46, 51, 55, 56, 88, 89, 99, 103, 106, 107, 111, 119, 134, 137, 140, 160, 178, 179, 180, 181, 183, 194, 202, 205, 226, 227, 243, 298, 299
Maher, Joseph 229
Mahon, John 62, 63
Mahoney, John 216
Mailer, Lev 123
Major Howard, Kevyn 150, 187
Makaro, J.J. 257
"Make the Sun Shine" 80
Mako 126, 148
Malave, ChuChu 80
Malet, Arthur 252
Malick, Wendie 214
Malinder, Jim 78
Malkin, Sam 257
Mallari, Melinda 311
Mallory, Carole 85, 125
Malone, Dorothy 84
Malone, Maureen 229
Malone, Nancy 58
Malone, Patrick 255
"The Maltese Cow" 149

A Man Called Hawk 275
A Man Called Sloane 99, 116
The Man from Atlantis 118
The Man from UNCLE 99, 116, 135, 145, 146, 155, 237
"Man in a Glass House" 35, 163
"The Man in the Full Toledo" 30, 104, 160
Man of the People 57, 320
"The Man Who Saw the Alligators" 52, 53, 68
Manard, Biff 220
Mancini, Michael 78, 126
Mancini, Ric 61, 77, 154
Mancuso, Nick 11, *11*, 106, 221–222, *222*, 223, 225, 227, 228, 273
Mancuso FBI 9, 30, 31, 177, 286, 326
Mandan, Robert 62, 230
Mandell, Alan 78
Mandingo 177
Mandrell, Barbara 69
Manduke, Joe 165
Manetti, Larry 8, 35, 69, 88, *89*, 91, 99, 100, 104, 111, 112
Mangiardi, Robert 272, 288
Mangrum, Dawn 151
Manimal 3, 137, 142, 221, 300
Mankuma, Blu 287, 290, 316
Mann, Andrea 256, 316
Mann, Michael 140, 198, 200, 270, 280, 283, 284, 286, 301
Manners, Kim 166, 167, 168, 188, 189, 210, 212, 228, 229, 248, 249, 250, 251, 253, 254, 255, 289, 297, 303
Manning, Don 100
Mannix 50, 97, 101, 120, 140, 178
"The Mansion" 75
Manson, Alan 67, 69
Mansour, Philip 76, 84
Mantee, Paul 149, 201, 207, 217
Mantegna, Joe 124
Manza, Ralph 312
Mara, Adele 40
March, Alex 79
Marciano, David 35, 262, 280, 285, 287, 308, 311
Marcovicci, Andrea 25, 78
Marcus, Bill 153
Marcus Welby MD 44, 83, 120
Marden, Adrienne 64
Marder, Eli 188
Margolin, Janet 60
Margolin, Stuart 19, 41, 43, 48, 53, 57, 58, 59, 64, 101
Marie 274
Marie-Johnson, Anne 211
Marinelli, Joe 220
Maris, Ada 210, 294
Mark, D. Neil 256
Mark VII 37, 39
Marker 329, 333
"The Marker" 81
Markham, Monte 149
Markland, Ted 66, 81, 148, 212, 220
Markle, Stephen 294
Markley, Andrew 256

Marko, Zekial 60
Marks, Jennifer 65
Marks, Marianne 155
Marley, John 72, 75, 163
Marlow, Lorri Gay 81
Marlowe 44
Marlowe, Nora 64
Marlowe, Scott 68, 217
Maross, Joe 63, 68
Marquette, Jacques 106
Marquez, Vanessa 294
Marquez, William 123
"The Marriage of Heaven and Hell" 262, 263, 268, 284, 287
Married ... with Children 30, 158, 239, 247, 273, 280
Mars, Kenneth 93, 166, 168, 233, 235
Marsac, Maurice 65, 155
Marsh, Michele 77, 79, 215
Marsh, Walter 257, 289, 292
"The Marshal of Sladetown" 170, 173
Marshall, Ken 219
Marshall, Peter 256, 293, 294
Marshall, Steve 249
Marta, Darcy 254
Marta, Lynn 67
Martell, Jay 319
Martell, Tasha 98
Marth, Frank 151
Martika 283, 285, 294
Martin, Anne-Marie 194
Martin, Barney 248, 249
Martin, Damon 253
Martin, Dean 277
Martin, Jared 212
Martin, Mary 166
Martin, Pepper 62, 63, 64, 66, 68, 84, 85, 184, 208
Martin, Quinn 1, 38, 39, 48, 52, 54, 82, 83, 175, 233
Martin, Ross 79
Martin, Sandy 209
Martin, Strother 23, 64, 74, 76, 79, 80
Martin, Todd 85
Martinez, A. 80
Martinez, Claudio 81
Martorano, Vince 76, 78
Maruzzo, Joe 255, 313
Marvel Comics 34, 325
Marvel super-heroes 120, 325
Mary 180
The Mary Tyler Moore Show 17, 39, 238
Masak, Ron 65
Mascolo, Joseph 64, 212
*M*A*S*H* (feature film) 45, 82
*M*A*S*H* (television series) 3, 24, 27, 39, 45, 82, 90, 103, 180, 196, 226, 238, 246, 309
Mason, Eric 66
Mason, Madison 209
Mason, Marlyn 169
Masquerade 140, 160, 221, 228
Masset, Andrew 168, 211, 312
"Match Point" 85
"A Material Difference" 68

Matheny, Charles 294
Matheson, Richard Christian 30, 32, 103, 105, 134, 143, 144, 148, 149, 150, 153, 154, 160, 161, 165, 166, 167, 199, 208, 209
Matheson, Tim 94
Mathews, Walter 152
Matlin, Marlee 266, 267
Matlock 203, 281, 297, 301, 326
Matt Houston 179, 190, 295, 298, 302
Matt Lincoln 237
"A Matter of Policy" 182, 188
Matthew, Patrick 215
Matthews, Brian 188
Matthews, Dakin 303
Matthews, Douglas 85
Matuszak, John 155, 199, 210
Maura, Ralph 123
Maverick 39, 40, 41, 43, 44, 47, 50, 56, 57, 99, 106, 200, 232
Maverick Square 325
Max, Ron 81, 208, 220
Maxwell, Daphne 100, 104, 151
Maxwell, Don 151
Maxwell, Frank 61
Maxwell, Vicki 316
Mayberry, Russ 58, 60, 61, 62, 63, 65, 75, 91, 92
Mayberry RFD 237
Mayne, Ferdy 123, 126
Mayo, Whitman 77, 78
"The Mayor's Committee from Deerlick Falls" 20, 54, 65
Mayot, France 208
Mays, Deborah 126
Mazmanian, Marius 155
McAllister, Chip 309, 311
McAlpine, James 59
McArthur, Alex 185
McBeath, Tom 287, 292
McBrearty, Dan 256
McBride, Harlee 68
McBride, Lilyan 85
McBroom, Amanda 105
McCabe and Mrs. Miller 45
McCain, Frances Lee 66, 214
McCallum, David 146, 155
McCalman, Macon 214
McCann, Chuck 65, 118, 125, 172, 173
McCannon, Dianne 209
McCarren, Fred 168
McCarthy, Annette 189
McCarthy, Frank 123, 124, 155, 166, 184, 190, 229, 248
McCarthy, Jeff 219
McCarthy, Joe 269
McCarthy, Julianne 229
McCarthy, Kevin 143, 145, 153, 174
McCary, Rod 84, 186
McCaslin, Maylo 152, 166, 184, 207
McClosky, Leigh 309, 311
McCloud 3, 39, 44, 49, 72, 101, 102, 103, 192, 300
McClure, Doug 107, 108, 165
McClure, Marc 211
McCoo, Marilyn 312

McCord, Kent 92, 250, 299, 303, 313
McCormick, Kathy 219
"McCormick's Bar and Grill" 159, 168
McCown, Cort 219
McCrane, Paul 290, 291
McCullem, Kathy 91
McCulley, Sandra 125
McCullough, Linda 78
McDaniel, George 126, 153, 174, 210, 230
McDonald, Christopher 185, 189, 208
McDonnell, Terrence 172, 174, 187
McDonough, Mary 217
McDormand, Fran 208
McDougall, Jane 249
McEachin, James 59, 214
McElroy, Alan 255
McEveety, Bernard 68, 148
McEveety, Vincent 59
McEvoy, Anne Marie 167
McFadden, Barney 64, 153
McFadden, Gates 329
McFadden, Tom 147, 188, 220
McFee, Dwight 289
McGavin, Darren 40, 71
McGee, Jack 311
McGeehan, Mary Kate 148
McGillin, Howard 64
McGinley, Lori 209
McGinn, Russ 62
McGonagle, Richard 153, 187, 250
McGoohan, Patrick 271
McGovern, Terrence 147
McGrath, Derek 230
McGrath, Douglas 78
McGreevey, Thomas 186, 216
McGregor, Richard 256
McGuire, Betty 165
McGuire, Bryan 151
McGuire, Maddy 112
McGuire, Michael 68
McIntire, James 125
McKane, Brendan 212
McKay, Peggy 303
McKenzie, Richard 104, 249
McKeon, Doug 252
McKeon, Nancy 102, 104
McKewin, Vince 186
McKinney, Bill 75, 76, 144, 145, 147, 152, 187, 219
McKinney, John 66
McKnight, David 312
McKnight, Fred 205, 215, 216
McKrell, Jim 98, 148, 166, 229, 249
McLaughlin, Bill 215
McLeod, Shelagh 153
McLerie, Allyn Ann 75
McLiam, John 85, 155, 187, 209
McManus, Michael 217
McMartin, John 62
McMillan, Kenneth 320
McMillan and Wife 44, 72, 298
McMullan, James 66, 152, 166
McMurray, Sam 251
McNally, Terrence 126

McNamara, J. Patrick 303
McNulty, Kevin 257, 287, 292
McPeak, Sandy 81, 154, 211
McPherson, Stephen 103, 104
McQueen, Neile 66
McQueen, Steve 23, 49
McRaney, Gerald 59, 60, 65, 80, 178
McShane, Ian 130
McWilliams, Caroline 98, 212
McWilliams, Paul 84
"Me, Myself, and Die" 216
Meadows, Jayne 110, 111
Meadows, Kristen 148, 152, 184, 312
"The Mean, Green Love Machine" 181, 182, 184
Mean Streets 111
"Mean Streets and Pastel Houses" 249
Mears, Deann 79
"Meatball Circus" 92
Medford, Don 74, 75, 78, 79, 80, 81, 83, 84
Media Access Awards 266
Medical Center 172
Medina, Benny 123, 126
Medina, Julio 75, 126
Mee, Kirk 68
"Meet Mike McPike" 281, 293
Megill, Sheelah 256
Megna, Frank 281, 289, 292
Meixel, Steve 79
Mejia, Gerardo 253
Melcher, Manfred 250
"Meltdown" 293
Melton, Sid 215
Melville, Sam 149, 153
"Members Only" 143, 153
Memmoli, George 63
Men 203
The Men 88, 99
Men at Law 237
Mena, Chaz 294
Mendelsohn, Carol 160, 168, 169, 227, 228, 229, 230, 266, 272, 273, 287, 288, 298, 303, 304
Mendenhall, Marissa 208
Menghi, Umberto 287
Menick, Jon 213
Menosky, Joe 213, 214, 215, 216, 217, 316
Mental Health Foundation 140
Menyuk, Eric 292, 293
Menzies, Rod 291
Mercado, Hector Jaime 154, 211, 213
"The Merchant of Death" 272, 288
Merlin, Jan 188
Merrill, Don 244, 261, 264
Merrow, Jane 124
Meshekoff, Matthew 292
Meszaros, Ronald 149
Metcalfe, Robert 254, 255
Metrano, Art 75, 79, 80, 153, 220, 230, 252
Mettey, Lynette 59
Meyer, Janice 212
Meyers, Richard 49, 102

MGM 71, 83
Miami Herald 273
Miami Vice 12, 36, 71, 137, 140, 181, 183, 198, 199, 200, 201, 202, 203, 205, 221, 223, 234, 244, 260, 271, 275, 279, 280, 283, 284, 285, 286, 313, 325, 326
Miano, Robert 155, 212, 312
Miceli-Sanchez, Paul 214
Michael, Ralph 128, 129
Michael, Ryan 129
Michaels, Corrine 66, 69, 84, 213
Michaels, Gregory 104
Michaels, Jeanna 213, 216
Michaels, Kerry 153
Michaels, Margaret 229
Michan, Cherie 150, 152
Michelman, Tony 168
Mickelson, Barry K. 257
Midnight Caller 273, 325, 326
Midwood, Ramsey 219
Mignini, Carolyn 250
Miguel, Nigel 254
Mike Hammer 4, 8, 8, 45, 120, 137, 180, 194, 196, 221, 265
"Mike's P.O.V." 254
Miles, Rosalind 78
Milford, John 149
Milford, Kim 311
Milius, John 29, 101
Millar, Doug 254
Millennium 314
Miller, Allan 59, 250
Miller, Barry 80
Miller, Beth 186
Miller, Denny 65, 67, 104, 106, 111, 169
Miller, Dick 311, 312
Miller, Frank 100
Miller, Gene 287, 316
Miller, Ivy 243
Miller, Joshua 125, 249
Miller, Mark Thomas 312
Miller, Robert 78
Miller, Ron 263
Miller, S. Marc 216
Miller, Stephen E. 230, 251, 255, 291, 292
Milligan, Deanna 256, 257
Milligan, Spencer 84
Milligan, Tuck 219
"Million Dollar Misunderstanding" 195, 199, 201, 209
"The Millionaire's Life" 112
Mills, Donna 84
Milmore, Jennifer 257
"La Mina" 294
Minardos, Nico 126, 147
"Mind Games" 134, 144, 153
Minn, Haunani 154, 250
Minor, Bob 113, 122
Minton, Faith 168
"Mirage" 159, 185
"Mirage a Trois" 159, 168
Miranda, John 124
Miranda, Robert 152, 216, 230, 235, 248, 287, 292
Miss Marple 297
Missing Persons **328–329**

Mission: Impossible 16, 37, 38, 132, 135, 136, 140, 162, 231, 320
"Mission of Peace" 154
"Mr. Cool" 235
Mr. Ed 22
"Mr. Hardcastle Goes to Washington" 164
Mr. Sardonicus 282
Mr. Smith 133
Mister T 16, 132, *133,* 135, 139, *142,* 146
Mister Terrific 118
Mitchell, Cameron 165
Mitchell, Channing 256
Mitchell, Dallas 68
Mitchell, Donna 214, 302
Mitchell, Elvis 260, 261, 264
Mitchell, Herb 151
Mitchell, Jake 92, 98
Mitchell, Phil 257
Mitchell, Scoey 79, 81
Mitchell, Thomas 257
Mix, Tom 170
Mlodinow, Leonard 217
Mockus, Tony 100, 214, 248
The Mod Squad 72, 237, 238, 239, 241, 247
Modern Screen 243, 244, 247
Moessenger, David 96, 98
Moffat, Donald 317
Moffat, Katherine 212, 302
Moffat, Kitty 147
Moffet, D.W. 326, 327, *327*
Mohica, Victor 164, 185
Monaco, Ralph 312
Monroe, Del 62
Montarastelli, Art 317
Montero, Tony 213
Montesi, Jorge 253, 254, 255, 256, 257, 281, 291, 293, 294, 316
Montgomery, Belinda J. 84, 187
Montgomery, Jo 159, 201, 210, 211, 214
Montgomery, Julia 216
Monty Python's Flying Circus 23
Moody, Lynne 112, 250
Moonlighting 4, 7, 10, 36, 98, 170, 183, 194, 203, 204, 227, 260, 301, 325, 326, 327
Moore, Alvy 168
Moore, Clayton *11*
Moore, Lisa 79
Moore, Roger 57
Moore, Terry 289
Moosekian, Vahan 184, 230
Mora, Danny 79, 153
Moratti, T. 69
Mordente, Tony 32, 149, 150, 151, 152, 153, 154, 158, 164, 165, 166, 167, 168, 186, 189, 198, 208, 209, 211, 215, 216, 217, 218, 219, 220
More, Arnie 124
More, Erwin 270
Moreno, Luis 126
Moreno, Melinda 151
Moreno, Rita 47, 58, 66, 67, 69
Morey, Bill 166, 216
Morgan, Cindy 214, 220
Morgan, Darin 253

Morgan, Glenn 252, 253, 254, 255, 326
Morgan, Read 151
Morgan, Sean 287
Morgan, Shelley Taylor 207, 212, 213
Moriarty, Cathy 292
Moriarty, James 169
Morita, Pat 328
Moritz, Louisa 67
Morley, Christopher 220
Morley, Natasha 293
Moroff, Mike 210, 213
Morris, Garrett 200, 207
Morrisey, Glenn 187
Morrison, Barbara 85
Morrison, Jim 241
Morrow, Byron 65, 67, 69, 123, 130, 186
Morrow, Vic 104
Morse, Richardson 214
Mortifee, Jane 257
Mortil, Janne 256
Moschitta, John, Jr. 151
Moses, Harry 94
Mosley, Irving, Jr. 311
Mosley, Roger E. 8, 64, 76, 105
Moss, Stewart 61, 92, 187, 229
"The Most Crucial Game" 116, 133
Moultrie, Emily 125
Mountain, Johnny 188
"Moving Targets" 152
Moye, Michael 239
Moyer, Tawny 151
Moynahan, Dennis 219, 251
MTM 1, 3, 4, 8, 10, 26, 28, 31, 32, 53, 54, 102, 163, 179, 237, 271
MTV 198, 236
Muellerleile, Marianne 123
Muhammed Ali 132
Mukai, Marcus 92, 94
Muldaur, Diana 60
Muldoon, Dan 287
Mulholland Falls 328
Mulkey, Chris 79
Mullavey, Greg 59, 165, 220
Mulligan, Jim 235
Mulligan, Richard 298, 303
Mullinax, Gary 274, 275
Mumy, Bill 53, 58
Munic, Robert 255
Munro, Lochlyn 256, 293
Munson, Warren 124
The Munsters Today 298
Muntner, Simon, 219, 220
Murcott, Derek 112
"Murder by Design" 303
"Murder by the Book" 297, 298
"Murder for Me" 73, 77
"Murder He Wrote" 215
"Murder in E Minor" 297, 298, 299, 302
Murder One 278
Murder, She Wrote 36, 96, 104, 138, 163, 177, 203, 297, 298, 310
Murdoch, Rupert 238, 239
Murdock, George 66
Murnick, Peter 317
Murphy, Charlie 312

Murphy, Timothy Patrick 211
Murphy Brown 35, 276, 301, 325
Murphy's Law 203, 282
Murray, Jan 166, 209
Murtaugh, James 67, 69, 111
Musante, Tony 40, 60, 71, 264
Muser, Wolf 166, 212, 303
"Mute Witness" 101
"My Future's So Bright, I Gotta Wear Shades" 255
"My Heroes Have Always Been Cowboys" 11, 118, 123, 159
My Living Doll 17
My Mother, the Car 17
My Secret Identity 12, 118
My Two Dads 26, 175
My World and Welcome to It 116
Myers, David 293
Myerson, Alan 219
Myrow, Jeff 256, 257
Mystery Movies 1, 39, 40, 132, 296

Nadder, Robert 75
Naff, Lycia 168, 208
Nagel, Don 63
Nahan, Stu 253
Nail, Joanne 65
Nairn, Gerry 257
Nakahara, Kellye 208
The Naked City 53, 163
The Naked Gun 233
"Naked Justice" 203, 214
Namath, Joe 155
The Name of the Game 26, 38, 39, 40, 237
Nancy Drew 177
Napier, Charles 27, 28, 61, 76, 92, 134, 146, 148
Napier, Chris 64
Naples, Toni 215
Narita, Richard 94
Nash, Gela 213
Nashville 45
Nasty Boys 239
Nathan, Stephen 106
National Coalition on Television Violence 140
National Lampoon's Animal House 231, 234
Natwick, Mildred 166
Naud, Melinda 93, 108
Navarro, Anne 212
Naxos, Michael 287
Nazarian, Randall 125
NBC 37, 38, 44, 50, 51, 57, 87, 88, 91, 121, 134, 136, 137, 140, 141, 144, 145, 156, 163, 173, 177, 179, 183, 197, 198, 203, 204, 205, 221, 223, 234, 237, 238, 239, 240, 263, 283, 301, 306, 307, 310, 313, 333
Neame, Christopher 153, 189, 220
Neely, Ted 187
"Negative Reaction" 298
Negrete, Rudy 213
Negron, Olivia 254
Neidorf, David 219
Neil, Tim 312
Neill, Bob 93

Neilsen, Lucinda 229
Nelkin, Stacy 152, 220
Nelson, Barry 298, 304
Nelson, Christopher 126
Nelson, Clair 100
Nelson, Craig Richard 230
Nelson, Dick 212
Nelson, Ed 64, 69, 298, 304
Nelson, Gary 203
Nelson, Jessica Lee 214
Nelson, Lisa 189, 303
Nelson, Terry 146, 155, 160, 188, 189, 213, 214, 216, 217, 218, 219, 220
Nelson, Willie 67
Nemes, Scott 188
"Nemesis" 247, 252
Nemo, Gina 243, 247, 251
"The Neniwa" 227
Neski, John 290, 293
Network 50
Neufeld, Sigmund 78
Neufeld, Sigmund, Jr. 84, 167, 168, 172, 174
Neukirch, Rob 214
Neumann, Frederick 290
Neumann, Jenny 148
"Never Cross a Vampire" 235
"Never Go to Your High School Reunion" 36, 160, 310, 312
"Never My Love" 161, 165
"Never Send a Boy King to Do a Man's Job" 68, 97
"Never Trust a Crystal Ball" 174
Neville, Kimberly 220
Nevins, Claudette 25, 64, 168
"New Blood" 262, 287
"New Girl in Town" 79
"New Georgia on My Mind" 92
New Jack City 310
"New Life, Old Dragons" 64
The New Maverick 56
The New Odd Couple 129
The New People 237
New Statesman 136
New York 136, 139, 326
New York Daily News 263, 270, 314
New York Herald Tribune 23
New York Post 244, 245, 247, 326
New York Times 138, 192, 206, 277
New York Woman 261
Newell, James 229
Newhart 53, 103
"The Newlywed Game" 119, 125
Newman, Kim 21, 22, 170
Newman, Robert 191
Newman, Robert Connor 219
Newmarch, Johannah 256
Newsday 263
Newsweek 260, 277
Newton, Richard 154
Newton, Sandy 66
"Next Generation" 249
"Next of Kin" 279, 290
"Next Victim" 253
Nguyen, Andrew-Huy 252
Nguyen, Dustin 155, *240*, 243, 246, 248, 255

"Nice Guys Finish Dead" 69, 196, 299
"A Nice Place to Visit" 148
Nichols 32, 43, 44, 47, 50, 51, 52, 57, 101, 127
Nicholson, Jack 193
Nielsen, Leslie 233
Night Court 89, 119, 178, 264
Night Gallery 33, 50
"Night Manoeuvres" 227
Night Moves 46
"Night of the Dragons" 201, 209
"Night on Bald Mountain" 213
Night Rider 107
"The Nightmare" 218
Nightmare on Elm Street 199, 241
"Nights in White Satin" 268
Nightside 107
Nightwing 227
"The Ninja" 73, 77
Nipar, Yvette 248
Nirvana, Yana 5, 232, *232*, 235
Nisbet, Lindy 255
Nisbet, Stuart 85
Nixon, Richard 44, 193, 236, 237, 240, 286
"The No Cut Contract" 62
"The No Fault Affair" 69
"No Good Deed Ever Goes Unpunished" 215
No Holds Barred 270
"No-One Gets Out of Here Alive" 262, 288
No Way Out 274
Noble, Trisha 68, 104
"Nobody in a Nothin' Place" 77
Noel, Hubert 107
Nolan, Jeanette 214
Nolan, Kathleen 64
Nolan, Lloyd 84
Nono, Claire 104, 168, 187, 213, 215
Noone, Kathleen 218
Norman, Maide 78
Norman, Renda Rae 257
Norman, Zack 152
Norris, Chuck 330
North, Hope 155
North, Sheree 79, 217
Northrup, Wayne 78
Norton, Ken 147
Norton, Randy 187
"Not for Nothin'" (*Wiseguy* ep.) 272, 288, 305
"Not Just Another John Doe" 215
Not of This Earth 273
"Not on Our Block" 79
Not Quite Beverly Hills 318
"Nothin' 'Cept Noise" 100
"Nothin' for Nothin'" (*Baretta* ep.) 78
Novak, James 257
Novak, John 252, 290
"The November Plan" 27, 84, 106
"Now You See It..." 119, 124
Nugent, Kelbe 148, 185, 228
"Number One with a Bullet" (*Riptide* ep.) 22, 23, 25, 159, 185
"Number One with a Bullet" (*21, Jump Street* ep.) 256

Nunez, Andre 312
Nunez, Miguel 230
Nunn, Alice 188
Nunn, William 287
Nuss, Bill 143, 144, 145, 152, 153, 154, 155, 160, 186, 246, 248, 249, 250, 251, 252, 253, 254, 321, 332
Nutter, David 249, 253, 255
Nyby, Chris 63, 126, 134, 147, 148, 184
NYPD Blue 145, 160, 198

Oakland, Simon 47, 58, 63, 66, 69, 70, 71, 90, 91, 97
Oberman, Milt 187
Obregon, Ann 152
O'Brian, Hugh 170
O'Brien, Edmond 260, 261
O'Brien, Kenneth 81
O'Brien, Richard 65
O'Brien, Tom 229, 249
O'Byrne, Sean 288, 289
O'Casey, Ronan 155
Ocean, Ivory 255
O'Connell, James 78
O'Connell, John 213
O'Connell, Patrick 215
O'Connor, John J. 138, 192
O'Connor, Raymond 212, 303, 311
O'Connor, Terry 62, 155
O'Connor, Tim 59, 150, 168
Odessa, Devon 219
O'Farrell, Conor 216, 253
O'Halloran, Jack 208
O'Hara, Jenny 61
O'Hara, Shirley 66
O'Hara, Terrence 124
O'Hara, U.S. Treasury 38
O'Herlihy, Michael 134, 143, 144, 145, 149, 150, 151, 152, 154, 155, 167, 185, 186, 210, 215
Ohta, Bennett 167
"Oil Bets Are Off" 187
O'Keefe, Dennis 151
O'Keefe, Michael 154
O'Keefe, Raymond 62, 67, 69
Okie, Richard 211, 213
Okumoto, Yuji 215
Olandt, Ken 34, 152, 178, 184, 254, 308
O'Laughlin, Gerald S. 185
"Old Haunts in a New Age" 253
The Oldest Rookie 325, 326
O'Leary, John 77, 312
Olfson, Ken 250
Oliu, Ingrid 218
Oliver, David 249
Oliver, Jason 249
Olkewicz, Walter 67, 153, 169, 188, 292
Olson, Glen 93, 94
Olson, Tracey 303
O'Malley, J. Pat 66, 80
O'Malley, Kathleen 75, 151
The Omega Syndrome 273, 274
Omen, Judd 79, 80, 124, 148, 153, 167, 185, 209
"On Air" 217

"On the Road" 74, 76
"One More Time" 147
Once a Hero 12, 118
"Once More for Free" 31
"Once More with Vigorish" 164
Once Upon a Time in America 207
One Day at a Time 16
"A One Horse Town" 293
One Life to Live 320
The 100 Lives of Black Jack Savage 163, 242, **323**
"One More Time" 9
"One of the Girls from Accounting" 158, 166
"One on One" 262, 287
"One Small War" 92
"The One That Got Away" 242, 291
"One Way Ticket to the End of the Line" 227
O'Neal, Ryan 111
O'Neil, F.J. 123
O'Neil, Tony 149
O'Neill, Dick 77, 158, 172, 173, 318
O'Neill, Ed 30, 158, 208, 280
O'Neill, Robert 219
O'Neill, Tricia 26, 144, 147, 150, 164, 185, 213
"The Only Church in Town" 148
"Only Rock and Roll Will Never Die" 69
Ontiveros, Bill 251, 288
Opatoshu, David 165
"Open Season" 73, 79
"The Opera" 197
"Operation: Spoilsport" 27, 118, 123
"Operation: Stand-Down" 94
Opper, Don Keith 254, 317
"The Oracle Wore a Cashmere Suit" 24, 54, 62, 160
"The Orange Grove" 9, 181, 185, 309
Orbach, Jerry 218
The Oregon Trail 74
O'Reilly, Cyril 219
O'Reilly, Robert 164, 186, 210
Orend, Jack 289
Oringer, Annie 250
O'Rourke, P.J. 90
O'Rourke, Tom 249
"Orpheus Three Point Three" 246, 251
Orsatti, Ernie 122
Oshry, Suzanne 281, 290, 291, 292
Osterhage, Jeffrey 186
Osterwald, Bibi 230
O'Sullivan, James 215
The Other Glass Teat 236
Otherworld 265
Our Gang 71
Our Miss Brooks 17
"Out of Control" 254
Out of This World 267
"The Out of Towners" 147
The Outer Limits 116
Outerbridge, Peter 256
"Outlaw Champion" 159, 161, 165
Outlaws 134
The Outsider 40

Overbey, Kelly 215
"Overnight Sensation" 211
Overton, Bill 184
Ow, Julie 218
Owen, Jack 100
Owen, Timothy 252
Owens, Edwin 111

Pac-Man 13
Pacino, Al 261, 275
Padhora, Roman 230
Page, Harrison 252
Page, Kevin 220
Page Camp, Helen 98
Pagliaro, Eddie Ross 287
Paige, Janis 67
Palace Guard **325, 326–327,** *327*
"Paladin of the Lost Hour" 300
Palillo, Ron 147
Pallone, Jon 287
"The Palm Springs Answer" 84
Palmer, Chris 68
Palmer, Gretchen 250
Palmer, Peter 62
Palminteri, Chazz 292
Palter, Lew 147
Panas, Alex 285, 294
Pankin, Stuart 229
Pantoliano, Joe 164, 191
Panych, Morris 256, 287
"Papa Rotzi" 310, 312
Paper Moon 127
"The Paper Palace" 18, 66
Papier, Frank 216
"Paradise Cove" 69, 143, 159
Paramount 329
Paraventi, Kit 215, 216
Pare, Michael 117, 122
"Parental Guidance Suggested" 254
Parfrey, Woodrow 81
Paris 31, 306, 326
Parke, Dorothy 248, 250, 251
Parker, F. William 124, 188
Parker, Lara 59, 81, 83, 84
Parker, Ray, Jr. 255
Parkes, James 112
Parkinson 15
Parks, Catherine 216
Parks, Charles 167
Parks, James 65
Parks, Michael 75
Parr, Stephen 60
Parrish, Fran 167
Parrish, Larry 303
Parry, George 100
Parry, Harvey 75, 76
Parsons, Kelly 174
Parsons, Nancy 167
"The Parting Shot" 84
Partington, David 215, 311
"The Partner" 103, 104, 160
"Partners" 216
Parton, Reg 62
Partridge, Derek 130
The Partridge Family 114
Pasternak, Michael 210
Pastorelli, Robert 164, 208, 230
"Pastoria Prime Pick" 61
Pataki, Michael 77

Paterson, Sheila 290
Paton, Angela 216
Patrick, Alan 85
Patrick, Dennis 61
Patterson, Florence 316
Patterson, John 69, 111
Patterson, Lee 150, 184, 207
Patterson, Neva 60
Paul, Don Michael 303, 328
Paul, Lee V. 111
Paulin, Scott 229
Paull, Morgan 94
Paulsen, Albert 107
Pavan, Marisa 68
Pax, James 230
"Pay or Die" 77
"Payback" (*Hunter* ep.) 215
"Payback" (*Stingray* ep.) 227
Paymer, David 126, 167, 249, 326
Payne, Charles 248, 256
Peaker, E.J. 60, 123, 218
Pearcy, Patricia 65
Pearl 103
Pearl, Burt 152, 154, 155, 161, 162, 168, 177, 182, 186, 188, 189, 227, 230, 298, 299, 303
Peck, Clare 154
Peckinpah, Sam 51, 162
Pedi, Tom 104
Peerless, Donna 256
Pellegrino, Mark 218
Pellegrino, Nick 125
Pellow, Cliff 80
Peluce, Meeno 112, 147
Peluso, Lisa 212
"Pen Pals" 208
Pena, Anthony 214
Pendleton, Austin 256
Penghlis, Thaao 112
Penhale, David 187
Penn, Arthur 46
Penn, Leo 165
Pennell, Jon Maynard 255
"Pennies from a Dead Man's Eyes" 166
Pennock, Christopher 150, 174, 189
Penny, Joe *14, 175, 176,* 177, 180, 301
Pentecost, George 230
Pento, Joey 208
People 232, 240, 324, 326, 327
"People Do It All the Time" 281, 292
Peppard, George 7, 16, 23, 132, *133,* 135, 141, *142,* 146
Pepper, Paul 81
Perak, John 65, 98, 147
Percelay, David 216
Peretz, Susan 213
Perez, Rosie 254
Perez, Tony 214
Performance 45
Perlich, Max 251
"Permanent Hiatus" 303
Perpich, Jonathan 5, 186, 231, *232,* 234, 235
Perry, Chuck 257
Perry, Felton 227, 230
Perry, Freda 257

Perry, Jo 256, 257
Perry, John Bennett 215
Perry, Joseph 68
Perry, Tom 256, 257
Perry, William 142, 154
Perry Mason 106, 114, 281, 295, 297, 301
Perryman, Clara 186
Persoff, Nehemiah 78, 98, 219, 303
"Peter Pan Is Alive and Well" 175, 186, 231
Peterman, Steve 126, 210
Peters, Brock 75, 76
Peters, Gerald 62
Peters, Jan 78
Peters, Virginia 211
Petersen, David 290
Petersen, Eugene 61, 65, 85, 123, 125, 126
Petersen, Paul 155
Peterson, Dan 217
Peterson, David 230
Peterson, Robyn 186
Petri, Donald 92
Petrie, George O. 289, 290, 291, 292, 294
Petrovna, Sonia 124
Pettus, Ken 92, 93
Petty, Lori 229, 321
Pevney, Brian 69
Pevney, Joseph 69, 172, 173
Peyser, John 92
Peyser, Penny 148
Peyton Place 298
Phalen, Robert 98
Phantom of the Opera 199
"Phantom Pain" 272, 288
The Philadelphia Experiment 117
Philbin, John 292
Phillips, Ethan 211
Phillips, Gary Houston 185
Phillips, Mackenzie 74, 76
Phillips, Robert 104
Phillips, William 96
Phinney, David 216, 217
Phipps, William 77, 85
"Photography by John Doe" 76
Phyllis 17
Piazza, Ben 70, 150
Picardo, Robert 168, 249
Picerni, Charles 167, 169, 193, 210, 211, 212, 213, 228, 230, 303
Picerni, Paul 167
Pierce, Robert 173
Pickens, Slim 74, 76, 79
Pickett, Cindy 184
"A Picture's Worth a Thousand Dollars" 173
"Piece Work" 63
Pierce, Barry 155
Pierce, Denny 255
Pierson, Frank 44
"A Pigeon Ripe for the Plucking" 98
Pike, Robert 101
Piland, Sheryl 250
Pileggi, Mitch 219, 312
Pillow, Mark 288
Pine, Philip 78, 104

Pinero, Miguel 80
Ping Wu 153, 254
Pinkett, Jada 257
Pino, Mariangela 291, 292
Pinter, Mark 218
Pinvidic, Margo 256
"The Pirate and the Princess" 189
"The Pit" 216
Pitt, Brad 247, 251
Piven, Byrne 100, 154, 212
"The Plague" 124
Plana, Tony 208, 209, 253
Planet Earth 127
Planet of the Apes (television series) 53
Platoon 241
Platt, Oliver 294
"Player to Be Named Now" 272, 288
"Playin' Police" 79
"Playing God" 213
"Playing Hardball" 189
"The Play's the Thing" 189
Pleasure, Fred 287
Pleshette, John 25, 66, 67, 111, 218
Pleshette, Suzanne 96, 98
Pletts, Tom 123, 184
Plutzig, Roberta 268
Pniewski, Michael 255
Pock, Bernie 153
Podell, Rick 77
Podhora, Roman 251, 293
"Point of No Return" (*A-Team* ep.) 155
"Point of No Return" (*Wiseguy* ep.) 294
Pointer, Priscilla 59, 85, 104
"Poison" 256
"Poker Night" 169
Polanski, Roman 82
Police Academy 108, 224, 231, 234
Police Squad 54, 233, 234
Police Story 72, 101, 102, 108, 160, 205, 326
Police Woman 53, 102, 160, 205, 306
Polito, Jon 288
Polizos, Vic 154, 210, 287
Pollak, Cheryl 251
"Polly Want an Explanation" 187, 189, 270
Polster, James 210
Pomerantz, Jeff 218
Ponce, Danny 209
Ponzini, Anthony 70, 164, 168, 220, 230
"Poor Little Lambs" 93
Pope, Catherine 289
Poppe, Herman 151, 174
Popwell, Albert 144, 147
"Por Nada" 80
Porter, Brett 210
Porter, Don 84
Porter, Rick J. 216
Portnow, Richard 289
"A Portrait of Elizabeth" 35, 62
Post, Markie 119, 123, 148, 151
Post, Mike 106, 145, 172, 183, 198, 333, 334

Post, Ted 76, 101
"Postcard from Morocco" 290
Potter, Jerry 188
Potts, Cliff 229
Pouget, Ely 155
Pousette, Lina 154, 188, 303
Powell, Darren 216
Powell, Mark 255
Powell, Randolph (Randy) 185
Powers, Alexandra 248, 255, 256
Powers, Ben 125
Powers, Stefanie 61
The Powers of Matthew Star 129
Pownall, Leon 287
Prange, Laurie 77, 93, 168, 217
Pratt, Deborah 213
Pratt, Dennis 151, 186
Pratt, Jordan 256
Preece, Michael 188, 208, 209, 210, 211, 212, 213, 214, 215, 216, 217, 218, 229
Prelutsky, Burt 65
Prendergast, Gerald 186, 312
Prentice, Ernie 287
Prentiss, Ann 75
Prescott, Judy 256
Prescription: Murder 296
Presley, Elvis 88, 89, 134, 308
Preston, J.A. 154, 168, 215, 250
Preston, Kelly 184
Preston, Mike 150, 152, 212
"Presumed Dead" 92
"Presumed Guilty" 215
"The Price Is Right" 125, 310
Priestley, Jason 247, 249
Prime Cut 46
Primus, Barry 219, 253
Prince, Dinah 310, 311
Prince, Michael 105, 125, 150
Prince, William 61, 126
"Prince of Fat City" 164
Princi, Elaine 66
Prine, Andrew 75, 78
The Prisoner 271
"The Prisoner of Rosemont Hall" 66
"Prisoner of War" (*Riptide* ep.) 183, 186
"Prisoners of War" (*Black Sheep Squadron* ep.) 92
Private Eye 116, 203, 247
Private Resort 241
"Privateers and Public Schools" 251
"The Prodigal Son" 266, 287
Profit 18, 329
"Profit and Loss" 59
The Projectionist 118
"Pros and Cons" 138, 142, 147
The Protectors 146
Pruett, Harold P. 249
Prutting, Steve 252
Pryor, Nicholas 188, 312
Pryor, Richard 128, 270
Prysirr, Geoff 186, 219
P.S. I Luv You 115
Pugh, Willard E. 208
Pugliese, Al 189, 219
The Punisher 121
Purcell, James 189, 257

Purcell, Lee 59
"Pure Dee Poison" 149
The Pursuit of Happiness 162
Putch, John 254
Puttonen, Michael 256
Pyper-Ferguson, John 256

Quade, John 32, 60, 81, 144, 145, 149, 151, 216
Quaid, Dennis 80
Quantum Leap 32, 88, 103, 127, 283
Quarry, Al 65
Quarry, Robert 68
"Quarterback Sneak" 155
Que Pasa USA 284
"Queen of Peru" 26, 65
The Quest (Cannell series) 4, 7, 52, 55, 109, 110, 127–130, 131, 156, 175, 177, 179, 224
"The Quest" (pilot) 129
The Quest (western series) 162
Quick, Eldon 68
"Quickie Nirvana" 24, 65
Quigley, Kevin 294
Quijada, Alfonso 257
Quillan, Eddie 80
Quincy 32, 53, 177
Quine, Richard 116, 296
Quinn, Alison 256
Quinn, Bill 55, 58, 61, 65, 67, 124, 125, 186, 207
Quinn, Daniel 216
Quinn, J.C. 229
Quo, Beulah 85, 215

"The Rabbit Who Ate Las Vegas" 7, 35, 139, 147
Rabkin, William 217
Rachford, Thom 229
Rachins, Alan 24, 298, 303
Racimo, Victoria 94
Rader, Jack 78, 164
Rafel, Lisa 166, 229
Rafield, Felecia 294
"Rag Doll" 300, 304
Ragin, John S. 85, 188
Raging Bull 326
Rags to Riches 320
"Ragtime Billy Peaches" 75
The Raiders 116
Raiders of the Lost Ark 128
"Raiders of the Lost Sub" 19, 143, 185
Raines, Christina 187, 218
Rainey, Ford 60, 93, 292, 293
Ralph, Sheryl Lee 95, 211
Rambo (films and character) 45, 137
Rambo, Dack 215
Ramirez, Frank 188
Ramos, Rudy 63, 201, 207
Ramsey, Anne Elizabeth 216
Ramsey, Logan 78, 214
Ramus, Nick 230
Randall, Ann 63
Randall, Tony 39
Randolph, John 98
The Range Rider 334

Ranito, George 78
Rankin, Steve 218
Rapagna, Anna 155
"Rape and Revenge" 30–31, 45, 203, 209
Rapiel, Ron 288
Rappaport, David 169
Rasche, David 194, 234
Raskind, Richard 216
Rasulala, Thalmus 124, 230
"Ratman Can" 310, 312
"Rattlers' Class of '63" 54, 63, 310
Raven 119, 333
Raven, Elsa 145, 151, 191, 210, 266, 287, 288, 289, 290, 291, 292, 294, 330
Rawnsley, Ben 100, 168, 214, 311
Ray, James 80
Ray, Jeff 124, 126, 134, 149, 150, 159, 168, 172, 174
Ray, Robert 63
Rayburn, Gene 186
Raymond, Lina 107
Raynr, David 230, 249, 254
Raz, Kavi 152, 168
Reagan, Ronald 43, 45, 113, 286
"The Real Easy Red Dog" 54, 61
"Really Neat Cars and Guys with a Sense of Humor" 165
Reason, Tom 112
Reasonable Doubts 268, 273, 325
Reavey, Liz 215
"Recipe for Heavy Bread" 148
Red Ryder 71
Redanty, Marisa 214
Redecker, Quinn 65
Redford, Robert 71
Redina, Victor 79
Redmond, Marge 68, 214
Redmond, Markus 257
Reed, Lance 311
Reed, Robert 213
Reed, Tracy 129, 149, 188
Reese, Della 143, 152
Reese, Jed 257
Reeves, Perrey 256
Reeves, Philip 254
Regalbuto, Joe 167, 303
Regasner, Ron 312
Regher, Duncan 123
Regina, Paul 218, 303
Register, Meg 214
Reid, Marc 290
Reid, Ric 289
Reimer, Max 289
"The Reincarnation of Angie" 61
Reiner, Rob 62
Reinhardt, Ray 155, 168
Reisel, Robert 62
Reisner, Allen 84, 164
Reisner, Dean 101
Reiss Martin, Eda 212
Remington Steele 4, 8, 10, 12, 17, 46, 129, 177, 179, 180, 194, 325, 326, 327
Remsen, Kerry 249
Renaldo, Duncan 12
Renalia, Pat 52

Renegade 201, 226, 310, 327, 329, **330–333**, *331, 332,* 333, 334
"Renegade" (*Hunter* ep.) 214
Rennard, Deborah 168
Renteria, Joe 76, 218, 228
"The Reporter" 220
Republic Serials 107, 309
"Requiem for a Funny Box" 65
"Requiem for Icarus" 177, 188
"Requiem for Sergeant McCall" 193, 211
"Resada Rose" 123
Rescher, Dee Dee 212
Rescue 911 239, 318
"Research and Destroy" 254
"Resurrection in Black and White" 61
"The Resurrection of Carlini" 126
The Return of Captain Invincible 118
"The Return of Russell Buckins" 252
The Return of Sam McCloud 103
"The Return of the Black Shadow" 68, 123
Return of the Greatest American Hero aka *The Greatest American Heroine* 224
Return of the Man from UNCLE 146, 222
Return of the Prince 239, 318
Return of the Six Million Dollar Man 222
"Return to the 38th Parallel" 63
"The Return of Typhoon Thompson" 200, 201, 211
"Return of White Cloud" 217
Reuben, Gloria 251
"The Reunion" (*Baretta* ep.) 79
"The Reunion" (*Wiseguy* ep.) 281, 292
The Revenge of Al Capone 268
"Revenge of the Mud People" 275, 288
Revenge of the Nerds 183
Revere, Ann 76, 78
Revill, Clive 218
Rey, Alejandro 155
Reynolds, Burt 195
Rhoades, Barbara 102, 104
Rhoda 17, 233, 235, 277
Rhodes, Andrew 288, 289
Rhodes, Jennifer 70, 312
Rhue, Madlyn 72, 75
Rhys-Davies, John 128, 129
Ricard, Adrian 63
Rice, Ed 76
Rich, Allan 61, 76, 106, 164
Rich, Katie 321
"Rich Girl" 30, 201, 202, 209
The Richard Boone Show 74
Richards, Beah 207, 211, 214
Richards, Kim 63
Richards, Lou 169, 210
Richardson, Catherine 214
Richardson, Lee 228
Richardson, Regina 210
Richert, Wanda 168
Richie Brockelman, Private Eye 4, 8, 9, 17, 18, 19, 35, 36, 46, 47, **96–98,** 99, 109, 110, 118, 159, 183, 233, 271
"Richie Brockelman, Private Eye" (pilot) 98
Richman, Josh 249, 254
Richman, Peter Mark 78, 156, 168
Richmond, Branscombe 69, 152, 210, 330, *331,* 332
Richmond, Steve 91
Richter Debi, 79, 165, 185
Rickenbacker, Eddie 86
Rickles, Don 220
Riddle, Hal 84
Rider, Michael 149, 167
Rider from Tucson 22
Ridgely, Robert 213
Riegart, Peter 299
Riffon, Marc 220
Rifkin, Ron 60, 63
Rigby, Peter 33
Right On 306
"A Rightful Place" 291
Riker, Robin 70, 92, 118, 123, 149, 187, 189
Riley, Edward 215
Riley, Jack 63, 186
"Ring of Honor" 216
Rings, Mary 76
"The Rip-Off Stick" 291
Rippy, Leon 215
Riptide 3, 4, 7, 8, 9, 12, 13, 14, *14,* 15, 17, 18, 19, 22, 23, 24, 25, 26, 27, 34, 36, 46, 48, 54, 91, 97, 108, 110, 118, 119, 128, 132, 133, 134, 135, 141, 143, 144, 156, 159, 160, 172, **175–189,** *176,* 194, 196, 197, 223, 224, 228, 231, 234, 270, 284, 298, 299, 300, 301, 308, 309, 310, 316, 318, 323, 330, 334
"Riptide" (pilot) 184
"The Rise and Fall of Joe Piermont" 304
Ritter, John 118
Rivas, Geoffrey 292
Rivers, Victor 220
"Road Game" 151
"The Road to Hope" 34, 143, 153
The Road Warrior 136
The Roaring Twenties 45
Roat, Richard 228
Robelo, Mike 168
Roberts, Arthur 64
Roberts, Cindy 150
Roberts, Doris 76
Roberts, Eve 186
Roberts, Jeremy 220, 252, 312
Roberts, J.N. 77
Roberts, Joan 152
Roberts, Mark 66
Roberts, Michael D. 75, 107, 215, 300
Roberts, Pernell 66, 79, 97, 107
Roberts, Randolph 85, 149
Roberts, Randy 216, 312
Roberts, Stephen 209
Robertson, Dale 7, 295, *297,* 299, 301, 302
Robertson, Dennis 191

Robin, Diane 174, 208
"Robin and Marian" 177, 188
Robin Hood (character) 10, 120
"The Robin Tucker's Roseland Roof and Ballroom Murder" 111
Robinette, Dale 67, 174
Robins, Dale 249, 290
Robinson, Andy 126, 144, 148, 149, 174
Robinson, Chris 74
Robinson, Edward G. 261
Robinson, Holly *240,* 242, *242,* 244, 245, 246, 247, 248, 256, 321
Robinson, Leroy 64
Robinson, Mike 250, 252
Robinson, Roger 77, 79
Robinson, Whitney Wherret 215
Robocop 322
Roboz 34, 179
Roca, Fernando 104
Roche, Eugene 57, 229
Roche, Mitchell 255
Rochon, Lela 254
Rocket, Charles 167
The Rockford Files 1, 3, 4, 6, 7, 8, 9, 12, 13, 15, 16, 17, 18, 19, 20, 21, 22, 23, 24, 25, 26, 27, 28, 29, 32, 35, 36, 37, 40, 41, **43–70,** *47,* 71, 74, 82, 83, 88, 90, 96, 97, 99, 101, 102, 103, 106, 107, 109, 110, 118, 120, 123, 127, 128, 131, 133, 134, 135, 142, 143, 145, 157, 158, 159, 160, 172, 173, 175, 178, 180, 182, 183, 195, 196, 197, 198, 199, 200, 202, 221, 226, 227, 233, 239, 258, 260, 263, 271, 277, 284, 298, 299, 305, 306, 308, 309, 310, 316, 317, 329, 330, 333, 334
Rockwell, Robert 209
Rocky II 132
Rocco, Alex 64, 79, 145, 151, 165, 214
Roche, Eugene 167, 227
Roche, Sean 94
Rockwell, Robert 191
Rocky, Kati 255
Rocuzzo, Mario 75, 79, 104, 112, 215
Rodd, Marcia 219, 248, 250, 253
Roddenberry, Gene 127
Rodine, Alex 124, 126
Rodriguez, Dennis 211
Rodriguez, Marco 211, 216, 228
Rodriguez, Percy 100, 107
Rodriguez Pagan, Saida 216
Roeves, Maurice 216
Rodgers and Hammerstein 334
Rogers, Gayle 84
Rogers, Ira 100
Rogers, Melody 304
Rogers, Michael 257
Rogers, Mimi *171,* 172, 173
Rogers, T. 253
Rogers, Timmie 84
Rogers, Wayne 82, 83, 84
Rokk, Rene 294
Roland, Christopher 167

Roley, Sutton 78
Rolfe, Sam 135
Rolike, Hank 5, 164, 208, 231, 235, 299, 303
Rolling Stone 198, 200, 206, 241, 260, 261, 264, 319
"Rolling Thunder" 159, 163
Rollins, Bernard 64
Rolston, Mark 287
Romano, Andy 151, 168, 312
Romano, Jason 249
Romano, Tony Michael 290, 291, 292
Romanus, Richard 32, 35, 67, 111, 112, 144, 145, 147, 155, 164, 208
Romanus, Robert 252, 253
Rombola, Ferde 79
Romero, Carlos 66, 152
Romero, Cesar 187, 189
Romero, Robby 230
"The Romp" 281, 293
Ronard, Jason 208
Rondeau, Charles 76
Rondell, Ron 76
"Room Service" 220
Room 222 237
Root, Stephen 294
Roots 111, 132
Roots II 111
Rosario, Bert 66
Rosas, Michele 151
Rosato, Tony 294
Rose, Barbra 65
Rose, Jamie 193
Rose, Margot 215, 253
Roseanne 239, 274
Roselius, John 69, 208
Rosen, Gary 246, 254, 255
Rosen, Milt 30, 78, 92, 151
Rosenberg, Arthur 48, 124, 186, 201, 207
Rosenberg, Meta 43, 44, 50, 51, 52, 57, 62, 63, 65, 68, 106
"Rosendahl and Gilda Stern Are Dead" 67
Rosengren, Clive 155
Rosetti and Ryan 158
Ross, Andrew 251
Ross, Donald 161, 168
Ross, Gene 185
Ross, Joe 214
Ross, Kimberly 150
Rossi, Leo 169, 209, 230, 251
Rossito, Angelo 77
Rossovich, Tim 147, 149, 218
Roswell, Maggie 216
Rothwell, Robert 185
"The Rough Rider Rides Again" 12
"Round Up the Old Gang" 168
"Roundabout" 60
"Rounding Third" 255
Roundtree, Richard 255
Roush, Matt 263, 277, 279, 314
Rousseau, Gerry 293
Rousters 4, 22, 35, 119, 135, 141, 156, 162, *170–174, 171*, 175, 181, 195, 224, 301, 317
Route 66 45
Rowe, Hansford 126

Rowe, Misty 230
Rowe, Stephen 220
Rowe Baker, Jordan 318, *319*
Roy, Rob 289
Rozakis, Gregory 77
Rubenstein, Phil 168, 187, 209
Rubenstein, Scott 217
Rubin, Andrew 165
Rubin, Mann 68, 77
Rubio, Edie Marie 148
Rudolph, Alan 46
Ruggiero, Alphonse, Jr. 24, 273, 280, 281, 289, 290, 291, 292, 293
Ruiz, Isaac, Jr. 66
Rukeyser, Louis 4
Run for Your Life 40, 52
"Runaway Cowboy" 78
"The Runaways" 79
Running Scared 207
Ruppenthal, Chris 211
Ruprecht, David 189
Ruscio, Al 62, 65, 145, 151, 169, 189, 207, 219, 312
Ruscio, Elizabeth 293
Ruskin, Bud 238
Ruskin, Joseph 106, 189, 230, 235
Russ, Tim 209, 251
Russ, William 187, 209, 269, 270, 272, 282, 288, 289, 293
Russell, Betsy 150, 153, 325
Russell, Forbsey 208
Russell, Jane 201, 210
Russo, Gianni 32, 66, 68, 98, 122, 178, 184, 214, 259, 287
Russo, Jodean 65
Russom, Leon 256
Ruth, Daniel 261, 263
Ruymen, Ayn 75, 98
Ryan, Fran 169
Ryan, John P. 64
Ryan, Mitchell 61, 77, 152, 165, 187, 215, 220
Ryan, Steve 282, 293
Ryan, Thomas 249
Ryan's Hope 163
Rydell, Mark 45
Ryder, Eddie 79
Ryon, Rex 125, 154, 311

Sabella, Ernie 168, 214, 235
Sabin, David 62
Sadoff, Fred 59, 60, 92
Sagal, Jean 250
Sagal, Liz 250
Sage, David 129, 209
Saget, Bob 126
Sailor, Charles 60
St. Clair, Michael 212
St. David, Martyn 216
St. Elsewhere 4, 9, 53, 107, 120, 137, 197, 224, 226, 246, 267, 282, 317
St. Elwood, Jon 212
St. Esprit, Patrick 216, 220
St. Jacques, Raymond 167, 213
St. James, Susan 106
St. John, Jill 298, 303
St. John, Thania 254
St. Louis Dispatch 202

Saito, Bill 85
Saito, James 92, 94, 155
Sajak, Pat 142, 153
Salamon, Jeff 286
Salazar, Leonard 213
Salcedo, Linda 228
Saldana, Theresa 212, 325, *325*, 326
Salem, Kario 312
Sallin, Robert 187, 188
Salmi, Albert 79, 144, 148
Salvin, Pedro 290
"Sam at Eleven" 195
Sampler, Philece 211
Samples, William 249
Sampson, Robert 147, 167, 184, 253
"Sam's Private Eye" 311
Sanchez, Frank, Jr. 253
Sanchez, Mario Ernesto 294
"Sanctuary" 293
Sanderford, John 164, 167, 186, 209
Sander, Casey 220
Sanders, Henry G. 112, 210
Sanders, Richard 188
Sanders, Shepard 75
Sandlund, Deborah 215, 250
Sandomirsky, Kerry 274, 287, 289, 290, 313, 316
Sandor, Steve 80, 149, 151, 167, 208
Sandoval, Miguel 216
Sanford, Garwin 251, 288, 290
Sanford and Son 53
San Francisco Examiner 261
Sanger, Jonathan 292, 293
San Jose Mercury News 263
San Juan, Guillermo 76
Santa Barbara 326
Santidrian, Raul 294
Santon, Penny 68
Santoni, Reni 168
Santoro, Dean 125
Santos, Bert 148
Santos, Joe 32, 48, 49, 53, 58, 76, 94, 126, 145, 151, 160, 163, 197, 207, 219
Santos, Vanessa 303
Santucci, John 278, 290
Sarafian, Richard 291
Sargent, Dick 80
Sargent, Richard 289
Sari Chang 254
Sarradet, Richard 92
"Satan, Cyanide, and Murder" 45
Satlof, Ron 147, 148, 164, 165, 166, 172, 174, 181, 184, 185, 186, 196, 207, 210
Sattels, Barry 168
Saturday Night Live 269
"Saturday Night Special" 25, 201, 211
"Saturday on Sunset Boulevarde" 123
Saulsberry, Rodney 155
Saunders, Alvin Lee 288
Saunders, Dusty 33
Saunders, J. Jay 208
Saunders, Lew 184
Sauter, Van Gordon 216
Savage, Brad 129

Savage, Elizabeth 214
Savage, Nick 212
"Savage Says That's What Friends Are For" 111
"Savage Says the Most Dangerous Bird Is the Jailbird" 112
"Savage Says There's No Free Lunch" 111
Savalas, Candace 303
Savalas, Telly 73, 299, 303
Savant, Doug 230
Sawyer, Toni 151
Saxon, John 62, 144, 145, 147, 152, 163, 190
"Say Goodbye to Jennifer" 54, 60
"Say Goodbye to Yesterday" 85
"Say It Ain't So, Pete" 253
"Say It with Bullets" 149
"The Say Uncle Affair" 146, 155
Scaglione, Al 77
Scandals 234, 318
Scandals II 318
Scanlon, John 150
Scannell, Susan 153
Scarber, Sam 148, 168, 184, 312
Scarbury, Joey 198
Scarecrow and Mrs. King 17, 127, 163, 173, 180, 205, 326
"Scared Stiff" 158, 160, 165
Scarface 269, 284
Scarfe, Alan 217
The Scarlet Pimpernel 107
Scene of the Crime 324, 330
Schaal, Richard 59, 167
Schaal, Wendy 152
Schaeffer, Craig 125
Schaeffer, Laurie Lee 69
Schaeffer, Nicholas 312
Schafer, Ross 250
Schaffer, Todd 257, 287, 317
Schedeen, Anne 80
Schell, Maximillian 20, 284, 286, 294
Schell, Tom 249
Schembri, Anthony J. 291, 316
Schenk, George 127
Scherer, Gene 66, 153
Schiavelli, Vincent 167
Schiffer, Paul 213
Schilling, William 207
Schneider, Mark 209
Schneider, Michael 187
Schneider, Scott 168
"School of Hard Knox" 289
"School's Out" 251
Schramm, David 290
Schreiber, Avery 63
Schruers, Fred 200, 206
Schuch, Robert 220, 311
Schuck, John 298, 303
Schulian, John 273, 275, 276, 289, 290, 291
Schull, Richard B. 61
Schulman, Benji 311
Schultz, Dwight 132, *133*, 135, *142*, 144, 145, 146
Schultz, Jacqueline 217
Schultz, Jeff 249
Schultz, Michael 58, 75
Schulz, Leroy 288
Schuman, Felix 100
Schwartz, Lloyd 154
Schwartz, Scott 249
Schwarzenegger, Arnold 10, 259
Schweitzer, S.S. 78, 79
Scoggins, Tracy 147, 149, 164
Scorpio, Jay 153
Scorsese, Martin 111, 277, 305, 326
Scott, Carey 251
Scott, George C. 329
Scott, Jacqueline 186
Scott, Jim 66
Scott, Judson 126, 152
Scott, Kathryn Leigh 81, 107
Scott, Simon 63
Scott, Timothy 81, 164
Scott Free 106
Scott Lynn, Meredith 255
Scotta, K.J. 245
Scotti, Vito 79
"Scrap Metal" 201, 210
Screaming Mimi 179
Scruggs Bogart, Linda 93
Scruples 222
Seago, Howie 214
Seale, Douglas 215
Seales, Franklyn 288
seaQuest DSV 120, 243
Sears, Steven 152, 154, 155, 161, 162, 168, 177, 182, 186, 188, 189, 227, 229, 299
"The Second Chance" (*Rockford Files* ep.) 65
"Second Chances" (*21, Jump Street* ep.) 257
"The Second Finest Man Who Ever Lived" 227
"Second Sight" 218
"The Secret of Terry Lake" 75
See No Evil, Hear No Evil 270
Seff, Richard 67
Segal, George 282
Segall, Pamela 253, 290, 291
Segall, Stuart 310, 332
Seibel, Deborah 257
Seigel, Don 101
Seinfeld 197
Selburg, David 167
Selko, Warren 252
Sellecca, Connie 15, 114, *115*, 117, 122, 173
Selleck, Tom 7, 8, 54, 55, 56, 58, 67, 69, 88, 106, 107, 178, 299
Selman, Karole 303
Seltzer, Milton 61, 66
Semi-Tough 277
"Semper Fi" 9, 309, 311
Senensky, Ralph 85
Serling, Rod 50, 237
Serna, Pepe 62, 77, 80, 125, 155, 214
Serpico 71
Serrano, Nestor 214, 287, 312, 327
Serrao, Maria 255
Server, Eric 60, 62, 92, 123, 154, 185, 302, 311
Sesame Street 143, 242
"The Set-Up" 31, 201, 210

"Set-Up City" 76
Seven, Johnny 66
"Seventh Avenue Freeze-Out" 279, 290
77, Sunset Strip 39, 99, 232
Severance, Joan 269, 270, 277, 288, 289, 322
Seymour, Carolyn 126
Sgarro, Nicholas 151
Shack 106
"Shades" 212
Shadow Chasers 98
"Shadows of the Past" 220
Shaft (television series) 306
Shalet, Diane 105
Shamata, Chuck 78
Shaner, Michael 217
Shanklin, Doug 302
Shannon, Michael 155
"The Shark Affair" 116
Sharkey, Ray 259, 260, 261, 263, *267*, 268, 269, 270, 273, 277, 287, 288, 290, 325
Sharpe, Thom 189
"Sharper Than a Serpent's Tooth" 76
Shaw, Larry 228, 230, 248, 250, 251, 262, 287, 297, 302
Shaw, Paula 290
Shaw, Stan 292, 293
Shay, John 77
"She Ain't Deep, But She Sure Runs Fast" 161, 167
Shea, Jack 185
Shea, Joe 210, 287, 288, 292, 305, *307*, 308, 311
Shear, Barry 84, 93
Shearin, John 11, 57, 168, 200, 207
"Sheep in the Limelight" 91, 94
Sheiner, David 78
Shelby, LaRita 254
Sheldon, Les 32, 123, 154, 167, 169, 212, 230, 248, 263, 275, 286, 289, 293
Shell Game 243
Shellen, Stephen 255
Shelley, Dave 81, 111, 123, 124, 151, 208
Shelley, Joshua 79, 80, 216
Shelly, La Rita 216
Shelton, Deborah 111, 184
Shelton, Reid 210
Shelyne, Carole 98
Sherbanee, Maurice 66, 152
Sheridan, Liz 148, 152, 186
"Sheriffs of Rivertown" 145, 151
Sherlock Holmes 295
Sherman, Gary 329
Sherman, Jenny 67, 80
Sherman, Vince 77, 78
Sherrill, David 249
The Shield 326
"Shield of Honor" 217
Shields, Nick 124, 150
Shigeta, James 67, 120, 124
"Shillelagh" 217
Shilton, Gilbert 148, 149
Shimoda, Yuki 92

Shimono, Sab 94
Shirriff, Cathie 187
"Shirts and Skins" 255
"The Shock Will Kill You" 34, 120, 124, 194
"Shoes" 73
Shoop, Pamela Susan 173
"Shoot to Kill" 216
"The Shooter" 193, 199, 208, 212
Shore, Pauly 250
Short, John 254
Shortridge, Stephen 125, 167, 209
"The Show Must Go On... Sometimes" 94
"Showdown" 30, 151
Sibbett, Jane 252
Sicari, Joe 213
Sidley, Robert 257
Siebert, Charles 61, 64, 98
Siegel, Charles 254, 257, 289
Siegel, Howard 229
Sierra, Gregory 123, 213, 221, 228
Signor, Gordon 229
Sikes, Cynthia 62
Sikking, James B. 67, 216
"Silent Stalker" 316
Silk Stalkings 317, 324, 325, 329
Silkwood 277
Silliphant, Stirling 101
Silva, Geno 155, 188, 213
Silva, Kathy 62
Silva, Trinidad 200, 210
Silver, Borah 80
Silver, Johnny 312
Silver, Robert 219, 312
Silver, Ron 37, 62, 277, 278, 279, 290
"Silver Bullet" 11, 200, 203, 215
Silver Spoons 172, 239, 283
Silvera, Frank 212
Silverman, Fred 297, 299
Silverman, Jeff 33, 189, 220, 311
Silvern, Bea 66
Simcox, Tom 81
Simon and Simon 4, 8, 12, 27, 32, 36, 46, 48, 51, 88, 102, 103, 178, 180, 181, 183, 194, 326
Simpson, Freddie 317
Simpson, Michael 76
The Simpsons 12, 24, 239
Sims, Tasha 257
Sinatra, Frank 334
Sinise, Gary 100, 218
Singer, Alex 65, 215
Singer, Raymond 123, 165, 229
"Sins of the Father" 292
Sinutko, Shane 80
Sirens 318
Sirola, Joseph 32, 68, 70, 145, 151, 185
Sirtis, Marina 212
Sister Kate 266
Sivertsen, Mark 214
The Six Million Dollar Man 54, 118, 144
"The Six Percent Solution" 303
"16 Blown to 35" 245, 248, 249
"The Sixteen Byte Data Chip and the Quick Brown Fox" 112

"67 Hours, 24 Minutes, and Counting" 104
"62 Hours of Terror" 201, 210
Skaff, George 64, 208
Skaggs, Jimmie F. 152, 166, 208, 311
Skatula, Kathryn 187
Skeen Hall, Gary 250
Skelton, Patrick 92
The Skin Game 44, 47
"Skins" 151
Skipper, Pat 217
Skomarovsky, Vladimir 155
"The Sky Is Falling" 80
Sky TV 239
Slack, Ben 154, 167, 210
Slade, Betsy 94
Slade, Jon 288, 311
"Slade vs. Slade" 174
Slater, Shirley 150
Slaughter, Lance 249
Slaughterhouse Five 177
Slavin, Millie 60, 187
Sledge Hammer 108, 194, 233, 234
"Sleepwalk" 280, 292
"Sleight of Hand" 59
"Slippin' Into Darkness" 251
Sloan, Michael 11, 131, 222
Slow Burn 241
Sloyan, James 112, 129, 186
"A Small and Deadly War" 7, 134, 138, 147, 158
Smaney, June 79
"Smiles We Left Behind" 189
Smith, Alison 217
Smith, Cotter 168
Smith, Donegan 229
Smith, Ebbe Roe 292
Smith, Forry 212, 250, 312
Smith, Garnett 124, 152
Smith, Jim 66, 293
Smith, Kurtwood 144, 149, 185, 229, 248, 249
Smith, Lane 60, 68
Smith, Norwood 66
Smith, Patricia 58
Smith, R. David 149
Smith, Reid 185, 312
Smith, Sam 79
Smith, Sandy 61
Smith, Scott, 250
Smith, Shelley 112, 212
Smith, T.D. 216
Smith, William 52, 58, 84, 147, 153, 184, 207, 210, 215, 217
Smith Boucher, Savannah 252
Smithers, William 219
"Smokey Mountain Requiem" 269, 271, 272, 288
"The Snake Chaser" 81
"Snake Eyes" 174
Sneed, Maurice 209
"Sniper" 199, 209
"A Snitch'll Break Your Heart" 219
"The Snow Queen" 35, 198, 208
Snyder, Arlen Dean 219
Snyder, Drew 255
Snyder, John 280, 291, 311, 313, 316
Snyder, Suzanne 187

"So Help Me God" 63
Soap 158, 298, 322
Soares, Sylvia 76
Sobel, Barry 250
Soble, Ron 59, 75, 81
Solar Warriors 243
Solari, Rudy 77
Solarz, Ken 327
"Soldier in the Jungle" 78
Soles, P.J. 167
Solin, Harvey 126
Solomon, Bruce 153
Solomon, George 188
Somack, Jack 61
"Someone Is Killing the Great Geeks of America" 18, 182, 184
Somers, Suzanne 59
"Something Fishy" 19, 183, 185
Something Is Out There 119, 127, 190, 199, 201, 224, 239, 258, 322
Something So Right 195
"Something's Going On on This Train " 160, 167
"Sometimes You Gotta Sing the Blues" 227
Sommars, Julie 58, 133
"The Son Also Rises" 45
"Son and Heir" 218
"A Song from the Sequel" 303
Sonny Spoon 7, 8, 9, 21, 23, 25, 35, 36, 143, 160, 203, 226, 234, 266, **305–312**, *307*, 313, 314, 318, 322, 327, 333, 334
Sonski, Steve 273
Sontoro, Dean 62
Soon-Teck Oh 93, 94, 126, 155
The Sopranos 10, 20, 32, 51, 53, 333
Sorel, Ted 185
Sorensen, Paul 66, 104
Soric, Vojo 208
Sotanoma Salsedo, Frank 230
Soul, David 200, 209, 313, 314, *314, 315*
"The Sound of Thunder" 134, 154
"South By South-East" 66
Southern, Daniel 219
Southern Comfort 36
Southwick, Shawn 151, 187
Souza, Sylvia 33
Space Patrol 120
"Space Ranger" 126
Spacek, Sissy 114, 274
Spacey, Kevin 269, 270, 272, 273, 277, 288, 289, 313, 316
Spackman, Tom 214
Sparv, Camilla 62, 112
Specht, Robert 78
Speer, Martin 125, 212
Spelling, Aaron 1, 3, 17, 28, 38, 39, 53, 55, 56, 115, 139, 173, 175, 190, 196, 200, 237, 238, 247, 295, 296, 297, 298, 305, 313
Spelman, Sharon 59, 61, 68
Spencer, Alan 194, 233
Spencer, Brenton 256, 257
Spencer, Sally 218
Spenser: For Hire 202, 203, 223, 275

Spider-Man (character) 113, 120
Spider-Man (comic-strip) 121
Spielberg, David 58, 60, 98, 102, 104, 166, 215, 270, 271, 284, 288, 289
Spielberg, Steven 38, 113, 309
Spielman, Jeff 76
Spies, Adrian 77
Spillane, Mickey 4, 8, 45, 55, 97, 118, 180
Spin City 313
Spiner, Brent 212
Spinks, Leon 132
Spinner, Anthony 78
Spotnitz, Frank 244
Spradlin, G.D. 85, 122
"Spring Break" 254
Springfield, Rick 66
"The Spy Who Mugged Me" 155
"Squeeze" 262, 272, 288
Stack, Robert 38
Stacy, James 266, 293
Stacy, Michele 98
Stadd, Leonard 81
Stafford, Nancy 186, 208
Stafford, Tamara 184
Stagecoach West 82
"Stairway to Heaven" 290
Staley, James 189, 250
Staley, Lora 155, 302
Stallone, Sylvester 10, 137, 177, 259, 264
Stamm, Raimund 257, 289
"Stand by Your Man" 254
Standing, John 214
Stanhope, Warren 215
Stanley, Paul 78, 79, 80, 81, 104
Stanley, Rebecca 149, 219
Stanley, Richard 94
Stanton, Valerie 166
The Star Chamber 29, 30, 158
Star Trek 1, 38, 120, 127, 129, 237, 313
Star Trek: The Next Generation 132, 310, 329
Starbuck see *J.J. Starbuck*
Stargate SG-1 271, 321
Stark, Anthony 250
Starlog 18, 28, 29, 36, 37, 119, 121, 128
Starman 201
Starr, Beau 148, 150, 153, 167, 168, 184, 208, 219, 230
Starr, Don 124
Starr, Mike 291
Starrett, Jack 154, 173, 209
Starsky and Hutch 19, 71, 73, 83, 181, 196, 200, 238, 305, 313
Stavola, Charlie 208
Steadman, John 60
Stebbings, Peter 256
Stechulte, Tom 111
Steedman, Tony 155
"Steel" 35, 149
Steel, Amy 147
Steele, Cynthia 126
Steele, Mike 52
Steen, Jessica 287, 317, *317*
Stein, Ron 76

Stenn, David 246, 253, 254
Stephens, James 250
Sterling, Jan 187
Sterling, Philip 66, 82, 83, 84, 97, 106, 147, 172, 174
Stern, Erik 189, 208
Stern, Leonard 44, 234
Stevan, Robyn 249
Stevens, Kate 49
Stevens, Paul 61, 63, 76
Stevens, Shadoe 312
Stevenson, Al 61
Stevenson, Valerie 153
Stewart, Catherine Mary 224
Stewart, Charles 166
Stewart, Dennis 126, 154, 208
Stewart, James/Jimmy 10, 39
Stewart, Kay 77
Stewart, Larry 208
Stewart, Mel 104, 123
Stewart, Paul 65
"Sticks and Stones May Break Your Bones..." 63
Still, Dana 289
"Still Going Steady" 160, 188
Stingray 11, *11*, 19, 23, 32, 106, 131, 191, 194, 199, 201, 203, **221-230**, *222*, 234, 242, 258, 259, 273, 298, 329, 334
Stir Crazy 266
Stirdivant, Mark 79
Stitch, Patricia 63
Stiteler, Elena 255
Stock, Alan 148, 173
Stockwell, Dean 144, 147, 212
Stoddart, Alexandra 104
Stoddart, Patrick 136
Stolow, Henry 214
Stone 4, 8, 9, 28, 30, **101-105**, 106, 107, 117, 127, 134, 158, 160, 192, 205
"Stone" (pilot) 104
Stone, Christopher 152, 185, 216
Stone, Harold J. 58
Stone, Oliver 241, 284
Stone, Rob 250
"The Stone Conspiracy" 81
The Storefront Lawyers 237
Story, Howard 230, 257
"The Story of Daring Dick Darling" 35, 308, 309, 311
Stovitz, Ken 167
Stowe, Madeleine 81
"Straight to the Heart" 212
Straightaways 34
Strand, Robin 149, 188, 216
Strangis, Judy 149
"Strangle Hold" 162, 168
Strano, Carl 152, 154, 188, 220, 235, 312
Strasberg, Lee 177
Strasberg, Susan 58, 62, 71
Strasser, Michael 217
Strassman, Marcia 69, 84, 229, 321
Strathairn, David 293
Stratton, Bill 20, 65
Stratton, Charles 251
Stratton, Jan 80

Stratton, W.K. 67, 68, 69, 89, *89*, 91, 105, 150, 151
The Street 278
Street, Elliott 64
Street, Rebecca 168
"Street Edition" 25, 78
Street Justice 324, *324*
"Street Wise" 218
Streeter, Tim 255
Streethawk 22
Streets of Fire 117
Streets of San Francisco 24, 73, 82, 280
Strickland, Gail 164
Stricklyn, Ray 289, 292, 293
Strong, Brenda 311
Strong, Deborah 218
"Stronger Than Steele" 12
Stroud, Don 144, 145, 148, 151, 173, 201, 209, 215
Struyken, Carel 213
Stryker, Jack 212
Stryker, Rod 153
Stuart, Maxine *171*, 172, 173
Stuart, Whitney 256
Studd, Big John 212
Stuillin, Marie 257
"Stupid Macho Guy Time" 175
Stuthman, Fred 112, 125
Stuyck, Joris 220
"Subterranean Homeboy Blues" 31
"A Sudden Silence" 85
"Sudden Withdrawal" 218
Sugarfoot 232
Sullivan, K.T. 168
Sullivan, Liam 151
Sullivan, Maggie 213
Sullivan, Susan 57
Sunset 170
Sunset Beat 239
Super Force 178
Super-Friends 114
Superman (character) 113, 118, 308
Superman (comic-book) 121
Superman (movie franchise) 29, 117
"Surprise on Seagull Beach" 143, 159, 167
"Survival" 200
Suspicion 52
Sussman, Joshua 294
Sussman, Mark 252
Sussman, Todd 230
Sutorius, James 166, 174, 218, 252
Sutton, Lisa 215
Sutton, Robert Raymond 84
Svenson, Bo 158, 207
Swackhamer, E.W. 111, 173
"Swallowed Alive" 252
Swan, Michael 66, 148, 165, 185
Swan, Robert 100, 230
Swann, Dale 216
Swanson, Robert 96
Swanson, Scott 257
Swarbrick, Carol 215
Swayze, Don 217
Sweeney, Bob 235
Sweeney, Joan 166, 186, 207
Sweet, Dolph 104

Swerling, Jo, Jr. 36, 51, 52, 59, 83, 127, 149, 172, 181, 310, 312
Switch 3, 51, 83
Switzer, Michael 168, 187, 188
Swofford, Ken 32, 35, 53, 60, 63, 65, 69, 106, 145, 152, 167, 172, 173, 174, 188, 310, 312
Sylvan, Paul 64, 155
Sylvester, Harold 98, 218
Symonds, Robert 59, 81, 187
Szigeti, Cynthia 215
Szwarc, Jeannot 61, 63, 64, 74, 76, 80, 92
Szollosi, Thomas 30, 32, 103, 105, 134, 143, 144, 148, 149, 150, 153, 154, 160, 161, 165, 166, 167, 199, 208, 209

Tabori, Kristoffer 69, 80, 211, 253
Taggart, Rita 209
Taglang, Tom 216
Takei, George 92
The Taking of Beverly Hills 282
Talbot, Nita 52, 58
Tales of the Gold Monkey 88, 127
Tales of the Wells Fargo 177, 295
"Tall Woman in a Red Wagon" 24, 59
Tan, C.K. 250
Tanaka, Toru 155
Tank Girl 321
"Tanks for the Memories" 27
Tannen, Steve 79, 94, 150, 153, 186
Tanzini, Philip 250
Tarbuck, Barbara 214, 253
Tarkington, Rockne 81, 84, 112
Tartikoff, Brandon 136, 141, 198, 223, 283, 306, 307, 310
Tasmanian Devil 308
Tata, Joe E. 58, 60, 62, 65, 67, 151, 220
Tate, Larenz 252, 312
Tatiana 312
Tattingers 264
Tatum, Brad 219
Taxi 137, 226, 228, 238, 276
"The Taxi Cab Wars" 148
Taxi Driver 305
Taxier, Arthur 151, 152, 166, 168, 189, 250
Taylor, Curtis 151, 212
Taylor, Darin 151
Taylor, David 64
Taylor, Dub 169
Taylor, Holland 293
Taylor, Lee 288, 291
Taylor, Mark L. 218, 229, 235, 312
Taylor, Rod 134
Taylor, Ron 291, 312
Taylor, Tammy 104
Taylor, William 249, 251, 289
Teague, Marshall 151, 185, 210
Tedrow, Irene 59
"Teen Dreams" 216
Television Viewers vs. Media Snobs 140
Telfer, Frank 213
Tell Them Willie Boy Is Here 71
Temple, Renny 230

"The Ten Percent Solution" 298
Tenafly 306
"Ten'll Get You Five" 94
Tenspeed and Brownshoe 4, 6, 7, 9, 13, 18, 25, 28, 35, 44, 46, 54, **109–112**, 117, 127, 128, 131, 183, 258, 300, 301, 305, 308, 318, 334
"Tenspeed and Brownshoe" (pilot) 111
Teodorescu, Ion 123
Terhune, Shannon 104
Termo, Lenny 292
Terry, Joe Michael 184
Terzo, Venus 256, 287
Tesh, John 115
Tessier, Robert 147, 152, 174, 312
Tewes, Lauren 211
The Texas Wheelers 53
Thames, Byron 249
That Girl 17
"That Sister Ain't No Cousin" 79
Thayer, Brynn 211
Then Came Bronson 237
"The Theory of Revolution" 155
"There Goes the Neighborhood" (*A-Team* ep.) 143, 153, 160
"There Goes the Neighborhood" (*Hardcastle and McCormick* ep.) 160, 166
"There's Always a Catch" 148
"There's Just No Accounting" 125, 196
"There's One in Every Port" 63
"They Don't Make 'em Like They Used To" 78
Thieves Like Us 45
Thigpen, Lynn 219
Thin Ice 163
"Things Get Ugly" 12
"Things We Said Today" 254
"Think Blue" 210
"Think Mink" 79
Thinnes, Roy 104, 271
"Third Down and Twenty Years to Life" 159, 164
"Thirty Seconds Over Little Tokyo" 126
"Thirty Six Hours to Dawn" 187
thirtysomething 280, 285
"This Ain't My Bag" 76
"This Ain't No Summer Camp" 256
"This Case Is Closed" 59
"This Is My Gun" 219
This Is Spinal Tap 178
"This Is the One the Suit Was Made For" 119, 125
"This One's Gonna Kill Ya" 112
"This Town Ain't Big Enough for the Twelve of Us" 174
Thomas, Christopher 69, 123, 187, 289
Thomas, Ernest 78
Thomas, Philip Michael 71
Thomas, Robin 207, 220
Thomas, Rosemarie 167
Thomerson, Tim 167, 208, 211, 215, 253

Thompkins, Anthony 253
Thompson, Fred Dalton 273, 274, 275, 277, 289
Thompson, Gene 78
Thompson, Robert (director) 122, 123, 124
Thompson, Robert (writer) 9, 10, 12, 16, 138
Thompson, Ron 77, 125
Thompson, Shawn 219
Thompson-Jenner, Linda 189
Thor, Cameron 187
Thorne, Geoffrey 257
Thoroughgood, Myles 254
Thorpe, Jerry 46
Thorsden, Kelly 59
"A Three Day Affair with a Thirty Day Escrow" 54, 67, 159, 298
Three Men and a Baby 275
"Three Ring Circus" 235
Three's Company 91, 118
The Thrill of It All 44
Thriller 52
Throne, Malachi 65
Thrower, Jean 19
Thunderboat Row 172, 310, 317, 323, 325
Tickner, French 293
Ticotin, Rachel 228
Tiefer, George 76
Tiefer, Gregory 76
Tierney, Lawrence 214
"Ties My Father Sold Me" 161, 165
Tiffe, Angelo 250, 252
Tigar, Kenneth 107, 211, 229, 312
Til, Roger 69
"'Til Death Us Do Part" 35, 147
"Timber" 134, 150
Time Out 12, 21, 37, 43, 44, 51
The Time Tunnel 201
Timecop 277
Tinder, Paul 153
Tippit, Wayne 61, 62, 215, 294
Tippo, Patti 210
"A Title on the Door and a Carpet On the Floor" 17, 98
Titus, Christopher 252
Tizon, Art 155
T.J. Hooker 137, 177, 190, 202
"To Die in Bettendorf" 281, 293
To Live and Die in L.A. 207
"To Protect and Serve" 53, 64
Tobeason, Hans 271, 288
Tobey, Kenneth 63, 66, 213
Tobin, Michele 213
Toby, Doug, Jr. 70
Todd, Beverly 294
Todd, Russell 187, 189
Todd, Tony 250
"Toe Hold" 235
Tokuda, Marilyn 207
Toland, Michael 216
Tolkan, James 327, 329
Toma 4, 40, 44, 45, 52, 55, 90, 127, 264, 283
Toma, David 71
Tomasina, Jeana 150
Tomlin, Lily 46
Tomlinson, Michael 220

Tompkins, Angel 167, 174
The Tonight Show 302
"Too Good to Be True, Too Good to Get Caught" 308, 311
"Too Rich and Too Thin" 166
Toolan, Rebecca 257
Top of the Hill 8, 114, 135, 158, 225, 310, 317, **318–320**
Topping, Lynn 167, 208
Torgov, Sarah 125
Torn, Rip 191
Tornatore, Joe 66
Toronto Globe and Mail 83
Toronto Star 306
Torppe, Danil 210, 211, 213, 216
Torres, Liz 211
Tortora, Oz 215
Toub, Shaun 214
Tough Guys 207
"The Tough Habit" 309, 311
Tour of Duty 90, 273
Toussaint, Beth 257
Towers, Constance 69
Towers, Robert 81
Townsend, Barbara 212
Toy, Alan 215
Tozzi, Giorgio 76
Tracey, Ian 252
Trackdown 116, 121
Trager, Sol 154, 188
"Train of Thought" 124
Trainor, Saxon 220
Trapper John 97, 196
Traps 329
Travanti, Daniel J. 328
Travolta, Joey 235
Travolta, John 114, 264
Traylor, William 59, 77, 78, 186
The Treasure of Sierra Madre 71
"The Treasure of Sierra Madre Street" 112
"The Trees, the Bees, and T.T. Flowers" 23, 64
Tremblett, Ken 256
Trent, Daniel 229
Tress, David 68, 123, 124
Treutelaar, Barbara 213
"Trial By Fire" 154
Trigger, Sarah 255
Trikonis, Gus 220, 290, 291, 294
Trinidad, Arsenio Sonny 167, 209, 215
Triska, Jan 219
Tritter, Wes 256
"Trouble at Fort Apache" 28, 93
"Trouble Brewing" 152
"Trouble in Chapter Thirteen" 25, 64
"Trouble on Wheels" 145, 150
"The Trouble with Harry" 154
"The Trouble with Warren" 63
Truby, John 247, 252, 254
"True Confessions" 211
Truman, Harry S. 86
Trusel, Lisa 173
Trustman, Alan 101
Tsu, Irene 65
Tubert, Marc 154
Tucci, Stanley 278, 290

Tuckahoe, Paul 79
Tucker, French 256
Tucker, Ken 326
Tucker, Louie 216
Tucker's Witch 129, 177
Tuell, John 311, 312
Tull, Eric 216
Tullis, Dan 155
"Tunnel of Love" 255
Tupou, Manu 155
Tureaud, Lawrence 132
Turich, Felipe 76
Turk 182 116
Turkel, Ann 186
Turley, Jack 77
Turley Travis, Diane 208
Turman, Glynn 124, 186, 300, 302
Turner, Arnold 125, 185, 207, 213
Turner, Brad 256, 257
Turner, Frank C. 293
Turner, Frantz 312
Turner, Janine 151
"Turning Point" 213
Turrentine, Rogers 68, 200, 201, 209, 210, 211, 212, 214
Tuthill, Bruce 60, 65, 112, 123, 174, 184, 209
TV Comic 1, 142
TV Detectives 49, 102
TV Guide 4, 12, 16, 23, 88, 91, 175, 206, 242, 243, 244, 247, 248, 261, 263, 264, 268, 298, 305, 306, 308, 333
TV 101 266
Tweed, Shannon 230, 250
20th Century–Fox 39
21, Jump Street 3, 7, 8, 9, 12, 13, 32, 35, 120, 135, 145, 163, 191, 225, 233, 234, **236–257**, *240*, 258, 264, 273, 310, 313, 320, 321, 323, 324, 326, 330, 331
"21, Jump Street" (pilot) 248
"2245" 254
The Twilight Zone (1960s) 50, 56, 178
The Twilight Zone (1980s) 32, 88, 177, 300
Twin Peaks 36, 237, 247, 281, 322
"The Twisted Cross" 183, 187
"The Two and a Half Days of the Condor" 174
"Two for the Road" 250
"The 200mph Fast Ball" 119, 123
"The 200 Pound Gorilla" 94
"Two into 5.56 Won't Go" 1, 27, 61, 309
Tyner, Charles 85, 189
Tyrell, Susan 76

Uda, Hatsuo 92
UFO 128
Ullrick, Sharon 93
Ulrich, Kim 154, 211, 303
"Unacceptable Loss" 218
Uncle Buck 239
"Uncle Buckle-Up" 142, 153
Under Siege 259
"Under Suspicion" 220
"Under the City" 78

"Under the Influence" 257
"Undercover McCormick" 158, 167
Underwood, Blair 247, 249, 310
Underwood, Jay 254, 302
"Unfinished Business" 194, 218
Unger, Joe 151
Universal 4, 33, 37, 38, 39, 40, 48, 51, 73, 91, 103, 104, 107, 110, 131, 132, 199, 296, 313
The Unofficial Making of a Wiseguy 261
Unsolved Mysteries 239, 318
Unsub 8, 200, 223, 225, 234, 273, 275, 299, **313–316**, *314, 315,* 318, 323
"Untitled" 112
The Untouchables 38, 53, 83, 260, 261
"Up for Grabs" 92
UPN 329
Urseth, Bonnie 166
Ursitti, Susan 250
US magazine 33, 244, 308, 321
U.S. Customs Classified 330
U.S.A. Today 158, 206, 247, 263, 265, 266, 277, 279, 306, 314
U.S.A. Weekend 308
"The Usual Suspects" 219
Utay, William 209

V 117, 177, 178, 241, 333
Vacarro, Tracy 209, 213, 216
Vahanian, Mark 79
Vahimagi, Tise 40
Valentine, Karen 76
Valentine, Kim 253
Valenza, Tasia 155, 213, 249
Van Ark, Joan 53, 59, 61, 63
Van Bergen, Lewis 81, 219
Van Buskirk, Leslie 308
Van De Vere, Trish 165
Van Der Velde, Nadine 174
Van Dusen, Granville 76, 104, 106, 218
Van Dyke, Barry 150
Van Dyke, Jerry 237
Vanering, Nathan 288
Vandever, Michael 104
Vandis, Titos 75, 76, 129, 153
Van Hoffman, Brant 185, 214
Van Horne, Toni 81
Vanity Fair 261, 264, 270, 273
"Vanity, Says the Preacher" 121, 122, 126
Van Ness, Jon 80, 94, 187
Van Norden, Peter 167
Van Patten, Joyce 64
Van Peebles, Mario 246, 247, 252, 253, 254, 292, 306, *307,* 310, 311, 312
Van Peebles, Melvin 306, 308, 310, 311
Van Riesen, Wendy 254
Van Scoyck, Robert 77
Varela, Jay 78, 125, 168
Varela, Migdia 79
Vargas, Jacob 210
Vargas, John 152
Variety 6, 13–15, 25, 40, 47, 57, 83,

88, 101, 106, 110, 136, 139, 143, 190, 223, 273, 285, 305, 306, 313, 320, 321, 323, 327, 330, 333
Varney, Jim *171*, 172, 173
Vath, Richard 209
Vatsula, Tony 220
Vaughn, Edward 228
Vaughn, Ned 250
Vaughn, Robert 116, 145, 146, 147, 155, 216, 229
Vaughn, Vince 247, 254
Vega, Isela 126, 228
Vegas 3, 74, 177, 182, 196, 238
Vejar, Mike 150, 186
Velez, Eddie 145, 146
Vennera, Chuck 76
Ventura, Jesse 209, 219, 330
Venture, Richard 62, 64
Vera, Billy 287
Verbois, Jack 148, 155
Verdier, Paul 288
Vereen, Ben 18, 109, 111, 300, 301, 302, 318, 325
Verkaar, Maurice 256
Vernon, Harvey 188
Vernon, John 126, 144, 148
Verrell, Cec 216, 230
Verroca, Joe 292, 293
Victor, James 152, 208
Victor, Paula 155
Video Today 49
Vietnam War 4, 10, 11, 36, 44, 90, 131, 136–137, 141, 183, 236, 241, 243–244, 269, 273
Vignon, Jean-Paul 69
Vigoda, Abe 58, 67
Viharo, Robert 81, 154, 164, 184
Village Voice 6, 12, 139, 286
Villalobos, Ray 262, 287, 292, 316
Villard, Tom 154, 218
Villaverde, Manolo 283, 284, 294
Vincz, Melanie 126
Vinnechenko, Leeza 235
Vinovich, Steve 228, 287, 311
Vint, Alan 80
Vint, Jesse 154
"Violence" 195
V.I.P. 332, 333
Viper 329
The Virginian 38, 40
Viscuso, Sal 186, 220
Visitor, Nana 209
Vitte, Ray 128, 129
Vlahos, Sam 209
Vogel, Carol 61
Voland, Herb 98
Volstadt, John 112
Volz, Nedra 154
Von Leer, Hunter 58, 65, 66
Voyage to the Bottom of the Sea 133, 144
Voyagers 116, 129
Vreeland, Mary 214
Vujovic, Steve 100

Wacks, Jonathan 252
Wagenheim, Charles 80
Waggoner, Lyle 168
Wagner, Lindsay 52, 53, 58, 59

Wagner, Lou 216
Wagner, Michael 68, 98
Wagon Train 52
Wagrowski, Gregory 311
Wahl, Chuck 264
Wahl, Corinne 154
Wahl, Ken 9, 10, 24, 146, 258, *259*, 263, 264, 265, *267*, 273, 274, 278, 279, 280, 281, 282, 285, 286, 287, 292, 293, 329
Wainwright, James 63, 165, 213, 228
Waite, Ric 83
Waite, Todd 256
"Waiting for Insane Wayne" 30, 35, 143, 154, 308
"Waiting for Mr. Wrong" 201, 210
Wakeham, Deborah 153, 208, 250
Wakely, Marge 63
Walberg, Garry 164
Walcott, Gregory 80
Walcutt, George 209
Walden, Robert 26, 62
"Walk Like You Talk" 72, 75
Walk on Water 317
Walker, Charles 123, 149, 168, 219, 311
Walker, Kasey 211, 214, 219
Walker, Kim 219
Walker, Marcy 326, 327, *327*
Walker, Matthew 290, 294
Walker, Robert 188
Walker, Scott 77
Walker, Steve 230
Walker, Tonja 209
Walker, Will 78
Walker, Texas Ranger 330
Walking Tall 158
Wall Street 261, 275
Wall Street Week 4, 13
Wallace, Earl 77
Wallace, Jack 100
Wallace, Marjorie 75
Wallace, Randall 24, 25, 200, 201, 210, 230, 296, 299, 300, 303, 304, 308, 309, 310, 311, 312, 316
Walsh, Edward 68
Walsh, M. Emmet 60, 76, 77, 313, *314*
Walsh, Sydney 210
Walston, Ray 249, 312
Walter, Jessica 298, 303
Walter, Sherilyn 147
Walter, Tracey 208
Walter and Emily 162
Walters, Arnie 293, 294
Walters, Dale 257
Walton, Brian 252
Walton, Jess 60, 78
Walton-Walker, Peggy 168, 189
The Waltons 265
Waltz, Lisa 291, 292
Wambaugh, Joseph 57, 101, 102, 108, 205
Wanted—Dead or Alive 82
"War Biz Warrior" 93
"War Zone" 201, 210
Ward, John 75, 79
Ward, Lyman 155

Ward, Richard 75
Ward, Robert 68
Ward, Sandy 59, 63, 78, 111, 123, 148, 167
Ward, Skip 62
Warfield, Marsha 178, 184
Warhit, Doug 126
Warhol, Andy 260
Warlock, Billy 247, 253, 327
Warner, Julie 253
Warner Bros. cartoons 34, 308, 311
Warners/Warner Bros. 39, 43, 56, 88, 99, 232
Warren, Aimee and Danielle 215
Warren, Celia 289
Warren, Joseph 123
Warren, Marcie 252
Warwick, Dionne 65
Washington: Behind Closed Doors 145, 146
Washington Post 243, 244
"WASPS" 93
Wasserman, Allan 216
Wasserman, Jerry 249, 251, 287, 289, 293, 316
Wasson, Craig 64, 94
"Waste 'Em" 152
"Wasted" 257
"Water, Water, Everywhere" 149
Watergate 3, 10
Waters, Ed 80, 81
Waters, Harry 260, 277
Waters, John 255
Watkins, James Louis 229, 303
Watson, James A., Jr. 61, 230
Watson, Mills 32, 59, 60, 66, 68, 92, 144, 148, 151, 155, 210
Watson, William 60
Wayland, Len 149
Wayne, John 90, 334
We Got It Made 195
Weary, A.C. 111
Weatherley, Shawn 208, 300, 301, 302
Weathers, Carl 324, *324*
Weaver, Dennis 39, 101, 102, 104, 192, 328
Weaver, Robby 102, 103, 104, 117, 122, 318
Weaver, Trevor 251
Webb, Jack 32, 37, 38, 39, 40, 48, 88, 118, 231, 299
Webber, Robert 20, 24, 32, 53, 59, 61, 62, 68, 110, 111
Webber, Timothy 256, 324
"The Wedding Bell Blues" 188
Weddle, Vernon 167, 229
Weidergott, Karl 255
Wein, Dean 185, 187
Weis, Don 73, 77
Weisser, Norbert 125, 211
Weldon, Ann 208
Weldon, Charles 104
Weller, Mary Louise 80
Welles, Gwen 80
Welles, Jesse 60, 61, 69, 215
Wells, Danny 108, 125, 129, 150, 173, 185, 189, 209, 220
Wells, Jack 188

Wells, Julienne 67
Wells, Vernon 210
Welsh, John 229
Wendkos, Gina 262, 272, 288
Wendle, Kevin 247
Werewolf 36, 103, 119, 127, 134, 199, 201, 239, 247, 258, 317, 333
Werner, Laurie 308
Werntz, Gary 311
Wesley, John 230, 287
Wessburg, Wendy 125
West, Adam 5, 12, 231, 232, *232*, 234, 235
West, Caryn 304
West, Red 32, 88, 91, 99, 100, 104, 112, 123, 125, 126, 144, 145, 147, 154, 155, 165, 220
"West Coast Turnaround" 147
The Westerner 162
Westley, William 107
Weston, Ellen 78
Westworld 114
Wettig, Patricia 228
Whaley, Michael 218
"What About Love?" 252
"What Do You People Want from Me?" 102, 104
"Whatever Happened to Guts?" 166
"What's So Funny?" 166
What's Up, Doc? 110, 111
"Wheel of Fortune" 144, 153, 160
Wheeler, Ellen 219
"Wheels and Deals" 254
"When Dues Come Down" 72, 73, 76
"When I Look Back on All the Things" 168
"When the Shark Bites" 219
"When You Comin' Back, Range Rider?" 12, 134, 165
"Where Echoes End" 219
"Where Is the Monster When You Need Him?" 143, 151
"Where the Girls Are" 144, 185
"Where's Houston?" 62
"Where's the Money?" 290
Whinnery, Barbara 186, 235
Whipp, Joseph 124, 251
Whirlybirds 45
"Whistler's Pride" 164
White, Al 123, 147, 185, 208, 249
White, Bradley 215
White, David 62, 154, 189
White, Dee 230
White, Hollace 211, 212
White, John Sylvester 75
White, Peter 123, 165, 212
White, Vanna 142, 153
"The White Ballot" 149
"White Bone Demon" 316
White Heat 260, 261, 266
"White Noise" 24, 281, 290
"White on White and Nearly Perfect" 55, 67, 109, 128, 299
Whitehead, Paxton 154
Whitman, Stuart 12, 144, 145, 147, 152, 168, 201, 209, 303
Whitmore, James 183, 188

Whitmore, James, Jr. 23, 32, 47, 48, 55, 58, 64, 69, 88, 89, *89*, 91, 98, 107, 112, 123, 125, 126, 164, 167, 172, 174, 183, 188, 196, 197, 204, 207, 208, 209, 211, 212, 213, 214, 216, 218, 246, 249, 251, 253, 254, 255, 290, 303
Whitney, John 141
Whittemore, L.H. 75
Whitworth, James 112
"Who Killed Cock Robin?" 80
"Who Really Watches the Sunset?" 188
Whoops Apocalypse 118
"Who's Got Tonsillitis?" 25, 311
Who's the Boss? 320
"Who's Woo in America" 114, 125
"Whose Choice Is It Anyway?" 251
"Why Me?" 80
Wiard, William 59, 60, 61, 62, 64, 65, 66, 67, 68, 69, 93, 106, 129, 130
Wicking, Chris 12, 40, 43
Widmark, Richard 39, 192
Wiederhorn, Ken 247, 251, 255
Wieland, Bob 266, 305, 311
Wilbee, Codie Lucas 316
Wilcox, Larry 165
Wilcox, Lisa 168
Wilcox, Mary 75
Wilcox, Nina 208
The Wild Bunch 136
The Wild Party 177
Wild West Movies 21, 22, 170
The Wild Wild West 87, 99, 116, 308
Wilder, Gene 270
Wilder, Glenn 123, 124
Wilding, Chris 255
Wildman, Valerie 155, 214
Wiley, David 167, 209
Wilhelm, Jeff 208
Wilkes, Elaine 186, 251
Wilkinson, Ann 229
Wilkinson, Lisa 209
Wilkinson, M. Scott 253
Wilkof, Lee 189, 208
Willcox, Pete 5, 232, 235
Willens, Shel 30, 69, 111, 126, 158, 165
Williams, Allen 210, 250
Williams, Barbara 229, 230
Williams, Billy Dee 264, 294
Williams, Brandon 112
Williams, Chino 75
Williams, Clarence, III 237
Williams, Darnell 215
Williams, Dick Anthony 65, 112, 229
Williams, Frances E. 251
Williams, Gail 162, 190
Williams, Greg Kean 252
Williams, Paul 76
Williams, Peter 256, 291
Williams, R.J. 252
Williams, Rugg 219
Williams, Steven 9, 145, 150, 163, 207, 208, 229, *240*, 241, 242,

245, 247, 248, 256, 257, 291, 321, 323
Williams, Taylor 100
Williams, Tom 61, 187
Williams, Van 107
Williamson, Doug 257
Williamson, Mykel T. 299, 303
Willingham, Noble 63, 154
Willis, Bruce 7, 170
Willis, Hope Alexander 79
Wills, Sheila 216
Willson, Paul 165, 188
Wilrich, Rudolph 75
Wilson, Dale 248, 257
Wilson, David 290
Wilson, Jeannie 149
Wilson, Jody 294
Wilson, Kim 292
Wilson, Melanie 151
Wilson, Ned 62, 63, 98, 122
Wilson, Pat 125
Wilson, Rita 174, 312
Wilson, Teddy 169
Windom, William 32, 50, 96, 98, 126, 147, 167, 197, 207
Windsor, Jane 249
Winer, Harry 104, 112
Winfield, Paul 279, 291
Wingreen, Jason 63
Winikoff, Ken 223
Winkler, Henry 177
Winkler, K.C. 151, 184
Winlaw, Mike 287
Winn, David 124
Winner, Michael 222
Winslow, Michael 108
Winston, Dayna 253
Winter, Chuck 85
Winter, Ed 25, 32, 85, 144, 145, 147, 151, 164, 172, 174, 177, 185
Winter, Gary 30, 209, 210, 229, 248
Winters, Chuck 62, 63
Winters, Time 218
"Wipeout" 25, 159, 183, 187
Wired 269, 325
Wirth, Billy 291
Wise, Ray 152, 186, 211, 228
Wiseguy 3, 4, 7, 8, 9, 10, 12, 13, 19, 20, 24, 25, 31, 32, 35, 36, 37, 45, 98, 102, 119, 131, 133, 135, 140, 145, 146, 156, 172, 175, 178, 191, 195, 198, 203, 207, 223, 225, 226, 233, 234, 242, **258–294**, *259*, *267*, 297, 298, 299, 305, 308, 310, 313, 314, 322, 323, 324, 325, 326, 329, 330, 331, 334
"Wiseguy" (pilot) 287
Wiseguys 268
Wiseman, Joseph 120, 123, 151
"With the French Heel Back, Can the Nehru Jacket Be Far Behind?" 26, 54, 68
Withers, Mark 123, 211
Without a Trace 328
"Without Reservations" 155
"Witness Protection for the Archangel Lucifer" 294

Witt, Howard 68, 98
Witt, Kathy 152, 184
Wittner, Meg 216
Wixted, Kevin 251
Wixted, Michael 220
"Wizards and Warlocks" 121, 126
Wizards and Warriors 196
Woessner, Hank 213, 312
Wogan 23
Wohl, David 215
Wohl, Jack 290
Wolcott, James 261, 264, 270, 273
Wolf, Marsha 129
Wolfe, Nancy 77
"Woman in the Harbor" 75
"Woman Trouble" 81
Wonder Woman 118, 329
Wong, James 252, 253, 254, 255, 326
Wong, Russell 252
Wood, Andy 126, 212
Wood, Gary 187, 218, 220
Woodard, Charlaine 289
Woodburn, Danny 220
Woodruff, Robert 293
Woods, James 58
Woods, Lauren 216
Woods, Lesley 112, 126, 149, 166, 217
Woodson, William 123
Woodville, Kate 60, 62
Woodward, Bob 269
Woodward, Edward 138, 222, 226
Woodward, Meredith 289
Woodward, Morgan 144, 145, 148, 151, 207, 255
Woody, Russ 276
"Wooly Bullies" 246, 252
"Works for Me" 34, 194, 200, 202
"The Worst Night of Your Life" 249
Worth, Nicholas 77, 111, 123, 125, 208
Worthen, Warren 81
Wren, Clare 216
Wren, Michael 211
Wright, Bruce 167
Wright, Herbert 199, 201, 209, 210, 228

Wright, Janet 289, 290
Wright, Ken 186
Wukovitz, John 87
Wulff, Kai 123, 124, 155, 166
"Wyatt Earp to the Rescue" 174
Wycherley, Margaret 266
Wyllie, Meg 84
Wynant, H.M. 60
Wyndham, Anne 249
Wyner, George 53, 60, 61, 65, 150
Wynn, Keenan 5, 32, 50, 78, 125, 164, 231, 235
Wynter, Dana 69, 85, 112

The X-Files 195, 226, 242
Xena—Warrior Princess 88, 332, 333

Yaegher, Jeff 241
Yah-Ling Sun, Irene 64
Yama, Michael 95
"The Yankee Clipper" 167
Yarmy, Dick 112
Yasbeck, Amy 302
Yashima, Momo 77
Yates, Cassie 80, 85, 111
Yates, Jack 215
Yates, Peter 101
Yea, Helena 288, 289
The Yellow Rose 173, 313
"Yellow Rose of Texas" 295
"Yesterday's Child" 217
Yniguez, Richard 30, 148, 209, 219
Yohn, Erica 229
York, Francine 187
York, John J. 211, 247, 255, 317
"You and the Horse You Rode in On" 166
"You Don't Hear the One That Gets You" 166
"You Oughtta Be in Prison" 250
"You Would Cry Too If It Happened to You" 161, 165
Young, Ben 68
Young, Bruce 249
Young, Buck 66
Young, Burt 63, 74, 75, 77, 78
Young, David 85
Young, Gail 213
Young, Keone 250

Young, Richard 207
Young, Robert (director) 163
Young, Stephen 215
Young, Victoria 165
Young Evans, Michael 152
The Young Lawyers 237
Young Maverick 57
The Young Rebels 237
The Young Riders 26, 247
Youngs, Jim 293, 294
"You're Sixteen, You're Beautiful, and You're His" 161, 168
Yue, Marion 69
Yulin, Harris 76, 107
Yung Sun 186
Yunker, Peter 256, 288, 291, 293
Yuro, Robert 62

Zabriskie, Grace 316
Zacha, W.T. 84, 85, 98, 122, 123, 208
Zachery, James R. 294
Zahrn, Will 288
Zakarian, Ruth 210
Zammit, Eddie 208, 287
Zand, Michael 210
Zane, Lora 293, 294, 316
Zano, Muni 92
Zapata, Carmen 213
Zapp, Peter 255
Zarchen, John 253
Zastrzembska, Christine 291
Zee, John 76, 111
Zeitlin, Erica 168
Zemrus, Dasha Lee 81
Zenda, John 111
Zentall, Kate 207, 210, 213
Zepeda, Jorge 147
Zerbe, Anthony 66
Zimbalist, Efrem, Jr. 165, 215
Ziskie, Daniel 212
Zohar, Rita 211
"The Zoo Under the Wacker Street Bridge" 100
Zorro 107, 333
Zucker, David and Jerry 233
Zuckert, Bill 61
Zwerling, Darrell 111

www.ingramcontent.com/pod-product-compliance
Lightning Source LLC
Chambersburg PA
CBHW081534300426
44116CB00015B/2622